THE
TAITTIRĪYA-PRĀTIŚĀKHYA

With its Commentary the Tribhāshyaratna : Text, Translation and Notes

WILLIAM D. WHITNEY

MOTILAL BANARSIDASS
DELHI :: PATNA :: VARANASI

Head Office : BUNGALOW ROAD, JAWAHARNAGAR, DELHI-7
Branches : 1. CHOWK, VARANASI (U.P.)
2. ASHOK RAJPATH (OPP. PATNA COLLEGE), PATNA-4 (BIHAR)

First Edition : New Haven, 1868
Reprint : Delhi. 1973

Printed in India

BY SHANTILAL JAIN, AT SHRI JAINENDRA PRESS, BUNGALOW ROAD, JAWAHARNAGAR, DELHI-7 AND PUBLISHED BY SUNDARLAL JAIN FOR MOTILAL BANARSIDASS, BUNGALOW ROAD, JAWAHARNAGAR, DELHI-7

ARTICLE I.

THE TÂITTIRÎYA-PRÂTIÇÂKHYA,

WITH ITS COMMENTARY,

THE TRIBHÂSHYARATNA:

TEXT, TRANSLATION, AND NOTES.

BY WILLIAM D. WHITNEY,

PROFESSOR OF SANSKRIT IN YALE COLLEGE.

Presented to the Society October 14th, 1868.

INTRODUCTORY NOTE.

THE manuscript material on which is founded this edition of the Tâittirîya-Prâtiçâkhya and Tribhâshyaratna is as follows:

1. **T.** A copy of the text of the treatise alone, in a modern hand, on light-colored paper. It was sent me by Prof. Fitz-Edward Hall, from Benares, in 1857, and appears to be a copy made for him from some older manuscript: but it contains no intimation of its own date or of that of its original; presenting at the end, in place of the usual colophon, the beginning of a list of words which in *pada*-text show a final *n*. It is distinctly and correctly written. On the back is inscribed "Krishna-yajuh-prátis'ákhya, by Kártikeya." On what ground this ascription of authorship is made, I do not know; it does not, so far as I am aware, find support from any other quarter.

2. **W.** A copy of the text and commentary together, each separate rule being followed by its own comment. This manuscript, like the preceding, I owe to the kindness of Prof. Hall. It is handsomely written, in a large clear hand, and fills 146 leaves (numbered 1–89, 100, 1–56), measuring about four and a half by nine and a half inches. To the end of 25*a*, seven lines are written on a page; thenceforward, nine lines. It has no statement of scribe, place, or date; but I imagine that a final leaf, with the end of the colophon, had been lost or destroyed some time before it was sent to me. The part remaining reads as follows: *çrîkṛshṇârpabhastu çrîkâlabhâiravaprasann oṁ yâyakâṁḍavidhâyordhvaṁ ṛshayo ṛshayo ṛshiḥ: ity âçîsraçîmal:âpûrvaṁ ṛshaṁ ce ti svataṁtratâ:* 1 *kramyâdhvano bhavaty agre pâvako rpayatîti ca.* This just fills up the leaf; but another hand has written below, at its edge, what purports to be the ending of the second verse: *visha-*

*yeṅgira ity evâpy agra ity âdi lupyate.*2., and has added as final benediction, *çrîviçveçvaraprasann.*

This is a virgin manuscript, containing neither erasures, insertions, nor alterations. Considering that it thus presents every first fault of its scribe unamended, it is very good and correct. Through the first twelve chapters, the rules of the Prâtiçâkhya are distinguished from the commentary by being rubbed over with a red powder.

3. **B**. This authority comes from the west of India, where (see Dr. Bühler, in Zeitsch. Deut. Morg. Ges., xxii.319) the Tribhâshyaratna is said to be not very rare. From a manuscript there collected, a copy was made under direction of Dr. Bühler for the Berlin library, and forwarded to Prof. Weber, at whose friendly suggestion and instance it was transcribed for me, in roman letters, by Dr. Siegfried Goldschmidt, to whom I desire here to express my gratitude for a service so valuable and so kindly rendered. The manuscript contains more inaccuracies of reading than any of the others which I have used, yet they are in the main superficial, and the text given is a pretty complete and correct one.

4. **O**. Through the kind offices of Prof. Max Müller, I have been enabled to procure a collation (made with a copy of my own manuscript, "W.") of the incomplete Oxford manuscript (MS. Bodl. W. 478), first described by Roth (Zur Lit. und Gesch. des Weda, pp. 54, 62 seq.), and used also by Weber (Ind. Stud. iv.77 seq.). It begins in the middle of the comment upon iii.12, thus lacking somewhat less than a quarter of the entire work.

5. **G**. This is a romanized copy of a manuscript which belongs to the Royal Asiatic Society of Great Britain and Ireland, and is written on strips of palm leaf, in the Grantham character. The copy was made for me by Dr. Julius Eggeling, who has thus laid me under deep obligation, and contributed most essentially to the success of my work. Hardly less than to him is my indebtedness to Dr. Reinhold Rost, Secretary of the Royal Asiatic Society, who notified me of the existence of the manuscripts in the Society's library soon after their discovery, and who suggested and aided their transcription. There are doubtless few other Sanskritists in Europe, besides these gentlemen, to whom works written in the southern Indian characters are not sealed books, and there can be none, I am sure, who evince a more liberal readiness to make their peculiar knowledge of service to the rest. The catalogue which Dr. Rost is preparing to publish of the Royal Asiatic Society's collection of manuscripts will give such other particulars respecting age, condition, etc., as I am compelled here to omit.

6. **M**. The library of the same Society also contains a second copy of the Prâtiçâkhya and its commentary, written on paper, in the Malayâlam character. Of this, Dr. Eggeling has taken the pains to note the various readings as compared with the Grantham manuscript, in his transcript of the latter.

Both these manuscripts from southern India are so arranged

that the rules of the Prâtiçâkhya are given first, in a body, and are followed by the commentary, also in bulk

As regards the text of the Prâtiçâkhya itself, all these authorities agree very closely: there are but two or three cases of well-established variations of reading among them. In respect to the text of the commentary, their accordance, as was to be expected, is much less: they fall, in fact, into three well-marked classes; or, as one might say, present three different recensions of the work. The two codices belonging to the Royal Asiatic Society, the Grantham ("G.") and the Malayâlam ("M."), stand in the nearest possible relation to one another, having almost all their errors, omissions, and orthographical peculiarities in common, and only by comparatively rare and inconspicuous differences proved not to be copied the one from the other. My own manuscript ("W.") and that sent by Dr. Bühler from Bombay ("B.") also offer substantially the same text, although their differences are much more frequent, and of a more important character, than those of G. and M. As for the Oxford manuscript ("O."), it is, in its earlier portions, pretty closely accordant with W. and B., having an especially near relationship to B., with whose slight variations of the text given by W. it almost uniformly agrees; later, however, it strikes off upon a track of its own, and comes to differ from both the other recensions in a much greater degree than they differ between themselves.

Such being the case, I have thought it best to adopt for publication the version offered by W., partly because this is the only one for which I possess an original manuscript (and a tolerably old and correct one), partly because it is, upon the whole, better supported than that of G. and M.—which, as I have shown above, can hardly be reckoned, both together, as constituting more than a single manuscript. I have accordingly, avoiding the making up of an eclectic text from the various recensions, followed W. as closely as I could; and especially, when it was supported by the joint authority of B. and O., or of B. alone—thus sometimes, undoubtedly, rejecting an intrinsically preferable and perhaps more original reading given by one or another of the remaining authorities, if that offered by W. was of a character to be endured. At the end of the comment to each rule are given the various readings of all the manuscripts, with sufficient fullness, I hope, to answer the desirable ends of critical comparison. Obvious and trifling errors of transcription, of course, I have not noted, but only those which made a false reading or tended to become such: I have been most liberal in overlooking the blunders of B., as being, on the whole, of least consequence.

In regard, however, to the two matters of punctuation and euphonic combination, I have taken liberties with the text of which I have given no account. The various manuscripts are in no slight degree discordant with one another, inconsistent with themselves, and careless of the requirements of the sense, in the use they make of the signs of interpunction: they offer absolutely no standard to follow. For the occurrence of the signs as printed, therefore, I am alone responsible; and no one who can anywhere make a better division of clauses than I have made need be restrained from so doing by the belief that he is running counter to manuscript authority. Again, I have (except in certain cases at the end of a cited rule or passage, where a reference follows) put all the words of the commentary in euphonic combination according to the usual rules; while in the manuscripts (as is common in exegetical writings) they are very frequently, for the sake of greater clearness, separated from one another.* Here, too, the usage of the various authorities is too discordant and irregular to be followed. And to report their readings in these two particulars would burden the critical notes with a mass of useless and wearisome details.

In the same manner are treated such orthographical peculiarities of the several manuscripts as that G. and M. regularly write a final sibilant instead of *visarjanîya* before an initial sibilant, and often, where a *m* is assimilated to a following mute, write the nasal mute corresponding to the latter, instead of *anusvâra*. Moreover, in the representation of the nasal sounds, by the nasal consonants, *anusvâra* (*n̐*), or *ṁ*, I have followed a consistent method, with disregard of the manuscript usage.

The text given at the foot of the page contains the whole comment, with two exceptions: citations from the Tâittirîya-Sanhitâ, being written out in full, with references, in the notes to the rules, are indicated below only by first words or letters, with signs of omission added; and again, where lists of affected words are given in a rule, in euphonic combination, and repeated, separate, at the beginning of the comment, they are replaced by signs of omission, as having been sufficiently presented uncombined in the translation of the rule. Errors of reading in the cited passages themselves are passed without notice, unless of such importance as to cast doubt upon the identity of the passage; but, on the other hand, the frequent differences of the versions as regards the extent of the illustrative passage cited are fully noted in the sequel of the reference.

I have preferred, instead of giving an express and direct translation of the commentary, to work its substance fully into my own notes upon the rules, somewhat as in my edition of the Atharva Prâtiçâkhya (Journ. Am. Or. Soc'y, Vol. vii., 1862). The different conditions of the case, however, impress quite a different character upon the present work. The completeness and elaborateness of the Tribhâshyaratna make its working-up by far the larger and more important part of what is to be done in illustration of the Prâtiçâkhya. Possessing no *index verborum* to the Tâittirîya-Sanhitâ, nor even a manuscript of its *pada*-text, I have not been able to try the Prâtiçâkhya by it with anything like the same

---

* Thus, to instance an extreme case, at the end of the comment on iv.10, the manuscripts read (for once, with almost perfect unanimity): *iṅgyasya antaḥ iṅgyántaḥ na iṅgyántaḥ aniṅgyántaḥ.*

thoroughness as in the case of the similar treatise to the Atharvan. What could be done in the way of testing and supplementing the rules given, by a careful reading and excerption of the Sanhitâ in a single good *saṁhitâ*-manuscript (also procured for me in India by Dr. Hall, and with one or two slight deficiences in it made up from Berlin, by Prof. Weber), I have endeavored to do. I have been able to refer points of interest connected with the text, in its *saṁhitâ* or *pada* readings, to friends in Europe owning or having access to fuller manuscript material, namely to Professors Weber of Berlin and Haug of München, and have received from them important aid, which I desire here gratefully to acknowledge. Of references to the teachings of the other Prâtiçâkhyas I have been much more sparing in this than in the former work, in order to avoid repetition: and, for the same reason, some matters of theory which were pretty fully discussed there receive here a more compendious treatment. The present work, in short, to a certain extent presupposes the other—not, however, in such a manner or degree as should interfere with its independence and separate intelligibility.

In making reference to the Tâittirîya-Sanhitâ, I have used only three principal numbers, to designate book, chapter, and section, or *kâṇḍa*, *praçna*, and *anuvâka*. The further division of the sections or *anuvâkas*, where they are of more considerable length, into parcels of fifty words each, is so artificial, destructive of the natural connection of passages, detrimental to the proper phonetic form of the text, and wholly ignored by the Prâtiçâkhya (see notes to the rules of chapter iii.), that I have preferred to express it by the use of "superior" figures attached to that which indicates the *anuvâka*. Of course, where such attached figure is wanting, the *anuvâka* is to be understood as composed of a single division.

In the notes of various readings, each figure refers only to the single word to which it is attached, unless a passage of more than one word is included between two repetitions of the same figure; in which case the reference figure, in the notes, is put within parentheses. The abbreviation "om." means 'omit,' and "ins." means 'insert.'

In all transliterated passages of Sanskrit, a colon stands in place of a single stroke of interpunction, and a full stop in place of a double stroke. The general method of transliteration is the same with that which I have hitherto used in the Journal of the American Oriental Society; it will be sufficiently understood from the alphabet given in the note to i.1 (p. 10).

CHAPTER I.

Contents: 1–11, enumeration and classification of sounds composing the alphabet; 12–14, surd and sonant consonants; 15, list of prepositions; 16–21, 27, names of letters and classes of letters; 22–24, 28, terminology of cited words, etc.; 25, 26, 29, 30, respecting the interpretation of rules; 31–37, quantity of simple sounds; 38–40, the three accents; 41–47, details respecting the circumflex accent; 48, 49, compound words; 50–53, respecting cited words; 54–55, words consisting of a single vowel; 56–61, further specifications respecting the interpretation of rules.

The commentator begins his work with a couple of rather awkwardly-constructed verses, as follows: "I, bowing low with devoted affection to the two feet of Gaṇeça, as also to the *gurus* and to divine Voice, shall proceed to utter this comment; which, made upon examination of the exposition of the Prâtiçâkhya given by Vararuci etc., shines, a Treasure of Threefold Comment (*tribhâshyaratna*), approved of Brahmans." He adds an exposition of their meaning, explaining *giraṁ devîm*, 'divine Voice,' by *vâgdevîm*, 'Goddess of Voice,' and *bhûsura*, 'Brahman' (literally 'earth-god'), by *vidvat*, 'learned man, sage.' On *lakshaṇa*, which, as name of a comment, is least in accordance

---

[1]*bhaktiyuktaḥ praṇamyâ 'haṁ gaṇeçacaraṇadvayam:*
gurûn api giraṁ[2] *devîm idaṁ vakshyâmi lakshaṇam.*1
vyâkhyânam prâtiçâkhyasya vîkshya vârarucâdikam[3]*:*
*kṛtaṁ tribhâshyaratnaṁ yad bhâsate bhûsurapriyam.*2.

çlokayor anayor ayam[4] *arthaḥ. bhaktiyukto 'haṁ gaṇeçacaraṇadvayaṁ gurûn giram*[5] *api devîm:* [6]*vâgdevîm ity arthaḥ: tâṁ ca*[6] *praṇamya lakshaṇam idaṁ vakshyâmi yal*[7] *lakshaṇaṁ tribhâshyaratnanâmakam bhûsurapriyaṁ vidvatpriyam bhâsate: kîdṛçaṁ lakshaṇam: prâtiçâkhyasya vyâkhyânarûpakaṁ*[8] *vârarucâdikam*[9] *bhâshyajâtaṁ vîkshya*[10] *nyûnâtirekaparihâreṇa kṛtaṁ viracitam: âdiçabdenâ "treyamâhisheyâu gṛhyete: ata eva tribhâshyaratnam iti nâmna upapattiḥ: trayâṇâm bhâshyâṇâṁ samâhâras tribhâshyam: tasya*[11] *ratnam bhûshaṇam.*

[1] W prefaces with *çrigaṇeçâya namaḥ. çrigaṇeça prasanno 'stu. oṁ.* B. prefaces with *çrigaṇeçâya namaḥ. çrisarasvatyâi namaḥ. çridattânnayâya namaḥ:* and the additional verse

çuklâmbaradharaṁ devaṁ çaçivarṇaṁ caturbhujam:
*prasannavadanam dhyâyet sarvavighnopaçântaye.*1.

'The white-raiment-bearing god, moon-hued, four-armed, propitious-faced, must one meditate on, in order to the surcease of all disturbance.' It then numbers the other verses "2" and "3;" but proceeds to confess the ungenuineness of the inserted verse by reading, like the other MSS., *anayoḥ çlokayoḥ*.

[2] G. M. *girân.* [3] B. *var-.* [4] G. M. om. [5] G. M. *girâm.* [(6)] G. M. om. [7] G. M. *tal.* [8] G. M. *-rûpam;* B. *-pûrvakaṁ.* [9] B. *var-;* W. *-ka.* [10] G. M. *samikshya.* [11] W. om.

with common usage, he makes no remark. To *vîkshya*, 'having examined,' he adds *nyûnâtirekaparihârena*, 'with avoidance of deficiency and redundancy.' The "etc." after "Vararuci" is declared to refer to Âtreya and Mâhisheya, these three being the authorities upon which the present work is founded, and from which it derives its name. Vararuci and Mâhisheya are, indeed, often (about ten times each: see Index) referred to in the sequel, and their discordant views sometimes set forth and discussed: Âtreya has only once (under v.1) the honor of being mentioned. Who is the digester of their three works, and author of the present commentary, which has taken their place and crowded them out of existence, we are not informed; nor, so far as I am aware, has any evidence bearing upon the point been anywhere brought to knowledge. Notice of the different authorities cited by our commentator will be put together in an additional note at the end of this work, for the sake of the light cast by them upon his age.

अथ वर्णसमाम्नायः ॥ १ ॥

1. Now the list of sounds.

The commentator first gives himself a great deal of trouble to explain the meaning of *atha*, 'now,' in the rule. He quotes Amara's definition of *atho* and *atha* (Amarakosha iii.4.32.8; p. 349 of Deslongchamps's edition), and points out that, as a variety of meanings is there attributed to *atha*, it is necessary to fix upon a single meaning for it here. In the first place, then, a propitiatory significance is claimed for it, by reason of its equivalence with *om*; "since the Çikshâ-makers declare, '*om* and *atha* are deemed propitiatory.'" Or, again, it indicates something coming next after another; "the implication being that, next after the reading of the Veda, one should gain a knowledge of the *lakshana*: there hav-

---

1. *mañgalânantarârambhapraçnakârtsnyeshv atho athe 'ti mañgalâdyanekârthatvâd athaçabdasyâ "rthanirṇayârtham eko 'rtho*[1] *niçcetavyaḥ: tatra prathamam tâvan mañgalârthatvam ucyate: tasya praṇavasâdharmyât: tathâ hi samâcakshate çikshâkârâḥ*[2]*:*

omkâraç ca 'tnaçabdaç ca mañgalâv iti kîrtitâv

iti: âho[3] *svid ânantaryârthatâ*[4]*: vedâdhyayanânantaram lakshaṇajñânam kuryâd iti sâpekshatvâl lakshaṇasya pûrvam vedâdhigame saty atha lakshaṇaparîkshâvasaraḥ: atha vâ 'dhikârârtho 'thaçabdaḥ: tv athai 've 'ti vinivartakâdhikârakâvadhârakâḥ* (xxii.6) *iti vidyamânatvât: atha varṇasamâmnâyaḥ pâṭhakramo*[5] *'dhikriyata iti sûtrânvayaḥ: sam ity ekîbhâve: âñ iti maryâdâyâm: mnâya ity ânupûrvyeṇo 'padeçaḥ*[6]*: ekîbhûtâ akârâdayo varṇâḥ svarabhaktiparyavasânâ ânupûrvyeṇa pûrvaiḥ çishṭâir*[7] *upadishṭâḥ.*

ing been study of the Veda before the *lakshaṇa*, now comes the occasion for the investigation of the *lakshaṇa*." Here, *lakshaṇa* appears to be used to designate the Prâtiçâkhya itself, as above it denoted the commentary to the latter. Once more, *atha* is declared to have the force of an introduction or heading, according to rule xxii.6, below: "*tu*, *atha*, and *eva* are respectively exceptive, introductory, and limitative;" and the connection of the rule is that *now* the list of sounds, the order of reading (*pâṭhakrama*), is made the subject of treatment.

The composition of *samâmnâya*, 'list, rehearsal,' is next pointed out, and the word is stated to mean "the collective sounds, beginning with *a* and ending with the *svarabhakti*, in their order, as taught by former learned men."

The catalogue itself follows, as understood by the commentator to be taught or implied in the rules of the treatise. First come the vowels, of which only sixteen are reckoned (see rule 5, below): *a*, *i*, and *u* have each a short, a long, and a protracted value, *ṛ* only a short and a long, *ḷ* only a short (W. and B. take the pains to write a figure 2 after the long *ṛ*, and a 1 after the *ḷ*, to point out clearly the number of *moras* they respectively contain; and B. adds after the *âi* and *âu* a 2, for the same purpose); second, the twenty-five mutes (see rule 7); third, the four semivowels (rule 8); and fourth, the six spirants (rule 9). This makes fifty-one sounds, clearly specified and counted in their order in the next succeeding rules. Of the rest, there is no so direct enumeration; the commentator has to infer them from their recognition by rules found in later portions of the treatise. Thus, he finds *anusvâra* acknowledged as an alphabetic element in rule 34 of this chapter, which teaches that it has the quantity of a short vowel; for, he says, "since it is made the substrate of a specific quantity, it is itself a concrete thing, and not, like nasalization, a quality." A passage from the Çikshâ, it is true, appears inconsistent with this, but finds its sufficient explanation in the circumstance that that work includes in one expression the concrete thing and its quality. The cited passage is not to be found in the known text of the

---

tathâ hi: a â â3 i î î3 u û û3 ṛ ṝ ḷ e âi o âu iti svarâḥ shoḍaça: ka kha ga gha ńa ca cha ja jha ña ṭa ṭha ḍa ḍha ṇa ta tha da dha na pa pha ba bha ma iti sparçâḥ pañcaviṅçatiḥ: ya ra la va iti catasro 'ntasthâḥ: ça sha sa ha ḥka[8] *ḥpa*[9] *iti shaḍ ûshmâṇaḥ: anusvâraç ca* (i.34) *iti sûtreṇâ 'nusvâra uktaḥ: kâlaviçeshâçrayatvâd asâu* [11]*dharmî na tv*[10] *anunâsikavad*[11] *dharmaḥ: vidher.*[12] *madhyasthanâsikya*[13] *iti çikshâvacane*[14] *sati*[15] *dharmadharmiṇor abhedavivakshayo 'papadyate: atha visarjanîyaḥ* (viii.5) *ity anena*[16] *visarjanîya uktaḥ: nâsikâvivaraṇâd ânunâsikyam* (ii.52) *ity anena*[16] *rańga uktaḥ: pṛktasvarât paro lo ḍam* (xiii.16) *ity anena*[16] *lakâra uktaḥ: sparçâd anuttamâd* (xxi.12) *iti catvâro yamâ uktâḥ: rephoshmasaṁyoge rephasvarabhaktir* (xxi.15) *iti svarabhaktir uktâ: anena krameṇa*

Çikshâ (and the same is the case with several of the passages quoted later: see the additional notes): it is given again, with more fullness, under viii.15. Next, for the *visarjanîya*, which our Prâtiçâkhya does not count among the spirants, is given as authority rule 5 of the eighth chapter, a rule introductory to the euphonic changes of a final *ḥ*. The commentator brings in as next constituent of the alphabet an element which he calls *rañga*, and for which he cites the rule (ii.52) that "nasal quality is given by the unclosing of the nasal passage." The word *rañga*, 'coloring,' though a common name for the nasal tinge of utterance, is not found in our Prâtiçâkhya, nor even used in the commentary excepting here and under ii.52. What is described in the latter rule is in fact a "quality" (*dharma*), and not a "qualified" or concrete thing (*dharmin*); and its inclusion in the alphabet would stultify the argument with which the inclusion of *anusvâra* was but just now supported. It would seem that the commentator ought to be aiming here at the *nâsikya*, or euphonic insertion between *h* and a following nasal mute, and should quote for it rule xxi.14; he does not otherwise take account of it in his list, while yet it is precisely as well entitled to a place there as are the *yamas*. The nasalized semivowels, it is true, into which *n* and *m* are directed to be converted before *y*, *l*, *v* (v.26–8), are also left out of the enumeration, unless we suppose the *rañga* to be meant to apply to their nasality; and I think it altogether likely that the commentator had them in view in its definition: but this is only avoiding one difficulty by running into two worse ones—namely, by omitting the *nâsikya*, and by reckoning as a member of the alphabet what is really only one of the constituent elements of certain sounds. Further, rule xiii.16 is made the warrant for the lingual *l*, rule xxi.12 for the four *yamas*, and rule xxi.15, finally, for the *svarabhakti:* and the conclusion is reached that "by this process, the number of sixty is clearly derivable from the rules themselves as that of the letters in the Yajur-Veda."

---

yâjurvedikavarṇânâṁ[17] *shashṭisaṁkhyâ sûtrata eva vispashṭâ drashṭavyâ. nanu*

trishashṭiç catuḥshashṭir vâ varṇâḥ çambhumate[18] *matâḥ:*

iti çikshâvacane sati kathaṁ shashṭisaṁkhyâ niyamyate: etal[19] *laukikavâidikasarvavarṇavishayam*[20] *iti* [21] *çikshâvacane na virodhaḥ: atra tu*[22] *sûtrâir etâvatâṁ varṇânâm*[23] *evo 'palambhâd esha eva*[24] *nirṇayo varṇitaḥ*[25].

varṇânâṁ samâmnâyo varṇasamâmnâyaḥ.

(1) G. M. *mañgalâdyanekârtho.* [2] W. G. M. *çiksh-*. G. and M. always write *çikshâ*, B. and O. always *çikshâ*; W. has *çi-* only in one other place (under xiv.28). [3] W. B. *aho.* [4] G. M. *-ryatâ;* W. adds *vâ.* [5] G M. *paṭhe kramo.* [6] W. B. om. [7] W. *çishyâir.* [8] B. *shka.* [9] B *shpa.* [10] G. M. om. (11) B. *dharmâṇatvâd anunâsikaḥ.* [12] G. ins. *ddharma.* [13] G. M. *-kâd.* [14] G. M. *-naṁ.* [15] B. om.; G M. *tu.* [16] B. G. M. om. [17] W. *-vâid-*. [18] B. *aṁçumate.* [19] G. M. *tal.* [20] G. M. *-savarṇavarṇa-*. [21] G. M. ins. *na.* [22] G. M. om. [23] G. M. om. [24] G. M. om. [25] B. *nirṇitaḥ.*

An objection is now raised and removed. "Considering that the Çikshâ says 'the letters are regarded as sixty-three or sixty-four, in the opinion of Çambhu' (Çikshâ, verse 3; see Weber's edition of the treatise, in his Indische Studien, iv.348–9), how is the number sixty established? Answer: there is no inconsistency with the *dictum* of the Çikshâ, seeing that the latter has in view the whole body of sounds, as used both in the Veda and in common life; while here the determination (of sixty) is derived from the assumption of just so many letters by the rules of the treatise."

The alphabetic scheme is, then, as follows:

Vowels	simple,	*a â â3 i î î3 u û û3*	9	
	impure and dipthongs,	*ṛ ṝ ḷ e âi o âu*	7	16
Mutes	guttural,	*k kh g gh ṅ*	5	
	palatal,	*c ch j jh ñ*	5	
	lingual,	*ṭ ṭh ḍ ḍh ṇ*	5	
	dental,	*t th d dh n*	5	
	labial,	*p ph b bh m*	5	25
Semivowels,		*y r l v*		4
Spirants,		*ẖ ç sh s ɸ h*		6
Anusvâra,		*ṅ̇*		1
Visarjanîya,		*ḥ*		1
Lingual *l*,		*ḷ*		1
Nâsikya,		(not written)		1
Yamas,		do.		4
Svarabhakti,		do.		1
	whole number of letters			60

With the exception of the nasal *y, l, v*, already referred to, this list includes all the alphabetic sounds treated of by the Prâtiçâkhya. For what concerns the peculiarities of their character or classification, see the special rules of which they are the subject; as also, for the differences between the teachings of this and of the other kindred treatises with reference to them. Only the Vâjasaneyi-Prâtiçâkhya includes in its text a complete list and enumeration of letters, and that by an afterthought, in a later and less genuine chapter (viii.1–31).

अथ नवादितः समानाक्षराणि ॥ २ ॥

2. Now the nine at the beginning are simple vowels.

---

2. *athe 'ti saṁjñâdhikârârthaḥ: asmin*[1] *varṇasamâmnâya âdita ârabhya nava varṇâḥ samânâksharasaṁjñâ bhavanti:* [2]*yathâ: a â â3 i î î3 u û û3*[2]. *saṁjñâyâḥ*[3] *prayojanam: dîrghaṅ samânâkshare savarṇapare* (x.2) *ity âdi. nanv îdṛçî mahatî saṁjñâ kimarthâ*[4]*: çikshâdiçâstraprasiddhyanurodhâye*[5] *'ti brûmaḥ.*

[1] B. *tasmin.* (2) W. B. *a â â3 ity* [3] G. M. *-jñâ.* [4] G. M. *-tham.* [5] G. M. om. *-di-*.

Literally, 'are homogeneous syllables;' *samânâkshara* and its correlative *saṁdhyakshara*, 'syllable of combination,' being the current names for simple vowel and for diphthong; the latter, however, is not used in this treatise. The nine intended are, as shown in the preceding list, *a â â3 i î î3 u û û3*. The *ṛ* and *ḷ* vowels are denied the quality of simplicity or homogeneity, although their structure as composed of heterogeneous elements is not further described; the Rik Pr. (xiii.14), the Vâj. Pr. (iv.145), and the Ath. Pr. (i.37–9) give the details of their formation, while nevertheless the two first expressly include *ṛ* and *ṝ* among the *samânâksharas* (omitting *ḷ*, apparently, because no case anywhere occurs that should test its quality), and the same classification is inferribly recognized by the last.

The commentator explains the *atha* of this rule as signifying the introduction of the subject of names or technical appellations (*saṁjñâ*), and cites, as example of the use of the term, rule x.2, respecting the coalescence of two similar simple vowels into a long vowel. Finally, the unwieldiness of the long word *samânâkshara* striking his mind, he asks "why such a big name?" and relieves himself by the answer "we say, in order to correspond with the established usage of the Çikshâ and other text-books." The Çikshâ as we know it, it may be remarked, does not employ the term.

द्वे द्वे सवर्णे ह्रस्वदीर्घे ॥ ३ ॥

3. Two and two, short and long, are similar.

That is to say, as the commentary explains, of these simple vowels, two and two short, two and two long, or a long and a short, are called "similar." The meaning seems rather to be that, of the three triplets which make up the category of simple vowels, the first two in each triplet, the short and the long, will be designated as "similar"—to the exclusion, namely, of the *pluta* or protracted vowels. The term is used but once in the treatise (namely in x.2, the rule last above quoted), as applied to vowels, and nothing is practically gained by denying its inclusion of the protracted vowels, since these are specially protected from coalescence by the rule x.24. The *ṛ*-vowels are here again shut out, as in the preceding rule; and, in fact, no case occurs in the Vedic text in which two of them are fused into one.

---

3. *teshu*[1] *samânâkshareshu dvedve hrasve dvedve dîrghe*[2] *hrasvadîrghe*[3] *dîrghahrasve vâ 'kshare parasparaṁ savarṇasaṁjñe bhavataḥ. iyam anvarthasaṁjñâ: savarṇatvaṁ nâma sâdṛçyam ucyate: tasmâd akârâdînâm ikârâdibhir na savarṇasaṁjñâçaṅkâ bhinnasthânaprayatnatvâd*[4] *anayoḥ. saṁjñâyâh prayojanam: dîrghaṅ samânâkshare savarṇapare* (x.2) *iti.*

hrasvaṁ ca dîrghaṁ ca hrasvadîrghe.

[1] G. M. *eteshu.* [2] G. M. ins. *vâ.* [3] B. om.; G. M. ins. *vâ.* [4] B. *-tnâd.*

The word translated 'similar' means literally 'of identical color' (i. e. sound), and is several times applied later to identity of consonantal sound. It is, as the commentator points out, a self-explaining term, or one whose application is directly in accordance with its natural meaning (*anvartha*); and hence no suspicion is to be entertained of the inclusion of *a* and *i*, for instance, as "similar," because of their different mode of organic production. As example of the use of the term is again cited x.2.

न प्लुतपूर्वम् ॥ ४ ॥

4. Not so, when a protracted vowel precedes.

This is an arbitrary exclusion, made to fit a particular case, which might with more evident propriety have been provided for later, where such cases are under treatment, rather than here in the preliminary definition of terms (compare a somewhat similar case in the Rik Pr., i.1, r. 4). The commentator paraphrases the rule "a simple vowel having a protracted one before it is not termed 'similar;'" and goes on to cite and explain in full the case to which it applies. In the phrase *ágne: íti: âha* (vi.5.8⁴), the word *ágne* has its final diphthong protracted, and becomes *ágnâ'3i*. By the rule (x.2) for the coalescence of two similar simple vowels into the corresponding long vowel, this would then unite with the following word to form *ágnâ'3î 'ti*. The quality of similarity, however, being denied by the present rule to the final *i*, it is treated as a dissimilar vowel, being first converted into *y* by rule x.15, the *y* dropped by x.19, and the coalescence of the remaining *â3* with the following *i* (as prescribed by x.4) prevented by x.24: thus is assured the reading *ágnâ'3 íty âha*.

षोडशादितः स्वराः ॥ ५ ॥

5. The sixteen at the beginning are vowels.

Namely, says the commentator, the sixteen beginning with *a* and ending with *âu*. As example of the use of the technical term

---

4. *plutapûrvaṁ samânâksharaṁ savarṇasaṁjñaṁ na bhavati. plutam asmât pûrvam iti plutapûrvam. yathâ: agnâ3 ity âhe 'ty atra dîrghañ samânâkshare savarṇapare* (x.2) *ity ekâdeçaḥ prasaktaḥ: tac câ 'nishṭam: pratishiddhâyâṁ tv evaṁ savarṇasaṁjñâyâm pâriçeshyâd ivarṇokârâu yavakârâv* (x.15) *iti pûrvasye 'kârasya yatvaṁ syât*[1]*: sa ca yakâro lupyete tv avarṇapûrvâu yavakârâv* (x.19) *iti lupyate: yakâre lupte sati ivarṇapara ekâram* (x.4) *ity ekâraḥ*[2] *prasaktaḥ: so 'pi*[3] *nishidhyate na plutapragrahâv* (x.24) *ity anena: tasmâd agnâ3 ity âhe 'ti prasidhyati*[4].

[1] W. om. [2] G. M. *ekâdeçaḥ*. [3] G. M. *vi*. [4] G. M. *sidhyati*.

svara, 'vowel,' he quotes the rule (ix.10) prescribing the conversion of *visarjanîya* into *y* before a vowel.

Our Prâtiçâkhya is to be commended for not including in its list of vowels the long *ḷ*, and for postulating no useless protracted forms of *ṛ* and *ḷ*.

शेषो व्यञ्जनानि ॥ ६ ॥

6. The rest are consonants.

As example of the term *vyañjana*, 'consonant,' rule xxi.1, which pronounces the consonant a member of the adjacent vowel, is cited in the commentary, according to the two manuscripts from northern India; those from the south substitute for it the opening rule of the third chapter, and also omit the explanatory statement "beginning with *k* and ending with *svarabhakti*," which is given by the others.

आद्याः पञ्चविंशति स्पर्शाः ॥ ७ ॥

7. The first twenty-five are mutes.

The commentator explains: "among the consonants, the first twenty-five letters are called mutes" (*sparça*, literally 'contact'). The northern manuscripts add, as under the last rule, "beginning with *k*, and ending with *m*." It is next pointed out that rules 2 and 5 contain the specification *âditaḥ*, 'at the beginning,' and that the different phraseology of this rule, namely *âdyâḥ*, 'first,' indicates a difference of meaning: it signifies that the sounds referred to

---

5. *varṇasamâmnâyasyâ*[1] *'"dita ârabhya shoḍaça varṇâḥ svarasaṁjñâ bhavanti: akârâdaya âukâraparyantâ ity arthaḥ. saṁjñâyâḥ prayojanam: atha svaraparo yakâram* (ix.10) *ity âdi.*

[1] G. M. *varṇânâṁ sam-*.

6. *svarebhyaḥ çesho varṇarâçir vyañjanasaṁjño bhavati:* [1]*kakârâdisvarabhaktiparyantâ ity ârthaḥ*[1]. *saṁjñâyâḥ prayojanam:* [2]*vyañjanaṅ svarâṅgam*[2] (xxi.1) *iti.*

(1) G. M. om. (2) G. M. *athâ '"dâv uttare vibhâge hrasvaṁ vyañjanapara* (iii.1).

7. *vyañjaneshv âdyâḥ pañcaviṅçativarṇâ sparçasaṁjñâ bhavanti:* [1]*kakârâdayo makârântâḥ*[1]. [2]*saṁjñâyâḥ prayojanam: sparça sparçaparaḥ* (xiv.27)[2]. *atha navâ '"ditaḥ samânâksharâṇi* (i.2)*: shoḍaçâ '"ditaḥ svarâḥ* (i.5) *itivad âdita iti vaktavya âdyâ iti çabdântaraprayogo 'rthântarasûcakaḥ: vyañjaneshv âdyâ na tu svareshv âdyâ iti vijñeyam*[3].

(1) G. M. om. (2) G. M. remove to end of exposition, and for *sparçaparaḥ* read *sparça ity âdi.* [3] G. M *jñeyam.*

are first among the consonants, not first among the vowels (better, we should say, not first in the whole list). Of this style of interpretation, which forces a special significance into very innocent variations of phraseology, we shall meet with other and more striking examples farther on.

Rule xiv.27 is given as instance of the employment of the technical term here defined

पराश्चतस्रो ऽन्तस्थाः ॥ ८ ॥

8. The next four are semivowels.

The four semivowels are *y*, *r*, *l*, *v*. The rule cited by the commentary in illustration of the use of the term "semivowel" (*antasthâ*, i. e. *antaḥ-sthâ*, 'standing between, intermediate [between consonant and vowel]:' see note to Ath. Pr. i.30) is one (v.28) prescribing the treatment of final *m* before an initial semivowel.

परे षडूष्माणः ॥ ९ ॥

9. The next six are spirants.

Namely, the three sibilants, *ç*, *sh*, and *s*, the *jihvâmûlîya*, *χ*, the *upadhmânîya*, *φ*, and the aspiration, *h*. As regards the sounds to which the name *ûshman*, 'flatus,' shall be given, the phonetic treatises are greatly at variance. The Vâj. Pr. (viii.22) limits the class to the sibilants and *h*; the Ath. Pr. (see note to i.31) apparently adds the guttural and labial spirants and the more indistinct *visarjanîya*; the Rik Pr. (i.2), these and the *anusvâra*. We have an equal right to be surprised at the inclusion of this last in the class, and at the exclusion from it, by our treatise, of the *visarjanîya*.

To instance the employment of "spirant," the comment cites the rule (xiv.16) forbidding the duplication of a spirant before a vowel.

स्पर्शानामानुपूर्व्येण पञ्चपञ्च वर्गाः ॥ १० ॥

10. Of the mutes, the successive fives are the series.

The commentary paraphrases: "among the mutes, five and five sounds, in their order, have the designation 'series;' they begin respectively with *k*, *c*, *ṭ*, *t*, *p*, and end with *ṅ*, *ñ*, *ṇ*, *n*, *m*." This

---

8. *sparçebhyaḥ pare catvâro varṇâ antasthâsaṁjñâ bhavanti. saṁjñâyâḥ prayojanam:* [1]*antasthâparaç ca savarṇam anunâsikam* (v.28) *ity âdi.*

[1] A *lacuna* in W., extending to the word *prayojanam* in the commentary to the next rule.

9. *antasthâbhyaḥ pare shaḍ varṇâ ûshmasaṁjñâ bhavanti. saṁjñâyâḥ prayojanam: ûshmâ svaraparaḥ* (xiv.16) *ity âdi.*

exposition is in accordance with the requirements of the context, the treatise being here engaged in defining its technical terms. Otherwise, we might divide ---- *pañca pañcavargâḥ*, and translate, like the corresponding rule in the Rik Pr. (i.2), 'there are five series, of five each.'

The illustrative rule (xiv.20) cited in the comment teaches the non-duplication of a mute of the lingual series before one of the dental series.

प्रथमद्वितीयतृतीयचतुर्थोत्तमाः ॥ ११ ॥

11. And are called first, second, third, fourth, and last.

Each series of five mutes, that is to say, is composed of a surd, a surd aspirate, a sonant, a sonant aspirate, and a nasal, as *t*, *th*, *d*, *dh*, *n*; and these classes are named according to their order in the several series. The commentator makes no note here of the physical difference of the classes, but says "In each series, the sounds, in their order, are styled first, second, third, fourth, and last. Even though a name founded on enumeration obviously belongs to them [is assured them, without a special rule to that effect], yet, for the purpose of denying appellation on the ground of any other enumeration, the technical terms 'first' and so on are prescribed, to enjoin a certain enumeration.(?) How so? Why, to establish the designation 'first' and so on for *k* and its successors alone, and to deny to the vowels, semivowels, spirants, etc., designations founded on their enumeration." And he proceeds to cite four rules (ii.9; xiv.12, 24; viii.3: but the southern MSS. cite v.38 instead of ii.9) as examples of the use of the five terms defined.

---

10. *sparçânâm madhya ânupûrvyeṇa pañcapañca varṇâ*[1] *vargasaṁjñâ bhavanti: ka-ca-ṭa-ta-pâdayo*[2] *ṅa-ña-ṇa-na-mântâ ity arthaḥ. saṁjñâyâḥ prayojanam: ṭavargaç ca tavargaparaḥ* (xiv.20) *iti.*[3]

[1] B. om. [2] G. M. *-pâdyâḥ.* [3] W. om. the cited rule; G. M. *ity âdi.*

11. *ekâikasmin varge yathâkrameṇa*[1] *varṇâḥ prathamadvitîyatṛtîyacaturthottamasaṁjñâ bhavanti: siddhe 'pi saṁkhyânimitte nâmani*[2] *saṁkhyântarânabhidhânârthaṁ*[3] *saṁkhyântaraṁ*[4] *kathayituṁ prathamâdisaṁjñâvidhânam: tat katham: kakârâdînâm eva*[5] *prathamâdisaṁjñâpratyayârtham: svarântasthoshmaprabhṛtishu tatsaṁkhyâsaṁjñâpratishedhârthaṁ*[6]. *saṁjñâyâḥ prayojanam: prathama ûshmaparo dvitîyam* (xiv.12): *tṛtîyañ svaraghoshavatparaḥ* (viii.3): *hakâro hacaturtheshu* (ii.9)[7]: *nâ 'nuttama uttamaparaḥ* (xiv.24): *ity âdi.*

[1] G. M. *-kramam.* [2] G. M. *nâmni.* [3] B. *saṁkhyântarâbh-*; G. M. *saṁkhyâbh-*. [4] M. *saṁjñântaram*: as to the true reading and interpretation of this clause I am by no means confident. [5] G. M. om. [6] G. M. *tu saṁkh-*. [7] G. M. substitute for this rule part of v.38, viz. *prathamapûrvo hakâraç caturtham tasya sasthânam.*

The other Prâtiçâkhyas employ the same designations for the mutes (save that the Vâj. Pr. also calls the nasals *pañcama*, 'fifth'), but without taking the trouble to define them or prescribe their use by a rule.

ऊष्मविसर्जनीयप्रथमद्वितीया अघोषाः ॥ १२ ॥

12. The spirants, *visarjanîya*, and the first and second mutes, are surd.

The Rik Pr. gives (i.2,3) a similar statement; the Ath. Pr. uses the terms "surd" and "sonant" without defining which consonants form each class; the Vâj. Pr. (i.50–53) substitutes for the terms arbitrary formulas.

The physical peculiarity of the surd utterance is defined in the next chapter (rules 5,10).

The commentator illustrates the use of the term by the rule (ix.2) concerning the treatment of *visarjanîya* before a surd.

न हकारः ॥ १३ ॥

13. But not *h*.

"*H* is not styled a surd; this is an exception rendered necessary by the circumstance that *h*, being [by i.9] a spirant, would otherwise be included [by the last rule] in the class of surds," says the comment.

All the phonetic treatises treat *h* as a sonant. For further definition of its character, see rules ii.6,9,46,47, below.

व्यञ्जनशेषो घोषवान् ॥ १४ ॥

14. The rest of the consonants are sonant.

The commentary enters into a rather lengthy defense of the propriety of this rule, which reads literally as follows: "The remainder of the consonants other than the surds is styled sonant. Even though, when the surds have already been stated in rule 12, the sonant quality of the rest, on the principle of 'remainder,' is assured—just as, when it is said, 'of Devadatta and Yajñadatta,

---

12. *ûshmâṇaç ca visarjanîyaç ca prathamadvitîyâç*[1] *câ 'ghoshasaṁjñâ bhavanti. saṁjñâyâḥ prayojanam: aghoshaparas tasya sasthânam ûshmâṇam*[2] (ix.2) *ity âdi*[3].

[1] B. *prathamaç ca dv-*. [2] W. B. omit the last two words of the rule. [3] G. M. om.

13. *na bhavaty aghoshasaṁjño*[1] *hakâraḥ: ûshmatvâd aghoshatve prâpte tadapavâdo 'yam.*

[1] W. *-jñiko*

Devadatta owns no kine,' the conclusion is assured that Yajñadatta is a kine-owner—nevertheless, the indication of the technical term is made in the text-book, for the sake of practical convenience (?). Also, because of the superiority of express mention over inclusion in a remainder. Otherwise—the name of surd is denied to *h* by rule 13, nor is *h* sonant, there being no rule to that effect; and so with the rest of the consonants; the vowels are also in like manner not sonant and not surd—this being the case, when the rule shall be given (ix.8) 'also when followed by a sonant,' the doubt would arise, 'followed by a sonant' means followed by what? Let not this be so: in this view the present rule is undertaken." It is added "In this rule, the distinctive meaning, in the form of objection and replication, is set forth by Mâhisheya." And the rule ix.8, already referred to, is quoted again by way of illustration of the use of the term "sonant."

The Rik Pr. (i.3), after specifying the surd letters, leaves the sonants to be inferred *pâriçeshyât*, 'by the remainder-principle,' as is expressly pointed out in the commentary on the passage (see Regnier's edition, note to rule i.12).

The vowels are not included under the designation *ghoshavant*, 'sonant,' although (as is explained in rule ii.8) formed of the same material with the sonant consonants.

Our treatise does not, like the other Prâtiçâkhyas (R. Pr. i.3; V. Pr. i.54; A. Pr. i.10), define the "first" and "third" mutes as *soshman*, 'aspirated.'

---

14. *aghoshebhyo*[1] *vyañjanaçesho ghoshavatsaṁjño bhavati: yady apy ûshmavisarjanîyaprathameshv*[2] *aghosheshû 'kteshu vyañjanaçeshasya pâriçeshyâd ghoshavattvaṁ siddham: yathâ*[3] *devadattayajñadattayor*[4] *apaçur devadatta ity ukte 'paraḥ paçumân iti siddham: tathâ 'pi çâstre saṁvyavahârârthaṁ*[5] *saṁjñânirdeçaḥ kriyate: pâriçeshyâd api kanṭhokter viçeshât*[6]*: anyathâ na hakâraḥ* (i.13) *iti hakârasyâ 'ghoshasaṁjñâ nishidhyate: nâ 'pi hakâro ghoshavân: vidhyabhâvât: tathâi 'va vyañjanaçeshaḥ: svarâ api tathâ*[7] *na ghoshavanto nâ 'py aghoshâḥ: tathâ sati ghoshavatparaç ca* (ix.8) *iti yatra*[8] *vakshyati tatra*[9] *saṁdehaḥ syât: ghoshavatparo nâma kimpara iti: tan mâ bhûd itî 'daṁ sûtram*[10] *ârabhyate*[11].

vyañjanarûpaḥ çesho vyañjanaçeshaḥ[12].

atra sûtre codyaparihârarûpa[13] *esha viçesho mâhisheyabhâshitaḥ.*

saṁjñâyâḥ prayojanam: ghoshavatparaç ca (ix.8) *ity âdi.*

[1] G. M. ins. *'nyo.* [2] G. M. *ûshmavisarjaniye 'ty.* [3] B. ins. *ca.* [4] W. *-dattaitiyor* [5] W. *saṁhâr-.* [6] G. M. *viçeshatvât.* [7] G. M. om. [8] G. M. *yatrayatra.* [9] G. M. *tatratatra.* [10] B. *çâstram.* [11] G. M. repeat the rule itself here. [12] W. om.; B. adds *yaḥ çeshaḥ.* [13] G. M. om. *rûpa.*

आप्रावोपाभ्यधिप्रतिपरिविनीत्युपसर्गाः ॥ १५ ॥

15. *Â, pra, ava, upa, abhi, adhi, prati, pari, vi, ni*—these are prepositions.

These ten words are but half the number which are reckoned as prepositions by the Rik and Vâj. Prâtiçâkhyas (R. Pr. xii.6; V. Pr. vi.24) and by Pâṇini (see the *gaṇa prâdayaḥ*). The commentator notes the discordance with Pâṇini, and inquires why the maker of this rule presumingly cuts short the list of prepositions with the word *iti* in it. His reply is, that only so many are recognized by the Yajur-Veda. Another objection which he raises and removes, arriving at the comfortable conclusion "therefore there is no discordance whatever," I do not see the point of. The discordance is a real one, and difficult to explain. The term preposition (*upasarga*) is used in three of the rules of the treatise, viz. vi.4 (which is the cited instance in the commentary), x.9, and xiv.8: for the bearing of the restriction in number, see the notes on those rules.

वर्णः कारोत्तरो वर्णाख्या ॥ १६ ॥

16. A sound followed by *kâra* is the name of that sound.

That is, for example, *akâra* is the name of *a*, *ekâra* of *e*, and so on. The Vâj. Pr. (i.37) is the only other treatise which takes the trouble to prescribe this usage, common to them all. Our own refers to it also in a later rule (xxii.4). The word *kâra* means 'making, producing.' It is in the rules of the Prâtiçâkhya added not only to simple alphabetic sounds (*varṇa*) as their names, but also to syllables like *aḥ* and *an* (see below, rules 23, 53), and the

15. ---- *ity ete çabdâ upasargasaṁjñâ bhavanti. nanu praparâpasamanvavanirdurvyâṅ ityâdi pâṇinîyâ viçeshena bhaṇanti*[1]*: katham atra sûtrakṛtâ nirargalam upasargâ itiçabdena saṁkucitâ ucyante. yajurvedavishaya etâvanta eve 'ti mantavyam. tarhi praparâpasam*[2] *iti samuccaye viçeshapâṭhaḥ*[3] *katham upalabhyate*[4]*. itiparatvavidhâne tasya tâtparyaṁ na tû 'pasargasaṁjñâvidhâne viçeshapâṭhaḥ*[5]*: tasmân na kenacid virodhaḥ. saṁjñâyâḥ prayojanam: upasarganishpûrvo 'nudâtte pade* (vi.4). *itiçabdaḥ prakâravâcî.*

[1] W. B. and G.p.m. *bhavanti.* [2] B. *prâpaparâvasaṁ;* G. M. *prâpasam.* [3] G. M. *viçeshaḥ;* W. *viçeshaṁp-.* [4] B. *-lakshyate.* [5] W. B. *viçeshaḥ p-.*

16. *kârottaro varṇo varṇasyâ "khyâ bhavati. yathâ: athâi 'kârekârâv* (iv.8) *iti.*[1] *kâraçabda uttaro yasmâd asâu kârottaraḥ.*

[1] G. M. *ity âdi.*

commentator very frequently uses it to make names for brief words, like *ca*.

Rule iv.8, respecting *e* and *î*, is the chosen illustration of the combination here taught.

अकारव्यवेतो व्यञ्जनानाम् ॥ १७ ॥

17. But with an *a* interposed, in the case of the consonants.

That is, the name of *k*, for instance, is (*k-a-kâra*) *kakâra*. Compare the equivalent rule, Vâj. Pr. i.38.

The commentator cites rule v.22, respecting the conversion of *t* to *c*.

न विसर्जनीयजिह्वामूलीयोपध्मानीयानुस्वारनासिक्यानाम् ॥ १८ ॥

18. Not of *visarjanîya*, *jihvâmûlîya*, *upadhmânîya*, *anusvâra*, and the *nâsikyas*.

The term *nâsikya* designates here, of course, the nasal figments taught in rules xxi. 12–14. All these indistinct, hardly articulate, sounds must be spoken of by their descriptive titles, not by any name founded upon their form. The commentator explains that the appending of *kâra* to the sounds here specified—which would otherwise be regular, since they come under the category of *varṇa*, 'alphabetic elements'—is annulled by the rule: adding as a reason, that they are nowhere met with thus treated. He then

---

17. *akâravyavahito*[1] *varṇaḥ kâraçabdottaro vyañjanânâm âkhyâ bhavati. yathâ*[2]*: takâraç cakâram* (v.22) *ity âdi. akâreṇa vyavahito*[3] *'kâravyavetaḥ.*

[1] W. *-vyaveto.* [2] W. B. put this word after the cited rule. [3] G. M. *vyaveto.*

18. *visarjanîyâdînâṁ varṇatvâviçeshât kârottaratvam prâptam anena nivartyate: na khalu visarjanîyâdînâṁ kârottaratâ bhavati: kutaḥ: sarvatra*[1] *prayogânupalambhât. nanu yathâ varṇaḥ kârottaro varṇâkhyâ* (i.16) *iti varṇaçabdavâcyasyâi 'va kârottaratvaṁ nakâro ṇakâram* (vii.1 or xiii.6) *ity âdi: na tu vâcakasyâi 'va*[2]*: anyathâ varṇakâra iti syât: tadvad*[3] *visarjanîyâdînâm*[4] *atrâ 'pi vâcyagrahaṇam eva yuktam: nâ 'nyathâ: tathâ sati vâcakaparatayâ vararucyâdiviracitam*[5] *udâharaṇam avasâne ravisarjanîya* (xiv.15) *ity âdy aruciram: iti cet: mâi 'vaṁ maṅsthâḥ: vâcyânâm*[6] *kevalânâm aprayogâd atra vâcyavâcakayor abhedavivakshayâ sûtrasaraṇir ity udâharaṇaga manikâ.*[7]

[1] G. M. ins. *tatha.* [2] G. M. om. *eva.* [3] W. *tad.* [4] G. M. ins. *ity.* [5] W. B. *vararucâd-*; G. M. *vâraruсâd-*. [6] W. B. *vâcyâdinâṁ.* [7] W. *-ṇaṁ gam-*.

goes on to raise and refute a very subtile and hair-splitting objection. In rule 16, he says, *kâra* is prescribed to be added not to the vocable (*vâcaka*) *varṇa*, 'sound,' itself, but only to the thing designated (*vâcya*) by that vocable; so likewise in this rule it is proper to understand by *visarjanîya* etc. the things designated by those words, and nothing else (and hence, the rule must not be interpreted as implying that *visarjanîya* and the other names given are, in default of those formed with *kâra*, the accepted designations for the sounds in question). This being the case, the illustration given under the rule by Vararuci and others—namely, rule xiv.15, speaking of *r* and "*visarjanîya*" as not liable to duplication—is an unsuitable one. Such is the objection. The reply is: you must not think so; since the sounds designated by the terms in the rule are actually nowhere employed by themselves (as designations), the rule simply intends to include designation and thing designated in one expression; and the quoted example is proper enough.

रेफस्तु रस्य ॥ १९ ॥

19. Of *r*, however, *epha* forms the name.

That is to say, the technical designation of *r* is *repha*; *ra* being also admitted, by rule 21, below: *rakâra* is not found anywhere in the Hindu grammatical literature. This peculiarity of treatment of *r*, as compared with the other consonants, is to be paralleled with the way in which it is written in consonant groups, almost as if a vowel.

The Vâj. Pr. has an equivalent rule (i.40).

The word *tu*, 'however,' in this rule, according to the commentator, is meant to deny the application to *r* of both the rules 16 and 17. Some, he says, hold that it denies only rule 17, or the insertion of *a* between *r* and the appended *kâra*: but this is wrong; for it would imply that the name of *r* was made sometimes by appending *kâra* and sometimes by appending *epha*, just as an alternation is in fact allowed by rule 21 below between *ra* and *repha*, and exemplified by rules vii.11 and xxi.15; while no

---

19. *rasya tv ephaçabda*[1] *âkhyâ bhavati. yathâ: rephoshmaparaḥ*[2] (xiii.2) *iti. rephasya vyañjanatvâviçeshât prâptaṁ kârottaratvam akâravyavetatvaṁ ca: tad ubhayaṁ tuçabdo nivârayati. anye tv anyathâ manyante: akâravyavetatvam eve 'ti: tad asâdhu: tathâ sati kadâcid ephottaratâ*[3] *kadâcit kârottaratâ ce 'ti vikalpaḥ syât: yathâ 'kâro vyañjanânâm* (i.21) *iti vidhânâd vikalpaḥ: tathâ hi*[4] *rephoshmasaṁyoge rephasvarabhaktiḥ*[5] (xxi.15)*: rashaḥpûrvo havanî* (vii.11) *ity âdi: na tv evaṁ kârottaratvam api vikalpena*[6] *svîkṛtaṁ*[7] *kutracit: tasmâd asmadukta eva yuktas tuçabdârthaḥ.*

[1] G. M. *reph-*; and M. reads *rephas* in the rule itself. [2] W. *-shmaçabda.* [3] B. *rephaksharatâ*; W. *reph-*. [4] W. B. *'pi.* [5] W. B. om. [6] G. M. *naka.* [7] G. M. *-taḥ.*

instance of a name formed with *kâra* is anywhere to be met with. This is a very easy demolition of a very insignificant man of straw.

ह्रस्वो वर्णोत्तरस्त्रयाणाम् ॥ २० ॥

20. The short vowel, with *varṇa* after it, is the name of the three vowels.

The "three vowels" referred to are the three quantities—short, long, and protracted—of the vowels *a*, *i*, *u*, respectively; *varṇa*, in this case, indicating only the 'color,' or phonetic complexion, of the vowel, without regard to its length. The Ath. Pr. has the same usage of this term, but without defining it by rule. As our treatise acknowledged no protracted *ṛ*, and neither a long nor a protracted *ḷ*, it does not admit the compounds *ṛvarṇa* and *ḷvarṇa:* of the other three it frequently avails itself. The instance selected by the commentator is rule x.4, which directs the combination of *a* with a following *i*, *î*, *î3* into *e*.

अकारो व्यञ्जनानाम् ॥ २१ ॥

21. An *a* forms the names of consonants.

This rule allows us to call a consonant not only, as prescribed in rules 16 and 17 above, by a name formed by adding *kâra* with *a* interposed, but also by one formed with *a* alone. The commentator's example is rule v.22, where *t* and *c* are referred to as *takâra*, *cakâra*, and *ç*, *c* again, and *ch*, as *ça*, *ca*, and *cha*. If something merely additional to the *kâra*, instead of alternative with it, were intended in the rule, we are told, rule 17 would be made meaningless. But, says an objector, why use *kâra* at all for the purpose, when even along with it the *a* has to be brought into requisition? let this alone furnish the name. The reasonableness of the objection is conceded, but the commentator alleges as sufficient justification of the practice followed, that it is in accordance with that of the Çikshâ and other text-books.

He continues: others assert that the *a* added to a consonant indicates (not that consonant pure and simple, but) a syllable composed of the consonant and any following vowel; as for instance in rule ix.3, "*visarjanîya* followed by *ksha* is not assimilated;" where the examples are *manaḥ ksheme* (v.2.1[7]), *ghanâghanaḥ kshobhaṇaḥ* (iv.6.4[1]: so all the MSS., both here and under ix.3; my MS. of the Sanhitâ reads *kshobhaṇiḥ*), and *ukthaçâsaḥ kshâma* (ii.6:12[4]). This is unsound; for then we should have to read *ishe ṭvâ* (for *ishe tvâ*, i.1.1 et al.), by the rule vii.13, "after *vâghâ* and *sha*, *t* becomes *ṭ*;" which is wrong. Moreover, in the rule (xii.

---

20. *varṇottaro hrasvo* [1] *hrasvadîrghaplutânâm âkhyâ bhavati. yathâ: ivarṇapara ekâram* (x.4) *ity âdi. varṇaçabda uttaro yasmâd asâu varṇottaraḥ.*

[1] G. M. ins. *trayâṇâṁ.*

4) "*ya, va, na, ha*, when followed by vowels," the final specification would be useless, because already implied in the names given to the letters. Hence the opinion referred to is wrong, and the name taught by the rule indicates the consonant alone.

As for the actual usage of the treatise, it is somewhat equally divided between the two modes of designation of the consonants: names formed with *a* alone occur nearly sixty times; with *akâra*, nearly eighty times. This is exclusive of *r*, which is called *ra* four times, *repha* fifteen times.

Compare rule i.39 of the Vâj. Pr.

ग्रहणस्य च ॥ २२ ॥

22. As also, of a cited word.

The term *grahaṇa* is used in only two other rules of the Prâtiçâkhya (i.24,50), but occurs in the commentary times innumerable, in the sense of 'citation, word taken or extracted from the Sanhitâ to be made the subject of some prescription' (root *grah*, 'seize, take'). The commentator, however, gives it an artificial and false etymology: it denotes, he says, either a word respecting which something is to be enjoined (*lakshya*), or one which is the cause (*nimitta*) of an effect produced in some other word. The former is called *grahaṇa* because it is "seized" (i. e. "affected"); the latter, because something is "seized" or "affected" by it. It is, he continues, a part of a word, a theme or base. The *ca*, 'also,' of the rule brings forward, or indicates the continued implication of, the *a* of the preceding rule. The meaning is, then, that *a* forms the name of a citation, a theme, in whatever situation it may occur.

---

21. *vyañjanânâm akâra âkhyâ bhavati. yathâ: takâraç cakâran*[1] *çacachaparaḥ* (v.22) *ity adi. kâraçabdottaratvam idaṁ ca vikalpyate: samuccaye tv akâravyaveto vyañjanânâm* (i. 17) *iti vyarthaṁ syât. nanu tarhi kârottaratâ*[2] *kimarthâ*[3]*: tadânîm api svarûpeṇâ*[4] *'kâralâbhât: sa evâ "khyâ bhavatu. satyam: çikshâdiçâstraprasiddhasaṁketânusâreṇe*[5] *'ti parihâraḥ. apare tu saṁgirante: akâraḥ sarvasvarântasya vyañjanasya grâhaka iti: yathâ*[6]*: man-....: ghan-....: ukth-....: ity âdi na kshaparaḥ* (ix.3) *iti nishedhasyo 'dâharaṇaṁ syâd iti. tad asâram: kutaḥ*[7]*: vâghâshapûrvas tash ṭam* (vii.13) *iti shapûrvatvât*[8] *takârasya ṭatve kṛte ish-.... iti syât: tac câ 'nishṭam: kiṁ ca: yavanahasvarapareshv*[9] (xii.4) *iti atra svaraparaçabdo vyarthaḥ syât: bhavanmate sarvasvarântasya*[10] *svîkâraniyamât: tasmâd anupapannam eva*[11] *tan matam manmahe: kiṁ tu varṇamâtrasyâ "khyâ.*

[1] W. B. omit these first two words of the rule. [2] G. M. *-tvaṁ.* [3] G. M. *-tham.* [4] G. M. *avyavâyarû-.* [5] G. M. *-sârâya.* [6] W. om. [7] G. M. om. [8] G. M. *shatvapû.* [9] W. *yavanahaparasvar-.* [10] G. M. *-ntamâtrasya.* [11] G. M. *evâi.*

That is to say, if a word be cited in the text of a rule by its theme-ending *a*, all its cases or other derivative forms are to be regarded as equally had in view by the rule. Reference is twice made to this principle hereafter by the commentator (under rules vi.13 and x.14), to justify such inclusions. The latter of the cases he here brings up, as example of a *nimitta*, or citation of an affecting cause; the cited word is *oshṭha*, which is declared to occasion the loss of a preceding *a* or *â:* the only two instances of this combination which the Sanhitâ contains are quoted in illustration, viz. *svâh" oshṭhâbhyâm* (vii.3.16[1]), and *upayâmam adhareṇ' oshṭhena* (v.7.12). As example of a *lakshya*, or citation of a word to be determined by rule, he quotes the end of rule xvi.26, with its illustrative citations, *kiñçilaç caturthaḥ* (v.5.9[2]), and *kiñçilâya' cakshayaṇâya ca* (iv.5.9[1]). This latter example is not very well chosen, as the case is a somewhat difficult and anomalous one (see the note on xvi.26).

This rule, like some of those that follow, is of very small value, since final *a* is not the necessary sign of a cited theme in which other cases are included; and, on the other hand, parts of words not ending in *a* are often cited "for the sake of the inclusion of many words" (*bahûpâdânârtham*).

अःकार आगमविकारिलोपिनाम् ॥ २३ ॥

23. *Aḥ* makes the name of an increment, or of an element suffering alteration or elision.

Here, again, is a precept hardly called for, as the construction and connection of each rule shows in what way any nominative it contains is to be understood, without such an explanation as this, which applies only to a part of the cases, and is unable to teach us which of the three possibilities it contemplates is the actuality in any given case. Moreover, it is faultily expressed, and the commentator is obliged to explain that *aḥ* here stands for the ending of the nominative case, in the dual and plural as well as the singular. He quotes in illustration five rules: xiv.5 exemplifies a singular increment; vii.1, a singular altered element; v.19, a singular elision; v.25, two-fold altered elements; xxi.12, plural increments.

---

22. [1]*lakshyaṁ nimittaṁ ca grahaṇam ity ucyate: gṛhyata*[2] *iti grahaṇam: gṛhyata anene 'ti nimittam api grahaṇam: padâikadeçaḥ prâtipadikam iti yâvat: cakâraḥ pûrvasûtroktam akâram âkarshati: grahaṇasya prâtipadikasya sarvâvasthasyâ 'kâra' âkhyâ bhavati. yathâ: kiñçilakiñçilâ* (xvi.26) *iti parakiñçilaçabdo lakshyam udâharaṇam: yathâ: kiñç- cat-....*[3]*: kiñç- caksh-....: oshṭhevaḥparo lupyate* (x.14) *iti tu*[4] *nimittam: yathâ: svâ-....: upay-....*

(1) W. inserts this passage out of place, between rule 19 and its commentary [2] G. *grahaṇyata.* [3] G. M. omit this example. [4] G. M. om.

Rule 28, below, is very intimately connected with this, and the insertion of rules 25–27 between is quite unaccountable.

Rik. Pr. i.14 includes the second of the three specifications here made, along with rule 28.

ग्रहणं वा ॥ २४ ॥

24. Or the simple citation.

The commentator says: "Of these—namely the increment etc.—there is in some cases, alternatively, citation; the meaning is, without any *aḥ*." And he goes on to quote three rules, in which increment (xvi.29), alteration (vii.3), and elision (v.15) are taught otherwise than as prescribed in the preceding rule—which is not, however, thus amended into acceptableness.

ग्रासन्नं संदेहे ॥ २५ ॥

25. In case of doubt, citation is made of the next.

This rule, occurring where it does, appears to have been interpolated by an afterthought, attaching itself to the word *grahaṇam*, 'citation,' of the preceding rule, without regard to the connection in which that word is used. The meaning is, that when the mere citation of a word from the Sanhitâ would leave a doubt as to which occurrence of the word is intended, some part of the context, a word or part of a word, is cited along with it. But the commentator's first example and its exposition are quite peculiar. He quotes *svayamâtṛṇṇâṁ ca vikarṇîm co 'ttame* (v.3.7[3]), and remarks: "There being a doubt, owing to the occurrence of two *ca*'s in this passage, which of them is to be taken to give the *pragraha*-character [to *uttame*], the one next to the proper subject of the rule [*kâryabhâj*, 'the word undergoing the prescribed

23. *âgamâdînâm aṅkâra âkhyâ bhavati: aṅkâra iti prathamâvibhakter upalakshaṇam. âgamasya yathâ: [1]dvitîyacaturthayos tu vyañjanottarayoḥ pûrvaḥ* (xiv.5)*: vikâriṇo yathâ[1]: atha nakâro ṇakâram* (vii.1)*: lopino yathâ: tishṭhantyekayâ sapûrvaḥ* (v.19)*: ity ekavacanâni: laparâu lakâram* (v.25)*: iti dvivacanam: ânupûrvyân nâsikyâḥ* (xxi.12)*: iti bahuvacanam. âgamaç ca vikârî ca lopî câ "gamavikârilopinaḥ: teshâm.*

(1) B. om.

24. *teshâm âgamâdînâṁ kvacid grahaṇaṁ vâ bhavati: aṅkâreṇa vinâ 'pî 'ti[1] tâtparyam. âgamasya yathâ: âdirañhatir* (xvi.29) *ity âdi: vikâriṇo yathâ: hanyâdupyamânaṁ ca* (vii.3) *ity âdi: lopino yathâ: eshasasya* (v.15) *ity âdi.*

[1] G. M. om. *iti.*

effect'] is to be assumed, in the rule reading *co 'ttame* [iv.11]!" He seems to suppose that the "doubt" referred to in the rule concerns the point, which of the two preceding *ca*'s is joined with *uttame* in the precept that establishes the latter's character as a *pragraha* word, and that we need authority for understanding that the latter of the two is taken. This is little less than silly. His other example is taken from rule iv.15, where *â pṛshatî* is made *pragraha*, the *â* being the final letter of the preceding word *yuñjâ* (*yuñjâ pṛshatî*, iv.6.9[4]).

Under a later rule (iv.23) this principle is twice referred to, and very curiously and artificially applied. See the note to that rule.

अनेकस्यापि ॥ २६ ॥

26. Even of more than one.

The genitive in this rule is grammatically inconsistent with the accusative of the one preceding, which I had to translate inaccurately in order to make the connection evident. The commentator declares the "even" (*api*) here to continue in force the word *saṁdehe*, 'in case of doubt,' which is hardly to be approved. He interprets: "When there is ambiguity, citation is made of more than one word or sound," and quotes *tishṭhanty ekayâ* (v.19) and *evo 'ttare* (iv.11) as examples. But in these we have only one additional word cited, though more than one additional letter; so that both are properly examples under the preceding rule. There is no case, I believe, where more than one word requires to be cited along with that at which the rule aims; of a part of a word containing more than one letter we have instances in vi.2,5 etc. I see no good reason, however, why these should not be regarded as authorized by the preceding rule, and this one, accordingly, omitted as superfluous.

प्रथमो वर्गोत्तरो वर्गाख्या ॥ २७ ॥

27. A first mute, followed by the word "series," is the name of the series.

---

25. *saṁdehe saty*[1] *âsannaṁ* [2]*varṇam padaṁ*[2] *vâ gṛhṇîyât: svay-.... ity atra cakâradvayasambhavât pragrahanimittatvena katarasyo 'pâdânaṁ kartavyaṁ iti saṁdehe yad*[3] *âsannaṁ kâryabhâjas tad eva svîkartavyaṁ co 'ttame* (iv.11) *iti sûtre*[4]. *varṇasya yathâ: â pṛshatî* (iv.15) *ity âdi.*

[1] W. om. [(2)] G. M. *padaṁ varṇaṁ.* [3] G. M. *yadi.* [4] W. B. *sarvatra.*

26. *saṁdeha anekasya padasya varṇasya vâ grahaṇam bhavati: apiçabdaḥ saṁdeha ity anvâdiçati*[1]. *yathâ*[2]*: tishṭhanty ekayâ sapûrvaḥ* (v.19)*: evo 'ttare* (iv.11) *ity âdi.*

[1] G. M. *âdiçati.* [2] W. B. om.

The commentator's example is rule xiv.20, "the *ṭ*-series, followed by the *t*-series;" that is to say, a lingual mute followed by a dental. Compare Vâj. Pr. i.64.

अं विकारस्य ॥ २८ ॥

28. *Am* makes the name of a product of alteration.

This is the correlative rule to 23, above, from which it has become strangely separated. The commentator explains, as before, that *am* stands here as representative of the accusative case in any number; but the two examples he gives (v.38 and vii.1) are both of them such as the rule might strictly apply to without any such extension of its meaning.

पूर्वं इति पूर्वः ॥ २९ ॥

29. By preceding is meant preceding.

A rule expressed in the form of an identical proposition cannot be claimed to cast much light of itself, but demands a comment as its essential part. Our commentator explains: "Whatever word is pointed out by the qualification 'preceding,' that word is to be understood as designated by its own form in that situation alone; but not, on account of identity of form, another word standing in a different situation. Thus, by the rules (iv.12,13) '*dyâvâpṛthivî* is *pragraha;* also the preceding word,' the word *yâvatî* is made a *pragraha* in the passage *yâvatî dyâvâpṛthivî mahitvâ* (iii.2.6[1]); but it is not therefore *pragraha* in the passage *yâvatî vâi pṛthivî* (v.2.3[1])."

पर इत्युत्तरः ॥ ३० ॥

30. By following is meant succeeding.

---

27. *vargaçabdottaraḥ prathamaḥ svavargasyâ*[1] *'"khyâ bhavati: ṭavargaç ca tavargaparaḥ* (xiv.20) *iti. vargaçabda uttaro yasmâd asâu vargottaraḥ.*

[1] W. om. *sva.*

28. *am iti çabdo vikârasyâ '"khyâ bhavati: am iti dvitîyâvibhakter upalakshaṇam. yathâ: prathamapûrvo hakâraç caturtham* (v.38)*: atha nakâro ṇakâram* (vii.1).

29. *yaḥ pûrvaçabdena nirdishṭaḥ*[1] *sa tatrâi 'va svena rûpeṇo 'palakshito jñâtavyaḥ: na tu rûpasâmânyâd anyo bhinnadeçasthaḥ. yathâ*[2]*: dyâvâpṛthivî: pûrvaç ca* (iv.12,13) *iti*[3] *pragraho bhavatî*[4] *'ti vakshyati: pûrvatvâd yâv-.... iti yâvatîçabdaḥ pragrahaḥ: yâv-.... iti tu*[5] *na syât pragrahaḥ.*

[1] G M. *viçishyate.* [2] W. om. [3] G. M. om. [4] G. M. *-vishyati.* [5] G. M. *atra.*

This is the counterpart of the preceding rule, and is explained by the commentator in corresponding terms. His illustration is taken from rules iv.49,50, where *dve* and the word following it are declared *pragraha*. In the passage, then, *dve jâye vindate* (vi.6.4[3]), *jâye* is *pragraha*, but not in the passage *yonir asi jâya e 'hi* (i.7.9[1]: G. M. omit *e 'hi*).

The rule is only once referred to hereafter, namely under iv.52; and there for a purpose which it was not intended to answer.

ऋकारऌकारौ ह्रस्वौ ॥ ३१ ॥

31. *Ṛ* and *ḷ* are short.

As examples of short *ṛ* and *ḷ*, the commentator cites *ṛtavo vâi* (vii.2.6[1]), and *akḷptasya kḷptyâi* (v.4.8[5]).

अकारश्च ॥ ३२ ॥

32. Also *a*.

"Also" (*ca*), says the commentator, brings forward the implication of "short" from the preceding rule. His example of short *a* is *ayam puraḥ* (iv.3.2[1] or 4.3[1]).

तेन च समानकालस्वरः ॥ ३३ ॥

33. Also any vowel having the same quantity with the latter.

Here again, the "also" continues the implication of the predicate of rule 31, we are told. The only vowels contemplated by the rule, further, are *i* and *u*, since there is an absence of the attribute of like quantity with *a* in the diphthongs. As examples from the Sanhitâ are quoted *ishe tvâ* (i.1.1 et al.), *upaprayanto adhvaram* (i.5.5[1] or 7[1]: W. B. omit *adhvaram*), and *atrâ "ha tad urugâyasya* (i.3.6[2]: but see the various readings below).' The commentator then raises the objection (without introducing it, as usual,

---

30. *yaḥ para ity anena viçishyate so 'pi tatrâi 'va svena rûpeṇa pratyetavyaḥ. yathâ: dve: paraç ca* (iv.49,50) *iti*[1] *pragraho bhavatî 'ti vakshyati: paratvâd dve jâ-.... ity atra jâye iti*[2] *pragrahaḥ:* [3]*yo-.... ity atra*[4] *na pragrahaḥ*[3].

[1] G. M. om. [2] G. M. ins. *çabdaḥ*. [(3)] B. om. [4] G. M. ins. *tu*.

31. *ṛkâraç ca ḷkâraç ca hrasvasaṁjñâu bhavataḥ. yathâ*[1]: *ṛt-....: ak-.....*

[1] W. B. om.

32. *akâraç ca hrasvasaṁjño bhavati: cakâro hrasvatvam*[1] *anvâdiçati. yathâ: ay-.... iti.*

[1] G. M. *-svam.*

with *nanu*), that the matter of tne three rules should have been put into this form: "*A* is short: also any vowel having like quantity with it;" because, as actually stated, they are liable to the reproach of saying the same thing over twice (since *ṛ* and *ḷ* are of the same quantity as *a*, and are therefore included in the prescription of the present rule). But he replies that the statement is right in its present shape; for *r* and *l* inhere in *ṛ* and *ḷ;* and one might therefore suppose that, being letters of more than one articulating position, they suffered an extension of quantity, and were not short: hence the special rule concerning them. The treatise, as was noticed above (under i.2), nowhere describes the formation of *ṛ* and *ḷ*, though it excludes them from the category of simple vowels.

The rule of the Vâj. Pr. (i.55) is nearly the same with this.

अनुस्वारश्च ॥ ३४ ॥

34. Also *anusvâra.*

The implication being the same as in the preceding rules, *anusvâra* is here defined as having the quantity of a short vowel. The commentator explains the occasion for the rule as follows: rule xxi.6, which teaches that *anusvâra* and *svarabhakti* are to be attached to the preceding vowel in syllabication, implies the consonantal character of the former; whence, by rule 37, below, it would have the quantity of a half-mora, and its true quantity of a mora requires special definition.

The Vâj. Pr. (iv.147,148) allows *anusvâra* to make with a preceding vowel, either long or short, two moras, oddly enough distributing the time between the two elements, vowel and nasal, in such a way that the latter has a mora and a half after a short vowel, the vowel being itself shortened to a half-mora, while after a long vowel the nasal is itself cut down to a half-mora, and a mora and a half are assigned to the vowel—a highly artificial ar-

---

33. *tenâ 'kâreṇa yas tulyakâlaḥ svaraḥ sa ca hrasvo bhavati: atrâ*[1] *'pi cakâro hrasvâdeçakaḥ*[2]*: ikâra ukâraç ce*[3] *'ty arthaḥ: saṁdhyaksharâṇâṁ samânakâlatvâbhâvât*[4]. *yathâ*[5]*: ish-....: up-....: 'atr-....*[6] *akâro hrasvas tena ca samânakâlasvara ity ârabdhavyam: ṛkâralkârâu hrasvâv iti tu*[7] *nâ "rabdhavyam: evam ârabhyamâṇe punaruktatayâ gâuravam bhaved iti. ucyate: ârabdhavyam evâi 'tat: kutaḥ: ṛkâralkârayor antarâ*[8] *rephalakârâu staḥ: tattatsthânatvâd*[9] *anayoḥ kâlavyabhicâraḥ syât: hrasvatvaṁ na*[10] *gamyeta*[11]*: tan mâ bhûd ity evam ârabhyate: ṛkâralkârâv* [12] *iti.*

[1] G. M. *tatrâ.* [2] G. M. *hrasvatvâdeçakaḥ samânakâla svara iti.* [3] G. M om. [4] G. M. *-kâlasvaratvâ-.* [5] W. om. [6] B. *atrâ "ha* only; G. M. *atra hy;* both as if the introduction to what follows. [7] G. M. om. [8] G. M. *anantare.* [9] G. M. *tatsth-.* [10] B. om. [11] G. M. *avagamyate.* [12] G. M. ins. *hrasvâu:*

rangement. The Rik Pr. gives no special statement respecting the quantity of the nasal element, but leaves it to be included among the other consonants, which have half a mora of time each.

All the "short" elements being now enumerated, the commentator quotes, as example of the employment of the term "short," rule iii.1. As example of *anusvâra*, he quotes *tâñ haste* (vi.1.3[7]).

द्विस्तावान्दीर्घः ॥ ३५ ॥

35. An element of twice that quantity is long.

The literal meaning of this rule is, says the commentator, that one of the before-mentioned short vowels, when doubled, is long: but its virtual intent is that a vowel having twice the quantity of a short is long. I have translated in accordance with the latter interpretation. As example of the use of the term "long" is quoted rule x.2, respecting the coalescence of two similar simple vowels into the corresponding long vowel.

त्रिः प्लुतः ॥ ३६ ॥

36. An element of three times that quantity is protracted.

The commentator explains the virtual meaning of this rule in the same manner as that of the preceding, and quotes in illustra-

---

34. *bhavaty anusvâraç ca*[1] *hrasvasaṁjñaḥ. yathâ: tâñ*..... *cakâro hrasvânvâkarshakaḥ*[2]*: anusvâraḥ svarabhaktiç ca* (xxi.6) *iti svarapratyañgatvavidhânâd*[3] *anusvârasya vyañjanatvam: tathâ sati hrasvârdhakâlaṁ vyañjanam* (i.37) *ity atrâ*[4] *'rdhamâtratvam*[5] *prâptam*[6]*: tan mâ bhûd iti hrasvatvaṁ vidhîyate. hrasvasaṁjñâyâḥ prayojanam: vibhâge hrasvaṁ vyañjanaparaḥ* (iii.1) *iti.*

[1] G. M. *api.* [2] G. M. *hrasvâk-.* [3] MSS. *svaraṁ pr-;* W. *-ṅgavidh-.* [4] G. M. om. [5] G. M. *-tve.* [6] G M. *-te.*

35. *tâvân iti prakṛto hrasva ucyate: dvir iti dvirûpaḥ*[1]*: tâvân hrasvo dîrghasaṁjño bhavatî*[2] *'ti sûtrayojanâ: tâtparyaṁ tu hrasvadviguṇakâlaḥ*[3]*. svaro dîrghasaṁjño bhavatî 'ti.*[4] *saṁjñâyâḥ prayojanam: dîrghañ samânâkshare savarṇapare* (x.2) *ity âdi.*

[1] G. M. *-pam.* [2] W. inserts here, out of place, *saṁjñâyâh prayojanam.* [3] B. *-la;* W. om. *laḥ.* [4] W. om. *iti.*

36. *atrâ 'pi*[1] *hrasvo 'nuvartate sâṁnidhyât: trir iti trirûpaḥ*[2]*: trirûpo hrasvaḥ plutasaṁjño bhavatî 'ti: *[3]*tâtparyaṁ tv atrâ 'pi brûmaḥ: hrasvatriguṇakâlaḥ svaraḥ plutasaṁjño bhavatî*[3]*. saṁjñâyâḥ prayojanam: na plutapragrahâv* (x.24) *iti.*

[1] G. M. ins. *sa.* [2] G. M. om. (3) G. M. om.

tion of the term "protracted" rule x.24, which directs that a protracted and a *pragraha* vowel are not liable to combination.

All the treatises agree closely in their definitions of vowel quantity; see Ath. Pr. i.59–62, and the notes upon those rules.

ह्रस्वार्धकालं व्यञ्जनम् ॥ ३७ ॥

37. A consonant has half the quantity of a short vowel.

This, the comment reminds us, is a rule defining the length of a consonant, not one giving the meaning of the term consonant. For, if it were the latter, the word "time" in rule xvii.5, which speaks of "the time of a consonant," would be open to the charge of redundancy. We hardly need so trifling and technical a proof of a thing so obvious. As example of a consonant, the word *vâk* (e. g. i.3.9[1]: but G. M. read instead *vâ*) is given us.

Of the other treatises, the Ath. Pr. (i.60) alone differs from this by giving to a consonant a whole mora as its quantity.

उच्चैरुदात्तः ॥ ३८ ॥

38. A syllable uttered in a high tone is acute.

The commentator enters into no explanation of the meaning of the definition of the acute tone or accent here given, but simply refers us to a later rule (xxii.9), where the action of the organs in producing the higher tone is more particularly described. He adds as example of an acute vowel *sá idhânáḥ* (iv.4.4[5]: but all the MSS. save W. read *sá iti*), and quotes rule xiv.29 as exemplifying the use of the term *udâtta*, 'acute' (literally 'elevated'). I have explained in the note to Ath. Pr. i.14–16 why I prefer, instead of transferring the terms *udâtta*, *anudâtta*, and *svarita*, to translate them by 'acute,' 'grave,' and 'circumflex,' respectively.

नीचैरनुदात्तः ॥ ३९ ॥

39. In a low tone, grave.

---

37. *vyañjanaṁ hrasvârdhakâlam bhavati: na tu vyañjanam iti saṁjñâ: anyathâ*[1] *vyañjanakâlaç ca svarasyâ 'trâ 'dhikaḥ*[2] (xvii.5) *iti.*[3] *kâlaçabdasya pâunaruktyâpatteḥ. yathâ: vâk. hrasvasyâ 'rdho*[4] *hrasvârdhaḥ*[4]*:* [5]*hrasvârdhakâlaḥ*[6] *parimâṇaṁ yasya*[5] *tat tatho 'ktam.*

[1] G. M. om. [2] G. M. omit the last two words of the rule. [3] G. M. ins. *atra*. [4] G. M. *-dhaṁ*. [(5)] G. M. *hrasvârdhaṁ kâlaḥ parimâṇakâlo yasya*—a good and consistent reading; B. is corrupt. [6] W. *-laṁ*.

38. *âyâmo dâruṇyam* (xxii.9) *iti lakshaṇalakshitaḥ*[1] *svara udâtta ucyate. yathâ: sá..... saṁjñâyâḥ prayojanam: udâttât paro 'nudâttaḥ svaritam* (xiv.29) *iti.*[2]

[1] G. M. *-ta.* [2] G. M. *ity âdi.*

We are again referred to the rule in one of the last chapters (xxii.10) which defines the action of the organs in producing the lower tone. The example for the accent is *avadatâm* (i.7.2[2]: but G. M. read *avadâtâm*), of which, in *pada*-text, all the syllables are grave; that for the term *anudâtta*, 'grave' (literally, 'not elevated'), is, in W. B., rule iv.43; but in G. M., rule xiv.29.

समाहारः स्वरितः ॥ ४० ॥

40. Their combination is circumflex.

The commentator explains *samâhâra*, 'combination,' as from *samâhriyate*, 'it is taken together, collected, combined;' and adds, "the accent arising from the mixing of those two is the circumflex (*svarita*). This is a precept concerning the peculiar nature of the accent; its occurrence is taught further on, in one and another place:" and he quotes not less than three of the rules (xiv.29, x.16, and xii.9) which teach under what circumstances the circumflex arises. His example of a circumflexed syllable is *tè 'bruvan* (iii.2.2[3] et al.).

This rule is so far ambiguous that it does not tell us in what order the acute and grave tones are to be combined to produce the circumflex accent—whether acute and grave, or grave and acute; but we may perhaps assume that the treatise consciously intends them to be taken in the order in which they are defined by the two preceding rules.

All the authorities practically agree in their general definition of the three kinds of accent (see note to Ath. Pr. i.14–16); and Pâṇini's rules (i.2.29–31) are precisely the same with those here given. As regards the details which form the subject of the following rules of our treatise, the accordance is not so perfect (see note to Ath. Pr. i.17).

तस्यादिरुच्चैस्तरामुदात्तादनन्तरे यावदर्धꣳ ह्रस्वस्य ॥ ४१ ॥

41. Of this circumflex, in case it immediately follows an

---

39. *anvavasargaḥ* (xxii.10) *iti*[1] *sûtralakshitaḥ*[2] *svaro 'nudâtta ucyate*[3]. *yathâ: av-. saṁjñâyâḥ prayojanam: anudâtto na nityam* (iv.43) *iti.*[4]

[1] W. B. om. [2] G. M. *-ta.* [3] B. *lakshyate.* [4] G. M. give xiv.29, and *ity âdi.*

40. *tayor udâttânudâttayor yaḥ samâhâraḥ sa*[1] *svarita ucyate. yathâ: tè..... samâhriyata iti samâhâraḥ: tayor melanajanyasvaraḥ*[2] *svarita*[3] *ity arthaḥ. svaritasvarûpavidhir ayam: uparishṭât tu* [5]*tatratatra svarito lakshyate*[4]*: yathâ: udâttât paro 'nudâttaḥ svaritam* (xiv.29)*: udâttayoç ca paro 'nudâttaḥ svaritam* (x.16)*: tasminn*[5] *anudâtte*[6] *pûrva udâttaḥ svaritam* (xii.9) *ity âdi.*

[1] M. om. [2] W. *-ra:* B. *-nyaḥ svara.* [3] G. M. om. [4] G. M. *vak-.* [(5)] W. om. [6] W. *tannudâtte.*

acute, the first part, to the extent of half a short vowel, is uttered in a yet higher tone.

That is, higher than the tone of acute, which properly forms its first element; one is tempted to give the word *udâttât* a double construction, as belonging in idea to *uccâistarâm* as well as to *anantare.*

The subject of the more particular definition of the circumflex accent occupies the six following rules, and any comments upon the doctrines laid down will be better reserved until the last rule.

As example of the circumflex, the commentator cites the words *sá idhânáh* (iv.4.4[5]), already once given (under rule 38); the first syllable of the second word has the enclitic circumflex, by rule xiv.29, under which the same quotation is repeated.

उदात्तसमः शेषः ॥ ४२ ॥

42. The remainder has the same tone with acute.

The plain meaning of this rule is distorted by the commentator, in an attempt to avoid a seeming inconsistency. He claims, namely, that the word "same with" here signifies "a trifle lower than," "because otherwise there would be no circumflex"—the circumflex having been defined in rule 40 as including both the higher and lower tone. But the inconsistency is not evaded by claiming for the last portion of the circumflex any thing short of the actual "grave" tone which rule 40 prescribes: if, indeed, giving to its first portion a higher tone than "acute" be not an equal offense against the same rule.

सव्यञ्जनो ऽपि ॥ ४३ ॥

43. Along with the consonant, too.

Says the commentator—"the rule as formerly given applied to a pure vowel; now the same thing is taught of the circumflexed vowel even in case of its combination with a consonant. The circumflexed vowel along with its consonant, either the one which directly follows an acute or another, is as defined. The 'too' (*api*) continues the implication of the circumflexed vowel." To this explanation of *api*, as simply equivalent with *ca*, we must demur. As any one may see by referring to the various rules in

---

41. *udâttâd anantare yaḥ svaraḥ svaryate tasyâ "dis tâvad uccâistarâm udâttataro bhavati yâvad dhrasvasyâ 'rdham. yathâ: sá - - - - -*

42. *hrasvârdhakâlâc chesha udâttasamo bhavati: 'na tû 'dâtta eva: samaçabdaprayogât kiṁcin nyûnatvam pratîyate*[1]*: anyathâ svaritâbhâvât. pûrvoktam evo 'dâharaṇam.*

(1) W. repeats these clauses in the comment of the preceding rule, after *bhavati.*

which it occurs, it is always best translated by 'even,' as pointing out something which is to a certain degree anomalous, or not to have been naturally expected.

As examples of circumflexed syllables containing consonants, the commentary offers *sákhâ sákhibhyo v̀árivaḥ kṛṇotu* (iii.3.11[1]: all the MSS. except W. give only the second and third words, which are the ones to which the rule applies; the second syllabl of each has the enclitic *svarita*, and they are to be read ano divided *sá-kh̀ib-bhyo vá-r̀i-vaḥ*), and *tishyàḥ* (ii.2.10[2] et al.: but G. M. omit this example).

I have not observed that any other of the treatises deems it necessary to lay down in terms the principle that the consonant shares in the accentuation of the vowel to which it is attached. Though the rule may be regarded as in a manner superfluous, it is less to be objected to in itself than on account of the place where it is thrust in, so wholly out of connection. It ought to be somewhere where it can be made to apply to all the three accents, and not to the circumflex alone.

अनन्तरो वा नीचैस्तराम् ॥ ४४ ॥

44. Or the part following is uttered in a lower tone.

The comment explains *anantara* in this rule as equivalent to *çesha* (in rule 42), and paraphrases by saying that "the remainder of this circumflexed syllable, after the half-mora [of which the character was defined in rule 41] is in a lower tone; that is, is *anudâttatara* ('lower than grave')." Whether this is the true meaning, and not rather that the last part of the syllable, instead of being "of the same tone with acute" (rule 42), is "of lower tone (than acute)," may well be made a question. It would be, I should think, an exaggeration of the circumflex of which hardly any theorist would be guilty, to begin it higher than acute, and end it lower than grave. The latter of the two interpretations suggested is also (though not unequivocally) supported by the next rule, which may most naturally be regarded as letting down the concluding tone of the syllable one degree farther than the present rule, as this than the preceding.

---

43. *kevalasyâ 'yaṁ vidhiḥ purastâd uktaḥ: idânîṁ vyañjanasahitatve 'pi [1]svaritasya tathâtvam ucyate: [1]savyañjano 'pi[1] svarita [2]udâttâd anantaro[2] 'nyo [3]vo 'ktavidhir[3] bhavati: api-[4] çabdaḥ[4] [5]svaritam âkarshati[5]. yathâ: sakhâ....: ti-.*

(1) W. om. (2) W. *-ttânant-*. (3) W. *vâ mukhyâ vi-*. (4) B. om. (5) G. M. *-tâkarshakaḥ*.

44. *tasya svaritasya hrasvârdhakâlâc chesho nîcâistarâm anudâttataro[1] bhavati: anantaraḥ çesha ity arthaḥ: tad evc 'dâharaṇam.*

[1] W. *-dâttaro*.

अनुदात्तसमो वा ॥ ४५ ॥

45. Or in the same tone with grave.

The commentator does not attempt this time, as under rule 42, to show that "same" means in reality "a little different," but simply paraphrases (taking no account of the *vâ*, 'or'): "That same remainder of this circumflexed syllable is the same with *anudâtta.*"

आदिरस्योदात्तसमः शेषो ऽनुदात्तसम इत्याचार्याः ॥ ४६ ॥

46. Its beginning is the same with acute; its remainder is the same with grave: so say the teachers.

Or, it may be, 'so says the teacher,' the plural being used in token of respect: the word *acârya* is not elsewhere found in the treatise (save at xxiv.6) except in the expression *ekeshâm âcâryâṇâm*, 'of certain teachers,' which occurs several times. The commentator does not give us his opinion upon the point, but he declares this to be the only rule that is approved or of force (*ishṭa*, literally 'desired') in the net-work (*jâla*) of alternative views here adduced, commencing with rule 41. It may, in fact, be looked upon as identical in meaning with the fundamental rule 40, and as presenting the only reasonable and sensible view of the true character belonging to the circumflex accent. The elaboration of the theory of the circumflex, the classification of its varieties, and the determination of their relations to one another, appear to have been quite a favorite weakness with the Hindu phonetists. The subject occupies the whole of one of the later chapters of this treatise (xx.), together with sundry rules in other chapters; and a more detailed examination of it, and criticism of the views taken respecting it, will be necessary in connection with some of those rules.

While approving this rule, for the reason that it is in accordance with the last two rules of chapter xx., which define the relation of

---

45. *tasya*[1] *svaritasya sa eva çesha anudâttasamo bhavati.*

[1] G. M. om.

46. *tasyâi 'va svaritasyâ "dihrasvârdhakâla udâttasamo bhavati:* [1]*çeshas tv anudâttasamo bhavati*[1]*: çeshas tv anudâttasama ity âcâryâ bruvate. yathâ: sakh-..... tasyâ "dir* (i.41) *ity âdyabhyâhite*[2] *'smin vikalpajâle*[3] *sûtram etad eve 'shṭam: praçlishṭaprâtihatayor mṛdutaraḥ* (xx.11)*: tâirovyañjanapâdavṛttayor* (xx.12) *iti lakshaṇânukûlyât: na tû 'paritanam api sûtram ishṭam: etallakshaṇaprâtikûlyâd eva.*

(1) G. M. omit, which is better. [2] G. M. *ârabhyâ 'bhihite;* B. *ábhyahita* (?—corrupt). [3] W. B. *-lpya-* (*lppa?*); W. *-jâte.*

four of the kinds of circumflex to one another in respect to hardness of utterance, the commentator rejects in advance the next following rule, as being discordant with them. The ground of the asserted accordance and discordance I am not able to discover.

सर्वः प्रवण इत्येके ॥ ४७ ॥

47. It is all a slide, say some.

The commentator says: "The word 'slide' (*pravaṇa*) is a synonym of 'circumflex:' the circumflexed vowel, along with its consonants, starting from its beginning, is all of it a slide: so some teachers have said." And he adds the same example already more than once given, *sákhibhyo várivaḥ* (iii.3.11[1]). We have seen that, in his exposition of the preceding precept, he has rejected this one, upon grounds of inappreciable value. The view here taken is one that might well enough be held by any one, as virtually equivalent with the one before presented: the voice somehow makes its descent from the higher to the lower pitch within the compass of the accented syllable; whether by a leap or a slide, is a proper theme for hair-splitting argumentation, but of the smallest practical consequence.

नानापदवदिंग्यमसंख्याने ॥ ४८ ॥

48. A separable word is treated like separate words, except in an enumeration.

The meaning and application of this precept may be best exhibited by means of the examples which the commentator quotes. We have a rule (iv.40) that *te* and *the* at the end of a word of more than two syllables are *pragraha* if preceded by *â* or *e*. In the passages *oshatât tigmahete* (i.2.14[2]) and *tat pravâte* (vi.4.7[2]), then, the final syllables would be *pragraha*, but that the words in which they occur are separable compounds, written in the *pada*-text *tigma-hete* and *pra-vâte*, and so are exempted by this rule from the

---

47. *pravaṇaçabdaḥ*[1] *svaritaparyâyaḥ: savyañjana eva svarita âdita ârabhya sarvaḥ pravaṇo bhavatî 'ty eka*[2] *âcâryâ ûcire. yathâ: sakh-*[3] ----.

[1] B. has *praṇava* for *pravaṇa* everywhere. [2] G. M. om. [3] M. *sarvebhyo.*

48. *iṅgyapadaṁ nânâpadavad bhavati: asaṁkhyânavishaye*[1]*: nânâpadavad iti kim: osh-*----*: tat*---- *ity âdâv âkârâikâ-rapûrvas tu bahusvarasya te the* (iv.40) *ity atra*[2] *pragrahatvam mâ bhûd iti: asaṁkhyâna iti kim: dve: paraç ca: ekavyaveto 'pi* (iv.49–51)*:* [3] *dve sav-*---- *ity atra pragrahatvam bhavatv*[4] *iti vadâmaḥ. nânâpadam iva nânâpadavat.*

[1] G. M. *-ne vish-.* [2] G. M. om. [3] G. M. ins. *iti.* [4] G. M. *prabhavatu.*

operation of iv.40: the *te* is in each case the ending of a dissyllabic word. What is meant by "enumeration" is not, in itself, very clear, as the case already cited is, in a certain sense, one of enumeration—namely, of the syllables of a word. The commentator shows its intent by pointing out that, by rules iv.49–51, the word *dve*, the next word to it, and the next but one, are made *pragraha:* hence, in the passage *dve savane çukravatî* (vi.1.6[4]), *çukravatî* (*pada*-text *çukra-vatî*) must be counted as a single word only, or the *î* of *vatî* would not be *pragraha*.

In this, as in the Rik and Atharva Prâtiçâkhyas, the word *iṅgya* T. W. B. and O. more usually write *îṅgya*, or *îṅya*) means a compound word, treated as separable into its constituents in the *pada*-text. The St. Petersburg lexicon erroneously explains it as signifying a single member of such a compound.

Compare Rik Pr. i.25, and Vâj. Pr. i.153.

तस्य पूर्वपदमवग्रहः ॥ ४९ ॥

49. Of such a word, the former member is called *avagraha.*

The example quoted is *devâyata iti deva-yate* (iii.5.5[3])—an instance of *carcâ*, or repetition with *iti* interposed, such as is usual in the *krama*-texts, and, to a certain extent, in the *pada*-texts also. The existing *pada*-texts of the Rik and Atharvan would write this word simply *deva-yate*, reserving the repetition with *iti* for words which are *pragraha* and separable at the same time: but that of the Tâittirîya-Sanhitâ treats all separable compounds in the latter method (see, for the varying usages of different texts, the note to Ath. Pr. iv.74). In *deva-yate*, the part *deva* is denominated *avagraha.* As instance of the use of this technical term is given the rule (iv.2) which exempts all first members of compounds from the action of the rules prescribing *pragraha.*

The commentator, finally, calls attention to the mutual relation, or apposition, of the words *pada* and *avagraha* in the rule, each in its own gender (the former being neuter, the latter masculine): compare under ii.7 and v.2.

The other Prâtiçâhkyas use the term *avagraha* in this sense, but without taking the trouble to define it.

पदग्रहणेषु पदं गम्येत ॥ ५० ॥

50. In citations of a word, that word is to be understood.

That is to say, the cited word itself, and not a part of a word

---

49. [1]*tasye 'ṅgyapadasya pûrvapadaṃ avagraha*[1] *ity ucyate. yathâ: dev-..... avagrahasaṃjñâyâḥ*[2] *prayojanam: nâ 'vagrahaḥ* (iv.2) *ity âdi. padâvagrahaçabdayor niyataliṅgatvâ-nyonyânvayaḥ*[3] *sambhavati.*

(1) G. M. om. [2] G. M. om. *avagraha.* [3] W. *niyama-.*

identical in form with it. Thus (to take the commentator's example), *tve* is later (iv.10) declared *pragraha* except at the end of a separable word, as in the passage *tve kratum* (iii.5.10[1]); the exception specified is necessary, because the *tve* of a word like *adititve* (p. *aditi-tve*) is also a *pada* or vocable;—but it is not therefore to be inferred that the *tve* of *kratve*, in the passage *kratve dakshâya* (iii.2.5[2]; 3.11[4]), is also *pragraha*.

As the commentator had formerly derived *grahaṇam* (i.22) from *gṛhyate*, so now he derives *grahaṇâni* from *gṛhṇanti*, 'they seize, take.'

The principle here taught is appealed to several times (under iv. 11,38; vii.2) hereafter, in order to the settlement of doubtful points.

It would seem possible to be still made a question whether the citation in any particular rule were a *pada*, 'a full word,' or a *padâikadeça*, 'part of a word,' since citations of the latter kind are also frequently made. Perhaps the commentator would settle the difficulty by asserting that no combination of articulate sounds which actually occurs in the Sanhitâ as a *pada* is ever cited in any other character.

अपि विकृतम् ॥ ५१ ॥

51. But that word, even when phonetically altered.

The commentator gives two examples. The word *vâhana*, he says, is cited later (vii.6) as one whose *n* is liable to conversion into *ṇ*: this conversion, then, still holds good, though the final syllable of the word have become *o*: thus, *pravâhaṇo vahniḥ* (i.3.3). Again, *syaḥ*, by v.15, loses its final *visarga*; and it does so, even when its *s* is changed to *sh*, as in *ayam u shya pra devayuḥ* (iii.5.11[1]). As regards the former of these examples, it might seem to be provided for by rule i.22, above: but the commentator would doubtless plead that the rule would apply to *vâhanaḥ*, but not to *vâhano*.

---

50. *padagrahaṇeshu sûtreshu gṛhîtam padam eva gamyeta:*[1] *jñâtavyam: na padâikadeçaḥ*[2]. *yathâ: tve ity aniñgyântaḥ*[3] (iv.10) *iti vakshyati: tathâ sati tve---- iti pragraho bhavati: kra----- iti padâikadeçân*[4] *na bhavati. gṛhṇantî 'ti grahaṇâni: padânâṁ grahaṇâni padagrahaṇâni: teshu.*

[1] M. ins. *tad.* [2] G. M. *-çaṁ.* [3] W. *aniṁñy-*; B. *aniñy-*. [4] G. M. *-çatvân.*

51. *apiçabdaḥ padam anvâdiçati: padagrahaṇeshu vikṛtam api padam avagantavyam. yathâ: ṇatvâpattâu vâhana* (vii.6) *iti grahîshyate: padam iti kṛtvâ visarjanîya otvam âpanne 'pi ṇatvaṁ nâi 'va nivartate: pra-----: eshasasyaḥ* (v.15) *iti visarjanîyalopagrahaṇam paṭhishyate: ay----- ity atra sakâre shatvam âpanne*[1] *visargalopo bhavaty eva.*

[1] G. M. ins. *'pi.*

अप्यकारादि ॥५२॥

52. And even when preceded by *a*.

The evident occasion of this rule is the frequent occurrence of words with the negative prefix *a* attached to them. But, it being once established, its sphere is not restricted to that class of compounds, as is shown in the very example chosen by the commentator to illustrate its working. By iii.2, *çvâ* is included among the words whose final *â* is liable to be shortened; then, by this rule, *açvâ* is also included: e. g. *açvâvantañ* (p. *açva-vantam*) *sahasriṇam* (iii.3.11[1]).

Application of this principle is quite frequently made below (under iii.2,8; v.13,16; vi.5,14; viii.8,13; xi.16; xvi.6,19).

अन्कारादि च ॥५३॥

53. And when preceded by *an*.

The origin and aim of this rule are obviously the same with those of the preceding, but the instances of its application are less frequent: it is appealed to but three times in the sequel (under rules iii.7, viii.8, and xvi.29). The last case is the one selected by the commentator as his example. The word *añçu*, by xvi.29, contains *anusvâra;* hence the same word preceded by *an* is to be regarded as included with it, as in the passage *anañçu kurvantaḥ* (iii.2.2[1]).

The commentator now raises the question: how comes *kâra* to

---

52. *atrâ 'py apiçabdaḥ padânvâdeçakaḥ: padagrahaṇeshv akârâdy*[1] *api*[2] *padaṁ vijñeyam:* [3]*çvartâvayunâ* (iii.2) *iti hrasvâdeçe vakshyati: akârâder api tasya grahaṇasya hrasvatvam bhavati. yathâ: açv-..... akâra âdir yasya tat tathoktam.*

[1] G. M. *-diç.* [2] G. M. *ca.* [3] G. M. prefixes the preceding three words of the cited rule.

53. *cakâraḥ padam iti bodhayati: padagrahaṇeshv ankârâdy api padaṁ vijñeyam: añçu* (xvi.29) *ity anusvârâgame vakshyati: ankârâder api tasyâ 'nusvârâgamaḥ syât. yathâ: an-..... ankâra âdir yasya tat tathoktam.*

nanv atra sûtre 'n ity asya kârottaratvaṁ kathaṁ kriyate: varṇaḥ kârottaraḥ (i.16) *iti* [1]*sûtre varṇasya*[1] *kârottaratvavidhânabhaṅgaprasaṅgat. ucyate: satyam*[2] *etacchâstrabalân* [3]*na kriyate: kiṁ tu çâstrântarabalât*[3] *kriyate: yathâ: pâṇinîyâ* [4]*evakâra apikâra*[4] *ityâdînâṁ sâdhutvaṁ kathayanti: evam atrâ 'pi evam aḥkâra âgama* (i.23) *ity atra*[5] *codyaparihârâu vijñeyâu.*

(1) G. M. *varṇaçabdasya.* [2] G. M. *tasya.* (3) B. om. (4) G. M. *evakâre 'pi-.* [5] G. M. *atrâ 'pi.*

be added here to the syllable *an?* since offense is thus committed against the precept in rule 16, above, that *kâra* is added to an alphabetic sound to form its name. His answer is: true enough that it is not done by authority of this text-book; but it is done by the authority of other text-books; for example, Pâṇini's followers establish the propriety of such expressions as *evakâra*, *apikâra* (for the words *eva* and *api*). So likewise in this very treatise (in rule 23, above) we have *aḥkâra* for *aḥ*; and the same objection and answer are to be understood as applying there. See the note under rule 16.

एकवर्णः पदमपृक्तः ॥ ५४ ॥

54. A single sound composing a word is called *apṛkta.*

The commentator explains *ekavarṇaḥ* after the fashion usual with him in treating a *karmadhâraya* or determinative compound: "that is both single (*eka*) and a sound (*varṇa*); hence, a single sound." The term *apṛkta* means, he says, 'uncombined with a consonant.' As example of an *apṛkta* word, he quotes *sa uv ekaviñçavartaniḥ* (iv.3.3[2]), where *uv* is, by rule ix.16, representative of the particle *u*; and, as counter-example, to illustrate the force of the specification "composing a word," *yajñapatâsv iti* (vi.6.2[3]), where *v*, though in a manner isolated, is not *apṛkta*, being only a fragment of a word. Rule ix.16 exemplifies the use of the term.

आद्यन्तवच्च ॥ ५५ ॥

55. And is treated both as initial and as final.

As an instance of the treatment of an *apṛkta* word as initial, the commentary again cites the passage *sa uv ekaviñçavartaniḥ* (iv.3.3[2]), and declares that in it is to be seen the effect of rule 41, above (G. M. have here a *lacuna*, and omit the reference to the rule, along with the other instance). This is quite unintelligible to me, since

---

54. *ekaç câ 'sâu varṇaç câi*[1] *'kavarṇaḥ: sa cet padam bhavati so 'pṛktaḥ*[2] *syât. yathâ: sa..... padam iti kim: yaj-..... saṁjñâyâḥ prayojanam: ukâro 'pṛktaḥ prakṛtyâ*[3] (ix.16) *iti. apṛkta iti vyañjanenâ 'saṁyuta*[4] *ity arthaḥ*

[1] B. ins. *sa.* [2] G. M. *-ktasaṁjña.* [3] G. M. add the remaining two words of the cited rule. [4] G. M. *-yukta.*

55. *cakârânvâdishṭaṁ tad apṛktasaṁjñam padam âdyantavac*[1] *ca kâryabhâg bhavati. âdivad yathâ: sa.... ity atra 'tasyâ "dir uccâistarâm* (i.41) *iti kâryam bhavati: antavad yathâ: o te.... ity atrâ*[2] *'ntaḥ* (iv.3) *iti pragrahakâryam*[3] *bhavati. âdiç câ 'ntaç câ "dyantâu: tâv ivâ "dyantavat.*

[1] G. M. *âdivad ant-.* ([2]) G. M. om. [3] G. M. *-ho.*

the rule referred to teaches nothing whatever that is characteristic of an initial sound,—indeed, teaches no *kâryam*, 'effect,' at all. For the treatment of such a word as a final, we have as an example the passage *o te yanti* (i.4.33), in which *o* is *pragraha;* with reference to rule iv.3, which teaches that only a final vowel is *pragraha.*

With this rule and the preceding compare Vâj. Pr. i.151–2, which are nearly identical with them in form and meaning. The Rik Pr. does not define the term *apṛkta*, but gives respecting it a rule corresponding with the present one. Both give in illustration the same passage, *indre" 'hi* (*indra: â: ihi*), analogous with the one (*bhakshe" 'hi:* iii.2.5[1]) quoted below, under v.3

वर्णस्य विकारलोपौ ॥ ५६ ॥

56. Alteration and omission are of a single sound.

That is to say, not of a whole word. Where, as by v.19, more than one letter is omitted, each is specified. The cited examples are, of alteration, *dhûrshâhâu* (i.2.8[2]: by rule v.10); of omission, *sa te jânâti* (i.2.14[2-3]: by rule v.15).

I find this rule expressly appealed to but once in the sequel (under ix.7).

विनाशो लोपः ॥ ५७ ॥

57. Omission is complete loss.

As example of *lopa*, 'omission,' the commentator quotes the passage *sa îm 'andrâ suprayasaḥ* (iv.1.8[1-2]), where the initial *m* of *mandrâ* is lost after *îm* (by rule v.12: see the note there given). As example of the use of the term, he gives rule v.11, which is introductory to the subject of omissions. He then proceeds to state a very curious reason why such a precept as this should seem called for: "some have maintained the eternity of sound: in order to the confutation of that doctrine, this rule hath been uttered, in conformity with general grammar." Pânini's corresponding precept (i.1.60) is *adarçanaṁ lopaḥ*, 'omission is disappearance from view.'

---

56. *varṇamâtrasya vikâralopâu syâtâṁ na tu sarvasya padasya. vikâras tâvat: dhû- iti: 'lopas tu': sa* ....

[1] W. om. B. omits this whole comment, along with the following rule.

57. *varṇavinâço*[1] *lopasaṁjño bhavati. yathâ: sa* .... *saṁjñâyâḥ prayojanam: atha lopaḥ* (v.11) *ity âdi. varṇasya nityatâṁ kecid âhuḥ: tannirâkaraṇâya vyâkaraṇânusâreṇa sûtram etad abhâṇi.*

[1] G. M. *varnasya v-*.

अन्वादेशो ऽन्त्यस्य ॥५८॥

58. Continued implication is of that which was last.

The term *anvâdeça*, 'after-indication,' with its corresponding verbal forms, and other equivalent expressions (especially *anvâkarshaka, âkarshaka*, etc.), is constantly employed in the commentary to signify the continued force in a given rule of some specification made in a preceding rule. And the simple meaning of the present precept appears to be, that such a bringing forward is of the predicate last used, the word last cited, or the like. The commentator's first example is entirely accordant with this understanding: in rule vii.3, namely, to the effect that the *n* of *hanyât* and *upyamânam* is changed to *ṇ*, the implication is "after *niḥ*," *niḥ* being the last mentioned in a list of altering words given in the preceding rule. But he goes on to make another application of the precept: rule xv.8 says "*a*, however, even in *sam̃hitâ* [is protracted and nasalized];" and it is to be understood that only a "last" or "final" *a* is intended—as in *suçlokâñ3* (i.8.16[2]), protracted from *suçloka;* while in *brahmâ3n tvañ râjan* (i.8.16[1,2]), *agnâ3 ity âha* (vi.5.8[4]), *vicityaḥ somâ3 na vicityâ3 iti* (vi.1.9[1]), where the words protracted are *brahman, agne, somaḥ*, and *vicityaḥ*, and the *a* is not a final, there is no nasalization. Evidently, this is a wholly forced and false interpretation: no rule can mean two things so utterly different. Compare the notes to iv.3 and xv.8, where the principle is appealed to.

The comment seeks a kind of support for its double interpretation by calling attention to the distinction between an "affecting cause" (*nimitta*), like the *niḥ* brought forward from vii.2 to vii.3 in the first example, and an "affected" word or element (*nimittin*, 'having a cause'), such as is concerned in the second example. The latter (nearly synonymous with *lakshya*, used in the comment to i.22) he defines as "something original (? *pradhâna* seems to be taken here in the sense of *prakṛti*) suffering a prescribed effect."

No one of the other Prâtiçâkhyas attempts to lay down any rules as to the *anvâdeça* (or *anuvṛtti*); and its usages are, in fact, wholly irreducible to rule—a circumstance which involves the condemnation of the *sûtra* style of composition, because the *sûtras* are not and cannot be self-explanatory, or intelligible without an authoritative comment.

---

58. *nimittasya nimittino vâ 'ntyasyâ 'nvâdeço bhavati: nimittî 'ti pradhânam*[1] *kâryabhâg iti yâvat. nimittasya yathâ: hanyâd upyamânam ca* (vii.3) *ity asyâ 'tra*[2] *niḥçabdasya. nimittino yathâ: akâras tu sañhitâyâm api* (xv.8) *ity atra suçlokâñ3*[3] *ity antyasyâ 'kârasya: antyasye 'ti kim: brah-....: ag-....: vic-.....*

[1] W. *-nâm̃*; G. M. *-na.* [2] G. M. om. [3] B. om. all the signs of protraction.

उपबन्धस्तु देशाय नित्यम् ॥ ५९ ॥

59. An *upabandha*, however, is for that particular passage, and of constant effect.

The commentator etymologizes *upabandha*, 'connection, tie,' as representing the meaning *upabadhyate*, 'it is tied up, bound to;' and he farther defines it as signifying a passage pointed out by the indication "in that," and one which is designated by an enumeration—referring to rules iv.22,23,48,52 as examples. An *upabandha*, then, is a connected part of the Sanhitâ, pointed out and defined by the rules of the Prâtiçâkhya in various ways: by citing the first words of a single verse (iv.20) or of an *anuvâka* (iv.25,48; xi.3); by the accepted title of a number of *anuvâkas*, either succeeding one another or otherwise (ii.9,11; iv.52; ix.20; xi.3); by giving the first and last words of a passage (iv.22,23); or by fixing a limit within a certain number of words from a specified word (iv.52). Respecting such a passage, we are told, this rule is intended to teach two things: first, that what is prescribed for it does not hold good in other passages—this is signified by the word *tu*, 'however,' in the rule;—second, that an exception which applies in other passages does not apply in it—this is signified by the word *nityam*, 'constantly, in all cases.'

Both prescriptions, as thus stated, the commentator undertakes to illustrate by quoted cases of their application. But his first illustration is imperfectly and obscurely set forth, and is, besides, of a very questionable character. He tells us that the passage *ity âha devî hy eshâ devaḥ somaḥ* (vi.1.7[7]) is brought, by the principle laid down in the next rule but one (i.61), under the action of rule iv.25—and this is all that he deigns to say about it. The meaning is this: the passage quoted contains a series of four words, *ity âha devî hi*, which are also found at ii.6.7[5] (*devî devaputre ity âha devî hy ete devaputre*); and, as the *î* of *devî* in the latter passage is *pragraha* by iv.25, so, under the operation of i.61, it should be *pragraha* also in the other. Such, however, is not the case; for *devî* in *devî hy eshâ* is singular, while in *devî hy ete* it is dual. It would seem, then, as if we ought to understand the commenta-

---

59. *upabandhas tu svadeçâyâi 'va nityaṁ nirdeçako bhavati: upabadhyata*[1] *ity upabandhaḥ: etasminn ity*[2] *adhikaraṇarûpaḥ saṁkhyânavishayaç ca pradeça upabandha ity ucyate. yathâ: irâvatî* (iv.22) *ity âdi sûtradvayam: somâya svai 'tasmin* (iv.48)*: gamayato bhavataḥ* (iv.52) *iti ca. upabandhe yad uktaṁ tad anyatra na bhavatî 'ti tuçabdârthaḥ*[3]*. yathâ*[4]*: ity----: atra tripadaprabhṛtinyâyena* (i.61) *pûrvajeprabhṛty â 'yam* (iv.25) *iti prâptiḥ. anyatra yo nishedhaḥ sa upabandhe na bhavatî 'ti nityaçabdârthaḥ. yathâ: sadohavirdhâne* (iv.11) *iti pragraho grahîshyate: kevalahavirdhâna*[5] *iti sarvathâ*[6]

tor to maintain that the present rule annuls the application of i.61, and, through it, of iv.25, to the case in question. But this is wholly inadmissible: for rule 61, below, is directly intended as a limitation to the present one, and has no force or value except as it applies to just such passages as the one here instanced; and with the latter are closely analogous a part of the examples adduced for its illustration, and leading to an opposite conclusion to the one here apparently arrived at. I cannot account for the way in which the commentator treats the matter. So far as I can see, *devî* at vi.1.7[7] is *pragraha* according to the rules of the Prâtiçâkhya, and has only by some oversight escaped being specially excepted: and the first restriction is of a general character, meaning that directions given for an *upabandha* passage are intended for that passage alone, and have no wider bearing—except as they receive it from i.61. The same, as will be seen below, limits also the other restriction, that expressed by *nityam.*

Further, the citation in rule iv.11 of the compound *sadohavirdhâne* as *pragraha* implies that the simple word *havirdhâne* would always be of a contrary character, as it in fact is in the passage *havirdhâne khyâyante* (vi.2.11[1]); but this implication does not hold in the passage *havirdhâne prâcî pravartayeyuḥ* (iii.1.3[r]), because of the inclusion of the latter among the *upabandhas* of rule iv.52. Here, however, is brought up an objection: the explanation given is not satisfactory, because an exception made elsewhere is sometimes of force also in an *upabandha* passage. For instance, in the passage *atha mithunî bhavataḥ* (vi.5.8[6]), the word *mithunî*, which would else be *pragraha* by iv.52, is made otherwise by iv.53. Again, an example of a similar class is afforded by *vâyava ârohaṇavâhâu* (v.6.21), where *vâyave* ought to be *pragraha*, because occurring in the *anuvâka* to which iv.48 refers, while it is deprived of that character by iv.54. The answer is made, that, in the case of *grâmî, vâyave, manave,* and the like, the exception must be allowed to have force because those words are excepted by specific mention; while the exception of *havirdhâne* is inferential only, and therefore does not hold good: specific mention being of more force than mere inference.

---

na pragraho gṛhyate: yathâ[7]*: hav-.... ity ayam atra*[8] *nishedhaḥ: hav-.... ity atra na prasarati: gamayato bhavataḥ* (iv.52) *ity âdinâ prâptiḥ. nanv etad anupapannam: anyatra nishedhasya kvacid upabandhe 'pi darçanât: yathâ: atha.... ity atra gamayato bhavataḥ* (iv.52) *ity upabandhaprâptir na grâmî* (iv.53) *ity âdinâ 'nyatra*[9] *nishedhena nishidhyate: tathâ*[10]*: vây-.... ity atra somâya sva* (iv.48) *iti prâptir ate samânapada* (iv.54) *ity anenâ 'nyatra nishedhena nishidhyate. atro 'çyate: grâmî vâyave manava ity âdînâṁ kaṇṭhoktatvâd esha nishedhaḥ prasaratu*[11] *kevalahavirdhâne*[12] *pragraho*[13] *ne 'ty ârthiko nishedho na prasaraty eva: ârthikakaṇṭhoktayoḥ kaṇ-*

But this suggests a further objection: why then is not the specific mention of *ate* and *ave* in rule iv.54 enough, and what is the use of adding the word *nityam*, 'in all cases,' in that rule? This, replies the commentator, is for the purpose of making the exception yet more strongly binding: the specific mention merely annuls the application of the *upabandha* rule; the addition of *nityam* avoids the application of any other rule. For example, in *dve jâye vindate* (vi.6.4[3]), *vindate* should be *pragraha* (by rule iv.51), because separated by only one word from *dve;* and in *vanaspate vîḍvañgaḥ* (iv.6.6[5]), the same character would belong to *vanaspate* (by iv.38) because followed by *vîḍ*—and we are left to infer that the *nityam* renders rule iv.54 capable of reaching these passages, and taking away the *pragraha* character of the two words in question. This, adds the commentator, may be still further pursued; it has been thus drawn out in accordance with the view of Mâhisheya.

In all this exposition is to be seen something of the artificial and hair-splitting character which is apt to belong to a Hindu comment, while upon the whole it is sound and to the point. The term *upabandha* is doubtless better understood actively, as representing *teno 'pabadhyate*, 'that whereby there is binding up:' the presence of *deçâya* in the rule is hardly reconcilable with the other interpretation. The intent of the specification *nityam* is to exclude general exceptions, made in view of other passages, or of the text at large, but not at all to deny the possibility of exceptions made expressly for the *upabandha* passages: and such are iv.53 and others, referred to by the objector, and refuted by an inapplicable special pleading. The force which the commentator ascribes to the *tu* of the rule belongs rather to *deçâya*, and the *tu* has the value of a general disjunctive, bringing in a precept not connected with what has gone before.

Any additional instances of the application of the principles here laid down I have not searched for or chanced upon. The rule is appealed to but once in the sequel (under iv.54).

नानापदीयं च निमित्तं प्रग्रहस्मादिषु ॥ ६० ॥

60. Also a cause belonging to another word, in the case of a *pragraha* or of a word containing *anusvâra.*

ṭhoktasya prâbalyât. nanv ate ave (iv.54) *ity anayoḥ kaṇṭhoktyâi 'vâ 'lam: tatra nityagrahaṇena kim. ucyate: nitarâm parihâraḥ: kaṇṭhoktir upabandhaprâptim eva nivartayati nityaçabdas tu prâptyantaram api pariharati: yathâ: dve---- ity atra ekavyaveto 'pi* (iv.51) *iti prâptiḥ: van----- iti* " *vîḍ* (iv.38) *âdiprâptiḥ: evam âdy ûhanîyam*[15]. *mâhisheyamatânusâreṇai 'vam prapañcitam.*

[1] B. *upanibadhyata.* [2] W. *itya.* [3] G. M. om. *tu.* [4] W. B. om. [5] G. M. *kevalaṁ hav-.* [6] G. M. *sarvadhâ.* [7] W. om. [8] G. M: *anyatra.* [9] G. M. om. [10] G. M. *yathâ.* [11] G. M. *-rati.* [12] B. *kevalaṁ h-.* [13] W. *-he.* [14] G. M. ins. *atra.* [15] G. M. *-niyamam.*

The intent of this rule is made sufficiently clear by the commentator, but he is unable to show satisfactorily its connection, or the implication in virtue of which it comes to mean what it does. He puts, however, a bold face upon it, and declares that the *ca*, 'also,' implies the negative (*nañ:* compare Pâṇini ii.2.6 etc.) meaning signified by *tu* (that is to say, the *tu* of the preceding rule). This is quite unintelligible. More defensible would be the continuance of *nityam*, 'constantly:' this, indeed, I conceive to be the real interpretation of the *ca;* although the rule is even thus left insufficiently explained by its context. The term *srâdishu* points us to the sixteenth chapter, where is to be found an enumeration of all the cases in the Sanhitâ exhibiting an *anusvâra* which is not a consequence of the phonetic rules of the treatise—of all the words which in their *pada* form contain an *anusvâra*—and this enumeration is led off (xvi.2) with the syllable *sra.* Many of this class of words are pointed out, as elsewhere in the Prâtiçâkhya, by mentioning the words which they precede or follow; which latter, then, become in the view of the treatise their *nimitta*, or 'cause' (taking the *post hoc* or *ante hoc* for a *propter hoc*). Inasmuch, now, as the *pragraha* quality and the occurrence of this *anusvâra* belong to the word itself, independently of its surroundings, it becomes necessary to teach that, when a word has been defined by means of its surroundings as thus characterized, it retains its character even when separated from them, as it is in the *pada*-text. Or, in the language of the rule, the defined occasion of a *pragraha* or of a constituent *anusvâra* is of force, even when it is, or is in, another *pada.*

The commentator, in illustration of the action of the rule, refers us first to iv.28, where *ghnî* and *cakre* are declared *pragraha* when immediately followed by *p;* these words are *pragraha* also in the *pada*-text of the same passages, when there is a pause between them and the *p.* Again, he quotes rule xvi.11, where *mâ* is declared to have no *anusvâra* after it when preceded by an *avagraha;* that is, when it begins the second member of a compound, as in *ardhamâse devâḥ* (ii.5.6[6]): here, too, the precept holds when

---

60. *cakâras tuçabdanigaditaṁ*[1] *nañartham anvâdiçati: pragraheshu srâdishu ca nânâpadasambandhi*[2] *nimittam asaṁhitâyâm api svakâryam*[3] *upadiçatî 'ti pragrahânusvârakâryaṁ*[4] *na nivartate. yathâ: vakshyati: ghnî cakre papare* (iv.28) *pragrahâu bhavata ity: atra pragrahatve paparaṇo*[5] *'padishṭe padakâle*[6] *tathâi 'va. srâdishu ca*[7] *yathâ: nâ 'vagrahapûrvaḥ* (xvi.11) *ity avagraheṇâ 'nusvârâgame nishiddhe padakâle 'pi tathâi 'va: yathâ*[8]*: ardh-..... shatvaṇatvâdâu*[9] *tu nânâpadîyaṁ*[10] *nimittaṁ saṁhitâyâm eva kâryaṁ karotî 'ty ayam ârambhaḥ: yathâ*[11]*: çuc-....: prav-.....*

[1] G. M. *-bdena ni-.* [2] G. M. *-dha.* [3] G. M. *svik-.* [4] W. *-sârak-;* B. *-hanusvak-.* [5] G. M. *pakâreṇa.* [6] G. M. ins. *'pi.* [7] G. M. om. [8] W. om. [9] G. M. ins. *ca.* [10] G. M. *-ya.* [11] W. om.

the *avagraha* pause intervenes between the two parts of the compound: as, *ardha-mâse.* On the other hand, the cause (*nimitta*) of nasalization of a sibilant or nasal, if in a different *pada* from the letter it affects, is efficient only in *saṁhitâ:* for example, *çucishad iti çuci-sat* (iv.2.1[5]), and *pravâhaṇa iti pra-vâhanaḥ* (i.3.3): and this is the occasion of the rule.

I see no reason why this rule does not need to apply also to the cases of an original lingual nasal (*ṇ*) enumerated in the thirteenth chapter.

यथोक्तं पुनरुक्तं त्रिपदप्रभृति त्रिपदप्रभृति ॥ ६१ ॥

61. A repeated passage, of three or more words, is as already established.

That is to say, the reading of any connected passage is as established by the rules for the first place where it occurs: if repeated in a later part of the Sanhitâ, where other rules, there applicable, would change its reading, it is exempted from their influence.

Several examples are given in illustration by the commentator. In the third chapter (*praçna*) of the first book (*kâṇḍa*) of the Sanhitâ occurs the phrase *devasya tvâ savituḥ prasave 'çvinoḥ* (i.3.1[1]: but the same phrase is found also twice before, at i.1.4[2],6), and the initial *a* of its last word is cut off by the general rule xi.1; hence, when it occurs again in a *vâjapeya* passage (namely at i.7.10[3]), where, by xi.3, the elision of the *a* is forbidden, the effect of the latter rule is suspended, and the passage reads as before. Again, the words *supathâ râye asmân* are first found at i.1.14[3], where, as the *anuvâka* is a *yâjyâ*, the *a* of *asmân* remains unelided by xi.3; and when they occur again at i.4.43[1], that letter still maintains its place. Once more, the phrase *sa jâto garbho asi rodasyoḥ* is read at iv.1.4[2], and again at v.1.5[3-4]; the former time in an *ukhya* passage, where the *a* of *asi* is retained by xi.3; and it is therefore retained in the other passage also.

The commentator applies to the rule the restriction that in the repeated passage the word respecting whose form there is question must hold the third place (that is to say, doubtless, that it must have not less than two other words before it). In support of this limitation, he cites a case: at iv.ii.8[3], in an *ukhya* passage, occur

---

61. *trayâṇâm padânâṁ samâhâras tripadam: kâryabhâjaḥ padasya tṛtîyatvaṁ vijñeyam: îdṛçaṁ tripadam: tat' prabhṛty âdir yasya tat tripadaprabhṛti yathoktam pûrvoktaṁ vidhiṁ karoti svaviçeshaṇaṁ*[2] *yatra*[3] *tripadaprabhṛti punaruktaṁ cet. tathâ: 'lupyate tv akâra ekârâukârapûrvaḥ* (xi.1) *ity anena prathamakâṇḍatṛtîyapraçne dev---- ity atrâ 'kâre lupte tad eva vâkyaṁ vâjâpeye 'py alopam bâdhitvâ tathâi 'va bhavati: tripadaprabhṛtitvât. ubhâ vâm* (i.1.14[1]) *ity atra sup---- ity etad ud u tyaṁ jâtavedasam* (i.4.43[1]) *ity atrâ 'pi tathâi*

the words *pṛthivîm anu ye antarikshe ye divi tebhyaḥ* (W. B. omit the first two words of the citation), and the *a* of *antarikshe* is left unelided by xi.3; but at iv.5.11[2] (in the last *anuvâka* of the chapter called *rudra:* see rule xi.3) we read *ye pṛthivyâṁ ye 'ntarikshe ye divi* (W. B., again, omit the first two words quoted, and also give *ye ant-*)—which, but for his restriction, would be a violation of the rule. I cannot but question, however, the right of the commentator thus to limit the rule, for I have noted at least three cases where, if it be admitted, the retention of an initial *a* in a repeated passage would be left without authority: they are *pâvako asmabhyam* (v.4.4[5] and iv.6.1[3,5]), *preddho agne* (v.4.7[3] and iv.6.5[4]), and *dadhikrâvṇo akârisham* (vii.4.19[4] and i.v.11[4]). Whether there are other cases like that to which the commentator appeals, I am unable to say: but I cannot help suspecting that he devised this modification of the rule to suit that particular passage, without sufficient regard to what might be required by other parts of the text.

But he is guilty of another piece of arbitrary interpretation which is still more unjustifiable, and which he makes yet lamer work of defending. The term *tripadaprabhṛti* means, according to him, a series of words beginning with three words of which the third is the one whose form is in question—that is to say, a series of at least four words, of which one follows the word of doubtful reading. The case to which he appeals to establish this is as follows: the words *divas pari prathamaṁ jajñe agnir asmat* (W. B. omit *asmat*) occur at i.3.14[4], in a *yâjyâ* passage, where *agniḥ* keeps its initial vowel by xi.3; again, the words *itaḥ prathamaṁ jajñe agniḥ* are found at ii.2.4[8]: there seems to be a repetition, and a reading of *agniḥ* founded upon it; but it is not proper to claim that the retention of *a* here has this ground; it is due to the inclusion (in rule xi.16) of *jajñe* among the words which do not cause the elision: for such inclusion would otherwise be to no purpose (since there is in the Sanhitâ no other passage to which the prescription should apply). Any other case seeming to require the interpretation here in question I have not noticed; and we have the right to presume that, if the commentator had knowledge of one which supported his view more unequivocally, he would not have failed to refer to it. So far as appears, then, the sole object of this forced

---

'*va.* [5] *saṁ te vâyur* (iv.1.4[1]) *ity atra sa---- ity etat krûram iva* (v.1.5[1]) *ity atrâ 'pi tathâi 'va. brâhmaṇavâkyeshu tu*[6] *tripadamâtrâd vâ kâryam bhavati: brâhmaṇavâkyeshu pûrvasthalasyâi*[7] *'vo 'kteḥ*[8]*: yathâ: imâm agṛbhṇan raçanâm*[9] (iv.1.2[1]) *ity atra mar-.... ity etad vâkyam*[10] *ut krâma* (v.1.3[1]) *ity atrâ 'pi tathâi 'va bhavati. kâryabhâjaḥ padasya tṛtîyatvam iti kim: pṛth-.... ity* [11] *ukhye: ye.... iti rudrottamânuvâke. prabhṛtî 'ti kim: tvam agne rudraḥ* (i.3.14[1]) *iti yâjyâyâṁ divas.... iti vâkyam agnaye 'nnavate* (ii.2.4[1]) *ity atra*

interpretation of the word *tripadaprabhṛti* (one which the word may be said decidedly not to admit of) is to save rule xi.16 from the charge of repetition in a single point: we shall presume with much greater plausibility that, when the rule was made, the fact that this particular case was already covered by i.61 was overlooked.

But the commentator virtually admits the unsoundness of his own work by acknowledging that in the *brâhmaṇa*-passages (*brâhmaṇavâkya*) of the Sanhitâ a simple phrase of three words is enough to justify the application of the rule, "because," he says, "of the quotation in the *brâhmaṇa*-passages of a previously-occurring phrase:" that is to say, because the prose part of the Sanhitâ is to so great an extent occupied with citing and commenting on the phrases and words of other parts—a fact which has, doubtless, been the special occasion and suggestion of the present rule. Thus, the words *maryaçrî spṛhayad varṇo agniḥ* are quoted at v.i.3³ (with the customary addition, *ity âha*), from the previous passage iv.1.2⁵; and although the *nâbhim* which follows *agniḥ* at its first occurrence is not also quoted, and the quotation is not therefore a *tripadaprabhṛti* according to the commentator's construction of this term, the rule holds good, and the *a* of *agniḥ* has a right to stand.

The general value of this rule is that of a limitation to the last but one; it points out a class of cases in which a rule given for a particular passage is not limited to that passage, but also acts elsewhere; in which, moreover, such a rule does not govern *nityam*, 'against all opposition,' the reading of the passage to which it relates.

The commentator notices the fact that the repetition of the final word of the rule indicates the conclusion of the chapter. Such repetition is made at the end of each chapter, and by all the manuscripts; and, as it is thus farther ratified by the comment, I have not hesitated to admit it as an authentic part of the text of the Prâtiçâkhya. G. M. repeat the whole rule in this case.

---

itaḥ .... *iti punaruktam: tat*[12] *tathâi 'vâ 'bhavad*[13] *iti cet: mâi 'vam: tripadamâtrâd*[14] *eva tathâbhâva*[15] *iti* [16] *vaktuṁ na yuktam: kiṁ tu jajñe sañsphânaḥ* (xi.16) *iti jajñegrahaṇasâmarthyât:* [17]*anyathâ tasya*[18] *vâiyarthyât*[17].

padavîpsâ[19] *'dhyâyaparisamâptiṁ dyotayati.*

iti tribhâshyaratne prâtiçâkhyavivaraṇe
prathamo 'dhyâyaḥ.

[1] G. M. om. [2] W. *-ṇdya;* G. M. *-sheṇa.* [3] G. M. *idaṁ.* [4] G. M. ins. *hi.* [5] G. M. ins. *tathá.* [6] G. M. om. [7] G. M. *pûrvasyâi.* [8] G. M. *'ktaḥ.* [9] G. M. om. [10] G. M. om. [11] G. M. ins. *ebhya.* [12] G. M. om. [13] G. M. *syád.* [14] G. M. *tripadád.* [15] G. M. *tathâ bhavatu.* [16] G. M. ins. *atra.* (17) W. om. [18] G. M. *tasyâi 'va.* [19] G. M. *padávṛttyá.*

CHAPTER II.

Contents: 1–11, general mode of production of articulate sounds, distinction of surd and sonant sounds, etc.; 12–29, special rules for the production of vowels and diphthongs; 30, nasals; 31–34, difference of vowels and consonants; 35–39, mode of production of mutes; 40–43, of semivowels; 44-45, of spirants; 46–48, of *h* and *ḥ*; 49–52, of nasal sounds.

अथ शब्दोत्पत्तिः ॥ १ ॥

1. Now for the origin of sound.

For the word *atha* in this rule the commentator allows us our choice between two interpretations: it either indicates immediate succession—thus, the list of articulate sounds having been given, there next arises the desire to know what is the cause of these sounds, or how they become apprehensible by the sense, and then follows the explanation here to be given—or it is introductory, signifying that from this point onward the subject of the origin of sound is the one had in hand. Compare the similar and yet more lengthy discussion under rule i.1. He then goes on to draw out the significance of the rule itself. *Çabda* he explains by *dhvani:* both, when used thus distinctively, mean audible sound in general, rather than articulate sound or voice (compare xxii.1,2; xxiii.3). He paraphrases: "of the articulate sounds, *a* etc., the cause of perception, or their origin, their birth, their apprehension by the sense—just as, even before water is seen, there is moisture in the ground, and that becomes visible in consequence of digging—this is the subject of description." We seem to catch here a glimpse of that same doctrine of the eternity of sound to which reference was made above, under i.57: our organs do not properly produce it, but their action brings it to the cognizance of the senses, as the action of digging brings water to light.

---

1. *ukto varṇasamâmnâyaḥ: teshâṁ varṇânâṁ kîdṛk*[1] *kâraṇaṁ*[2] *kathaṁ vâ tadupalabdhir ity âkâṅkshânantaraṁ*[3] *nirûpyata ity ânantaryârtho 'thaçabdaḥ. atha vâ: ita uttaraṁ yad vakshyate tac chabdotpattir ity etad*[4] *adhikṛtaṁ veditavyam ity adhikârârthaḥ. çabdo nâma dhvaniḥ: varṇânâm akârâdînâm upâdânakâraṇaṁ*[5] *tadutpattir*[6] *janma upalabdhir vâ: yatho 'dakasya*[7] *darçanât pûrvam eva bhûmâu jalam asty eva tat khananâd*[8] *dṛçyate tadvat*[7]*: se 'yam ucyata*[9] *iti sûtrârthaḥ.*

[1] G. M. *kidṛçam.* [2] W. *karaṇam.* [3] G. M. ins. *tan.* [4] G. M. om. [5] B. *-karaṇam.* [6] G. M. *tasya ut-.* (7) W. B. om. [8] MSS. *khananâ.* [9] G. M. *ârabhyata.*

वायुशरीरसमीरणात्कण्ठोरसोः संधाने ॥ २ ॥

2. By the setting in motion of air by the body, at the junction of throat and breast.

The first part of this rule (literally, 'from air-body-impulsion') is obscurely expressed, and of ambiguous meaning. The commentator gives three explanations of it, the first of which is also itself obscure. Agni ('fire, warmth'—'heat of the body'?), he says, impels Vâyu ('air, wind'); that is what "air-body" means (but how?). From such an impulsion—that is to say, expulsion, effort at utterance—at the junction of, or between, throat and breast, comes the origination of sound. And he quotes a verse from the Çikshâ (verses 8–9 of the Yajus version, verses 6–7 of the Rik version: see Weber's Ind. Stud., iv.350–1): "the mind impels the body-fire; that sets in motion air; and air, moving in the breast, generates a gentle tone." Again (or rather, apparently, as a part of the same explanation: but its inconsistency with the rest is palpable), he makes a copulative compound of *vâyu-çarîra*, namely 'air-and-body:' "from the impulsion of those two." Once more, he quotes as the opinion of other authorities that *vâyu-çarîra* means 'the air in the body,' the compound being of such a sort that that which should be its first member is put last, after the analogy of *râjadanta*, 'upper incisor' (literally, 'king-tooth'—that is, as the Hindu etymologists explain it, 'tooth-king, chief among the teeth'), and the other words composing that *gaṇa* (to Pâṇ. ii.2.31). And he adds the remark that, in this interpretation, the air is understood as the cause of the impulsion, not its product.

In the translation of the rule given above, the primary division of the compound is regarded as to be made after *vâyu*; *çarîra-samîraṇa* meaning an 'impulsion by the body,' and *vâyu* being prefixed in a genitive relation, 'of the air.' This is harsh, but appears to me more acceptable and less violent than the other constructions proposed. Practically, the point is of small consequence.

2: *vâyum agniḥ samîrayatî 'ti vâyuçarîram: tathâbhûtât samîraṇât: preraṇâd abhighâtâd*[1] *ity arthaḥ: kaṇṭhorasoḥ saṁdhâne madhyadeçe çabdotpattir bhavatî 'ti*[2]*: çikshâ câi 'vaṃ astî 'ti*[3]*:*

manaḥ kâyâgnim[4] *âhanti*[5] *sa*[6] *prerayati mârutam*[7]*:*
mârutas tû 'rasi caran mandraṁ janayati [8]*svaram*

iti[8]. *vâyuç ca çarîraṁ ca vâyuçarîre: tayoḥ samîraṇam: tasmât*[9]. *anye tv âhuḥ: vâyoḥ çarîre sataḥ samîraṇam:* [10]*tasmâç chabdotpattir iti: tatre*[11] *'tthaṁ samâsaḥ: râjadantâditvâc charîrasya*[12] *paranipâtaḥ: çarîre vâyur*[13] *vâyuçarîram: tasya samîraṇaṁ*[10]*: tasmât. asmin mate vâyoḥ samîraṇakartṛtvam eva na tu karmatvam.*

[1] G. M. *abhipâ-*. [2] G. M. om. [3] G. M. om. [4] G. M. *-gni*. [5] G. M. *kânti*. [6] G. M. *sam*. [7] G. M. om. [(8)] G. M. om. [9] G. M. ins. *vâyuçarîrasamîraṇât*. [(10)] B. om. [11] G. M. *atre*. [12] G. M. *-raçabdasya*. [13] G. M. om.

Compare with what is taught by our treatise here and later (xxii.1,2; xxiii.1–3) Vâj. Pr. i.6–9; Rik Pr. xiii.1.

तस्य प्रातिश्रुत्कानि भवन्त्युरः कण्ठः शिरो मुखं नासिके इति ॥ ३ ॥

3. The parts which give it audible quality are breast, throat, head, mouth, and nostrils.

The commentator explains *prâtiçrutkâni* as signifying 'the places of production' (*sthânâni*), having to do with the resonance (*pratiçrut=pratidhvani*, 'resonance'), of the aforesaid sound (*çabda*).' He offers no remark upon the organs enumerated, but leaves their various offices to be derived from the rules which follow. But, in anticipation of the next three rules, he observes that they teach the three-fold quality of sound, as sonant, surd, and *h*-sound, rule 4 giving the definition of the first kind.

The Çikshâ (v.13: Weber's Ind. Stud. iv.351) makes an enumeration of eight *sthânas*, or places of production of articulate sounds, dividing the "mouth" of our list into root of the tongue, teeth, lips, and palate.

संवृते कण्ठे नादः क्रियते ॥ ४ ॥

4. When the throat is closed, tone is produced.

The commentator treats this rule as a definition of the technical term *nâda*, 'tone,' and cites rule 8, below, as an example of the use of the term.

The Rik Pr. (xiii.1) gives a corresponding definition of sonant utterance, but specifies the aperture (*kha*) of the throat as the part whose contraction or closure produces the tone. Compare also Vâj. Pr. i.11. It is greatly to the credit of the ancient Hindu phonetists that they had gained by acute observation so clear an idea of the manner in which the intonation of the breath is effected in the throat; but precisely how accurate a knowledge

---

3. *tasya prakṛtasya*[1] *çabdasyo 'raḥprabhṛtîni sthânâni* [2] *bhavanti: pratiçrut*[3] *pratidhvaniḥ:* [4]*tatsambandhîni prâtiçrutkâni*[4]. [5]*saṁvṛte kaṇṭhe nâdaḥ kriyate* (ii.4) *etadâdinâ sûtratrayeṇa çabdatrâividhyam*[6] *ucyate: nâdaḥ*[7] *çvâso hakâraç ce 'ti: tâvan nâdalakshaṇam âha*[8] [5].

[1] G. M. *prakṛti.* [2] G. M. ins. *prâtiçrutkâni.* [3] G. M. *-çrutkâ.* [(4)] W. om. [(5)] G. M. insert this (excepting the rule) at the beginning of the commentary to the next rule. [6] G. M *çabdasya tr-.* [7] MSS. *nâda.* [8] G. M. *ucyate.*

4. *saṁvṛte kaṇṭhe yaḥ çabdaḥ kriyate sa nâdasaṁjño bhavati. saṁjñâyâḥ*[1] *prayojanam: nâdo 'nupradânam* (ii.8) *iti*[2].

[1] G. M. *nâdasaṁ-.* [2] G. M. *ity âdi.*

they had of the nature and action of the vocal chords, whose tension produces the closure, we, of course, cannot say.

विवृते श्वासः ॥५॥

5. When it is opened, breath is produced.

The explanation given of this rule corresponds with that of the preceding, and the rule cited for the use of the term *çvâsa*, 'breath,' is ii.10.

मध्ये हकारः ॥६॥

6. When in an intermediate condition, the *h*-sound is produced.

Madhye is explained as meaning 'in a method intermediate between closed and opened:' the rest of the comment agrees with the two preceding, and the cited rule is ii.9.

Of the other Prâtiçâkhyas, only that of the Rig-Veda sets up a third kind of articulated material, besides tone and breath; and that (xiii.2) derives the material from a combination of the two others, rather than their mean. I have already (note to Ath. Pr. i.13) expressed my opinion that the attempt to establish this distinction is forced and futile, and I see at present no reason for changing it. That intonated and unintonated breath should be emitted from the same throat at once is physically impossible. In loud stridulous whispering, there is a tension of the vocal chords only short of that which gives rise to sonant vibration; and if any one chooses to claim that the aspirations used in loud speaking partake of such a character, sometimes or always, we need not be at the pains to contradict him.

ता वर्णप्रकृतयः ॥७॥

7. Those are the materials of alphabetic sounds.

That is to say, the three kinds of material just described—tone, breath, and *h*-sound, some letters having one of these as the material out of which they are made, and others another. Just so, it is added, jars and dishes have clay for their material, and thread is the material of cloth.

The commentator then goes on to raise and answer a grammatical objection to the form of the rule. Since it is the office of a

---

5. *vivṛte kaṇṭhe yaḥ çabdaḥ kriyate sa çvâsasaṁjño bhavati. saṁjñâyâḥ prayojanam: aghosheshu çvâsaḥ* (ii.10) *iti.*

6. *saṁvṛtavivṛtayor madhye madhyaprakâre yaḥ çabdaḥ kriyate sa hakârasaṁjño bhavati. saṁjñâyâḥ prayojanam: hakâro hacaturtheshv* (ii.9) *iti.*

pronoun to call to mind things already mentioned, and the words *nâda*, *çvâsa*, and *hakâra*, which are referred to by the pronoun in this rule, are masculine, why is the pronoun feminine (*tâḥ*, instead of *te*)? The reply is: "by the *dictum* of the Mahâbhâshya, 'pronouns effecting the equivalence of the thing pointed at and of that which is pointed out respecting it assume at pleasure the gender of either of the two,' is established the propriety of the form used in the rule; therefore there takes place a mutual accordance, or apposition." The passage referred to is apparently that found, not in the Mahâbhâshya itself, but in Kaiyyaṭa's Mahâbhâshya-pradîpa, nearly at the beginning of the work (I owe this reference to the kindness of Prof. Goldstücker): in Ballantyne's edition (p. 7) it reads, with several variations from the text given by our commentator, *uddiçyamânapratinirdiçyamânayor ekatvam âpâdayanti sarvanâmâni paryâyeṇa tallin̄gam upâdadata iti.* Reference is again made to this passage for a similar purpose under v.2.

The Rik Pr. (xiii.2) has this rule also, in nearly identical form.

नादो ऽनुप्रदानः स्वरघोषवत्सु ॥ ८ ॥

8. In vowels and sonant consonants, the emission is sound.

The term *anupradâna* is etymologized as representing *anupradîyate 'nena varṇaḥ*, 'therewith is given forth an articulate sound;' and *anupradîyate* is farther explained by *upâdîyate*, 'is obtained,' and *janyate*, 'is generated.' As synonym for the same term is given *mûlakâraṇa*, 'radical cause.'

I have already (note to Ath. Pr. i.13) called attention to the praiseworthy unanimity with which the Hindu phonetists define

---

7. *varṇânâm prakṛtayo varṇaprakṛtayaḥ: tâ varṇaprakṛtayo bhavanti ye nâdaçvâsahakârâ uktâḥ: nâdaprakṛtayaḥ kecid varṇâḥ: çvâsaprakṛtayo 'nye: hakâraprakṛtayo 'nye: yathâ mṛtprakṛtayo ghaṭaçarâvâdayaḥ: yathâ vâ*[1] *tantuprakṛtayaḥ paṭâḥ. nanu sarvanâmnaḥ prakṛtaparâmarçitvân*[2] *nâdaçvâsahakâreshu puṁlin̄geshu*[3] *satsu tâ iti strîlin̄gaprayogaḥ kathaṁ sâdhuḥ. ucyate: nirdiçyamânapratinirdiçyamânayor*[4] *ekatâm âpâdayanti sarvanâmâni kâmacâreṇa tallin̄gam*[5] *upâdadata iti mahâbhâshyavacanât prayogasâdhutvam adhyavasîyate: tasmâd anyonyânvayaḥ*[6] *sambhavati*[7].

[1] G. M. om. [2] G. M. *-rçakatv-*. [3] G. M. ins. *parâmarçârheshu.* [4] W. *-prakṛtinird-*. [5] W. *-n̄gatâm;* G. M. *tattall-*. [6] G. M. *-yasambhavaḥ.* [7] G. M. om.

8. *svareshu ghoshavatsu ca*[1] *varṇeshu nâdo 'nupradânam bhavati: anupradîyate 'nena varṇa*[2] *ity anupradânam mûlakâraṇam: anupradîyata upâdîyate janyata ity arthaḥ.*

[1] W. om. [2] W. B. *-ṇâ.*

the true ground of the distinction between surd and sonant letters. European phonetists, after long perplexing the subject with such false distinctions as are expressed by the terms "soft" and "hard," "weak" and "strong," and the like, seem now at last to be coming to a universal accordance in the correct view.

हकारो हचतुर्थेषु ॥ ९ ॥

9 In *h* and in sonant aspirate mutes, it is *h*-sound.

For the quality of this *h*-sound, see rule 6, above. The Rik Pr. (xiii.2,5: rules 6,17) connects in the same manner *h* and the "fourth" mutes. Our treatise evidently regards the peculiar *h*-sound belonging to the sonant aspirates not as something that follows the breach of contact, but as inhering in the letter, in the same manner as tone in the simple sonants. Whether the Rik Pr. hints at a difference of opinion on this point may be made a matter of question. But the failure on the part of the Prâtiçâkhyas to recognize the essentially compound character of the aspirate mutes, the fact that these differ from the unaspirated mutes by interposing something between the mute and the following vowel, is one of their marked weaknesses.

The commentator enters into no labored exposition of the rule, but spends his strength, rather, in defending its situation. He first suggests the objection that it is not in proper place, as offending against the order observed in the definition of the three kinds of material (the *h*-sound is defined last, and we should therefore expect the letters containing it to be specified last); but claims in reply that it is, after all, in place, being intended to obviate an undue extension of the preceding rule, which would otherwise be liable to be made, since *h* and the "fourth" mutes are included (by i.13,14) among the sonant consonants, to which that rule applies.

अघोषेषु श्वासः ॥ १० ॥

10. In surd consonants, it is breath.

Which are the surd consonants, was taught us in rule i.12.

---

9. *hakâraç*[1] *ca caturthâç ca hacaturthâḥ: teshu varṇeshu*[2] *hakâro 'nupradânam bhavati. nanu saṁjñâvidhânakramabhañgaprasañgân*[3] *nâ 'tre 'daṁ sûtram avatarati. ghoshavatsv iti sâmânyân nâdo hacaturtheshu ca*[4] *prasajyata*[5] *ity atiprasañgaparihârârthatvâd avataraty eve 'ti vadâmaḥ*[6].

[1] W. *haç.* [2] W. om. [3] G. M. B. *-bhañgân.* [4] G. M. om. [5] G. M. *-jyeta.* [6] G. M. *vâdaḥ.*

10. *aghosheshu varṇeshu çvâso 'nupradânam bhavati*[1].

[1] B. omits rule and comment.

भूयान्प्रथमेभ्यो ऽन्येषु ॥ ११ ॥

11. And more of it in the other surd letters than in the simple surd mutes.

Here *çvâsa*, 'breath,' is continued by implication from the preceding rule "in virtue of vicinage" (*sâṁnidhyât*), as the commentator says (there being no *ca*, 'and,' in the rule, to indicate it directly). The other surd letters are the surd aspirate mutes and the spirants (excepting *h*). There is no separation made of these two classes upon the important ground that in the spirants the greater expenditure of breath inheres in the whole character of the sound, as being fricative, while in the aspirate mutes it consists in a brief emission between the explosion of the contact and the following vowel.

The Rik Pr. (xiii.6: rule 19) says "some regard the breath in the aspirates as quicker"—an ambiguously indefinite expression.

अवर्णे नात्युपसंहृतमोष्ठहनु नातिव्यस्तम् ॥ १२ ॥

12. In forming the *a*-vowels, the lips and jaws must not be too nearly approximated, nor too widely separated.

The plain intent of this rule appears to be to guard against an excess either of openness or of closeness in the utterance of *a* and *â*, while at the same time these two sounds are considered as alike in quality. Such is not, however, the understanding of the commentator; he declares it impossible to follow both directions in forming one sound, and directs that a division be made: excessive approximation is to be avoided in the case of *a*, and excessive separation in those of the long *â* and protracted *â*s. If his intention had been to recognize the same difference in quality between *a* and *â* which is taught by the Ath. Pr. and Vâj. Pr. and by Pâṇini (see note to Ath. Pr. i.36), he would have been likely to apply the two directions of the rule in a contrary manner, warning against over-openness in *a* and over-closeness in *â*.

---

11. *sâṁnidhyâc chvâsa iti labhyate: prathamebhyo 'nyeshu aghosheshu çvâso*[1] *bhûyân adhiko bhavati.*

[1] G. M. om.

12. *avarṇa uccâryamâṇa oshṭhahanv atyupasaṁhṛtam atisaṁçlishṭaṁ na bhavati: ativyastam ativivṛtaṁ 'ca na*[1] *bhavati. oshṭhâu ca hanû c' oshṭhahanu: dvandvaç ca prâṇitûryasenâṅgânâm* (Pâṇ. ii.4.2) *ity ekavadbhâvaḥ: tad etad*[2] *ekasminn ubhayathâ na çakyate kartum iti yogavibhâgaḥ kâryaḥ*[3]*: akâre nâ*[4] *'tyupasaṁhṛtam âkâre ca*[5] *plute ca nâ 'tivyastam iti.*

[1] W. *na ca.* [2] W. *eva tad;* G. M. om. [3] G. M. B. om. [4] W. G. *nâ.* [5] W. B. om.

The term *oshṭhahanu*, though singular, is declared to signify the two lips and the two jaws, and a rule of Pâṇini (ii.4.2) is quoted in justification of such treatment of a copulative compound.

ओकारे च ॥ १३ ॥

13. Also in uttering *o*.

The "also" (*ca*) of this rule, we are told, brings forward only the action of the jaws prescribed in the preceding rule: this appears from the fact that the one following gives a special direction with regard to the action of the lips. In forming an *o*, then, the jaws are not to be too widely separated.

ओष्ठौ तूपसंहृततरौ ॥ १४ ॥

14. But the lips are more nearly approximated.

"Vicinage" is here again made the sufficiently obvious ground of assuming that the direction applies to the utterance of *o*. The "but" (*tu*) of the rule, according to Vararuci, one of the three authorities from whom our comment is principally derived (see the introduction), annuls the direction formerly (in rule 12) given as to the position of the lips: but Mâhisheya, another of the same authorities, has explained it as exempting from the widely separated condition the *o* of such words as *bandhoḥ* (ii.5.8[7]). This latter interpretation is quite absurd, or else I am very obtuse with regard to it.

As regards the precise tone of the *o*, such directions as these can teach us nothing satisfactory. The only valuable conclusion which we derive from them is that the authors of the Prâtiçâkhya looked upon the sound as a simple homogeneous tone—not phonetically diphthongal, although in classification excluded (by rule i.2) from the category of simple vowels. The same, we shall see, is the case with *e* also.

ईषत्प्रकृष्टावेकारे ॥ १५ ॥

15. In uttering *e*, they are slightly protracted.

---

13. *cakâro hanumâtrakâryânvâdeçakaḥ: oshṭhakâryasya parasûtreṇa viçeshavidhânât. okâra uccâryamâṇe hanû ativyaste na bhavataḥ.*

14. *sâṁnidhyâd okâra iti labhyate: okâre kârya oshṭhâv*[1] *upasaṁhṛtatarâu syâtâm: tuçabda oshṭhayoḥ pûrvoktavidhiṁ nivârayatî*[2] *'ti vararucir uvâca. mâhisheyas tu babhâshe: bandhor ity âdikam okâraṁ savyañjanaṁ*[3] *vyastato*[4] *nivârayatî 'ti.*

[1] W. B. om. [2] G. M. *vâr-*. [3] G. M. *vyañj-*. [4] W *vyes-*.

That "they" means the lips is, we are told, sufficiently indicated by the dual number of the adjective. *Prakṛshṭa*, 'protracted,' is glossed by *saṁnikṛshṭa*, 'drawn down together, brought near'

उपसंहृततरे हनू ॥ १६ ॥

16. The jaws are more nearly approached.

The force of the comparative is explained by the usual term *atiçayena*, 'with excess.'

In the utterance of *e*, the position of the tongue is also a matter of importance, and is explained in the next rule.

जिह्वामध्यान्ताभ्यां चोत्तराञ्जम्भ्यान्त्स्पर्शयति ॥ १७ ॥

17. And one touches the borders of the upper back jaws with the edges of the middle of the tongue.

The "and" (*ca*) in this rule we are directed to regard as bringing forward the *ekâra* of rule 15, "on the frog-leap principle"—that is to say, by overleaping the intervening rule. The terms descriptive of the organs concerned I have translated in accordance with the directions of the commentator, although much tempted to render *jambhyân* by 'jaw-teeth, grinders.' I cannot doubt that *jambhyân* is the true reading here, although the MSS. give a curious and perplexing variety of forms to the word, and *uttarâñ jambhyânt* is not once read: T. comes nearest to it, giving *uttarân jaṁbhyâṁ*; W. has *uttarâ jaṁbhyâṁt* in the rule, and *uttarâ jabhyân* and *jabhyân* in the comment; B., *uttarâñ jabhyât* in the rule, *uttarâ jabhyân* and *jaṁbhyân* in the comment; G. and M., *uttarâñ jabhyâṁ* in the rule; G., *uttarâṁ jabhyâṁ* and *jaṁbhyâm*; and M., *uttarâñ jabhyâṁ* and *jabhyâm*, in the comment. The verb *sparçayati* is equivalent to *spṛçet*, the causative ending *ṇic* being added without altering the meaning of the simple verb (compare Pâṇ. iii.1.25), as in *pâlay* for *pâ*, and other like cases.

---

15. *prakṛshṭâv ity atra dvivacanena prakṛtâv oshṭhâu gṛhyete: ekâre kârya oshṭhâv îshatprakṛshṭâu syâtâm. prakṛshṭatâ saṁnikṛshṭatâ.*

16. *sâṁnidhyâd ekâra iti labhyate: ekâre kârye hanû upasaṁhṛtatare bhavataḥ. atiçayeno 'pasaṁhṛte upasaṁhṛtatare.*

17. *ekâre kârye jihvâmadhyântâbhyâm uttarâñ jambhyânt sparçayati spṛçed ity arthaḥ: pâlayatî*[1] *'ty âdivat svârthe ṇic: jambhyân iti hanûmûlaprântadeçân*[2] *ity arthaḥ: maṇḍûkaplutinyâyena*[3] *cakâra ekâram âkarshati. jihvâyâ 'madhyaṁ jihvâmadhyam: tasyâ 'ntâu*[4]*: tâbhyâṁ jihvâmadhyântâbhyâm.*

[1] G. M. *palây-*. [2] G. M. *-çam*; W. *-ntaprade-*. [3] G. M. *-kagatiny-*. [(4)] W. *madhya antâu*; B. *madhyasya anân.*

In order to complete the definition of the mode of production of *e*, rules 20 and 23, below, have yet to be applied; but they add nothing essential to the description of the present rule, which assures to the vowel, as clearly as any such description could do, the "continental" sound of *e*, or that which it has in *they*, short in *met*. There is no hint of a composite or diphthongal utterance, any more than in the case of *o*. A diphthongal utterance, however, as *ai*, *au* (in *aisle*, *house*), we must assume them to have had originally (compare note to Ath. Pr. i.40).

उपसंहृततरे च जिह्वाग्रमृकारर्कारल्कारेषु बर्स्वे-
षूपसंहरति ॥ १८ ॥

18. The jaws, also, are more closely approximated, and the tip of the tongue is brought into close proximity to the upper back gums, in *ṛ*, *ṝ*, and *ḷ*.

The construction of this rule is very harsh; the subject *hanû*, 'jaws,' comes into its first member again with a flying leap from rule 16, drawn by the *ca*, 'also;' while the second member starts off independently, "one approximates," with no connective to bind it to the other. These roughnesses are unremarked by the commentator, and I have smoothed them over in the translation. The word *upasaṁharati*, 'approximates,' is glossed in the comment by *nikshipet*, 'let one throw down (or apply),' and *barsvâs* is explained as 'the high places behind the row of teeth'—that is, the swelling of the inner gums.

The commentator starts a question as to the propriety of the conversion of *ṝ* and *ḷ* in this rule into *r* and *l* after *a* (*ṛkârarkâralkâra*, from *ṛkâra-ṝkâra-ḷkâra*), the cases not being covered by the prescription given below (at x.8: no case of the combination of *ṝ* and *ḷ* occurring in the Sanhitâ, the Prâtiçâkhya makes no provision for it): he is compelled to acknowledge that this treatise does not teach the conversion, but claims that it is justified by the authority of other text-books; and that the same explanation applies to an earlier case (rule i.31) of a like combination.

This wholly insufficient direction is all that our treatise gives

---

18. *caçabdo hanvor*[1] *anvâdeçakaḥ: ṛkâra ṝkâra ḷkâre ca kârye hanû*[2] *upasaṁhṛtatare bhavataḥ: jihvâgraṁ ca barsveshû 'pasaṁharati nikshipet: barsveshv iti dantapañkter uparishṭâd uccapradeçeshv ity arthaḥ. nanv aram ṛkârapare* (x.8) *iti lakshaṇâsambhavâd*[3] *ṛkârarkâralkâreshv iti kathaṁ saṁdhiḥ sâdhuḥ. satyaṁ nâi 'tallakshaṇât: kiṁ tu çâstrântarabalât*[4]*: evam ṛkâralkârâu hrasvâv* (i.31) *iti vijñeyam*[5].

[1] W. *hanvár;* B. *h;* G. M. *hanor.* [2] W. om. [3] G. M. -*ṇas-;* B. -*ṇâsaṁjñavâdâd.* [4] G. M. ins. *sâdhuḥ.* [5] G. M. *jñeyam.*

us for the utterance of the difficult *r* and *l* vowels. By i.2, they are excluded from the category of simple homogeneous vowels. For the teachings of the other Prâtiçâkhyas respecting them, see note to Ath. Pr. i.37. However they may have been pronounced at the period of grammatical treatment of the Vedic texts, we have no good reason to doubt that, at the time when those texts were composed, they were phonetically the same with the semi vowels *r* and *l*, differing from them only as, for example, the *l* of *able* differs from that of *ably*, the *r* of (French) *aigre* from that of *aigri*. For a theoretical discussion of this double value of the articulated sounds which lie nearly upon the boundary line between vowels and consonants, see Journ. Am. Or. Soc. viii.362 seq.

एकेषामनुस्वारस्वरभक्त्योश्च ॥ १९ ॥

19. As also, according to some, in *anusvâra* and *svarabhakti*.

In this case, we are told, the "also" (*ca*) brings down the whole of the preceding rule, and the meaning is, that there is approximation of the jaws in uttering *anusvâra*, and approach of the tip of the tongue to the gums in uttering the *svarabhakti*, according to the opinion of some; while others hold that *anusvâra* is simply nasal, and the *svarabhakti* (see xxi.15) equivalent to *ṛ*. This, the commentator adds, is Vararuci's explanation, and its truth is questionable. We, in our turn, may regard it as matter for question whether this attribution and expression of doubt apply to the whole interpretation of the rule, or only to its concluding part, the statement of the opinion of "others." The latter is perhaps most probable.

So far as regards *anusvâra*, we can hardly ascribe any value or propriety to this rule; the definition of *svarabhakti* in connection with that of the *ṛ*-vowels is natural enough.

अनादेशे प्रण्यस्ता जिह्वा ॥ २० ॥

20. In the absence of special direction, the tongue is thrust down forward.

When no such direction as "with the point of the tongue," "with

---

19. *cakâraḥ pûrvoktavidhim anvâdiçati: yathâsaṁkhyenâ*[1] *'nusvârasvarabhaktyoḥ pûrvoktavidhir bhavati: anusvâre hanvor upasaṁhâraḥ: svarabhaktâu jihvâgrasya barsveshû 'pasaṁhâraḥ: etad ekeshâm matam. anyeshâṁ tu matam anusvârasyâ 'nunâsikamâtratvam: svarabhakter ṛkâratulyatvam. iti vararucimatam*[2]*: tac cintyam*[3].

[1] G. M. *-khyo.* [2] G. M. *-ciracitam.* [3] W. *cityam;* B. *cânityam.*

the middle of the tongue" is given, then its position is to be understood as here directed. To explain *praṇyastâ*, the commentator gives, besides an ordinary analysis, the expression "in a quiescent state;" as example, he cites *upa mâ* (iii.2.4[1]: G. and M. spoil the citation by adding the following word, *dyâvâpṛthivî*), in the utterance of which words the tongue is not called perceptibly into action. But this interpretation evokes a difficulty: "since the position of quiescence is assured to all the articulating organs in the absence of any direction respecting them, of what use is this precept?" The reply is: *e* (as taught by rule 17, above) is to be produced with the edges of the middle of the tongue, and the *a* contained in that letter is of the same character; hence it might be inferred, from the identity of the *a*-quality, that *a* was to be so uttered in other situations, as in words like *atha* (i.1.13[1] et al., if the word is to be regarded here as a citation)—a misapprehension which the rule removes. To this reply the objection may be raised that our treatise acknowledges the presence of no such element as *a* in *e*, and that an *a* uttered with the middle of the tongue is a phonetic impossibility. The direction respecting the tongue may well enough be regarded as a not entirely negative one; or it may have been deemed desirable to fix so very mobile and unruly a member by a special law.

अकारवदोष्ठौ ॥ २१ ॥

21. The lips are as in the utterance of *a*.

We are directed to include in this rule, by vicinage, "in the absence of special direction." The proper position of the lips for uttering *a* was given in rule 12, above. As illustration is added, quite needlessly, the word *indraḥ* (*passim*); the southern manuscripts read instead *indriyâvaḥ* (vi.5.8[3]).

---

20. *yatra jihvâgreṇa jihvâmadhyene 'ty âdir*[1] *anâdeças*[2] *tatra vishaye jihvâ praṇyastâ tûshṇîmbhûtâ*[3] *bhavati: prakarsheṇa nyastâ praṇyasta*[4]. *yathâ: upa..... nanv anâdeçe sarvakaraṇânâṁ tûshṇîmbhâvasiddheḥ kimartho 'yam ârambhaḥ. ucyate: ekârasya jihvâmâdhyântanishpâdyatvam*[5] *asti*[6]*: tadavayavasyâ*[7] *'kârasya tathâtvam asti: akâratvasâmyâd anyatrâ 'py athe 'ty âdâu tathâtvam prasajyeta: tac câ 'nishṭam: tan mâ bhûd iti parihâraḥ.* [8]*nâ "deço 'nâdeçaḥ*[8]*: tasmin: upadeçâbhâva ity arthaḥ.*

[1] G. M. *âdinâ.* [2] G. M. ins. *anupadeçaḥ.* [3] W. B. *-ṇibh-.* [4] W. B. om. [5] G. M. *-dyamânatvam.* [6] G. M. *asti 'ti.* [7] G. M. ins. *'pi.* [(8)] W. *anvâdeçaḥ;* B. *anâdeçaḥ.*

21. *sâṁnidhyâd anâdeça iti labhyate: oshṭhayor yatrâ 'nâdeças tatrâ 'kâravad akâre yathâ tath'*[1] *oshṭhâu bhavataḥ: nâ 'tyupasaṁhṛtatarâv*[2] *ity arthaḥ. yathâ: indra*[3] *iti.*

[1] MSS. *tathâ.* [2] G. M. *-hṛtâv.* [3] G. M. *indriyâva.*

तालौ जिह्वामध्यमिवर्णे ॥ २२ ॥

22. In the *i*-vowels, the middle of the tongue is to be approximated to the palate.

The comment supplies, without remark, the predicate "to be approximated," and gives as example *ishe tvâ* (i.1.1 et al.).

एकारे च ॥ २३ ॥

23. Also in *e*.

Here the "also" (*ca*) brings down the whole of the preceding precept, both the specification of the active organ (*karaṇa*) and that of the passive organ or place (*sthâna*). The exposition of the meaning of the rule is very simple and easy; but the commentator does not fail to notice that its necessity is open to objection upon two grounds, and enters into its defense at considerable length. The first objection is, why make two separate rules (22 and 23) for a single direction?—that is to say, if the *i*-vowels and *e* are all produced by the approximation of the middle of the tongue to the palate, why not include them in one rule together? The answer given is that the degree of approximation is not the same in the two cases, but is less in the *e* than in the *i*-vowels. If it be asked, why is this so? the reply is made, because the *e* is mixed with *a*, and production of this *a* with the middle of the tongue is on account of its constituting a part of *e*, and not by reason of its own natural character (compare the comment to rule 20, above)—which special qualification is sufficient ground for the less degree of approximation. The second difficulty is stated thus: both place and organ of *e* have been already defined in rules 15–17, above; but here is laid down for the same letter something different: and it is not possible that both directions should be followed

---

22. *ivarṇe kârye jihvâmadhyaṁ tâlâv upasaṁhartavyam. yathâ: ishe..... [1]jihvâyâ madhyaṁ[1] jihvâmadhyaṁ[2].*

[1] W. om. [2] B. om.

23. *cakâraḥ pûrvavidhim anvâdiçati: ekâre kârye [1]jihvâmadhyaṁ tâlâv[1] upasaṁhartavyam[2]. nanu vidhâu samâne pṛthaksûtrârambhaḥ kimarthaḥ[3]. ucyate: ivarṇe yathâ jihvâmadhyopasaṁhâro na khalv evam ekâre kiṁ tu tato[4] nyûna ity arthaḥ: kutaḥ: akâramiçritatvâd ekârasya: akârasya ca tadekadeçatvâj jihvâmadhyântanishpâdyatvaṁ[5] na tu svataḥ: ata eva sopâdhikatvân nyûnatvopapattiḥ. îshatprakṛshṭâv* (ii.15) *ity atra[6] sûtratrayeṇâi 'kârasya sthânakaraṇe nirdishṭe: iha tu tato [7]'nyat tasyâi[7] 'va nirdiçyate: tad ekasminn ubhayathâ kartuṁ na çakyate: virodhât tasmâd atra yogavibhâgaḥ kartavyaḥ[8]: avyañ-*

in the production of one sound. To get rid of this difficulty, a division must be made; the former description must be understood as applying to *e* by itself, and the present one to *e* combined with a consonant. How is this determination made? Why, when we say in a general way "the letter *e*," it lies nearest, or is most natural, to understand that letter itself, without a consonant; hence, because of its prior suggestedness, the first definition belongs to it; and the other is left, to be applied to the same sound as combined with a consonant.

The utter artificiality of the answer to the second objection is too obvious to need pointing out; and even the first evokes more difficulties than it removes. There is no inconsistency whatever between rules 17 and 23, and we have reason to be surprised only at the repetition in the latter of what is implied already in the former. Rule 23 has the air of being an afterthought, slipped in, because of the really close relationship between *e* and *i*, with disregard of what had been taught before. The alleged difference of degree of approximation exists clearly enough, but would be very insufficiently intimated by a mere separation of one rule into two.

ओष्ठोपसंहार उवर्णे ॥ २४ ॥

24. In the *u*-vowels, there is approximation of the lips.

After his paraphrase of the rule, the commentator enters here upon an exposition, the intent of which is not altogether clear to me. "Here, he says, approximation is as formerly, and not mere drawing down together" (that is, of the same kind as was taught in rule 14, above, and not the *prakṛshṭatâ*, 'protraction,' of rule 15, which is there glossed by *saṁnikṛshtatâ?*). "However, 'the lips drawn down together may be long'—this will be said hereafter" (by this phrase some direction given later in the treatise is

---

jane tal lakshaṇaṁ savyañjane tv etad iti. kuto 'yaṁ niyamaḥ. ucyate: [9]ekâra iti[9] sâmânyoktâu satyâm [10]prathamam avyañjanasyâi[10] 'va grahaṇaṁ mukhyam[11]: tathâ sati prathamapratîtes[12] tasmin prathamaṁ lakshaṇaṁ yujyate: savyañjane [13] pâriçeshyâd etad iti vijñeyam.

([1]) W. G. M. *-dhyántâv.* [2] G. M. *-vyâu.* [3] G. M. *-thaṁ.* [4] G. M. *ato.* [5] B. *-dhyântábhyâṁ nish-*; G. M. *-dhyanish-.* [6] G. M. om. ([7]) W. *ṅyasyâi*; B. *nye t-.* [8] G. M. om. ([9]) G. M. *ekârasya.* [10] B. *pratham av-*; G. M. *-maṁ vy-.* [11] W. *sukaram.* [12] G. M. *-maṁ pra-.* [13] G. M. ins. *tu.*

24. *uvarṇe kârya oshṭhopasaṁhâro bhavati: atro 'pasaṁhâraḥ pûrvavan na saṁnikṛshṭatâmâtram: kiṁ tu: saṁnikṛshṭâv oshṭhâu dîrghâu syâtâm iti vakshyate: evam oshṭhâu tû 'pasaṁhṛtatarâv* (ii.14) *ity atrâ 'pi vijñeyam. yathâ: ul-.... oshṭhayor upasaṁhâra oshṭhopasaṁhâraḥ*[1].

[1] W. B. om.

wont to be cited; but there is no sucn direction as this, either in text or in commentary); "the same is to be understood in rule 14, above" (compare a similar reference to a preceding rule in the comment to ii.18). A phrase is then cited from the Sanhitâ, containing *u* and *û*, namely *ulûkhalabudhno yûpaḥ* (vii.2.1[3]).

एकान्तरस्तु सर्वत्र प्रकृतात् ॥ २५ ॥

25. But, in all cases, with an interval of one from the preceding.

The commentary on this very obscure rule reads as follows:

By vicinage, "labial approximation" is here implied: everywhere, in the case of labial vowels, after the preceding labial approximation, a separate labial approximation is to be made, provided it have an interval of one: by this is understood having the quantity of a *mora* interposed: that, namely, has an interval of one whereof one *mora* is the interval or interposition. This is the distinctive condition of the separate labial approximation. The word "but" (*tu*) denies the necessity of the interval of one in a case where *o* [W. says, where *âu* or *v*] follows. Examples are: *utpûtaçushmam* (i.6.1[1]); *sûnnîyam iti su-unnîyam* (vi.2.4[1]); *atho oshadhîshu* (iii.5.5[2] and vi.3.9[5]); *bâhuvor balam* (v.5.9[2]); *tanuvâu ghorâ 'nyâ* (v.7.3[3]: G. M. omit the last word); *caturhotâ* (not found in the Sanhitâ: occurs Tâitt. Brâh. ii.2.3[2]).

Objection: in *yo 'n̐çum* (iii.3.4[3]), the *anusvâra* has a *mora* [by i.34] and the *ç* a half-*mora* [by i.37]; since, then, the quantity being a *mora* and a half, there is not an interval of one, how is the separate labial approximation assured?

Answer: it is assured by the principle "a hundred includes fifty." Where there is a *mora* and a half, there is *à fortiori* a *mora;* in virtue of this the prescribed effect is produced, but its excess does not vitiate the rule, because the word "one" excludes what does not belong to itself (?) For the same reason, the occurrence

---

25. *sâṁnidhyâd oshṭhopasaṁhâra iti labhyate: sarvatr' oshṭhyasvareshu prakṛtâd oshṭhopasaṁhârât pṛthagoshṭhopasaṁhâraḥ* [1]*kartavyaḥ: sa ced ekântaraḥ*[1]*: ekântara iti mâtrâkâlavyavâya*[2] *iti labhyate*[3]*: ekamâtrâ 'ntaraṁ vyavadhânaṁ yasyâ 'sâv ekântaraḥ: iti pṛthagoshṭhopasaṁhârasya viçeshaṇam. tuçabda okâraparatva*[4] *ekântaratvaniyamaṁ*[5] *nivartayati. udâharaṇâni: ut-:*[6] *sûn-....: atho....: bâh-....: tan-....: cat-.... nanu yo.... ity atrâ 'nusvârasya mâtrâkâlaḥ* [7]*çakârasyâ 'rdhamâtrâkâlaḥ:*[7] *evam adhyardhamâtratve saty ekântaratvâbhâvât*[8] *katham pṛthagoshṭhopasaṁhârasiddhiḥ. ucyate: çatepañcâçannyâyena sidhyati: adhyardhamâtratve 'py*[9] *ekamâtratvaṁ sutarâm*[10] *asti; tena kâryam bhavaty adhikaṁ tu na nishidhyate: svâyogavyavachedakatvâd ekaçabdasya: ata eva bâh-.... ity âder*[11] *na*

of the double labial in such passages as *bâhuvor balam ûruvor ojaḥ* (v.5.9[2]: G. M. omit the last word) is not primary (or original), but its quality as *sphurita*, 'quavered,' is shown by the likeness of the example (?).

Second objection: then why is there not a separate labial approximation in the two *u*'s following the *k* and *r* of *kusurubindaḥ* (vii. 2.2[1]), since there occurs more than a *mora* and a half of interval between them?

Answer: not so; here there is denial of separate labiality only for the two *u*'s that follow *k* and *s*, because of the absence of its necessary condition; but to that following the *r* this rule does not apply, because it is not a case of separateness from the preceding, but of separateness from the *u* that follows the intermediate *s*; this being so, there is no occurrence of the interval of one for a letter in this situation: thus there is no offense against the rule.

So far the comment; but either I have failed to apprehend its true meaning, or it has given a false interpretation to the rule, or the rule itself is destitute of intelligible significance. I must confess myself unable to see what peculiarity there should be in the utterance of two labial vowels following one another in two successive syllables with not less than a *mora*'s interval between them. No precept, so far as I know, in any of the other Prâtiçâkhyas, is analogous with this, or casts light upon it.

It appears to be intimated, in the course of the answer to the first objection, that the peculiar utterance of the *u* in such words as *bâhuvoḥ* for the usual *bâhvoḥ* and *ûruvoḥ* for *ûrvoḥ* is denominated *sphurita*. The term does not occur elsewhere; nor is any notice taken of the phenomenon, if not here. It is a well-known characteristic of Tâittirîya texts, but is found in fewer words than one would be apt to imagine. Besides the two just given, I have noted in the Sanhitâ only the cases of *tanû* (*tanuvam*, e. g. i.1.8; *tanuvâ*, e.g i.1.10[2]) and the word *suvar*, which are often met with. Of similar resolutions of an *i*-vowel into *iy*, the cases are more nu-

---

dviroshṭhyam[12] *mukhyam: kiṁ tu sphuritatvam*[13] *udâharaṇatvâbhâsatayâ*[14] *darçitam. tarhi kus- ity atra kakârarephâbhyâm uttarayor ukârayoḥ katham pṛthagoshṭhopasaṁhâro na bhavati: adhyardhamâtravyavâyasambhavât*[15]. *mâi 'vam: atra*[16] *kakârasakârottarayor*[17] *ukârayos tâvad*[18] *apṛthagoshṭhatâ*[19]*: etallakshaṇâsambhavât: rephâd uttarasya tu*[20] *prakṛtât pṛthaktvâbhâvân nâ 'yaṁ vidhiḥ:* [21]*kiṁ tu*[21] *madhyasthasakârottarâd ukârât pṛthaktvam: tathâ saty ekântarâbhâvaḥ*[22]*: tadavastha*[23] *eve 'ti lakshaṇam idam avyabhicaritam*[24].

(1) W. om. [2] G. M. *-labhedavy-*. [3] G. M. *arthaḥ*. [4] W. *âukâravakârap-*. [5] G. M. *ekamâtrânantaratva-*. [6] G. M. om. (7) B. om. [8] G. M. *ekâratv-*. [9] G. M. om. [10] W. *muttarâm*. [11] G. M. *âdâu*. [12] G. M. *-ṭhyatvam*. [13] G. M. *svar-*. [14] W. *-haratvâ-*; B. *-tvabh-*; G. M. *-ṇan tu âbh-*. [15] G. M. *-vyavadhânas-*. [16] G. M. om. [17] G. M. *-râbhyâm utt-*. [18] G. M. *-van*. [19] G. M. *na pṛthagoshṭhasaṁhâratâ*. [20] W. *u*; B. om. (21) W. B. om. [22] G. M. *-vât*. [23] W. *-sthay*; B. *-sthâ*. [24] G. M. *vyabh-*.

merous, but less frequent. I have collected the following (without exhausting the Sanhitâ, especially of themes in *iya*): *ágriya* (iv.5.5[2]), *aghniya* (i.1.1), *áçviya* (ii.2.12[8]), *asmadríyañc* (i.4.21), *îdhríya* (iv.5.7[2]), *dhíshṇiya* (iii.1.3[1]); *pâ'triya* (iii.2.3[3]), *budhníya* (i.3.3), *réshmiya* (iv.5.7[2]), *viçvápsniyâ* (i.5.3[3]), *viçvadríyañc* (i.7.13[3]), *vr̥'shṇiya* (iii.2.5[3]), *çî'ghriya* (iv.5.5[2]), *sadhríyañc* (i.2.14[5]); and, of oblique cases from themes in *i* or *î*, *indrâgniyóḥ* (i.3.12), *gâyatriyâ'* (iii.2.9[1]), *pâ'rshṇiyâ* (iv.6.9[2]), *pr̥'çniyâi* (ii.2.11[4]), *râ'triyai* (iv.4.1[1]), *lakshmíyâ* (ii.1.5[2]), *viçpátniyâi* (iii.1.11[4]), *svâdhíyam* (i.3.14[6]). None of the consonantal combinations which are thus avoided by the resolution of the *u* are such as the euphony of the Tâittirîyakas does not tolerate: but of those which are avoided by the resolution of the *i*, only three are met with in the text—namely, *try* (e. g. i.8.22[1]: ii.4.3[1]), *tny* (iv.4.2[2]), and *çny* (v.5.6[3]). I have not entered deeply enough into the investigation to deduce the law, if law there be, by which the resolution is made.

अकारार्धमैकारौकारयोरादिः ॥ २६ ॥

26. The beginning of *âi* and *âu* is half an *a*.

Rules 28 and 29, below, tell of what constitutes the remainder of these diphthongs.

संवृतकरणतरमेकेषाम् ॥ २७ ॥

27. Which, in the opinion of some, is uttered with the organs more closed.

We have here another indication that, as intimated above (under ii.12), our Prâtiçâkhya does not recognize the close or neutral pronunciation of the short *a;* for, if it did so, there would obviously be no reason for referring to the opinion held by certain authorities respecting its assumption of that utterance in diphthongal combination. Some phonetists (without sufficient reason, as it appears to me) have in like manner defined the first element in our English diphthongs ("long *i*" in *aisle*, *isle*, and *ou* or *ow* in *house*, *down*) to be the neutral vowel (*u* in *but*), rather than the open *a* (of *far*). But, whatever may have been the case with the Sanskrit diphthongs, our own cannot be truly described as composed of two elements each: they are slides; and to allow the organs to remain in

---

26. *âikârasyâu "kârasya câ "dir akârârdham bhavati. akârasyâ 'rdham akârârdham.*

27. *sâṁnidhyâd akârârdham iti labhyate: ekeshâm mate tad akârârdhaṁ saṁvr̥takaraṇataram bhavati. saṁvr̥tâni saṁnikr̥shṭâni karaṇâni yasya tat saṁvr̥takaraṇam: atiçayena saṁvr̥takaraṇaṁ saṁvr̥takaraṇataram.*

B. reads *saṁvr̥tta* throughout.

either their first or last position long enough to make the initial or final element distinctly audible, would be an error of pronunciation.

The commentator glosses *saṁvṛta*, 'enveloped, shut up, closed,' with *saṁnikṛshṭa*, 'drawn down together, approximated.'

इकारो ऽध्यर्धः पूर्वस्य शेषः ॥२८॥

28. Of the former, the rest is one and a half times *i.*

Of the former—that is, of *âi ; âi* and *âu* having been mentioned together in a preceding rule (ii.26), says the commentator.

उकारस्तूत्तरस्य ॥२९॥

29. But, of the latter, *u.*

That is to say, the remainder of *âu* is one and a half times *u.* To account for the word "but" (*tu*) in the rule, the commentator notes that, as the beginning of both diphthongs is the same sound, *a*, it might seem to follow that their end would be the same sound, *i:* this the "but" denies. This explanation merely intensifies and makes too precise the actual meaning of the word.

For the teachings of the other Prâtiçâkhyas as to the pronunciation of *âi* and *âu*, see the note to Ath. Pr. i.40. As there remarked, the euphonic treatment which they receive proves their first element to have had originally more than a half-*mora* of quantity. If they must be limited to two *moras*, a better description of them would have been $1\frac{1}{2}a+\frac{1}{2}i$, and $1\frac{1}{2}a+\frac{1}{2}u$. If, as we may presume to be the case, the authors of these treatises defined their own pronunciation pretty accurately, then the *âi* and *âu*, not less than the *e* and *o*, had by their time taken on a value notably different from that which belonged to them when the euphonic rules of the language were the faithful representation of living processes.

अनुस्वारोत्तमा अनुनासिकाः ॥३०॥

30. *Anusvâra* and the last mutes are nasal.

As example of *anusvâra*, the comment cites *yo 'ñçum* (iii.3.4[3]);

---

28. *pûrvasyâi "kârasye 'ty arthaḥ: adhastâd[1] âikârâukârayoḥ sahoccaritatvât[2]: adhyardha ikâra âikârasya çesho bhavati. adhikam ardhaṁ yasyâ 'sâv adhyardhaḥ.*

[1] W. *adhyardhas tâvad.* [2] G. M. *uccar-.*

29. *uttarasyâu "kârasye 'ty arthaḥ: adhyardha ukâra âukâraçesho[1] bhavati: yathâ 'nayor ubhayor apy âdir akâra eva tadvad ikâra eva çeshaḥ[2] prasaktaḥ: tan[3] nishedhati tuçabdaḥ.*

[1] G. M. *-rasya çe-.* [2] W. B. om. [3] W. B. *taṁ.*

of the "last" or nasal mutes, *pratyañ hotâram* (vi.3.1[5])—to which G. M. add *prâñcam upa* (v.2.7[3]), and *maṇinâ* (vii.3.14).

The term *anunâsika* is interpreted by the commentator as signifying *nâsikâm anuvartate*, 'it goes after the nostril'—that is to say, doubtless, 'it finds exit by the nasal passages:' an accurate definition of this class of sounds. As employed in this Prâtiçâkhya, *anunâsika* means simply, as adjective, 'nasal,' and its derivative noun, *ânunâsikya*, signifies 'nasality, nasal utterance.' Rule 52, below, describes how such mode of utterance is produced, and in chapter xvii. (rules 1–4) is made an attempt to define the degree of nasality in the various sounds of the class. "Nasal," or *anunâsika*, by the present rule, are the *anusvâra* and the five nasal mutes, *ṅ*, *ñ*, *ṇ*, *n*, *m*; the same term is applied later to the nasal semivowels into which *n* and *m* (v.26–28) are under certain circumstances convertible; and at v.31, x.11, xv.1,6, xxii.14, we also hear of nasal (*anunâsika*) vowels. The other nose-sounds, the *yamas* and *nâsikya* (ii.49,50, xxi.8,12–14), do not anywhere receive this title.

It is desirable to put together somewhere a comprehensive statement of the doctrines held by the Tâittirîya-Prâtiçâkhya respecting the nasal constituents of the alphabet it recognizes, and no more suitable place is likely to present itself than is offered here.

All nasal (*anunâsika*) sounds are uttered (ii.52) by the mouth and nose together. An *uttama*, a "last" or nasal mute, is a sound in the production of which the intonated breath escapes through the nose, while the organs of the mouth form one of those same contacts which give rise to the corresponding non-nasal mutes of the series. In *anusvâra*, on the other hand (including under that designation the nasal semivowels, of which more further on), the mouth-organs are not wholly closed, but the intonated breath finds exit through them at the same time that it passes through the nasal cavities. In all cases, then, in which the character of the nasal of a syllable is determined by that of the following consonant, the nasal will be a mute if the latter is a mute, but an *anusvâra* if succeeded by a letter not forming a contact—by a semivowel or a spirant. Respecting the phonetic character and occurrence of the nasal mutes, there has been no difference of opinion, so far as we have any information, among the Hindu phonetists of the period represented by the Prâtiçâkhyas; none of them has allowed a final *anusvâra* before a pause, or an *anusvâra* before a mute, either in the same or a following word. As to the phonetic value, however, of the real *anusvâra*, the nasal uttered with open mouth-organs, there was by no means the same accordance among those ancient grammarians. Some held it to be a pervading nasalisation of the preceding vowel; others, a nasal addition to

---

30. *anusvâraç co 'ttamâç câ 'nunâsikâ bhavanti: nâsikâm anuvartanta ity anunâsikâḥ. yathâ: anusvâraḥ: yo....: uttamâ ca*[1]*: pra-....:* [2]*prâ-....: maṇ-*[2].

[1] G. M. ins. *yathâ.* [2] W. B. om.

that vowel. The former view is adopted and consistently maintained by the Atharva-Prâtiçâkhya, which acknowledges nasal consonants and nasalized vowels, but no *tertium quid.* The Prâtiçâkhyas of the Rik and White Yajus are equally consistent in their recognition of an *anusvâra* as nasal appendage to the vowel, and the latter of them gives (Vâj. Pr. iv.147–8) detailed directions as to the quantity belonging to each element. The Tâittirîya-Prâtiçâkhya adopts prevailingly the same view, but lets the other appear distinctly in some of its rules. Thus, at v.31, it is stated to be Âtreya's opinion that, when a nasal mute becomes *l*, the preceding vowel is nasalized; and, in conformity with this, xv.1 directly teaches that, after the various conversion of *m* and *n*, the vowel before them becomes nasal, the following rules adding (xv.2,3) that some authorities deny this, and direct *anusvâra* to be inserted instead: here the commentary has to reverse the obvious intent of the text, and declare the latter rules approved, and the first disapproved. Further, x.11 directs that when a vowel is combined with a nasalized vowel the result is nasal (the commentary, however, gives a different interpretation: see the rule). Once more, in xxii.14, among "heavy" syllables is reckoned one that is *anunâsika*, 'nasal.'

I very much doubt whether this difference of views is founded upon an actual difference of pronunciation; it is probably due rather to a discordant apprehension and analysis of a single mode of utterance. The same point might divide into two parties our phonetists at the present day—just as they have long been divided upon the question whether a *b* differs from a *p* in being sonant, or in being soft, or weak, or of inferior aspiration, or something of that kind. Without entering into any detailed discussion of the subject, I will simply say that I incline to side with the Atharvan school, and to believe in nasal vowels rather than in *anusvâra.* No one of the Prâtiçâkhyas gives an intelligible definition of the phonetic character of *anusvâra*, considered as an independent alphabetic element; if it is to be so considered, we shall hardly be able to make of it anything but a bit of the neutral vowel (*u* of *but*) nasalized, or the sound of the French *un*, and shall have to regard it as attached to the vowel much in the same way as, by us who speak English, the same sound not nasalized is attached to most of our long vowels before an *r*—for example, in *there, here, oar, cure, fire, sour* (see Journ. Am. Or. Soc'y, viii.353).

Which of the two views is originally favored by the Devanâgarî alphabet does not admit of much question; the writing of *aṅça*, for example,* with a nasal sign over the vowel of the first syllable, is an unequivocal recognition of the quality as something affecting the vowel itself. If it had seemed to the framers of this alphabet to be a something interposed between the vowel and the following consonant, they would doubtless have

---

* Namely, अंश, or अँश

found for it a sign to stand between those of the other elements. This has actually been done, out of a true regard for consistency, by the writers of the Vâjasaneyi and Tâittirîya texts: for lack of a better device, they have brought down one of the usual signs of nasality from above the syllable to a position between the syllables, giving it an addition which enables it to maintain its place there*—in the Tâittirîya texts, we have the dotted crescent, with the *virâma*, the usual mark for a consonant not graphically combined with a following consonant, beneath it. The scribes of the Rig-Veda seem to have been less solicitous to make their practice square with their theory. It may well be made a question, however, whether the habit, now so common, of writing *aṁka*, *aṁta*, *aṁbâ*, for *añka*, *anta*, *ambâ*, etc.,† could have grown up until the opinion had become prevalent that the nasal sign in *aṁça* also represented a nasal sound which followed the vowel, and was accommodated in its special mode of utterance to its successor.‡

One more point in the theory of the nasal sounds calls for notice. The assimilation of *n* to a following *l*, and of *m* to a following *l*, *y*, or *v* (v. 26-8), is treated by the Tâittirîya, the Vâjasaneyi, and the Rik Prâtiçâkhyas as resulting in the production, not of *anusvâra*, but of a nasal counterpart to the semivowel—that is, the case is made analogous with that of a nasal before a mute, instead of before a spirant. Here, also, the Atharva-Prâtiçâkhya pursues an independent course, and accepts no nasal *y* or *v*, but only a nasal *l*, as product of both *m* and *n* (see Ath. Pr. ii.35). In this case, as well as in the other, we have to assume merely a difference in the theoretical explanation of an identical mode of pronunciation; and I should not only favor the Atharvan view, but should be willing to give up the nasal *l* itself, as not worth distinguishing from an ordinary case of *anusvâra*—or of nasalized vowel, if we accept this understanding of the matter. Thus much, indeed, may be allowed—that, while the absence of sonant utterance in the spirants cuts them off from sharing in a nasal quality, it might be difficult to prevent the nasality of the preceding vowel from infecting at least

---

* Thus, for अंश or अँश, the Vâj. S. writes अꣳश, the Tâitt. S. अँ्श.

† That is, अंक, अंत, अंबा, for अङ्क, अन्त, अम्बा.

‡ No valid objection can be raised against the, practically so convenient, imitation of this habit on the part of modern European scholars, so far as concerns the representation of an original *m* assimilated to a following consonant. To go farther than this, however, and write the *anusvâra* sign in the interior of a word for a nasal mute which is equally radical or thematic with the succeeding non nasal, and, yet more, to write it for a final *m*, which no Prâtiçâkhya allows to be pronounced otherwise than *m*, seems an indefensible practice, and one wholly to be disapproved and rejected. Of Müller's seemingly elaborate defense of his adherence to it, given in the Preface to his Hitopadeça, absolutely the whole point lies in the phrases (p. xi.): "it is easier to write *aṁkitâ* than *añkitâ*. What applies to writing applies with still greater force to printing"—which latter consideration must be pronounced destitute of weight; since, on the contrary, we *do* expect our printing to be superior in accuracy to ordinary writing.

the beginning of the sonant semivowels. For the exclusion of *r* from the same treatment with the other semivowels I can discover no good reason.

The usage of the manuscripts is pretty nearly in accordance with the theories of the Prâtiçâkhya. For an assimilated *m*, the distinctive *anusvâra* sign is always written before *r*, as before the spirants; but before *l*, *y*, and *v* is written the sign of nasality above the preceding syllable, as before a mute. But as regards *n* before *l*, my manuscript varies with complete irregularity between treating it like *m*, as required by the Prâtiçâkhya, and writing the *n* unchanged, either with *virâma* or conjoined with the *l* (instances of the latter mode of treatment are about twice as frequent as of the former). The edited text more usually follows a third method, supported neither by my manuscript nor by the Prâtiçâkhya: it writes the *l* double, and puts a sign of nasality over the preceding syllable. This is nonsense: if two *l's* are written, the first should be separated from the other, and should have the sign of nasality written above it. But there is no reason why this should be done in the case of a combination of *l* with *n* any more than with *m*, or than in the combination of *m* with *y* and *v*.

It only remains to add that, in my manuscripts (T. and W.) and those at Berlin and Oxford (B. and O.), the text of the Prâtiçâkhya follows, in regard to the treatment of the nasals as to other points of euphony, the usages of the Tâittirîya text, and that the citations from the latter in the commentary are also written accordingly; while the body of the commentary itself follows the methods of ordinary Sanskrit texts. In this edition, therefore, their example is followed as closely as possible: the proper *anusvâra* being represented by ṅ, and the *m*-assimilated to a mute or semivowel, by ṁ. The two South-Indian manuscripts (G. and M.) do not distinguish these two from one another.

स्वराणां यत्रोपसंहारस्तत्स्थानम् ॥ ३१ ॥

31. In the case of the vowels, that is their place of production, to which approximation is made.

The term *upasaṁhâra*, 'approximation,' is glossed by *upaçleshaviçeshaḥ*, 'a sort of embrace'—unless, indeed, we are to read, with G. and M., *saṁçleshaviçleshaḥ*, 'disunion of embrace,' i. e., 'embrace which does not come to actual contact.'

The terms *sthâna*, 'place,' and *karaṇa*, 'organ,' denote, as in the other Prâtiçâkhyas (see note to Ath. Pr. i.18), the more passive and the more active of the two parts of the mouth whose concurrence gives birth to a sound.

---

31. *svarâṇâṁ tat sthânam bhavati*[1] *yatro 'pasaṁhâraḥ syât: upasaṁhâro nâmo 'paçleshaviçeshaḥ*[2].

[1] B. om. [2] W. *'paçlosh-;* G. M. *saṁçleshaviçleshaḥ.*

यदुपसंहरति तत्करणम् ॥ ३२ ॥

32. That is producing organ, which makes the approximation.

Here, "in the case of the vowels" is declared to be implied from the preceding rule; *upasaṁharati*, 'approaches,' is explained by *prâpayati*, 'attains;' and, as example of a *karaṇa*, or producing organ, reference is made to the "tip of the tongue," spoken of in rule 18 of this chapter.

अन्येषां तु यत्र स्पर्शनं तत्स्थानम् ॥ ३३ ॥

33. But in the case of the other letters, that is place of production, where contact is made.

By this expression, the commentator says, simple embrace or union is predicated of the consonants, while above a sort of embrace (or disunion of embrace) was predicated of the vowels. The difference, he adds, between approximation and contact will be inferred by any knowing person from the force of the terms themselves. The word "but" (*tu*) is meant to exclude the vowels; or, as Mâhisheya explains it, annuls for *anusvâra* and *svarabhakti* the quality of being produced by contact merely, like the other consonants. This last is a precious bit of pregnant construction; and the whole comment is more obscure than the rule itself, whose meaning and implication are sufficiently obvious.

येन स्पर्शयति तत्करणम् ॥ ३४ ॥

34. That is producing organ, whereby one makes the contact.

The commentator supplies, as subject of the verb, the noun *adhyetâ*, 'reader'—or, rather, 'repeater.'

---

32. *svarâṇâm iti sâṁnidhyâl labhyate: svarâṇâṁ tat karaṇam bhavati: yat svarân upasaṁharati prâpayati: 'tat karaṇam'*[1]. *yathâ: jihvâgram ṛkâra* (ii.18) *ity âdi.*

[1] B. *tat sthânam;* G. M. om.

33. *svarebhyo 'nyeshâṁ varṇânâṁ tat sthânaṁ yatra sparçanam bhavet: atra vyañjanânâṁ saṁçleshamâtraṁ*[1] *kathyate: svarâṇâṁ tu*[2] *purastât saṁçleshaḥ*[3] *kathitaḥ: upasaṁhârasparçanayoḥ*[4] *çabdaçaktyâ viçesho*[5] *vidushâ vijñeyaḥ*[6]*: tuçabdaḥ*[7] *svaranivṛttyarthaḥ: athavâ*[8]*: anusvârasvarabhaktyor vyañjanavat*[9] *sparçanamâtrakatvanivartaka*[10] *iti mâhisheyabhâshitam*

[1] W. *-çlosh-;* G. M. *-mâtratvam.* [2] W. om. [3] G. *-shaviçeshaḥ;* M. *-shaviçleshaḥ.* [4] G. M. *-hâra iti sparçana.* [5] G. M. ins. *eva.* [6] G. M. *jñâtavyaḥ.* [7] G M. *çabda.* [8] G. M. om. [9] W. *-nave;* B. *-na.* [10] B. *sparçakamnamâ-;* G. M. *sparçamâtrakâlan niv-;* M. *-vartata.*

In these four rules is implied that distinction of opener and closer position between vowel and consonant which constitutes their essential difference (see Journ. Am. Or. Soc'y, viii.367 seq.), and which the Ath. Pr. states more fully (i.29–35:—where, in rule 33, we should read *eke 'spṛshṭam*), with specifications of degree of openness and closure which are here omitted (save so far as represented by rule 45, below).

हनूमूले जिह्वामूलेन कवर्गे स्पर्शयति ॥ ३५ ॥

35. In the *k*-series, one makes contact with the root of the tongue at the root of the jaws.

Compare Ath. Pr. i.20, and the references to the other Prâtiçâkhyas there given.

The locative and instrumental cases, in this and the following rules, correspond with the *yatra*, 'where,' and *yena*, 'whereby,' of rules 33 and 34, above, and point out respectively the place and organ of production of the different classes of sounds.

The singular number of *hanûmûla*, 'root of the jaws,' the commentator accounts for as used generically (*jâtyapekshâyâm*, 'with reference to the whole kind or class').

तालौ जिह्वामध्येन चवर्गे ॥ ३६ ॥

36. In the *c*-series, with the middle of the tongue, upon the palate.

Compare Ath. Pr. i.21, and the note upon it. The sonant aspirate of this series, *jh*, is not met with in the text.

जिह्वाग्रेण प्रतिवेष्ट्य मूर्धनि टवर्गे ॥ ३७ ॥

37. In the *ṭ*-series, with the tip of the tongue, rolled back, in the head.

Compare Ath. Pr. i.22, and the note upon it. Our commentary says, "by the word 'head' (*mûrdhan*) is intended the upper part

---

34. *sâṁnidhyâd anyeshâm iti labhyate: svarebhyo 'nyeshâṁ varṇânâṁ tat karaṇam bhavati: adhyetâ yena vyañjanâni sparçayati prâpayati tat karaṇam.*

35. *kavarga uccâryamâṇe jihvâmûlena*[1] *hanûmûle sparçayati prâpayed ity arthaḥ. hanvor mûlaṁ hanûmûlam*[2]*: tasmin*[3]*:*[4] *jâtyapekshâyâm*[5] *ekavacanam.*

[1] G. M. ins. *varṇaṁ.* [2] B. G. M. om. [3] W. B. om. [4] G. M. ins. *mûlam iti.* [5] W. *-ksham.*

36. *çavarge kârye*[1] *jihvâmadhyena varṇân*[2] *tâlâu spṛçet*[3].

[1] G. M. put *tâlâu* here. [2] M. *-naṁ.* [3] B. *spṛçayet;* G. M. *sparçayet.*

of the mouth-cavity." Perhaps we shall best remove the difficulties attaching to the use of the word "head" in describing this class of sounds, by assuming that the name *mûrdhanya*, 'capital,' had become firmly established in use as designating them, at an earlier period of phonetic science in India, when their mode of production was less accurately understood and defined; and was therefore retained by the later grammarians, who gave to it a new definition. For, that *mûrdhan* should have been taken directly and without ceremony to signify the 'dome of the palate' does not appear to me possible. As in the notes to the Atharva-Prâtiçâkhya, I shall take the liberty of speaking of the *ṭ*-sounds as "lingual"—a term, on the whole, as unobjectionable and as commonly accepted as any other.

The commentator glosses the word *prativeshṭya*, 'having rolled it back,' by "having done what? having rolled back (G. M. add in explanation *âveshṭya*, 'having rolled up') the tip of the tongue, on account of its suitableness" (i. e. of the adaptedness of this position to produce the contact aimed at).

जिह्वाग्रेण तवर्गे दन्तमूलेषु ॥ ३८ ॥

38. In the *t*-series, with the tip of the tongue, at the roots of the teeth.

Compare Ath. Pr. i.24, and the note upon it.

ओष्ठाभ्यां पवर्गे ॥ ३९ ॥

39. In the *p*-series, with the two lips.

The commentator explains that here the upper lip is the place of production, as the various places of production mentioned have been the upper organ; and that the under lip is the organ of production.

Compare Ath. Pr. i.25, and the note upon it.

---

37. *ṭavarge kârye jihvâgreṇa*[1] *mûrdhni*[2] *varṇaṁ spṛçet*[3]*: kiṁ kṛtvâ: yogyatvâj*[4] *jihvâgram prativeshṭya*[5]*: mûrdhaçabdena vaktravivaroparibhâgo vivakshyate*[6].

[1] G. M. put *varṇaṁ* here. [2] B. G. M. *mûrdhani.* [3] B. *spṛçayet.* [4] W. *-tvâ;* B. *-tvât taj;* G. *-tvâñ;* M. *-tvâyogyatvâñ.* [5] G. M. *-shṭyâveshṭya.* [6] G. M. *-kshitaḥ.*

38. *tavarge kârye jihvâgreṇa varṇaṁ dantamûleshu sparçayet*[1].

[1] G. M. *spṛçet.*

39. *pavarge kârya oshṭhâbhyâm anyonyaṁ sparçayet: atro*[1] *'ttaroshṭha sthânam uttaratvasâmyâd*[2] *eshâṁ sthânânâm: adharoshṭhaḥ karaṇam.*

[1] W *tatro.* [2] B. *-râtvât sâmânyâd;* G. M. *oshṭhatva-.*

तालौ जिह्वामध्यान्ताभ्यां यकारे ॥ ४० ॥

40. In *y*, with the two edges of the middle of the tongue, upon the palate.

The Tâittirîya-Prâtiçâkhya stands alone in omitting to rank the semi-vowels along with the mutes, as palatal, etc., and in describing their formation throughout by special rule. Respecting *y*, see the note to Ath. Pr. i.21.

The description of the mode of production of *y*, here given, is quite accurate and sufficiently distinctive. The "edges" are mentioned, as being the parts which form contact with the palate, the central part remaining open, as taught for *i* in rule 22, above.

रेफे जिह्वाग्रमध्येन प्रत्यग्दन्तमूलेभ्यः ॥ ४१ ॥

41. In *r*, with the middle of the tip of the tongue, back of the roots of the teeth.

Pratyak is explained by the phrase, "in the interior upper portion"—that is, 'within and above'—the equivalence of *pratyagâtman* and *antarâtman*, 'inner soul,' being pleaded as justification.

The somewhat discordant teachings of the Prâtiçâkhyas with reference to this sound are detailed in the note to Ath. Pr. i.28. The most note-worthy circumstance in their common treatment of the letter is that they so ignore its special relationship with the lingual mutes, and in part with the *ṛ*-vowels: although in this treatise the definition of the latter (ii.18) is, essentially, nearly accordant with that here given for the semi-vowel. *R* could not possibly have the value which belongs to it in the Sanskrit euphonic system, if it were not a lingual semi-vowel, like the English *r*, uttered with the tip of the tongue reverted into the dome of the palate.

दन्तमूलेषु च लकारे ॥ ४२ ॥

42. Also in *l*, at the roots of the teeth.

According to the commentator, the "and" (*ca*) of this rule brings down by implication from the preceding both *jihvâgramadhya*, 'middle of the tongue-tip,' and *pratyak*, 'back from.' It

---

40. *yakâre kârye jihvâmadhyântâbhyâṁ tâlâu sparçayet. jihvâyâ madhyam: tasyâ 'ntâu: tâbhyâṁ jihvâmadhyântâbhyâm*[1].

[1] G. M. om.

41. *rephe kârye jihvâgramadhyena dantamûlebhyaḥ pratyak sparçayet: pratyag ity* [1]*abhyantara uparibhâga*[1] *ity arthaḥ:* [2]*yaḥ pratyagâtme 'ty*[2] *antarâtmâ pratîyate.*

[1] G. M. *-ntaropari-*. [(2)] G. M. *yathâ pratyagâtmani.*

appears obvious, however, if only from the locative case of *dantamûleshu*, that the latter item is not intended, and that we are to regard the roots of the teeth themselves (more properly, the gums close upon them) as the *sthâna*, or 'place of production,' of *l*. This, indeed, is nearly enough intimated by the final paraphrase of the comment. The really distinctive characteristic of the *l*, that it forms a contact in front, but allows the breath to escape at the sides of the tongue, is here by no means clearly brought out: rather, we are left to infer that it and the *r* are produced in the same manner, only the *r* a little further back. No one of the other treatises gives a better description (see note to Ath. Pr. i.24, where I have given the Tâittirîya definition more credit than really belongs to it).

ओष्ठान्ताभ्यां दन्तैर्वकारे ॥४३॥

43. In *v*, with the edges of the lips, along with the teeth.

This rule cannot be commended for distinctness. The commentator gives it not a little of additional precision, by his paraphrase "with the two edges of the lower lip, along with the points of the upper teeth." But how comes the lower lip to have two edges? He adds, that the teeth are the place, and the lips the organ, of production. But then why does not the rule read *danteshu*, instead of the instrumental *dantâih?* It gives us two instrumentals, as if teeth and lips were joint organs, and neither of them any more "place" than the other. The lower lip, being the more passive organ, should be the "place" on which the teeth, as "organ," make their contact; but from taking this view the treatise and its comment appear to be hindered by the analogy of the other *sthâna*'s, which have uniformly been the upper of the two parts concerned in the contact. To make a good definition, the rule should read *adharoshṭhânte* for *oshṭhântâbhyâm*.

Of the other treatises (as pointed out in the note to Ath. Pr. i.25), the Vâj. Pr. gives the *v* a description corresponding with this, and showing the letter to have had the precise phonetic value of our English *v*. This, of course, should not in the least stand in the way of our fully recognizing the fact that its original sound was that of our *w*. The *w* is a semi-vowel, standing in the same relation to *u* as *y* to *i*; but to call *v* a semi-vowel is a sim-

---

42. *cakâro 'jihvâgramadhyapratyaktvam anvâdiçati*[1]*: lakâre kârye jihvâgramadhyena*[2] *dantamûleshu pratyak sparçayet*[3]*: ayam arthaḥ: lakârasya* [4]*dantamûlapratyâsannam pratyagantarapradeçasthânam*[4] *iti vijñeyam*[5].

(1) G. M. *jihvâmadhyaṁ pratyaktvaṁ cá "karshati.* [2] G. M. *-hvâmadh-.* [3] W. B. put after *vijñeyam.* (4) G. M. *-sannapradeça sthânam.* [5] G. M. *jñeyam.*

43. *vakâre kârye 'dharoshṭhântâbhyâm uttaradantâgrâiḥ saha sparçayet. dantâir iti sthânanirdeçaḥ: oshṭhântâbhyâm iti karaṇanirdeçaḥ.*

ple abuse of terms. We might nearly as well call our *j* a semivowel, because it is written with an originally vocalic sign, and represents in the majority of cases a sound which the Romans pronounced as *y*.

स्पर्शस्थानेषूष्माण आनुपूर्व्येण ॥ ४४ ॥

44. The spirants, in their order, are produced in the places of the mutes.

By rule i.9, there are six spirants, and as there are but five "places" of mutes, these belong to the first five spirants, as is signified by the expression "in their order:" *h*, therefore, is omitted, and its rules will be given hereafter (rules 46, 47). To this effect the commentator, who also allots the spirants to their respective mute-classes, and cites from the Sanhitâ an example for each: namely, for *jihvâmûlîya*, uttered in the place of a *k*-mute, *yaḥ kâmayeta* (ii.3.2⁴ et al.: I follow the example of all the MSS., and do not attempt to distinguish the guttural and labial spirants from *visarjanîya* by different signs); for *ç*, in the place of a *c*-mute, *madhuç ca mâdhavaç ca* (i.4.14, or iv.4.11¹: W. B. omit the last two words of the citation, and W. reads *manyuç ca*, which is found at iv.7.2¹); for *sh*, in the place of a *ṭ*-mute, *ashṭâbhyaḥ svâhâ* (vii.2.15); for *s*, in the place of a *t*-mute, *stanâ uparavâḥ* (vi.2.11⁴); and for *upadhmânîya*, in the place of a *p*-mute, *yaḥ pâpmanâ* (ii.3.13²).

To make this rule a definition of the mode of utterance of the spirants, the one next following is to be applied to modify it. Unfortunately, both together are insufficient to give us any clear idea of the two problematical sounds, *jihvâmûlîya* and *upadhmânîya;* and there is room for us to suspect them of being, like the long *l*-vowel, an artificial fabrication of the Hindu grammarians. As for the *s*, there is no question as to its value. Nor ought there to be respecting that of the *sh*, which both the explanations of the phonetists and the phenomena of Sanskrit euphony show to have been that particular sibilant (more nearly resembling our *sh* than *s*, but sufficiently distinct from either) which is uttered with the tongue reverted into the dome of the palate. It passes my comprehension how European grammarians should continue to identify

---

44. *ûshmâṇa ânupûrvyeṇa yathâkrameṇa sparçasthâneshû 'ccâraṇîyâ bhavanti. yathâ: jihvâmûlîyaḥ kavargasthâne: yaḥ k-: çakâraç cavargasthâne*[1]*: madhuç*[2] *----: shakârash ṭavargasthâne: ashṭ-----: sakâras tavargasthâne: stanâ----: upadhmânîyaḥ pavargasthâne: yaḥ p-: ity ânupûrvyeṇa*[3]*: ânupûrvyân*[4] *niyamât pañcasû "shmasû 'kteshu hakâro viçishṭaḥ*[5]*: tasya vidhim uparishṭâd âcashṭe.*

[1] W. *cavargıyas-;* B. *cakâras-.* [2] W. *manyuç.* [3] G. M. *-vyâ vijñeyâḥ.* [4] G. M. *-vya.* [5] B. *-çeshaḥ;* G. M. *vasishṭhaḥ.*

it with our *sh;* and, yet more, how that absurd distinction of the lingual and palatal sibilants (of which, so far as I know, Wilson was the originator) which defines the former as the same with our *sh* in *shun*, and the latter with our *ss* in *session*, can still be repeated in the latest Sanskrit grammars. Absurd I call it, because there is really no difference at all between the pronunciation of *sh* in *shun* and *ss* in *session.* If our *sh* be found in the Sanskrit alphabet, it is the palatal sibilant *ç*, not the lingual, *sh.* The question of the value of *ç* is connected with and depends upon that of the palatal series of mutes; and upon this I have nothing more to say than I said in the note to Ath. Pr. i.21.

करणमध्यं तु विवृतम् ॥ ४५ ॥

45. But the middle of the producing organ is unclosed.

The "but" (*tu*) of this rule, we are told, is intended to annul (so far) the similarity of organ of the spirants with the mutes. This prescription of an unclosure of the middle of the organ is a rather artificial device for saving the credit of the general prescription of actual contact in all the consonants. It is nearly equivalent with the rules of the Ath. Pr. (i.30,31) upon the same subject.

कण्ठस्थानौ हकारविसर्जनीयौ ॥ ४६ ॥

46. The throat is place of production of *h* and *visarjanîya.*

And, the commentator adds, they have no *karaṇa*, or organ of production. As example of *h*, he cites *aharahar havirdhâninâm* (ii.5.6[3]), but leaves *visarjanîya* uninstanced.

The other Prâtiçâkhyas give a corresponding definition of the utterance of these two sounds (see note to Ath. Pr. i.19). It is too indefinite to be of any particular use to us in determining their phonetic value. But the two rules which next follow in our treatise are very interesting and instructive.

उदयस्वरादिसस्थानो हकार एकेषाम् ॥ ४७ ॥

47. In the opinion of some authorities, *h* has the same position as the beginning of the following vowel.

Our commentator first offers the simple paraphrase of this rule

---

45. *teshâm ûshmaṇâṁ karaṇamadhyaṁ tu vivṛtam bhavati: sparçânâṁ karaṇasâmyanivṛttiparas*[1] *tucabdaḥ. karaṇânâm madhyaṁ karaṇamadhyam.*

[1] B. *-ttyarthaṁ.*

46. *hakâravisarjanîyâu kaṇṭhasthânâu syâtâm. kaṇṭha sthânaṁ yayos tâu tathoktâu. anayoḥ karaṇâbhâvaḥ. ah-....*

which he finds given by one of his three chief authorities, Vararuci, and then proceeds to exhibit his own superior acuteness by a very long, but not very important, discussion of it: a loose version is as follows:

The expression "the same position as the beginning," etc., implies a difference of position in the remainder of the vowel; but there is none such in *a*, *i*, *u;* as a vowel has but a single position, the word "beginning" is superfluous, and the desired result would be secured by saying simply "of the same position with the vowel." That is not so: a difference of position does in fact belong to the remainder of the diphthongs: the two rules (ii.28, 29) which teach that *i* and *u* form the final elements of *âi* and *âu* assure the difference of position for those two sounds; in like manner, a difference of position is to be remarked as prescribed in general grammar [though not in this treatise] for the final elements of *e* and *o*, they being included in the category of diphthongs. But again: even granting that, the utterance in the throat of this very *a* which makes the initial element of the diphthongs is taught by the rule, "the throat is the place of production of *a*, the *k*-mutes, *h*, and *visarjanîya;*" hence, as sameness of position [with the *a*, as throat-sound] is prescribed by the preceding rule, this rule is open to the charge of superfluous repetition. You must not think so, is the reply; there is a difference between the *a* which forms the beginning of *e* and *o* and an *a* standing by itself: to the latter belongs the description given above in rule 12, "the lips and jaws not too widely separated," etc.; to the other, that of rule 27, "with the organ of production more closed;" therefore, as place and organ correspond to one another, the expression "of the same position as the beginning" is to be understood as meaning "of the same place and organ as the beginning." Moreover, in the former rule the absence of an organ of production was taught, but here is implied also the presence of such; hence a difference of opinions comes to light, and not merely a superfluous repetition.

---

47. *ekeshâm mate hakâra*[1] *udayasvarâdisasthâna âtmana upari svarâdisasthâno*[2] *bhavatî 'ti vâraruc oktam*[3] *syâd etat. âdinâ*[4] *sasthâna ity ukte çeshasya sthânântaratvaṁ*[5] *vaktavyaṁ tad epy akârekârokâreshu nâ 'sti:* [6] *svarasyâi* [7]*'kam eva* [8]*sthânam*[7] *ity âdiçabdavâiyarthyaṁ syât: svarasasthâna*[9] *ity etâvatâi 'vâ 'rthasiddhir*[10] *iti: mâi 'vam: sandhyakshareshu çeshasya*[8] *sthânântaropapatteḥ: ikâro 'dhyardhaḥ* (ii.28) *iti sûtradvayena çeshabhûtavarṇavyaktâu*[11] *tayo*[12] *sthânântaram api prasiddham eva: evam*[13] *ekârâukârayor api vyâkaraṇe*[14] *çeshasya sthânântaraṁ vihitaṁ vijñeyam: sandhyaksharatvâviçeshâd anayoḥ. nanv evam apy akuhavisarjanîyânâṁ kaṇṭha iti sandhyaksharâdâv akârasyâ 'pi kaṇṭhasthânatvât tena samânasthânatve*[15] *kathyamâne*[16] *pûrvasûtroktena*[17] *pâunaruktyam asya*[18] *sûtrasya*

Any detailed criticism of this cunning argument would certainly be open to the charge of superfluity, and I shall not attempt it.

A few further examples of the occurrence of *h*, before the various diphthongs, are added: *tigmahete* (i.2.14²), *yâvatîr vâsâmahâi* (vii.5.2¹), *agnihotraṁ juhoti* (i.5.9¹), *samprayatîr ahâu* (v.6.1²).

The acuteness of observation of the "some authorities" who have made this definition of the character of a *h* certainly deserves respectful, if not admiring, acknowledgment. It is the peculiarity of the aspiration, that it is an emission of unintonated breath through the same position of the mouth organs by which the following intonated sound receives its character: thus, the *h* of *ha* is a surd *a*, so to speak; that of *he*, a surd *e*; that of *who*, a surd *u*; that of *hue*, a surd *y*; and so on (see Journ. Am. Or. Soc'y, viii.370 seq.). The rule would have been made better by reading *udayavarṇa*, instead of *udayasvarâdi*—'the following sound,' instead of 'the beginning of the following vowel'—for the assimilation is not less true of the semi-vowels and nasals than of the vowels.

पूर्वान्तसस्थानो विसर्जनीयः ॥ ४८ ॥

48. *Visarjanîya* has the same position as the end of the preceding vowel.

The commentator does not tell us whether this definition is to be looked upon as, like the preceding, expressing the opinion of "some authorities," or as having the unqualified approval of the Prâtiçâkhya. From his silence we should infer the latter, but the connection gives reason for presuming the former. He paraphrases: "*visarjanîya* is of like position—that is, of like place and organ—with the end of the vowel that precedes itself;" and adds that

---

syâṭ. mâi 'vam maṅsthâḥ: ekârâukârâdivartino[19] *'kârasya kevalasya ca viçesho 'sti: kevalasya*[20] *karaṇam oshṭhahanu nâ 'tivyastam* (ii.12) *iti*[21]*: sandhyaksharâdâu vartamânasya tu saṁvṛtakaraṇataram* (ii.27)*: tasmât sthânakaraṇayoḥ sahacaritatvâd*[22] *âdisasthâna ity ukta âdisamânasthânakaraṇa*[23] *iti vijñeyam. kiṁ ca: pûrvasûtre karaṇâbhâva ity*[24] *uktaḥ: atra tu karaṇavattvam api*[25] *vidyata iti matântaram upapadyate: na pâunaruktyaṁ ca. tathâ*[26]*: tig-: yâv-....: agn-....: sam-..... udayaçabda uttaraparyâyaḥ*[27]*: udayaç câ 'sâu*[28] *svaraç ca*[29] *: tasyâ "diḥ: tena sasthânaḥ.*

[1] G. M. put before *ekeshâm*. [2] G. M. *udayasvar-*. [3] W. B. *var-*. [4] W. *âdi*. [5] G. M. *-taraṁ*. [6] G. M. ins. *tathâ sati*. [(7)] W. *'kasthânam evam*. [(8)] B. om. [9] G. M. *svarasya sa-*. [10] G. M. om. *artha*; G. M. *-ddher*. [11] G. M. *-bhûtaṁ v-*. [12] G. M. *tasyâ*. [13] G. M. om. [14] G. M. *-ṇa*. [15] G. M. *sthâ-*. [16] G. M. *kalpy-*. [17] G. M. *-vok-*. [18] G. M. *eva tasya*. [19] G. M. *-rayor âdi-*. [20] W. ins. *tu*. [21] G. M. *nâ 'tyupasaṁhṛtaṁ ca*; B. *no 'pasaṁhṛtaṁ*. [22] W. B. *-ritvâd*. [23] W. *-sthâna*. [24] G. M. om. [25] G. M. om. [26] G. M. om. [27] G. M. *udayasvarâdisasthânah*. [28] G. M. om. *asâu*. [29] G. M. ins. *udayasvaraḥ*.

here too the language of the rule is aimed at the diphthongs, since no other vowel exhibits any difference of position between its end and its beginning. His examples, again, are only of *visarjanîya* after a diphthong: they are *agneḥ* (i.1.10^{3} et al.), *brâhmaṇâir âyushmat* (ii.3.10^{3}), *bâhuvor balam* (v.5.9^{2}), and *â 'yaṁ gâuḥ* (i.5.3^{1}). In the second and third of these passages, only the first word should have been quoted, in order to exhibit the *visarjanîya.*

The teachings of the other Prâtiçâkhyas respecting the *visarjanîya* are rehearsed in the note to Ath. Pr. i.19. All are so indefinite as really to teach us nothing respecting the phonetic value of the sound. The present rule alone gives us positive and precise information, teaching us to regard it as, like the *h*, a simple uncharacterized breathing, a kind of final *h*.

नासिक्या नासिकास्थानाः ॥४९॥

49. The nose-sounds have the nose as their place of production.

The "nose-sounds," the commentary says, are the *yamas* (xxi. 12,13); but why the *nâsikya* (xxi.14) should not be regarded as included among them I do not see. Any discussion of their phonetic character may be best deferred until the chapter where the rules for their occurrence are given. As examples of the nose-sounds are quoted *rukmam antaram* (v.i.10^{3}: but G. M. B. give instead *rukmantam*, ii.2.3^{3}), *yâcñâ* (i.5.7^{4}; but G. M. give instead *râjñâ*, ii.6.2^{2} et al.), *âtnârah* (v.6.5^{3}), *ratnam abhajanta* (ii.6.12^{1}: but G. M. give instead, if it be not merely a corrupted reading, *uccâ ratnam ayajanta*, which I have not found in the Sanhitâ), and *pâpmânam* (i.4.41 et al.).

मुखनासिक्या वा ॥५०॥

50. Or they are produced by the mouth and nose.

Respecting this alternative explanation nothing need be said at present.

---

48. *visarjanîya âtmanaḥ pûrvasvarântena sasthânaḥ samânasthânakaraṇo bhavati: atrâ 'pi pûrvasvara iti sandhyaksharam ucyate: svarântarasya*[1] *hi*[2] *sthânântaratvâbhâvât. yathâ: ag-:*[3] *brâḥ-....: bâḥ-....:*[4] *â..... pûrvasyâ 'ntaḥ: tena sasthânaḥ pûrvântasasthânaḥ*[5].

[1] W. B. *-ntasya.* [2] B. om; G. M. *bhinna.* [3] B. om. [4] B. om. [5] B. om.

49. *nâsikyâ yamâ nâsikâsthânâ bhavanti. yathâ: ruk-....: yâ-: âṭ-: rat-....: pâp-.*

50. *ta*[1] *eva nâsikyâ mukhanâsikâbhyâm*[2] *uccâraṇîyâ bhavanti. mukhaṁ ca nâsikâ*[3] *ca mukhanâsike*[4]*: tatsambandhino mukhanâsikyâḥ.* [5]*uktâny evo 'dâharaṇâni*[5].

[1] G. M. *eta.* [2] G. M. *mukhena nâsikâbhyâṁ ca.* [3] G. M. *-ke.* [4] G. M. *-kam.* [(5)] G. M. put after *bhavanti.*

वर्गवच्चैषु ॥५१॥

51. And, in them, the organ of production is as in the series of mutes.

The "and" (*ca*) of this rule, the commentator says, brings forward, on the principle of 'the lion's look' (a distant glance backward: the phrase is used several times later in like cases), the already defined organs of production of the various mute series.

If the mouth be regarded as bearing a part in the production of the nose-sounds or *yamas*, in a way which is determined by the mode of formation of the mutes to which they are attached, it is difficult to see how their number can be restricted to four, as it is in the "list of sounds" given at the beginning of the treatise, and in the comment on rule xxi.12.

नासिकाविवरणादानुनासिक्यं नासिकाविवरणादानुनासिक्यम् ॥५२॥

52. Nasal quality is given by the unclosing of the nose.

Ânunâsikya is the quality of being *anunâsika* or 'nasal;' and this name, as prescribed by rule 30, above, and fully supported by the usage of the treatise elsewhere, belongs to *anusvâra* and the various nasal consonants. The definition of the manner in which the quality is communicated is quite unexceptionable; the organs of the mouth remaining in the positions already given for the various classes and single sounds, the opening of the nasal passage, and the utterance through it of a part or the whole of the emitted material, makes the corresponding nasal sound.

The commentator explains *nâsikâvivaraṇa* by *ghrâṇabila*, 'hole of the nose, nasal passage,' as if *vivaraṇa* signified the opening or cavity, instead of the act of opening or unclosing. His choice of an example also seems to betray a want of appreciation of the true scope of the rule: it is *suçlokâ3ñ sumañgalâ3ñ* (i.8.16[2]).

---

51. *siṅhâvalokanena*[1] *vargasyo 'ktaṁ karaṇaṁ cakâro 'nukarshati: eshu*[2] *nâsikyeshu vargavat karaṇam bhavati. vargasye 'va vargavat.*

[1] G. M. *kananyâyena*. [2] G. M. (as also in the text of the rule itself) *eteshu*.

52. *nâsikâvivaraṇâd ghrâṇabilâd*[1] *ânunâsikyaṁ rañgâdi kartavyam. yathâ*[2]*: suç---- ity âdi.*

iti tribhâshyaratne prâtiçâkhyavivaraṇe dvitîyo 'dhyâyaḥ.

[1] G. M. *nâsikâb-*. [2] B. *tathâ;* W. om.

CHAPTER III.

CONTENTS: 1, introductory; 2–6, cases of *á* at the end of the first member of a compound, requiring to be shortened in divided text; 7, of *í* and *ú*; 8–12, of final *á* of verbal forms and particles; 13–14, of final *í* and *ú*; 15, of initial *á*.

अथादावुत्तरे विभागे ह्रस्वं व्यञ्जनपरः ॥ १ ॥

1. Now then—at the beginning or end of a word, a vowel, in case of separation, if followed by a consonant, becomes short as hereinafter set forth.

Matters of introductory explanation, of interpretation of the rules of the treatise, and of phonetic theory, being now for the present disposed of (for they are resumed, in a supplementary way, in some of the concluding chapters), the task of determining the readings of the Sanhitâ is taken up. And the first subject dealt with is that of the irregular prolongations of vowels—chiefly final *a*, *i*, and *u*—which are so frequent in all the Vedic texts. In the other treatises (Rik Pr. vii.–ix., Vâj. Pr. iii.95–128, Ath. Pr. iii.1–25), the rules tell us in what situations a vowel originally short is lengthened: this is more in accordance with the general method of the Prâtiçâkhyas, which take for granted, upon the whole, the existence of their *çâkhâs* in the analyzed condition of the *pada*-text, and proceed to construct the *saṁhitâ* from it. Here, on the contrary, we are told what vowels, long in the ordinary text, are to be shortened when thrown out of combination with their surroundings. Such dissolution of the continuity of the text takes place, first, in *pada*, whenever a pause—either the *avagraha* separating the two members of a compound, in its repetition after *iti*, or the longer pause that divides between two words—comes to stand between the vowel in question and the consonant which was its next neighbor in *sanhitâ*: thus, *devâyata iti deva-yate; ava: naḥ* (s. *avâ naḥ*). Second, it is made in the so-called *jaṭâ*-text, examples of which are often quoted in the sequel, and to which the rules of the treatise are in more than one instance adapted; this text is constructed by thrice repeating each pair of words—first in

---

1. *athe 'ty ayam adhikâraḥ: âdâu padâdâv uttare padânte ca vartamânaḥ saṁhitâyâṁ yo dîrgho 'sâu vibhâge vibhâgasamaye vyañjanaparo hrasvam âpadyate:* [1] *vyañjanaparatvam*[2] *atra yathâsaṁhitâsthaṁ vijñeyam. nanu dîrghaḥ kathaṁ labhyate.* [3]*hrasvânantarabhâvitvâd devâçîkâ* (iii.2) "*digrahaṇeshu plutâdarçanâc ce*[4] *'ti brûmaḥ. saṁhitâyâm ity asyâ 'yam arthaḥ*[5]*: kâryabhâjaḥ padasyo 'ttarapadena saha sambandhaniyamaḥ*[5]*: na tu pûrvapadena saha sambandhaniyamaḥ*[6]*. vibhâgo 'tra*

their natural order, then inverted, then in the natural order again: for example, *âpo hi shṭhâ mayobhuvaḥ* would become *âpo hi hy âpa âpo hi: hi shṭha stha hi hi shṭha: sthâ mayobhuvo mayobhuva stha sthâ mayobhuvaḥ: mayobhuva iti mayaḥ-bhuvaḥ:* the treatment of the *â* of *sthâ* here illustrates the conditions of the restoration of the short vowel in such cases. Third, the same restoration takes place in the *saṁhitâ*-text of the existing manuscripts and in the edition founded upon them, when the lengthened vowel happens to come at the end of one of those passages, of just fifty words each, into which the *anuvâkas* or sections of the Sanhitâ are divided. This division the Prâtiçâkhya does not recognize—or, at any rate, does not notice—not infrequently quoting in *sandhi*, without remark, words which are separated by it (for example, under rule 13, below, *uçmasî gamadhye*, i.3.6$^{1-2}$, where the edited text reads correctly *uçmasi: 1: gamadhye*).

The comment upon this rule may be loosely translated, or paraphrased, as follows:

Here *atha*, 'now then,' is an introductory heading; *âdâu* [literally, 'at the beginning'] means 'at the beginning of a word' [including, also, a separable part of a compound word]; *uttare* [literally, 'in the latter part'] means 'at the end of a word:' a vowel occupying such a position, if it be long in *saṁhitâ*, becomes short *vibhâge*, i. e. 'in case of separation,' when followed by a consonant—that is to say, when so followed in *saṁhitâ*. But whence is derived the limitation to a "long" vowel? We answer, from its conversion into a short, and from the non-occurrence of any protracted (*pluta*) vowels among the instances included in the rules. The limitation "in *saṁhitâ*" implies that the word whose form is in question is placed in euphonic connection with the word that follows it; not, however, with the word that precedes it [unless, as should be excepted, its initial vowel, instead of its final, is the one liable to change of quantity]. "Separation" (*vibhâga*) is to be understood as division from the words with which it stands in natural or original connection—that is, according to the reading of the fundamental text: otherwise, in the *jaṭâ*-text of the two words *sthâ mayobhuvaḥ* (see above), the *stha* would retain its long *â* in its second repetition, because of its standing in euphonic connection with the following word: and that should not be so. The sense of the word *vibhâga* is, in case of a long initial vowel, separation from the preceding word; in case of a long final, from the

---

prakṛtipadâir ucyate: prakṛtir nâma yathâpâṭhaḥ: prakṛtipadâir iti kim: sthâ m- ity atra jaṭâyâṁ sthaçabdasya dvitîyoccâraṇe 'pi dîrghaḥ prasajyeta[7]*: uttarapadena vibhâgâbhâvât: sa*[8] *mâ bhûd iti parihâraḥ. vibhâgapadasyâ*[9] *'yam arthaḥ: padâdâu*[10] *dîrghasya pûrvapadena vibhâgaḥ: padânte*[11] *dîrghasyo 'ttarapadena vibhâgaḥ. vibhâge vyañjanapara iti kim: ṛt-.... ity atra mâ bhûd iti: nâdhâmâdhârayâ* (iii.8) *iti prâptiḥ. saṁhitâyâṁ*[12] *dîrgha iti kim: esha.... ity atra prâptisampâdanârtham:*

following word. The limitation "in case of separation, if followed by a consonant" is for the sake of excluding such cases as *ṛtadhâmâ 'si* (i.3.3: in separated form, *ṛtadhâmâ. asi*), which would otherwise come under the rule iii.8 [among the specifications of which, *dhâmâ* is included]. The limitation "a long vowel in *saṁhitâ*" is intended to bring *esha vo bharatâ râjâ* (i.8.10² et al.; *pada*-text, *bharatâḥ*) under the action of the rules; since thus, and not otherwise, is pertinence given to the word *yâjyâ* in rule 11 of this chapter. Undue extension of the prescription to such cases as *tvâ vâyavaḥ* (i.1.1) is provided against by the rules that follow [since these specify all the cases in which it is to be applied].

The only difficulty arising in connection with the understanding of this rule, or of the interpretation of it given by the commentator, grows out of the specification *vyañjanapara*, 'followed by a consonant.' Respecting this, we are explicitly told, near the beginning of the exposition, "the being followed by a consonant is to be understood here of the condition of things in the *saṁhitâ*-text"—that is to say, any long vowel which appears in *saṁhitâ* as a final, with a consonant following it, is to be regarded as falling under the rules of the chapter. This specification, then, makes the rules apply to such cases as *bharatâ râjâ* (the example quoted by the commentator: the *pada*-reading is *bharatâḥ: râjâ*) and *adhâ mâ* (quoted under rule 9; *pada*-reading *adhâḥ: mâ*), and they have to be specially allowed for and excepted—as is done in rules 9 and 11. It seems very strange, now, to have this implication made, requiring as a consequence that all the words which by euphonic processes come to exhibit in *saṁhitâ* a long final vowel (*â*) should be taken into consideration: but the number of cases actually needing to be guarded against in the rules on account of it is very small. For, in the first place, the question can arise only in regard to the words specially mentioned in the rules; and among these there are not many for which homophonous forms in *âḥ* or *âi* occur; and of these, again, only a part would occur otherwise than before a vowel, in which situation the hiatus would betray the omission of the former final element. The makers of the treatise, then, appear to have thought it safer to avoid a possible confusion of *adhâ* from *adhâḥ* with *adhâ* from *adha*, and so on, by making the rules apply in general to both cases, and specially excepting the former. And this is what they have attempted to do: and it has cost them only two additional words—*agniyâjye* in rule 9, and *yâjyâsu* in rule 11—together with an artifice of

---

tathâ sati bharatâ yâjyâsv (iii.11) *iti yâjyâpadaṁ sârthakaṁ nâ 'nyathâ. vyañjanam asmât param*[13] *iti vyañjanaparaḥ. tvâ---- ity âdâv etallakshaṇasambhavâd*[14] *ativyâptim*[15] *uttarasûtrâiḥ pariharati.*

[1] G. M. ins. *padâdâu ca padânte ca yo dirgho vyañjanottaro vibhâge kriyamâṇe hrasvaṁ saṁyâti.* [2] G. M. *-nam.* (3) M. om.; G. *hrasvânt-.* [4] G. om. *ca.* [5] G. M. *-dhah.* (6) W. om. [7] G. M. *-yate.* [8] G. M. om. [9] G. M. *-gaçabd-.* [10] W. *-dâdi.* [11] W. *-nta.* [12] G. M. ins. *yo.* [13] G. M. *-ra.* [14] G. M. *eva tal-.* [15] W. *atiprâ-.*

construction under rule 8, in connection with the word *prâṇâḥ*. Without a complete *index verborum* to the Sanhitâ, or a laboriously minute examination of the whole text with reference to this particular point, I cannot tell just how nearly successful their attempt has been; but I have, I believe, discovered at least one case which they have overlooked. At i.4.24, namely, we read *rakshâ mâkiḥ* (p. *rakshâḥ*), and, by rule 8, the *â* of *rakshâ* should be shortened. That the section containing these words was really a part of the text for which the Prâtiçâkhya was constructed is proved by the fact that two of its peculiarities of reading are provided for in later rules (vi.5 and xi.13).

But with the interpretation thus given appears to be quite at variance the phrase containing the illustration *ṛtadhâmâ 'si*, where *vibhâge* and *vyañjanaparaḥ* are immediately connected, and made to mean 'followed by a consonant in separated text' (not *ṛtadhâmâ: asi*). This I can hardly believe to be a genuine part of the commentary. The second *â* of *ṛtadhâmâ 'si* cannot be said to be either final or initial: it is a combination of both: it does not furnish a case to which the rules of the chapter apply with any propriety, as the *saṁhitâ* reading cannot be affected by them. If not some later meddler, then the commentator himself, has suffered himself to be scared by an imaginary difficulty, and has unnecessarily twisted the rule a little awry in order to its removal.

The specification *vibhâge*, 'in case of separation,' applies in the Tâittirîya *pada*-text more generally and more strictly than in those of the other Vedas. Where the separation of a compound is suspended on account of its further composition, the restoration of its natural form is suspended also; and we read, for example, *vîrya-vat*, but *vîryâvat-tara; viçva-mitra*, but *viçvâmitra-jamadagnî; anu-yâja* and *ananu-yâja*, but *prayâja-anûyâja*, and so on—and we shall find illustrations hereafter in connection with other changes than prolongation of vowels. Thus, also, in the full *pada*-readings, the word is given first, before *iti*, in its *saṁhitâ* form, without change (except euphonic combination with the *iti*); and this part of the reading I shall accordingly usually omit in quoting the *pada*-text, setting down only the separated and restored form which follows *iti*, or the part which corresponds to the entire reading of the Rik and Atharvan *pada*-texts.

देवाशीकासुम्नाश्वर्तावयुनाहृदयाघोक्थाप्सुद्धा ॥ २ ॥

2. *Devâ, çîkâ, sumnâ, çvâ, ṛtâ, vayunâ, hṛdayâ, aghâ,*

---

2. ------ *ity eteshu grahaṇeshv avagraheshv*[1] *antyasvaro vibhâge vyañjanaparo hrasvam âpadyate. yathâ: dev-----: çîk-----: sumn-----: dyâv-----:* [2]*apy akarâdi* (i.52) *iti vacanâd*[3] *idam apy udâharaṇam*[4]*: açv-----: ṛt-----: vay-----:*[2] *hṛd----: agh-----: ukth-----: âpo-----.*

[1] G. M. om. [(2)] B. om. [3] G. M *sûtrâd* [4] G. M. *-hartavyam.*

ukthâ, and *çuddhâ*, as first members of a compound, shorten their final when separated.

This and the following rules, including the seventh, properly form one connected passage, with the specification *ity avagrahaḥ*, 'these, as former members of a compound,' which applies alike to them all, standing at the end.

The examples quoted from the Sanhitâ in illustration of the rule are as follows. For *devâ: devâyate yajamânâya çarma* (iii.5.5[3]: G. M. omit the last word of the citation), the only case, so far as I have noted, for *devâyant;* we have *devayate* (with short vowel) twice, at i.2.12[3] and ii.5.9[3]; *devâyuvam* occurs ii.5.9[6] and iv.1.1[3], but *devayuḥ*, iii.5.11[1]. For *çîkâ, çîkâyate svâhâ* (vii.5.11[2]), the only case. For *sumnâ, sumnâyanto havâmahe* (i.5.11[4]), also alone. For *çvâ, dyâvâpṛthivyâ çvâvit* (v.5.20): *çvâ*, however, by rule i.52, includes *açvâ*, for which is quoted *açvâvatîñ somavatîm* (iv. 2.6[4]); I have noted farther only iii.3.11[1], but feel less than usual confidence in the completeness of my excerption. For *ṛtâ, ṛtâyavaḥ purâ 'nnam akshan* (ii.2.5[5]: G. M. omit the last word of the citation): there are more than twenty such cases in the text, for the themes *ṛtâyu* (e. g. i.4.5: but *ṛtayu* once, ii.2.12[4]), *ṛtâyant* (e. g. iv.2.9[3]), *ṛtâvan* (e. g. i.3.14[2]) and its feminine *ṛtâvarî* (e. g. i.1. 3), *ṛtâvṛdh* (e. g. i.4.5), and *ṛtâsah* (iii.4.7[1]: but this word reads in *pada* as in *saṁhitâ*). For *vayunâ, vayunâvid eka it* (i.2.13[1] and iv.1.1[1]). For *hṛdayâ, hṛdayâvidhaç cit* (i.4.45[1]). For *aghâ, aghâyavo mâ gandharvo viçvâvasur âdadhat* (i.2.9: G. M. omit after *gandharvaḥ*): other cases of *aghâyu* are found at iii.3.11[1]: iv.1.10[3]; 5.10[4]: v.7.3[1]; and of *aghâyant*, ii.3.14[1]. For *ukthâ, ukthâmadânâṁ dhenuḥ* (ii.4.11[6]): the same compound occurs again at iii.3.2[1] and v.6.8[6], and *ukthâyu* at i.4.12, twice. For *çuddhâ, âpo devîḥ çuddhâyuvaḥ* (i.3.8[2] and vi.3.8[4]).

इन्द्रा वद्वन्वान्परः ॥ ३ ॥

3. Also *indrâ*, when followed by *vat*, *van*, and *vân*.

One example is quoted by the commentator for each of the three cases enumerated: *indrâvatîm apacitîm ihâ "vaha* (v.7.4[3]: G. M. omit after *apacitîm*), *indrâvanto marutaḥ* (iv.7.14[1]), and *indrâvânt svâhâ* (i.1.12); and I have noted no others. As counter-examples, he quotes: first, to show that not every long *â* is to be shortened before the three syllables named, *ûrṇâvantam prathamaḥ sîda yonim* (iii.5.11[1]: G. M. give only the first two words), *asura prajâvân* (iii.1.11[1]: but B. reads, I presume only by an

---

3. *indre 'ty asminn*[1] *avagrahe 'ntyasvaro vad van vân ity evamparo vibhâge hrasvam âpadyate. yathâ*[2]*: ind-....: ind-....: ind-..... indre 'ti kim: ûrṇ-....: as-....: praj-..... evampara iti kim: ind-....*

[1] G. M. *etasminn.* [2] G. M. om.

error, *pratâpavân*), and *prajâvatîr anamîvâ ayakshmâḥ* (i.1.1: but omitted in G. M.); second, to show that *indrâ* is not altered except under the circumstances specified, *indrâvaruṇayor aham* (ii.5.12[2]). This last is a case in which no *vibhâga*, or 'separation,' would be made in any text of the other Vedas; but the Tâittirîya *pada* reads *indrâvaruṇayor itî 'ndrâ-varuṇayoḥ*, and the example is therefore to the purpose.

चित्रा वपरः ॥ ४ ॥

4. Also *citrâ*, when followed by *v*.

The illustrative passage cited is *citrâvaso svasti te pâram açîya* (i.5.5[4] and 7[5]: G. M. omit after *te*). As counter-examples, are given *mitrâvaruṇâv eva* (ii.1.7[3] et al.: p. *mitrâ-varuṇâu*), and *citrâpûrṇamâse dîksheran* (vii.4.8[2])—the former to show the necessity of the restriction to *citrâ*, the latter, of the restriction to sequence by a *v*. I have found no farther instances falling under the rule.

प्रस्थेन्द्रियाद्रविणाविश्वदेव्यादीर्घावीर्याविश्वावातात्वा-भङ्गुराकर्णकावृष्णियासुगोपर्कसामाघासत्रावर्षापुष्पामेघाप्रास्वा ॥ ५ ॥

5. Also *prasthâ*, *indriyâ*, *draviṇâ*, *viçvadevyâ*, *dîrghâ*, *vîryâ*, *viçvâ*, *vâtâ*, *tvâ*, *bhangurâ*, *karṇakâ*, *vṛshṇiyâ*, *sugopâ*, *ṛksâmâ*, *aghâ*, *satrâ*, *varshâ*, *pushpâ*, *meghâ*, *prâ*, *svâ*.

For each of these words, the commentator cites a single example. For *prasthâ*, *prasthâvad rathavâhanam* (iv.2.5[6]), the only case. For *indriyâ*, *indriyâvate puroḍâçam* (ii.2.7[1]): half a dozen cases of this word occur in the text, and several of *indriyâvin* (e.g. i.6.2[4]: ii.1.6[3]: vi.2.10[6]); the latter word, however, is not separated in the *pada*-text. For *draviṇâ*, *draviṇâvataḥ kurute* (v.3.11[2]), the only case. For *viçvadevyâ*, *viçvadevyâvate çvâtrâḥ* (i.4.1[1]): the word occurs also at iv.1.6[1,2]. For *dîrghâ*, *dîrghâdhiyo rakshamâṇâḥ* (ii.1.11[4]), the only case. For *vîryâ*, *vîryâvantam abhimâtishâham* (i.2.7): the same theme is found in other passages, as are also its comparative, *vîryâvat-tara* (e.g. i.7.6[3]), and superlative, *vîryâvat-tama* (ii.4.2[1]), in which the shortening of the *â* is not authorized by the Prâtiçâkhya, since, in the division, it does not stand next before the pause: and the *pada*-text reads accordingly. For *viçvâ*, *viçvâmitrasya sûktam bhavati* (v.2.3[3-4]: G. M. omit

---

4. *citrâ ity asminn*[1] *avagrahe 'ntyasvaro vakâraparo*[2] *vibhâge hrasvam âpadyate. yathâ*[3]*: cit-.... citre 'ti kim: mitr-....: vapara iti kim: citr-....*

[1] G. M. *etasminn*. [2] G. M. *vap-*. [3] G. M. om.

the last word): the same word occurs in other passages (iv.3.2[2]: v.2.3[3,4],10[5]; 4.2[2]), as also in the compound *viçvâmitrajamadagnî* (v.4.11[3]), where, as the division is *viçvâmitra-jamadagnî*, the *â* is not shortened; and we have further the themes *viçvâvasu* (e. g. i.1.11[1]), *viçvâvant* (iii.5.6[2]), *viçvârâj* (i.3.2[1]), and *viçvâsah* (i.4.17; p. *viçva-sâham*). For *vâtâ*, *vâtâvad varshan* (ii.4.7[1]), the only case. For *tvâ*, *tvâvato maghonaḥ* (ii.2.12[8]; p. *tva-vataḥ*): the Rik *pada*-text does not shorten the *â* of this word. For *bhañgurâ*, *bhettâram bhañgurâvatah* (i.5.6[4] and iv.1.2[5]). For *karnakâ*, *sûrmî karnakâvaty etayâ* (i.5.7[6] and v.4.7[3]: G. M. omit the first word, W. B. the last). For *vṛshṇiyâ*, *vṛshṇiyâvatas tava* (iii. 5.6[2-3]). For *sugopâ*, *sa sugopâtamo janaḥ* (iv.2.11[2]; p. *sugopa-tamaḥ*: G. M. omit the first word): the Rik *pada* writes *su-gopâtamaḥ*. For *ṛksâmâ*, *ṛksâmâbhyâm yajushâ* (i.2.3[3] and iii.1.1[4]). For *aghâ*, *aghâçvâd evâi 'nam antar eti bhûtam* (iii.1.7[2]; p. *agha-çvât*: G. M. omit the last two words); the Rik and Atharvan *pada*-texts write *agha-açva*: the themes *aghâyu* (e. g. i.2.9[1]) and *aghâyant* (ii.3.14[1]) are also found in the Saṁhitâ. For *satrâ*, *satrâjitaṁ dhanajitam* (iv.1.1[3]; p. *satra-jitam* : the word *satrâ* occurs repeatedly (e. g. i.6.12[1]) uncompounded, and maintains its long final in the *pada*-text also. For *varshâ*, *varshâhvâṁ juhoti* (ii.4.10[3]; p. *varsha-hvâm*). For *pushpâ*, *pushpavatîḥ supippalâḥ* (iv.1.4[4] and v.1.5[10]). For *meghâ*, *meghâyate svâhâ* (vii.5.11[1]; p. *megha-yate*; in the same division occurs also *meghâyishyate*, which is not divided: *meghayantî* is found at iv.4.5[1]). For *prâ*, *prâvaṇebhiḥ sajoshasah* (iv.2.4[3]; p. *pra-vanebhih*); the Rik *pada*-text writes this word *pravaṇa*, without separation: other words beginning with *prâ* are *prâsah* (e. g. i.3.14[6]; p. *pra-sahâ*), *prâçṛñga* (ii.1.3[4,5]), *prâsaca* (vii.5.11[1]; not divided in *pada*-text), *prâkâça* (i.8.18; also not divided), and *prâvṛta* (iv.6.2[2] et al.; also not divided). And for *svâ*, *svâdhiyaṁ janayat sûdayac ca* (i.3.14[6]; p. *sva-dhiyam*): but this the Rik *pada*-text writes *su-âdhyam*.

लोकरवेष्टा ॥ ६ ॥

6. Also *ishṭâ*, after *loke* and *eva*.

The commentator cites the two cases: *sam amushmiṅ loka ishṭâpûrtena* (iii.3.8[5] twice: G. M. omit the first word), and *sa tv eve 'shṭâpûrtî* (i.7.3[3]; p. *ishṭa-pûrtî*). Then, to show that *ishṭâ* after other words remains unchanged, he quotes *prati jâgṛhy enam ishṭâpûrte saṅ sṛjethâm ayaṁ ca* (iv.7.13[5]; p. *ishṭâ-pûrte*: W. B.

---

5. ------ *ity eteshv avagraheshv antyasvaro vibhâge vyañjanaparo hrasvam âpadyate. yathâ: pras-----: indr-----: drav-----: viçv-----: dîr-----: vîr-----: viçv-----: vât-----: tvâ-----: bhett-----: sûr-----: vṛsh-----: sa-----: ṛks-----: agh-----: satr-----: varsh-----: pushp-----: megh-----: prâv-----: svâ-----.*

omit before *enam*, G. M. after *-pûrte*); and the same mode of treatment is followed by the *pada*-text at v.7.7[2], which is the only other case I have noted. The ground of this difference does not appear. To show, further, that only *ishṭâ* shortens its *â* in the defined position, the passage *sâkshâd eva prajâpataye* (v.1.2[5]) is given.

शक्तीरथीत्विषीवाशीरात्र्योषध्याहुतीव्याहृतीस्वाहा-कृतीह्रादुनीशचीचितीश्रोणीपृष्टीपूत्यभीचर्षणीपर्यधीपा-रीशत्रूविषूवसूअनूहनूसूविभू इत्यवग्रहे ॥७॥

7. Also *çaktî, rathî, tvishî, vâçî, râtrî, oshadhî, âhutî, vyâhṛtî, svâhâkṛtî, hrâdunî, çacî, citî; çroṇî, pṛshṭî, pûtî, abhî, carshaṇî, parî, adhî, pârî, çatrû, vishû, vasû, anû, hanû; sû, vibhû*—all these, as first members of a compound.

To the passages cited by the commentator I add, as above, notice of other cases which I have found in the text. For *çaktî*, the sole instance is *çaktîvanto gabhîrâḥ* (iv.6.6[3]). For *rathî*, *rathîtamâu rathînâm* (iv.7.15[3]). For *tvishî*, *saspiñjarâya tvishîmate pathînâm* (iv.5.2[1]: W. B. omit the last word, G. M. the first). For *vâçî*, *te vâçîmanta ishmiṇaḥ* (ii.1.11[2] and iv.2.11[2]: G. M. omit the last word). For *râtrî*, *râtrîbhir asubhnan* (ii.4.1[1]): if there are other cases, I have failed to note them. For *oshadhî*, *oshadhîbhyo vehatam âlabheta* (ii.1.5[3]: G. M. omit the last word): I have noted half a dozen other cases, but they are not worth reporting. For *âhutî*, *âhutîbhir anûyâjeshu* (ii.6.9[4]). For *vyâhṛtî*, *etâbhir vyâhṛtîbhiḥ* (i.6.10[2] and v.5.5[3]). For *svâhâkṛtî*, *svâhâkṛtîbhyaḥ preshye 'ty âha* (vi.3.9[5]: G. M. omit the last two words). For *hrâdunî*, *svâhâ hrâdunîbhyaḥ svâhâ* (vii.4.13: G. M. omit the first word, W. B. the last). For *çacî*, *viçvâ rûpâ 'bhi cashṭe çacîbhiḥ* (iv.2.5[4-5]: W. B. omit before *cashṭe*). For *citî*, *citîbhyâm upâyan* (v.7.5[7]). For *çroṇî*, *çroṇîbhyâñ svâhâ* (vii.3.16[2]): another case is found at v.7.15. For *pṛshṭî*, W. B. give *pṛshṭîbhir divam* (v.7.17), but G. M. read *pṛshṭîbhyaḥ svâhâ* (vii.3.16[1]). For *pûtî*, *pûtîgandhasyâ 'pahatyâi* (ii.2.2[4]). For *abhî*, *abhîvṛto ghṛṇîvâñ cetati tmanâ* (iii.5.11[1]: G. M. omit the last two words): we have also *abhîshah* at ii.3.2[6] (p. *abhi-sahâ*). For *carshaṇî*, *mitrasya carshaṇîdhṛtaḥ* (iii.4.11[5] and iv.1.6[3]): another case at i.4.16. For *parî*, *vîravantam parînasam* (ii.2.12[6]; p. *pari-nasam*: compare rule vii.4). For *adhî*, *adhîvâsam yâ hiraṇyâny asmâi* (iv.6.9[2]: G. M. omit the last word). For *pârî*, *pârînahyasye "çe* (vi.2.1[1]; p. *pâri-nahyasya*: compare rule vii.4). For *çatrû*, *ça-*

6. *loke: eva: ity evampûrva ishṭe 'ty asmin*[1] *grahaṇe*[2] *'ntyasvaro vibhâge vyañjanaparo hrasvam âpadyate. yathâ: sam----: sa----. evampûrva iti kim: prati----: ishṭe 'ti kim: sâk-----.*

[1] G. M. *etasminn.* [2] G. M. *avagrahe.*

trâyato hantâ (i.6.5[3] and iv.2.1[2]). For *vishû*, *vishûvân vishûvantaḥ* (vii.4.3[4]): another case at vii.4.8[2]. For *vasû*, *aramatir vasûyuḥ* (iv.3.13[6]). For *anû*, *anûrâdhâ nakshatram* (iv.4.10[2]); we have it also in the compounds *anûyâja* (e. g. ii.6.9[4]), *anûbandhya* (e. g. ii.2.9[7]), *anûkâça* (e. g. v.4.1[3]), and *anûvṛj* (v.7.23). In the further compound of the first, *prayâjânûyâja* (e. g. i.7.1[1]; p. *prayâja-anûyâjân*), the shortening is not authorized, since in it there is no division after *anu.* Appealing to rule i.53 as his authority, the commentator adds, as contemplated by the present rule, *ananûyâjam prâyaṇîyam* (vi.1.5[3]; p. *ananu-yâjam*). For *hanû*, *hanûbhyâñ svâhâ* (vii.3.16[1]). For *sû*, *sûyavasinî manave yaçasye* (i.2.13[2]): *sûyavasa* occurs more than once (e. g. i.7.5[2,3]). For *vibhû*, *vibhûdâvne* (iii.5.8,9[2]).

The commentator notes that the specification at the end of this rule defines the whole mass of words thus far enumerated as collectively *avagraha* (i.49), 'first members of compounds.'

अवासचस्वानुदामृडावर्धाशिक्षारक्षाद्याभवाभजायत्रा-
चरापिबानाधामाधारयाधर्षाघावर्धयाबोधात्रातत्रामुञ्चाश्व-
स्यापृणस्वाहिष्ठात्वतराजनिष्वायुक्ष्वाच्छा ॥ ८ ॥

8. Also *ava*, *sacasvâ*, *nudâ*, *mṛḍâ*, *vardhâ*, *çikshâ*, *rakshâ*, *adyâ*, *bhavâ*, *bhajâ*, *yatrâ*, *carâ*, *pibâ*, *nâ*, *dhâmâ*, *dhârayâ*, *dharshâ*, *ghâ*, *vardhayâ*, *bodhâ*, *atrâ*, *tatrâ*, *muñcâ*, *açvasyâ*, *pṛṇasvâ*, *hi shṭhâ*, *tvaṁ tarâ*, *janishvâ*, *yukshvâ*, *achâ*.

Henceforth we have to do only with independent words, the category of *avagrahas*, or former members of compounds, having been exhausted by the foregoing rules. There is cited in illustration, for *avâ*, *avâ no devyâ kṛpâ* (iv.1.4[1]). For *sacasvâ*, *sacasvâ naḥ svastaye* (i.5.6[2]). For *nudâ*, *pra nudâ naḥ sapatnân* (iv.3.12[1] thrice, and v.3.5[1]). For *mṛḍâ*, W. B. give *mṛḍâ jaritre* (iv.5.10[4]), but G. M. read *mṛḍâ no rudra* (iv.5.10[2]): I have noted no other case. For *vardhâ*, *vardhâ no amavac chavaḥ* (ii.6.11[3]). For *çik-*

---

7. ------ *ity eteshv avagraheshv*[1] *antyasvaro vibhâge vyañjanaparo hrasvam âpadyate. yathâ: çak----: rath----: sa----: te----: râ----: ôsh----: âh----: et----: svâ----: svâhâ----: viç----: cit----: çro----: pṛsh----: pût----: abh----: mitr----: vîr----: adh----: pâr----: çatr----: vish----: ar----: anû----: ankârâdi ca*[2] (i.53) *iti vacanâd*[3] *anan---- ity etad*[4] *udâharaṇam bhavati: han----: sûy----: vibh----: ity avagraha ity anena prakâreṇo 'ktiḥ*[5] *padasamudâye*[6] *'vagraho vijñeyaḥ*[7].

[1] G. M. om. [2] G. M. om. [3] G. M. *sûtrât.* [4] G. M. ins. *apy.* [5] G. M. *'ktaḥ.* [6] G. M. *-muccayaḥ.* [7] B. *viçeshaḥ.*

shâ, çikshâ no asmin puruhûta yâmani (vii.5.7[4] : W. B. omit the last two words): it is found again at iv.6.2[5]. For *rakshâ, rakshâ ca no adhi ca deva brûhi* (iv.5.10[3] and vii.5.24 ; G. M. omit the last two words): the form occurs also at ii.3.14[1]. I have pointed out in the note to the first rule of the chapter that a passage (i.4.24) in which *rakshâ* appears as euphonic alteration of *rakshâḥ* before a sonant consonant ought to be somehow excepted here. For *adyâ, adyâ devâñ jushṭatamaḥ* (iv.6.7[5]): also at ii.1.11[6]: iii.4.11[2] : iv.6.2[6]. For *bhavâ, bhavâ pâyur viço asyâ adabdhaḥ* (i.2.14[1] : G. M. omit the last two words): other cases are not infrequent; see i.1.14[4]; 4.32: iii.2.5[3]; 4.10[1]: iv.1.7[2]; 2.5[1],7[4]; 4.4[7]; and likewise ii.6.12[1], where *bhavâ*, standing at the end of the first division of the *anuvâka*, is situated *vibhâge*, and loses its *â* even in the *saṁhitâ*-text. For *bhajâ, â gomati vraje bhajâ tvaṁ naḥ* (i.6.12[1] : W. B. begin at *vraje*): another case at iii.3.9[2]. For *yatrâ, yatrâ naro marutaḥ* (iii.1.11[8]): other cases at iv.4.4[1]; 6.6[4],7[2]. For *carâ, pra carâ soma duryân* (i.2.10[1]). For *pibâ, pibâ somam indra mandatu* (ii.4.14[3] : G. M. omit the last word): another case at i.4.19. For *nâ, ripavo nâ ha debhuḥ* (i.2.14[5-6]): in connection with this word, the commentator runs off into a lengthy discussion, which I defer to the end of the note. For *dhâmâ, dhâmâ ha yat te ajara* (iii.1.11[6]): we have *dhâma*, plural, in *saṁhitâ* also, at iv.6.5[5]; 7.13[4]. For *dhârayâ, bṛhaspate dhârayâ vasûni* (i.3.7[1] and vi.3.6[1]): other cases at iv.1.5[4],7[2]. For *dharshâ*, W. B. have *dharshâ mânushân adbhyaḥ* (i.3.8[1]), but G. M., *dharshâ mânushân iti ni yunakti* (vi.3.6[3]). For *ghâ, uta vâ ghâ syâlât* (i.1.14[1]): there is another case, if my manuscript reads correctly, at iii.4.11[6]. For *vardhayâ, tam agne vardhayâ tvam* (iv.6.3[1]): other cases are at i.5.5[2]: iv.2.4[4]; 7.13[5]. For *bodhâ, bodhâ no asya vacaso yavishṭha* (iv.2.3[4]: G. M. omit the last two words). For *atrâ, atrâ te rûpam* (iv.6.7[3]): other cases are at iv.6.7[2],8[2]. For *tatrâ, tatrâ ratham upa çagmam* (iv.6.6[3]). For *muñcâ, pra muñcâ svastaye* (iii.2.8[3]): again at iv.7.15[7]. For *açvasyâ, ekas tvashṭur açvasyâ viçastâ* (iv.6.9[3]). For *pṛṇasvâ, sapta yonîr â pṛṇasvâ ghṛtena* (i.5.3[3] and iv.6.5[5]). For *sthâ* after *hi, âpo hi shṭhâ mayobhuvaḥ* (iv.1.5[1]: v.6.1[4]: vii.4.19[4]); and, as counter-example, to show that the correption takes place only after *hi, pratishṭhâ vâ ekaviñçaḥ* (v.2.3[6] et al.). For *tarâ* after *tvam, agne tvam tarâ mṛdhaḥ* (iv.1.9[3]), with the counter-example *antaratarâ taptavrato bhavati* (vi.2.2[7] : G. M. omit the last word). For *janishvâ, janî-*

---

8. ------ [1] *eteshv anavagraheshv antyasvaro vibhâge vyañjanaparo hrasvam âpadyate. yathâ: avâ----: sac----: pra----: mṛ----: var----: çiksh----: rak----: adyâ----: bhav----: â go----: yat----: pra----: pibâ----: rip----. api vikṛtam* (i.51) *apy akârâdi* (i.52) *iti dvâbhyâṁ*[2] *vacanâbhyâm prâ---- ity atra hrasvâdeçaḥ kiṁ na syât: mâi 'vam: api vikṛtam* (i.51) *iti vacanaṁ kaṇṭhoktapadavishayaṁ*[3] *na tv akârâdipadavishayaṁ*[4]*: prâṇâ* [5] *ity asyâ 'py akârâditvân nâ*

shvâ hi jenyo agne (iv.1.3^{4} and v.1.4^{5}: G. M. omit *agne*). For *yukshvâ, yukshvâ hi devahûtamân* (ii.6.11^{1} et al.): other cases at iv.2.9^{5}: v.5.3^{1,2}. For *achâ, achâ nakshi dyumattamaḥ* (i.5.6^{3} and iv.4.4^{8}): other cases at i.7.10^{2}: ii.2.12^{8}; 6.11^{1}: iv.2.4^{2} twice; 4.4^{2} (if my MS. is correct; the Rik reads *acha*); 5.1^{2}; 6.7^{5}: but the compound *achâvâka* (vii.1.5^{5}) is left undivided and unchanged.

The occasion of the commentator's delay and discussion over the word *nâ* is given by the fact that the *pada*-text of the Tâittirîya Sanhitâ (unlike that of the Rik and Atharvan: see note to Ath. Pr. iv.39) divides the word *prâṇâḥ* thus: *pra-anâḥ*. Hence, when we read in the Sanhitâ, as in the passage which he quotes, *prâṇâ vâ añçavaḥ* (vi.4.4^{4}: W. B. read simply *prâṇâ vâi*, which occurs in various other places; e. g. v.3.8^{2}), he fears that, having this division in mind, we shall be misled into believing that the specification *nâ* of the present rule applies to *prâṇâ*, because we are taught in the first chapter (i.51,52) that a word cited in any rule comes equally under that rule when phonetically altered, or preceded by *a*. He sets aside this difficulty, however, by the arbitrary *dictum* that it is not permitted to vary the same word in both ways at once—that we may accept the altered form only of a vocable which is actually quoted entire, not of one made by the prefixion of an *a* to one so quoted: hence, he infers, the present rule does not apply to [the *aṇâ* of] *prâṇâ*, as it begins with *a*. But a further objection is interposed: in that case, why does it not apply to the part *anâ* of the compound, in which is no altered *ṇ*? He replies, because of the absence of a long vowel in *saṁhitâ*, in a word wearing this form—or, as would seem a better statement, because of the absence of any such word in *saṁhitâ* as *anâ* (for *anâḥ*) with a long vowel as its final. The second objection, in fact, is a wholly futile one, scarcely worth the trouble of bringing up and setting aside. The original difficulty is one growing out of the extension of the leading rule in the chapter to cases of final *â* in *saṁhitâ* where a *visarjanîya* has been lost after it (see note to rule 1). The answer has a somewhat quibbling aspect, but the rule of interpretation which it involves is in accordance with that adopted in one or two analogous cases elsewhere.

अधाग्नियाज्ये ॥ ९ ॥

9. Also *adhâ*, in *agni* and *yâjyâ* passages.

'yaṁ vidhiḥ. tarhi vikṛtatvâbhâvâd[6] *anâ ity asye*[7] *'ṅgyâñçasya*[8] *kiṁ na syâd ayaṁ vidhiḥ. evaṁrûpasya saṁhitâyâṁ dîrghâbhâvât. dhâ-....: bṛh-....: dhar-....: uta....: tam....: bodhâ....: atrâ....: tat-....: pra....: ek-....: sap-....: âpo....: hî 'ti kim: pra-....: agne....: tvam iti kim: ant-....: jan-....: yuk-....: achâ....*

[1] G. M. ins. *ity.* [2] G. M. om. [3] W. *-ktip-*; B. om. *pada.* [4] B. om. *pada.* [5] W. ins. *vd.* [6] G. M. *vâikṛtasyâ 'bh-.* [7] B. G. M. om. [8] B. G. M. *-yâç-.*

The commentator's first care is to define what parts of the Sanhitâ are styled *agni* and *yâjyâ*. The former name, he says, designates those *mantras* which celebrate Agni—namely, the fourth *kâṇḍa:* by the latter are intended the concluding *anuvâkas*, or sections, of every *praçna*, or chapter, from the beginning of the Sanhitâ to the third *praçna* of the fourth *kâṇḍa*, inclusive; and, besides, the eleventh *anuvâka* of *praçna* six, *kâṇḍa* two (i. e. i.1.14; 2.14; 3.14; 4.46; 5.11; 6.12; 7.13; 8.22: ii.1.11; 2.12; 3.14; 4.14; 5.12; 6.11,12: iii.1.11; 2.11; 3.11; 4.11; 5.11: iv.1.11; 2.11; 3.13—in all, twenty-three *anuvâkas*). The name *agni* does not occur again: the *yâjyâs* are the subject of further prescription below, in rules iii.11, ix.20, xi.3. The compound *agniyâjya* (neuter singular) is justified by a simple reference to Pâṇini's rule (ii.2.29) defining a copulative compound.

The passages cited in illustration of the rule are *adhâ hy agne kratoḥ* (iv.4.4[7]), *adhâ ca naḥ çarma yacha dvibarhâḥ* (iv.5.10[3]: G. M. omit the last word), *adhâ te sumnam îmahe* (ii.6.11[4]), and *adhâ yathâ naḥ pitaraḥ* (ii.6.12[4]: W. B. omit the last word): I have noted no other cases. As counter-example, to show the necessity of the restriction imposed in the rule, is quoted *adhâ me 'ti tad vishṇave 'ti prâyachat* (ii.4.12[4]: W. B. omit *prâyachat*), where *adhâ* stands for *adhâh:* see, for the bearing of the exception, the note upon the introductory rule of the chapter.

कुत्रादक्षिणेनास्वेनाहन्तनाजगामारुहेमाविद्मर्ध्यामाच-
कृमाक्षामास्तरीमाभरेमावर्षयथेरयथारिथापाथाथासिञ्चथा-
जनयथाजयतोक्षतावतायाताशृणुताकृणुताबिभृता ॥ १० ॥

10. Also *kutrâ, dakshiṇenâ, svenâ, hantanâ, jagâmâ, ruhemâ, vidmâ, ṛdhyâmâ, cakṛmâ, kshâmâ, starîmâ, bharemâ, varshayathâ, îrayathâ, ârithâ, pâthâ, athâ, siñcathâ, janayathâ, jayatâ, ukshatâ, avatâ, yâtâ, çṛṇutâ, kṛṇutâ, bibhṛtâ.*

The commentator's illustrative passages are: for *kutrâ*, *kutrâ cid yasya samṛtâu* (ii.1.11[3]: G. M. omit the last word). For *dak-*

---

9. *agniç ca yâjyâ câ 'gniyâjyam*[1]*: tasmin*[2]*: câ 'rthe dvandva iti*[3] *samâsaḥ. agnir ity agniprakâçakamantrâ*[4] *lakshyante: caturthakâṇḍa ity arthaḥ: ubhâ vâm indrâgnî* (i.1.14[1]) *prabhṛty agnir vṛtrâṇi* (iv.3.13[1]) *paryantâḥ praçnottamânuvâkâ yâjyâsaṁjñâ bhavanti yukshvâ hi* (ii.6.11[1]) *ity anuvâkaç ca.* [5]*atra vishaye*[5] *'dhe ty asmin*[6] *grahaṇe 'ntyasvaro vibhâge*[7] *vyañjanaparo hrasvam âpadyate. yathâ: adhâ hy----: adhâ ca----: adhâ te----: adhâ y-----. agniyâjya iti kim: adhâ m-----.*

[1] G. M. -*jye.* [2] G. M. -*inç.* [3] G. M. om. [4] B. -*çaman-.* [(5)] G. M. om. [6] G. M. *etasmin.* [7] G. om.

shinenâ, dakshinenâ vasûni patiḥ sindhûnâm asi (iii.4.11⁴ : G. M. omit after *vasûni*). For *svenâ, svenâ hi vṛtrañ çavasâ jaghantha* (vii.4.15 : B. omits the last word; G. M. the last two). For *hantanâ, tapasâ hantanâ tam* (iv.3.13⁴). For *jagâmâ, â jagâmâ parasyâḥ* (i.6.12⁵). For *ruhemâ, asravantîm â ruhemâ svastaye* (i.5.11⁵). For *vidmâ, vidmâ te agne tredhâ trayâṇi vidmâ te* (iv.2.2¹ : G. M. stop at *agne*, thus instancing only one of the two cases; there are two more in the same verse): also at i.7.13³: ii.6.11⁴. For *ṛdhyâmâ, ṛdhyâmâ ta ohâiḥ* (iv.4.4⁷). For *cakṛmâ, cakṛmâ kac canâ "gaḥ* (iv.7.15⁶): other cases at i.8.3: ii.6.12²: iv.1.11¹; 6.8³. For *kshâmâ, kshâmâ rerihad vîrudhaḥ* (i.3.14²: iv.2.1²,2²: G. M. omit the last word): other cases at ii.6.12⁴: iv.7.12³. For *starîmâ, sushṭarîmâ jushâṇâ* (v.1.11²): here the application of rule i.51 becomes necessary. For *bharemâ, añhomuce pra bharemâ manîshâm* (i.6.12³ : G. M. omit the last word). For *varshayathâ, yûyam vṛshṭim varshayathâ purîshiṇaḥ* (ii.4.8² : W. B. omit the first word). For *îrayathâ, ud îrayathâ marutaḥ* (ii.4.8²). For *ârithâ, yoner udârithâ yaje tam* (iv.6.5⁴). For *pâthâ, kshaye pâthâ divo vimahasaḥ* (iv.2.11²). For *athâ, athâ somasya prayatî yuvabhyâm* (i.1.14¹ : G. M. omit the last word): other cases are numerous, namely i.1.13¹ twice; 5.5²,11³; 6.4² twice; 7.13⁴: ii.3.14³; 6.12²: iii.1.11²; 4.11⁶: iv.2.1⁴,4⁴,5³,6¹·²; 6.3⁴ twice; 7.13⁵; and, as I doubt not, at the end of iii.2.11², where, however, the present *saṁhitâ*-text reads *atha*, because the word stands *vibhâge*. For *siñcathâ, yatrâ naro marutaḥ siñcathâ madhu* (iii.1.11⁸). For *janayathâ, âpo janayathâ ca naḥ* (iv.1.5¹: v.6.1⁴: vii.4.19⁴). For *jayatâ, upa pre 'ta jayatâ nara sthirâḥ* (iv.6.4⁴ : G. M. omit the last word). For *ukshatâ, â ghṛtam ukshatâ madhuvarṇam* (iv.3.13⁸). For *avatâ, asmân u devâ avatâ haveshu* (iv.6.4⁴): another case at iv.2.6³. For *yâtâ, devâ rathâir yâtâ hiraṇyayâiḥ* (iv.7.12¹ : G. M. omit the first word). For *çṛṇutâ, marutaḥ çṛṇutâ havam* (iv.2.11²). For *kṛṇutâ, saṁvatsarâya kṛṇutâ bṛhan namaḥ* (v.7.2⁴). Finally, for *bibhṛtâ, mâte 'va putram bibhṛtâ sv enam* (iv.2.3² : W. B. begin at *putram*).

भरता याज्यासु ॥ ११ ॥

11. Also *bharatâ, in yâjyâ* passages.

---

10. ...... *ity*[1] *eteshv anavagraheshv*[2] *antyasvaro vibhâge vyañjanaparo hrasvam âpadyate. yathâ: kutrâ....: daksh-....: svenâ....: tap-....: âj-....: asr-....: vidmâ....: ṛdhy-....: cakṛ-....: kshâ-....: susht-....: añh-....: yûyam....: ud....: yoner....: kshaye....: athâ....: yatrâ....: âpo....: upa....: â....: asmân....: devâ....: mar-....: saṁ-....: mâ-.....*

[1] G. M. om. [2] W. *avag-*; G. M. om.

Which are the sections called *yâjyâ* has been pointed out above, under rule 9.

The cited passages are: *bharatâ vasuvittamam* (iii.5.11[4]), *bharatâ jâtavedasam* (iii.5.11[1]), and *pûrvyaṁ vaco 'gnaye bharatâ bṛhat* (iii.2.11[1]: G. M. omit the first two words), which are all that the text contains. As counter-example, to show the necessity of restricting the change to *yâjyâ* passages, is quoted *esha vo bharatâ râjâ* (i.8.10[2],12[2]), where *bharatâ* stands for *bharatâḥ*. If the text contained a *bharatâ* as instrumental of the participle *bharant*, it would come more properly under the action of the rule, and would have a better right to be specifically excluded; but I have not found such a form anywhere. Respecting *bharatâ* as standing in *saṁhitâ* for *bharatâḥ*, see what is said in the note to the first rule of this chapter.

अत्ताभवतानदतातरतातपताजुहुतावोचतामुञ्चताकृ-ताघुष्याजनयावर्तयासादयापारयादीयाहराभरापाससादा-सृजातिष्ठायेना ॥ १२ ॥

12. Also *attâ, bhavatâ, anadatâ, taratâ, tapatâ, juhutâ, vocatâ, amuñcatâ, cṛtâ, ghushyâ, janayâ, vartayâ, sâdayâ, pârayâ, dîyâ, harâ, bharâ, apâ, sasâdâ, sṛjâ, tishṭhâ,* and *yenâ.*

The cited passages are: for *attâ, attâ havîṅshi* (ii.6.12[2]). For *bhavatâ, âdityâso bhavatâ mṛḍayantaḥ* (i.4.22 and ii.1.11[4]). For *anadatâ, samprayatîr ahâv anadatâ hate* (v.6.1[2]: W. B. omit the first word). For *taratâ, suvo ruhâṇâs taratâ rajâṅsi* (iii.5.4[2]: G. M. omit the first word). For *tapatâ, gharmaṁ na sâmaṁ tapatâ suvṛktibhiḥ* (i.6.12[2]: W. B. O. [O. begins in the comment to this rule] omit before *tapatâ*). For *juhutâ, pitre juhutâ viçvakarmaṇe* (iv.6.2[6]). For *vocatâ, viçve devâso adhi vocatâ me* (iv.7.14[2]: G. M. omit to *adhi*). For *amuñcatâ, padi shitâm amuñcatâ yajatrâḥ* (iv.7.15[7]). For *cṛtâ, ayasmayaṁ vi cṛtâ bandham etam* (iv.2.5[3]). For *ghushyâ, parushparur anu ghushyâ viçasta* (iv.6.9[3]). For *janayâ, manur bhava janayâ dâivyaṁ janam* (iii.4.2[2],3[7]). For *vartayâ, tâbhir â vartayâ punaḥ* (iii.3.10[1]). For *sâdayâ, sâdayâ yajñaṅ sukṛtasya yonâu* (iii.5.11[2] and iv.1.3[3]). For *pârayâ, agne tvaṁ pârayâ navyo asmân* (i.1.14[4]: all but W. omit the last word). For *dîyâ, bṛhaspate pari dîyâ rathena* (iv.6.4[1-2]: the text reads *dîya*, as the word stands before the division between the first and second fifty of the section): another case is iii.1.11[6]. For *harâ, nihâram in ni me harâ nihâram*

---

11. *bharatâ ity asmin*[1] *grahaṇe*[2] *'ntyasvaro yâjyâvishaye*[3] *vibhâge vyañjanaparo hrasvam âpadyate. yathâ: bhar-....: bhar-....: pûr-.... yâjyâsu iti kim: esha....*

[1] G. M. *etasmin.* [2] B. *avagraheshv.* [3] G. M. *yâjyâyâm*, and put before the preceding word.

(i.8.4[1]). For *bharâ*, *mâ no, mardhîr â bharâ dadhi tan naḥ pra dâçushe* (i.7.13[3]: O. omits after *bharâ;* B. G. M. after *dadhi*): there is no other case, *bharâ* at i.3.14[3] in the Calcutta edition being an erratum. For *apâ*, *duro na vâjañ çrutyâ apâ vṛdhi* (ii.2.12[6]: W. B. omit the first two words). For *sasâdâ*, *agnir hotâ ni shasâdâ yajîyân* (i.3.14[1] and iv.1.3[4]: G. M. omit the first word): there is another case at iv.6.2[1], requiring, like the others, the application of rule i.51. For *sṛjâ*, *sṛjâ vṛshṭiṁ divaḥ* (ii.4.8[2],10[3]): there are other cases at ii.4.8[2]: iii.5.5[2],10[1]: iv.1.8[3]. For *tishṭhâ*, *tishṭhâ devo na savitâ* (iv.1.4[2]): other cases at iii.1.4[1]: v.2.1[4], and perhaps also at iv.1.2[3], where the word ends a division of the *anuvâka*. For *yenâ*, *yenâ sahasram vahasi* (iv.7.13[4] and v.7.7[3]).

उश्मसीक्रयीकृधीश्रुधीयदी ॥ १३ ॥

13. Also *uçmasî*, *krayî*, *kṛdhî*, *çrudhî*, and *yadî*.

The quoted examples for these words, being the only ones which the text contains, are as follows. For *uçmasî*, *te te dhâmâny uçmasî gamadhye* (i.3.6[1-2]: W. B. O. omit the first three words): here, as *uçmasî* stands at the end of a division, or *vibhâge*, its *i* is short in the accepted text. For *krayî*, *rudra yat te krayî paraṁ nâma* (i.8.14[2]). For *kṛdhî*, *kṛdhî sv asmân aditeḥ* (iv.7.15[7]: W. B. O. omit the last word). For *çrudhî*, *imam me varuṇa çrudhî havam* (ii.1.11[6]). For *yadî*, *yadî bhûmiṁ janayan* (iv.6.2[4]).

सूतूनूमिथूमक्षू ऊ ॥ १४ ॥

14. Also *sû*, *tû*, *nû*, *mithû*, *makshû*, and *û*.

The cited passages are as follows: for *sû*, *mo shû ṇa indra* (i.8.3). For *tû*, *â tû na upa gantana* (i.5.11[4-5]): there are two other cases, i.7.13[3]: ii.2.12[7], both after *â*. For *nû*, *etaçasya nû raṇe* (iv.6.1[2]). For *mithû*, *gâtrâṇy asinâ mithû kâḥ* (iv.6.9[4]: G. M. omit the first word). For *makshû*, *makshû devavato rathaḥ* (i.8.22[3]). For *û*, a part of the manuscripts give two examples,

---

12. ------ *eteshv anavagraheshv*[1] *antyasvaro*[2] *vibhâge vyañjanaparo hrasvam âpadyate. yathâ: attâ----: âd-----: sampr-----: suvo----: ghar-----: pitre----: viçve----: padi----: ayas-----: par-----: man-----: tâbh-----: sâd-----: agne----: bṛh-----: nih-----: mâ----: duro----: agnir----: sṛjâ----: tish-----: yenâ----.*

[1] W. *av-;* G. M. *grahaṇeshu.* [2] O. begins here.

13. ------ *ity*[1] *eteshv*[2] *anavagraheshv*[3] *antyasvaro vibhâge vyañjanaparo hrasvam âpadyate. yathâ: te----: rudra----: kṛdhî----: imam----: yadî----.*

[1] G. M. om. [2] G. M. *eshv.* [3] W. *av-;* G. M. om.

asmâbhir â nu praticakshyâ 'bhût (i.4.33: wanting in G. M.), and *ûrdhva â shu na utaye* (iv.1.4[2]: W. B. O. omit the first word, G. M. the last): other cases are found at i.5.11[5]: ii.5.12[2]: iii.5.10[1]: iv.1.10[3]; 6.5[6]: v.1.5[3]: vii.1.18[2]; 6.17[2].

व्युत्पूर्व आननुदात्तो ऽनूष्मवत्यनूष्मवति ॥ १५ ॥

15. Also *ân*, when unaccented, and preceded by *vi* or *ut*, in a word containing no spirant.

This rule applies simply to the compounds *vyâna* and *udâna*, in which the long *â* of the radical syllable is treated by the *pada*-text as the effect of an irregular prolongation. The words are instanced by the commentator in their full *pada*-form, *vyânâye 'ti vi-anâya* (iii.5.8 et al.), and *udânâye 'ty ut-anâya* (iv.2.9[1] et al.). In the same manner, *prâṇâya* and *apânâya* are divided into *pra-anâya* and *apa-anâya*. As regards the treatment of this group of compounds, the different *pada*-texts are somewhat inconsistent and somewhat conflicting. The Atharvan *pada* (see Ath. Pr. iv.39) divides *vi-âna* and *sam-âna*, without correption of the radical *â*, but leaves *prâṇa* and *apâna* undivided. The Rik *pada* does not divide *prâṇa*: I do not know that any of the others are Rik words. The White Yajus, again (Vâj. Pr. v.33,36), divides *apa-âna* and *sam-âna*, but not *prâṇa*. The consistency of the Tâittirîya *çâkhinah* is to be commended; less, perhaps, their assumption that the *â* of *âna* is a mere Vedic irregularity, requiring restoration to a correcter form. They also, it may be remarked, divide *prâṇatha* (iv.1.4[1]) into *pra-anatha*.

The commentator goes on to cite counter-examples, proving the necessity of the restrictions imposed by the rule. To show that *ân* is to be shortened only after *vi* and *ut*, he gives *yad ânṛcus tene 'yam* (vii.3.1[3]: W. B. O. omit the last word), and *paryâṇîyâ havanîyasya* (vii.1.6[6]). To show that only *ân*, not *â* followed by any other consonant, is shortened, he quotes *yad rukmam vyâghârayati* (v.2.7[5]), and *udâdâya pṛthivîm jîradânuḥ* (i.1.9[3]: G. M. omit the last word). To show that the *ân* must not be accented, he gives *viçvákarmâ vyâ'nat* (iv.2.10[4]), and *néshṭaḥ pátnîm udâ'naya* (vi.5.8[6]). Finally, to show that the presence of a spirant in the word prevents the correption, we have *pathâ madhor dhârâ vyânaçuḥ* (v.7.7[3]: all but W. omit the first word), and *ud ânishur mahîr iti* (v.6.1[3]).

The question is now in point, how complete is this rehearsal of the cases of prolonged vowels occurring in the Sanhitâ; or, how closely does the *pada*-text which it assumes correspond with that

---

14. ...... *ity*[1] *eteshv*[2] *anavagraheshv*[3] *antyasvaro vibhâge vyañjanaparo hrasvam âpadyate. yathâ: mo....: â....: eta-....: gâ-....: mak-....: asm-....: ûrdhva....*

[1] G. M. om. [2] G. M. *eshv.* [3] W. *av-;* G. M. om.

found in the existing *pada*-manuscripts? As regards the latter point, I am unable to speak with certainty, of course, without the possession of a *pada*-manuscript, and its careful examination throughout; but so much as this I can say—that, having referred a liberal selection of the most questionable cases to Dr. Haug at Munich, for verification in his *pada*-texts, no instance of a discordance between these and the Prâtiçâkhya has come to light. Among the cases referred were several in regard to which I was beforehand very confident that I had caught the authors of the Prâtiçâkhya in fault. Thus *yojâ*, in the refrain *yojâ nv indra te harî* (i.8.5[1,2]) which is shortened to *yoja* in the *pada*-texts both of the Rik (by Rik Pr. vii.7) and the White Yajus (by Vâj. Pr. iii.106), remains *yojâ* in that of our Sanhitâ. Again, *eva* occurs six times in our text with its final lengthened (viz. at i.8.22[2]: ii.1.11[3]: iv.2.9[2]; 3.13[3]; 7.15[7]: v.2.8[3]), as it does also not infrequently in the other Vedic texts (as noticed and provided for in their Prâtiçâkhyas: see Rik Pr. vii.12,19; viii.20: Vâj. Pr. iii.123: Ath. Pr. iii.16, note, I.l.*c*.): but the Tâittirîya *pada* reads in each case *evâ*. Once more, in the passage *tava dharmâ yuyopima* (Rig-Veda vii.89.5; Ath. Veda vi.51.3; Tâitt. Sanh. iii.4 11[6]), the *pada*-texts of the Rik and Atharvan read *dharma* (I do not find that the case is noted in the Rik Pr.; in the Ath. Pr. it would fall under the comprehensive rule iii.16), while that of our Sanhitâ has *dharmâ*, like the *saṁhitâ*-reading.

I will add, as received from the same quarter, a few words respecting which a question might naturally arise as to how they were treated in the *pada*-text. Separated, without correption of the long vowel at the end of their first member, are *uttarâ-vat* (v.4.8[5]), *sahasâ-van* (i.6.12[6]), *malmalâ-bhavant* (i.4.34), *vṛshâ-kapi* (i.7.13[2]), such copulative compounds as *indrâ-varuṇayoḥ* (ii.5.12[2]) and *agnâ-vishṇû* (i.1.12), and *ûrṇâ-mradas* (i.1.11[1]: while, nevertheless, we have *ûrṇa-mradas* at i.2.2[2], the *pada*-reading agreeing in both cases with that of the *saṁhitâ:* where the Calcutta edition gets its authority for reading *ûrṇâmmradas* and *ûrṇammradas* is more than I can imagine).

---

15. *vî 'ty evampûrva upûrvo vâ "n ity esha*[1] *svaro nudâtto 'nûshmavaty*[2] *ûshmarahite pade vartamâno vyañjanaparaḥ padâdâu vartamânatvât pûrvapadena*[3] *vibhâge sati hrasvam âpadyate. yathâ: vyânâye 'ti vi-anâya: udânâye 'ty ut-anâya. evampûrva iti kim: yad----: pary-----: nakâraḥ kimarthaḥ: yad----: udâ-----: anudâtta iti kim: viçv-----: nesh-----: anûshmavatî 'ti kim: pathâ----: ud-----.*

iti tribhâshyaratne prâtiçâkhyavivaraṇe tṛtîyo 'dhyâyaḥ[4].

[1] G. M. ins. *âkâra.* [2] W. *ûshm-.* [3] G. M. *-de.* [4] G. M. add *çrikṛshṇâya namaḥ.*

Not separated, and therefore, of course, without correption of the vowel, are such words as *ṛtâshâṭ* (iii.4.7[1]) and *turâshâṭ* (i.7.13[4]), also *tvashṭîmant* (i.2.5[2]), *anyâdṛç* (i.8.13[2]), *ubhayâdat* (ii.2.6[3]), *arâtîyant* (i.6.1[1]) and *arâtîvan* (vii.4.15), *atîkâça* (i.2.2[2]) and *prâkâça* (i.8.18), *avâçṛnga* (ii.1.8[5]) and *prâçṛnga* (ii.1.3[1]: I doubt not: my information is deficient for this word), *upânah* (v.4.4[4]), *nîvâra* (iv.7.4[2]) and *nîhâra* (iv.6.2[2]), and *purûravaḥ* (i.3.7[1]).

There is not, as in the other Vedic texts, any restoration of a theoretically correct short vowel which is not strictly a final or initial: thus we read in *pada*-text, for example, *vâvṛdhe* (i.4.20), *sâsahat* (i.3.14[7]), and *ushâsam* (iv.4.4[2]).

Many of these items constitute striking peculiarities of the Tâittirîya *pada*, and its careful study and comparison with the other works of its class would undoubtedly bring to light much that is curious.

CHAPTER IV.

CONTENTS: 1–4, introductory; 5–54, rehearsal of cases of *pragrahas*, or uncombinable final vowels.

अथ प्रग्रहाः ॥ १ ॥

1. Now the *pragrahas*.

A simple heading to the chapter, and explained as such by the commentator. The same subject is treated by the other Prâtiçâkhyas, at Rik Pr. i.18–19, Vâj. Pr. i.92–98, Âth. Pr. i.73–82. It occupies here a great deal more space, because the Tâitt. Pr. avoids on principle the mention of grammatical categories in its rules, and is at infinite pains to catalogue, word by word, what the other treatises dispose of summarily, by classes. A rule in a later chapter (x.24) teaches that all the vowels here rehearsed and defined as *pragraha* are exempt from euphonic combination. The term *pragraha* is peculiar to this treatise, the rest using instead *pragṛhya*.

नावग्रहः ॥ २ ॥

2. No former member of a compound is *pragraha*.

As the former member of a separable compound (*avagraha*: i.49) is regarded and treated as an independent *pada*, the rules declaring certain final vowels *pragraha* would apply to the finals

1. *athe 'ty ayam adhikâraḥ: pragrahâ ucyanta ity 'etad² adhikṛtaṁ veditavyam ita¹ uttaraṁ yad vakshyâmaḥ.*

(1) W. om. ² G. M. om.

of such members, but for this prescription to the contrary. The commentator cites rules 5, 6, 36, 37, 49 of the chapter as needing the restriction of their application here made, and quotes from the Sanhitâ in illustration *tanûnapâd asuraḥ* (iv.1.8[1]: the *tanû* of *tanû-napât* would otherwise be *pragraha* by rule 5), *agoargham yajamânam* (vi.1.10[1]: *ago-argham* would fall else under rule 6), *agnîshomâu mâ* (ii.5.2[2]: it is implied that the *pada*-text would write *agnî-somâu*, bringing the word within the sphere of rule 36; such compounds are not divisible in the other Vedic texts), and *dvedve puronuvâkye kuryât* (ii.2.9[2]: the *pada* writes *dve-dve*, so that both members would be declared alike *pragraha* by rule 49). The present precept is therefore declared to be one making exceptions in advance to the rules specified.

अन्तः ॥ ३ ॥

3. Only a final is *pragraha.*

Or, as the commentator paraphrases, the end of a word is entitled to the designation *pragraha.* He cites, as example, the phrase *devate samṛddhyâi* (ii.1.9[3]). The necessity of the rule, he explains, arises out of the fact that the following rules, in part—for example, rules 5, 6, 33—describe certain letters or syllables as *pragraha* without farther limitation, and it is desirable to specify that they bear that character only when final. This in answer to the criticizing inquiry "whether a letter not final can also be *pragraha?*"—that is, as I understand it, whether this predicate is not in the nature of things restricted to finals? But now a yet more troublesome objection is raised. The limitation to finals, urges the interpellator, is otherwise assured; for the word *api* of the next rule, in the sequel of this one, brings into action the principle "continued implication is of that which is last" (i.58). The objection is wholly futile and inept, both as implying that false interpretation of the rule appealed to to which attention was directed in the note upon it, and as attributing to *api* a mysterious force to which it can lay no claim whatever. Instead, however, of showing the

---

2. *avagrahaḥ pragraho na bhavati: ûkâraḥ* (iv.5)*: okâro 'sâñhito 'kâravyañjanaparaḥ* (iv.6)*: gnî* (iv.36)*: na hiparaḥ* (iv.37)*: dve* (iv.49) *iti vakshyate*[1]*: etad*[2] *uddiçya purastâdapavâdo 'nena vidhîyate. yathâ*[3]*: tan-....: ago-....: agn-....: dve-....: avagraha*[4] *iti jâtyapekshâyâm ekavacanam.*

[1] W. *-ti;* B. O. om. [2] G. M. *tad.* [3] G. M. om. [4] G. M. *nâ 'v-.*

3. *padasyâ 'ntaḥ pragrahasaṁjño bhavati. yathâ: dev-.... atrâ "ha: kim apadânto 'pi pragrahaḥ syât. atro 'cyate: ûkâraḥ* (iv.5) *ity aviçesheṇa vakshyati: okâro 'sâñhito 'kâravyañjanaparaḥ* (iv.6) *iti: cî yatpraparaḥ* (iv.33) *iti ca: apadântasyo "kârasyâu 'kârasya cîçabdasya vâ pragrahatvam*[1] *mâ bhûd iti.*

objector to the door, the commentator proceeds elaborately to confute him. "We reply, not so: specification of finality is appropriate where there is a congeries of several letters; here, on the other hand, there is indication of a single letter. If the matter in question were the euphonic alteration or elision of *û* and the other letters treated of, a final would be designated in virtue of the principle quoted: but here it is a simple case of application of the term *pragraha*, not of an affected nor an affecting letter: hence continued implication has no force."

इतिपरो ऽपि ॥४॥

4. It is followed by *iti*.

This is the interpretation of the commentator, who declares that the "also" (*api*) brings in by implication, from the first rule of the preceding chapter, the specification *vibhâge*, 'in case of separation,' or in the *pada* and other artificially divided texts. As example, he cites *ubhe iti* (i.4.22 et al.: G. M. add *devate iti*, ii.1.9[3] et al.).

If such be its real meaning, the rule is a very anomalous one, as giving a single direct prescription respecting the mode of construction of the secondary texts. These are elsewhere only referred to or implied, in a more indirect manner. I should therefore prefer to translate 'even when followed by *iti*'—that is to say, a word here defined as *pragraha* in the ordinary text has that character also in the other texts before *iti*, not being combined with the latter.

ऊकारः ॥५॥

5. A long *û* is *pragraha*.

---

nanu siddham evâi 'tat: etatsûtraçeshabhûta[2] *uttarasûtre*[3] *'piçabdenâ 'nvâdeço 'ntyasya* (i.58) *eva kâryanirvâhât*[4]. *ne 'ti brûmaḥ: anekavarṇasamudâye hy antyatvam*[5] *upapannam: ayam punar ekavarṇanirdeçaḥ: ûkâraḥ* (iv.5) *ity âdivarṇasya yâu vikâralopâu tayor* [6] *anvâdeço 'ntyasya* (i.58) *ity anenâ 'ntyaḥ: pragraha ity uktam*[7] *pragrahasaṁjñâmâtram*[8]*: na tu*[9] *nimittaṁ nimittî vâ: tasmâd anvâdeço na prasarati.*

[1] G. M. *grahaṇam.* [2] B. O. *-çeshe;* G. M. *-bhût.* [3] G. M. *ottarasya sû-.* [4] G. M. *-vâhakaḥ.* [5] B. O. *anta-.* [6] G. M. ins. *eva.* (7) G. M. *'ntyapratyaya uktaḥ.* [8] G. M. *-ha iti saṁ-.* [9] B. O. om.

4. *apiçabdaḥ siṅhâvalokanenâ 'thâ "dâv uttare vibhâge* (iii.1) *ity atra vibhâgapadam*[1] *anvâdiçati: so 'yam pragraho vibhâga itiparo bhavati. yathâ:* [2] *ubhe iti. itiçabdaḥ paro yasmâd asâv itiparaḥ.*

[1] G. M. *-gam.* [2] G. M. ins. *devate iti.*

The commentator adds the limitation "if long in *pada*-text," the final *ū* is universally *pragraha;* referring, in justification, to the cases treated of above, in rule iii.14, of an *u* irregularly lengthened in *saṁhitā*. His examples are *hanū vā ete yajña-sya* (vi.2.11^{3}: W. B. O. omit the last word), *vāsantikāv ṛtū çukraç ca* (iv.4.11^{1}: W. B. O. omit after *ṛtū*), and *hariṇasya bāhū upastutaṁ janima tat te arvan* (iv.2.8^{1}: G. M. omit the last four words; the others, the first word).

ओकारो ऽसांहिता ऽकारव्यञ्जनपरः ॥ ६ ॥

6. Also an *o* which is not the product of euphonic combination, if followed by *a* or a consonant.

Of words exhibiting in *pada*-text, as well as in *saṁhitā*, a final *o*, there are (apart from the theme *go*, which occurs only as first member of a compound, and therefore, by rule 2 of this chapter, does not require to be regarded in the determination of *pragrahas*) two classes, the one composed of vocatives from themes in *u*, the other of words whose final *a* or *ā* is combined with the particle *u*. The present rule deals, in general, with the former class; the one next following, with the latter class. The right of the vocatives in *o* to be treated as *pragrahas* is a very dubious one, and is not unequivocally supported by the Prâtiçâkhya; for to say that such words are *pragraha* before *a* or a consonant is not to distinguish them perceptibly from the euphonic *o* which comes from a final *as;* since this also is not capable of combination with a consonant, and does not necessarily absorb a following initial *a*. The only instances in which a vocative in *o* exhibits a *pragraha* character are the three which are cited under the next rule (i.4.27: v.7.2^{4}: vi.5.8^{3}); the cases in which it is regularly changed to *av* before other vowels than *a* are much more numerous: namely, before *ā*, at i.4.39: ii.2.12^{4}; 6.11^{1}: vi.4.3^{3}; before *i*, at ii.2.12^{8}; before *u*, at i.2.13^{2} twice; 6.12^{3}: iii.2.10^{1}; before *e*, at ii.4.12^{3}. I have noted but two cases in the text where such an *o* stands before initial *a* without absorbing it; they are found at i.3.8^{1},14^{7}. And there are the same

---

5. *ūkāraḥ padāntaḥ sarvatra pragraho bhavati: padasamaye vartamānaḥ. yathā: hanū----: vās-----: har-----. padasamaye vartamāna iti kim: sūtānūmithūmakshūū*[1] (iii.14) *ity ādi.*

[1] G. M. omit after *mithū*.

6. *asāṁhita okāro 'kāraparo vā' vyañjanaparo vā pragrahaḥ syāt. yathā: vad-----: vish------. asāṁhita iti kim: so-----: 'pra-----. evampara iti kim*[2]*: vish-----. saṁhitānimittaḥ sāṁhitaḥ: na sāṁhito 'sāṁhitaḥ: akāraç ca vyāñjanaṁ cā 'kāravyañjane: te pare yasmāt sa tatho 'ktaḥ.*

[1] G. M. om. [2] W. B. O. om.

number of cases—namely, at ii.5.12[5] and vi.4.3[4]—in which it causes the elision of a following *a*.

The commentator's citations in illustration of the rule are *vadmâ hi sûno asi* (i.3.14[7]), and *vishṇo havyañ rakshasva* (i.1.3). To show the necessity of the limitation *asâṁhitaḥ*, he cites *so 'bravît* (ii.1.2[1] et al.), and *pra so agne* (iii.2.11[1]: omitted, however, by W. B. O.), where *so* is the *saṁhitâ* reading for *saḥ;* and, to show that the prescribed quality belongs to the vowel only before *a* or a consonant (the *lacuna* of W. B. O. extends through this explanation), he gives us *vishṇav e 'hî 'dam* (ii.4.12[3]).

For the teachings of the other Prâtiçâkhyas respecting this class of asserted *pragrahas*, see the note to Ath. Pr. i.81.

समम्हृदथपित्पूर्वश्च ॥ ७ ॥

7. As also, when preceded by *s*, *m*, *h*, *d*, *th*, and *pit*.

The *anuvṛtti* of this rule is even more blind and equivocal than usual. Instead of bringing down either the subject or predicate of the one preceding, we are to bring down both, only with the exclusion of one of the modifications included in the former. The meaning is, that an original *o*, preceded as here specified, is *pragraha* even when followed by other vowels than *a*. The commentator is in error in saying that *ca* implies *okâraḥ* from above; he should have said *okaro 'sâṁhitaḥ*.

As above remarked, this rule chiefly concerns the class of *pragrahas* composed of words whose final vowel, *a* or *â*, is combined with the particle *u*. Of these, *atho* is vastly the most numerous, occurring about two hundred and fifty times in the Sanhitâ. Before *a* it is met with twenty times, always without occasioning elision; before other vowels, twenty-nine times, always uncombined. Along with it, *tatho* is had in view by the rule, as presenting a final *o* after *th:* it is found but once, in the passage cited by the commentator (see below). The only word showing *o* after *s* is *so*, found only in two passages, as noted below. After *m*, we have *o* both in *mo* (in two passages, once before *sh*, at i.8.3; the other is cited by the commentator) and in *imo*, which latter is found only before *a* (iv.3.13[6]), and so does not necessarily come within the purview of the rule. The other words of the class occur before consonants alone, and are, therefore, here made no account of: they are *o* (once, i.4.33), *to*

---

7. *pûrvoktaparanimittâbhâve 'pi kâryavidhânârtham okâraṁ viçinashṭi: cakâra okâram anvâdiçati. sa: ma: ha: da: tha: pit: evampûrvo 'sâṁhita okâro 'kâravyañjanâbhyâm anyaparo 'pi pragraho bhavati. yathâ: so----: mâ----: upa-----: indo ----: tatho----: sa-----. evampûrva iti kim: 'çat-----: asâṁhita iti kim'[1]: pra-----.*

(1) B. om.

(i.2.5[2] and vi.1.8[5]) and *uto* (five times), *upo* (four times), and *pro* (i.7.13[5]).

Of the remaining specifications of the rule, the *h* is made for but a single case of the exclamation *ho*, which the commentator quotes: *upahûtâñ3 ho ity âha* (ii.6.7[3]); the *d* is for the vocative *indo*, which occurs twice: *indo indriyâvataḥ* (i.4.27), and *indo ity âha* (vi.5.8[3]): the commentator quotes the latter passage; the *pit* is for the vocative *pito*, only found once, as cited: *sa no mayobhûḥ pito â viçasva* (v.7.2[4-5]: W. B. O. omit the first three words). These three, as was noted under the preceding rule, are the only instances which the Sanhitâ affords of vocatives in *o* showing an uncombinable quality.

The commentator's explanation of the rule is "the *o* is here specially distinguished in order to the prescription of its quality even in the case of absence of the sequent determining circumstances before stated." As examples of words whose ending is combined with *u*, after the consonants specified, he gives *so evâi 'shâi 'tasya* (ii.2.9[7]; 5.5[5]), *mâ bher mâro mo eshâm* (iv.5.10[1]), and *tatho evo 'ttare nir vapet* (iii.4.9[7]: W. B. O. omit after *uttare*). His counter-examples are *çatakratav ud vañçam iva* (i.6.12[3]: G. M. omit *iva*), and *pra so agne* (iii.2.11[1]): but G. M., which have given the latter passage under the preceding rule, here substitute for it *mâ so asmâñ avahâya* (v.7.9[1]); their separate application is manifest.

The treatment by the Prâtiçâkhya of words ending in *o* is awkward and bungling to a degree quite rare or wholly unknown elsewhere in its rules. We should be justified in inferring from its statements that *o*, *to*, *uto*, *upo*, and *pro* were not regarded as *pragrahas* at all, nor the vocatives in *o* except under the conditions and in the places specified, and that (if the commentator's explanation of rule 4 is accepted) they are not written with *iti* in the *pada*-text: while, doubtless, in every *pada*-text of the Black Yajus, as in those of the other Vedas, each word is treated uniformly, whether it happen to exhibit its uncombinable quality in *saṁhitâ* or not. Through the rest of the chapter, it will be noticed, the words mentioned are defined as *pragrahas*, without regard to the circumstances in which they may stand in the text.

अथैकारेकारौ ॥ ८ ॥

8. Now follow cases of *e* and *î*.

This is a heading for the remainder of the chapter, excluding all other vowels than final *e* and *î* from the action of its rules. The words exhibiting such finals are, of course, mainly duals, and are by the other treatises simply defined as such, with immense saving of trouble.

---

8. *athe 'ty ayam adhikâraḥ: ekârekârâu*[1] *pragrahatvena vidhîyete*[2] *ity etad*[3] *adhikṛtaṁ veditavyam.*

[1] G. M. *ekâra ikâraḥ.* [2] W. O. *-yate;* B. *-yayate;* G. M. *viçishyata.* [3] G. M. om.

अस्मे ॥ ९ ॥

9. *Asme* is *pragraha.*

The example cited by the commentator is, according to W. B. O., *asme te bandhuḥ* (i.2.7); according to G. M., *sampatte gor asme candrâṇî* (also i.2.7). Neither exhibits in *saṁhitâ* the *pragraha* quality of the word, as is done at i.7.13[5] and elsewhere: *asme* is not uncommon in the Sanhitâ, occurring twenty-nine times.

त्वे इत्यनिंग्यान्तः ॥ १० ॥

10. Also *tve,* when not the final member of a separable compound.

The office of the word *iti* in this rule is differently explained by the two versions of the commentary: W. B. O. say that it indicates the quality of a separable cited word (they mean, doubtless, of an inseparable); G. M., that it indicates *pragraha* quality. Each interpretation is as good, and as worthless, as the other. The commentary is not infrequently at much pains to put some special, even wonderful, significance into *iti* when found in a rule; and generally with as little acceptable result as here.

The pronoun *tve* occurs seven times in the Sanhitâ (at i.3.14[2]; 4.46[1]: iii.1.11[7]; 5.10[1]: iv.2.7[3]; 6.5[4]: vi.1.8[5]), exhibiting its *pragraha*-quality in *saṁhitâ* only once (at iv.2.7[3]). The commentator's instance is *tve kratum api* (iii.5.10[1]: G. M. omit *api*); and his counter-instance, to show the necessity of the restriction imposed in the rule, is *anâgâstve adititve turâsaḥ* (ii.1.11[6]: G. M. omit *turâsaḥ*), where the *pada*-text reads *anâgâḥ-tve : aditi-tve.*

देवतेउभेभागधेऊर्ध्वेविशाखेभृङ्गेएन्नेमध्येतृष्णेतृप्येकनी-
निकेग्राव्णेशिवेचोत्तमेएवोत्तरेशिप्रेरथंतरेवत्सरस्यरूपेवि-
रूपेविषुरूपेसदोहविर्धानेअधिषवणेअहोरात्रेधृतव्रतेस्तुत-

---

9. *asme ity asmin*[1] *grahaṇe 'ntyasvaraḥ pragraho bhavati. yathâ: asme.....*

[1] G. M. *etasmin.*

10. *itiçabda iṅgyagrahaṇatvaṁ*[1] *dyotayati: aniṅgyântas tve ity esha çabdaḥ pragraho bhavati. yathâ: tve..... aniṅgyânta iti kim: anâ-..... iṅgyasyâ 'nta iṅgyântaḥ: ne 'ṅgyânto 'niṅgyântaḥ.*

[1] G. M. *pragrahatvaṁ.* T. W. B. O. write *iṅgy-* throughout.

शस्त्रेऋक्सामेअक्तेअर्पितेरैवतेपूर्तेप्रत्तेविधृतेअनृतेअच्छिद्रे-
बहुलेपूर्वजेकृणुध्वंसदने ॥ ११ ॥

11. Also *devate, ubhe, bhâgadhe, ûrdhve, viçâkhe, çṛṅge, ene, medhye, tṛṇne, tṛdye, kanînike, pârçve, çive, co 'ttame, evc 'ttare, çipre, rathaṁtare, vatsarasya rûpe, virûpe, vishurûpe, sadohavirdhâne, adhishavaṇe, ahorâtre, dhṛtavrate, stutaçastre, ṛksâme, akte, arpite, râivate, pûrte, pratte, vidhṛte, anṛte, achidre, bahule, pûrvaje, kṛṇudhvaṅ sadane.*

For the *pragrahas* catalogued in this rule—all of them dual cases of feminines and neuters—the commentator quotes illustrative passages as follows. For *devate, devate samṛddhyâi mâitram* (ii.1.9^{3}: the last word in G. M. only). For *ubhe*, G. M. have *achidre bahule ubhe: vyacasvatî saṅvasâthâm* (iv.1.3^{2}); but W. B. O., blunderingly, *ime eva rasenâ 'nakti* (vi.3.11^{3}: B. O. have *ubhe* for *ime*): the word occurs also in other passages. For *bhâgadhe, bhâgadhe bhâgadhâ asmâi* (ii.5.6^{6}): also in the preceding division of the same *anuvâka*, and at v.5.9^{2}. As counter-example, to show that *dhe* (itself a *pada*, *bhâga-dhe*) would not have answered the purpose alone, we have *agna udadhe* (v.5.9^{1}: *pada*-text, *uda-dhe*). For *ûrdhve, ûrdhve samidhâv â dadhâti* (ii.6.6^{3} and vi.2.1^{6}). For *viçâkhe, viçâkhe nakshatram* (iv.4.10^{2}): and as counter-example, to show the necessity of including the *vi* (of *vi-çâkhe*), we have *tasmint sahasraçâkhe*, stated to be found "in the text of another school." About a score of such alleged citations from "another text," assumed to have been had in view by the authors of the Prâtiçâkhya in constructing their rules, are given in various parts of the commentary (five of them in the comment upon this rule): they will be put together, and their bearing discussed, in an additional note at the end of the work. For *çṛṅge, antarâ çṛṅge taṁ devatâḥ* (vi.2.8^{4}: only G. M. have *devatâḥ*): the word also occurs at i.2.14^{7}. The next two words, *ene* and *medhye*, occur in the same passage, *medhye evâi 'ne karoti* (vi.2.9^{1}), which the comment quotes, in W. O. giving *medhye* last, after the rest, by way of justifying the order in which the two words stand in the rule: but B. G. M. read the whole passage as it stands in the text, and G. M. make the rule read correspondingly *medhye ene* (T. has, like the others,, *ene medhye*). *Ene* is also found in one or

---

11. ------ *etâni padâni pragrahasaṁjñâni*[1] *syuḥ*[2]. *yathâ: dev-----: achid-----: bhâg-----: bhâge*[3] *iti kim: agna----: ûr-----: viç-----: vî*[4] *'ti kim: tas----- iti çâkhântare*[5]*: ant-----: ev-----: me-----: asaṁ-----: saṁ-----: yad----: pâr-----: pit-----: vik-----: ce 'ti kim: saṁ-----: tatho----: eve 'ti kim: nâi----: pît-----: yad----: saṁv-----: sam-----: vish-----: vatsarasyavivishv*[6] *iti kim: arû-----:* [7]*rûpaçabdasya*

two other passages (iv.6.2[4]: vi.2.9[1] again; 3.9[6]). For *tṛṇne, asaṁtṛṇne hi hanû atho khalu* (vi.2.11[3]: only G. M. have the last two words). For *tṛdye, saṁtṛdye dhṛtyâi* (vi.2.11[3]). For *kanînike, yad atirâtrâu kanînike agnishṭomâu yat* (vii.2.9[1]: W. B. O. begin at *kan-*): the same word occurs twice more in the next division. For *pârçve, pârçve paraḥsamânaḥ* (vii.3.10[3]): it is found a second time in the same division. For *çive, pitaraḥ somyâsaḥ çive no dyâvâpṛthivî* (iv.6.6[4]: W. B. O. begin at *çive*). For *co 'ttame, vikarṇîṁ co 'ttame upa dadhâti* (v.3.7[3]: only G. M. have the last two words): and, to show the necessity of the *ca*, *saṁvatsaraṅ saṁpâdyo 'ttame mâsi* (vii.5.3[1]). For *evo 'ttare, tatho evo 'ttare nirvapet* (iii.4.9[7]): and, to show why *eva* had to be included in the rule, *nâi 'ti shoḍaçy uttare tena* (vii.1.4[3]: only G. M. have *tena*). For *çipre, pîtvâ çipre avepayaḥ* (i.4.30: W. B. O. begin with *çipre*). For *rathaṁtare, yad bṛhadrathaṁtare anvarjeyuḥ* (vii.5.3[2]: only G. M. have *yad*): the same compound occurs in several places elsewhere. For *vatsarasya rûpe, saṁvatsarasya rûpe âpnuvanti* (vii.5.1[4]). For *virûpe, samanasâ virûpe dhâpayete* (iv.1.10[4]; 6.5[2]; 7.12[3]). For *vishurûpe, vishurûpe ahanî dyâur ivâ 'si* (iv.1.11[3]: W. B. O. stop with *ahanî*). The necessity of including in the rule, besides the *pada rûpe*, the words *vatsarasya*, *vishu* (of *vishu-rûpe*), and *vi* (of *vi-rûpe*) is proved by the citation of *arûkshitaṁ dṛça â rûpe annam* (iv.3.13[2]), where *rûpe* is locative: and the commentary adds the remark (wanting, however, in the South-Indian MSS.), "the separate specification of the word *rûpa* is to be looked upon as for the sake of distinct enunciation." For *sadohavirdhâne, sadohavirdhâne eva sam minoti* (ii.5.5[5]): the compound occurs twice more, at vi.2.6[2]; 5.1[5]. To justify the 'inclusion of *sadaḥ*, the commentator quotes *uparavâ havirdhâne khâyante* (vi.2.11[1]); but the case appears to him one not to be so easily disposed of, and he enters into an elaborate discussion of it, which I defer to the end of this note, in order not to interrupt the connection. For *adhishavane, hanû adhishavane jihvâ* (vi.2.11[4]): it is also found in the preceding division of the same section, and at iv.7.8[1]. The *adhi* is justified by reference to *sâvanesavane 'bhi gṛhṇâti* (vi.4.11[4]; 6.11[3]). For *ahorâtre, ahorâtre prâ 'viçan* (i.5.9[7]): the word occurs not infrequently elsewhere. The passage *atirâtre paçukâmasya* (vi.6.11[4]) is given to account for the inclusion of *ahaḥ*; this implies, of course, that the Tâittirîya *pada*-text treats the word as a separable compound, *ahaḥ-râtre*. For *dhṛtavrate, dyâvâpṛthivî dhṛtavrate âvinnâ devî* (i.8.12[2]: G. M. omit the last

---

prativiçeshaṇam uccâraṇavispashṭârthaṁ[9] drashṭavyam[7]: sad-----: sada iti kim: up-----. nanu padagrahaṇeshu padaṁ gamyeta (i.50) *iti sâmarthyâd 'dhavirdhâne ity ekapadasyâi 'va kâryasiddhiḥ: sadaḥpadaṁ vyartham. mâi 'vam: padagrahaṇe sthalântare[10] bhinnarûpasya[11] sambhâvanâyâṁ[9] viçeshaṇaṁ sârthakam bhavati[12]: bhinnarûpatvâbhâve tu codyam etad bhavet[13] nanu tarhi devate iti padagrahaṇasya sthalântare[14]*

word); and, to account for the inclusion of *dhṛta*, *yasya vrate pushṭipatiḥ* (iii.1.11[3]). For *stutaçastre*, *stutaçastre evâi 'tena duhe* (v.6.8[6]: G. M. omit the last word): it occurs again at vii.3.13. This time, resort is had to "another text" (*çâkhântaram*) for a passage to explain why the rule does not say simply *çastre:* it is *ûrdhve çastre pratishṭhite.* For *ṛksâme*, *ṛksâme vâi devebhyaḥ* (vi.1.3[1]): the word is found twice in this division, and also at vi.5.9[2]; 6.7[4]. Here, again, a passage in "another text," *brahma sâme pratishṭhite* (G. M. omit the last word, and B. O. omit the *sâ* of *sâme*), is appealed to in justification of the *ṛk.* For *akte*, *purûravâ ghṛtenâ 'kte vṛshaṇaṁ dadhâthâm* (i.3.7[1] and [except *purûravâḥ*] vi.3.5[3]: W. B. O. omit the first word, B. also the last). For *arpite*, *dyâvâpṛthivî bhuvaneshv arpite* (iv.7.13[2]: only G. M. have the first word). For *râivate*, *çâkvararâivate sâmanî* (i.8.13[2] and iv.4.2[3]): the same compound is found again at iv.3.2[3]. For *pûrte*, the different recensions give different examples: W. B. O. have *ishṭâpûrte saṅ sṛjethâm* (iv.7.13[5]); G. M., *ishṭâpûrte kṛṇutât* (v.7.7[2]): I have noted no other cases: for the treatment of the word in the *pada*-text see the note to iii. 6. For *pratte*, *pratte kâmam annâdyaṁ duhâte* (v.4.9[3]: G. M. omit the last word). For *vidhṛte*, again, W. B. O. have *vidhṛte sarvataḥ* (vi 4.10[3]), and G. M. *tasmân nâsikayâ cakshushî vidhṛte samânî* (ii.3.8[2]), and the *vi* is justified by an alleged citation from "another text," *agnidhṛte* (G. M., however, omitting the *agni*, thus leaving it to be understood that the simple word *dhṛte* is found elsewhere not *pragraha*). For *anṛte*, *satyânṛte avapaçyan* (v.6.1[1]). For *achidre*, *achidre bahule ubhe* (iv.1.3[2]: only G. M. have *ubhe*), which answers also for *bahule:* it is the only passage containing either word. For *pûrvaje*, *pûrvaje pitarâ navyasîbhiḥ* (iv.1.11[4]: W. B. O. omit the last word): another passage beginning with the same word is the subject of rule 23 of this chapter. Once more a word, *prathamaje*, is cited from "another text," in order to explain why the rule does not say simply *je* (since the *pada*-text writes *pûrva-je*). For *kṛṇudhvaṅ sadane*, finally, we have the sole passage in which it occurs, *gîrbhiḥ kṛṇudhvaṅ sadane ṛtasya* (iv.1.11[4]: G. M. omit *ṛtasya*), with the counter-example *apâṁ tvâ sadane sâdayâmi* (iv.3.1: G. M. omit the last word), to show the necessity of *kṛṇudhvam.*

To return, now, to the long word *sadohavirdhâne.* The objection is raised, that its part *sadaḥ* is unnecessary, and that it would

---

soma.... iti bhinnarûpatvâd[15] viçeshaṇena bhavitavyam: tac ca nâ 'sti. ucyate: devate ity akhaṇḍapadasyai 'va kâryavidhânâd atra viçeshaṇaṁ na yujyate: akhaṇḍavidhânam[16] iti katham pratîyate: te ity asya te mâ patam (iv.42) *ity âdinâ pṛthakkaraṇâd iti brûmaḥ: nâi[17] 'vaṁ havirdhâne[18] ity asyâ[19] 'khaṇḍatvadyotakaṁ [20] kiṁcid apy[21] asti yena sadaḥpadavâiyarthyam âlambate[22]. hanâ....: adhî 'ti kim: sav-....: aho-....: ahar iti kim: ati-....: dyâv-....: dhṛte 'ti kim: yasya....: stu-*

have been sufficient to say *havirdhâne* simply; for rule i.50 teaches us that, in citations of *padas*, the cited *pada* alone is to be understood, not any collocation of words or letters phonetically equivalent with it: and *havirdhâne* is here a single *pada* (the compound being divided *sadaḥ-havirdhâne*, while its latter member, occurring by itself as a non-*pragraha*, is written *haviḥ-dhâne*, and so is a congeries of two *padas*). It is replied: not so; a distinctive addition is properly made to a cited *pada*, in case of its occurrence in a different form in another passage; though the objection would hold good, were it not for such occurrence in a different form. But this explanation is not suffered to pass without challenge. In that case, retorts the objector, a distinction ought to be added to *devate*, because it occurs elsewhere in a different form (made up of two independent words), as in *soma deva te matividaḥ* (iii.2.5[2,3]); and no such addition is made. The answer is, that no distinction need here be applied to *devate*, because its treatment is defined as of an undivided word: and, if you ask how its indivisibility is established, we reply that rule 42, below, treats of *te* as a separate *pada* in the various situations in which it is *pragraha* [whence the inference is clear that it is here an inseparable part of the word *devate*]; while there is nothing whatever to show in like manner the indivisibility of *havirdhâne*, and so to prove the addition of *sadaḥ* superfluous. The implication is, that if the *pada dhâne* happened to be described elsewhere as *pragraha* after certain other *padas*, of which *haviḥ* was not one, then we could be sure that *havirdhâne* here meant a single undivided *pada*, and its mention by itself would be enough; while, as things are, one cannot be certain that its part *haviḥ* is not, like the *vi* and *vishu* of *virûpe* and *vishurûpe*, a distinctive addition.

अमीचक्षुषीकार्ष्णी देवताफल्गुनीमुष्टीधीनाभीवपाश्रपणीश्रद्धनीजन्मनीसुम्निनीसामनीविष्णावीरिन्नवीदर्वीद्यावापृथिवी ॥ १२ ॥

----: *stute 'ti kim: ûrdh-.... iti çâkhântare: ṛks-....: ṛg iti kim: brah-.... iti çâkhântare: pur-....: dyâv-....: çâkv-....: isht-....: prat-....: vidh-....: vî 'ti kim: agn- iti çâkhântare:* [22]*saty-....: ach-....: pûrv-....: pûrve 'ti kim: prath- iti çâkhântare:*[23] *gîr-....: kṛṇudhvam iti kim: apâṁ* ----.

[1] O. *pragṛhyas-.* [2] G. M. *bhavanti.* [3] G. M. *bhâgadhe.* [4] G. M. *viçâkhe.* [5] G. M. *-raṁ.* [6] W. O. *vatsaraviv-.* (7) G. M. om. [8] B. *-ṇaṁ vi-*; W O. *-tha.* (9) G. M. om. [10] MSS. *sthâl-.* [11] W. *-patraṁ.* [12] B. G. M. om. [13] G. M. om. [14] B. *sthâl-* [15] W. B. O. *abh-.* [16] B. O. *-ṇḍitavi-.* [17] W. B. O. *mâi.* [18] W. B. O. *sadoh-.* [19] W. *asâ*; B. *â*; O. om. [20] W. B. O. ins. *na.* [21] W. B. O. *tathâ.* [22] B. *-ṁbyate*; O. *-ṁbhyate*; G. M. *âpadyate.* (23) B. om.

12. Also *amî, cakshushî, kârshṇî, devatâ phalgunî, mushṭî, dhî, nâbhî, vapâçrapaṇî, ahanî, janmanî, sumninî, sâmanî, vâishṇavî, âikshavî, darvî, dyâvâpṛthivî.*

The illustrative passages cited under this rule are as follows. For *amî*, according to W. B. O., *amî vâ idam abhûvan* (iii.3.7[1]); but according to G. M., *amî tvâ jahati* (iii.2.11[3]): I have noted elsewhere only vi.1.5[4]. For *cakshushî, cakshushî vâ ete yajñasya* (ii.6.2[1] et al.: G. M. omit *yajñasya*): the word occurs about a dozen times. For *kârshṇî, kârshṇî upânahâv upa muñcate* (v.4.4[4]; 6.6[1]: G. M. omit the last two words). For *phalgunî, pitaro devatâ phalgunî nakshatram* (iv.4.10[1]): again in the next division of the same section. To show the necessity of including *devatâ* in the rule, is given *yad dvitîyañ sâ phalgunî* (ii.1.2[2]). For *mushṭî, mushṭî karoti vâcam* (v.2.1[7] and vi.1.4[3]: G. M. omit *vâcam*). For *dhî, pradhî tâv ukthyâ madhye* (vii.4.11[2]: G. M. omit *madhye*). For *nâbhî, rajatanâbhî vâiçvadevâu* (v.5.24). For *vapâçrapaṇî, vapâçrapaṇî pra harati* (vi.3.9[6]): it occurs also in the fourth division of the same section. As counter-example, to explain the presence of *vapâ* in the rule, is given, "from another text," the compound *paçuçrapaṇî* (or, as G. M. read, *bhasmaçrapaṇî*): our Sanhitâ has *paçuçrapaṇam* at iii.1.3[2]. For *ahanî, ahanî dyâur ivâ 'si* (iv.1.11[3]). For *janmanî, ubhe ni pâsi janmanî* (i.4.22). For *sumninî, sumnâya sumninî* (i.1.13[3]). For *sâmanî, sâmanî pratishṭhityâi* (iv.4.2[3]): also at i.8.13[2]. For *vâishṇavî, valagahanâu vâishṇavî bṛhann asi* (i.3.2[2]: only G. M. have the last two words). For *âikshavî, âikshavî tiraçcî* (vi.2.1[5] twice). For *darvî, darvî çrînîsha âsani* (ii.2.12[7] and iv.4.4[6]). For *dyâvâpṛthivî, dyâvâpṛthivî eva svena* (ii.1.4[7]): the word is frequently found elsewhere. The commentator gives us here also a counter-example, *mahî dyâuḥ pṛthivî ca naḥ* (iii.3.10[2] et al.: G. M. omit *ca naḥ*), as if the inclusion of *dyâvâ* required justification: but, in ordinary Vedic usage (I have omitted to inform myself in season respecting that of the Tâittirîya *pada*-text), *dyâvâpṛthivî* is inseparable, and therefore itself a single *pada.*

पूर्वश्च ॥ १३ ॥

13. As also, the preceding word.

That is to say (by the application of rule i.58), the word preceding the last one mentioned in the rule next above, or *dyâvâpṛthi-*

---

12. ...... [1] *etâni padâni pragrahasañjñâni syuḥ*[2]. *yathâ*[3]: *amî....: caksh-....: kârsh-....: pit-....: devate 'ti kim: yad....: mush-....: pra-....: raj-....: vap-....: vape 'ti kim: paç-.... iti çâkhântare: ah-....: ubhe....: sum-....: sâm-....: val-....: âiksh-....: dar-....: dyâv-....: dyâve 'ti kim: mahî....*

[1] G. M. ins. *iti.* [2] G. M. O. *bhavanti.* [3] W. B. O. om.

vî. The examples given are *yâvatî dyâvâpṛthivî mahitvâ* (iii.2.6[1]), and *âvinne dyâvâpṛthivî* (i.8.12[2]: G. M. invert the order of the two citations): I have noted only two other cases of the application of the rule, at ii.2.12[6]; 6.7[5].

न रुन्धे नित्यम् ॥ १४ ॥

14. But not *rundhe*, in any case.

The case intended to be excluded is quoted by the commentator: *paçûn evâ 'va rundhe dyâvâpṛthivî gacha svâhâ* (vi.4.1[3]: W. B. O. omit the first three words and the last). The specification *nityam*, 'constantly, in all cases,' is intended to exclude also the operation of any other rule under which *rundhe* might chance to fall: for example, in *rundhe yadâ sahasram* (ii.1.5[2]), where, as preceding *yadâ*, it would otherwise be *pragraha* by rule 38 of this chapter. I have noted no other case.

हरीसहुरीसहूतीकल्पयन्तीआपृषतीआहुती ॥ १५ ॥

15. Also *harî*, *sahurî*, *sahûtî*, *kalpayantî*, *â pṛshatî*, and *âhutî* are *pragraha*.

The cited examples are as follows. For *harî*, *harî te yuñjâ pṛshatî abhûtâm* (iv.6.9[4]: G. M. omit the last two words): it occurs in toward a dozen other passages. For *sahurî*, *sahurî saparyât* (iv.2.11[1]); and the counter-example, to show the necessity of the *sa*, *tam âhurî hvayante* (but O. reads *tâm*, B. *hvayate*, and G. M. *ahurî vâcayati*), claimed to be found "in another text." This would imply, of course, that the *pada*-text reads *sa-hurî*—as is in fact the case. For *sahûtî*, *sahûtî vanataṁ giraḥ* (ii.3.14[1]); and, as counter-example, for the same purpose as the last, *hûtî punar juhoti* (but G. M. read *manur* for *punar*), also from "another text." For *kalpayantî*, *adhvaraṁ kalpayantî ûrdhvaṁ yajñam* (i.2.13[2]: G. M. omit the first word, and W. B. O. the last): another case is found at vi.2.9[3]. For *â pṛshatî*, the passage already quoted for *harî*, *yuñjâ pṛshatî abhûtâm* (iv.6.9[4]); and, to justify the *â*, the counter-example *pṛshatî sthûlapṛshatî* (v.6.12). For *âhutî*, *puroḍâçam ete âhutî juhoti* (i.5.2[3-4]: G. M. omit the first two words, W. B. O. the last): nearly the same phrase occurs again at

---

13. *cakâreṇâ 'nvâdishṭadyâvâpṛthivî ity asmât*[1] *pûrvo 'pî "kâra ekâro*[2] *vâ padântaḥ pragraho bhavati. yathâ: yâv-.....: âv-.....*

[1] G. M. *etasmât.* [2] G. M. put before *îkâraḥ.*

14. *rundhe ity antyasvaro*[1] *dyâvâpṛthivî ity etasmât pûrvo 'pi na pragraho bhavati: paçûn..... nityaçabdaḥ prâptyantaranishedhârthaḥ: rundhe.....: vîḍâdi*[2] (iv.38) *prâptiḥ.*

[1] W. *antasv-*; B. O. *antaḥ sv-*. [2] O. *viḍdvârâv iti.*

i.5.4[4]. To account for the *â* in this word, G. M. simply cite *hutî* as found in "another text:" but W. B. O. give the phrase *hutî tasmâd evâḥ* (but W. O. read *hûtî*, and B. *ddhatî:* W. also has *vivâ iti* instead of *evâ iti*).

पूर्वश्च ॥ १६ ॥

16. As also, the preceding word.

Namely *ete*, occurring before *âhutî* in the passage already quoted: *puroḍâçam etè âhutî* (i.5.2[3]: W. B. O. here omit the first word).

वाससीतपसीरोदसी ॥ १७ ॥

17. Also *vâsasî*, *tapasî*, and *rodasî*.

The examples are: *vâsasî iva vivasânâu* (i.5.10[1]: the word is also found at i.8.18); *sâkshâd eva dîkshâtapasî ava rundhe* (vi.1.1[2]: the compound occurs again in the same division: only G. M. have the first two words); and *ime vâi rodasî tayoḥ* (v.1.5[4]: G. M. have dropped out *vâi*): the word is not rarely met with elsewhere.

परश्च ॥ १८ ॥

18. As also, the following word.

The passage contemplated by the rule is, as cited in the comment, *anv indrañ rodasî vâvaçâne* (i.7.13[1]): there is, I believe, no other falling under it.

---

15. ------ [1] *eteshv antyasvaraḥ*[2] *pragrahaḥ syât*[3]: *harî----: sah-----: se 'ti kim: tam---- iti çâkhântare: sah-----: se 'ti kim: hûtî---- iti çâkhântare: adhv-----: yuñjâ----:* [4]*e 'ti*[4] *kim: pṛsh-----: puro-----: e 'ti kim: hutî---- iti çâkhântare.*

[1] G. M. ins. *ity.* [2] B. O. *antyaḥ sv-.* [3] G. M. *bhavati.* [(4)] G. M. *âkâreṇa.*

16. *cakârânvâdeçâd*[1] *âhutî ity etasmât pûrva* [2]*îkâra ekâro vâ padântaḥ*[2] *pragraho bhavati. yathâ: pur-----*

[1] G. M. *-anvâdishṭa.* [(2)] G. M. om.

17. [1]------ *ity etâni pragrahasaṁjñâni bhavanti*[1]. *yathâ: vâs-----: sâk-----: ime----.*

[(1)] G. M. *eshv antyasvaraḥ pragraho bhavati.*

18. *cakârânvâdishṭarodasî*[1] *ity etasmât para* [2]*îkâra·ekâro vâ padântaḥ*[2] *pragraho bhavati. yathâ: anv-----.*

[1] G. M. *-ṭâd ro-.* [(2)] G. M. om.

व्यचस्वतीभरिष्यन्तीनःपृथिवी ॥ १९ ॥

19. Also *vyacasvatî*, *bharishyantî*, and *naḥ pṛthivî*.

The examples are: *vyacasvatî saṁ vasâthâm* (iv.1.3²); *agnim antar bharishyantî jyotishmantam* (iv.1.3²: G. alone has the last word); and *dyâvâ naḥ pṛthivî imaṅ sidhram* (iv.1.11⁴). The needed counter-example for the last is supplied by *rejate agne pṛthivî makhebhyaḥ* (iv.1.11⁴).

येअप्रथेतामुर्वी तेअस्यंयंक्रन्दसीछन्दस्वतीतेआचरन्तीअन्तरैतासु ॥ २० ॥

20. Also in the verses beginning *ye aprathetâm*, *urvî*, *te asya*, *yaṁ krandasî*, *chandasvatî*, *te âcarantî*, and *antarâ*.

The commentator cites only the beginning of each verse, as a word with *pragraha* final occurs at or near the beginning in every case. Thus: *ye aprathetâm amitebhiḥ* (iv.7.15⁶: there are three other cases of *pragrahas* in the verse): with the counter-example *ye te panthânaḥ* (vii.5.24), to show that *ye* alone would not have defined the verse; *urvî rodasî varivaḥ* (iv.7.15⁶: G. M. omit the last word: three cases, besides *rodasî*, already disposed of by rule 17); *te asya yoshaṇe* (iv.1.8²: one more case: the *te* is therefore made no account of in rule 42, below): with the counter-example *te 'vardhanta svatavaso mahitvanâ* (iv.1.11³), to show the necessity of *asya*; *yaṁ krandasî avasâ* (iv.1.8⁵: contains two other cases): and, as counter-example, for a like purpose, *yam agne pṛtsu martyam* (i.3.13²); *chandasvatî ushasâ* (iv.3.11¹: it contains seven cases); *te âcarantî* (iv.6.6²: also seven cases): with *te no arvanto havanaçrutaḥ* (i.7.8²) as counter-example, to prove that *te* alone would not be enough; and, finally, *antarâ mitrâvaruṇâ carantî* (v.1.11²: with four cases).

नोपस्थे ॥ २१ ॥

21. But not *upasthe*.

---

19. ------ *'eteshv*[1] *antyasvaraḥ*[2] *padântaḥ*[3] *pragraho bhavati. yathâ: vyac----: agn----: dyâvâ----*[4]*: na iti kim: rej----.*

[1] G. *eshv.* [2] B. *-tyaḥ sv-.* [3] G. om. [(4)] M. om.

20. ------ *etâsv ṛkshv îkâra ekâro*[1] *vâ padântaḥ pragraho bhavati. yathâ: ye----: aprathetâm iti kim: ye te----: urvî----: te----: asye 'ti kim: te 'v----: yaṁ----: krandasî iti kîm: yam----: chand----: te â----: âcarantî iti kim: te no----: ant-----.*

[1] G. M. put before *ikâro.*

That is to say, *upasthe* is exempted from the action of the preceding rule: it occurs but once in the verses forming the subject of that rule, namely in *mâte 'va putram bibhṛtâm upasthe* (in the verse beginning *te âcaranti*, iv.6.6²: W. B. O. give only the last two words). To show that *sthe* would not have sufficiently defined the exception (*upa-sthe*), the commentator quotes *ye pratishṭhe* (*prati-sthe*) *abhavatâm* (from the verse beginning with *urvî*, iv.7.15⁶).

इरावतीप्रभृत्या दाधार ॥ २२ ॥

22. Also in the passage beginning with *irâvatî*, and ending with *dâdhâra*.

The passage in question is found at i.2.13², and contains six *pragrahas*, whereof one, *rodasî*, needs no further provision than was made in rule 17, above; it also contains a word in *e*, *manave*, which is not *pragraha*, being excepted by rule 54. The commentator quotes its beginning, *irâvatî dhenumatî hi bhûtam.*

पूर्वजेप्रभृत्यायम् ॥ २३ ॥

23. And in the passage beginning with *pûrvaje* and ending with *ayam*.

Of this passage, found at ii.6.7⁵, the commentator quotes the first four words. In order to the better understanding of the following discussion, I set it down here in full, along with the word that precedes it: *hvayate pûrvaje ṛtâvarî ity âha pûrvaje hy ete ṛtâvarî devî devaputre ity âha devî hy ete devaputre upahûto 'yam.* It contains ten *pragraha* endings, of which, however, two (*pûrvaje*) fall under rule 11, above. The word *â*, 'as far as,' in the rule, is declared here to exclude the two limiting words mentioned (com-

---

21. *etâsu ṛkshû 'pasthe ity antyasvaraḥ*[1] *padântaḥ*[2] *pragraho na bhavati. yathâ: mât-.... upe 'ti kim: ye....*

[1] B. O. *antaḥ sv-*. [2] G. M. om.

22. *irâvatîprabhṛtî 'râvatî iti*[1] *çabdam ârabhyâ" dâdhâra dâdhâraçabdaparyantam*[2] *îkâra ekâro vâ padântaḥ pragraho bhavati. yathâ: irâ-....*

[1] G. M. om. [2] W. B. O. *paryantam*.

23. *pûrvajeprabhṛtyayamparyantam*[1] *îkâra ekâro vâ padântaḥ pragraho bhavati. yathâ*[2]*: pûrv-.... âṅpadam*[3] *maryâdâyâṁ vartate. nanu pûrv-.... ity ârabhyâ 'yam.... ity etatparyantaṁ sthalam*[4] *etatsûtravishayaḥ*[5] *kiṁ na syât. ucyate: bharatpaksha upabandhântaḥpâtitvât*[6] *kṛṇudhvaṅ sadane* (iv.11) *iti grahaṇasya*[7] *vâiyarthyaṁ*[8] *'syât: tan*[8] *mâ bhûd iti: tasmâd*

pare Pâṇini ii.1.13)—an arbitrary restriction, directly opposed by the analogy of the preceding rule; intended, doubtless, to relieve the treatise of the reproach of declaring the word *pûrvaje* a *pragraha* by two separate rules; but this is a small gain, since the same word occurs a second time in the passage, and cannot there be reached by any such device.

A protracted, not to say tedious, discussion now arises, respecting the sufficiency and propriety of the rule as stated. The first objection is: how do we know that the passage had in view by the rule is not that which begins with *pûrvaje pitarâ* (iv.1.11[4]) and ends with *ayam purobhuvaḥ* (iv.3.2[1]: B. O. omit *bhuvaḥ*). Because, it is answered, the special citation (in rule 11) of *kṛṇudhvañ sadane* (iv.1.11[4]), which occurs within the limits mentioned, would in that case be rendered superfluous. Objection second: the word *pûrvaje*, at any rate, is useless, it having been already made *pragraha* by rule 11; the rule should read "beginning with *varî*" (the concluding *pada* of the separable compound *ṛta-varî*). This, too, is repelled: the rule reads as it stands because *varî* occurs twice in the passage, and the question would arise where the defined limit should be understood to be: moreover, as we are taught (i.25) in case of doubt to take the nearest, we should have to assume as intended the latter of the two, as being nearer to the other specified limit: in which case we should arrive at the untoward result that the *pragraha* character of the first *varî* would not be established at all. But now the objector triumphantly retorts, that there are also two instances of *pûrvaje*, and a like doubt as in the supposition last made would arise as to the identity of the one cited, and a like untoward result as was pointed out in connection therewith. Not so, is the defense: *pûrvaje* is not desig-

---

etat[9] *sthalam etatsûtravishayo na bhavati. nanu atra pûrvajegrahaṇam anarthakam: pûrvajekṛṇudhvañsadane* (iv.11) *iti tatrâi 'vo 'ktatvât:* [10]*kiṁ tu*[10] *varîprabhṛty*[11] *etâvatâi 'vâ 'lam. ne 'ti brûmaḥ: varîgrahaṇadvayasambhavât: kutra vâ 'vadhiniyamatvena*[12] *svîkâra*[13] *iti saṁdehaḥ syât: kiṁ ca: âsannañ saṁdehe* (i.25) *iti vacanâd uttarâvadhisaṁnikṛshṭo*[14] *dvitîyavavarîçabda eva svîkartavyaḥ: tathâ sati pûrvavarîçabdasya*[15] *pragrahatvaṁ na syât: tac câ 'nishṭam. nanu bhuvanmate 'pi pûrvajedvayasambhavât kutra vâ grahaṇam iti saṁdehaḥ samânaḥ: kiṁ ca: yuktyuktam*[16] *anishṭaṁ ca*[17] *samânam*[18]. *mâi 'vam: pûrvaje iti padam atra kâryabhâktveno*[19] *no 'cyate* [20]*yena pâunaruktyam bhavet: kiṁ tu pûrvaç câ 'sâu jeçabdaç ca pûrvaje: etatprabhṛtî 'ty*[21] *upalakshakatveno*[22] *'cyate*[20]. *nanu tarhy*[23] *upahûta iti padam atikramyâ 'yam ity avadhitvena kimartham*[24] *ucyate:* [25]*upahûta iti padânâm bâhulye* [26] *'py âsannañ saṁdehe* (i.25) *iti vacanât prâthamikasyâi 'va grahaṇasiddhiḥ*[27]. *mâi 'vam*[25]: *upahûta iti padagrahaṇe*[28] *tatra*[29] *gâuravadoshaḥ:*

nated by the rule as a word possessing the defined quality—which would indeed be a superfluous repetition (in view of rule 11); but it means 'the former *je* of the two,' and is given merely as a convenient limit to count forward from! Again: why, at the end of the passage, is *ayam* pitched upon as limit, to the neglect of *upahûtaḥ*; for, though this word is found several times in the immediate sequel, yet, in virtue of the principle already appealed to, "in case of doubt, take the nearest" (i.25), its first occurrence would be distinctly enough the one intended. This also is disallowed: to quote the whole compound word *upahûtaḥ* (*pada*-text, *upa-hûtaḥ*) would be to incur the charge of excess; and as for *upa* by itself, the first member of the compound, though it be a *pada*, its *pada* quality is of secondary rank, while that of *ayam* is primary [the latter being a complete word, but the former only a somewhat artificially separated portion of such]; hence, on the principle "where there is a primary, a secondary is not in place," it was proper to cite *ayam*. The answer, however, suggests the further objection that, on the same principle, the first limit is unsuitable [*je* being also a fragment of a word; and its predecessor *hvayate* should have been taken instead]. That cannot be made good, is the reply; for there is a want of suitableness in the primary word suggested: if you take the primary *hvayate*, then, on the supposition that the definition of limits is to be understood inclusively [*â* being susceptible of both an inclusive and an exclusive interpretation], this word [as it ends in *e*] will appear to be cited as a *pragraha*: which is wrong. And if you urge that rule 54 of the chapter annuls this false inference, we reply that, on the principle "not to touch filth is far better than to wash it off," it is better not

---

upe 'ty etâvanmâtrasyâ "dibhûtasyâ[30] *'ṅçasya*[31] *padatvaṁ gâuṇam: ayam ity asya tu*[32] *mukhyam: mukhye sambhavati na gauṇam iti nyâyâd ayam iti yuktaṁ grahaṇam. nanv etenâi 'va nyâyenâ "dyâvadher*[33] *anupapannatâ. nâ 'yam pakshaḥ: mukhyasambhavâbhâvât*[34]*: tathâ hi: hvayata iti mukhye svîkṛte 'bhividhinyâyena tasyâ 'pi grahaṇaṁ*[35] *syât: tac câ 'nishṭam: ate samânapade* (iv.54) *iti vacanâd etad*[36] *anishṭaṁ na*[37] *bhavatî 'ti*[38] *cet: prakshâlanâd dhi paṅkasyâ dûrâd asparçanaṁ varam iti nyâyâd dhvayata ity uccârya tasya nishedhakathanâd api tadanuccâraṇam eva ramaṇîyam*[39]. *iti mukhyasambhavâbhâvo 'vastha*[40] *eva: tasmâd asmint sûtre 'nupapattileço nâ 'sti.*

[1] W. O. *-ti â ayam-*; B. *-ti âyam-*. [2] B. O. G. M. om. [3] G. M. ins. *idam*. [4] B. O. om. [5] B. O. *sûtr-*; G. M. *-yaṁ*. [6] W. ins. *pûrvaje*. [7] W. *pragrahasya*. (8) W. B. O. om. [9] G. M. om. (10) B. om. [11] W. B. *ṛtâvarî-*. [12] W. *vidhi-*; G. M. *-dhitvena*. [13] G. M. *svikriyata*. [14] G. M. *uktâv-*. [15] G. M. ins. *ca*. [16] W. O. *yuktiyuktam*: G. M. *yad uktam*. [17] G. M. om. [18] B. O. *tulyam*. [19] B. O. *-tve*. (20) B. om. [21] G. M. om. [22] G. M. *-kshaṇat-*. [23] G. M. om. [24] G. M. *kim*. (25) B. om. [26] G. M. ins. *iti*. [27] G. M. *-dheḥ*. [28] G. M. om. *pada*. [29] G. M. *sûtra*. [30] W. G. M. om. [31] W. *'ṅçabdasya*; G. M. *iṅgyâṅç-*. [32] G. M. om. [33] B. O. *-dyapadasya*. [34] O. G. M. *-khye s-*. [35] G. M. *pragrahatvaṁ*. [36] G. M. *tad*. [37] G. M. om. [38] G. M. om *iti*. [39] W. *svar-*; B. O. *varam*. [40] G. M. *tadav-*.

to quote *hvayate* at all than to quote it and then make it the subject of an exception. The case, then, is one where no suitable primary word is to be found; and not the slightest charge of impropriety can be maintained against the rule as given.

Both parties to this controversy are about equally open to the charge of hair-splitting absurdity; but the objector must be acknowledged to have the right of it so far as this—that the rule is really ambiguous, considering the presence of the two words *pûrvaje.* That *pûrvaje*, as used in it, means 'the former *je*,' I do not at all believe.

इमे गर्भमुपैवरसेनपरः ॥ २४ ॥

24. Also *ime*, when followed by *garbham*, *upa*, and *eva rasena.*

The passages referred to are: *yad ime garbham adadhâtâm* (iii.4.3²: G. M. omit the last word), *ime upâvartsyataḥ* (vi.1.3¹), and *ime eva rasenâ 'nakti* (vi.3.11³). Two counter-examples are given: one to show the necessity of *rasena* after *eva*, *ima evâ 'smâi lokâḥ* (ii.4.10³), and one to show in general the need of specifying the situations in which *ime* is *pragraha*, *adhvartavyâ vâ ime devâḥ* (iii.2.2³).

क्रूरमापःसजूर्ब्रह्मजैतेषु च ॥ २५ ॥

25. As also, in the sections beginning with *krûram*, *âpaḥ*, *sajûḥ*, and *brahma ja.*

That is to say, *ime* in the sections specified is always *pragraha*, even when otherwise followed than by the words mentioned in the preceding rule. The commentator quotes the beginning words of each section, and a single example from each: thus, from the section *krûram iva vâi* (v.1.5: only G. M. have the last two words), *rodasyor ity âhe 'me vâi rodasî* (v.1.5⁴: the only case in the sec-

---

24. *ime ity antyasvaro garbhaḥ: upa: eva rasena: evamparaḥ padântaḥ*[1] *pragrahaḥ syât. yathâ: yad----: ime----: ime ----. rasene 'ti kim:*[1] *ima----: evampara iti kim: adhv-----.*

[1] G. M. om.

25. *ime iti caçabdo*[1] *'nvâdiçati: krûram: âpaḥ: sajûḥ: brahma ja:* [2]*eteshv anuvâkeshv ime ity antyasvaraḥ pûrvoktaparanimittâbhâve*[2] *'pi pragraho bhavati. krû---- ity atra yathâ*[4]*: rod- ----. âpo----. ity atre 'me----.*[3] *saj---- ity atra yathâ*[5]*: etaça----. brah---- ity atra yathâ: na----: je 'ti kim: brah---- ity atra traya---- ity asya*[6] *pragrahatvam mâ bhûd iti.*

[1] G. M. put before *ime.* (2) W. *jñâneshu.* [3] G. M. om. *para.* [4] B. O. om. [5] B. O. G. M. om. [6] B. om.; G. M. *atra.*

tion: B. O. begin the citation at *ime*); from the section *âpo varuṇasya patnayaḥ* (v.5.4: G. M. omit the last word), *ime evo 'pa dhatte* (v.5.4[1]: there are two more cases in the following divisions); from the section *sajûr abdaḥ* (v.6.4: G. M. omit the last word), *etaça ime açvinâ saṁvatsaraḥ* (v.6.4[1]: the only case: only G. M. have the first word); from the section *brahma jajñânam* (v.2.7), *na hî 'me yajushâ "ptum arhati* (v.2.7[4]: the only case: B. O. omit the last word). The last calls for a counter-example, to show the need of including in the rule the syllable after *brahma:* there is another section beginning *brahmavâdino vadanty adbhiḥ* (ii.6.5: B. O. omit *adbhiḥ*), which contains an *ime* not *pragraha: traya ime lokâḥ* (ii.6.5[3]: only G. M. have *trayaḥ*).

पूर्णे च ॥ २६ ॥

26. As also *pûrṇe.*

The *ca*, 'and,' in this rule merely brings down the heading of the last *anuvâka* named in the one preceding. In that *anuvâka*, *pûrṇe* is *pragraha:* to wit, in *pûrṇe upa dadhâti pûrṇe evâi 'nam* (v.2.7[4]); but not elsewhere, as for example in *yo vâi pûrṇa âsiñcati* (vii.5.6[1]).

दृढे ॥ २७ ॥

27. Also *dṛḍhe* is *pragraha.*

The restrictions imposed in previous rules no longer hold good: *dṛḍhe* is *pragraha* wherever met with. The example given is *yena dyâur ugrâ pṛthivî ca dṛḍhe* (iv.1.8[5]). There is another case at iii.2.4[3].

घ्नीचक्रे पपरे ॥ २८ ॥

28. Also *ghnî* and *cakre,* when followed by *p.*

---

26. *caçabdo brahmajajñânam ity anvâdiçati: pûrṇe ity antyasvaro brahmajajñânam ity anuvâke pragraho bhavati. yathâ[1]: pûrṇe.... [2]asminn anuvâka[2] iti kim: yo....*

[1] B. O. G. M. om. [2] B. O. *brahmaja.*

27. *dṛḍhe ity asminn[1] antyasvaraḥ sarvatra[2] pragraho bhavati. yathâ[3]: yena....*

[1] B. O. om. [2] B. O. om. [3] B. O. G. M. om.

28. *ghnî: cakre: ity[1] ete pade papare pragrahe[2] bhavataḥ. vâr-....: cakre.... papare iti kim: yad....: sam-.... ghnîcakre iti kim: çak-....: ye-.... pakâraḥ[3] paro yâbhyâṁ te papare.*

[1] G. M. om. [2] G. M. *-gṛhye.* [3] W. *paḥ.*

The examples are: *vârtraghnî pûrṇamâse* (ii.5.2[5]); *cakre pṛshṭhâni* (vi.6.8[1]): I have noted no other cases. We have then two pairs of counter-examples, to show that these words are *pragraha* before *p* only, and only these words before *p:* the first pair are *yad virûpayâ vârtraghnî syât* (vi.1.6[7]) and *samidhâna cakre nîcâ tam* (i.2.14[2]: only W. has *tam*); the second, *çakâ bhâumî pântraḥ* (v.5.18) and *yeshâm îçe paçupatiḥ* (iii.1.4[1-2]).

न्वती ॥ २९ ॥

29. Also *nvatî.*

Two examples are cited: *omanvatî te 'smin* (ii.6.9[5]: G. M. omit the last two words), and *vṛdhanvatî amâvâsyâyâm* (ii.5.2[5]): also a counter-example, proving that *vatî* alone would not have been sufficient: *karṇakâvaty etayâ* (v.4.7[3]).

पपरो न ॥ ३० ॥

30. But not when followed by *p*

The case here excepted—the only one, so far as I have noticed—is *mûrdhanvatî puronuvâkyâ bhavati* (ii.6.2[2]: G. M. omit the last word).

समीची ॥ ३१ ॥

31. *Samîcî* is *pragraha.*

For this word, G. M. cite *samîcî retaḥ siñcataḥ* (v.5.4[2]); B. O. cite *paçcât samîcî tâbhiḥ* (v.2.3[5]); W. gives both passages. The word is met with a dozen times or more in the Sanhitâ.

नपरो न ॥ ३२ ॥

---

29. *nvatî ity antyasvaraḥ*[1] *pragraho bhavati. yathâ*[2]*: om-.....: vṛdh-..... nakâreṇa kim: karṇ-.....*

[1] B. *antaḥ s-*; O. *antas-*. [2] B. O. G. M. om.

30. *sâṁnidhyân nvatî iti*[1] [2]*labhyate: paparo nvatî ity*[3] *antyasvaraḥ*[3] *pragraho na bhavati. yathâ*[4]*: mûr-.....*

[1] O. om. [(2)] B. om. [3] B. *antaḥ s-*; O. *antas-*. [4] B. O. G. M. om.

31. *samîcî ity antyasvaraḥ*[1] *pragraho bhavati. yathâ*[2]*: sam-.....: paç-.....*

[1] B. *antas-*; O. *antyaḥ s-*. [2] B. O. G. M. om.

32. *sâṁnidhyât samîcî iti labhyate: na khalu samîcî ity antyasvaro nakâraparaḥ*[1] *pragraho bhavati. yathâ*[2]*: sam-.....*

[1] G. M. om. [2] W. G. M. om.

32. **But not when followed by** ***n.***

The case excepted is *samīcī nāmā 'si* (v.5.10[1]). I have noted no other.

चो यत्प्रपरः ॥ ३३ ॥

33. *Cī* is *pragraha,* when followed by *yat* or *pra.*

The passages had in view by this rule are: *āikshavī tiraçcī yad āçvavālaḥ* (vi.2.1[5]: W. O. omit the first word, G. M. B. the last; and B. has the citation out of place, after the next but one), and *prācī pretam adhvaram* (i.2.13[2] and vi.2.9[3]); besides two other cases before *pra* at vi.2.1[5]; 3.9[6]. The commentator gives in addition a number of counter-examples: to show that *cī* is not always *pragraha, prācī diçām* (iv.3.3[1] et al.: but W. B. O. read instead *yā prācī dik,* which is not to be found in the Sanhitâ: *prācī dik,* without *yā,* occurs at several places, e. g. iv.3.6[2]); to prove the necessity of the *t* of *yat* and the *r* of *pra, gāur ghṛtācī yajño devāṅ jigāti* (ii.5.7[4]: only G. M. have the last two words) and *tasmāt paçcāt prācī patny anv āste* (v.3.7[3]: only G. M. have the first two words); to indicate that other endings than *cī* are not *pragraha* in the situations specified, *yad agnir vajra ekādaçinī yad agnāu* (v.5.7[1]: only G. M. have the first three words) and *prajanane prajananañ hi vāi* (i.5.9[1]: only G. M. have the last two words).

आन्मह्री ॥ ३४ ॥

34. Also *ān mahī.*

The passage is *mahān mahī astabhāyat* (ii.3.14[6]). Elsewhere, *mahī* is not *pragraha:* e. g. in *mahī dyāuḥ pṛthivī ca naḥ* (iii.3.10[2] et al.: G. M. omit the last two words); and even after *n* preceded by any other vowel than *ā:* e. g. in *vayunāvid eka in mahī devasya* (i.2.13[1] and iv.1.1[1-2]: G. M. omit the last word).

पत्नी श्रुतिः ॥ ३५ ॥

---

33. ***cī ity antyasvaro yatparaḥ praparo vā pragrahaḥ syāt***[1]. ***yathā***[2]***: āiksh-***. . . . . ***prā-***. . . . . ***evamparu iti kim: prā-***. . . . ***: tukārarephābhyāṁ kim: gāur***. . . . ***: tas-***. . . . ***: cī 'ti kim: yad***. . . . ***: praj-***. . . . .

[1] G. M. *bhavati.* [2] G. M. om.

34. ***ān ity etadviçishṭe mahīgrahaṇe 'ntyasvaraḥ pragrahaḥ syāt***[1]. ***yathā: mah-***. . . . . ***ān iti kim: mahī***. . . . ***: ākāreṇa kim: vay-***. . . . .

[1] G. M. *bhavati*

35. Also the combination of sounds *patî.*

The commentator explains: wherever there is *çruti*, i. e. 'hearing,' of *patî*, there we are to understand a case of *pragraha*-quality. Hitherto we have been dealing only with *padas*, or complete individual words; but the *î* of *patî* is uncombinable, even when that audible combination is only a part of a *pada.* The selected examples are, first, *dvâu patî vindate* (vi.6 4³) and *çubhas patî idam aham* (iii.2.10²: only G. M. have the last word), where *patî* is a *pada;* then *yam âçirâ dampatî vâmam açnutaḥ* (iii.2.8⁴: only G. M. have the first two words) and *priyam indrâbṛhaspatî* (iii.3.11¹), where it is part of a *pada:* there are a few other cases. It is remarked at the end of the comment, that, from this rule on, parts of words are also subjects of prescription of *pragraha*-quality.

ग्नी ॥ ३६ ॥

36. Also *gnî.*

I have noted a number of cases of *gnî* as dual of *agnî* and its compounds. The commentator gives two: *antarâgnî paçûnâm* (i. 6.7¹), and *viçvâmitrajamadagnî vasishṭhena* (iii.1.7³ and v.4.11³).

न ह्रिपरः ॥ ३७ ॥

37. But not when followed by *hi.*

The case excepted is that of *gnî* occurring as nominative singular feminine of *âindrâgna: âindrâgnî hi bârhaspatyâ* (v.5.6²). The commentator pleads the occurrence of *indragnî havâmahe* "in another text," as justification of the rule, in saying "by *hi*," instead of "by *h*." But we may question whether the justification is not officious and uncalled for.

वीड्वारीकृष्णाश्वरावीयदापरः ॥ ३८ ॥

---

35. *patî ity asya yatra yatra çrutiḥ*[1] *çravaṇam asti tatra tatra pragrahatvaṁ vijñeyam. yathâ: dvâu----: çubh-----. çrutir iti kim: yam----: priy-----. ity âdâv api*[2] *padâikadeçe pragrahatvâya*[3].

[1] G. M. om. [2] G. M. om. [3] G. M. *-tvam.*

36. *gnî iti pragraho bhavati*[1]. *yathâ*[2]: *ant----: viçv-----.*

[1] G. M. om. [2] G. M. om.

37. *gnî iti sâṁnidhyâl labhyate: na khalu gnî iti*[1] *padânto hiparaḥ pragraho bhavati*[2]. *yathâ: âindr-----. evampara iti kim: indr---- iti çâkhântare.*

[1] G. M. ins *api.* [2] G. M. om.

38. Also an *î* or *e* followed by *vîḍ, dvârâu, kṛshṇaḥ, carâvaḥ,* and *yadâ.*

The quoted passages under this rule have each its counter-example. The first is *dhishaṇe vîḍû satî vîḍayethâm* (i.4.1[2]), a double case; and, to show that *vî* alone would not have been enough, *âpaç ca me vîrudhaç ca me* (iv.7.5[1]). Next, *devî dvârâu mâ mâ* (iii.2.4[4]), with *dvâdaça sam padyante dvâdaça* (i.5.7[3]), to prove the need of the *râu* of *dvârâu.* Again, *yajñâyâ "tishṭhamâne kṛshṇo rûpaṁ kṛtvâ* (vi.1.3[1]: only G. M. have the first word; they also omit the last two words; while B. O. omit *kṛtvâ*); and *câtvâle kṛshṇavishâṇâm prâ 'syati* (vi.1.3[8]: G. M. omit the last two words) justifies the *ḥ* of *kṛshṇaḥ.* Again, *vivasânâu ye carâvaḥ* (i.5.10[1]), with *râye ca naḥ svapatyâya deva* (v.5.4[4]: G. M. omit *deva*) to show that *ca* alone would not have been enough: to prove that more than *car* or *carâ* is needed, the commentator does not attempt. Finally, we have *ajanan nannamâne: yade 'daṁ tâḥ* (iv.6.2[4]: only G. M. have *ajanan*). To this is raised the question whether *yatante,* as coming before *yad â-* in *çreṇiço yatante yad âkshishur divyam* (iv.6.7[4]: only G. M. have the first word), is not also *pragraha?* The answer is an appeal to rule i.50, "in citations of *padas,* a *pada* only is to be understood:" but how we are to know that an integral *pada* is meant to be signified by *yadâ,* any more than by *vîḍ,* the commentator does not inform us.

न ज्ञे ऽह्ने नित्यम् ॥ ३९ ॥

39. But not *jñe* and *ahne,* under any circumstances.

The passages quoted in illustration of the rule are *varuṇâya râjñe kṛshṇaḥ* (v.5.11), and *vanaspatînâm enyahne kṛshṇaḥ* (v.5.15: only G. M. have the first word): these are both exceptions to the preceding rule, and are the immediate occasion of the

---

38. ------ [1]*ity evampara*[1] *îkâra ekâro vâ* [2] *pragraho bhavati*[3]. *yathâ*[4]: *dhish-----: ḍakâreṇa*[5] *kim: âpaç----: devî----: râv iti kim: dvâd-----: yaj-----: visargeṇa kim: cât-----: viv-----: râva iti kim: râye----: aj-----. nanu*[6] *çre----- ity atra pragrahatvaṁ kiṁ na syât. padagrahaṇeshu padaṁ gamyeta* (i.50) *iti*[7] *vacanân na bhavati*[8] *'ti brûmaḥ.*

[1] G. M. *eshu pareshu.* [2] G. M. ins. *padântaḥ.* [3] G. M. om. [4] W. G. M. om. [5] G. M. *vid iti.* [6] G. M. om. [7] G. M. *atra.* [8] W. *pravartate;* G. M. om.

39. *jñe: ahne: ity*[1] *etayor antyasvaro nityam pragraho na syât. yathâ: var-----: van-----: vîḍâdi* (iv.38) *prâptir anayoḥ. nityaçabdaḥ prâptyantarapratibandhakaḥ*[2]. *yathâ*[3]: *yaj-----: gamayatobhavataḥ* (iv.52) *ity âdinâ praptiḥ: sva-----: somâyasva* (iv.48) *iti prâptiḥ.*

[1] G. M. om. [2] B O. *-pratishedh-;* G. M. *prâptyânishedhaprayojanakaḥ.* [3] G. M. om.

introduction here of this one. But the addition of *nityam*, 'constantly, in all cases,' excepts the same words from the action of any other rule: for example, of rules 52 and 48, which would otherwise apply in the passages *yajñe 'pi kartor iti tâv abrûtâm* (ii.6.7[1]) and *svarâjñe 'novâhâu* (v.6.21).

आकारैकारपूर्वस्तु बहुस्वरस्य ते थे ॥४०॥

40. *Te* and *the*, however, are *pragraha* in a word of more than two syllables, if preceded by *â* or *e*.

The class of words here aimed at, of course, is composed of second and third persons plural of present and perfect tenses middle of verbs. The commentator quotes several instances: *etasmin vâ etâu mṛjâte yo vidvishâṇayoḥ* (ii.2.6[1-2]: only G. M. have the first three words, and they omit the last word); *çukrâ manthinâu gṛhyete* (vi.4.10[1]); *pra pṛthivyâ riricâthe divaç ca* (iv.2.11[1]: only G. M. have the first and the last two words); and *dṛñhanâ yaṁ nudethe* (iv.7.15[2]). Then, to justify the requirement of a preceding *â* or *e*, we have given us *â vṛçcyate vâ etad yajamânaḥ* (iii.3.8[1]: G. M. omit the last word); of a polysyllabic word, *tat pravâte vi shajanti* (vi.4.7[2]: see under i.48) and *yad ete gṛhyante* (iii.3.6[1]); the restriction to the endings *te* and *the*, *anûcyamâna â sâdayati* (ii.2.5[7],11[1]).

As to the special significance of *tu*, 'however,' in this rule, two of our commentator's three chief authorities, Vararuci and Mâhisheya, are reported by him as at variance. The former maintains that it indicates the cessation of regard had to the words specified in rule 38 as occasions of *pragraha*-quality; the latter, that it prescribes the annulment of continued implication of the exceptions mentioned in rule 39, and of what was there signified by the word *nityam*. Vararuci's view is declared the better one, and with good reason—unless, indeed, we prefer to ascribe to the word a general change of subject, from mention of individual words to the description of a class.

---

40. *bahusvarasya padasya sambandhî*[1] *te iti the iti vâ*[2] *"kârapûrva ekârapûrvo vâ pragraho bhavati. yathâ; et-....: çuk-....: pra....: dṛñh-..... evampûrva iti kim: â vṛç-....: trîṇi....: bahusvarasye 'ti kim: tat....: yad....: tethe iti kim: anûc-..... vîḍâdi* (iv.38) *nimittasâpekshatânivartakas tuçabda iti vararucipakshaḥ: mâhisheyapakshas tu vakshyate*[3]*: pûrvasûtroktanishedhanityaçabdajñâpitânuvṛttiṁ*[4] *nivârayatî*[5] *'ti*[6]*: tatra*[7] *vararucimataṁ ruciram. bahavaḥ svarâ yasmin tad bahusvaram: tasya. atra svaraçabdopâdânâc*[8] *ca*[9] *bahuçabdena vyaktibhedo vijñeyaḥ.*

[1] W. *-dhiya.* [2] G. M. ins. *çabdaḥ.* [3] G. M. *ucyate.* [4] G. M. *-dhaṁ nit-.* [5] G. M. *vâr-.* [6] G. M. om. [7] G. M. *atra.* [8] W. *bahusvaraçabdopâdânatâ;* B. O. *bahusvararûpaçabdena upâdânatâ.* [9] W. B. O. om.

The commentator's final remark as to *bahusvarasya* is obscure to me.

न शार्यते ॥ ४१ ॥

41. But not *çâryâte*.

Namely, in the passage *çâryâte apibaḥ sutasya* (i.4.18: G. M. omit the last word). An exception to the preceding rule, by express mention of the excepted word.

ते मापातंनमएनमभिवायुर्गर्भमुपाह्नस्तुपरः ॥ ४२ ॥

42. *Te* is *pragraha* when followed by *mâ pâtam*, *namaḥ*, *enam abhi*, *vâyuḥ*, *garbham*, *upa*, *ahas*, and *tu*.

The passages, as quoted by the commentator, are: *vâm â rabhe te mâ patam â 'syâ* (i.2.2[1-2]: only G. M. have the first three words), with *te mâ 'smin yajñe* (iii.2.4[1]), to show the necessity of including *pâtam* in the rule; *punas te: namo 'gnaye 'pratividdhâya* (i.5.10[1]: only G. M. have the last word), with *te na vy ajayanta* (v.4.1[1]), to prove that *na* alone would not have been enough; *te enam abhi sam anahyetâm* (ii.5.6[5]), with *ta enam bhishajyanti brahmaṇaḥ* (ii.3.11[4]: W. omits the last word), to justify the inclusion of *abhi*; *te vâyur vy avât* (iii.4.3[1]), with *te vâcañ striyam* (vi.1.6[5]), to show why the *yuḥ* of *vâyuḥ* was needed; *te garbham adadhâtâm* (iii.4.3[1]), without any counter-example to prove that *ga* would not have answered the purpose; *te upâ 'mantrayanta* (vi.1.3[1]); *te ahorâtrayoḥ* (vi.1.3[1]); *te tv âva no 'tarjye ity âhuḥ* (vii.5.7[1]: G. M. omit the last two words), with *te te dhâmâny uçmasi* (i.3.6[1]), to show that *t* not followed by *u* is not enough to determine the *pragraha* quality. Then, as further counter-examples, we have *te devâḥ* (i.4.10[1] et al.) in proof that *te* is not *pragraha* before other words than those here mentioned; and *bṛhad ukshe namaḥ* (i.4.26), *amushmiñ loka upa çere* (v.3.7[2]), and *yanti*

---

41. *çâryâta ity antyasvaraḥ*[1] *pragraho na*[2] *bhavati. yathâ: çâr-..... pûrvasûtraprâptâu*[3] *satyâm kaṇṭhoktanishedho*[4] *'nena*[5] *vidhîyate.*

[1] B. *-yaḥ s-*. [2] O. om. [3] G. M. *-treṇa pr-*; B. *-tre pr-*. [4] G. M. *-ktyâ n-*. [5] G. M. om.

42. [1]...... *evamparas te iti çabdaḥ pragrahaḥ syât. yathâ*[2]: *vâm....: pâtam iti kim: te....: punas....: ma iti kim: te ....: te e-....: abhî 'ti kim: ta....: te v-....: yur iti kim: te v-....: te ga-....: te u-....: te ah-....: te tv....: ukâreṇa kim: te te.... evampara iti kim: te d-....: te iti kim: bṛh-....: am-....: yanti....*

[1] W. B. O. ins. *te*. [2] G. M. om.

vâ ete savanâdye 'haḥ (vii.5.6[3]), showing that only *te* is *pragraha* in the situations defined.

These are not all the instances found in the Sanhitâ of *te* as *pragraha;* one was disposed of by rule 20 above, and at least one or two others come under the action of other rules of this chapter.

अनुदात्तो न नित्यम् ॥ ४३ ॥

43. But not when unaccented, under any circumstances.

That is to say, even in such a situation as would bring it otherwise under the preceding rule. The example quoted is *bâhubhyâm uta te namaḥ* (iv.5.1[1]): if the text contains others, I have failed to notice them. The specification *nityam* has its usual force, as suspending the application of all rules to the contrary, wherever found: for example, that of rule 52, below, in the passage *namas te astv âyudhâya* (iv.5.1[4]).

एते तनुवौवैसमेवह्यियज्ञपदिष्टकपरः ॥ ४४ ॥

44. *Ete* is *pragraha* when followed by *tanuvâu, vâi sam, eva, hi, yajña, pad*, and *ishṭak*.

The passages, as quoted by the commentator, are: *tasyâi 'te tanuvâu* (v.7.3[3]); *ete vâi saṁvatsarasya cakshushî* (ii.5.6[1]: G. M. omit the last word), with *ete vâ iḍâyâi stanaḥ* (i.7.1[2]: G. M. omit the last word) as counter-example, showing that before *vâi* not followed by *sam* the word is not *pragraha; sa ete eva namasyann upâ 'dhavat* (ii.5.6[5]: only G. M. have the first word, and they omit the last two); *ete hi devânâm* (ii.5.6[6]: another case at vii.5.7[1]); *cakshushî vâ ete yajñasya* (ii.6.2[1] et al.: compare also the nearly identical passage vi.2.11[3]); *yajñasya hy ete pade atho* (v.1.6[3-4]: W. omits the first word); and *yad ete ishṭake upadadhâti* (v.3.5[2]). Counter-examples would have been in place to show that, in citing the last three fragments of words, the rule had taken no more than just what was sufficient for its purpose; but

---

43. *mâ pâtam ityâdiparo 'pi te ity antyasvaro*[1] *'nudâtto nityam pragraho na bhavati. yathâ*[2]*: bâh-.... nityam iti kim: lakshaṇântaraprâptasyâ 'pi pratishedho*[3] *yathâ syât: na-....: gamayatobhavataḥ* (iv.52) *ity âdinâ*[4] *prâptiḥ.*

[1] O. *-yaḥ sv-.* [2] G. M. om. [3] G. M. *nish-.* [4] O. G. M. om.; B. *antya.*

44. [1]*...... ity evampara ete ity antyasvaraḥ*[2] *padântaḥ*[3] *pragraho bhavati. yathâ: tas-....: ete-....: sam iti kim: ete-....: sa-....: ete-....: cak-....: yaj-....: yad-....*. [4]*evampara iti kim: atha-....: ete iti kim: man-....: push-....: agre-....: sapt-....*[4]

[1] B. O. ins. *ete.* [2] O. *-yaḥ s-.* [3] G. M. om. ([4]) W. B. O. om.

they are not furnished. The general counter-examples under this rule, like those under the last but one, proving that only *ete* is *pragraha* before the words specified, and *ete* itself before them only, are given by G. M., but omitted in the other manuscripts: they are *atha katama ete devâ iti* (ii.6.9³), *manuta evâi 'nam etâni* (v.5.6¹), *pushkaraparṇe hy enam upaçritam* (v.1.4⁴: MSS. *-çrutam*), *agre yajñapatiṁ dhatta* (i.1.5¹), and *saptame pade juhoti* (vi.1.8¹).

परश्च द्वयोः ॥४५॥

45. As also, the letter following the two last mentioned.

The "two" of the rule are *pad* and *ishṭak;* and the commentator makes the further obvious specification that the letter following them is *pragraha* only when they themselves follow *ete*, as prescribed in the preceding rule. He quotes the passages referred to: *yajñasya hy ete pade atho* (v.1.6.³⁻⁴: W. omits to *pade*, B. O. to *ete*), and *yad ete ishṭake upadadhâti* (v.3.5²); adding, to show the necessity of the limitation made by him, the counter-examples *saptame pade juhoti* (vi.1.8¹), and *tasyâs te devî 'shṭake* (iv.2.9²).

स्थःपरः ॥४६॥

46. Also one followed by *sthaḥ*.

There is a natural reason for this rule, *sthaḥ* being a dual verb, and so, apt to be preceded by a dual noun. I have noted near a dozen cases in the text; the one cited in illustration by the commentator is *vishṇoḥ çnyaptre sthaḥ* (i.2.13³). To show that *stha* instead of *sthaḥ* would not answer, is given *etasmiṅ loke stha yushmâñs te 'nu* (iii.2.5⁶: only G. M. have the first two words, and they omit the last three).

परश्चोभयोः ॥४७॥

47. As also, one following them both.

Following, namely, a *sthaḥ* and a preceding *pragraha* word: for example, *çilpe sthas te vâm â rabhe* (i.2.2¹: but this citation is wanting in G. M.), and *dṛḍhe sthaḥ çithire samîcî* (iii.2.4³). A counter-example, of a word following *sthaḥ* only, is *vṛshaṇâu stha urvaçî* (i.3.7¹).

---

45. *nimittina upari vartamânayoḥ padishṭakçabdayoḥ*[1] *para*[2] *'îkâra ekâro vâ*[3] *pragraho bhavati. yathâ: yaj-....: yad-.... nimittina upari vartamânayor iti kim: sapt-....: tas-.....*

[1] B. O. *dvayoḥ padishṭak ity etayoç cakârânvâdishṭayoḥ;* G. M. *pat ishṭaka ity etayoḥ cakârânvâdishṭayoḥ dvayoḥ.* [2] B. O. *parata.* [(3)] G. M. om.

46. *stha ity evampara îkâra ekâro vâ padântaḥ pragraho bhavati. yathâ: vish-..... visargeṇa kim: et-.....*

The commentator then proceeds to point out that the difference in phraseology between this rule and the last but one—*dvayoḥ*, 'two,' being used in the one, and *ubhayoḥ*, 'both,' in the other—indicates a difference of meaning. Above, the two affecting causes (*nimitta*) specified in the preceding rule, each along with the word affected by it (*nimittin*), were intended; here, on the other hand, the two aimed at are an affecting and an affected word.

सोमायस्वेतस्मिन् ॥ ४८ ॥

48. Also in the section beginning *somâya sva.*

The section in question is v.6.21: it was necessary to add *sva*, in order to distinguish it from that beginning *somâya pitṛmate* (i.8.5). It contains thirteen *pragrahas*, of which the commentator cites several together: *avî dve dhenû bhâumî* (v.6.21[1]: G. M. omit *bhâumî*): three of these, however, would be disposed of by the three rules next following.

द्वे ॥ ४९ ॥

49. Also *dve*.

This word, which occurs about forty times in the Tâittirîya text, is, of course, always *pragraha*. The commentator cites two instances: *dvedve sam bharati* (i.6.8[2]), and *yad dve naçyetâm* (ii.6.3[5]).

परश्च ॥ ५० ॥

---

47. *cakârânvâdishṭayoḥ pûrvasûtroktanimittanimittinor*[1] *ubhayoḥ para îkâra ekâro vâ padântaḥ pragraho bhavati. yathâ: çil-....: dṛḍhe..... ubhayor iti kim: vṛsh-..... paraç ca dvayor* (iv.45) *iti*[2] *vâcya ubhayor iti çabdântaram*[3] *arthântarajñâpakam*[4]*: nimittisahitayoḥ*[5] *pûrvasûtroktayor nimittayoḥ paraḥ pragraho bhavati: paraç ca dvayor* (iv.45) *iti sûtrârthaḥ: atra tu*[6] *sûtre nimittanimittinor*[7] *ubhayoḥ paraḥ pragrahaḥ syâd iti viçeshâd*[8] *bhedo vijñeyaḥ.*[9]

[1] G. M. *pûrvokta-*. [2] B. ins. *kiṁ ca*, O. ins. *ca*. [3] G. M. *-taraprayogaḥ*. [4] G. M. *-kaḥ*. [5] G. M. *-ttas-*. [6] G. M. om. [7] G. M. *-ttinimittayoḥ*. [8] B. *-shaṇa*; O. *-sheṇa*; G. M. *vishaya*. [9] G. M. *drashṭavyaḥ*.

48. *somâya svarâjñe* (v.6.21) *ity asminn anuvâka îkâra ekâro vâ padântaḥ pragraho bhavati. yathâ: avî.... ity âdi. sve 'ti kim: somâya pitṛmate* (i.8.5) *ity atra mâ bhûd iti.*

49. *dve ity antyasvaraḥ padântaḥ*[1] *sarvatra pragraho bhavati*[2]. *yathâ*[3]*: dve-....: yad.....*

[1] G. M. om. [2] G. M. om. [3] G. M. O. om.

50. As also, the following word.

The comment instances but one case, a double one: *dve çukle dve kṛshṇe mûrdhanvatîḥ* (v.3.1⁴: G. M. omit the last word). Of such the text contains more than a dozen, but they are not worth referring to in detail.

एकव्यवेतो ऽपि ॥५१॥

51. Likewise the next but one.

The *api*, 'likewise,' in this rule is explained as bringing forward *dve* from the last rule but one; another application of the "principle of the frog's leap." The cited examples are *dve hy ete devate* (ii.1.9³: but G. M. omit this citation), and *dve vâva devasatre* (vii 4.5¹). By rule i.48, *devasatre*, though a divisible compound (*pada*-text, *devasatre iti deva-satre*), is reckoned as but a single *pada* for the purposes of this precept: another like case, *dve savane çukravati* (vi.1.6⁴), was expressly quoted as an illustration under the former rule. At vi.6.4³ (*dve jâye vindate*) is a case where the action of the rule is suspended by a later one, iv.54.

गमयतोभवतोऽनूकारात्परं तनूयदकरोत्कुर्यादिष्टिष्वब्रूतां प्रवर्तास्ताᳪस्तभ्नीतां वाचयतिबिभृतस्तामिंगायत्रं ताभ्यामेवोभाभ्यामवान्तरं पर आ षष्ठात् ॥५२॥

52. Before, and within six words of, *gamayataḥ*, *bhavataḥ* (except when it follows *û*), *tanû yât*, *akarot*, *kuryât* (in *ishṭi* passages), *abrûtâm*, *pra varta*, *âstâm*, *stabhnîtâm*, *vâcayati*, *bibhṛtas ta*, *agniṁ gâyatram*, *tâbhyâm eva*, *ubhâbhyâm*, and *avântaram*.

Of the words here specified, some are duals, and so would naturally have other duals, with *pragraha* endings, in their vicinity; in other cases, the collocation is purely accidental.

The *â* in the rule is declared to be intended this time "inclusively" (*tena saha*, 'along with the specified limit:' compare the scholiast to Pâṇini ii.1.13); and the necessity of the specification

---

50. *cakâro dve ity anvâdiçati: dve ity etasmât*[1] *para îkâra ekâro vâ padântaḥ pragraho bhavati*[2]. *yathâ*[3]*: dve*....

[1] O. *asmât.* [2] B. O. *syât;* G. M. om. [3] G. M. om.

51. *ekavyaveto*[1] *'pi dve ity etasmât para îkâra ekâro vâ padântaḥ pragraho bhavati*[2]. *yathâ*[3]*: dve*....*: dve*.... *ekena padena*[4] *vyaveta*[5] *ekavyavetaḥ. apiçabdo dve ity anvâdiçati maṇḍûkaplutinyâyena.*

[1] B. O. *-vahito.* [2] G. M. om [3] G. M. om. [4] G. M. om. [5] W. *vyavahita.*

"within six words" is explained as arising from rule i.30, which would limit the meaning of "before" to 'the word standing next before.' This involves a misinterpretation of the rule referred to, which was made for quite another purpose (see the note upon it). No such special and technical ground is needed to justify the terms of the present rule, which are of obvious and incontestable propriety.

The commentator's example for *gamayataḥ* is *te evâi 'nam pratishṭhâṁ gamayataḥ* (ii.1.4[7]): I have noted no other case. For *bhavataḥ*, he gives *uttarâvatî bhavataḥ* (v.4.8[5]); with the counter-example *dîkshante 'ntanâmânâv ṛtû bhavataḥ* (vii.4.8[1]); to show the necessity of the restriction imposed by the rule in the case of this word. There are quite a number of other passages where *bhavataḥ* assures the *pragraha*-quality to words in its neighborhood: I have noted ii.2.2[3],11[4-5]; 3.2[9],3[5],4[3.4],8[2]: iii.1.7[2],9[3]; 5.4[4]: v.4.6[3]; 5.1[2]: vii.1.4[3]; 2.1[3] twice. With regard to the limitation *anûkârât*, the commentator remarks that although simple absence is the primary significance of its negative prefix, yet another meaning is here assumed, in accordance with the requirements of the case: that is to say, "after a not-*û*" is to be understood as 'after any letter but *û*.' For *tanû yat*, we have *ete vâi mahâyajñasyâ 'ntye tanû yat* (ii.2.7[5]: I have found no other case); and, as counter-example, to justify the inclusion of *yat*, *paripataye tvâ gṛhṇâmi tanûnaptre tvâ* (i.2.10[2]: only W. has the last word). For *akarot*, *budhnavatî agravatî yâjyânuvâkye akarot* (ii.3.4[3]: another case at ii.2.8[5]). For *kuryât*, *mânavî ṛcâu dhâyye kuryât* (ii.2.10[2]: another case at ii.3.3[5]); with the counter-example *agnaye dâtre puroḍâçam ashṭâkapâlaṁ kuryât* (ii.5.5[2]), to explain the restriction to *ishṭi*-passages. The *ishṭis* are defined as being "the three *praçnas* beginning with the tenth, but excepting their final *anuvâkas*" (which have before received the designation *yâjyâ*): that is to say, ii.2.1–11; 3.1–13; 4.1–13. There are other passages besides the one quoted proving the necessity of the restriction in question: thus v.4.7[7]: vii.5.5[1]. For *abrûtâm* is cited *te abrûtâṁ varaṁ vṛṇâvahâi* (ii.5.2[5],6[5]: another case at v.2.3[3]). For *pravarta*, *havirdhâne prâcî pravartayeyuḥ* (iii.1.3[1]); with the counter-

52. *gamayataḥ: bhavato 'nûkârât: ûkâravyatiriktavarṇât param bhavata iti*[1]*: yady apy abhâvo mukhyârthas tathâ 'pi tadanyârthatâ*[2] *svîkṛtâ*[3] *lakshyânusârât: tanû yat: akarot: kuryâd ishṭishu: ishṭayo*[4] *daçamâdayas trayaḥ praçnâ uttamânuvâkavarjitâḥ*[5]*: abrûtâm: ...... ity evampara â shashṭhât padât pûrvo vartamâna îkâra ekâro vâ padântaḥ pragraho bhavati*[6]*. abhividhâv ayam âkâraḥ: tena sahe 'ty abhividhiḥ. yathâ: te....: utt-....: anûkârât param iti kim: dîksh-....: ete....: yad iti kim: pari....: budh-....: mân-....: ishṭishv iti kim: agn-....: te....: hav-....: varte 'ti kim: te....: ime....: vâiç-....: utt-....: te....: te*[7] *'ti kim: manm-....: ete....: gâya-*

example *te 'dityâñ sam adhriyanta tvayâ pra jânâme 'ti* (vi.1.5[1]: G. M. end at *pra*), to show why *varta* was added to *pra*. For *âstâm*, *ime vâi sahâ "stâm* (iii.4.3[1]: another case at iv.3.10[2]). For *stabhnîtâm*, *vâiçvadevâgnimârute ukthe avyathayantî stabhnîtâm* (iv.4.2[3]). For *vâcayati*, *uttame âudumbarî vâcayati* (v.1.10[2-3]). For *bibhṛtas ta*, *te eva yajamânasya reto bibhṛtas tasmât* (v.6.8[4]); with the counter-example *manmahe yâv âtmanvad bibhṛto yâu* (iv.7.15[3]), to show that *bibhṛtaḥ* alone would not have answered the purpose of the rule. Doubtless the single case is provided for in this rule rather than in 42, above, because there are cases of *ta eva* in the Sanhitâ which it would have made trouble to distinguish properly from this one. For *agniṁ gâyatram*, *ete dadhâte ye agniṁ gâyatram* (vi.3.5[3]); with the counter-example *sadhasthe 'gnim purîshyam* (iv.1.3[1]), to show that the addition of *gâyatram* was needful. For *tâbhyâm eva*, *ete vâi yajñasyâ 'ñjasâyanî srutî tâbhyâm eva* (vii.2.1[2]; 3.5[3],7[3],9[3]; 4.1[3],2[4],4[3]). With reference to this passage, the commentator raises the difficulty that *ete*, one of the words intended to be determined as *pragraha*, is not within six words of *eva*, one of the two words specified in the rule as conditioning its *pragraha*-character within that distance; but he declares it of no account, since what is within reach of any part of the assigned cause (*nimitta*) is within reach of that cause in its entirety. For, he says, in common life also, a quality belonging to a part is ascribed to the whole which contains that part: for example, people say "Devadatta has an ear-ring," when it is really his ear that has the ring. Truly a most lucid and convincing illustration! The necessity of the *eva* is proved by the counter-example *apa hañsy agne tâbhyâm patema* (iv.7.13[1]: G. M. omit the last word). For *ubhâbhyâm*, *ye dve ahorâtre eva te ubhâbhyâm* (vii.4.4[4]). Finally, for *avântaram*, *utsṛjye ity âhur ye avântaram* (vii.5.7[1]); with the counter-example *saṁ te 'va te heḍaḥ* (ii.5.12[1]), to prove that *ava* would not have been enough alone.

न ग्रामीवर्चसीमिथुनीमासेलोकेधत्ते ॥ ५३ ॥

53. But not *grâmî*, *varcasî*, *mithunî*, *mâse*, *loke*, *dhatte*.

---

tram iti kim: sadh-....: ete.... atra padadvayam ekaṁ[8] *nimittam ity*[8] *etepadam*[10] *uddiçyâ "shashṭhaniyamabhañgaprasañga iti cet:* [11]*nâ 'yam bhañgaprasañgaḥ*[11]*: nimittâikadeçasya shashṭhatvopapatteḥ sakalasyâ 'pi nimittasya*[12] *shashṭhatvam upapadyate: loke 'py avayavadharmeṇâ 'vayavino 'pi*[13] *viçeshasiddheḥ: tathâ hi: karṇe kuṇḍalaṁ dhârayantaṁ kuṇḍalî devadatta iti vadanti. eve 'ti kim: apa....: ye....: ut-....: antaram iti kim: saṁ....: â shashṭhâd iti kim: para ity uttaraḥ* (i.30) *iti paribhâshayâ 'nantarasyâi 'va paratvaṁ syât: tan mâ bhûd iti.*

[1] G. M. ins. *padaṁ naño.* [2] G. M. *-tâṁ.* [3] G. M. *-kârya.* [4] G. M. ins. *nâma.* [5] G. M. *-karahitâh.* [6] G. M. om. [7] W. B. O. *ste.* [8] G. M. *etan.* [9] O. *eve 'ty.* [10] O. *etat p-.* [(11)] B. O. *nâi 'vam pras-*; G. M. om. *bhañga.* [12] W. O. *-syâ 'pi.* [13] B. O. G. M. om.

These are words which, occurring within six of those mentioned in the last rule, would be *pragraha* if not thus specially excepted. The commentator quotes the passages in which they occur, as follows: *gramy eva bharati ganavatî yâjyânuvâkye bhavataḥ* (ii.3.3[5]: another nearly identical case is found at ii.2.11[4]); *brahmavarcasy eva bhavaty ubhayato rukmâu bhavataḥ* (ii.3.2[3]); *atha mithunî bhavataḥ* (vi.5.8[6]); *pûrṇamâse prâ 'yachat târ abrûtâm* (ii.5.2[3]); *loke pratitishṭhanto yanti dvâu shaḍahâu bhavataḥ* (vii.4.11[3]); and *dhatte jyotishmantâv asmâ imâu lokâu bhavataḥ* (ii.6.2[4]).

अते समानपदे नित्यमवे चावे च ॥५४॥

54. Nor *ate*, in a single word, nor *ave*, under any circumstances.

After paraphrasing the rule, in a way which shows that he regards the specifications "in a single word" and "under any circumstances" as both alike referring to each of the "parts of words" mentioned, the commentator proceeds to cite illustrative passages, as follows: *ava rundhate 'tirâtrâv abhito bhavataḥ* (vii.2.6[3]; 4.1[3], 2[5],3[6]: another nearly identical case is found at vii.4.5[4]); *abhyâhvayate vajram enam abhi pra vartayati* (iii.2.9[1,7]); and *anâtatâya dhṛshṇave: ubhâbhyâm uta te namaḥ* (iv.5.1[4]: B. O. omit the last word, and G. M. the last two). To show the necessity of specifying that *ate* should form part of a single word, he quotes *eva te ubhâbhyâm* (vii.4.4[3]). The limitation *nityam*, 'under any circumstances,' is explained in the usual manner, as intended to exclude the operation of other rules besides the one (iv.52) here especially aimed at: for the appropriate examples we are referred to the comment upon rule i.59, where they are given in connection with the illustration of another point.

---

53. ...... *eteshv*[1] *antyasvaro gamayato bhavata ityâdiparo 'pi pragraho na bhavati. yathâ*[2]*: grâ-....: brah-....: atha....: pûr-....: loke....: dhatte....*

[1] G. M. *eshv.* [2] G. M. om.

54. *nishedhaṁ cakâro 'nvâdiçati. ate: ave: ity anayoḥ padâikadeçayor antyasvaraḥ samânapade vartamâno gamayato bhavata ityâdiparo 'pi nityam pragraho na bhavati. yathâ*[1]*: ava ....: abhy....: anâ-.... samânapada iti kim: eva.... atra nityaçabdaḥ prâptyantaraparihârârthaḥ. udâharaṇam*[2] *upabandhas tu deçâya* (i.59) *iti sûtre*[3] *prasañgâd uktam. samânaṁ ca tat padaṁ ca samânapadam: tasmint samânapade*[4].

iti tribhâshyaratne prâtiçâkhyavivaraṇe caturtho 'dhyâyaḥ.

[1] O. om. [2] G. M. *iti sodâ-.* [3] W. *sûtreṇa.* [4] G. M. om.

This finishes the rehearsal of the words with *pragraha*-endings contained in the Sanhitâ. As to the economy of the method of their rehearsal—whether it would have been possible to state the facts in fewer or briefer rules—I cannot speak with confidence: it would be, certainly, a thankless task to endeavor to recast them in an improved form. Nor can I, without a *pada*-manuscript, or a much more thorough and detailed study of the text, with the aid of a commentary, than it has been in my power to make, judge absolutely the success of the method followed. It appears, however (with exception of the equivocal treatment of the words in *o*, pointed out under rule 7), to be complete: my excerption of the text has shown me no *pragraha*-endings in *î* and *e* which are not duly taken account of, nor any case of final *î* or *e* not *pragraha* as involved in the general rules of the chapter without being duly excepted by special precept. One or two words whose endings are treated as uncombinable without being *pragraha* are disposed of in another chapter (x.18).

CHAPTER V.

Contents: 1–2, introductory, relation of *pada* and *saṁhitâ* texts; 3, order of application of rules; 4–8, anomalous insertions of a sibilant and *d;* 9–10. anomalous conversions of *ṛ* and *ḥ;* 11–19, anomalous omissions of *v*, *s*, *ḥ*, *m*, and *yâ;* 20–24, treatment of final *n* and *t* before palatal letters; 25–26, before *l;* 27–31, of final *m* before a consonant; 32–33, of final *ṅ*, *ṭ*, *n* before sibilants: 34–37, of initial *ç* after consonants; 38–41, of initial *h* after consonants.

अथ सꣳहितायामेकप्राणभावे ॥ १ ॥

1. The following rules apply in combined text (*saṁhitâ*), within the compass of a single breath.

This is an introductory heading to the main part of the Prâtiçâkhya—the rules for the construction of the euphonically combined text (*saṁhitâ*) from its presupposed material, the *pada*-text, where

---

1. *athe 'ty ayam adhikâraḥ: saṁhitâyâm ekaprâṇabhâva ity etad adhikṛtaṁ veditavyam ita uttaraṁ yad vakshyâmaḥ. saṁhite 'ti ko 'rthaḥ: nânâpadasaṁdhânasaṁyogaḥ*[1] (xxiv.3) *iti* [2]*sûtreṇo 'ktaḥ*[2] *saṁhitârthaḥ*[3]*: paraḥ saṁnikarshaḥ saṁhite 'ti vâiyâkaraṇâḥ*[4] *paṭhanti*[5]. *ekasamutthaḥ prâṇa ekaprâṇaḥ: tasya bhâvas tadbhâvaḥ*[6]*: tasmin: ity âtreyamatam. anyathâ 'pi samâsaḥ saṁgachate: ekaprâṇena bhâvyate janyata uccâryata ity ekaprâṇabhâvaḥ: ekeno 'chvâsena yâvân uccâryate vedabhâgas tâvân ekaprâṇabhâva ity arthaḥ: ata evâ 'vasâne padavi-*

each word stands separate, as if occurring independently. It is a rule of far-reaching force, applying through many chapters (for an attempt to define precisely how far, see the comment to xxiv.2). The matters treated in the first two chapters—the mode of utterance of elementary sounds, definitions, general explanatory precepts, and the like—were with propriety first disposed of; the separate rehearsal of the *pragraha*-endings, made in chapter iv., is more questionable, but defensible on the ground that those endings exhibit their *pragraha* character also in the *pada*-text, before *iti*: but the exclusion of the vowels irregularly protracted in *saṁhitâ*, as rehearsed in the third chapter, is quite anomalous (see note to iii.1).

The commentator defines *saṁhitâ* by quoting a later rule (xxiv.3), which declares it to be "the union of separate words in euphonic combination;" referring at the same time to the rule of Pâṇini (i.4.109), as the account of it given by "the grammarians." For *ekaprâṇabhâve* he first gives us Âtreya's simple paraphrase; but then goes on to explain it more fully, as 'that which is brought about, generated, uttered, with a single breath; such portion of the Veda, namely, as is uttered by the help of one expiration'—the condition of *pada*, or separated and euphonically independent words, recurring with the pause that follows the expiration. That is to say, if the repeater of the text has to pause to take breath where there is no regular *avasâna*, or pause of interpunction (such as separates the *pâdas* of a verse: its length is taught in rule xxii.13), his last word is thrown out of *sandhi* with the next, and the end of the one and the beginning of the other must assume their *pada* form.

Now is interposed an objection: of what use are the two specifications "in combined text" and "within the compass of a single breath"? the former is enough by itself. To this it is replied: if the latter specification were not made, then no pause after a *pada* would be authorized in the continuous *saṁhitâ* arrangement: and if the other were not made, then that respecting the single breath would apply also to the *padas*; hence doubt would arise as to where any direction to be given would have force: there is, therefore, good reason for the double specification.

---

dhiḥ. nanu saṁhitâyâm ity etâvatâi 'vâ[7] *'lam: ekaprâṇabhâva iti vâ ubhayârambhaṇena*[8] *kim. ucyate*[9]*: ekaprâṇabhâva ity anârabhyamâṇe pravṛttasya saṁhitâvidheḥ padâvasânatvaṁ ne 'shyate: saṁhitâyâm ity anârabhyamâṇe tu padeshv apy ekaprâṇabhâva upapadyata iti*[10] *vakshyamâṇaṁ*[11] *kâryaṁ kva*[12] *bhavatî 'ti saṁdehaḥ syât: tasmâd*[13] *asminn*[14] *ubhayârambhaṇe*[15] *prayojanam asti.*

[1] B. O. *-nayoga.* (2) G. M. *sûtrokta.* [3] G. M. *saṁhite 'ty ar-.* [4] W. B. G. *vâiyyâ-.* [5] G. M. *bhaṇanti.* [6] W. om. [7] B. O. om. *eva.* [8] B. O. *-bheṇa*; G. M. *-bhaṇe.* [9] G. M. om. [10] G. M. om. [11] B. G. M. *-ṇa.* [12] B. O. G. M. *kutra vâ.* [13] G. M. *tadâ.* [14] G. M. *tas-.* [15] O. G. M. *-bhe*; W. B. *-bheṇa.*

यथायुक्ताद्विधिः सा प्रकृतिः ॥२॥

2. Separation from the text as combined—that is the fundamental text.

I cannot but believe the intent of this precept to be the same with that of the rule which begins the second chapter of the Rik Pr., *saṁhitâ padaprakṛtiḥ*, 'the *pada*-text is the foundation of the *saṁhitâ*:' but such intent is not readily and distinctly deducible either from the rule itself or from its commentary. The latter explains that hereby is taught the *prakṛti*, or proper form, of *saṁhitâ*, the reason being that a later rule (xxiv.5) prescribes as necessary to be understood, among other things, "*prakṛti, vikrama, krama.*" An arrangement which does not deviate from the *pada*-text as constituted, taken as supreme, that is to be regarded as the fundamental text. By way of illustration is then quoted the whole series of passages falling under the action of rule x.13, below; passages in which the fundamental or *pada* form of certain words is maintained, against the ordinary rules of euphonic combination: they are *svadhâ asy urvî câ 'si* (i.1.9³), *dhanvann iva prapâ asi* (ii.5.12⁴), *sahasrasya pramâ asi* (iv.4.11³: G. M. put this citation before the preceding one), *pra budhniyâ írate* (iv.3.13⁶), *jyâ iyañ samane* (iv.6.6²), *â pûshâ etu* (ii.4.5¹: W. B. O. omit this), and *aminanta evâiḥ* (iii.1.11⁵). No explanation is attempted of the bearing of these examples upon the principle which is laid down in the rule now in hand: we may suppose it to be that, the application of the rules of *sandhi* being denied in the case of these particular words, they remain in *saṁhitâ* in their regular or natural shape as shown in *pada*-text—*prakṛtyâ*, as it is elsewhere termed. And in this office of the precept is to be seen the real ground of its statement, rather than in a provision against the requirements of xxiv.5.

The grand difficulty in this exposition lies in its quiet postulation of *avicalitaḥ*, 'unremoved, not deviating,' as connective between *vidhiḥ* and *yathâyuktât*. I would sooner recur to the etymologic meaning of *vidhi*, 'dis-posal, putting apart,' and empha-

---

2. *prakṛtiḥ saṁhitâsvarûpam aneno 'cyate: prakṛtir vikramaḥ kramaḥ* (xxiv.5) *iti vijñeyatvavidhânât*[1]. *yathâyuktâd yathâsthitât*[2] *padapâṭhât kûṭasthâd avicalito*[3] *yo vidhiḥ sâ prakṛtisaṁhitâ*[4] *vijñeyâ: vidhir vidhânam prakṛtir ity arthaḥ. yathâ*[5]*: sva-....: dhan-....: sah-....: pra....: jyâ....: â pû-....: ami-..... atra sûtre padânâm parasparânvayo mahâbhâshyavacanâc*[6] *ca*[7] *vijñeyaḥ: tac ca vacanaṁ tâ varṇaprakṛtayaḥ* (ii.7) *ity atra paṭhanti*[8]*: evam atrâ*[9] *'pi svaritayor madhye yatra nîcam* (xix.1) *ity âdâu mantavyam.*

[1] W. *rijñeyatvavidhât;* B. *-tvena vi-;* G. M. *jñeyatvena vi-.* [2] G. M. *-thâvas-.* [3] G. M. *-câline.* [4] W. B. O. *-tiḥ s-.* [5] G. M. om. [6] G. M. *-canena.* [7] G. M. om. [8] O. G. M. *paṭhitaṁ.* [9] G. M. *anyatrâ.*

size its prefix *vi* sufficiently to make it take an ablative adjunct, meaning 'separation from [the state] as combined;' and I have so translated above, though far from being confident that I have found the true solution of the difficulty. Neither *vidhi* nor its synonym *vidhâna* occurs elsewhere in the text, although both are frequent in the commentary (see Index), usually with the meaning 'rule, prescription;' not infrequently also 'arrangement, disposal.'

The commentator concerns himself finally with the gender of *sâ*, which, he says, comes under the rule already once quoted from the Mahâbhâshya in explanation of a like case (under ii.7); and he points out further that the same principle applies elsewhere—for example, in xix.1.

तत्र पूर्वंपूर्वं प्रथमम् ॥ ३ ॥

3. And here, that which comes first is first taken.

That is to say, in the construction of the *saṁhitâ* text, both the words to be treated and the rules to be applied must be taken up in their order, as they stand in the text and in the Prâtiçâkhya respectively. A variety of instances are given to illustrate the working of the principle. First, in *bhaksha: â: ihi* (iii.2.5[1]), the first two words are first combined, according to x.2, and then their result, *bhakshâ*, is combined with *ihi*, by x.4, making *bhakshe* " *'hi*, the true reading; whereas, if the second combination had been first made, forming *e 'hi*, this would have coalesced with *bhaksha* into *bhakshâi 'hi*—which (though in itself, as may well be claimed, the preferable reading) is unauthorized and incorrect. This exemplifies the application of the rule to the order in which words are to be treated; for its application to the use of rules there are three examples. The first concerns the production of the *saṁhitâ*-reading *shaṇṇavatyâi* (vii.2.15) from the *pada*-reading *shaṭ-navatyâi:* it is accomplished by the successive application of vii.2, which prescribes the conversion of *n* to *ṇ* after *shaṭ*, and of viii.2,

3. *tatra saṁhitâvidhâne pûrvampûrvam padaṁ sûtraṁ ca prathamaṁ kartavyam. yathâ: bhaksha : â : ihi : ity atra dîrghañ samânâkshare* (x.2) *iti dîrghaḥ:* [1] *bhakshâ : ihi : iti sthita ivarṇapara ekâram* (x.4) *ity ekâre kṛte bhakshe* " *'hî 'ti bhavati: anyathâi 'hî 'ti kṛtvâ bhakshaçabde*[2] *saṁdhîyamâne bhakshâi 'hî 'ti syât: tac câ 'nishṭam: pûrvapadakartavyatva etad udâharaṇam. pûrvasûtrakartavyatve 'pi*[3] *vadâmaḥ: yathâ*[4]*: shaṭtrigrâmanishpûrvaḥ* (vii.2) *iti nakârasya ṇatve kṛta uttamapara uttamañ savargîyam* (viii.2) *ity anena*[5] *ṭakârasya ṇatve kṛte*[6] *shaṇṇavatyâ iti bhavati: anyatho 'ttamapara uttamam* (viii.2) *iti sûtre prathamam*[7] *pravṛtte sati*[8] *shaṇṇavatyâ iti syât: tac câ 'nishṭam. tathâ*[9]*: vaṭth*[10] *svayamabhigûrtâye 'ty atra ṭanakârapûrvaç ca takâraḥ* (v.33)*:*

which changes *ṭ* before *ṇ* to *ṇ:* if, on the contrary, the latter rule had been applied first, changing *shaṭ* to *shaṇ*, the former would no longer have had force at all, and the reading would have stood *shaṇṇavatyâi.* The next case is that in which the words *vaṭ* and *svayamabhigûrtâya.* come together (iii.2.8[1] seven times: G. M. read *vashaṭ* for *vaṭ*, doubtless by a clerical error). Here, v.33 requires the insertion of a *t* between the *ṭ* and *s*, and this inserted *t* is then, by xiv.12, made *th ;* so that we are finally to read *vaṭth svay-:* if the latter conversion were first made, the reading would turn out instead *vaṭth svay-* (since v.33 would not then apply at all, but to the combination *ṭhsv* would be prefixed a *ṭ* of duplication, by xiv.1,5: the manuscripts, as usual in such cases, do not give these complicated readings altogether correctly: and W. B. even make the blunder of substituting at last *vaṭ svâhâ*, apparently having in mind *-vâṭ svâhâ*, in the same division). Once more, in the passage *imam: vi: syâmi* (iii.1.10[2] and iii.5.6[1]), we are first to convert the *s* of *syâmi* to *sh* by vi.4, and then to duplicate the *sh* by xiv.1, making *vi shshyâmi:* if the duplication were first performed, making *vi ssyâmi*, then, by rule vi.4, we should have to read *vi shsyâmi.* Of the three examples thus given, only the first has to do with the form of the text as given in the manuscripts, since these very sensibly ignore the rules for duplication which make up the bulk of the fourteenth chapter of our treatise.

So far as regards the taking up of words for combination in their natural order, the Rik Pr. (ii.2) and Ath. Pr. (iii.38) have rules of like force with the present one.

त्रपुमिथुपूर्वः शकारश्चपरः ॥ ४ ॥

4. After *trapu* and *mithu* is inserted a *ç* before *c.*

---

prathama ûshmaparo dvitîyam (xiv.12) *iti sûtradvayam prasaktam: tatra pûrvatvât ṭanakârapûrvaç ca takâra*[11] *ity etad eva prathamaṁ kartavyam*[12]*: anyathâ* [13]*vaṭth svayam iti*[13] *syât: tac câ 'nishṭam. athavâ: imaṁ vi shshyâmî 'ty atro 'pasarganishpûrvo 'nudâtte pade* (vi.4)*: svarapûrvaṁ vyañjanaṁ* [14]*"dvivarṇaṁ vyañjanaparam"*[14] (xiv.1) *iti sûtradvayam*[15] *prâptam: tatra dvitvasûtre* [16]*prathame kârye sati*[16] [17] *vi shsyamî*[18] *'ti syât: tan mâ bhûd iti shatvam eva prathamaṁ kartavyam.*

pûrvampûrvam iti [19]*vîpsâ sarvathâi*[20] *'vam arthaṁ samarthayati*[19].

[1] G. M. ins. *tena.* [2] W. *-dena na.* [3] G. M. om. [4] W. B. O. om. [5] G. M. om. [6] B O. *sati.* [7] W. O. *-ma.* [8] G. M. om. [9] W. B. O. om. [10] G. M. *vashaṭth ;* B. *vaṭa ;* O. *vaṭt.* [11] G. M. om. [12] O. M. put before *praihamam.* (13) W. B. *vaṭ svâhe 'ti ;* O. *vaṭ svayam iti ;* G. M. *vashaṭhth svayam iti.* (14) G. M. om. [15] G. M. *-traṁ.* (16) G. M. *prathamaṁ kṛte.* [17] G. M. ins. *imam.* [18] B. G. M. *shyâmi.* (19) G. M. *vîpsayâ sarvatrâi 'tad âha 'yam iti samarthanîyam ;* B. *vîpsâ sarvatrâi 'vam arthayati.* [20] O. *sarvatrâi.*

The passages are *sîsaṁ ca me trapuç ca me* (iv.7.5[1]), and *mithuç carantam upayâti* (iv.7.15[2]): the existing *pada*-text reads *trapu* and *mithu*, as this rule would lead us to expect. But the right of *trapus* to be recognized as an independent word by the side of *trapu* is assured by the derivative adjective *trâpusha*, and the close analogy of *manu*, *manus*, *mânusha*.

The commentator adds a couple of counter-examples: one, *vibhu ca me prabhu ca me* (iv.7.4[1·2]), to show that not every *u* has a *ç* added before *c*; the other, *asinâ mithû kaḥ* (iv.6.9[4]), to show that the insertion is only made before *c*, after the words specified.

सुपूर्वश्च चन्द्रपरः ॥ ५ ॥

5. As also after *su*, before *candra*.

The example quoted by the commentator is *suçcandra dasma viçpate* (iv.4.4[6]): the word occurs once more, at ii.2.12[7]. The *pada*-text reads *su-candra*. Counter-examples are: *pra candramâs tirati dîrgham âyuḥ* (ii.4.14[1]: G. M. omit the last two words), and *â mâ sucarite bhaja* (i.1.12): their application is obvious.

संपूर्वः सकारः कुरुपरः ॥ ६ ॥

6. After *sam* is inserted *s* before *kuru*.

The commentator's example is *yajamânaḥ sañskurute* (v.6.6[4] and vi.5.5[2]). The *pada*-text reads *sam : kurute*. Counter-examples are *puroḍâçâñ alaṁ kurv iti* (vi.3.1[2]: G. M. have a *lacuna* involving this passage), and *saṁkṛtya châvâkasâmam bhavati* (v.4.12[3]) The text has further *sañskṛtya* and *sañskṛta*, but (as is also implied in rule xvi.26) they are read in the *pada*-text as in *saṁhitâ*, without division, or ejection of the intruded *s*.

अकुर्वं च प्रत्ययात्परः ॥ ७ ॥

---

4. *trapu: mithu: evampûrvaḥ çakâra âgamo bhavati* '*caparaḥ*'. *yathâ: sîs-....: mith-..... evampûrva iti kim: vi-....: evampara iti kim: as-....*

[1] G. M. *cakârap-*.

5. *cakâraḥ çakâram anvâdiçati: supûrvaḥ çakâra âgamo bhavati candraparaḥ. yathâ*[1]*: suç-.... evampûrva iti kim: pra ....: evampara iti kim: â mâ..... sv ity esha çabdaḥ pûrvo yasmâd asâu supûrvaḥ.*

[1] G. M. om.

6. *sam ity evampûrvaḥ sakâra âgamo bhavati kuruparaḥ. yathâ*[1]*: yaj-..... evampûrva iti kim:* [2]*pur-....: evampara iti kim*[2]*: saṁ-..... kuruçabdaḥ paro yasmâd asâu kuruparaḥ.*

[1] G. M. om. [(2)] G. M. om.

7. And before *akurva*, after the augment.

The passage is, as quoted by the commentator, *ta ishuñ sam askurvata* (vi.2.3[1]); the *pada*-text reading *sam: akurvata.* The counter-example is *agnihotraṁ vratam akurvata* (iii.2.2[2]). As *pratyaya* occurs nowhere else in the treatise we cannot tell whether it signifies distinctively 'augment,' or, as in other of the Prâtiçâkhyas, 'affix' in general. The commentator gives a scholastic explanation of the term, as indicating "that whereby the consonants are added unto, are made distinct."

नीचापूर्वो दकार उच्चापरः ॥ ८ ॥

8. After *nîcâ* is inserted *d* before *uccâ*.

The passage is *madhyân nîcâd uccâ* (ii.3.14[6]); and the *pada*-text actually reads *nîcâ: uccâ.* This is a proceeding to which it would be hard to find a parallel in the *pada*-texts of the other Vedas. To write *madhyena* for *madhyât* just before would be in itself quite as defensible. As counter-examples, we receive *lokaṁ yanty uccâvacâ 'hni* (vii.4.3[6]), and *nîcâ taṁ dhakshi* (i.2.14[2]).

At the end of the comment is made the remark "the above are cases of insertion" (*âgama*, 'accession'). The matter of irregular conversions is next taken up.

असंपूर्वो ऽरमृकारः ॥ ९ ॥

9. After *asam*, *ṛ* becomes *ar*.

The passage in which this anomalous change is made is *gṛhâṇâm asamartyâi* (iii.3.8[2]), where the *pada*-text has, as the rule implies, *asam-ṛtyâi.* Here, again, we cannot praise the work of the *pada* text-maker. Nor is the rule of unexceptionable form, for the commentator is obliged to specify that the *asam* intended is one not made up of the parts of two words (not *-a sam*); else such passages as *kalyâṇî rûpasamṛddhâ* (vii.1.6[6]), and *vahî hy esha*

---

7. *cakâraḥ sampûrvatvam*[1] *âgamaṁ*[2] *câ*[3] *'nvâdiçati. akurva*[4]*ce 'ti*[4] *grahaṇe pratyayât paraḥ sakâra âgamo bhavati sampûrvaḥ. yathâ: ta*----- *pratyayo nâmâ 'kâra ucyate: pratîyanta*[5] *abhivyajyante vyañjanâny anene 'ti pratyayaḥ. sampûrva iti kim: agn*-----

[1] G. M. *-rvam.* [2] G. M. *sakârâg-.* [3] G. M. om. [(4)] W. *ca;* O. G. M. *iti.* [5] B. O. *pratyâyante;* G. M. *pratyayante.*

8. *nîcâpûrvo dakâra âgamo bhavaty uccâparaḥ. yathâ*[1]*: madh*----- *evampûrva iti kim: lok*----*: evampara iti kim: nîcâ*----

âgamâ ete.

[1] G.. M. O. om.

samṛddhyâi (ii.2.2[1]) would be included. As counter-example, to show that *ṛ*, not a syllable containing *ṛ*, is liable to the specified conversion, is quoted *asaṁtṛṇṇe hi hanû* (vi.2.11[3]: G. M. omit *hanû*).

अवग्रह आशीर्धूःसुवरिति रेफं परः सकारः षकारम् ॥ १० ॥

10. Of *âçîḥ*, *dhûḥ*, and *suvaḥ*, when first members of a compound, the *visarjanîya* becomes *r*, and a following *s* becomes *sh*.

The word *avagraha* in this rule is the locative *avagrahe*, says the commentator, and applies to each of the specified words taken separately. He supplies *visarjanîya*, the omission of which, or of some other word answering the same purpose, is rather a serious defect in the rule. The illustrative passages quoted are *ity âçîrpadaya rcâ* (vi.2.9[4]; the *pada*-text reads *âçîḥ-padayâ*), *dhûrshâhâv anaçrû* (i.2.8[2]; p. *dhûḥ-sâhâu*), and *dadhishe suvarshâṁ jihvâm agne* (iv.4.4[1]; p. *suvaḥ-sâm*: W. B. O. omit the first word of the citation, G. M. the last). The necessity of the specification "when first members of a compound" is shown by the counter-example *ye devâ devasuva stha te* (i.8.10[2]: p. *deva-suvaḥ*: G. M. omit the first two words and the last). *Âçîḥ* shows the same irregular combination also in *anâçîrkeṇa* and *sâçîrkeṇa* (i.6.10[4]), but these words are not treated as divisible by the *pada*-text. The commentator goes on to point out the rules to which exceptions are established by this one: viii.23 would require *âçîshpadayâ*, and ix.2

---

9. *asam ity evampûrva ṛkâro 'ram vikâram âpadyate. yathâ: gṛh-.... tatra*[1] *nimittam ekapadasthaṁ*[2] *vijñeyam: anyathâ kaly-....: vahî....: ity âdâv api bhavet. ṛkâra iti kim: asaṁ-....*

[1] G. M. O. *atra.* [2] B. *-dasaṁsthaṁ.*

10. *avagraha iti saptamyantam padam âçîḥprabhṛtibhiḥ pratyekam abhisambadhyate. âçîḥ: dhûḥ: suvaḥ: ity*[1] *eteshv avagraheshu visarjanîyo repham âpadyate: ebhyaḥ*[2] *paro yadi sakâro*[3] *vartate tarhi shakâram*[4] *âpadyate. yathâ*[5]*: ity....: dhûr-....: dadh-..... avagraha iti kim: ye..... kakhapakâraparaḥ*[6] (viii.23) *ity anenâ*[7] *"çîshpadaye 'ti prâptam:* [8]*aghoshaparas tasya sasthânam ûshmâṇam*[9] (ix.2) *iti dhûssâhâu*[10] *suvassâm*[11] *iti ca prâptam*[8]*: tadubhayabhañgâyâ 'yam ârambhaḥ. itiçabda eshâm evâi 'sha viçesho nâ 'nyeshâm iti prakâravâcî.*

[1] G. M. om. [2] G. M. *tebh-.* [3] G. M. put before *yadi.* [4] G. M. *so 'pi shatvam.* [5] G. M. om. [6] G. M. om. *paraḥ.* [7] G. M. om. [(8)] W. om. [9] B. O. om. [10] B. O. *dhûḥs-.* [11] B. O. *suvaḥs-.*

dhûssâhâu and *suvassâm* (or, as it is customary to write them, *dhûhsâhâu* and *suvahsâm:* only G. M. are conscientious about giving the double sibilant, as demanded by the Prâtiçâkhya). The *iti*, he remarks finally, signifies that only the words mentioned, and no others, are intended—that is to say, it has no particular meaning at all. It would be well if he always as frankly acknowledged the insignificance of this word where it occurs in the rules.

अथ लोपः ॥ ११ ॥

11. Now for cases of omission.

An introductory rule or heading, having force as far as rule 19, below, inclusive.

ईपूर्वो मकारः ॥ १२ ॥

12. A *m* is dropped, when preceded by *îm*.

The passage aimed at is *îm 'andrâ suprayasaḥ* (iv.1.8[2]: p. *îm: mandrâ*): it is the only one of its kind in the text. The Vâjasaneyi-Sanhitâ reads in the corresponding passage (xxvii.15) *îm mandrâ*. To treat the loss of a *m* here as suffered by the second word instead of the first is most arbitrary and unreasonable. The particle *îm* is reduced to *î* in quite a number of Rik passages, and before other letters than *m:* they are duly noted in the Prâtiçâkhya (Rik Pr. iv.36). A series of counter-examples is added by our commentator: *imam me varuṇa* (ii.1.11[6]) shows that *m* is not dropped after another *m* in general; *agnim mitraṁ varuṇam* (ii.1.11[1]), that *m* after short *i* does not exercise the specified effect; *îṁkârâya svâhe ''ṁkṛtâya* (vii.1.19[1]), that *îm* elides no other consonant than *m*. The yet farther restriction is applied, that *îm* here is a *padagrahana*, 'the citation of a complete *pada*;' for otherwise there would be an elision of a *m* in such cases as *pṛthivîm mâ hiṅsîḥ* (iv.2.9[1]): G. M. add the further example *uta çravasâ pṛthivîm mitrasya*, which I am unable to find in the Sanhitâ.

तुनुपूर्व उदात्तयोर्वकारः ॥ १३ ॥

---

11. *athe 'ty ayam adhikâraḥ: lopa ity etad adhikṛtaṁ veditavyam ita uttaraṁ yad vakshyâmaḥ. ayam adhikâras tishṭhanty ekayâ* (v.19) *itisûtraparyanto veditavyaḥ.*

12. *makâra îm ity evampûrvo lupyate. yathâ*[1]*: îm----. evampûrva iti kim: imam----: dîrgheṇa kim: agn-----. îm iti padagrahaṇam*[2]*: itarathâ*[3] *pṛth---- ity âdâu makâro lupyeta*[4]*. makâra*[5] *iti kim: îṁ-----.*

[1] G. M. om. [2] W. *-hacarṇaḥ.* [3] G. M. *anyathâ.* [4] G. M. *-yate;* and add *tac câ 'nishṭâ.* [5] W. *-rapara.*

13. A *v* is dropped when preceded by *tu* or *nu*, in case these are accented.

It is when the particle *vâi*, or *vâva*, follows *tu* and *nu* that this anomalous mutilation is made. The commentator quotes *sa tv 'âi yajeta* (ii.6.6[3] and vii.1.3[1]: p. *saḥ : tu : vâi*), and *in nv 'â upastîrṇam ichanti* (i.6.7[3]: p. *it : nu : vâi*). The same *sandhi* of *tu* and *vâi* is not infrequent elsewhere (the passages are i.7.1[4],6[2]: ii.2.4[8]; 5.4[1]: iii.2.9[2]; 3.9[2]; 5.1[3]: v.5.9[4]: vi.4.3[1]: vii.2.10[3]); that of *nu* and *vâi* is comparatively rare (only at i.5.9[6] twice); that of *tu* and *vâva* I have found only once, at vii.5.6[5]. Here, again, it would seem better to regard the final *u* as suffering elision, instead of the initial *v*. The specification "if accented" is explained as intended to exclude such passages as *anu vṛtrahatye* (i.6.12[1]; 7.13[1]), where *anu* would fall under this rule by i.52 (even if the *nu* here, like the *îm* in the preceding rule, were regarded as a *padagrahaṇam*). Other counter-examples, of obvious intent, are *idam vâm âsye haviḥ* (iii.3.11[1]), and *pra tu janayati 'ti* (i.7.2[4]) and *vidusho nu yajñam* (i.3.13[1-2]).

उत्पूर्वः सकारो व्यञ्जनपरः ॥ १४ ॥

14. A *s* is dropped after *ut*, when a consonant follows.

The commentator's example is *praty uttabdhyâi sayatvâya* (vi.6.4[6] : p. *ut-stabdhyâi*). This is, so far as I have discovered, the only case in the Sanhitâ from the root *stabh :* similar forms from *sthâ* occur variously (*anûtthâya*, iii.4.10[3] ; *upotthâya*, vii.1.6[8]; 5.15[1.2] ; *utthâsyant*, vii.1.19[3] ; *utthita*, vii.1.19[3]; 2.9[3]; and *utthâna*, vii.2.1[4] thrice). As counter-examples are given *jagatsthâ devâḥ* (ii.1.11[4]), *utkrañsyate svâhâ* (vii.1.19[3]), and *utsâdena jihvâm* (v.7.11).

This familiar *sandhi* is also the subject of Ath. Pr. ii.18, and Vâj. Pr. iv.95.

एषसस्य इति च ॥ १५ ॥

15. Also *eshaḥ*, *saḥ*, and *syaḥ*.

---

13. *tu : nu*[1]*: ity evampûrvo vakâro lupyate tayos tunvor udâttayoḥ sator iti vibhajya viyogo*[2] *vijñeyaḥ. yathâ : sa tv----: in nv----. udâttayor iti kim : anu----: apy akârâdi* (i.52) *iti prâptiḥ : evampûrva iti kim :* [3]*idam----: vakâra iti kim*[3]*: pra ----: vid----. tuç ca nuç ca tunû*[4]*: tâu pûrvâu yasmât sa tathoktaḥ.*

[1] B. O. *nú*, as also B. in the rule itself. [2] G. M. *viniy-*. [(3)] B. om. [4] G. M. *tunu*.

14. *vyañjanaparaḥ sakâra utpûrvo lupyate. yathâ : praty----. vyañjanam asmât param iti vyañjanaparaḥ. evampûrva iti kim : jag----: sakâra iti kim : ut----: evampara iti kim : ut-----*

Here the *ca*, 'also,' is declared to continue the implication of "when a consonant follows" from the preceding rule. The *iti* is added for the sake of clearness; it shows the final *visarjanîya* of *syaḥ*, and attributes it by analogy to each of the other words also. What indicates that this final *visarjanîya* is the letter which is to suffer elision is not so evident. The illustrative examples are *esha te gâyatraḥ* (iii.1.2[1]), *sa te jânâti* (i.2.14[2-3]: but G. M. substitute *sa tapo 'tapyata*, iii.1.1[1]), and *esha sya vâjî* (i.7.8[3]). The counter-example, showing that the omission occurs only before a consonant, is *dama evâ 'syâi 'sha upa tishṭhate* (i.5.7[4]), where, if the *ḥ* of *eshaḥ* were lost by this rule, x.5 would require the reading *esho 'pa.*

The corresponding rules in the other treatises are Rik Pr. ii.4, Vâj. Pr. iii.15,16, Ath. Pr. ii.57.

नासः ॥ १६ ॥

16. But not *asaḥ*.

Namely, in the passage *hṛtsvaso mayobhûn* (iv.2.11[3]; p. *hṛtsu-asaḥ*), which would otherwise fall under the preceding rule for *saḥ*, by i.52.

इदिदग्नइमांनएनौषधीःपरः सः ॥ १७ ॥

17. And *saḥ*, when followed by *id u, id agne, imâṁ naḥ, enâ, oshadhîḥ*.

These are the cases in the Sanhitâ where, after the regular loss of the final of *saḥ*, its vowel is irregularly combined with the one that follows, against rule x.25. Such cases in the other Vedic texts are treated at Rik Pr. ii.33,34, and Vâj. Pr. iii.14. The commentator quotes the passages affected, as follows: *se 'd u hotâ so adhvarân* (i.1.14[4]: B. O. omit the last word; G. M. the last two), *se 'd agne astu* (i.2.14[3]), *se 'mâṁ no havyadâtim* (iv.6.6[6]), *sâi 'nâ 'nîkena* (iv.3.13[2] and 6.1[5]) and *sâu 'shadhîr anu rudhyase* (iv.2.3[3], 11[3]). The first two need counter-examples, to show that *it* not followed by *u* or *agne* does not coalesce with *sa*: they are *sa ij*

---

15. *vyaktivishaya*[1] *itiçabdaḥ pratyekam esha ity âdîn*[2] *visarjanîyântân*[3] *dyotayati: cakâro vyañjanaparatâm anvâdiçati. eshaḥ: saḥ: syaḥ: eshu*[4] *visarjanîyo vyañjanaparo lupyate. yathâ*[5]*: esha....: sa....: esha.... evampara iti kim: dama ....*

[1] G. M. *-tiçishṭa;* O. *-tiviçishṭa.* [2] G. M. *-nâm.* [3] G. M. *-yântatân.* [4] G. M. ins. *padeshu.* [5] G. M. om.

16. *asa ity asmin*[1] *grahaṇe visarjanîyo vyañjanaparo na lupyate. hṛt-..... apy akârâdi* (i.52) *iti prâpter*[2] *nishedhaḥ*[3].

[1] G. M. *etas-.* [2] G. M. *-tiḥ.* [3] G. M. om.

janena (ii.3.14[3]) and *sa id deveshu gachati* (iv.1.11[1]). The third also wants a counter-example, to prove the need of *naḥ* after *imâm:* it is found in *sa imâm abhy amrçat* (v.5.2[4]). Finally, to show that only *sah* undergoes the prescribed effect before the words specified in the rule, we have *paro divâ para enâ* (iv.6.2[2]).

अवग्रह इत्येकम् ॥ १८ ॥

18. Also *ity ekam,* when *ekam* is the former member of a compound.

The passage aimed at is *pâpîyânt syâd ity ekâikaṁ tasya juhuyât* (v.1.1[2]: but as given by W. O., without the first two words, it is also found again at v.4.5[5]: G. M. omit *juhuyât*); and the *pada*-text actually reads *ekam-ekam.* The case is akin with that which forms the subject of the next rule. Two counter-examples are given, to justify the terms of the rule: they are *ardhukaṅ syâd ity ekam agre 'tha* (vi.2.3[5]: only G. M. have the first two words), and *yad ekamekaṅ sambharet* (i.6.8[2]).

तिष्ठन्त्येकया सपूर्वः ॥ १९ ॥

19. Also *tishṭhanty ekayâ,* along with the preceding letter.

The commentator quotes the passage: *tishṭhanty ekâikayâ stutayâ* (vii.5.8[4]); the *pada*-reading is *ekayâ-ekayâ.* As counter-example, where the same word remains unmutilated, is given *samânânâṁ karoty ekayâikayo 'tsargam* (vi.1.9[4]: only G. M. have the first word).

In this rule and the foregoing are noted, but at the same time ignored, the first occurrences of the compound *ékâika,* which (see the St. Petersburg Lexicon) is not very rare in the Çatapaṭha Brâhmaṇa and later.

---

17. ------ [1] *evamparaḥ saḥkâra*[2] *ity atra visarjanîyo lupyate. yathâ: se 'd----: se 'd---- v*[3] *agna ity âbhyâṁ*[4] *kim: sa ----: sa----: se----: na iti kim:* [5]*sa----: sâi----: sâu----: sa iti kim: paro----.*

[1] G. M. ins. *iti.* [2] W. B. O. *sakâra;* G. M. *sa.* [3] W. B. *id;* G. M. O. *u.* [4] B. O. *etâbhyâm.* [5] A *lacuna* in B., to near the end of the comment on rule 18.

18. *itiçabdaviçishṭa ekam ity asminn avagrahe makâro lupyate. yathâ*[1]*: pâp----. avagraha iti kim: ardh----: itiçabdaviçishṭa iti kim:*[2] *yad----.*

[1] G. M. om. [2] End of the *lacuna* in B.

19. *tishṭhantiçabdaviçishṭa ekaye 'ty asmin grahaṇe 'ntyo*[1] *varṇaḥ sapûrvaḥ pûrvasahito lupyate. yathâ*[2]*: tish----. tishṭhantî 'ti kim: sam----. pûrveṇa saha vartata iti sapûrvaḥ.*

[1] G. M. *-yasvaro.* [2] O. om.

The terms in which the rule is expressed show that, from rule 15 on, the implication has been of a "final" letter as liable to the effect prescribed. We have reason to be surprised that it was not distinctly stated when first made.

नकारः शकारं चपरः ॥२०॥

20. A *n*, when followed by *c*, becomes *ç*.

The commentator's illustrative examples are *ahîñç ca sarvâñ jambhayan* (iv.5.1²), *ṛtúñç ca tasya nakshatriyâñ ca* (vii.1.3²: G. M. omit *ca*), and *karṇâñç câ 'karṇâñç ca* (i.8.9³). The counter-examples, to show that only *n* is so changed, and *n* itself only before *c*, not before other palatal mutes, are *çaṁ ca me* (iv.7.3¹) and *tâñ chandobhir anu* (i.5.9⁷: G. M. omit *anu*).

The nature of the conversion taught in this rule, and of the kindred ones forming the subject of rules vi.14 and ix.20, as being a historical, not a euphonic process, has been sufficiently explained and illustrated in the note to Ath. Pr. ii.26. At the same place will be found noted the usage of the other Vedic texts as regards the *sandhi ñç:* the Atharvan and the Vâjasaneyi-Sanhitâ make it uniformly, the Rik only occasionally. In the Tâittirîya-Sanhitâ it is prevailingly usual: I have noted thirty-nine examples of it, against the eight exceptions mentioned in the next rule.

The definition of the *sandhi*, of course, is not complete without the aid of rules xv.1–3, which teach that, where *n* has been converted into a sibilant, the preceding vowel is nasalized, or has *anusvâra* added to it. A better course, according to our understanding of the history of the phenomenon, would be to teach the insertion of a *s* (or *visarjanîya*) and the change of *n* to *anusvâra* before it: but the makers of the Prâtiçâkhyas concern themselves much less about the theoretical accuracy than the mechanical aptitude of their rules.

नायन्नैरयन्नार्धुवन्ननड्वान्घृणीवान्वारुणानेवास्मिन् ॥२१॥

21. But not the *n* of *âyan*, *âirayan*, *ârdhnuvan*, *anaḍvân*, *ghṛṇîvân*, *vâruṇân*, and *evâ 'smin*.

The passages are: *lokam âyañ catasraḥ* (v.2.3⁴), *yâm âirayañ*

---

20. *cakâraparo*[1] *nakâraḥ çakâram âpadyate. yathâ*[2]*: ah-....: ṛt-....: kar-..... nakâra iti kim: çam-....: capara iti kim: tâñ-.... 'caḥ*[3] *paro yasmâd asâu caparaḥ.*

[1] G. M. *caparo.* [2] O. om. [3] G. M. O. *cakâraḥ.*

21. ...... *eteshu*[1] *grahaṇeshu nakâraḥ çakâram nâ "padyate caparo 'pi. yathâ*[2]*: lo-....: yâm-....: loka....: anaḍ-....: ghṛṇ-....: vâr-....: evâ.... *[3]*eve 'ti kim:*[3] *asm-.....*

[1] G. M. *eshu.* [2] G. M. O. om. [(3)] B. om.

candramasi (i.1.9[3]), *loka ârdhnuvañ caruṇâ 'smin* (v.5.1[5]: only G. M. have the first word), *anaḍvâñ ca me dhenuç ca me* (iv.7.10[2]), *ghṛṇîvâñ cetati tmanâ* (iii.5.11[1]), *vâruṇâñ catushkapâlân nir vapet* (ii.3.12[1]: only W. has the last two words), and *evâ 'smiñ cakshur dhattah* (ii.2.9[3-4]; 3.8[2]). *Evâ 'smiñ* is found once more, in a slightly different connection, at ii.3.8[1]: the others occur only in the passages cited. A counter-example, *asmiñç câ 'mushmiñc ca* (vii.3.4[1],5[2]) is given to prove the need of specifying *eva* before *asmin.*

By rule 24, below, the *n* in all these cases is assimilated to the *c*, and should be so written in the text. My own manuscript of t e Sanhitâ, in fact, follows the authority of the Prâtiçâkhya, and represents the assimilated nasal in the same manner as an assimilated *m*, except in a single case (*ârdhnuvan car-*). The Calcutta edition, however, in the part hitherto published, gives *ñ c* only once (i.1.9[3]), and everywhere else *n c.*

तकारश्चकारꣳ शचछपरः ॥ २२ ॥

22. A *t*, when followed by *ç*, *c*, or *ch*, becomes *c*.

The form assumed by initial *ç* after this assimilation is taught in rules 34–37, below.

The commentator's examples are: *tac chaṁyoḥ* (ii.6.10[2,2-3]), *tac câ 'daduḥ* (vii.1.5[3]), and *tac chandasâṁ chandastvam* (v.6.6[1]). He proceeds to point out that the *ç*, *c*, and *ch*, all mentioned in the rule as upon the same footing, are to be understood as original (not the products of previous euphonic processes), that being their chief or primary value: otherwise the mention of *ç* at all would be superfluous; since, the *ç* being (by v.34) ordered changed to *ch* after a mute, it would be enough for this rule to say "when followed by *c* or *ch*." Moreover, if the later rule were applied, then, after it, the application of the earlier rule would not be suitable (*svarasa*, 'having its own proper flavor;' the word is not used elsewhere), as it would constitute an offense against the third rule of this chapter.

---

22. *çacachaparas takâraç cakâram âpadyate. yathâ: tac....: tac....: tac..... atra çacachapara iti sâmânyoktânâṁ*[1] *nimittânâm*[2] *prakṛtitvaṁ*[3] *vijñeyam: mukhyatvât: tatra*[4] *prâkrtavâikṛtayoḥ prâkṛtam*[5] *mukhyam: anyathâ çakâragrahaṇavâiyarthyât*[6]*: kuto vâiyarthyam: sparçapûrvaḥ çakâraç chakâram* (v.34) *iti çakârasya chatve kṛte takâraç cakâraṁ cachapara*[7] *ity etâvatâi 'va siddher*[8] *iti brûmaḥ. kiṁ ca: parasûtre pravṛtte sati paçcât pûrvasûtraprasaraṇaṁ na svarasam*[9]*: tatra pûrvampûrvam prathamam* (v.3) *iti niyamabhañgaprasañgât*[10].

[1] G. M. B. O. *-nyeno 'kt-*. [2] W. O. *prani-*. [3] G. M. *prâkṛtatv-*. [4] G. M. om. [5] G. M. *-tatvam*. [6] G. M. *-yâc ca*. [7] G. M. B. *çacacha-*. [8] G. M. *sidhir*. [9] G. M. *bhavati*. [10] G. M. *nyâyabh-*.

जपरो जकारम् ॥ २३ ॥

23. When followed by *j*, it becomes *j*.

The cited example is *taj jayânâṁ jayatvam* (iii.4.4): rather superfluously, a counter-example is also given: *tat pravâte* (vi.4.7[2]).

नकार एतेषु ञकारम् ॥ २४ ॥

24. A *n*, before the same letters, becomes *ñ*.

As *eteshu* is plural, we are obliged, having recourse to that which lies nearest, to regard as implied the letters pointed out in the last two rules as requiring certain changes in those that precede them: that is to say, *ç*, *c*, *ch*, *j*. These are, in fact, the whole class of palatals, since *ñ* never occurs at the beginning of a word, nor, indeed, in any independent position, and since *jh* is found nowhere in any Vedic text. The dental *n*, then, never maintains itself before a palatal, but is assimilated to it. The other treatises teach virtually the same doctrine: see note to Ath. Pr. ii.11.

The commentator's illustrative example for *n* before *ç* (where, to complete the combination, rule 34 below has also to be applied) is *tenâi 'vâi 'nâñ chamayati* (iii.4.8[4]). As for *n* before *c*, he points out that the rule applies only to the cases where the *n* does not become *ç* by v.20, as excepted by v.21, and quotes again one of the examples given under the latter rule, *lokam âyañ catasraḥ* (v.2.3[4]). Before *ch*, he gives the phrase already quoted as counter-example under v.20, *tâñ chandobhir anu* (i.5.9[7]); and before *j*, *aparûpam âtmañ jâyate* (iii.5.7[3]). As general counter-example, finally, he gives *tânt subdhân* (ii.4.1[1]), where *n*, coming before *s*, is treated in a quite different manner.

The occurrence of *n* before *ch*, which does not once happen in the Atharvan, is found not less than nine times in the Tâittirîya-Sanhitâ. My own MS. reads every time *nch*, combining the dental nasal with the palatal aspirate. The Calcutta edition, at the only place which it contains as yet, reads *ñch*.

---

23. *sâṁnidhyât takâra iti labhyate: japaras takâro jakâram âpadyate. yathâ*[1]*: taj----. evampara iti kim: tat----.*

[1] G. M. om.

24. *eteshv iti bahuvacananirdeçât*[1] *pratyâsannam evâ 'napekshya*[2] *sûtradvayastheshu paranimitteshu sampratyayaḥ*[3]*: tasmâd eteshv iti: çacachajeshu*[4] *parata*[5] *ity arthaḥ: nakâro ñakâram âpadyate. yathâ*[6]*: te----: çatvâpattâu nishiddho*[7] *yo nakâraḥ so 'tra caparatvena vishayîkriyate. lok----: tâñ----: apa----. evampara iti kim: tânt----.*

[1] W. *-rdiç-*. [2] G. M. *'navek-*. [3] G. M. *praty-*. [4] W. O. *-chabhujeshu*. [5] W. *para*; G. M. *pareshv*. [6] G. M. om. [7] G. M. B. O. put after *yo*.

The combination of final *n* with initial *ç*, producing, according to all the phonetic text-books (with trifling exceptions: see note to Ath. Pr. ii.17), *ñch*, is decidedly of more common occurrence. But here, too, my own MS. reads, with but a single exception among the cases which I have noted, *nch*: the Calcutta text is inconsistent with itself, now giving *ñ* (as at ii.2.12³), now *n* as at i.3.9¹).

Final *n* is found yet more frequently before initial *j*, or some scores of times in all. As regards its method of writing the combination, my manuscript is about equally divided between *nj* and *ṁj*. The Calcutta text is equally wavering; and there is no approach to consistency between the two authorities, or to recognizable principle in either: in both alike, the variation seems wholly accidental and arbitrary.

Such being the case, I think it clear that a careful editor of the Tâittirîya-Sanhitâ ought to disregard, as of no authority or consequence, the variations, or the unanimity, of his manuscripts upon all these points, and to adopt uniformly the reading prescribed by the Prâtiçâkhya (either *ñ* or *ṁ*), wherever a final *n* comes to stand before a palatal mute.

लपरौ लकारम् ॥ २५ ॥

25. Both *t* and *n*, when followed by *l*, become *l*.

The dual *laparâu* indicates that the *t* and *n*, already treated of, are the letters aimed at in this rule, says the commentator. He cites as examples *yal lohitam parâpatat* (ii.1.7²: G. M. omit the last word), and *trîṅ lokân ud ajayat* (i.7.11¹: only G. M. have *ud ajayat*). The combination of *n* and *l* is finished by the next rule, and will be further remarked upon in the note thereto.

नकारो ऽनुनासिकम् ॥ २६ ॥

26. The *n* becomes nasalized *l*.

As the nasal quality of *n* itself is already established by rule ii.30, explains the commentator, it could not properly be defined here again as nasal. Hence the *anunâsikam* of the present precept must be understood as qualifying the *l* of like position into which the *n* is converted: this *l* is to be a nasal *l*. No additional example is given, the combination having been illustrated under the preceding rule.

There are in the Tâittirîya-Sanhitâ over a hundred cases of the meeting of final *n* with initial *l*, and in fully two-thirds of them

---

25. *dvivacanasâmarthyâd*[1] *gṛhîtâu prakṛtâu*[2] *takâranakârâu lakâram âpadyete*[3] *laparâv. yathâ*[4]*: yal....: trîṇ.... laḥ*[5] *paro yâbhyâṁ tâu laparâu.*

[1] G. M. *-thya.* [2] G. M. om. [3] MSS. *-yate.* [4] G. M. om. [5] G. M. *lakâraḥ.*

my MS. reads *nl* simply, without attempting any accommodation of the two sounds to one another. In the remaining cases, it treats the *n* in the same way as it would treat a *m*, substituting for it the ordinary *anusvâra*-dot over the preceding *akshara.* The Calcutta text varies between *nl* and *ṅll.* Here, as in the cases treated above, there seems to be every reason why an editor should follow one consistent method, as the irregularities of the manuscripts have no ground but accident—and, not less certainly, the method prescribed by the Prâtiçâkhya is the one better entitled to be followed. As to the way in which the nasal *l* shall be represented, there may be some question. As I have already mentioned (note to ii.30), I cannot think that the designation of the Calcutta edition is at all to be commended, since it properly implies the insertion of an *anusvâra* between the preceding vowel and a doubled *l*, and thus quite distorts the character of the combination—except as this is viewed by Âtreya, as noted in a later rule (v.31). The method followed in my MS., on the other hand, is theoretically unobjectionable, since there is no phonetic difference recognized, or to be recognized, by phonetic theory between the combination of *n* and *l* and that of *m* and *l:* it has only the practical inconvenience of not distinguishing to the eye these two combinations—and this is of very small account, since there can be few if any cases where the least ambiguity would result. If the nasal *l* is to be written separately, it should properly have the *virâma* beneath and the sign of nasality over it. That is to say, one ought always to print either अस्मिल्ँ लोके or अस्मिं लोके, not अस्मिँल्लोके.

In romanized text, as the assimilated *m* is represented by *ṁ*, so, by an analogous method and for the sake of convenient distinction, the assimilated *n* may be very suitably represented by *ṅ;* and this is the sign with which I have chosen to write it, both before *l* and before the palatals.

All the Prâtiçâkhyas (see note to Ath. Pr. ii.35) agree in converting both *n* and *m* before *l* into a nasal *l.*

मकार स्पर्शपरस्तस्य सस्थानमनुनासिकम् ॥ २७ ॥

27. A *m*, when followed by a mute, becomes the nasal of like position with it.

The commentator's examples are *yaṁ kâmayeta* (i.6.10[4] et al.), *çaṁ ca me* (iv.7.3[1]), *taṁ te duçcakshâḥ* (iii.2.10[2]), and *tam prat-*

---

26. *anusvârottamâ*[1] *anunâsikâḥ* (ii.30) *iti nakârasyâ 'nunâsikatve siddhe* [2] *punar atrâ 'pi tatkathanam anupapannam: tasmâd atra lakshaṇayâ nakâro nâma tatsthâno lakâra*[3] *ity arthaḥ: asâv* [4] *anunâsikam bhajate*[5]. *pûrvoktam evo 'dâharaṇam.*

[1] W. *nanu anunâsvâ-.* [2] G. M. ins. *'pi.* [3] G. M. *nak-.* [4] G. M. ins. *lakâro.* [5] G. M. *bhajeta.*

nathâ (i.4.9). Of *m* before a lingual he is able to give no example, as such a concurrence is not to be found in the Sanhitâ.

अन्तस्थापरश्च सवर्णमनुनासिकम् ॥ २८ ॥

28. Followed by a semivowel, it becomes a nasal of like quality with it.

From the class of semi-vowels is excepted *r*, by the next rule. Examples are given for the others, as follows: *saṁyattâ âsan* (i.5.1[1] et al.), *suvargaṁ lokam* (i.5.4[4] et al.), *saṁvatsaraḥ* (i.5.1[3] et al.: the *pada*-text, like that of the Atharvan, reads *sam-vatsaraḥ*, while that of the Rik leaves the word undivided). No attempt is made in the manuscripts or the printed text of the Sanhitâ to give a special representation to these nasal semi-vowels standing for an assimilated *m:* it is left to be understood that the sign of nasality over the preceding *akshara* stands for a nasal letter of like quality with the following consonant in the case of the semi-vowels, just as in that of the mutes, provided for by the preceding rule. Nor are the manuscripts of the Prâtiçâkhya and its commentary any more particular—saving that G. M. usually write, instead of *ṁy*, the combination *yy*, without any sign of the nasality of the first *y*.

Only the Ath. Pr. disagrees with our treatise in its treatment of *m* before the semi-vowels, acknowledging no nasal *y* or *v*, but a *l* alone (see note to Ath. Pr. ii.35).

The commentator explains the word *anunâsika*, 'nasal,' in the rule, by *anunâsikadharmaviçishṭa*, 'distinguished by nasal quality,' but afterward raises a difficulty over it, in terms which imply that he regards it as a noun, 'a nasal;' asking, how we are to understand it here as equivalent to *sânunâsika*, 'combined with nasality.' As it is, in fact, originally and properly an adjective, signifying 'possessed of nasal quality,' and is constant-

---

27. *sparçaparo makâras tasya sparçasya sasthânam anunâsikam*[1] *bhajate. yathâ*[2]*: yaṁ----: çaṁ----: taṁ----: tam----. samânaṁ sthânaṁ yasyâ 'sâu sasthânaḥ: tam*[3]*: sparçaḥ paro yasmâd asâu sparcaparaḥ.*

[1] W. om. [2] G. M. om. [3] B. G. M. om.

28. *cakâro makâram anvâdiçati: antasthâparo makâras tasyâ antasthâyâḥ savarṇaṁ sadṛçam anunâsikam*[1] *anunâsikadharmaviçishṭam bhajate. yathâ: saṁ----: suv----: saṁ----. nanv anunâsikam ity anena sânunâsikaṁ* [2]*kathaṁ labhyate*[2]. *ucyate:* [3]*nitarâm parihâraḥ*[3]*: yato dharmavâcakaḥ çabdo dharmiṇam*[4] *api*[5] *kathayati:* [6] *çuklaḥ paṭo nîlam utpalam ity âdivat*[7].

[1] B. O. om. [(2)] W. om.; O. *ity anena sânunâsikaṁ katham upalambhâmahe;* G. M. *sakalam upâlambhâmahe yathâ.* [(3)] O. om. [4] W. *dharmeṇa.* [5] W. *avika;* O. *avi.* [6] G. M. ins. *yathâ.* [7] G. M. *âdi.*

ly so used and applied in the Prâtiçâkhya, the difficulty is worse than hair-splitting; it is a downright perversion. The answer by which it is met is a quibble worthy of being matched with it: "because a word expressing a quality also designates the object possessing that quality; as, for example, when we say 'a white cloth,' 'a blue lotus.'" As if the words "white" and "blue" strictly applied to the color alone, and did not just as properly mean 'of white color,' 'of blue color'!

न रेफपरः ॥ २९ ॥

29. But not when followed by *r*.

R being also a semi-vowel, *m* would be converted into a corresponding nasal before it by the previous rule, but for this special exception. The instances given of the treatment of *m* before *r* are *pra samrâjam prathamam adhvarâṇâm* (i.6.12[3]: G. M. have only the first two words), and *sâmrâjyâya sukratuḥ* (i.8.16[1]). They are particularly ill selected, as neither case comes under the action of the preceding rule; they fall, rather, under xiii.4, and are, in fact, the two passages there given as examples of the peculiar treatment of *sam* before *râj*. We ought to have, instead, such passages as *pratyushtañ rakshaḥ* (i.1.2[1]), *vi vayañ ruhema* (i.1.2[2])—which, of course, are of exceedingly frequent occurrence in the Sanhitâ.

The omission of *m* before *r*, and the nasalization of the preceding vowel, or the insertion of *anusvâra* after the latter, are taught below, in rules xiii.2,xv.1–3. The written and printed texts are consistent in their recognition of the mode of combination thus prescribed, always setting the proper *anusvâra* sign before *r*, while before *y*, *l*, *v* they write the assimilated *m* just as before the mutes.

यवकारपरश्चैकेषामाचार्याणाम् ॥ ३० ॥

30. Nor, according to some teachers, when followed by *y* or *v*.

The authorities referred to, of course, would leave the *m* to be treated before these letters as before *r*, and would acknowledge no

---

29. *antasthâtvâd rephaparasyâ*[1] *'pi makârasya tatsavarṇânunâsikaprâptir*[2] *anena nishidhyate: na khalu rephaparo*[3] *makâraḥ pûrvoktam bhajate. yathâ*[4]*: pra.....: sâm-..... rephaḥ paro yasmâd asâu rephaparaḥ.*

[1] G. M. *rephasya tatp-.* [2] G. M. *-kâpattiḥ prâptâ.* [3] G. M. *-pakâro.* [4] G. M. om.

30. *cakâro nishedhânvâdeçakaḥ*[1]*: prakṛto*[2] *makâra ekeshâm âcâryâṇâm pakshe yakâraparo vâ*[3] *vakâraparo*[4] *vâ na savarṇam anunâsikam bhajate. yathâ*[5]*: saṁ- : saṁ-.*

[1] G M. *-âkarshakaḥ.* [2] W. B. *prâk-.* [3] B. O. om. [4] B. om. [5] G. M. om.

nasal semi-vowel save *l.* Their opinion is again quoted in connection with the rule respecting the actual treatment of *m* before *r* (xiii.3), and the commentator there calls attention to the fact that the "some teachers" spoken of are the same with those here noticed: who they are, he does not attempt to tell us. The view held by them is the same with that taken by the Atharva Prâtiçâkhya, as pointed out above (see Ath. Pr. ii.35, and the note upon it); but, until we know much more than we do at present of the history and mutual relations of these phonetic treatises, it would be highly venturesome to conclude that the authors of this Prâtiçâkhya had here in mind the other one and its authors.

I find it difficult to discover any good phonetic reason why the assimilation of *m* should not yield a like result before all the semi-vowels, and why, if we are to admit an *anusvâra* at all, it would not find a particularly appropriate place as representing the sound into which *m* might naturally pass before *y*, *r*, *l*, and *v*.

As examples, are repeated *saṁvatsaraḥ* and *saṁyattâḥ* (see under rule 28, above).

उत्तमलभावात्पूर्वो ऽनुनासिक इत्यात्रेयः ॥ ३१ ॥

31. Âtreya holds that, when a nasal mute becomes *l*, the previous vowel is nasalized.

As has been pointed out above, Âtreya's view of the combination is the one represented accurately by the mode of writing adopted in the Calcutta edition. It is not elsewhere supported in the Prâtiçâkhyas. Its quotation here seems a little unprepared, or the expression of it given in the rule imperfect, as we have been directed to convert *m* and *n*, not into *l*, but into a nasal *l*. One might think, too, that it would be in better place at the beginning of chapter xv., where certain other differences of opinion on kindred points are rehearsed.

The commentator gives Âtreya the title of *muni*, 'sage,' instead of *âcârya*, 'teacher.'

To illustrate the sage's style of making the combination, he cites *trîṅl lokân* (i.7.11[1]) and *suvargaṅl lokam* (i.5.4[4] et al.); but not one of the manuscripts of the commentary takes the pains to write the extracts as they should be written, to serve their purpose as illustrations. Finally, he adds the caution that "this rule and the preceding are not approved."

ङपूर्वः ककारः सषकारपरः ॥ ३२ ॥

---

31. *uttamasya nakârasya makârasya*[1] *vâ labhâvâl lakârâpatteḥ pûrvasvaro 'nunâsiko bhavatî 'ty âtreyo nâma munir manyate. yathâ*[2]*: trîṅ----: suv-----. uttamayor labhâva uttamalabhâvaḥ*[3]*: tasmât.*

sûtradvayam etad anishṭam.

[1] G. M. put before *nak-*. [2] G. M. om. [3] G. M. om.

32. After *ń* is inserted a *k* before *s* and *sh*.

The commentator's examples are *pratyańk somo atidrutaḥ* (i.8.21: but G. M. have instead *sadṛńk samânâiḥ*, ii.2.8[6]), and *pratyańk shaḍaho bhavati* (vii.4.2[5]: O. G. M. omit *bhavati*). As counter-examples, showing that the insertion is made only under the circumstances specified, he gives *pratyań hotâram* (vi.3.1[5]), and *tat savituḥ* (i.5.6[4] et al.) and *tat shodaçî* (vi.6.11[1]).

The combinations here treated of are not otherwise than rare in any Vedic text. In the Tâittirîya-Sanhitâ I have found no other instance of the meeting of *ń* and *sh* than the one quoted; of *ń* before *s*, besides the two here given, occur two others, at vi.3.1[6] and iv.4.4[7-8]; but, in the latter passage, the division of the section into half-centuries falls between the two letters, as the text is at present written, and prevents the exhibition of the *sandhi*. Neither the Calcutta edition (so far as yet printed) nor my manuscript makes in any of these passages the insertion required by the Prâtiçâkhya: and it may properly enough be considered a question whether the latter's authority ought to be followed in a matter of this character, any more than in regard to the duplications which form the subject of chapter xiv. Nevertheless, considering the phonetic reasonableness of this particular insertion, and its close analogy with that of *t* between *n* and *s* (see the next rule), I should myself decidedly incline to write *ńk s* and *ńk sh*. The manuscripts of the commentary, it should be remarked, try to follow the directions of the rule, W. B. O. reading *ńks*, and W. O. *ńksh* (with the *k* and *sh* united in the usual sign for *ksh*); while G. M. even yield to the requirement of xiv.12, and give us *ńkhs* and *ńkhsh*. This last is a refinement which no one, probably, would care to see introduced into our printed texts.

As is shown in detail in the note to Ath. Pr. ii.9, the teachings of the Ath. Pr. and Vâj. Pr. are virtually in agreement with those of our own treatise as regards the insertions prescribed in this rule and the next, while the Rik Pr. merely mentions them as enjoined by some authorities.

टनकारपूर्वश्च तकारः ॥ ३३ ॥

33. After *ṭ* or *n* is inserted a *t*.

The examples given for these combinations are *vashaṭt svâhâ* (vii.3.12 nine times), and *vidvânt somena yajate* (iii.2.2[3]); and, in order not to be without an illustration for the collision of *ṭ* with *sh*, one is dragged in from the *jaṭâ*-text: *anûyâjâu shaṭt shaḍ anûyâjâv anûyâjâu shaṭ* (vi.6.3[3]): to which G. M. even add, from the

---

32. *sakâraparaḥ* [1] *shakâraparo vâ kakâra âgamo bhavati ńapûrvaḥ. yathâ: praty-....: praty-..... evampara iti kim: praty-....: evampûrva iti kim: tat....: tat....*

[1] G. M. ins. *vâ*.

same source, *tânt subdhânt subdhâṅs tâṅs tânt subdhân* (ii.4.1[1]). Counter-examples are *shaḍ vâ ṛtavaḥ* (iii.4.8[6]), and *tân rudrâ abruvan* (v.5.2[6]).

The final lingual *ṭ* occurs before *s*, according to my notes upon the text, in ten other passages (iii.2.8[1] eight times: iv.4.8[1]; 6.1[4]: v.4.3[4], 4[2]; 5.2[6]: vi.2.3[4]; 6.3[3]: vii.1.5[1]; 4.10[2]); and my MS. does not once employ the intermediate *t*. The manuscripts of our commentary, however, all introduce it; and this time B. abets G. M. in converting it into *th*, by rule xiv.12. The combination is without doubt a very troublesome one, in the demand it makes upon the tip of the tongue: but whether the transition is helped by the intrusion of a *t* is a much more serious question—and one to exercise and gratify the subtlety of a Hindu phonetist. The Ath. Pr. also requires *ṭts* (ii.8), but the Rik Pr. (iv.6) only notices the mode of *sandhi* as enjoined by certain teachers.

It is indeed true that the strict letter of the rule requires a *t* to be inserted between a *ṭ* and *sh*, as illustrated by the commentator from the *jaṭâ*-text. But it would be wholly preposterous to suppose that the authors of the Prâtiçâkhya intended to teach any such insertion—which would convert the consonant combination from one wholly natural and easy to one in a high degree harsh and difficult, if not absolutely impossible. They evidently relied on the non-occurrence of *sh* after *ṭ* anywhere in the Sanhitâ for the annulling of that part of the rule's prescription—either having no regard to a *jaṭâ*-text, or overlooking the fact that in it the two letters would come in contact.

Twice in the Tâittirîya text we have a final *t* before an initial *sh* (at v.5.2[6]: vii.5.6[3]). Although their collision might seem to call for mediation in somewhat the same manner as that of *ṭ* and *s*, the Prâtiçâkhya makes no special provision for it, and the manuscript text simply combines the two letters.

The meeting of final *n* with initial *s*, the other case contemplated by the rule, is very frequent (there are sixty instances in the first two *kâṇḍas*: I have not collected them through the whole text). Neither the printed text nor my manuscript is absolutely faithful in inserting the prescribed *t*; yet I have found but six cases in the whole Sanhitâ in which the latter omits it; and out of the seven passages in *kâṇḍas* i. and ii. where the former leaves it out, my manuscript confirms the omission in only one. As the requirement of the Prâtiçâkhya receives so much support from the usage of the scribes, and also accords with the prescriptions of the Ath. Pr. (ii.9) and Vâj. Pr. (iv.14), there can be no question that it ought to be followed by an editor of the Tâittirîya Veda.

---

33. *cakâraḥ sashakârâv anvâdiçati: ṭakârapûrvo vâ*[1] *nakârapûrvo vâ takâra âgamo bhavati sashakâraparaḥ. vash-....: vid-....: anâ-....: tânt..... evampara iti kim: shaḍ....: tân.....*

[1] B. om.

स्पर्शपूर्वः शकारश्छकारम् ॥ ३४ ॥

34. A *ç* preceded by a mute becomes *ch.*

The commentator gives only an example of a *ç* converted into *ch* after *t*, the *t* at the same time becoming *c* by rule 22, above: *çarac chrâutrî* (iv.3.2²). He adds a counter-example, *âçuḥ çiçânaḥ* (iv.6.4¹). The occurrence of any other final mute than *t* and *n* (for which an example is given above, under rule 24) before initial *ç* is very rare (excepting *m*, for which see the following rule); and it is properly only after a dental, or after a dental or lingual, that the conversion here prescribed has good phonetic ground—namely, in the coalescence of a *t*-sound and a *sh*-sound into the compound sound of our *ch* in *church* (see note to Ath. Pr. ii.17). There is one case of a preceding *ṭ* (i.3.14⁶), where my MS. reads, as the Prâtiçâkhya directs, *ṭ ch*, while the Calcutta text has *ṭ ç*. A single case of preceding *p* is treated of below, in rule 36.

न मकारपूर्वः ॥ ३५ ॥

35. But not when preceded by *m.*

By this rule, says the commentator, is annulled the conversion of *ç* to *ch* after *m*, which would otherwise be in order (according to the preceding rule), since *m* is a mute. He instances *sañçitam me* (iv.1.10³ and v.1.10²) and *sañçravâ ha* (i.7.2¹). Being thus specially exempted from the operation of the foregoing rule, this combination, of course, falls under xiii.2 and xv.1–3, and the *m*, as before other spirants, becomes *anusvâra*. An objection is raised against the pertinence of the present precept, on the ground that xiii.2 directs the omission of *m* before a spirant, and that hence there could arise no occasion for any such conversion of *ç* into *ch* as is here contemplated and guarded against. The reply, however, is a very easy one; that, by rule 3 of this chapter, the requirement of the conversion into *ch*, as it is stated earlier, would have to be applied first, and that the result of so doing would be to pro-

---

34. *çakâraç chakâram âpadyate sparçapûrvaḥ*[1]. *yathâ*[2]: *çarac*..... *evampûrva iti kim: âçuḥ*..... *sparçaḥ pûrvo yasmâd asâu sparçapûrvaḥ.*

[1] G. M. puts first. [2] W. G. M. om.

35. *makârapûrvaḥ çakâraç chakâraṁ nâ "padyate. yathâ: sañ-.....: sañ-..... sparçatvân makârasya 'tatpûrve*[2] *çakâre*[3] *prâptaṁ chatvam*[4] *anena nishidhyate. nanv etad anupapannam:* [5]*atha makâralopaḥ*[5] (xiii.1)*: rephoshmaparaḥ* (xiii.2) *iti makârasya lopavidhânân na*[6] *çakârasya chatvâpattinimittam*[7] *astî 'ti. mâi 'vam:* [8]*chatvâpâdakam malopâpâdakât pûrvam: atas*[1,8] *tatra pûrvampûrvam prathamam*[9] (v.3) *iti nyâ-*

duce, in the passage already quoted, the reading *saṁchitam me brahma;* which is wrong.

पकारपूर्वश्च वाल्मीकेः ॥ ३६ ॥

36. Nor, according to Vâlmîki, when preceded by *p*.

There is but a single case in the Sanhitâ of *p* before *ç*, namely the one here quoted by the commentator, *anushṭup chāradî* (iv.3.2²): so my manuscript reads, according to the requirement of rule 34, above. Vâlmîki thinks it would be better to read *anushṭup çāradî*—and I presume we shall have little hesitation in approving his opinion.

व्यञ्जनपरः पौष्करसादेर्न पूर्वश्च अकारम् ॥ ३७ ॥

37. Nor, according to Pâushkarasâdi, when followed by a consonant; and a preceding *n*, in that case, does not become *ñ*.

This translation is made in accordance with the commentator's exposition. One might be tempted to understand the last part of the rule otherwise, not regarding the continuance of the negative as implied from the other part; translating 'and a preceding *n* becomes *ñ*;' but, besides the authority of the comment against it, this would be a mere repetitious enactment of the rule already given above (v.24). The inquiry is raised, how we know that *pūrvaḥ*, 'the preceding letter,' means here 'a preceding *n*.' The reply is, because only *n* is liable to conversion into *ñ*, and annulment is only made of that which would, without direction to the contrary, be liable to take place.

The examples given to illustrate this peculiar view of Pâushkarasâdi are *âdityân çmaçrubhiḥ* (v.7.12), and *pâpîyân çreyase* (i.5.7⁴). The edition has *pâpîyâñ chreyase* in the latter passage, in accordance with the approved rules of the Prâtiçâkhya; but my MS. seems to have been written by a sectary of Pâushkarasâdi at this point (namely, in the margin: a line or two of the context was omitted just here by the original scribe). In the former, I

---

yena chatvam eva pûrvaṁ[10] *kartavyaṁ syât: tathâ sati makâra sparças*[11] [12]*tatpare*[13] *çakâre chatvam*[12] *âpanne saṁ-.... iti syât: tan mâ bhûd ity etat sûtram upapannam eva.*

[(1)] B. om., excepting *lokavidhânân na.* [2] G. M. *-vasya.* [3] G. M. *-rasya.* [4] G. M. put before *prâptam.* [(5)] G. M. O. om. [6] G. M. put before *asti.* [7] G. M. *-ttatvân.* [(8)] G. M. *chatvâpâdakasya sûtrasya malopasya ca chatvâpâdakasyâi 'va sapûrvatvât.* [9] W. B. O. om. [10] G. M. om. [11] B. *-ça.* [(12)] G. M. *tasye 'ti makâre ñakaram.* [13] B. *pare.*

36. *cakâraḥ pratishedhârthakaḥ*[1]*: vâlmîker mate pakârapûrvaḥ*[2] *çakâraç chakâraṁ*[3] *nâ 'padyate. yathâ: an-....*

[1] B. G. M. *-dhâkarshakaḥ.* [2] G. M. *papû-.* [3] G. M. *chatvaṁ.*

find the reading *âdityân chmaçrubhiḥ*, which would satisfy neither side. There is one other case of the collision of *n* with *çr* (at v.6.7[3]), where I find read *n chr*. So also, at v.7.1[3] my MS. has *n chv;* and at vii.3.14, *n chy*. These are the only instances, I believe, which the text affords of the combinations contemplated by the rule.

The commentator, at the end, declares this rule and the preceding not approved, and with reason: the evident intent of the treatise is that the conversion of initial *ç* to *ch* shall take place in all the cases falling under rule 34.

प्रथमपूर्वो हकारश्चतुर्थं तस्य सस्थानं प्लाक्षिकौण्डिन्यगौतमपौष्करसादीनाम् ॥ ३८ ॥

38. According to Plâkshi, Kâuṇḍinya, Gâutama, and Pâushkarasâdi, a *h* preceded by a first mute becomes a fourth mute corresponding with the latter.

The examples of this, the approved and customary combination of an initial *h* with a final surd mute, are, as given by the commentator, *arvâg ghy enam* (vi.3.3[1]), *saraḍ ḍhavâ açvasya* (v.3.12[2]: G. M. omit *açvasya*), and *tad dhiraṇyam* (v.4.2[3] and vi.1.7[1]). In giving the first two quotations, W. O. G. M. (following a vicious and indefensible mode of combination, which occasionally appears even in carefully written Vedic manuscripts, and has incautiously been admitted into some edited texts) write *ghgh* and *ḍhḍh* instead of *ggh* and *ḍḍh;* and in the latter of them my MS. of the Sanhitâ does the same (see the note to xiv.5). As counter-examples, establishing the restrictions imposed by the rule, we have *pratyañ hotâram* (vi.3.1[5]), *vâk ta â pyâyatâm* (i.3.9[1]), *vashaṭ te* (ii.2.12[4]); and, in W., *â 'tishṭhipat te* (iv.6.9[4]), but in all the other MSS. *tat te* (i.3.9[1] et al.).

This is one of several instances in which the Prâtiçâkhya, instead of stating first, categorically, its own doctrine, and then mentioning others at variance with this, puts forward the conflicting views of different authorities, without appearing itself to decide in favor of any one against the rest. The commentator here points out (at the end of the chapter) that the present rule presents the accepted doctrine of the treatise, the three that follow being dis-

---

37. *pâushkarasâder mate vyañjanaparaḥ çakâra sparçapûrvo 'pi chatvaṁ nâ "padyate: çakârapûrvo nakâraç ca ñakâraṁ nâ "padyate. yathâ[1]: âd-....: pâp-..... pûrva ity ukte nakâra iti kathaṁ labhyate. ñakârâpattir asyâi 've 'ti brûmaḥ: prasaktasyâi 'va[2] hi[3] pratishedhât.[4] vyañjanam asmât param iti vyañjanaparaḥ.*

nâi 'tat sûtradvayam ishṭam.

[1] W. om. [2] G. M. om. *eva.* [3] B. O. om. [4] G. M. *-dhaḥ.*

approved; but this does not satisfy us. We might, to be sure, regard ourselves as justified in assuming that the doctrine of the authors of the work is first stated, with due and respectful mention of the authorities upon whom they especially rely in maintaining it: but such an assumption does not in all cases help us out of the difficulty.

अविकृत एकेषाम् ॥ ३९ ॥

39. According to some authorities, it remains unchanged.

That is to say, the authorities here referred to would read, for example, in one of the passages already quoted (vi.3.3[1]), *arvâk hy enam.*

As the euphonic treatment of *h* as a sonant instead of a surd letter is one of the most perplexing anomalies of the Sanskrit phonetic system, such indications as this of the fluctuating and antagonistic views of the old Hindu phonetists respecting it, and the willingness of some of them to give it the value of a surd in making combinations, are worth a great deal to us.

चतुर्थो ऽन्तरे शैत्यायनादीनाम् ॥ ४० ॥

40. According to Çâityâyana and others, a fourth mute is interposed.

These respectable authorities would, if their views are not misrepresented, approve the very strange-looking and hardly defensible reading *arvâkgh hy enam* (so writes W., with the utmost possible explicitness; B. reads *arvâk hya hy;* O. gives *arvâgh hy;* G. M. have *arvâghy*). The commentator tells us (one would like to know on what authority) that the "others" are Kâuhalîputra, Bharadvâja, Old Kâuṇḍinya, and Pâushkarasâdi. All are mentioned elsewhere (see Index) in the text itself.

---

38. *plâkshiprabhṛtînâm mate prathamapûrvo hakâras tasya prathamasya sasthânam caturtham bhajate. yathâ: arv-....: saraḍ....: tad..... evampûrva iti kim: prât-....: hakâra iti kim: vâk....: va-....: â 'ti-..... prathamaḥ pûrvo yasmâd asâu prathamapûrvaḥ.*

[1] G. M. om.

39. *ekeshâm mate prathamapûrvo hakâro 'vikṛto bhavati. yathâ: arv-.....*

40. *çâityâyanâdînâm mate hakâraprathamayor antare madhye prathamasasthânaç caturthâgamo bhavati. yathâ: arv-..... âdiçabdena kâuhalîputrabharadvâjasthavirakauṇḍinyapâushkarasâdayo[1] gṛhyante.*

[1] G. M. *-ṇḍinyânâm*, and then a *lacuna* to *pûjârtham* under the next rule.

मीमाꣳसकानां च मीमाꣳसकानां च ॥४१॥

41. As also, according to the Mîmâñsakas.

The especial mention, in a separate rule, of the agreement of this school with the view of Çâityâyana and his abettors, is made, says the commentary, with an honorific intent.

He adds, as was above remarked, that rules 39 to 41 are disapproved.

CHAPTER VI.

CONTENTS: 1–5, conversion of *s* and *h* into *sh;* 6–13, exceptions and counter-exceptions; 14, insertion of *s* between final *n* and initial *t.*

अथ षकारꣳ सकारविसर्जनीयौ ॥१॥

1. Now for conversions of *s* and *visarjanîya* into *sh.*

An introductory heading to the rules of this chapter—excepting the last rule.

स्वानासोदिव्यापोह्ययमुकमूमोप्रोत्रीमह्यिद्यविपद्यवग्रहपूर्वः ॥२॥

2. A *s* is converted into *sh* when preceded by *svânâso divi, âpo hi, ayam u, kam u, û, mo, pro, trî, mahi, dyavi, padi,* or a former member of a compound.

The illustrative passages, as given by the commentator, are as follows: *uta svânâso divi shantv agneḥ* (i.2.14[7]: only O. has *agneḥ;* B. omits both that and the preceding word): with the

---

41. *cakâraḥ pûrvoktavidhim anvâdiçati: mîmâñsakânâṁ câ 'ntarâgamamataṁ sammatam. pûrvoktam evo 'dâharaṇam. mîmâñsakânâm*[1] *pûjârtham pṛthaksûtrârambhaḥ.*

nâi 'tat sûtratrayam ishṭam.

iti tribhâshyaratne prâtiçâkhyavivaraṇe
pañcamo 'dhyâyaḥ.

[1] G. M. om. to here.

1. *athe 'ty ayam adhikâraḥ: sakâravisarjanîyâu shakâram âpadyete ity etad adhikṛtaṁ veditavyam ita uttaraṁ yad vakshyâmaḥ.*

counter-example *tṛtîyasyâm ito divi soma âsît* (iii.5.7[1]), to show the powerlessness of *divi* to effect the change except after *svânâsaḥ*. Then *âpo hi shṭhâ mayobhuvaḥ* (iv.1.5[1]: v.6.1[4]: vii.4.19[4]: only G. M. have the last word): the necessity of *âpo* is shown by the counter-example *na hi svaḥ svañ hinasti* (v.1.7[1]). Next *ayam u shya pra devayuḥ* (iii.5.11[1]), and *kam u shvid asya senayâ* (ii.6.11[2]): with the counter-example *tad u soma âha* (iv.2.8[1]), to prove that *u* changes *s* only after *ayam* and *kam*. For *û*, the example is *ûrdhva û shu ṇa ûtaye* (iv.1.4[2]: only G. M. have the first word): the other passages in which it exerts a like influence upon an initial *s* are i.5.11[5]: iii.5.10[1]: iv.6.5[6]: v.1.5[3]: vii.1.18[2]; 4.17[2]. For *mo*, the only passage is the one quoted, *mo shû ṇa indra* (i.8.3). For *pro*, only *pro shv asmâi puroratham* (i.7.13[5]). For *trî*, only *trî shadhasthâ* (ii.4.11[2] and iii.2.11[1]). For the three remaining words, also, the text affords only the single examples given by the commentator: *mahi shad dyumann namaḥ* (iii.2.8[2]), *ya upa dyavi shṭha* (ii.4.14[5]), and *padi shitâm amuñcatâ yajatrâḥ* (iv.7.15[7]: G. M. omit the last word). To the prescription conveyed in the last item of the rule, which seems to demand that every *s* beginning in *pada*-text the latter member of a compound should be changed to *sh*, rule 7, below, makes the very important general exception "not after a consonant or an *a*-vowel;" it means, then, that *s* is so changed after the *i*, *u*, and *ṛ* vowels and the diphthongs. The commentator illustrates only one or two of the cases in which the conversion would be required: *hañsaḥ çucishad vasuḥ* (iv.2.1[5]; p. *çuci-sat:* only G. M. have the first word), *ayâ vishṭhâ janayan* (i.7.12[2]; p. *vi-sthâḥ:* only G. M. have *ayâ*), and *goshṭomaṁ dvitîyam* (vii.4.11[1]).

I have collected from the Sanhitâ all the words coming under the operation of this part of the rule, concerning the initial *s* of the latter member of a compound (just about a hundred in number, and some of them of quite frequent occurrence), but I do not think the list worth the trouble of giving here. So far as regards the Prâtiçâkhya and its relation to them, the important point is to determine whether its rules and exceptions precisely cover them—and I have to say that I have not succeeded in discovering any want of exact adaptedness to them. There is a single participle, *anusthita*, whose unaltered *s* is unnoticed and unprovided for in the chapter, but it occurs only as final member of a compound, *vishṇvanusthitaḥ* (ii.4.12[3,4,5]; p. *vishṇu-anusthitaḥ*), and so, not being itself separated into its constituents, is exempted from the action of the present rule.

---

2. ...... *ity evampûrvo 'vagrahapûrvaç ca sakâraḥ shakâram âpadyate. yathâ: uta....: svânâsa*[1] *iti kim: tṛt-....: âpo ....: âpa iti kim: na....: ayam....: kam....: ayaṁkam iti kim: tad....: ûrdh-....: mo....: pro....: trî....: mahi....: ya....: padi....: hañs-....: ayâ....: go-..... avagrahaḥ pûrvo yasmâd asâv avagrahapûrvaḥ.*

[1] W. B. *svâna.*

असदामासिञ्चंश्च ॥ ३ ॥

3. Also *asadâma* and *asiñcan*.

The "also" (*ca*) in this rule implies, the commentator says, that the words mentioned are preceded by an *avagraha*, according to the final specification of the preceding rule: else such passages as *ajâyâṁ gharmam prâ 'siñcan* (v.4.3[3]) would fall under the prescribed action. The examples are *yena kâmena nyashadâme 'ti* (vii.5.2[1]; p. *ni-asadâma*), and *mitrâvaruṇâv abhyashiñcan* (i.8.11; p. *abhi-asiñcan*). The rule is given, we are told, for the purpose of ordaining that, in the case of these two words, the conversion into *sh* after an *avagraha* takes place even notwithstanding the interposition of an *a*. Why not, then, puts in an objector, say "even when *a* interposes," without specification of the words concerned? Because, is the reply, the rule would then apply to such cases as *hṛtsvaso mayobhûn* (iv.2.11[3]; p. *hṛtsu-asaḥ*).

उपसर्गनिष्पूर्वो ऽनुदात्ते पदे ॥ ४ ॥

4. Also in an unaccented *pada*, when a preposition or *nis* precedes.

This rule can apply only to unaccented verbal forms, since they alone can be technically *anudâtta* throughout, having the *anudâtta* sign written under every syllable. In any compound beginning with a preposition like *pári*, for instance, having an acute on the first syllable and an enclitic *svarita* on the second, the syllables of the other member of the compound would not have the *anudâtta* accent, but the *pracaya*: such would fall under rule 2 of this chapter. The word *pada* in the rule, we are told, is intended to specify the text: "a word which is *anudâtta* throughout in the *pada*-text" is what the Prâtiçâkhya means—it being, in fact, impossible that any word should be so accented in *saṁhitâ*-text.

The commentator's examples are, for prepositions, *açmann ûrjam iti pari shiñcati* (v.4.4[1]), *imam vi shyâmi* (i.1.10[2] and iii.5.6[1]), *sâmrâjyenâ 'bhi shiñcâmi* (i.7.10[3] twice, and v.6.3[3]: but B. O. read *shiñcati*, I presume by a copyist's blunder, as I find no such phrase in the text), *yajamâne prati shṭhâpayanti* (vi.1.4[2]), and *ni shasâda dhṛtavrato varuṇaḥ* (i.8.16[1]: only B. O. have *varuṇaḥ*);

---

3. *asadâma: asiñcan: ity etayoḥ sakâraḥ shakâram*[1] *âpadyate. yathâ: yena----: mitr-----. cakâro 'vagrahapûrvatvânvâdeçakaḥ*[2]. *anvâdeçenâ 'nena*[3] *kim: aj-----. avagrahapûrvatve 'py*[4] *akâreṇa vyaveta ity ayam ârambhaḥ. nanu lâghavâd akâravyaveto 'pî 'ty etâvatâi 'vâ 'lam: kaṇṭhoktyâ kim. ucyate: hṛt---- ity âdâu mâ bhûd iti.*

[1] G. M. *shatvam.* [2] W. B. and O. p. m. om. *pûrva.* [3] B. O. G. M. om. [4] G. M. *sati.*

for *nis, ni shṭanihi duritâ* (iv.6.6[7]: all the manuscripts of the comment, along with my manuscript of the Sanhitâ, read thus, as required by ix.1: compare the similar cases noted under rule 13, below). A number of counter-examples are given, showing the effect of absence of any one of the conditions contained in the rule: they are *sadane sîda samudre* (iv.3.1), *bṛhataḥ çarmaṇi syâm* (iv.1.5[1]), *vi sîmataḥ surucaḥ* (iv.2.8[2]: G. M. omit this example), and *abhi savanâ pâhi* (i.4.10,11).

The cases coming under this rule are not so numerous but that it may be worth while to report them. Of verbal forms after *adhi* I have found none; after *abhi*, I have noted *abhi shyâma* (i.4.46[3]), and forms of *abhi shiñcâmi* (i.7.10[3] et al.) and *abhi shuṇomi* (iii.1.8[2]); after *prati*, forms of *prati shṭhâpayâmi* (i.7.5[2] et al.), and *prati shṭobhanti* (ii.2.12[3]); after *pari*, forms of *pari shicye* (iii.3.11[1] et al.), and *pari shṭhât* (i.7.13[3]); after *vi* (besides that quoted under rule 13, below), *vi shajanti* (vi.4.7[2]), and forms of *vi shyâmi* (iii.4.11[6]); after *ni* (besides the one under rule 13), *ni shasâda* (i.8.16[1] et al.), and forms of *ni shîdâmi* (iii.5.11[4] et al.). Such cases as *ni-shâdáyati* (v.3.7[2]), where the preposition, losing its accent before the accented verbal form, is combined with the latter in the *pada*-text, belong under rule 2, above. The same is the case with *vyátishajet* (vi.6.4[2] et al.), where the verb has two prepositional prefixes, and is therefore written in combination with them (*vi-átishajet*), and with altered sibilant. But for this circumstance, we should require a separate and special treatment of the word; for *ati* is by this Prâtiçâkhya (i.15) excluded from the list of *upasarga*, 'prepositions,' and so could not by the present rule cause the alteration of an initial *s* of a root. *Anu* is also thus excluded, whence the passage *anu sthana* (v.6.1[3]) does not fall under the rule, and the retention of its dental sibilant needs no specific authorization. It is the only case, so far as I have discovered, in which the restriction of the class of prepositions to half its usual number has any bearing upon the objects of this rule.

रासःसप्तेऽग्निर्निर्विदुर्मीढुःपायुभिर्वैःसुमतिर्मािक रीयुरायुराभिःसधिर्नकिस्तकारपरो नित्यम् ॥ ५ ॥

5. Also the *visarjanîya*, when followed by *t*, of *agniḥ* preceded by *râsaḥ* or *sapte*, and of *niḥ, viduḥ, mîḍhuḥ, pâyubhiḥ*,

---

4. *sarvânudâtte pade vartamanaḥ sakâra upasargapûrvo nishpûrvo vâ shatvam âpadyate. yathâ: açm-....: imam....: sîm-....: yaj-....: ni....: etâny[1] upasargapûrvaṇi[2]. nishpûrvam api: ni sh-.... evampûrva iti kim: sad-.... bṛh-....: sarvânudâtta iti kim: vi....: abhi....: pada iti kim: kâlârtham: padakâle[3] 'nudâtta ity arthaḥ.*

[1] G. M *ete.* [2] G. M. *-rgâ.* [3] W. *-kâ a.*

veḥ, sumatiḥ, mâkiḥ, îyuḥ, âyuḥ, âbhiḥ, sadhiḥ, and *nakiḥ,* under all circumstances.

This is, the commentator remarks, a rule establishing exceptions in advance to rule 2 of the ninth chapter, which would require in every case *s* instead of *sh.* The examples are: for *agniḥ, avidushṭarâsaḥ: agnish ṭad viçvam* (i.1.14[4]) and *medhyaç ca sapte: agnish ṭvâ* (v.1.11[1]); with a counter-example, *varshishṭhe adhi nâke 'gnis te tanuvam* (i.1.8: only G. M. have the first two words), to show that *agniḥ* becomes *agnis* after other words than the two specified in the rule. For *nis, nish ṭapâmi goshṭham* (i.1.10[1]). For *viduḥ, vidushṭaraṅ sapema* (ii.5.12[5]; p. *viduḥ-taram*), and also, in virtue of rule i.52, *avidushṭarâsaḥ* (i.1.14[4]; p. *aviduḥ-tarâsaḥ*): *vidushṭaraḥ* occurs at ii.6.11[1]. For *mîḍhuḥ, mîḍhushṭama çivatama* (iv.5.10[4]; p. *mîḍhuḥ-tama*). For *pâyubhiḥ, pâyubhish ṭvaṅ çivebhiḥ* (i.4.24): with the counter-example *tasmâd açvas tribhis tishṭhaṅs tishṭhati* (v.4.12[1]: only G. M. have the first two words), to show that the quotation of *bhiḥ* (of *pâyu-bhiḥ*) alone as *nimitta* would not have answered the purpose. For *veḥ, çoce vesh ṭvaṅ hi yajvâ* (iv.3.13[5]). For *sumatiḥ, sumatish ṭe astu bâdhasva* (i.4.45[1]: only G. M. have the last word): and, to justify the text in quoting *sumatiḥ* (p. *su-matiḥ*) in full, instead of *matiḥ* simply, we receive an asserted quotation from "another text," *pramatis te devânâm.* For *mâkis, mâkish ṭe vyathir â dadharshît* (i.2.14[2]). For *îyuḥ, îyush ṭe ye pûrvatarâm apaçyan* (i.4.33). For *âyuḥ, âyush ṭa âyurdâ agne* (ii.5.12[1]: only G. M. have *agne*): we have *âyush ṭe* again at i.3.14[4]. For *âbhiḥ, âbhish ṭe adya gîrbhiḥ* (iv.4.4[7]: G. M. omit the last word). For *sadhiḥ, apsv agne sa-*

---

5. *râsaḥ: sapte:* [1]*ity etâbhyâṅ viçishṭe 'gnir ity asmin*[3] *grahaṇe: niḥ----*[1,2]*---- nakiḥ: ity eteshu visarjanîyas takâraparaḥ shakâram*[4] *âpadyate*[2]. *yathâ: avid----: medh----: etâbhyâṅ viçishṭa iti kim: varsh----: nish----: vid----: apy akârâdi* (i.52) *iti vacanâd avidushṭarâsa ity apy udâharaṇam: mî-----: pây----: pâyv*[5] *iti kim: tasm----: çoce----: sum----: sv iti kim: pram---- iti çâkhântare: mâk----: îyush----: âyush----: âbhish----: apsv----: nakish----. nityaçabdaḥ kimarthaḥ: ṛkârarephavati* (vi.8)*: avagrahaḥ* (vi.9) *iti nishedhaṅ*[6] *vakshyati: avidur*[7] *ity atra visarjanîyasyâ 'vagrahasthatvât shatvaṅ na syât: tan mâ bhûd iti: kaṇṭhoktir* [8] *vidurity asyâi 'va* [9] *na tv avidur ity asye 'ti dâurbalyât: tatsaṅrakshaṇârtho nityaçabdaḥ prayujyate.*

aghoshaparas tasya sasthânam (ix.2) *ity asya purastâd apavâdo 'yam.*

(1) (2) W. transposes, breaking *miḍhuḥ* in the middle. [3] G. M. *etasminn.* [4] G. M. *shatvam.* [5] W. O. *-yur;* G. M. *-yubhir;* B. corrupt. [6] G. M. *pratishedho.* [7] G. M. *vid-.* [8] G. M. ins. *api.* [9] G. M. ins. *shatvam.*

dhish ṭava (iv.2.3[2],11[3]). And for *nakiḥ*, *nakish ṭaṁ ghnanti* (ii.1.11[4]): *nakish ṭam* is found also at i.8.22[4].

The final specification of the rule, *nityam*, 'under all circumstances,' is explained as intended to assure the inclusion in the rule of the word *avidushṭarâsaḥ* (i.1.14[4]), already quoted, which would otherwise be liable to exclusion by the operation of rules 8 and 9, below. The word *viduḥ* itself, we are told, is all right, because of its specific mention in the text, but a little additional force is needed to bring in *aviduḥ* as its hanger-on. The explanation is by no means of the most satisfactory character, but I have nothing to suggest in its place. We have already once (see note to iii.8) had a case arising under i.52 treated as demanding a special handling

अथ न ॥ ६ ॥

6. Now for exceptions.

An introductory heading, of force in the rules that follow (through rule 13).

अवर्णव्यञ्जनशकुनिपत्न्यृतुमृत्युमलिम्लुबृहस्पतिपूर्वः ॥ ७ ॥

7. Excepted is a *s* preceded by an *a*-vowel, a consonant, *çakuni*, *patnî*, *ṛtu*, *mṛtyu*, *malimlu*, or *bṛhaspati*.

The bearing of the first two items of this rule on those which precede it has been noticed under rule 2. The commentator's examples are, for a preceding *a*-vowel, *antarikshasad dhotâ* (i.8.15[2] et al.: only G. M. have the second word) and *â siñcasva* (i.4.19: but G. M. omit the passage), of which one falls as an exception under rule 2, the other under rule 4; and, for a preceding consonant, *ṛksâme vâi* (vi.1.3[1]). Then, for the words specified, we have *çakunisâdena* (v.7.14), *patnîsaṁyâjânâm* (ii.6.10[4]: G. M. read *-yâjâḥ*, which is found twice in the same division of the same section, but not elsewhere), *ṛtusthâs tasya* (v.7.6[6]: the same compound is found at v.5.8[1]), *mṛtyusaṁyuta iva* (i.5.9[4]: only G. M. have *iva*), *nâi*

---

6. *athe 'ty ayam adhikâraḥ: ne 'ty etad[1] adhikṛtaṁ veditavyam ita uttaraṁ yad vakshyâmaḥ[2].*

[1] G. M. om. [2] W. *vadayâmaḥ.*

7. *avarṇapûrvo vyañjanapûrvaç ca çakuni.... bṛhaspati: ity[1] evampûrvaç ca[2] sakâraḥ shakâraṁ[3] nâ "padyate. yathâ: ant-....: avagrahapûrvatvât [4] prâptiḥ: [5]â siñ-....: upasargapûrvatvât prâptiḥ[5]: ṛk-....: çak-....: patn-....: ṛtu-....: mṛt-....: nâi....: bṛh-....: [6]avagrahapûrvatvâd eshâm prâptiḥ[6].*

[1] O. om. [2] G. M. om. [3] G. M. *shatvam.* [4] G. M. ins. *eshâm.* [(5)] G. M. om. [(6)] G. M. om.; W. adds *sa visrasyaḥ: avagrahapûrvatvât prâptiḥ.*

'ṅam malimlusenâ vindati (vi.3.2[6]: only G. M. have the first two and the last words), and *bṛhaspatisutasya te* (i.4.27 and vi.5.8[3]); all of which, as the commentator points out, are cases falling under the last specification of rule 2, respecting the conversion of initial *s* of the latter member of a compound.

ऋकाररेफवति ॥ ८ ॥

8. Also in a word containing *ṛ* or *r*.

The commentator gives one example of each case, the former constituting an exception under rule 4, the latter under the last specification of rule 2: *vi srjate çântyâi* (i.7.6[7]), and *tasmât sa visrasyaḥ* (vi.2.9[4],10[7]: only G. M. have *tasmât*).

Of other words falling under this rule, I have noted *parisrutam* (i.8.21), *visarjanam* (i.1.5[2]), *bahusûvarî* (iii.1.11[4]), and *gosatram* (vii.5.1[1]). Compare the nearly corresponding rules of the other treatises, Rik Pr. v.11, Vâj. Pr. iii.81, Ath. Pr. ii.102,106.

अवग्रहः ॥ ९ ॥

9. Also in the former member of a compound.

We should expect the word *avagraha* in this rule to be put in the locative case, so as to accord in construction with the preceding rule; and I have translated it as a locative. Its being a nominative makes the commentator some trouble: he declares *avagraha* here equivalent to *avagrahastha*, 'standing in *avagraha*,' and quotes as corresponding and customary expressions "the stages cry out," "the fat one knows," where "those occupying the stages," "the soul inhabiting a fat body," are really meant.

The occasion for such a precept as this arises out of rule 4, above, which provides for the conversion into *sh* of the initial *s* of a word wholly *anudâtta*, after a preposition. It was aimed, as is there pointed out, at unaccented verbal forms. But the former members of compounds which are accented on the latter member

---

8. *ṛkâraç ca rephaç ca ṛkârarephâu: tâv asmint sta ity ṛkârarephavat: tasmin pade vartamânaḥ sakâraḥ shakâraṁ*[1] *nâ "padyate. yathâ*[2]*: vi-----:* [3]*upasargapûrvatvât prâptiḥ*[3]*: tasm-----:* [4]*avagrahapûrvatvât prâptiḥ*[4].

[1] G. M. *shatvaṁ.* [2] G. M. om. [(3)] W. B. O. om. [(4)] W. om.

9. *avagrahasthaḥ sakâraḥ shakâraṁ*[1] *nâ "padyate: upasargapûrvaç*[2] *ca*[3]*: avagraha ity avagrahastho*[4] *lakshyate*[5]*: mañcâḥ kroçantî 'ty atra* [6] *mañcasthâḥ:* [7] *sthûlo jânâtî 'ti*[8] *sthûladehasthaḥ. udâharaṇâni: tasy-----: mukh-----.*

[1] G. M. *shatvaṁ.* [2] W. *-va;* G. M. *visarjanîyaç.* [3] W. *sat.* [4] G. M. change place with *avagraha.* [5] B. O. *labhy-.* [6] G. M. ins. *yathâ.* [7] G. M. ins. *yathâ.* [8] B. O. om. *iti.*

would also come under the rule, as being *anudâtta* throughout, and also entitled to the designation *pada*, 'word,' equally with completely independent vocables: hence the necessity of providing for their exclusion from its action. The commentator illustrates with a couple of examples: *tásyâṁ devâ' ádhi saṁvấsantaḥ* (iii.5.1[1]), and *múkhaṁ yajñâ'nâm abhí saṁvidấné* (v.1.11[2]: only G. M. have the first word). W. B. O. introduce a third, between the other two, namely *abhí sám agachanté 'ti* (ii.5.3[7]); but, as is shown by the accentuation and division, it does not fall under either the fourth rule or this, and has evidently come in by somebody's blunder.

It is very possible that the Sanhitâ contains other cases requiring the application of this rule; but if so, they have escaped my notice.

सवस्थानम् ॥ १० ॥

10. Also in *sava* and *sthânam*.

The cited passages are *agnisavaç cityaḥ* (v.6.1[5]), *anusavanam puroḍâçân* (vi.5.11[4] and vii.5.6[4]), *savanesavane 'bhi gṛhṇâti* (vi.4.11[4]; 6.11[3]), *prasavâya sâvitraḥ* (vi.6.5[2]: G. M. omit the last word; and the whole example is a blunder, since there is nowhere a rule requiring the lingualization of the sibilant in *prasavâya*), and *gacha gosthânam* (i.1.9[1,2]).

The word *sthânam* being cited with its special case-ending, the rule would not apply to such forms as *sthânaḥ*, *sthânî*, which in fact occur in the compound *pratishṭhâna* (e. g. i.7.6[6]: ii.4.4[1]), with their sibilant converted to *sh*. *Sava*, however, having no case-ending, falls under rule i.22, and is employed as "part of a word, in order to the inclusion of a variety of cases," as the comment duly points out, and as his selected examples illustrate.

न धिपूर्वे ॥ ११ ॥

11. But not when *dhi* precedes.

The examples are *adhishavaṇam asi* (i.1.5[2]: W. omits this example), *adhishavaṇe jihvâ* (vi.2.11[4]), and *adhishṭhânam âram-*

---

10. *sava: sthânam: ity[1] etayoḥ sakâraḥ shakâraṁ[2] nâ "padyate. save 'ti padâikadeço bahûpâdânârthaḥ[3]. agn-....: anus-....: sav-....: pras-....: gacha....*

[1] G. M. om. [2] G. M. *shatvaṁ*. [3] B. *bahûnâṁ padânâm arthaḥ.*

11. *sava: sthânam: ity ayoḥ[1] sakâre[2] dhipûrve[3] nishedho na prasarati. yathâ: adh-....: adh-....: adh-.... dhî 'ty ayaṁ varṇaḥ[4] pûrvo yasmâd asâu dhipûrvaḥ: tasmin.*

[1] B. G. M. *etayoḥ*. [2] G. M. *sakârasya pûrva*. [3] G. M. put first. [4] W. om.

bhaṇam (iv.6.2[4]). There are no other words illustrating the rule, although *adhishavaṇa* occurs in one or two other passages.

Considering that an appended specification constituting a rule often applies only to the last word given in the preceding rule (e. g. iv.13,16), it might well enough have seemed advisable to the authors of the Prâtiçâkhya to read here *dhipûrvayoḥ*, in the dual, instead of *dhipûrve.*

संतानेभ्यःसप्ताभिःसंमिताꣳस्तनाꣳसीतꣳस्पशःसक्सनि-
सनिःसनीःसभेयःसत्त्वासस्यायै ॥ १२ ॥

12. Also in *saṁtânebhyaḥ, saptâbhiḥ, sammitâm, stanâm, sîtam, spaçaḥ, sak, sani, saniḥ, sanîḥ, sabheyaḥ, sattvâ,* and *sasyâyâi.*

The examples, as quoted by the commentator, are as follows. For *saṁtânebhyaḥ, parisaṁtânebhyaḥ svâhâ* (vii.4.21). For *saptâbhiḥ, trisaptâbhiḥ paçukâmasya* (v.2.6[2]: G. M. have only the first word). For *sammitâm, vedisammitâm minoti* (v.6.8[2]). For *stanâm, dvistanâṁ karoti* (v.1.6[4]). For *sîtam, anusîtaṁ vapati* (v.2.5[5]). For *spaçaḥ, tanûpânaḥ pratispaçaḥ* (v.7.3[1]). *Sak* is declared a part of a word, implying a variety of forms: for example, *paççât pṛçnisaktho bhavati* (ii.1.3[3]), *pṛçnisakthâs trayo hâimantikâḥ* (v.6.23: G. M. omit the last word), *pṛçnisaktham â labheta grâmakâmaḥ* (ii.1.3[2]: G. M. O. omit the last word), and *pṛçnisakthâya svâhâ* (vii.3.18): I have noted no other cases, and should regard *saktha* as (by i.22) the preferable form for the *grahaṇa* in the rule. For *sani, tasmâd etad gosani* (vii.5.2[2]); for *saniḥ, asi stanayitnusanir asi* (iv.4.6[2]: G. M. omit the first word); for *sanîḥ, vṛshṭisanîr upa dadhâti* (v.3.1[3],10[1]): *gosaniḥ* is found also at iii.2.5[7], and *vṛshṭisaniḥ* at iv.4.6[2]. As it would satisfy all these cases to cite *san* alone, in the character of part of a word (like *sak*, above), the commentator inquires why that was not done, and the citation of whole words avoided; and he brings up in reply *mṛdhâ vâ esho 'bhishaṇṇo yasmât samâneshv anyaḥ çreyân uta* (ii.4.2[3]: all but W. stop at *-shaṇṇo*), and *nishaṇṇâya svâhâ*

---

12. ------ *eteshu*[1] *sakâraḥ shakâraṁ*[2] *nâ "padyate. yathâ: pari-----: tri-----: vedi-----: dvi-----: anu-----: tan-----: sag iti padâikadeço bahûpâdânârthaḥ: yathâ paçc-----: pṛç-----: pṛç-----: pṛç-----: tas-----: asi---. vṛsh-----:* [3]*sann ity*[3] *etâvatâi 'va*[4] *siddhe kim akhilapadarahaṇena*[5]*: mṛdhâ-----: nish-----: ty âdâu mâ bhûd iti: sus-----: abhis-----: sus-----.* [6]*sattvâsaṁtânebhya ity etayor upasargapûrvatvât prâptiḥ:*[6] [7]*sarveshâṁ*[8] *anyeshâm avagrahapûrvatvât prâptiḥ*[7].

[1] G. M. *eshu.* [2] G. M. *shatvaṁ.* (3) W. B. O. *san ity;* G. M. *sanî 'ty.* [4] G. M. om. *eva.* [5] G. M. om. *pada.* (6) W. *satvâsasyâyâ ity ayor upasargâvagrahapûrv-;* B. O. *saṁtânebhyaḥ svâhâ: ity etayor up-.* (7) W. om. [8] G. M. om.

(vii.1.19[1]), as examples of the alteration of *san*. *Sani* would not cover all the cases; and the treatise makes no provision for the citation of a theme ending in *i*, or any other vowel than *a*, as representative of all the forms derived from that theme. For *sabheyaḥ* is quoted *susabheyo ya evam* (vii.1.8[1]: G. M. omit *evam*). For *sattvâ*, *abhisattvâ sahojâḥ* (iv.6.4[2]: all the MSS. read everywhere, in text, commentary, and Sanhitâ, *satvâ*). And for *sasyâyâi*, *susasyâyâi supippalâbhyaḥ* (i.2.2[3]).

All these are exceptions under rule 2, being cases of compounds whose second member begins with *s*, after a vowel other than an *a*-vowel. The commentary tries (with much discordance between the different manuscripts: see the various readings below) to claim two of them as exceptions under rule 4; but there is no ground for so doing.

न स्वरस्पर्धास्तरीमसाहस्रसारथिस्फुरन्तीस्तुब्ज्योतिरायुश्चतुःपूर्वस्तो ॥ १३ ॥

13. But not in *svara*, *spardhâḥ*, *starîma*, *sâhasra*, *sârathiḥ*, *sphurantî*, *stubh*, and in *sto* when preceded by *jyotiḥ*, *âyuḥ*, or *catuḥ*.

Of these words, the first six constitute counter-exceptions under rule 8, which excepted words containing *ṛ* or *r* from the conversion of their initial *s* into *sh*. The examples, as quoted by the commentator, are as follows: *amba ni shvara* (i.4.1[2] and vi.4.4[3]); *vi shpardhâç chandaḥ* (iv.3.12[3])—these two, it is noted, are cases under rule 4, of unaccented verbal forms after a preposition—*sushṭarîmâ jushâṇâ* (v.1.11[2]); *dvishâhasraṁ cinvîta* (v.6.8[2]: G. M. omit *cinvîta*), and *trishâhasro vâ asâu lokaḥ* (v.6.8[3]: G. M. omit after *vâi*)—both forms are, we are made to observe, included in the citation of *sâhasra* by its theme-ending *a*, according to rule i.22: other forms do not occur in the Sanhitâ, nor these elsewhere than in the two divisions quoted from—*kâmayate sushârathiḥ* (iv.6.6[2]); and *vishphurantî amitrân* (iv.6.6[2]).

The next case is a very anomalous one, being the conversion of *s* into *sh* after *a*, contrary to the first specification of rule 7. The phrase is *sashṭup chandaḥ* (iv.3.12[2]; p. *sa-stup*). Compare similar cases as noted in Ath. Pr. ii.95.

The combination of *sto* with the three words mentioned, although

---

13. ...... *stup: ity eteshu sakâraḥ: jyotiḥ: âyuḥ: catuḥ: evampûrvaç ca*[1] *sto ity atra sakâra ṛkârarephavati* (vi.8)*: avarṇavyañjana* (iv.7) [2]*iti co 'ktaṁ*[2] *nishedhaṁ nâ "padyate: kiṁ tu shatvaṁ pratipadyate: iti pratiprasavârtho 'yaṁ nakâraḥ. yathâ: amba....: vi sh-....: upasargapûrvatvâd anayoḥ prâptiḥ: susht-....: grahaṇasya ca*[3] (i.22) *iti vacanâd akâragṛhîtaṁ* [4]*sâhasragrahaṇam anekârtham: yathâ*[4]*: dvish-....:*

not quite regular, has nothing strange in it. The final *visarjanîya* of the first member of the compound is lost by ix.1, and the sibilant is treated as it would be had no *ḥ* been present. The examples are *jyotishṭomam prathamam* (vii.4.10[1],11[1]), *âyushṭomaṁ tṛtîyam* (vii.4.11[1]), and *catushṭomo abhavat* (iv.3.11[2]): *jyotishṭoma* and *catushṭoma* occur in a number of other passages, which it is not worth while here to rehearse. The exception this time is to the second specification of rule 7, according to which the consonant *ḥ* at the end of the former member of the compound would prevent the lingualization of the sibilant. Of course, according to the theory of the Prâtiçâkhya (by v.3), the lingualization is first performed, giving *jyotiḥshṭoma* etc., and then, by ix.1, the *visarjanîya* disappears, making *jyotishṭoma*, as all the manuscripts, of comment and Sanhitâ, constantly read.

The commentator remarks the fact that, from *starîma* on, the cases are such as fall under the last specification of the second rule of this chapter. He then adds, as counter-examples under *sto*, *yad akshṇayâstomîyâḥ* (v.3.3[1]), *catustanâṁ karoti* (v.1.6[4]), and *jyotis tv 'â asya* (ii.2.4[8]: but G. M. omit this example).

There are a few other words which we might expect to see included among those forming the subject of this rule. Such is *barhishad* (iv.6.1[4] et al.), i. e. *barhiḥ-sad:* but the Rik and Atharvan *pada*-texts adopt the omission of the final *ḥ* as part of their own reading, and the Tâittirîya (p. *barhi-sad*) does the same, so that the irregularity of the word lies outside the Prâtiçâkhya. Such, again, are *dushṭara* (iv.4.12[2]) and *dushṭarîtu* (iv.4.12[1]), provided that, as seems to me probable (compare note to Ath. Pr. ii.85), they are regarded as compounds of *duḥ* with *stara* and *starîtu.* But these words are written by the *pada*-texts of the other Vedas *dustara* and *dustarîtu*, and the *pada*-text of the Tâittirîya-Sanhitâ reads *dushṭara* and *dushṭarîtu*, so that there is no reason for their peculiar phonetic form being noticed by the Prâtiçâkhya. Once more, *trishshamṛddhatvâya* (ii.4.11[5]) would call for inclusion here, but that the addition of the suffix *tva* at its end annuls the separation which would otherwise be made of the first element of the compound, *triḥ*, and the word stands in *pada*-text *trishshamṛddha-tvâya*, and so does not require alteration in *saṁhitâ*.

तर्कांꣳस्तस्मिंलोकान्विद्वांꣳस्तांꣳस्त्रीन्युष्मानूर्ध्वानम्बका-नॄतॄनश्मन्कृण्वन्पितॄननान्कपालांꣳस्तिष्ठन्नाव्युदात्तेनेमि-

---

trish-....: kâm-....: vish-....: sash-....: jyot-....: ây-....: cat-....: starîmâdînâm eshâm avagrahapûrvatvât prâptiḥ: jyotirâdipûrvatvena kim: yad-....: sto iti kim: cat-....: jyot-....

[1] G. M. om. [(2)] G. M. *ity âdi.* [3] W. B. om. [(4)] W. B. O. om.

देवान्त्सवनेपशूंस्तकारपरः सकारं प्राकृतो नित्ये प्राकृतो नित्ये ॥ १४ ॥

14. In *tarhân*, *tasmin*, *lokân*, *vidvân*, *tân*, *trîn*, *yushmân*, *ûrdhvân*, *ambakân*, *ṛtûn*, *açman*, *kṛṇvan*, *pitṝn*, *anân*, *kapâlân*, *tish'han* when accented on the first syllable, *nemir devân*, and *savane paçûn*, an original *n*, followed by a *t*, becomes *s*, when the *t* is a constant one.

There seems to be no particular reason why this rule is introduced here, instead of anywhere else in the work, as it has no relation with the rest of the contents of the chapter. It is a complete rehearsal of the cases in which the old *s*, with which most Sanskrit words in *n* originally ended, is retained under the protection of a following initial *t*. The combination, of course, is historically identical with that of *n c* into *ñçc*, treated of in the preceding chapter (v.20: see the note upon that rule). The "conversion" of *n* into *s*, as the treatise chooses to state the case, involves, by xv.1–3, the prefixion of *anusvâra* to the sibilant.

The examples quoted by the commentator are as follows. For *tarhân*, *çatatarhâñs tṛṇhanti* (i.5.7^{6} and v.4.7^{4}). For *tasmin*, *tasmiñs tvâ dadhâmi* (i.6.5^{1}; 7.5^{1}). For *lokân*, *imân eva lokâñs tîrtvâ* (iii.5.4^{3}): there is another case of *lokâñs* at ii.3.6^{1}. For *vidvân*, *ya evaṁ vidvâñs trâidhâtavîyena yajate* (ii.4.11^{4}: G. M. stop with *-yena*: the Tâittirîya-Sanhitâ has *paçukâmo* before *yajate*, which W. B. O. have doubtless dropped out by an oversight). For *tân*, *kaksheshv aghâyavas tâñs te dadhâmi jambhayoḥ* (iv.1.10^{3}: only G. M. have the first two words, and they omit the last one): *tâñs* is also found at ii.4.11^{4}: iii.1.9^{5}: iv.1.10^{2} twice: vi.3.1^{4} twice; 4.10^{3,4}. For *trîn*, *trîñs tṛcân anu* (ii.5.10^{1}). For *yushmân*, *yushmâñs te 'nu* (iii.2.5^{6}): we find *yushmâñs* again at vii.1.5^{2}. For *ûrdhvân*, *yân ûrdhvâñs tân upabdimataḥ* (iii.1.9^{1}: only G. M. have the first word). For *ambakân*, *tryambakâñs tṛtîyasavanam akurvata* (iii.2.2^{3}: G. M. omit the last word). For *ṛtûn*, *ṛtûñs tanvate kavayaḥ prajânatîḥ* (iv.3.11^{3}: G. M. omit after *tanvate*). For *açman*, *açmañs te kshut* (iv.6.1^{1} and v.4.4^{1}). For *kṛṇvan*, *punaḥ kṛṇvañs tvâ pitaraṁ yuvânam* (iv.7.13^{5}: only W. has the last word). For *pitṝn*, *oja iti pitṝñs tantur iti* (v.3.6^{1}:

---

14. ------ *âdyudâtte tishṭhangrahaṇe------ eshu*[1] *grahaṇeshu prâkṛto nakâraḥ padasamaye*[2] *vartamânas takâraparaḥ sakâram âpadyate. yathâ: çat----: tasm----: imân----: ya----: kaksh----: trîñs----: yush----: yân----: tryam----: ṛt----: açm----: punaḥ----: oja----: prâṇ----: api vikṛtam* (i.51) *iti vacanâd etad bhavati: dvâd----: tribh----: âdyudâtta iti kim: na----: apy akârâdi* (i.52) *iti prâptiḥ: nem----: nemir iti kim: jât----: mâdh----: savana iti kim:*

only G. M. have the first two words). For *anân*, *prаṇâṅs tasyâ 'ntar yanti* (vii.1.3[1]; p. *pra-anân*): here rule i.51 is invoked to show that the lingualized *n* does not render the citation inoperative. For *kapâlân*, *dvâdaçakapâlâṅs tṛtîyasavane* (vii.5.6[4]). For *tíshṭhan*, *tribhis tishṭhaṅs tishṭhati* (v.4.12[1]): as counter-example, proving the necessity of the requirement as to accent, we have *na praty atishṭhan tâ vasuko 'si* (v.3.6[3]: G. M. omit *na*), which would fall under the operation of the present rule by i.52. For *nemir devân*, *nemir devâṅs tvam paribhûr asi* (ii.5.9[3]: G. M. omit *asi*); with the counter-example *jâtavedo vapayâ gacha devân tvaṅ hi* (iii.1.4[4]: G. M. omit the first word), to show that *devân* is so treated only after *nemiḥ*. For *savane paçûn*, *mâdhyandine savane paçûṅs tṛtîyasavane* (iii.2.9[2]: G. M. omit the first word); with the counter-example *prajâm paçûn tenâ 'vardhata* (vii.4.3[2]), to prove the need of *savane* in the rule. Then, as general counter-example, to bring out the fact that *n* is thus converted into *s* only before *t*, we have *tasmin prajâpatir vâyuḥ* (vii.1.5[1]): G. M. add also *lokân dravinâvataḥ* (v.3.11[2]). And finally, the commentator proceeds to explain and illustrate the limitations "an original (*prâkṛta*) *n*" and "a constant (*nitya*) *t*," given in the rule. An original *n* is one which is not the product of euphonic processes, but is read in the *pada*-text: in *tâṁ tena çamayati* (v.7.3[3]), then, where the *ṁ* represents a *n*, produced by the assimilation of *m* to the following *t* (by v.27), the rule has no force. A constant *t*, in like manner, is one which is found in all forms of the text, and not in *saṁhitâ* alone: hence, in *vidânt somena yajate* (iii.2.2[3]), the *t* which is introduced (by v.33) between *n* and *s* does not cause the conversion of the *n* into *s*. The *t* in this case, to be sure, is (by xiv.12) to be turned into *th* (and is so written in the citation by W. G. M.); but, as the rules of the treatise (by v.3) have to be applied in their order, the danger of misapprehension upon the point in question requires to be guarded against: for a *t* inserted by authority of the fifth chapter might assibilate a nasal according to the sixth, before it was itself turned into an innocuous *th* by the fourteenth.

The cases in which the insertion of *s* between *n* and *t* is made in the Tâittirîya-Sanhitâ are thus seen to number only thirty-one. On the other hand, the cases of the collision of *n* and *t* without interposition of *s* are very numerous: I have noted about two hundred

---

praj-____: takârapara iti [2]*kim: tasmin____: lokân____: prâkṛta iti kim: tâṁ____: vâikṛto*[4] *'yaṁ nakâro* [5] *makâra sparçaparaḥ* (v.27) *iti prâptatvât: nitye takâra*[6] *iti kim*[3]*: vidv-____: anityo 'yam nakâro yataḥ padasamaye nâ 'sti.*
takâraḥ paro yasmâd asâu tathoktaḥ[7].

iti tribhâshyaratne prâtiçâkhyavivaraṇe
shashṭho 'dhyâyaḥ.

[1] B. O. *eteshu.* [2] G. M. *nitye pade.* [(3)] B. om. [4] G. M. *aprâkṛto.* [5] G. M. ins. *yataḥ padasamaye nâ 'sti.* [6] G. M. om. [7] G. M. *takâraparaḥ.*

and eighty, and presume that I may have overlooked here and there others, so that there would be in all ten times as many instances of the omission as of the insertion. In the Atharva-Veda (see second marginal note to Ath. Pr. ii.26) the condition of things is quite different: while the whole number of collisions is much less (only ninety-five), the sibilant is introduced in considerably more than two-thirds of them (in sixty-seven cases, against twenty-eight). The comparison is of some interest in its bearing upon the question of the relative age of the two texts.

CHAPTER VII.

CONTENTS: 1–12, cases of the conversion of *n* into *ṇ*; 13–14, of *t* and *th* into *ṭ* and *ṭh*; 15–16, exceptions to the conversion of *n* into *ṇ*.

अथ नकारो णकारम् ॥ १ ॥

1. Now for conversion of *n* into *ṇ*.

An introductory heading, stating the subject of the chapter (with the exception of rules 13 and 14). We have treated here all the cases with which the Prâtiçâkhya has properly to deal, as arising in the process of conversion of *pada*-text into *saṁhitâ:* chapter thirteen (rule 6 seq.) takes up the occurrence of *ṇ* in a different way, determining every instance in which that letter is found in the whole Sanhitâ.

षुषूकृधिसुवःसमिन्द्रास्थूर्युरुवाःषट्त्रिग्रामनिष्पूर्वः ॥ २ ॥

2. *N* becomes *ṇ* when preceded by *shu*, *shû*, *kṛdhi suvaḥ*, *sam indra*, *asthûri*, *uru*, *vâḥ*, *shaṭ*, *tri*, *grâma*, or *niḥ*.

The commentator's illustrative examples are as follows. For *shu*, *ûrdhva û shu ṇaḥ* (iv.1.4² and v.1.5³: O. omits the first word); and, as counter-example, *gṛheshu naḥ* (ii.4.5¹), where *shu*, not being a complete word, does not (by i.50) lingualize the nasal: but G. M. omit this passage and the accompanying explanation. For *shû*, *mo shû ṇa indra* (i.8.3). The commentator points out

---

1. *athe 'ty ayam adhikâraḥ: nakâro ṇakâram âpadyata ity etad adhikṛtaṁ veditavyam ita uttaraṁ yad vakshyâmaḥ.*

2. ...... *evampûrvo nakâro ṇakâram âpadyate. yathâ*[1]*: ûrdh-....: *[2]*gṛh-.... ity atra ṇatvaṁ na bhavati padagrahaṇeshv* (i.50) *iti vacanât:*[2] *mo....: susû*[3] *ity etayor yadâ shatvaṁ nâ 'sti tadâ ṇatvanishedhârthaṁ vâikṛtagrahaṇam: ya-*

that *shu* and *shû* are cited in the rule in their altered form (not as *su* simply, which, by i.51, would include them both) in order to indicate that where their consonant is not lingualized they do not lingualize the following nasal; and he quotes in illustration *su na ûtaye* (iv.1.4[2]) and *sû na indra* (i.8.3). Both these passages are the same which have been already quoted to illustrate the conversion, and G. M. O. very properly put them into the form of another text (apparently a *krama*), reading *su naḥ: na ûtaye*, and *sû naḥ: na indra*. *Shu* converts *n* to *ṇ* also at iv.6.5[6]. For *kṛdhi suvaḥ*, the passage is *brahmaṇâ kṛdhi suvar ṇa çukram* (ii.2.12[6]: O. omits the first word: the Calcutta edition has the false reading *na*); and the necessity of *kṛdhi* is shown by the counter-example *svâhâ suvar nâ 'rkaḥ svâhâ* (v.7.5[2]: O. omits the first word). For *sam indra*, *sam indra ṇo manasâ* (i.4.44[1]); and *vartaye 'ndra nardabuda* (iii.3.10[1]) shows that *indra* when not preceded by *sam* does not exercise the prescribed influence. For *asthûri*, *asthûri ṇo gârhapatyâni santu* (v.7.2[1]: only O. has *santu*). For *uru*, *uru ṇas kṛdhi* (ii.6.11[3] and vi.3.2[2]): there is another like case at iv.7. 14[2]. For *vâḥ*, *tasmâd vâr ṇâma vo hitam* (v.6.1[3]: G. M. omit the last two words). For *shaṭ*, *shaṇṇavatyâi svâhâ* (vii.2.15). For *tri*, *triṇava stomo vasûnâm* (iv.3.9[1]: G. M. O. omit the last word): the word *triṇava* is found in a considerable number of other passages. For *grâma*, W. B. give *grâmaṇî râjanyaḥ* (ii.5. 4[4]), but G. M. O. have instead *grâmaṇîyam prâ "pnuvanti* (vii.4. 5[2]): the word is found once more, at iv.4.3[1]. For *niḥ*, *nir ṇenijati tato 'dhi* (vii.2.10[2]: G. M. omit the last two words); and *ni no rayim* (ii.2.12[8]) is added, to show that *ni*, without *visarjanîya*, has no alterant force. *Nir ṇenikte* (vii.2.10[4]) and *nirṇij* (iv.6.8[1]) are the only other cases I have noted for *niḥ*.

हन्यादुप्यमानं च ॥ ३ ॥

3. Also in *hanyât* and *upyamânam*.

That is to say, after *niḥ*, the last of the words given in the preceding rule. The passages are: *yoner garbhaṁ nir haṇyat* (v.6.9[1]:

---

thâ: su----: sû----: brah----: kṛdhî 'ti kim: svâhâ----: sam----: sam iti kim: vart----: asth----: uru----: tasmâd----: shaṇ----: tri----: grâm----: nir----: visargeṇa kim: ni----.

[1] G. M. om. [(2)] G. M. om. [3] O. *shushû*.

3. *cakâro nishpûrvatvam anvâdiçati: niḥçabdottarayor*[1] *hanyâd upyamânam ity etayor grahaṇayor*[2] *nakâro ṇakâram*[3] *âpadyate. yathâ*[4]: *yon----: nir----. anvâdeçaḥ kimarthaḥ: na ----*

[1] G. M. *-bdasyo 'tt-*; O. *nishpûrvayor*. [2] G. M. om. [3] W. *ṇakâtvam*; B. *ṇatvam*. [4] G. M. om.

O. omits the first word), and *nirupyamâṇaṁ abhi mantrayeta* (i.6.8[3]: O. omits the last word). A counter-example, showing *hanyât* without altered *n*, is *na ni hanyân na lohitaṁ kuryât* (ii.6.10[2]).

पारीपरिपरीप्रपूर्वः ॥ ४ ॥

4. Also after *pârî*, *pari*, *parï*, and *pra*.

The illustrative citations of the commentator are *pârîṇahyasye ''çe* (vi.2.1[1]), *pari ṇo rudrasya* (iv.5.10[4]), *vîravantam parîṇasam* (ii.2.12[6]), and *pra ṇo devî sarasvatî* (i.8.22[1]: O. omits the last word). For *pârî* (p. *pâri-nahyasya:* compare iii.7) there is no other case; nor for *parî* (p. *pari-nasam:* compare iii.7); for *pari*, I find only *pari ṇayati* (ii.3.4[3] et al.). But for *pra* the examples are quite numerous: we have *pra ṇaḥ* at i.5.11[4]; 6.4[3]; 7.10[2] twice: ii.5.12[1]: iii.1.11[2]; 3.11[4]: iv.2.6[5]: v.5.7[5]: vii.4.19[4]; *pra ṇâmâni* at iv.3.13[6]; forms of *pra ṇayâmi* at i.6.8[1] et al., of *pra ṇude* at ii.1.3[5] et al.; *praṇinâya* at i.3.5; *praṇîyamânaḥ* at iv.4.9[1]; *pra ṇenekti* at vi.2.9[1]; *praṇî* at ii.5.9[2], *praṇîti* at i.4.18 and *supraṇîti* (but p. *su-praṇîti*) at i.5.11[5] et al., *praṇetar* at iii.5.11[3], and *praṇava* at iii.2.9[6]. *Parâṇutti* occurs only in composition (vi.2.3[2]; p. *bhrâtṛvya-parâṇuttyâi*).

अवर्णव्यवेतो ऽपि ॥ ५ ॥

5. And that, even when an *a*-vowel intervenes.

The word "even" (*api*) here brings down by implication, according to the commentator, the words in the preceding rule from *pari* on—that is to say, virtually, *pari* and *pra*, for there is no case of *parî* exercising such an effect. The examples for *pari* are *agram pary aṇayat* (ii.3.4[3]: all but O. omit *agram:* I find besides only *pary aṇayan*, at vi.5.7[2]), and *paryâṇîyâ ''havanîyasya* (vii.1.6[6]). For *pra*, we have *prâṇâya svâhâ* (vii.1.19[1]; p. *pra-anâya*), and *anu prâ 'ṇyât prathamâm* (v.5.5[2]; p. *pre 'ti: anyât:* only O. has *anu*). The occurrence of *prâṇa* is very frequent: of other cases, I have noted only *prâ 'ṇudata* at vi.2.3[2], and *prâ 'ṇudanta* at vi.4.10[3-4]—where, however, the lingualization of the *n* is suspended in our text, as at present constituted, by the intervention

---

4. ------ *evampûrvo nakâro ṇakâram âpadyate. yathâ*[1]*: pâr-*----*: pari*----*: vîr-*----*: pra*----.

[1] G. M. O. om.

5. *apiçabdaḥ paryâdy*[1] *anvâdiçati*[2]*: paryâdipûrvo*[3] *nakâro avarṇavyaveto 'pi ṇatvam bhajate*[4]*. yathâ*[5]*: agram*----*: pary-*----*: prâṇ-*----*: anu*----. *avarṇavyaveta iti kim: pari*----*: pra*----.

[1] B. *pâr-*. [2] G. M. O. *-âdeçakaḥ*. [3] B. *pâr-*. [4] G. M. *âpadyate*. [5] G. M. O. om.

between the preposition and the verb of the pause which separates the third and fourth divisions of the section.

A couple of counter-examples are given, to show us that the intervention of a letter of any other complexion than *a* prevents the change of nasal: they are *pari minuyât sapta* (v.2.6[3]: G. M. omit the last word), and *praminâma vratâni* (i.1.14[4]).

वाहनउह्यमानोयानमयन्यवेनवश्च ॥ ६ ॥

6. Also in *vâhanaḥ, uhyamânaṇ, yânam, ayan, yavena,* and *van.*

According to W. B. O., the *n* becomes *ṇ* in these words "when they are preceded as implied by the word 'also' (*ca*)," the commentary failing to tell us what this implication is. G. M., however, confess that *pra* only is brought forward (from rule 4): which is a marked departure from the ordinary usage of the treatise, since in the intermediate rule *pra* and *pari* were both distinctly understood. The commentator omits, not to say avoids, noticing the irregularity. Perhaps he would be justified in claiming that *pari* and *parî* are never found preceding the words specified in the rule, and that therefore it makes no difference whether they be regarded as implied or not: still, even that consideration would not wholly excuse the want of accuracy and consistency. The examples are: for *vâhanaḥ, pravâhaṇo vahniḥ* (i.3.3; p. *pra-vâhanaḥ*); to this, W. adds a counter-example, to show that, after any other word than *pra*, *vâhanaḥ* remains unchanged—namely *havyavâhanaḥ çvâtro 'si* (i.3.3): B. tries to do the same, but only succeeds in repeating one of the counter-examples of the last rule, *pari minuyât* (v.2.6[3]), which is not at all in place here. For *uhyamânaḥ, prohyamâṇo 'dhipatiḥ* (iv.4.9: p. *pra-uhyamânaḥ*. For *yânam, prayâṇam anv anya id yayuḥ* (iv.1.1[2]; p. *pra-yânam:* O omits the last three words, G. M. the last two). *Ayan* is declared a part of a word, including a number of cases, of which G. M. give only three, *tasmâd âdityaḥ prâyaṇîyaḥ* (vi.1.5[1]; p. *pra-ayanîyaḥ:* O. omits *tasmât*), *prâyaṇîyaṁ kâryam* (vi.1.5[3,5]), and *prâyaṇam pratishṭhâm* (i.6.11[1]: p. *pra-ayanam*); while W. B. O. add two others, *prâyaṇîyasya puronuvâkyâḥ* (vi.1.5[5]), and *prâyaṇîye 'han* (vii.2.8[1]). There are a number of other passages for *prâyaṇîya;* and *prâyaṇa* occurs again at i.6.11[2] and vii.1.13, besides its compounds,

---

6. ------ *eteshu*[1] *grahaṇeshu cakârâkṛshṭapûrveshu*[2] *nakâro ṇatvam bhajate. yathâ: prav-----:* [3]*pre 'ti kim: havy-----:*[3] *proh-----: pray-----: ayann iti padâikadeço bahûpâdânârthaḥ: tasm-----: prây-----: prây-----:* [4]*prây-----: prây-----:*[4] *pray-----:* [5]*vann iti padâikadeço bahûpâdânârthaḥ*[5]*:* [6]*yadi-----:*[6] *âhav-----: anvâdeçena kim: asi-----: uday-----.*

[1] G. M. *eshu.* [2] G. M. *-shṭaprapûrvo.* [(3)] G. M. om; O. om. the example. [(4)] G. M. *ity âdi.* [(5)] G. M. O. B. om. [(6)] O. om.

suprâyaṇa (v.1.11[2]; p. *su-prâyaṇâḥ*) and *agnishṭomaprâyaṇa* (vii.2.9[1]; p. *agnishṭoma-prâyaṇâḥ*). For *yavena, prayaveṇa pañca* (iv.3.11[2]; p. *pra-yavena*). *Van*, again, is (by W. alone) declared a part of a word, intended to include many cases: only two are given, *yadi vâ tâvat pravaṇam* (ii.4.12[1]), and *âhavanîyât pravaṇaṅ syât* (vi.2.6[4]), nor have I found any other, except the compound *purastâtpravaṇaḥ* (v.3.1[5]; p. *purastât-pravaṇaḥ*). Finally, we have a couple of counter-examples, showing the necessity of the implication from the preceding rule: they are *asi havyavâhanaḥ* (i.3.3), and *udayanaṁ veda* (i.6.11[2]).

प्रापूर्वश्च ॥ ७ ॥

7. As also, when preceded by *prâ.*

The "also" (*ca*) of this rule brings forward from the preceding rule only the word last mentioned there, namely *van.* The example is *prâvaṇebhiḥ sajoshasaḥ* (iv.2.4[3]; p. *pra-vaṇebhiḥ:* compare iii.5). I have noted no other case.

इन्द्रोऽयजुःपूर्वं एनंकेन ॥ ८ ॥

8. Also *enam* and *kena,* when preceded respectively by *indraḥ* and *ayajuḥ.*

There is nothing in the rule meaning 'respectively,' and if *enam* were found anywhere in the text preceded by *ayajuḥ*, or *kena* by *indraḥ*, their *n*'s would doubtless require lingualization: yet the evident intent of the precept is as translated. The passages are *indra eṇam prathamaḥ* (iv.6.7[1]), and *yad ayajushkeṇa krîyate* (v.1.2[1]; p. *ayajuḥ-kena:* G. M. O. omit *yat*). I find no other cases falling under the rule: there are, however, one or two other forms, analogous with the latter of those here contemplated, which we might expect to find treated in the same way, namely *anâçîrkena* and *sâçîrkeṇa* (i.6.10[4]); but they are written by the *pada*-text without division of *âçîrkena*, or restoration in it of the dental *n* (thus: *anâçîrkeṇa*, and *sa-âçîrkeṇa*).

Counter-examples are added: to show that *enam* and *kena*, when otherwise preceded, retain their dental nasals, *rudra enam bhûtvâ* (iii.4.10[3]), and *brahmavâdinaḥ kena tad ajâmî 'ti* (vii.4.10[2]: G, M. O. end with *kena*); to show that *indraḥ* does not exercise a lin-

---

7. *cakârâkṛshṭe*[1] *vann iti grahaṇe nakâraḥ pre 'ty evampûrvo ṇatvam bhajate. yathâ*[2]: *p r â v-* . . . . .

[1] W. B. *-shṭa;* O. *cakâro 'nvâdishṭo.* [2] G. M. om.

8. *indraḥ: ayajuḥ: pûrvayor*[1] *enam: kena: ity etayor nakâro ṇatvam bhajate. yathâ*[2]: *i n d r a* . . . . : *y a d* . . . . . *evampûrva iti kim: r u d r a* . . . . : *b r a h-* . . . . : [3]*enaṁkene*[4] *'ti kim: i n d r o* . . . . .[3]

[1] G. M. O. *ity evampûrva.* [2] G. M. O. om. [(3)] W. om. [4] B. *kene.*

gualizing effect upon other words, *indro neshad ati* (v.7.2^3: B. omits *ati;* W. omits the whole example).

नृश्रीपूर्वो मनाः ॥ ९ ॥

9. Also *manâḥ*, when preceded by *nṛ* or *çrî*.

The examples are *nṛmaṇâ ajasram* (i.3.14^5 and iv.2.2^1: W. reads *yantrî* instead of *ajasram*, but doubtless by a copyist's blunder, for *nṛmaṇâ yantrî* is not found in the Sanhitâ), and *çrîmaṇâḥ çatapayâḥ* (iv.6.3^2); with the counter-example *sumanâ upâgahi* (iii.3.11^5). Of *çrîmaṇâḥ* I find no other example; *nṛmaṇâḥ* occurs also at iv.2.2^1 (a second time) and vii.1.12.

अङ्गानामोनेगानिगानांग्यानियामेन ॥ १० ॥

10. Also *an̄gânâm*, *one*, *gâni*, *gânâm*, *gyâni*, and *yâmena*.

These words in *saṁhitâ*, says the commentator: that is to say, in the only cases in which they occur as *padas*, they take *ṇ* in the combined text. The passages are: *yat tryan̄gâṇâṅ samavadyati* (vi.3.10^6; p. *tri-an̄gânâm:* only G. M. O. have *yat*, and O. omits the last word), *âyushi duroṇe* (i.2.14^3; p. *duḥ-one:* the *pada*-texts of the Rik and Atharvan do not separate this word), *ati durgâṇi viçvâ* (i.1.14^4; p. *duḥ-gâni*, like the other Vedas), *purogâṇâṁ cakshushe* (iii.2.4^4; p. *puraḥ-gânâm*), *suvargyâṇy âsan* (v.3.5^3; p. *suvaḥ-gyâni*), and *antaryâmeṇâ 'ntar adhatta* (vi.4.6^1; p. *antaḥ-yâmena:* O. omits the last word). I have found no second example for any of these words, although there may be occurrences of *duroṇe* which I have overlooked.

रषःपूर्वो हवन्यह्नेहन् ॥ ११ ॥

11. Also *havani*, *ahne*, *han*, when preceded by *r* or *shaḥ*.

The cited examples are: *agnihotrahavaṇî ca* (i.6.8^3; p. *agnihotra-havanî*); *çarady aparâhṇe* (ii.1.2^5; p. *apara-ahne:* the Atharvan has *apara-ahnaḥ*); and further, for *han*, which is declared to be a part of a word, involving several cases, *rakshohaṇam* (i.2.14^6 et al.; p. *rakshaḥ-hanam:* O. omits this example), *vâish-*

---

9. *nṛ: çrî: ity*[1] *evampûrvo manâ ity atra nakâro ṇatvam bhajate. yathâ*[2]*: nṛm-....: çrîm-..... evampûrva iti kim: sum-....*

[1] G. M. om. [2] G. M. om.

10. ...... *eteshu*[1] *nakâraḥ saṁhitâyâṁ ṇatvam bhajate. yathâ*[2]*: yat....: ây-....: ati....: puro-....: suv-....: antary-....*

[1] G. M. O. *eshu.* [2] W. G. M. O. om.

navî rakshohaṇâu (i.3.2[2]: G. M. omit the first word), and *vṛtra-haṇaṁ puraṁdaram* (iii.5.11[4] and iv.1.3[3]; p. *vṛtra-hanam*: G. M. omit the last word). For *han*, besides the compounds here quoted, which are found repeatedly in other passages, the Sanhitâ affords us also *avîrahaṇâu* (i.2.8[2]; p. *avîra-hanâu*); for the other two words I know of no additional examples. Counter-examples are given, namely *sâhna evâ 'smâi* (vi.6.11[4]; p. *sa-ahne*), and *valagahanaḥ* (i.3.2[1] et al.).

There is good ground for questioning the correctness of the commentator's interpretation of *ra* in the rule as signifying the letter *r* (*repha*), and not the syllable *ra*. In none of the examples given are the words specified directly preceded by *r*, and it is not at all in accordance with the usage of the treatise to describe as "having *r* before it" a word preceded by another word containing *r*. All the versions of the comment, however, unite in this interpretation, and it is farther assured by the quotation of the rule above, under i.19, as a case in which *r* is called *ra*, instead of *repha*. It looks as if G. M. had made a blundering attempt to remedy the difficulty by reading the third word *ahan* instead of *han*, and also by understanding *shaḥ* to mean 'the letter *sh*' (see the various readings, below), thus parallelizing the two specifications. The attempt, however, is an abortive one, only issuing, if carried out, in a host of new difficulties. I have made the translation of the rule conform to the requirements of the comment, but with much misgiving, having hardly a doubt that the meaning properly is 'when preceded by *ra* or *shaḥ*.'

रुपूर्वौ मयान्यनी ॥ १२ ॥

12. Also *mayâni* and *anî*, when preceded by *ru*.

The passages are *dârumayâṇi pâtrâṇi* (vi.4.7[3]; p. *dâru-mayâni*: O. omits *pâtrâṇi*; G. M. omit the whole example), and *tve vasûni purvaṇîka hotaḥ* (i.3.14[2-3]; p. *puru-anîka*: O. omits the first two words, G. M. the last): *purvaṇîka* is found also at

---

11. *havani*[1]: *ahne*: *han*[2]: *eshu*[3] *grahaṇeshu nakâro rephapûrvaḥ* [4]*sha ity*[4] *evampûrvo*[5] *vâ ṇatvam bhajate. yathâ: agnih-----: çar-----: hann*[6] *iti padâikadeço bahûpâdânârthaḥ: raksh-----: vâish-----: vṛtr-----. evampûrva iti kim: sâhna -----: val-.*

[1] W. O. *havani*. [2] G. M. *ahan*. [3] W. *evaṁ*. [(4)] G. M. *shakâra*. [5] W. B. *ekamp-*; G. M. *pûrvo*. [6] G. M. *ahann*.

12. *mayâni*: *anî*[1]: *ity atra rupûrvo nakâro*[2] *ṇatvam bhajate. yathâ*[3]: [4]*dârum-----:*[4] *tve-----. evampûrva iti kim: yâni-----: agnaye-----: rephagrahaṇena kim: svan-.*

[1] W. O. *ani*, as also (with T.) in rule; G. M. *anîka*, as also in rule. [2] G. M. O. put after *atra*. [3] W. G. M. om. [(4)] G. M. om.

iv.4.4[5]. As counter-examples are given *yâni mṛnmayâni sâkshât tâni* (vi.4.7[3]: B. omits the last word, G. M. O. the last two), *agnaye 'nîkavate* (i.8.4[1] et al.), and *svanîkasaṁdṛk* (iv.3.13[1]).

वाघाषपूर्वस्तष्टम् ॥ १३ ॥

13. After *vâghâ* and *sh, t* is changed to *ṭ*.

The passage for *vâghâ* is given by O. as *dârvâghâṭas te* (v.5.15[1]); all the other MSS. have only the first word, in its complete *pada*-form, *dârvâghâṭa iti dâru-âghâtaḥ.* The same word forms the subject of Vâj. Pr. iii.47. As counter-example, showing that *ta* does not become *ṭa* after *ghâ* except when the latter follows *vâ*, we have *praghâta âdityânâm* (vi.1.1[3-4]). For the conversion of *t* to *ṭ* after *sh* is quoted *âyush ṭa âyurdâ agne* (ii.5.12[1]: G. M. omit the last word, O. the last two), whose *sh* depends on rule vi.5, above. O adds a counter-example for this second part of the rule also, namely *agnis te tejaḥ* (i.1.10[3] and vii.5.17).

थश्च ठम् ॥ १४ ॥

14. Also *th* to *ṭh*.

The cited example is *goshṭham mâ nirmṛksham* (i.1.10[1]: W. B. omit the last word); to which O. alone adds *prati shṭhâpayanti* (vi.1.4[2]). As counter-example is given *gacha gosthânam* (i.1.9[1,2]).

न तकारपरः ॥ १५ ॥

15. But not when *t* follows.

The commentator explains the connection of this rule by pointing out that the two preceding do not come under the introductory heading of the chapter—that is to say, that they deal with a subject unconnected with the rest of its contents—and that hence they are regarded as dropped out, and the present exception does not apply to them, but to the foregoing rules, for conversion of *n* into *ṇ*. This is well enough, though not a little awkward, as concerns the status of rule 15; but we should like to hear what he had to say in defense of the intrusion of rules 13 and 14 thus into

---

13. *vâghâ: ity evampûrvaḥ shakârapûrvaç[1] ca takârash ṭakâram bhajate[2]. yathâ[3]: dârv-....: âyush.... ve[4] 'ti kim: pragh-....: [5]shapûrva iti kim: agnis....[5]*

[1] G. M. om.; O. om. *kâra.* [2] O. *âpadyate.* [3] W. G. M. om. [4] W. *vâghâ;* B. *vâghâta.* [(5)] Only in O.

14. *cakâraḥ shapûrvatvâkarshakaḥ[1]: thakâraḥ shakârapûrvash[2] ṭhakâram bhajate. yathâ: gosh-....: [3]prati....[3] evampûrva[4] iti kim: gacha....*

[1] G. M. *shakârap-;* O. *-tvâdeçakaḥ.* [2] O. om. *kâra.* [(3)] Only in O. [4] O. *shap-*

a chapter where they do not belong, and where they sorely disturb the natural and desirable connection. Considering their near relation to the rules of the preceding chapter, they might better have been added there as an appendix; or else put at the head of chapter vii., before its general *adhikâra.*

Only a single illustrative example is quoted, namely *pary antarikshât* (iii.1.10²), where rules 4 and 5 of this chapter combined would require *aṇ* at the beginning of the second word, but for the exception here made.

This precept is an anticipation of one of the items of xiii.15, below, and might properly enough be looked upon as open to the charge of *punarukti*, or unnecessary repetition, which the treatise so carefully shuns, and the commentator not seldom labors hard to remove. It is characteristic of the method of the Tâittirîya-Prâtiçâkhya that it does not attempt to state the real *nimitta* or occasion of the lingual *ṇ* in the words rehearsed here, although it does so, fully and distinctly, in rule xiii.6, where the subject of the occurrence of *ṇ* in the interior of a word is taken up.

नह्यतिनूनंनृत्यन्त्यन्योऽन्याभिरन्यान्यन्तश्चान्तश्च ॥ १६ ॥

16. Nor in *nahyati, nûnam, nṛtyanti, anyaḥ, anyâbhiḥ, anyâni;* nor when final.

The *ca* in this rule indicates the continuance of the exception. These words, and a final *n*, are not subject to the rules given in the chapter for the substitution of lingual *ṇ*. The commentator quotes as follows. For *nahyati, vâsasâ paryânahyati* (vi.1.11²; p. *pari-ânahyati:* O. omits the first word): he notes that the case constitutes an exception to rule 5. For *nûnam, pra nûnam pûrṇavandhuraḥ* (i.8.5¹: O. omits the last word). For *nṛtyanti, pari nṛtyanti* (vii.5.10). For the three cases of *anya, prâ 'nyaḥ çañsati* (vii.5.9³), *prâ 'nyâbhir yachaty anv anyâi mantrayate* (v.1.6⁴: O. omits *pra* in all these three examples, and in this, along with G. M., the last three words; B. omits the last word), and *prâ 'nyâni pâtrâṇi* (vi.5.11¹,²): the commentator remarks that all these (since *nahyati*) are cases of exceptions under rule 4. He then proceeds to raise the question why the three complete words

---

15. *vâghâshâdividhir*[1] *anadhikṛtatvâd utpannapradhvañsî: tasmâd atra*[2] *nâ 'yañ nishedhaḥ*[3]*:* [4]*kiñ tu*[4] *prakṛto*[5] *ṇatvavidhir anena vishayîkriyate. takâraparo nakâro ṇatvañ nâ "padyate. yathâ: pary----: pârîparipârîprapûrvaḥ* (vii.4)*: avarṇavyaveto 'pi* (vii.5) *ity etâbhyâm*[6] *prâptiḥ.*

[1] W. O. *vâghâdi-*. [2] G. M. *tatra.* [3] B. *viçeshaḥ.* [(4)] O. om. [5] W. O. *prâk-*. [6] W. B. *âdibhyâm.*

16. *nishedhâkarshakaç cakâraḥ*[1]*: ------ eshu*[2] *grahaṇeshu nakâraḥ padântaç ca*[3] *ṇatvañ na bhajate*[4]*. yathâ*[5]*: vâs-----: avarṇavyaveto 'pi* (vii.5) *iti prâptiḥ: pra----: pari----: prâ*

are quoted in the rule, instead of the syllable *an*, which would include them all; and makes the very obvious answer, that it is on account of the passage *anu prâ 'ṇyât prathamâm* (v.5.5[2]), already quoted under vii.5. Finally, as example of final *n* exempt from conversion, he cites *vṛtrahañ chûra vidvân* (i.4.42), remarking that it is a case otherwise falling under rule 11.

The exception of a final *n* from becoming *ṇ* is also one of those made below, in rule xiii.15, for the class of cases to which that chapter relates.

I have not discovered in the Sanhitâ any case of a lingual nasal arising in the conversion of *pada*-text into *saṁhitâ* which is not duly provided for in this chapter.

CHAPTER VIII.

CONTENTS: 1–4, conversion of a final surd mute to sonant or nasal; 5–7, of *ḥ* to *r*; 8–15, conversions of *ḥ* to *r* after *a* and *â*; 16–22, treatment of *ḥ* before *r*; 23–35, conversion of *ḥ* to *s* or *sh* before *k*, *kh*, or *p*.

अथ प्रथमः ॥ १ ॥

1. Now for changes of first mutes.

That is to say, of surds unaspirated, or *k*, *c* (only *c* nowhere occurs as a final), *ṭ*, *t*, and *p*. The force of this heading only reaches, as the commentary points out, through rule 4—hardly far enough, one would think, to make a separate introductory rule necessary.

----: *prâ*----: *prâ*----: *pârîparipariprapûrvaḥ*[6] (vii.4) *ity eshâm*[7] *prâptiḥ. ann ity etâvatâ*[8] *siddhe 'nyonyâbhiranyânî 'ti kim pratipadapâṭhena*[9]: *anu*---- *ity atrâ 'nena*[10] *nishedho*[11] *na*[12] *prasarati*[13]. [14]*padânto nakâra ṇatvaṁ na bhajate: yathâ*[14]: *vṛtra*----: *rashaḥpûrvaḥ* (vii.11) *iti prâptiḥ.*

iti tribhâshyaratne prâtiçâkhyavivaraṇe
saptamo 'dhyâyaḥ.

[1] B. G. M. O. put first. [2] B. O. *eteshu.* [3] G. M. om.; O. adds *nakâro.* [4] G. M. *âpadyate.* [5] G. M. O. om. [6] W. B. om. *prapûrvaḥ.* [7] G. M. *eteshâṁ.* [8] G. M. O. *-vatâi 'va.* [9] O. puts before *kim.* [10] O. *nâi 'sha.* [11] G. M. *pratish-.* [12] G. M. O. om. [13] G. M. *-tv iti.* [(14)] B. O. om.; G. M. *padântaç ca.*

1. *athe 'ty* [1]*ayam adhikâraḥ*[1]: *prathama* [2]*ity etad*[2] *adhikṛtaṁ veditavyam ita uttaraṁ yad vakshyâmah:* [3] *visarjanîya* (viii.5) *paryanto*[4] *'yam adhikâraḥ.*

[(1)] W. *adhikârârthaḥ.* [(2)] G. M. om. [3] O. ins. *atha.* [4] O. *itisûtrapa-.*

उत्तमपर उत्तमः सवर्गीयम् ॥ २ ॥

2. A first mute, followed by a last mute, becomes a last mute of its own series.

The examples selected by the commentator to illustrate this mode of combination are *vâṅ ma âsan* (v.5.9[2]), *shaṇṇavatyâi svâhâ* (vii.2.15), and *tan mahendrasya* (vi.5.5[3]). For the conversion of *p* into *m* he is able to offer no instance, as none occurs in the Sanhitâ. As counter-examples, showing that only a nasal causes the conversion, and causes it only in a "first" mute, he brings up *vâk ta â pyâyatâm* (i.3.9[1]: only G. M. have the last word), and *imâṁ no vâcam* (vi.4.7[3]).

All the Prâtiçâkhyas join in treating this conversion as necessary, not as alternative with conversion into a sonant (see note to Ath. Pr. ii.5).

तृतीयः स्वरघोषवत्परः ॥ ३ ॥

3. Followed by a vowel or a sonant consonant, it becomes a third mute.

The examples are *ṛdhag ayâḍ ṛdhag uta* (i.4.44[2]), and *yad vâi hotâ* (iii.2.9[1]).

ककुच्च मकारपरः ॥ ४ ॥

4. Also in *kakut*, when *m* follows.

Namely, in the passage *kakudmân pratûrtir vâjasatamaḥ* (i.7.7[2]; p. *kakut-mân:* G. M. O. omit the last word). As counter-examples are given *ya unmâdyet* (iii.4.8[4]: G. M. O. omit *yaḥ*), and, according to W. B., *kakut trayastrinçaḥ* (vii.2.5[3]); for which G. M. O. substitute *kakuc chandaḥ* (iv.3.12[2]). The commentator

---

2. *uttamaparaḥ prathamaḥ* [1] *savargîyam uttamam âpadyate. yathâ*[2]*: vâṅ----: shaṇ-----: tan----. evampara iti kim: vâk ----: prathama iti kim: imâṁ----. uttamaḥ paro yasmâd asâv uttamaparaḥ.*

[1] G. M. O. ins. *âtmanaḥ*. [2] G. M. om.

3. *svaraghoshavatparaḥ*[1] *prathamaḥ savargîyaṁ tṛtîyam âpadyate. yathâ*[2]*: ṛdhag----: yad----: ity âdi. svarâç ca ghoshavantaç ca svaraghoshavantaḥ: te pare yasmâd asâu*[3] *sa tathoktaḥ.*

[1] B. om.; G. M. O. *svaraparo ghoshavatparaç ca.* [2] G. M. O. om. [3] G. M. om.

4. *kakud ity asmin grahaṇe 'ntyo varṇo*[1] *makâraparaç*[2] *cakârâkṛshtaṁ savargîyaṁ*[3] *tṛtîyam âpadyate*[4] *yathâ*[5]*: kakud-----*

notices, finally, that the present rule establishes an exception to rule 2 of this chapter.

अथ विसर्जनीयः ॥ ५ ॥

5. Now for changes of *visarjanîya.*

Departing a little from his stereotyped mode of explanation of *atha*, the commentary declares it in this rule to cause *visarjanîya* to be understood, in the character of that respecting which something is to be enjoined (*lakshya*), in the precepts that follow; and he adds that this understanding is to remain in force as far as rule 10 of the next chapter.

रेफमेतेषु ॥ ६ ॥

6. *Visarjanîya* becomes *r* before the classes of sounds last mentioned.

The examples are *tad agnir âha* (iv.2.8[1]), and *âçîr ma ûrjam* (iii.2.8[5]: O. omits *ûrjam*); with the counter-example *agniç ca ma indraç ca me* (iv.7.6[1]). The commentator points out that it is the plural form of the pronoun (*eteshu*, literally 'before those') in this rule that shows the implication of the vowels and sonant consonants, in the character of following causes (*paranimitta*), since those are the only things which have been mentioned above (namely, in rule 3). That is doubtless so; still, the reference must be regarded as an unusually blind one, involving a "frog-leap" (*maṇḍûkapluti*) over two intervening obstacles, of which one is a general heading, that changes entirely the subject under treatment.

---

kakud iti kim: ya----: evampara iti kim: kakut----. makâraḥ paro yasmâd asâu makâraparaḥ. uttamapara 'uttamaṅ savargîyam (viii.2) *ity asyâ 'pavâdo 'yam.*

[1] G. M. *takâro.* [2] W. *makâraḥ.* [3] G. M. O. put after *tṛtîyam.* [4] W. *prâpyate.* [5] G. M. om.

5. *athaçabdo visarjanîyaṁ lakshyatvenâ 'dhikarotî 'ta uttaraṁ yad ucyate*[1]. *atha svaraparo yakâram* (ix.10) *ity avadhibhûto 'yam adhikâraḥ.*

[1] G. M. *vakshyâmaḥ.*

6. [1] *svareshu ghoshavatsu ca*[2] *parato*[3] *visarjanîyo repham âpadyate. yathâ*[4]*: tad----: âçîr----. eteshv*[5] *iti bahuvacanântasya sarvanâmno*[6] *nirdeçât svaraghoshavatâm paranimittânâm upâdânam*[7]*: teshâm eva prakṛtatvât. eteshv iti kim: agniç----.*

[1] G. M. ins. *eteshu.* [2] G. M. om. [3] O. *pareshu.* [4] G. M. O. om. [5] W. B. *svareshv.* [6] W. O. *sarvânâma*; B. *-nâmino.* [7] G. M. *-nât.*

न रेफपरः ॥७॥

7. But not before *r*.

R, although a sonant consonant, and therefore included in the preceding rule, requires a different treatment in the final *visarjanîya* before it. What this different treatment is, is pointed out farther on in the chapter (rule 16 seq.). The examples here given are *suvo rohâva* (i.7.9[1]), and *ahorâtre* (i.5.9[7] et al.: W. O. add *pârçve*, but there is no such collocation of words in the Sanhitâ, and I suspect the word to be a corrupted reading for *prâviçan*, which follows next at the place referred to).

ह्वारभावार्हारबिभरजीगरकरनन्तर्विवःसुवःपुनरहरहः-प्रातर्वस्तःशमितःसवितःसनुतस्तनुतस्तोतर्होतःपितर्मा-तर्यष्टरेष्टर्नेष्टस्त्वष्टः ॥८॥

8. *Visarjanîya* becomes *r* in *hvâḥ*, *abhâḥ*, *vâḥ*, *hâḥ*, *abibhaḥ*, *ajîgaḥ*, *akaḥ*, *anantaḥ*, *vivaḥ*, *suvaḥ*, *punaḥ*, *aharahaḥ*, *prâtaḥ*, *vastaḥ*, *çamitaḥ*, *savitaḥ*, *sanutaḥ*, *stanutaḥ*, *stotaḥ*, *hotaḥ*, *pitaḥ*, *mâtaḥ*, *yashṭaḥ*, *eshṭaḥ*, *neshṭah*, and *tvashṭaḥ*.

With this rule begins the detail of the cases of an original *r* after *a* and *â*, which is protected and brought to light by a following sonant letter, being treated in quite a different manner from an original *s*, although both *r* and *s* are represented, as finals, by the indifferent *visarjanîya*. The commentator points out at the end the rules to which these cases constitute exceptions, namely ix.7,9,10. His illustrative examples are as follows. For *hvâḥ*

---

7. *rephaparo visarjanîyo repham nâ "padyate. yathâ*[1]*: suvo ----: ahor----: ghoshavattvâd rephasya pûrvavidhiprâptiḥ. rephaḥ paro yasmâd asâu rephaparaḥ.*

[1] G. M. om.

8. [1]*------ eteshu*[1] *visarjanîyo repham âpadyate svaraghoshavatparaḥ*[2]*. yathâ*[3]*: mâ----: yonâv----: vâr----: mâ me----: ab----: osh----: dev----:* [4]*karâvar anudâtte pade*[4] (viii.9) *iti*[5] *vakshyati: tenâi 'vâi*[6] *'tad*[7] *api sidhyaty*[8] *apy akârâdi* (i.52) *iti vacanât: iti cet: mâi 'vam: anudâtte kahçabde tad bhavati: idam tv anyasvarârtham iti*[9]*: yathâ*[10]*: arvâ----:* [11]*âdyudâttas tv idam*[11]*. yajña-----: antar anâdyudâtte* (viii.10) *iti vakshyati: tasmâd ankârâdi ca*[12] (i.53) *iti vacanât sidhyati: iti cet:* [13]*mâi 'vam*[13]*: anâdyudâtte tad bhavati: âdyudâttârtham*[14] [15]*idam grahaṇam*[15]*. ca ----: suvar----: punar----: ahar-*

according to W. B., *mâ hvâr mitrasya* (i.1.4[1]); but, according to G. M. O., *mâ hvâr vasûnâm* (i.1.3): I have found the word only in these two sections. For *abhâḥ*, *yonâv abhâr ukhâ* (iv.2.5[2]). For *vâḥ*, *vâr nâma vo hitam* (v.6.1[3]). For *hâḥ*, *mâ me pra hâr asti vâ idam* (ii.4.12[3,4]: vi.5.1[1,2]: only G. M. have the last two words): the word is found also at ii.4.12[5]; 5.2[3,5]. For *abibhaḥ*, as the only passage where it occurs (ii.5.1[2]) does not exhibit in *saṁhitâ* the final *r*, we have the *jaṭâ*-text quoted, namely *abibhas taṁ tam abibhar abibhas tam.* *Ajîgaḥ*, for the same reason, is treated in the same way in W. B. O., namely *oshadhîr ajîgar ajîgar oshadhîr oshadhîr ajîgaḥ : ajîgar ity ajîgaḥ* (iv.6.7[3]); but G. M. read simply *oshadhîr ajîgaḥ.* For *akaḥ*, *devatrâ 'kar ajakshîreṇa* (v.1.7[4]: G. M. omit the last word): it is found also at i.3.14[2] twice; 5.2[3]: ii.4.9[2]; 5.7[1]: iii.1.10[3]; 4.10[4]: iv.1.2[4]: v.2.1[4],8[7]: vi.4.8[1]. As for this *akaḥ*, the commentator supposes the objection raised that rule 9, which teaches that *kaḥ* and *ávaḥ* change *ḥ* to *r* in an unaccented word, combined with rule i.52, which would extend the force of that rule to *kaḥ* with *a* prefixed, is sufficient to cover the cases of its occurrence, without separate mention in the present rule; but he denies the pertinence of the objection, on the ground that the specification here made includes all instances of *akaḥ*, without regard to their accentuation—for example, *ákaḥ* at iv.1.2[4], which is accented on the first syllable, but exhibits *r* in its *jaṭâ*-reading, *árvâ' 'kar ákar árvâ' 'rvâ' 'kaḥ.* For *anantaḥ*, *yajñaparusho 'nantarityâi* (v.2.5[6]). A precisely similar objection is suggested to this word also, on the ground of rules viii.10 and i.53 combined; and it is similarly repelled, by reference to the difference of accent: *ánantar* has the acute on the first syllable, which rule 10 forbids. For *vivaḥ* is given, again in *jaṭâ*-text, *ca vivar vivaç ca ca vivaḥ : vivar iti vivaḥ* (iv.2.8[2]; only O. has the final repetition of *vivaḥ*: the Atharvan reads *vi vaḥ*, as two separate words, in the corres-

---

----: *ahârahar*[16] (viii.13) *ity aniṅgyânto nishidhyate*[17]: *evaṁrûpasya* [18]*nâ 'yaṁ niyamaḥ*[18]. *prâtar*----: *doshâ*----: [19]*çṛtañ*----:[19] *deva*----: *ârâc*----: *stanutar*[20] *iti çâkhântare: etañ*----: *hotar*----: *marut*----: *pṛthivi*----: *agne*----: *açîy'*----: *neshṭaḥ*----: *çivas*----. *svaraghoshavatpara iti kim: ab*----: *punas*----: *avarṇapûrvas tu lupyate* (ix.9) *iti kvacil lopaprâptiḥ:* [21]*atha svaraparo yakâram* (ix.10) *iti kvacid yatvaprâptiḥ: okâram aḥ sarvo 'kâraparaḥ* (ix.7) *iti kvacid otvaprâptiḥ*[21]: *tâ etâḥ prâptîḥ*[22] *pratisheddhuṁ hvârabhârâdyârambhaḥ.*

(1) O. ---- *eshu*; G. M. *hvár abhâr vár hár ity âdi.* [2] G. M. om. *svara.* [3] G. M. om. [4] W. om. (5) G. M. *kar anudâttatvena.* [6] O. om. *eva.* [7] W. *tad.* [8] O. puts after *vacanât.* [9] G. M. om.; O. *api.* [10] G. M. O. om. (11) W. *âdyudâttasvarârthaḥ*; G. M. O. *ayam* for *idam.* [12] O. om. (13) G. M. *na*; O. om. [14] B. *-âttam*; G. M. O. *-âttas.* (15) G. M. *tv ayam*; O. *tv ayam iti gr-.* [16] G. M. add *suvar.* [17] W. *-dhyeta*; G. M. *-shedhita ity.* (18) G. M. *ayaṁ nishedhaḥ.* (19) B. om. [20] G. M. *san-.* (21) O. om. [22] W. G. M. O. *-ptiḥ.*

ponding passage, iv.1.1). For *suvaḥ*, *suvar asi suvar me yacha* (v.7.6[2]: O. omits the last word): the numerous passages in which this word occurs it would be quite useless to rehearse. For *punaḥ*, *punar âsadya sadanam* (iv.2.3[3]: O. omits the last word): this, too, is of too frequent occurrence to be worth detailed reference. For *aharahaḥ*, *aharahar havirdhâninâm* (ii.5.6[3]): the same repetition of *ahaḥ* is found further at i.5.9[6] twice,[7]; ii.5.6[6]. In connection herewith is made the remark that *ahaḥ* when not at the end of a separable compound is the subject of rule 13, below; but that that rule does not apply to a case like the one here in hand. For *prâtaḥ*, *prâtar upasadaḥ* (vi.2.3[3]): *prâtaḥ* is found also at i.4.7: ii.1.2[5]; 5.6[3]: iii.1.7[1]; 3.8[4]; 4.10[1]: vi.4.2[1]. For *vastaḥ*, *doshâvastar dhiyâ vayam* (i.5.6[2]; p. *doshâ-vastaḥ*): also at i.2.14[4]. For *çamitaḥ*, *çṛtaṅ haviṣḥ çamitar iti trishatyâḥ* (vi.3.10[1]: only G. M. have the first word, only O. the last). For *savitaḥ*, *deva savitar etat te* (iii.2.7[1]): the word is found also in about a dozen other passages. For *sanutaḥ*, *ârâc cid dveshaḥ sanutar yuyotu* (i.7.13[5]). For *stanutaḥ* we are simply referred to "another text" (*çâkhântara*): but G. M. read *sanutar*, and omit *stanutar* in the rule itself. For *stotaḥ*, *etaṅ stotar etena* (vii.4.20). For *hotaḥ*, *hotar yavishṭha sukrato* (i.2.14[5]: O. omits the last word): also at i.3.14[3]; 6.2[2]: iv.3.13[2]: v.1.4[5]: vi.3.8[2]; 4.3[3]. For *pitaḥ*, resort is had to the *jaṭâ*-reading, since the only passage (iii.3.9[1]) in which the word occurs does not bring to view the *r*: thus, *marutâm pitaḥ pitar marutâm marutâm pitaḥ*. For *mâtaḥ*, *pṛthivi mâtar mâ mâ hiṅsîḥ* (iii.3.2[2]: O. omits the last word). For *yashṭaḥ*, *agne yashṭar idaṁ namaḥ* (i.1.12). For *eshṭaḥ*, again a *jaṭâ*-reading, *açîy' eshṭar eshṭar açîyâ 'çîy' eshṭaḥ* (i.2.11[1]): its treatment before the word which follows it in *saṁhitâ* is the subject of rules 18–22 of this chapter; that of the preceding word, of x.14. For *neshṭaḥ*, once more the *jaṭâ* is drawn upon, *neshṭaḥ patnîm patnîṁ neshṭar neshṭaḥ patnîm* (vi.5.8[6]). For *tvashṭaḥ*, finally, *çivas tvashṭar ihâ" gahi* (iii.1.11[2]: O. omits the last word): also at i.3.7[1],10[1]: iii.1.11[1]: vi.3.6[2],11[2].

The commentary adds a couple of counter-examples, illustrative of the fact that these words show their *r* only before a vowel or sonant consonant: they are *abibhas tam bhûtâni* (ii.5.1[2]), and *punas te mâi 'shâm* (iv.7.14[3]).

कावरनुदात्ते पदे ॥ ९ ॥

9. Also in *kaḥ* and *âvaḥ*, in an unaccented word.

The cited examples are: *mithuyâ kar bhâgadheyam* (i.3.7[2]), and

---

9. *kaḥ: âvaḥ: ity etayor visarjanîyaḥ padakâle 'nudâtte[1] pade vartamânaḥ svaraghoshavatparo repham âpadyate. yathâ[2]: mith-....: suruco..... anudâtta iti kim: ko....: [3]âvo....:[3] evampara iti kim: adhi.....*

[1] G. M. *-tta*. [2] G. M. om. [3] O. om.

suruco vena ávaḥ: ávar ity ávaḥ (iv.2.8[2]: G. M. O. omit *surucaḥ*). For *ávaḥ* I find no other example; *kaḥ* occurs further at i.4.45[1]: ii.2.12[1]. As counter-examples, *kò 'sye "çvaráh* (ii.6.7[1]), and *á'vo vá'jeshu yám̃ jundá'ḥ* (i.3.13[2]: G. M. omit the last two words; O. omits the whole passage) show the necessity of the specification respecting accent; while *adhipám akaḥ samashṭyái* (vi.1.7[6]) shows that the *r* appears only before a sonant letter. This last example, it may be remarked, is brought under the action of the rule by i.52: it would be an example also under the preceding rule; compare what is there said in connection with the cited word *akaḥ*.

अन्तरनाद्युदात्ते ॥ १० ॥

10. Also in *antaḥ*, except when accented on the first syllable.

The cited examples are: *antár agne rucá' tvám* (iv.1.9[3]; 2.1[5]), *agním antár bharishyántī* (iv.1.3[2]: O. omits the first word), and *antaryámé maghavan* (vi.4.6[3]: but O. omits the example—reasonably enough, since it is given again later in this very comment, in illustration of a special point). It were to no good end to rehearse the other cases of occurrence of so common a word. To show the necessity of the restriction respecting accent, the commentator quotes *eshó 'ntó 'ntam manushyáḥ* (vii.2.7[2]), where we have the noun *ánta*, which the rule was especially constructed to avoid including. To prove, again, the continued implication of "followed by a sonant letter," is given *antás te dadhámi* (i.4.3 and vi.4.6[1-2]). Then the comment proceeds to justify the form in which the restriction respecting accent is made in the rule: it might have been said, "when accented on the last syllable;" but then the rule would have applied only under those circumstances; whereas now is included the case when the word is not accented at all, as in *antarvedí mithuná'u* (vii.5.9[4]; p. *antaḥ-vedí*) and *antaryámé maghavan* (vi.4.6[3], as above: but G. M. omit). The mode of statement selected, however, it may be remarked, has this inconvenience—that it renders necessary the separate specification, in rule 8, of *anantaḥ*, because that combination, where it occurs, happens to be "accented on the first syllable" (see note to rule 8). It would appear to admit of question, in-

---

10. *antar ity* [1]*asmin pade*[1] *'nádyudátte visarjanīyaḥ svaraghoshavatparo repham ápadyate*[2]. *yathá*[3]*: antar----: agnim----: antar-----. anádyudátta iti kim: esho----: evampara iti kim. antas-----.* [4]*antodátta iti vaktavye*[4] *bahusvaratvam bahúpádánártham*[5]*: anyathá tv*[7] *antodáttasyái 'va syát:*[6] *antarv-----: antary-----. ádáv udátto yasya tad ádyudáttam: ná "dyudáttam anádyudáttam: tasmin.*

(1) G. M. *etasmin.* [2] G. M. *ápnoti.* [3] G. M. om. [4] G. M. om. [5] W. O. *-thaḥ.* (6) B. om. [7] G. M. *hy.*

deed, whether *ánantaḥ* was not fairly included in the present rule, since the *antaḥ* part of it, at any rate, is not "accented on the first;" but the treatise chooses to avoid so nice a question of interpretation, and to take the safe side.

आवृत्परः ॥ ११ ॥

11. Also a *visarjanîya* followed by *âvṛt.*

The quoted examples are *jinvar âvṛt svâhâ* and *ugnar âvṛt svâhâ* (both ii.4.7[1]: B. has *bhîmar* for *ugnar;* O. reads in each case *âvṛth*, according to the requirements of rule xiv.12). Other instances in the same and following divisions of the same section are *bhîmar âvṛt, tveshar âvṛt, çrutar âvṛt,* and *bhûtar âvṛt.* The anomalous combination does not occur elsewhere.

इतिपरो ऽपि ॥ १२ ॥

12. And likewise when *iti* follows.

The word *api* in this rule, we are told, brings forward the implication of "a *visarjanîya* followed by *âvṛt.*" According to the commentator's exposition, further, the rule is intended to apply to the *jaṭâ* repetition of *çrutaḥ* with its predecessor *iti:* as, *iti çrutaḥ çrutar itî 'ti çrutaḥ* (ii.4.7[2]). Nor do I see of what other interpretation it is capable, although it seems strange that the irregular conversion of *ḥ* into *r* should be retained in the *jaṭâ*-reading of this word only, and not of the others, where repeated with their respective predecessors. It is clearly implied that we are to read, for example, in the first case falling under the preceding rule, *varshaṅ jinvo jinvo varshan varshaṅ jinvaḥ.*

As counter-example, showing the necessity of the implication signified by *api*, we receive *ṛtubhir havanaçrutaḥ* (ii.4.14[5]: G. M. O. omit the first word; G. M. add *havam*, but no such word follows in the Sanhitâ, and the addition is doubtless a copyist's error—possibly growing out of the attempt to repeat the compound, in its *pada* or *jaṭâ* form). Here both the *pada*-text (as the word is a compound) and the *jaṭâ* (as it stands before a pause) would read *havanaçruta iti havana-çrutaḥ*, the ordinary *sandhi* being made of *çrutaḥ* and *iti.*

अह्वारह्वःसुवरनिंग्यान्तः ॥ १३ ॥

---

11. *âvṛd ity evamparo visarjanîyo repham âpnoti. jinv-....: ugn-.....*

12. *apiçabda âvṛtparaṁ*[1] *visarjanîyam anvâdiçati: asâu visarjanîya itiparo repham âpnoti. iti çr-..... anvâdeçaḥ kimarthaḥ: ṛtu-....: itiḥ*[2] *paro yasmâd asâv itiparaḥ.*

[1] W. O. *-paro;* G. M. *-para.* [2] W. B. *iti;* O. *itiçabdaḥ.*

13. Also in *ahâḥ*, *ahaḥ*, and *suvaḥ*, except at the end of a separable word.

There is a well-established difference of reading in the text itself of this rule. T. and W. read the last word *anîngyântâḥ*, as plural, to agree with the three words mentioned, or else with the three cases of *visarjanîya* which they present; and at the beginning of the comment, both in W. and in O., is seen an attempt to explain the word as a plural—not, however, consistently carried out in either. As both readings are equally acceptable, I have adopted the one which is best supported.

The examples given in illustration of the rule are *ahâr jâtavedâ vicarshaṇiḥ* (iii.2.5[4]: O. omits the last word), *ahar mâṅsena* (v.7.20: but G. M. substitute *aharbhâjo vâi*, vii.4.5[1]), and *suvar devâñ aganma* (i.7.9[2]: O. omits the last word): and, as counter-examples, first, to show that the *ḥ* in the words specified, when they stand as final members of compounds, is treated in the usual manner, *abhipûrvaṁ tryahâ bhavanti* (vii.3.9[2] et al.; p. *tri-ahâḥ*: O. omits the first word), *pratyañ tryaho bhavati* (vii.3.5[3] et al.; p. *tri-ahaḥ*: but B. has dropped out the whole example, and G. M. O. substitute, O. with omission of the first word, *pratyañ shaḍaho bhavati*, vii.4.2[5]), and *devasuva stha te* (i.8.10[2]: but W. B. O. give simply the *pada*-reading of *devasuvaḥ*, namely *devasuva iti deva-suvaḥ*, since thus alone is the word put into circumstances which show its *ḥ* not to be convertible into *r*); and second, to show that the conversion takes place only before sonant letters, *prâyaṇîyam ahas tasmât* (vii.2.8[1]: O. omits the first word), and *suvaç ca mûrdhâ ca* (i.7.9[1] and iv.7.11[2]).

The commentator then proceeds to give an explanation, so far as *ahâḥ* is concerned, respecting the virtual intent of the rule, which, he says, is meant to establish an exception for that word when the final member of a compound; since the inclusion of *hâḥ* among the words cited in rule 8 would, under the operation of the often-quoted rule i.52, be authority sufficient for turning *ahâḥ* into *ahâr* before a sonant letter. Upon this he next imagines the objection to be raised, that the reading in this rule also, as well as the other, should have been *hâḥ*, *ahâḥ* being then included along with it according to the principle referred to; and thus the liability to reproach for over-doing the explicitness of the rule would be avoid-

---

13. *ahâḥ: ahaḥ: suvaḥ: eteshu*[1] *visarjanîyo*[2] *'niṅgyântaḥ*[3] *svaraghoshavatparo repham âpnoti*[4]. *yathâ*[5]: **ahâr**----: **ahar**----: **suvar**----. *aniṅgyânta iti kim:* **abhip**----: **praty**----: **dev**----. *evampara iti kim:* **prây**----: **suvaç**----. **hvârabhâr** (viii.8) [6] *âdisûtre hâr ity anena grahaṇenâ 'hâḥçabdasyâ 'py* **akârâdi** (i.52) *iti vacanâd rephasiddhâu satyâm atra punarvacanam iṅgyântasyâ 'hâḥçabdasya pratishedhârtham. nanv atrâi 'va*[7] *hâr iti vaktavyam: apy* **akârâdi** (i.52) *iti vacanena kâryasiddheḥ: na tu tadgâuravâpatteḥ*[8]*: iti cet: mâi 'vam: aniṅg-*

ed. But he replies, reasonably enough, that, as the rule says "when not the final member of a separable word," it is to be inferred that the words specified do occur as such members: and with *hâḥ* that is not the case; wherefore the distinction would be meaningless with reference to *hâḥ*. And it would be a poor enough side to take, and altogether unworthy of approval, to give a direction which did not apply to a word itself, but only to that word with *a* prefixed. Hence the quotation is made in proper form.

Just as long a discussion might have been raised with equal reason over *ahaḥ* and *suvaḥ*, both of which are also included in the former rule. So far as *ahaḥ* is concerned, indeed, it is easy to see that this is the general rule, applying to the cases of occurrence of that word in the main, with a specific restriction; and that *ahar-ahaḥ* in rule 8 is a sort of exception in advance, made for a single case which would otherwise fall under this restriction (since, in *ahaḥ-ahaḥ*, the second *ahaḥ* is in fact the final member of a compound). But I am unable to discover any justification of the way in which *suvaḥ* is treated: it is made the subject of two general rules, to the one of which a needed restriction is attached, to the other, not. For *ahâḥ* and *suvaḥ*, the present rule should, it seems, have taken distinctly the form of an exception merely: *nâ 'hâḥ-suvar iṅgyântâu;* 'not, however, *ahâḥ* and *suvaḥ*, when final members of compounds;' and *ahaḥ* should have been separately treated, or else included with them and a further counter-exception added.

न भिर्भ्यांपरः ॥ १४ ॥

14. Not, however, when followed by *bhiḥ* or *bhyâm*.

There is violation of the ordinary usage of the Prâtiçâkhya in this rule also. The only one of the words mentioned in the preceding rule which is found with the case-endings *bhiḥ* and *bhyâm* following it is *ahaḥ;* and hence, to it alone the present precept applies. We should expect it, therefore, in accordance with the principle of which i.58 is an expression, to have been placed last in the trio of which it forms a member. The commentator does not remark upon the irregularity, but simply points out that the

---

yânta ity ukter[9] *iṅgyântatvam*[10] *iti*[11] *sambhâvanîyam: tac ca hâr ity evaṁrûpe*[12] *grahaṇe nâ 'stî 'ty*[13] *atre 'daṁ viçeshaṇam anarthakaṁ syât: tathâ 'py*[14] *evaṁrûpe mâ bhûd iti*[15]*:* [16]*kiṁ tv*[16] *akârâditve bhavatî 'ti jaghanyaḥ pakshaḥ: na tu saralaḥ: iti sûtre*[17] *'hâr*[18] *iti grahaṇam upayujyate.*

[1] O. *eshu padeshu.* [2] W. *-yâ.* [3] W. *aniṅgyântâḥ;* O. *-tâ.* [4] O. *âpnuvânti.* [5] G. M. O. om. [6] G. M. ins. *ity.* [7] G. M. *'vâ.* [8] O. *tatra gâuravadoshâp-;* G. M. *tatra gâugavadeshop-.* [9] W. *ukten;* G. M. O. *ukte.* [10] G. M. *-ântam.* [11] G. M. O. *api.* [12] G. M. O. *-pa.* [13] W. om. *iti.* [14] G. M. O. *sati:* a better reading. [15] O. om. (16) G. M. om.; O. *kiṁ tv apy.* [17] G. M. O. *sutarâm.* [18] MSS. *ahâr.*

circumstances of the case restrict the application of the rule to *ahaḥ*, and gives as examples *uttarâir ahobhiç caranti* (vii.5.1[4] : G. M. O. omit the last word), and *çam ahobhyâm iti ni nayati* (vi.3.9[1]).

अर्ंहश्च सर्वेषाम् ॥ १५ ॥

15. Also not in *aṅhaḥ*, as all agree.

Some authorities, namely, the commentator informs us, accept this word as containing an *anusvâra*, others not; but all alike regard it as an exception under rule 13 (and therefore not liable to have its final *visarjanîya* converted into *r* under any circumstances). Those who accept the *anusvâra* still regard the word as falling under the action of rule 13, in virtue of the principle "a nose-sound occurring in the interior of a word is no bar to the application of a rule; hence it performs the offices of letters while itself only a quality" (if this be, in fact, the meaning of the second line of the verse, of which I am by no means confident; the readings of the manuscripts are here somewhat discordant, without being mutually explanatory). The first words of this verse were quoted in the comment on rule i.1, in connection with the discussion as to whether *anusvâra* was a concrete thing or a quality (see p. 8), and were credited to the Çikshâ—which, however, in the form in which we now possess it, neither contains such a passage, nor seems to furnish a connection in which it should naturally be introduced. I should question the sober verity of the considerations whereby the commentator tries to justify the rule. It is hardly credible that *aṅhaḥ* and *ahaḥ* should be fairly identified by any authorities. And *anusvâra* is not a *nâsikya*, but an *anunâsika*, in the view of this treatise every where. It might be bet-

---

14. *sâṁnidhyena*[1] *labdhaḥ*[2] *pûrvasûtrokto visarjanîyo* [3] *bhirbhyâm* [4] *evamparo*[5] *na repham âpnoti. arthâd ahar ity atra visarjanîyaḥ parigṛhyate: itaratrasthitasyâi 'vamparatvâbhâvât. yathâ: utt-....: çam-....*

[1] G. M. O. *-dhyâl.* [2] W. *labhyaḥ.* [3] W. ins. *na.* [4] O. ins. *ity.* [5] G. M. *paro.*

15. *cakâro* [1]*nishedham âkarshati*[1]*: aṅha ity asmin*[2] *grahaṇe visarjanîyo na repham âpnoti: ahârahar* (viii.13) *iti prâptiḥ. atra*[3] *grahaṇe kecid anusvâram ichanti* [4]*kecin ne 'chanti: sarveshâṁ*[4] *teshâṁ esha*[5] *nishedho bhavati: anusvâram ichadbhir api prâptir evam pratipâdyate*[6]*:*

vidher madhyasthanâsikyo na virodho[7] [8]*bhavet smṛtaḥ*[8]*:*
tasmât karoti[9] *kâryâṇi varṇânâṁ* [10]*dharma eva*[10] *tv*

iti. yathâ[11]*: aṅha....: aṅho-..*

(1) G. M. O. *-dhâkarshakaḥ.* [2] G. M. *etasmin.* [3] O. *asmin.* (4) G. M. om. [5] G. M. *eva.* [6] G. M. *-pady-.* [7] B. *-dhi.* (8) B. *bhavet: sataḥ;* G. M. *bhaved yataḥ.* [9] B. G. M. *kurvanti.* (10) W. *dharmaṇas.* [11] G. M. om.

ter to regard the specific exception of *an̄haḥ* as simply a sort of supererogatory effort at extreme explicitness, intended to guard against the confusion with *ahaḥ*, even by a blunderer, of another word which was, indeed, definitely different from it, but different by only so inconspicuous an element as the nasalization of a vowel.

The illustrative examples are *an̄ha indram evâ 'n̄homucam* (ii.2.7[4]: but O. writes ---- *eva: an̄homucam*, as if the latter word were a separate citation: it is found in other passages), and *an̄homuce pra bharema* (i.6.12[3]: but O. substitutes *an̄homuce puroḍâçam*, ii.2.7[4]).

अनवर्णपूर्वस्तु रेफपरो लुप्यते ॥ १६ ॥

16. But, when not preceded by an *a*-vowel, *visarjanîya* followed by *r* is omitted.

The commentator's example in illustration of the action of this rule is *revatî ramadhvam* (i.3.7[1] et al.; p. *revatîḥ*); and he adds as counter-examples, first, to show the necessity of the restriction "not preceded by an *a*-vowel," *yo rudro agnâu* (v.5.9[3]), and again, to show that the omission takes place only before a *r*, *revatîr naḥ sadhamâdaḥ* (ii.2.12[8]; 4.14[4]). This exhausts the evident intent of the rule: the *tu*, 'but,' which the latter contains, merely indicates the transition to a new and diverse subject; it intimates no distinction between the classes of cases in which the *visarjanîya* represents a *s* on the one hand and an original *r* on the other; and all the cases of final *aḥ* and *âḥ* are left to be treated alike, as prescribed by the rules given hereafter (ix.7–10)—*aḥ* being changed to *o*, and *âḥ* to *â*. This truly represents the usage of the Sanhitâ: the latter does not contain (if the special case which forms the subject of rules 18–22, below, be excepted) a single instance of *aḥ* converted into *â* before *r:* the occurrence before *r* of *aḥ* standing for original *ar* is very rare, and the product is always *o:* besides the cases of *ahorâtre* (*pada*-text, *ahaḥ-râtre*), I have

---

16. *avarṇâd anyasvarapûrvo rephaparo visarjanîyo lupyate. yathâ*[1]*: rev----. evampûrva iti kim: yo----: evampara iti kim: rev----. tuçabdârambhâd avarṇapûrvo 'pi hvârabhâr* (viii.8) *âdînâṁ visargo lupyate pûrvasvaraç ca dîrgham âpadyate. yathâ*[2]*: rukmo----. tarhi suvo---- ity atra lopadîrghâu kiṁ na syâtâm. dviruktatvâd iti brûmaḥ. tat katham. hvârabhâr* (viii.8) *âdisutre* [3] *: ahârahaḥsuvar* (viii.13) *ity atra ca. nanv ahorâtre ity atra katham otvam. anyârthena grahaṇasâmarthyene 'ti brûmaḥ. tat*[4] *katham. ahorâtre dhṛtavrate*[5] (iv.11) *ity evaṁrûpasâmyâd*[6] *ahorâtrâbhyâm ahorâtrayor*[7] *ity âdi vijñeyam*[8]. [9]*evaṁ ced adhishavaṇe* (iv.11) *iti grahaṇasâmarthyenâi 'va*[9] [10]*shatve siddhe*[11] [12] *na dhipûrve* (vi.11) *iti* [13]*nishedhanishedhena virodhaḥ*[13]. *satyam: sa-*

only found four instances of *suvaḥ* before forms of *ruh;* namely *suvo ruhâṇâḥ* (iv.1.2[4]; 7.13[1]), *suvo rohâva* (i.7.9[1]), and *suvo rokshyâmi* (i.7.9[1]). The other Prâtiçâkhyas (Rik. Pr. iv.9, r. 28,29; Vâj. Pr. iv.34; Ath. Pr. ii.19, iii.20) convert *aḥ* to *â* in like circumstances; and at least the Rik and Atharvan afford several instances of the *sandhi.*

So much for the rule and its meaning. The commentator, unfortunately, has found occasion to give it a forced and false interpretation; it leads him into a nest of difficulties, through which he flounders as best he can, coming out at the end with much discredit. There happens to be a single passage (or, if there be another, I have not noticed it) where a word with original final *r* follows in the Sanhitâ a word beginning with *r*—namely *rukmo antaḥ* (iv.1.10[4-5]; 6.5[2]; 7.12[3])—and, of course, in the inversions of the *jaṭâ*-text, comes to stand before its predecessor. The accepted *jaṭâ*-reading, it appears (as given in full by the commentator), is *rukmo antar antâ rukmo rukmo antaḥ*, the analogy of the Rik and Atharvan usage being followed in the treatment of *antaḥ.* In order, now, to find authority for this reading, the commentator declares that *tu*, 'but,' in the rule signifies that, even when preceded by an *a*-vowel, the words specified in rule 8 and its successors lose their *visarjanîya* and lengthen the preceding vowel. This is an attribution of portentous pregnancy of meaning to the particle such as is not very infrequently made, rarely with more evident falsity than here. The objection is immediately suggested—why, in that case, does not *suvaḥ* in *suvo rohâva* (i.7.9[1]), lose its *ḥ* and lengthen its *a?* Because, is the acute reply, it has been mentioned twice, once in rule 8, and once in rule 13. What possible connection is to be discovered between this repetition and the use to which he would fain put it, he does not give himself the trouble to inform us: he takes care to raise only such difficulties as he conceives himself able to remove. The next which it pleases him to evoke is—how is the *o* of *ahorâtre* to be explained? We rather

---

vaçabdasyâ 'dhishavaṇe iti grahaṇasâmarthyena[10] *shatvaṁ sidhyatu: sthânaçabdasya kathaṁ sidhyet: grahaṇâdisâmarthyâbhâvât*[14]*: tasmât tadarthaṁ*[15] *tâvat*[16] *sûtraṁ sârthakam iti* [17]*tadarthaṁ ca drashṭavyam*[17]*: tadarthaṁ ce*[18] *'ti guḍajihvikânyâyaḥ*[19]*: tathâ hi: grahaṇasâmarthyâd*[20] *iti*[21] *gamanikâmâtram*[22]*: kaṇṭhoktis tu viçeshaḥ: tataḥ savaçabdârthaṁ*[23] *sûtram iti bhâvaḥ*[24].

avarṇâd anyo 'navarṇaḥ: asâu pûrvo yasmât sa tathoktaḥ. rephaḥ paro yasmâd asâu rephaparaḥ.

[1] B. G. M. O. om. [2] W. B. G. M. om. [3] W. B. ins. *aharahar iti.* [4] W. B. O. om. [5] O. *adhishavaṇe.* [6] G. M. *pragrahe evaṁrûpasâmarthyâd.* [7] G. M. *-tre.* [8] B. *jñeyam.* [(9)] O. *nanu anyârthena grahaṇenâi 'va.* [(10)] G. M. om. [11] O. *siddhiḥ.* [12] B. ins. *nishiddhe.* [(13)] O. *shatvanishedhanishedho na vidheyaḥ;* B. *nishedho na iti virodhaḥ.* [14] B. *-ṇâsâm-.* [15] B. *artham;* G. M. *tadavastham.* [16] G. M. *vâ tat.* [(17)] G. M. O. *saṁtoshṭavyam.* [18] G. M. *ve.* [19] G. M. *gula-.* [20] O. *-thyam.* [21] O. om.; G. M. *i.* [22] G. M. *kam-.* [23] G. M. *savasthânaçab-;* O. adds *api.* [24] G. M. *gâvaḥ.*

expect to hear him reply—because *ahaḥ* also is twice mentioned, in the same two rules with *suvaḥ*. But no; we do injustice to the tenderness of his exegetical conscience, in supposing him capable of such gross arbitrariness of interpretation, when in rule 8, instead of *ahaḥ*, *aharahaḥ* is read. He alleges instead the competency of a form cited for another purpose (compare Rik Pr. i.13, r. liv,55): we have read in rule iv.11 *ahorâtre*, where the *pragrahas* are under treatment, and this suffices, by analogy of form, to determine the reading also of *ahorâtrâbhyâm* and *ahorâtrayoḥ*. If this be so, it is next retorted, then, as the *sh* of *adhishavaṇe*, which is cited in the same rule, is assured by the citation itself, rule vi.11, prescribing the *sh*, in the way of an exception to an exception, is out of order. That is true, the commentator confesses: but, granting that the *sh* of *sava* is established by the previous mention of *adhishavaṇe*, how is that of *sthâna*, the other word specified in the same rule, established? the rule is therefore to be deemed of force so far as relates to that word, and to be regarded as intended for it. Of what follows, not all is clear to me: it appears that the rule is, after all, defended as it stands, on "the principle of sugar-candy and little tongue" (i. e. as merely giving more than is absolutely required of what one cannot receive too much of, as the palate of candy—?): for to establish the reading on the authority of a previous citation is only doing just what will answer (? *gamanikâ* occurs in only one other passage, the comment on i.18, and I find nowhere any thing that explains its use), while specific mention is a distinction; hence the rule has a meaning as applied to *sava* also: such is the understanding.

The commentator might much better, surely, have acknowledged that his text-book had omitted to provide for the special case of *jaṭâ*-reading which has caused all this trouble, than have forced it within the contemplation of the rules at such cost.

दीर्घं च पूर्वः ॥ १७ ॥

17. And the preceding vowel is made long.

The "and" (*ca*) in the rule is declared to signify that the lengthening of the vowel takes place only when *visarjanîya* has been omitted. The cited examples are *rurû râudraḥ* (v.5.19), *tittirî rohit* (v.5.16), and *vishṇû rûpaṁ kṛtvâ* (vi.2.4²: only G. M. have the last word). As was noticed in the comment upon the preceding rule, there is no such case of *aḥ* changed to *â* before *r*, except the one forming the special subject of the following rules.

---

17. *tasmâd rephaparavisarjanîyâl luptât pûrvo 'pi*[1] *yaḥ svaro hrasvaḥ sa ca dîrgham âpadyate. yathâ*[2]*: rurû ....: titti-....: vishṇû.... yadâ*[3] *visarjanîyasya lopas tadâi 'va dîrghatvaṁ yathâ syâd ity evamarthaç caçabdaḥ.*

[1] O. om. [2] G. M. om. [3] G. M. O. ins. *tasya*.

एष्टश्च ॥ १८ ॥

18. As also, in *eshṭaḥ*.

This word has been already mentioned, in rule 8, as one of those whose final *ḥ* is liable to become *r*. It is here made the further subject of a special rule, because it is the only case in the Sanhitâ of *aḥ* changed to *â* before *r* (see the note to rule 16). The passage in which it occurs is *eshṭâ râyaḥ* (i.2.11[1] and vi.2.2[6]).

We have seen, however, that the commentator has felt obliged to give a false interpretation to rule 16, and one which renders superfluous the present rule, as applying to a case already included under that one. He is well aware of the objection to his interpretation thence arising, and himself points out that *eshṭâ râyo râya eshṭar eshṭâ râyaḥ* (only W. gives this) is a case analogous with *rukmo antar antâ rukmo rukmo antaḥ* (W. B. omit the last two words), and that the loss of *ḥ* and lengthening of *a* in *eshṭaḥ* is an effect of the *tu* in rule 16; but he does what he can toward removing the objection by alleging that the detail of discordant opinions which is to follow (in the next four rules) renders it more desirable to cite the case specially, in order that it may be understood to what those opinions apply. This is a tolerably ingenious subterfuge—but, after all, only a subterfuge.

नैकेषाम् ॥ १९ ॥

19. Not so, according to some authorities.

The commentator gives two alternative explanations of this rule—both, however, as he notices, leading to the same reading of the phrase under question. Vararuci, namely, holds that, in the view of some, the rule denies the conversion of *ḥ* to *r* in *eshṭaḥ*, and therefore also the prolongation of the *a*; whence, by the general rule ix.8, the word would become *eshṭo* (in analogy with all the other cases in the text of *aḥ* before *r*). Mâhisheya, however, understands that some are said to deny that the *ḥ* of *eshṭaḥ* is liable to conversion into *r* before another *r*—that is to say, he makes the rule establish so far an exception under rule 8 rather than rule

---

18. *eshṭar ity asmin grahaṇe visarjanîyo rephaparo*[1] *'varṇapûrvo 'pi*[2] *lupyate*[3]. *yathâ*[4]: *eshṭâ* . . . . [5]*caçabdo lopadîrghayor âkarshakaḥ*[5]. *nanv etad anupapannam: hvârabhâr* (viii.8) *âdyantaḥpâtitvâd eshṭar ity asya:* [6]*eshṭâ* . . . . :[6] *rukmo* . . . . *itivat*[7]: *anavarṇapûrvaḥ tu* (viii.16) *ity atra tuçabdena*[8] *lopadîrghasiddhâu*[9]. [10]*mâi 'vam*[10]: *vakshyamâṇamatabhedâçrayatvajñâpanâya gṛhîtam etad upapannataram: iti parihâraḥ.*

[1] W. B. *rephaḥ*. [2] O. om. [3] G. M. ins. *pûrvaç ca dîrghaḥ*. [4] G. M. om. [(5)] G. M. *-ghâv âkarshati*, and put at the beginning. [(6)] B. G. M. O. om. [7] W. *iti*; G. M. *iti padam*. [8] G. M. *çabde*. [9] B. *-ghaçruteḥ*; G. M. O. *-ddhe*. [(10)] W. B. O. om.

18. There can be little question that Vararuci's explanation is the true one.

In rule 21, below, we have yet another mode taught of arriving at the same result as regards the reading.

द्वावुत्तमोत्तरीयस्य रेफम् ॥ २० ॥

20. According to Uttamottarîya, two become *r*.

Here, again, there are two interpretations, Vararuci giving one, Mâhisheya the other. The former says that, in the opinion of the specified authority (*çâkhin*, 'holder of a *çâkhâ* or recension of the sacred text'), the *visarjanîya* of *eshṭaḥ* and the following *r* both become *r*—that is, as I should think it ought to mean, both fuse together into a single *r:* thus, *eshṭarâyaḥ*—but none of the manuscripts give this reading in illustrating the case: see the various readings below. Mâhisheya, on the other hand, regards the individual referred to as owning the portentous name Dvâvuttamottarîya, and as holding that the *ḥ* of *eshṭaḥ* becomes *r* before *r*, making *eshṭar râyaḥ*.

Vararuci here maintains, in my opinion, his usual superiority over Mâhisheya, as regards both the plausibility of the name assumed and the admissibility of the reading taught; and I have accordingly made my translation conform with his interpretation.

It is interesting to note the uncertainty of the tradition within reach of the commentators as to the personality of the authorities quoted by the Prâtiçâkhya.

सांकृत्यस्योकारम् ॥ २१ ॥

21. According to Sâṁkṛtya, the *visarjanîya* becomes *u*.

And this *u*, by x.5, unites with the preceding *a* to form *o*, so that the reading of the passage is *eshṭo râyaḥ*, as it is according

---

19. *ekeshâm mata eshṭar iti visarjanîyo rephaparo na lupyate: ata eva pûrvasvaradîrghâbhâvaç ca: kiṁ tu ghoshavatparaç ca* (ix.8) [1]*ity otvam*[1]. *yathâ: eshṭo râyaḥ. vararuciviracitam etat*[2]*: mâhisheyabhâshitaṁ tv*[3] *evam: eshṭar iti visarjanîyo rephaparo* [4]*rephaṁ nâ*[5] [4]*padyata iti*. *siddharûpam ubhayoḥ samânam.*

(1) W. om. [2] G. M. om. [3] G. M. *ca.* (4) G. M. *na rephaṁ âpnoti.* [5] O. om. *na.*

20. *uttamottarîyasya çâkhino*[1] *mata eshṭar iti visarjanîyas*[2] *tatparo rephaç ca dvâv etâu repham âpadyete. yathâ: eshṭar*[3] *râyaḥ. ayam artho vâraruco ktaḥ*[4]*: mâhisheyoktas tu dvâvuttamottarîya iti kasya cin nâma: tanmata eshṭar*[5] *iti visarjanîyo rephaparo rephaṁ âpadyate:* [6] *eshṭar*[7] *râya iti*[8].

[1] O. *-nor.* [2] G. M. *-yaç ca.* [3] B. G. M. *-ṭâ;* O. *-ṭâr.* [4] W. B. O. *var-.* [5] W. B. *eshṭâ râya.* [6] O. ins. *yathâ.* [7] B. G. M. *-ṭâ.* [8] G. M. O. om.

to the "some authorities" quoted in rule 19, above. This is pointed out by the commentator; who, however, declares that the reference to Sâṁkṛtya in a separate place shows that he is not one of the people there spoken of. B. specifies (probably by a copyist's blunder) that the exposition given of the meaning of the rule is to be credited to Mâhisheya.

उख्यस्य सपूर्वः ॥ २२ ॥

22. And, according to Ukhya, along with the preceding letter.

That is, *eshṭar* becomes *eshṭu*, the *ḥ* and its predecessor *a* coalescing into *u.* This is the only exposition given by W. and O. But G. M. and B., strangely agreeing for once to differ from the rest, ascribe this understanding of the meaning of the rule to Mâhisheya, and report Vararuci as holding it to signify that the *ḥ* of *eshṭaḥ*, with its predecessor, becomes *r.* This last version of the *sandhi* seems little better than nonsense, and neither of the MSS. gives a reading to correspond.

The commentator declares, finally, that, in this net-work of alternative views, the first rule only (viii.18) is approved. In accordance herewith is the reading of the edited text and of my manuscript, *eshṭâ râyaḥ.*

The most interesting circumstance connected with this waste of half a dozen rules over the reading of a single word, is the indication afforded of the anomalousness of the combination as a phenomenon belonging to the Tâittirîya-Sanhitâ, while it is in other Vedic texts a natural and usual thing.

कखपकारपरः षमकारपूर्वः समवग्रहः ॥ २३ ॥

---

21. *sâṁkṛtyasya mata eshṭar iti visarjanîyo rephapara ukâram âpadyate*[1]. *tata*[2] *uvarṇapara okâram* (x.5) *iti otvam. yathâ*[3]: *eshṭo râyaḥ. asya ca nâi 'keshâm* (viii.19) *ity asya*[4] *deçabhedâd bhedaḥ: siddhodâharaṇaṁ*[5] *samânam.*

[1] B. adds *iti mâhisheyoktam.* [2] G. M. om. [3] W. B. G. M. om. [4] G. M. O. ins. *câ.* [5] G. M. O. ins. *tu.*

22. *ukhyasya mate rephapara*[1] *eshṭar iti visarjanîyaḥ pûrvavarṇena saho 'kâram âpadyate:* [2]*iti mâhisheyoktam*[2]. *yathâ*[3]: *eshṭu*[4] *râyaḥ.* [5]*vârarucoktaṁ*[6] *tv eshṭar iti visarjanîyo rephaparaḥ pûrveṇa saha repham âpadyata iti*[7]. *yathâ*[8]: [9]*eshṭâ*[10] *râyaḥ*[5,9] *pûrveṇa saha vartata iti sapûrvaḥ.*

asmin vikalpajâle[11] *prathamaṁ eshṭaç ca* (viii.18) *iti sûtram eve 'shṭam.*

[1] G. M. om.; O. puts after *iti.* (2) W. om.; O. *iti.* [3] G. M. om. [4] B. *ṭo;* G. M. *-ṭa.* (5) W. O. om. [6] B. *var-.* [7] G. M. om. [8] G. M. om. (9) M. om. [10] B. *-ṭrâ.* [11] W. *-jâte.*

23. **At the end of the former member of a compound, before *k*, *kh*, or *p*, *visarjanîya* becomes *sh*—or *s*, if preceded by *a*.**

The commentator notes the fact that, as a different following occasion is here introduced, the implication "followed by a vowel or a sonant consonant," which has so long been in force (namely, since rule 3 of this chapter), comes to an end. His illustrative examples are: *atho havishkṛtânâṁ eva* (vi.4.3[3]: O. omits *eva*), *grasitaṁ nishkhidati* (vi.1.9[1]: O. omits the first word), *bahishpavamâna upasadyaḥ* (vi.4.9[2]: O. omits the last word), *namaskârâir evâi 'nam* (v.5.7[4]: O. omits *enam*), and *pathaspathaḥ paripatim* (i.1.14[2]: O. omits the last word). As counter-example, to show that the *ḥ* must end the first member of a compound, not an independent word, we have *pushpâvatîḥ prasûvatîḥ* (iv.2.6[1]), and *namaḥ pitṛbhyo abhi* (iii.2.8[3]: only G. M. have *abhi*).

This is a general rule, applying to almost all the compounds in the Sanhitâ which show a final *ḥ* before an initial *k*, *kh*, or *p* of the second member. A few exceptions are mentioned farther on (rules 32,33).

आविर्निरिडःशश्वतोऽपसोत्विरिषोऽंहसोऽतिदिवोविश्वतोऽश्मनस्तामसः ॥ २४ ॥

24. **Also in *âviḥ*, *niḥ*, *iḍaḥ*, *çaçvataḥ*, *apasaḥ*, *deva rishaḥ*, *añhasaḥ*, *ati divaḥ*, *viçvataḥ*, *açmanaḥ*, and *tamasaḥ*.**

This rule, the commentator remarks, relates to words which are not first members of compounds. His examples are: for *âviḥ*, *âvish kṛnushva* (i.2.14[2]). For *niḥ*, *ghṛtaṁ nish pibati* (ii.3.11[5]):

---

23. *atra paranimittaviçeshaṇâd*[1] *etatparyantâ*[2] *svaraghoshavatparânuvṛttir*[3] *mantavyâ. avagrahântavartî*[4] *visarjanîyaḥ kakârakhakârapakâraparaḥ shakâram âpadyate: akârapûrvaç cet sakâram. yathâ*[5]: *atho*----: *gras*-----: *bahish*-----: *namas*-----. *pathas*-----. *avagraha iti kim: push*-----: *namaḥ*-----. *kakâraç ca khakâraç ca pakâraç ca kakhapakârâḥ: te*[6] *pare*[7] *yasmâd asâu*[8] *tathoktaḥ. akâraḥ pûrvo yasmâd asâv akârapûrvaḥ.*

[1] G. M. *-shâd.* [2] W. *ctâvatp-.* [3] G. M. *-paratvân-.* [4] W. *-havatara*; B. *-ha*; G. M. *-havarti.* [5] G. M. om. [6] O. *ete.* [7] G. M. *parâ.* [8] G. M. O. *sa.*

24. [1]------ *eshu*[1] *visarjanîyaḥ kakhapakâraparo* [2] *yathâvihitam*[3] *bhajate. yathâ*[4]: *âvish*----: *ghṛtaṁ*----: *iḍas*----: *çaçv*-----: *apasas*----: *uror*----: *deve 'ti kim: sa*----: *añhasas*----: *ati*----: *atî 'ti kim: divaḥ*----: *viçv*-----: *tvam* ----: *ud*-----.

anavagrahârtho 'yam ârambhaḥ.

(1) G. M. *âvirâdishu vidyamâno.* [2] G. M. ins. *hi shakâram akârapûrvaç cet sakâram iti.* [3] G. M. *-thâsaṁh-.* [4] G. M O. om.

of *nish* before *p*, I find besides only *nish padyerân* (vii.3.10²); before *kh*, *nish khidati* (ii.2.10⁵); before *k*, the cases are more numerous, with forms of *krî* (e.g.v.5.7²), and *kram* (vi.4.10²⁻³: doubtless; the separation of the divisions prevents the exhibition of the *sandhi*); cases of *niḥ* with accented forms of verbs in *k* are yet more frequent, but come under the preceding rule, not this one. For *iḍaḥ*, *iḍas paḍe sam idhyase* (ii.6.11⁴ and iv.4.4⁴: O. omits the last two words): on the other hand, we have *iḍâyâḥ pade* at vi.1.8². For *çaçvataḥ*, *çaçvatas kar haste* (ii.2.12¹). For *apasaḥ*, *apasas pâre asya* (iii.2.11²: O. omits *asya*). For *deva rishaḥ*, *uror â no deva rishas pâhi* (i.4.45²: O. omits to *deva*); with *sa rishaḥ pâtu naktam* (i.2.14⁷; 5.11¹⁻²) as counter-example, to show that the prescribed effect takes place only after *deva*. For *aṅhasaḥ*, *aṅhasas pâtu vâyuh* (iii.2.4³: only O. has *vâyuḥ*): another case is found in the same division, *aṅhasas pâtam*. For *ati divaḥ*, *ati divas pâhi samâvavṛtran* (i.8.14²: G. M. O. omit after *pâhi*); with *divaḥ pṛshṭhaṅ suvar gatvâ miçrâḥ* (iv.6.5¹: only B. has the last word; O. omits the last three) as counter-example, to show that the prescribed effect takes place only after *ati*. For *viçvataḥ*, *viçvatas pari havâmahe* (i.6.12¹: G. M. omit the last word): other cases occur at i.5.3³: ii.1.11¹; 3.14¹: iii.1.11⁴: iv.2.1³,3⁴; 3.13⁸ (in the various repetitions of only two phrases, always before *pari*); and, as first member of a compound, hence falling under the preceding rule, at iv.6.2⁴: an exception is noted in a later rule (viii.32). For *açmanaḥ*, *tvam açmanas pari* (iv.1.2⁵). For *tamasaḥ*, *ud vayaṁ tamasas pari paçyantaḥ* (iv.1.7⁴ and v.1.8⁶: only O. has the last word, and it omits the first two).

कृधिपिन्वपथेपरः ॥ २५ ॥

25. Also before *kṛdhi*, *pinva*, and *pathe*.

The examples are: *uru ṇas kṛdhi* (ii.6.11³), *apas pinva* (iv.3.4³), and *saprathâ namas pathe* (iv.7.13²: G. M. omit the first word). For *pinva* and *pathe* I find no further examples; but *s* before *kṛdhi* occurs also at i.4.2 (where the edition has the false reading *ḥ*), 3: iv.2.9⁴; 5.10²: v.7.6³⁻⁴: vi.3.2²; 4.5⁴.

न सक्रघकारपरे ॥ २६ ॥

26. But not when *s*, *kr*, or *gh* follows.

---

25. ...... *evamparo visarjanîyo yathâvidhim*¹ *bhajate. yathâ*²: *uru....: apas....: sapr-....*

¹ O. *-vihitaṁ.* ² G. M. O. om.

26. *sakraghe*¹ *'ty evampare sati kṛdhyâdâu*² *visarjanîyo yathâvihitaṁ*³ *nâ "padyate. yathâ*⁴: *tân....: çaṁ.... rephena kim: uta....: uru-....*

¹ W. adds *kâre sati.* ² O. *-âdi.* ³ G. M. *-vidhiṁ.* ⁴ W. B. G. M. om.

By its terms, the rule means that the prescription of the preceding rule becomes void when either of the words there mentioned is followed as here specified; but the cases of its application, so far as I am aware, all concern *kṛdhi.* The commentator's illustrations are: *tân ma âmanasaḥ kṛdhi svâhâ* (ii.3.9[1]: only W. has the first two words, and it omits the last one), *çaṁ ca naḥ kṛdhi: kratve dakshâya* (iii.3.11[4]: O. omits the last word), and *uru kshayâya naḥ kṛdhi: ghṛtaṁ ghṛtayone* (i.3.4[1]: G. M. O. omit the last word); and to the second of these there is a counter-example, *uta no mayas kṛdhi kshayadvîrâya* (iv.5.10[2]), to show that only *kr*, not *k* alone, gives occasion for retention of the *ḥ*. The words *âmanasaḥ kṛdhi svâhâ* occur again at ii.3.9[2]: I find no other cases to be specified in addition to those quoted by the commentator.

पत्नीवेपतीपतेपतयेपतिष्पतिंपरः ॥ २७ ॥

27. Also before *patnî ve, patî, pate, pataye, patiḥ,* and *patim.*

The examples are: first, *brahmaṇas patnî vedim* (iii.5.6[1]), with a counter-example, to show that the word *patnî* must be followed by *ve*, *retodhâḥ patnî va ity âha* (vi.5.8[4]: but O. reads *indriyâvataḥ patnîvantam*, i.4.27); further, *çubhas patî idam aham* (iii.2.10[2]: only O. has *aham*), *vâstosh pate prati* (iii.4.10[1]), *pra cyavasva bhuvas pate* (i.2.9 and vi.1.11[4]), *vâcas pataye pavasva* (i.4.2), *vâcas patir vâcam* (i.7.7[1]), and *vâcas patiṁ viçvakarmâṇam ûtaye* (iv.6.2[5]: G. M. O. omit the last word). The inquiry is now raised, why it was necessary to give all these words in detail, instead of comprehending them all in *pat*, and in reply is quoted the passage *divaṁ gacha suvaḥ pata* (iv.1.10[5] and v.1.10[5]).

The cases of retention of *s* before the cases of *pati* are so numerous, that it would be highly convenient to be able to dispose of them at once by quoting in the rule the theme *pati*; but such a proceeding is permitted (by i.22) only with themes ending in *a*. I add the other combinations of this class which I have noted from the Sanhitâ: *manasas pati* (i.1.13[3]; 4.44[3]), *pathas pati* (i.1.14[2]), *brahmaṇas pati* (i.5.6[4]: ii.1.57), *jyotishas pati* (i.5.11[1]: iv.4.4[6]), *çavasas pati* (ii.2.12[7]), *jagatas pati* (ii.4.5[1]), *sadasas pati* (ii.6.8[2]: iii.2.4[4]), *çatinas pati* (ii.6.11[1]: iv.4.4[1]), *nabhasas pati* (iii.3.8[3,6]), and *yas patiḥ* (iv.7.14[3]). We have the genitive *pateḥ* in *bṛhaspateḥ* (i.7.8[4]), but, as the *pada*-text reads *bṛhaḥ-pateḥ*, the word does not fall under this rule: *tapaspati* (i.2.10[2]; p. *tapaḥ-patiḥ*)

---

27. ------ *evamparo visarjanîyo yathâvihitam*[1] *bhajate. yathâ*[2]*: brah-----: va iti kim: reto-----: çubh-----: vâst----- pra-----: vâc-----: vâc-----: vâc----- pad ity etâvatâi 'va siddhe* [3]*pratipadapâṭhena kim*[3]*: divaṁ----- ityâdinishedhârthaḥ*[4].

[1] B. G. M. *-vidhiṁ.* [2] G. M. O. om. [3] G. M. *-ṭhaḥ kimarthaḥ;* O. *-ṭho.* [4] O. *-âdâu n-.*

belongs in the same category. Of the words quoted by the commentator, *bhuvas pati* occurs again at i.7.10[2], and *vâcas pati* at ii.6.8[1,2].

दिवःसहसस्परिपुत्परः ॥२८॥

28. Also in *divaḥ* and *sahasaḥ*, before *pari* and *put*.

The cited examples are *divas pari prathamam* (i.3.14[5] and iv.2.2[1]), *divas putrâya sûryâya* (i.2.9: O. omits the last word), and *sahasas putro adbhutaḥ* (iv.1.9[2]). We have *sahasas putram* also at iv.4.4[3], and *divas pari* at iii.3.3[3] and iv.2.10[4]; one case of *divaḥ pari* is excepted by rule 34, below. As counter-examples, are given *divaḥ pṛthivyâḥ pary antarikshât* (iii.1.10[2] et al.: W. B. O. omit *divaḥ*, which is better, as this is used just below to illustrate another point), *parushaḥparushaḥ pari* (iv.2.9[2]), and *puñsaḥ putrâñ uta viçvâyushañ rayim* (iv.6.9[4]: G. M. O. have only the first two words), to show that only the words specified show *s* before *pari* and *put*; and *divaḥ pṛthivyâḥ pari* (iii.1.10[2] et al.: G. M. omit *pari*, which is better this time), to show that those words show it only in the circumstances stated.

Put is declared a part of a word, involving more than one case.

रायस्पोपरः ॥२९॥

29. Also in *râyaḥ*, before *po*.

The commentator's examples are: *paçavo vai râyas poshaḥ* (v.4.6[2]), *sam ahañ râyas poshena* (i.7.9[2]), *çaṁtanutvâya râyas poshâya* (iii.2.5[1]: G. M. omit the first word and add *bṛhate*, which makes the reference belong to iv.1.10[2]), and *râyas poshasya daditâraḥ syâma* (iii.2.3[1]: only O. has the last word). As counter-examples, he gives *vibhuḥ posha uta tmanâ* (iii.1.11[2]), to show that the rule applies to no other word than *râyaḥ* before *po*, and *eshṭâ râyaḥ pre 'she bhagâya* (i.2.11[1]: G. M. omit the first word),

---

28. *divaḥ: sahasaḥ: ity ayor*[1] *visarjanîyaḥ pariputparo*[2] *yathâvidhim*[3] *bhajate. divas----: divas pu----: sah----. anayor iti kim: divaḥ----: par----: puñ----: evampara iti kim: divaḥ----. anekârthatvât*[4] *pud iti padâikadeçaḥ.*

[1] B. *anayoḥ;* G. M. *etayoḥ.* [2] G. M. *pari: put: ity evamparo;* O. do. except *ity.* [3] G. M. O. *-vihitam.* [4] B. G. M. O. *-rthaḥ.*

29. *râya iti atra visarjanîyaḥ po ity evamparo yathâvihitam*[1] *bhajate. yathâ*[2]*: paçavo----. po iti padâikadeço bahûpadâ-nârthaḥ: sam----: çaṁ----: râyas----. râya iti kim: vibhuḥ----:* [3]*po ity okâreṇa kim*[3]*:* [4]*eshṭâ----*

[1] G. M. *-vidhim.* [2] G. M. O. om. [(3)] G. M. *okâraḥ kimarthaḥ.* [4] B. om. to *yathâ* in comment to next rule.

to show that only *po*, not *p* when otherwise followed, calls out the prescribed effect in *râyaḥ*.

I have not attempted to note the numerous instances of the occurrence of *râyas posha* in the Sanhitâ. In the derivative *râyasposhavani* (i.2.12³; 3.1²), where the division is before *vani*, the *pada*-text, according to its custom, leaves the *s* of *râyas* unchanged (reading *râyasposha-vani*).

नमस्करोपरः ॥ ३० ॥

30. Also in *namaḥ*, before *karo*.

The examples illustrating the action of the rule are *saṁvatsareṇa namas karomi* (v.5.7³), and *ubhayîbhyo namas karoti* (ii.6.9⁸: O. reads *karomi*); counter-examples, showing the uselessness of either specification of the rule without the other, are *namaḥ kapardine ca* (iv.5.5¹,9¹: W. omits *ca;* O. omits the example), and *ekahâyanâd enaḥ karoti* (vi.6.3¹).

Other instances of *namas karoti* are found at v.5.5¹,7²: vi.3.8⁴; and of *-vatsareṇa namas karomi* at v.5.7³ twice, 7⁴ twice.

The printed text has *çreyasas karat* and *vasyasas karat* (but, by a strange inconsistency, immediately after, *paçumataḥ karat*) at i.8.6²; but, as these combinations are unauthorized by the Prâtiçâkhya, and not supported by my manuscript, I do not doubt that the readings are erroneous.

वसुष्ककारपरः ॥ ३१ ॥

31. Also in *vasuḥ*, before *k*.

The passage is *sa idhâno vasush kaviḥ* (iv.4.4⁵), and I have found no other. Counter-examples, of obvious application, are given: *vipraḥ çuciḥ kaviḥ* (i.3.14⁸; 5.5³), *mayi vasuḥ puro vasuḥ* (iii.2.10²), and *viçvâvasuḥ pary amushṇât* (vi.1.6⁵,11⁵: B., which is quite defective just along here, omits the first word).

नाधरंविश्वतोऽन्तर्जातोविविश्नुःपरुःपुनः ॥ ३२ ॥

---

30. *nama ity atra*[1] *visarjanîyaḥ karo ity evamparo yathâvihitam*[2] *bhajate. yathâ*[3]*: saṁv-....: ubhay-.....* [4]*karo iti kim: namaḥ....:*[4] [5]*nama iti kim: ekah-....*[5]

[1] G. M. O. om. [2] G. M. *-vidhim.* [3] G. M. O. om.; B. omits to here. (4) O. om. (5) G. M. put before *ubhay-*; B. puts after *ubhay-....*, and om. *karo iti.*

31. [1]*vasur ity atra visarjanîyaḥ kakâraparo yathâvihitam*[2] *âpadyate*[3]. *yathâ*[4,1]*: sa.... vasur iti kim: vipraḥ....: evampara iti kim: mayi....: viçvâ-....*

(1) B. om. [2] G. M. *-vidhim.* [3] G. M. O. *bhajate.* [4] G. M. O. om.

32. Not in *adhvaraṁ viçvataḥ, antaḥ, jâtaḥ, viviçuḥ paruḥ,* and *punaḥ.*

These words constitute exceptions under the foregoing rules. The commentator specifies in each case under which rule the exception falls. The first example is *yajñam adhvaraṁ viçvataḥ paribhûr asi* (iv.1.11[1]: O. omits the first word, W. B. the last): an exception under viii.24, which would require *viçvatas;* W. B. O. remark that the distinctive addition of *adhvaram* effects the exception, and W. O. add the counter-example *indraṁ vo viçvatas pari* (i.6.12[1]). For *antaḥ*, the example is *mahâdevam antaḥpârçvena* (i.4.36: O. omits the first word): an exception under rule 23, *antaḥ* being first member of a compound. For *jâtaḥ, bhûtasya jâtaḥ patir eka âsît* (iv.2.8[2]: O. omits the first word, and alone adds *âsît;* G. M. omit *ekaḥ* also): an exception under viii.27. For *viviçuḥ paruḥ, yâ âviviçuḥ paruḥparuḥ* (iv.2.6[4]); with the counter-example *parushparur anughushyâ viçasta* (iv.6.9[3]: only G. M. have the last word). For *punaḥ*, finally, *punaḥpunar hy asmât* (vi.5.1[3-4]: only G. M. have *asmât*). Both these last are exceptions under viii.23.

The versions of the comment to this rule are more than usually discordant, all being defective except W. and O., and even these having suffered considerable disarrangement. For the details, see the various readings below.

धषवति ॥ ३३ ॥

33. Nor before a word containing *dh* or *sh*.

"By vicinage," says the commentator, is understood a negative, in this and in the next following rule. The meaning of the rule is that, when a word containing either of the letters *dh* or *sh* follows the *visarjanîya*, the latter is not liable to conversion into *s* or *sh*, as required by the foregoing precepts. The examples given are

---

32. ------ *eteshâṁ*[1] *visarjanîyo yathâvihitaṁ*[2] *na bhajate*[3]. *yathâ*[4]: *yajñam----: âvirnir*[5] (viii.24) *iti prâptiḥ:* [6]*adhvaraviçeshanân nivṛttiḥ*[6]: [7]*adhvaram iti kim: indr----:*[7] *mahâ----:* [8]*kakhapakâra* (viii.23) *iti prâptiḥ: bhût----: patnîvepatî*[9] (viii.27) *iti*[10] *prâptiḥ*[8]: [11]*yâ----*[11]: *viviçur*[12] *iti kim: parush----: punaḥ----: kakhapakâraparaḥ*[13] (viii.23) *ity anayoḥ prâptiḥ.*

[1] G. M. *ity eteshu.* [2] G. M. *-vidhiṁ.* [3] G. M. O. *âpadyate.* [4] G. M. O. om. [5] G. M. add *iḍaḥ.* (6) G. M. om. (7) B. G. M. om.; W. O. put next before *viviçur iti kim.* (8) B. om. [9] O. om. *pati;* G. M. *patishpatim.* [10] O. *ity âdinâ.* (11) W. B. O. put after *mahâ----.* [12] G. M. *-çuḥ parur.* [13] G. M. O. om. *paraḥ.*

33. *sâṁnidhyâd atra*[1] *paratra ca*[2] *nañartho labhyate. dhaç*[3] *ca shaç*[4] *ca dhashâu: tâv asmint sta iti dhashavat: tasmin dhashavati*[5] *pade parabhûte sati* [6]*pûrvo visarjanîyo*[6] *yathâvihitaṁ*[7]

bahiḥparidhi skandât (ii.6.6[2] and vi.2.8[5]: the same divisions contain each a second example of the compound), *purushaḥpurusho nidhanam* (vi.6.3[2]: the same division contains a second example of the compound), and *ubhayataḥkshṇûr bhavati* (v.1.1[4]). I have noted besides only *parushaḥparushaḥ pari* (iv.2.9[2]). That the word containing *dh* or *sh* must follow the *visarjanîya*, not be the one that itself ends in that letter, is shown by the counter-examples *adhaspadaṁ kṛṇute* (iv.7.13[3]), and *ṛtasya jyotishas patim* (i.5.11[1]).

परिवाप्रपरः ॥ ३४ ॥

34. Not before *pari vâ* or *pra.*

The examples are *rocanâ divaḥ pari vâjeshu* (iv.2.11[1]: only G. M. have the first word)—with the counter-example *divas pari prathamam* (i.3.14[5] and iv.2.2[1]), to show the need of citing *vâ* after *pari*—and *tasmâd itaḥpradânam devâḥ* (iii.2.9[7]: O. omits *devâḥ*). Of these, the first is an exception under viii.28; the other, under viii.23. There is yet another passage, *bahiḥprâṇo vâi manushyaḥ* (vi.1.1[4]), which needs to be brought under the rule; and the commentator accordingly declares that the quotation of *pra* in this rule with short *a* is intended to connote *prâ* also—just as, in a rule of the next chapter (ix.24), *athâ* connotes *atha* also, by a converse principle. This, however, suggests a difficulty: why then is not rule vii.7, prescribing for *prâ* an effect which had already been

---

nâ "padyate. yathâ[8]*: bahiḥ-----: puru-----: ubhay-----: kakhapakâra*[9] (viii.23) *iti prâptiḥ. parabhûta iti kim: adhas-----: ṛtasya-----.*[10]

[1] G. M. ins. *ca.* [2] G. M. O. ins. *sûtre.* [3] G. M. O. *dhakâraç.* [4] G. M. O. *shakâraç.* [5] B. G. M. O. om. [(6)] O. om.; G. M. *pûrvav-.* [7] G. M. *-vidhiṁ.* [8] B. G. M. O. om. [9] B. *-rapara.* [10] W. adds *tasminn iti nidishṭe pûrvasya. parivâpravaraḥ.*

34. *pari vâ: pra:* [1] *evamparo visarjanîyo yathâvihitaṁ*[2] *nâ "padyate. rocanâ-----: ve 'ti kim: divas-----: tasmâd-----. pre 'ti hrasvagrahaṇaṁ dîrghasyâ 'py upalakshaṇam:* [3] *yatho 'dathâparaç ca* (ix.24) *iti dîrghagrahaṇaṁ hrasvasyo 'palakshaṇârtham*[4]*. tarhi prâpûrvaç ca* (vii.7) *iti sûtraṁ vyartham: praçabdasyâ* [5] *'nuvṛttasyâi 'va dîrghopalakshakatvâd*[6]*: iti cet: ucyate: pratyakshagṛhîtasyâi 'vo 'palakshakatvaṁ*[7] *nâ 'nukṛshṭasye 'ti vijñeyam:* [3]*tathâ hi: vâhanauhyamânaḥ* (vii.6)[3] *ity atra*[3] *cakâreṇa praçabdas tatrâ 'nukṛshṭaḥ: atra tu*[8] *parivâprapara*[9] *ity* [10] *upalakshakatvam*[11] *bhavati. tathâ satî 'dam apy udâharaṇam: bahiḥ-----.*

[1] G. M. ins. *ity.* [2] G. M. *-vidhiṁ.* [3] B. ins. [(3)] here, as well as below, in its place. [4] G. M. O. *-ṇam;* B. *hrasvop-.* [5] G. M. ins. *eva.* [6] G. M. *-kshaṇatvâd;* O. *dîrghagrahaṇasyop-.* [7] G. M. *-tvât.* [8] G. M. om. [9] G. M. *vâ-.* [10] G. M. ins. *prapara iti pratyakshagrahîtatvâd;* O. ins. *pratyakshagṛhîtatvâd.* [11] G. M. *-kshaṇam.*

prescribed for *pra*, a superfluity? Because, is the reply, such connotation is only proper in the case of a word directly cited, not of one that is brought forward by implication merely: and in rule vii.6 the *pra* was thus brought forward [from rule 4], in virtue of the *ca*, 'and,' contained in the rule: whereas here the *pra* is expressly mentioned. This seems a case of rather questionable interpretation.

न निर्णं निः ॥३५॥

35. Not so with *niḥ*.

That is, as the commentator explains it, the exception established by the preceding rule does not hold good in the case of *niḥ*, which is treated as prescribed in rule 24, even before *pra*. The cases instanced in illustration of the rule are both of a doubtful character: the one is a *jaṭâ*-reading, *prâñcâu nir ṇish prâñcâu prâñcâu niḥ* (vi.4.10²), the other an extract from the ending of the same *anuvâka* (vi.4.10), *âtmanâ parâ nish pra çukraçocishâ*, these words being those which end respectively the first four divisions of the *anuvâka*. We shall find other quotations of the endings later; and their appearance is at least decisive of the recognition by the commentator of the breaking up of the *anuvâkas* into divisions of fifty words each, whatever we may have to believe respecting its recognition by the Prâtiçâkhya. We are not, however, to take for granted that even the commentator accepted the division as now made in our manuscripts, involving a suspension of continuity of the *saṁhitâ*-text after each fiftieth word: there was probably at first a mere enumeration made, with an expression of its results at the end of the *anuvâka*. The endings, as may be seen in the Calcutta edition, are carefully accented, and written according to the rules of combination as laid down by the Prâtiçâkhya. The same rules are followed in the *jaṭâ*-text; and hence, as (by rule vii.2, above) *niḥ* converts the following initial *n* into *ṇ* in *saṁhitâ*, so does it also in the repetitions of the *jaṭâ* (*nir ṇish*). As a yet farther consequence, it has the same effect in the rules of the Prâtiçâkhya, and I have therefore accepted the reading *ṇa* instead of *na* in the repetition of the present rule, although it is supported only by T. and W

---

35. *nir ity atra visarjanîyasya*[1] *praparatve*[2] *'pi shatvanishedho na bhavati: shatvam eva bhavatî 'ty arthaḥ. prâñ-....: âtm-....*

iti tribhâshyaratne prâtiçâkhyavivaraṇe[3]
ashṭamo 'dhyâyaḥ.

[1] O. *-nîyaḥ.* [2] O. *prapare.* [3] O. ins. *prathamapraçne.*

CHAPTER IX.

CONTENTS: 1–6, treatment of final *ḥ* before initial surd letters; 7–10, treatment of final *aḥ* and *âḥ*; 11–15, of final diphthongs before initial vowels; 16–17, of the particle *u*; 18–19, duplication of final *ṅ* and *n*; 20–24, conversion of final *ân*, *în*, *ûn*, to *âṅ*, *îṅr*, *ûṅr*.

ऊष्मपरो ऽघोषपरे लुप्यते काण्डमायनस्य ॥ १ ॥

1. *Visarjanîya*, when followed by a spirant which has a surd letter after it, is dropped, according to Kâṇḍamâyana.

The commentator, after a brief paraphrase of the rule, gives a couple of examples to illustrate its working: namely, *catustanâṁ karoti* (v.1.6⁴; p. *catuḥ-stanâm*), and *vâyava stho 'pâyava stha* (i.1.1). The mention of Kâṇḍamâyana is declared to be made on account of a difference of views: others, namely, hold that *ḥ* is dropped before a spirant that is followed by a sonant letter as well, as *adbhya svâhâ* (i.8.13³), *ye çuklâ syus tam* (ii.3.1³: W. B. omit *tam*), *yo hatamanâ svayampâpaḥ* (ii.2.8³: O. omits *yo*; G. M. omit *pâpaḥ*), and *dânakâmâ me prajâ syuḥ* (ii.2.8³; 3.4¹: O. omits the first word; G. M., the first two). I am not sure that I understand the consideration further alleged, in view of which it is decided that "the rule is all right;" it appears to be that, reference having thus been made to a discordance of views, those words will be hereafter specified in which there is omission made under any other prescription—but what this refers to, I am unable to see.

Every MS. that I have reads *'ghoshaparo* as second word in the rule: but the comment so plainly implies the reading *-pare*, and the sense so obviously requires it, that I have ventured its adoption.

Although the prescription here given is put upon the authority of an individual, it is pretty evidently to be regarded as definitely

---

1. *ûshmaparo visarjanîyaḥ kâṇḍamâyanasya mate lupyate tasminn ûshmaṇy aghoshavatpare*[1] *sati. yathâ: catu-....: vây-.... kâṇḍamâyanagrahaṇaṁ*[2] *vikalpârtham: anyeshâm mate ghoshavatpare 'py ûshmaṇi visarjanîyo lupyate: yathâ: adbhya .... ye....: yo....: dâna-..... evaṁ ca vikalpâçrayaṇe*[3] *sati lakshaṇântaragataṁ*[4] *yeshu padeshu lupyate tâni padâni vakshyâma*[5] *iti vacanaṁ saralam bhavati.*

ûshmâ paro yasmâd [6]*asâv ûshmaparaḥ*[6]*: na ghoshavân aghoshaḥ. asâu*[7] *paro yasmât* [8]*sa tathoktaḥ*[8]*: tasminn aghoshapare.*

[1] G. M. O. om. *vat.* [2] G. M. *-yanasya gr-.* [3] W. *-çravaṇe*; O. *-çrayagrahaṇe* G. M. *-lpântare.* [4] W. O. *-ṇâtara-.* [5] G. M. O *prav-.* [(6)] G. M. *sa tatho 'ktaḥ* [7] G. M. om. [(8)] G. M. om.

adopted and taught by the Prâtiçâkhya, and is usually (not without occasional exceptions) conformed to by the edition of the Sanhitâ, and by my manuscripts both of that and of the Prâtiçâkhya and its commentary. I have, therefore, treated it as peremptory, and have everywhere governed by it the readings I have accepted. The same omission is prescribed by the Rik and Vâjasaneyi Prâtiçâkhyas, but not by the Atharvan (see Ath. Pr. ii.40, note).

अघोषपरस्तस्य सस्थानमूष्माणम् ॥ २ ॥

2. Followed by a surd letter, it becomes the spirant of like position with that letter.

The commentator's examples are: *yaχ kâmayeta* (ii.1.2[3] et al.; O. reads *-yate*); *agniç ca me* (iv.7.6[1]: O. omits this and the next example), *ulûkaç çaçaḥ* (v.5.18), *agnis te tejaḥ* (i.1.10[3] and vii.5.17: O. leaves out *te*), and *yaφ pâpmanâ gṛhîtaḥ* (ii.1.3[5],4[6]: W. leaves off the first word; G. M. O. omit the last).

The requirements of this rule are by no means complied with by the manuscripts, nor have I followed them in the present work. In the first place, no manuscript that I possess, or have ever seen, attempts to represent any such sounds as the *jihvâmûlîya* and *upadhmânîya* (see i.9), or *χ* and *φ*; for these, *visarjanîya* is universally substituted, as if the sect of Âgniveçya and Vâlmîki (see rule 4, below) had supplanted all its rivals; and, in the second place, the agreement to leave *visarjanîya* unchanged before a sibilant (according to the view of the authorities referred to below, in rule 5) is nearly as general. In my MS. of the Sanhitâ, I have noted about thirty cases of conversion to a sibilant, in place of unchanged retention, and they are nearly all in a single limited neighborhood (in iv.5), where a different scribe has developed his originality a little. As is hinted above, in the introduction, however, G. and M. make with great regularity the assimilation of *ḥ* to the following sibilant; O. does it not infrequently; the others, almost never.

I have put together, in the note to Ath. Pr. ii.40, a statement of the variously conflicting views respecting the treatment of *ḥ* before the different classes of surd letters held by the different Prâtiçâkhyas, or referred to in their rules; and it is unnecessary to repeat it here. The sole point upon which all authorities agree is the conversion into *ç* and *s* before palatal and dental mutes respectively—and this is also the only point left unquestioned by the rules which follow here in our treatise.

न क्षपरः ॥ ३ ॥

---

2. *aghoshaparo visarjanîyas tasyâ 'ghoshasya sasthânam ûshmâṇam bhajate.* yaχ....: [1]agniç....: ulû-....:[1] agnis....: yaφ....

(1) O. om.

3. But not when followed by *ksh.*

That is to say, *visarjanîya* remains unchanged before *ksh*, the preceding rule for its conversion to *jihvâmûlîya* being annulled. There is nothing corresponding to the usage here prescribed in either of the other treatises. The commentator quotes a number of examples: *manaḥ ksheme* (v.2.1[7]), *ubhayataḥkshṇûr bhavati* (v.1.1[4]: W. B. omit *bhavati*: the *visarjanîya* was exempted from conversion into *s* before the *k* by viii.33), *ghanâghanaḥ kshobhaṇaḥ* (iv.6.4[1]), *pûrvo 'rshṭuḥ kshîyate* (iii.1.7[1]), and *dyâuḥ kshâmâ rerihat* (iv.2.1[2]: O. omits the last word).

कपवर्गपरश्चाग्निवेश्यवाल्मीक्योः ॥ ४ ॥

4. Nor, according to Âgniveçya and Vâlmîki, when followed by a guttural or a labial mute.

The two authorities here specified (the commentator calls them "holders of a *çâkhâ*, teachers"), it appears, reject altogether the *jihvâmûlîya* and *upadhmânîya*, since they prescribe the retention of *visarjanîya* in the only situations where those problematical sounds are liable to arise. The commentator quotes a couple of illustrative passages: *yaḥ kâmayeta* (ii.1.2[3] et al.), and *agniḥ paçur âsît* (v.7.26: O. has dropped out what follows *agniḥ*). Then, to show that on other points these heterodox persons accept our rule 2, he cites *madhuç ca mâdhavaç ca* (i.4.14 and iv.4.11[1]), *manas tatvâya* (iv.1.1[1]: but B. substitutes *namas talpyâya*, iv.5.9[1]), *âçuç çiçânaḥ* (iv.6.4[1]), *yas somaṁ vamiti* (ii.3.2[6]).

ऊष्मपर एवैकेषामाचार्याणाम् ॥ ५ ॥

5. According to some authorities, not when followed by a spirant, and only then.

I believe there can be no real doubt as to the meaning of this rule, although it is not very explicitly interpreted by the commen-

---

3. *kshaparo visarjanîyaḥ pûrvavidhiṁ na bhajate. yathâ*[1]: *man-....: ubhay-....: ghanâ-....: pûrv-....: dyâuḥ.... kshakârasyâ 'ghoshavattvât praptiḥ.*

[1] G. M. O. om.

4. [1]*cakâro nishedham âkarshati. âgniveçyavâlmîkyoḥ*[1] *çâkhinor âcâryayor*[2] *mate* [3]*kavargaparaḥ pavargaparo vâ*[3] *pûrvavidhiṁ* [4]*nâ* "*padyate*[4]. *yaḥ....: agniḥ*[5].... *kakâraç ca pakâraç ca kapâu: tayor vargâu*[5] *kapavargâu: tâu parâu yasmât sa tathoktaḥ. evampara iti kim: madhuç....: manas....: âçuç ....: yas....*

(1) G. M. om.; O. *caçabdo nañâkarshakaḥ: âgn-.* [2] O. om. (3) O. *kapavargaparo visarjanîyaḥ.* (4) O. *na bhajate.* (5) O. *kavargaç ca pavargaç ca.*

tator, and although G. M. O. omit the negative in the interpretation (I presume, by a copyist's blunder only). Some authorities, who do not, like Âgniveçya and Vâlmîki, refuse to accept the *jihvâmûlîya* and *upadhmânîya*, nevertheless deny the doctrine of rule 2 to this extent—that they prescribe the retention of *visarjanîya*, not its assimilation, before a sibilant. Thus, they would write *âçuḥ çiçânaḥ* (iv.6.4[1]). G. M., as is their constant custom, write here *âçuç;* and so does O., as is its common, though far from invariable, usage: but this means nothing; for we have no good reason to expect the manuscripts of the commentary to conform themselves in any such case to a reading which will truly illustrate the matter in hand; they simply make the *sandhi* in the manner usual with them: for example, under rule 2, no MS. attempts to indicate the χ and φ, and W. B. give the ḥ instead of the sibilant before the sibilant.

If we reject this interpretation, our sole alternative is, so far as I can see, to hold that some authorities would accept rule 2 only so far as it relates to ḥ before a sibilant, but would retain ḥ every where else, even reading *agniḥ te tejaḥ, agniḥ ca me.* This seems altogether inadmissible. Yet we must acknowledge that it is to some extent favored by the commentator's selection of counter-examples, namely *manas tatvâya* (iv.1.1[1]: but B. substitutes again *namas talpyâya*, iv.5.9[1]) and *yaḥ kâmayeta* (ii.1.2[3] et al.). According to our preferred interpretation, there would be no particular reason for quoting the former of these, since the combination it illustrates has been made a question by no one: according to the other, it would be required (in the form *manaḥ tatvâya*), to show what these dissidents held should be done in such a case.

न प्लाक्षिप्लाक्षायणयोः ॥ ६ ॥

6. Not according to Plâkshi and Plâkshâyaṇa.

The natural interpretation of this rule would seem to be, that Plâkshi and Plâkshâyaṇa are not of the number of those who hold the objectionable doctrine of the last rule, or of the last two rules. If, however, I rightly apprehend the commentator, he declares it

---

5. *ekeshâm âcâryâṇâm mata ûshmapara eva visarjanîyaḥ pûrvavidhim na*[1] *bhajate. yathâ*[2]*: âçuḥ---- evakâreṇa kim: manas----:* [3]*yaχ----.*[3]

[1] G. M. O. om. [2] G. M. O. om. [(3)] G. M. om.

6. *kapavargapara*[1] *ûshmaparaç ca visarjanîyaḥ plâkshiplâkshâyaṇayoḥ çâkhinoḥ*[2] *pakshe na khalu pûrvavidhim bhajate. yaḥ----: yaḥ----: âçuç---- evampara iti kim: manas----.* [3]*kapavargâdi sûtratrayam anishṭam.*[3]

[1] O. *kavargaparaḥ pavargaparaç ca.* [2] G. M. om. [(3)] G. M. prefix *evaṁ*, and put the whole at the end of the comment on the preceding rule; they also omit rule 6.

to mean "in the opinion of these two authorities, it does not—that is, *ḥ* does not follow the prescription of rule 2 either before a guttural or palatal mute or before a spirant." This is equivalent to a ratification of rule 4, and a ratification or rejection of rule 5, according as we adopt the one or the other of the two interpretations proposed for the latter; and it is, in my view, quite unsuited to the connection. The discordant explanations of some of the other views of designated authorities given in the rules of the treatise show us that the commentators had not in all cases, at least, any certain knowledge by tradition of the matters referred to, but simply interpreted as well as they were able the notices of their text-book—and we have the same right as they in this respect. If the particular point here under discussion were of more practical consequence, I should be inclined to go into a fuller discussion of it; as the case stands, it has perhaps cost us already more words than it is worth.

The commentator illustrates by repeating several of the quotations already given—namely *yaḥ kâmayeta* (ii.1.2[3] et al.), *yaḥ pápmanâ* (ii.1.3[5] et al.), *âçuḥ çiçânaḥ* (iv.6.4[1]): these as direct examples; as counter-example, according to W. O., *manas tatvâya* (iv.1.1[1]), for which B. once more substitutes *namas talpyâya* (iv.5.9[1]), while G. M. read *agniç ca me* (iv.7.6[1])—the readings of which, as regards the *visarjanîya*, each manuscript gives in its usual fashion (except that W. has this time *âçuḥç çiçânaḥ*, by a blundering divergence in the wrong direction), so that we are deprived of any farther aid from that quarter to the understanding of the rule.

Finally, rules 4–6 are declared not approved.

ओकारमः सर्वो ऽकारपरः ॥ ७ ॥

7. *Aḥ*, the whole of it, when followed by *a*, becomes *o*.

The commentator's cited examples are *preddho agne* (iv.6.5[4] and v.4.7[3]), *samiddho añjan* (v.1.11[1]), and *so 'bravit* (ii.1.2[1] et al.). He then enters into a long exposition intended to prove the necessity of the specification *sarvaḥ*, 'the whole of it,' in the rule. Without it, we are told, the reading *samiddho añjan* (in the second example given) would not be established: for, by i.56, alteration and omission concern only a single letter; hence, if *sarvaḥ* were omitted, only the final *visarjanîya* would be converted to *o*; this, with the preceding *a*, would become *âu* by x.7; the *âu* would

---

7. *aḥsarvo visarjanîya*[1] *otvam*[2] *bhajate 'kâraparaḥ*[3]*: aḥsarva ity akâreṇa sahe*[4] *'ty arthaḥ. pre-....: sam-....: so-.... aḥsarva iti kim: samiddho aññjann iti na sidhyet*[5]*: kiṁ tu vârṇasya vikâralopâv* (i.56) *iti visarjanîyamâtrasya syâd otvam: tata okârâukâraparaḥ* (x.7) *ity âukâre kṛta âukâra âvam* (ix.15) *ity âvâdeçaḥ: tathâ sati*[6] *samiddhâv añjann iti syât.* [7]*yad vâ*[7]*:* [8] *svaraparo yakâram* (ix.10) *iti yatvam* [9]

be converted into *âv* by ix.15, and the final reading would be *samiddhâv añjan.* Or, again [supposing the present rule not to be given], the *visarjanîya* would become *y* by ix.10, the *y* would be dropped by x.19, the preceding *a* would be exempted from further combination by x.25, and the *saṁhitâ*-reading would turn out *samiddha añjan.*

The Ath. Pr. (ii.53) avoids the same difficulty by prescribing the conversion of the *ḥ* into *u*, which then combines with the preceding *a* into *o*. The other treatises (Rik Pr. ii.12; Vâj. Pr. iv.42) treat the combination in the same manner as our own. What becomes of the following *a* is taught in the eleventh and twelfth chapters.

घोषवत्परश्च ॥ ८ ॥

8. Also when followed by a sonant consonant.

Only one example of this combination is cited, namely *mâ no mitro varuṇaḥ* (iv.6.8[1]: G. M. O. omit the last word).

The commentator raises against this rule the objection that, as prescribing the same thing with the one preceding, it should not have been made a separate rule at all; and, in reply, he promises that the exposition of the meaning of *tu* in the next rule shall explain the reason of the proceeding.

अवर्णपूर्वस्तु लुप्यते ॥ ९ ॥

9. But *visarjanîya*, when preceded by an *a*-vowel, is omitted.

In these rules, from 7 to 10 inclusive, the *anuvṛtti*, or continuance of implication, is intricate and irregular in an unusual degree, and even beyond the measure of what ought to be tolerated. The implication of *visarjanîya* being made all the way from viii.5 to

---

bhavati: tasmiñç ca lupyete tv avarṇapûrvâu yavakârâv (x.19) *iti yakâre*[10] *lupte paraç ca paraç ca* (x.25) *iti*[11] *kâryântarâprasiddheḥ*[12] *samiddha*[13] *añjann ity syât: tan mâ bhûd ity*[14] [15]*evam arthaḥ*[15]*: aḥsarva*[16] *ity uktam.*

[1] G. M. om., and ins. *apy.* [2] G. M. *okâram.* [3] G. M. put at the beginning. [4] G. M. *sahito visarjaniya.* [5] O. *sidhyati.* [6] B. G. M. om. [(7)] G. M. *kiṁ ca;* O. *kiṁ tu.* [8] G. M. O. ins. *atha.* [9] G. M. O. ins. *vâ.* [10] G. M. O. om. [11] O. ins. *sûtreṇa.* [12] G. M. *-prasakte;* O. *-prasaktiḥ tathâ sati.* [13] W. *-ddho;* B. *-ddhâu.* [14] G. M. om. [(15)] G. M. O. om.; B. om. *evam.* [16] B. om. *aḥ.*

8. *cakâra*[1] *okâram aḥsarvaṁ câ 'nvâdiçati. aḥ*[2] *sarvo ghoshavatpara*[3] *otvam bhajate. yathâ*[4]*: mâ*----. *nanu vidhâu samâne pṛthakkaraṇam*[5] *anarthakam iti cet: uttarasûtre tuçabdavyâkhyânena*[6] *sphuṭîkarishyata*[7] *iti parihâraḥ.*

[1] G. M. put next before *anvâdiçati.* [2] O. om. [3] G. M. O. *-raç ca.* [4] G. M. O. om. [5] G. M. *-ksûtrak-.* [6] G. M. *-khyâne.* [7] W. O. *-shya.*

ix.10 (as pointed out in the comment to viii.5), rule 7 of this chapter ought to teach that "*visarjanîya*, when preceded by *a*, becomes *o* along with the latter, when *a* follows:" instead of which a new subject, "the whole syllable *aḥ*," is introduced there; and *visarjanîya*, being thus replaced by something else in rules 7 and 8, ought to drop out of view altogether, or, if needed further, to be distinctly specified over again. But we find it implied without specification in the present rule; and, farther, the being followed by a sonant consonant is brought down "by vicinage" from rule 8, while the *tu*, 'but,' the commentator says, merely annuls the being followed by *a*, as specified in rule 7. This is little less than absurd: if the sequence of *a* was to be annulled at all, it should have been so in rule 8—or, rather, it was annulled by rule 8, and needs to be made no further account of. The *tu* is here, as often elsewhere, a simple sign of a change of subject, and the commentator's attempt to give it a precise significance is—also, as often elsewhere—a failure. Our rule means, by its terms, that *aḥ*, *âḥ*, and *â3ḥ* lose their *ḥ* before a sonant consonant; only, as *aḥ* was already specially provided for by rule 8, it virtually applies only to *âḥ* and *â3ḥ*. The statement is thus made more general than is needed for the case in hand, because the whole implication of "preceded by any *a*-vowel" is needed for rule 10, which is to teach that *aḥ*, *âḥ*, and *â3ḥ* before a vowel—here, again, with the exception of *aḥ* before *a*, already provided for—convert their *ḥ* into *y*, preliminary to dropping it altogether, by x.19. But rule 10 presents a more anomalous combination of two heterogeneous matters into one precept than is easily to be paralleled elsewhere in the Prâtiçâkhya. It is really made up of two independent parts: one, *atha svaraparaḥ*, 'Now then, when followed by a vowel,' which is an introductory heading having force through this chapter and the next; the other, *visarjanîyo yakâram*, '*ḥ* becomes *y*;' and their combination is made in order that the implication of *visarjanîya* and also of *avarṇapûrva* may be made from what precedes, and may not require to be distinctly stated.

The commentator's examples of the application of the rule are *devâ gâtuvidaḥ* (i.1.13³; 4.44³: vi.6.2³), and *vicityaḥ somâ3 na vicityâ3 iti* (vi.1.9¹; *somâ3* for *somâ3ḥ*, by protraction from *somaḥ*: G. M. omit the last two words, O. the last three). He adds, as his exposition of the connection of the rule, that the express spe-

9. *avarṇapûrvo ghoshavatparas tu* [1] *visarjanîyo lupyate: hrasvapûrvasyâu 'kâra*[2] *eva dîrghapûrvasya*[3] *plutapûrvasya ca lopaḥ. yathâ: devâ----: viç-----. okâram aḥ sarvo 'kâraparaḥ* (ix.7) *ity akâraparatvam pratyaksham tuçabdena nivartyâ 'numânikam ghoshavatparatvam parigṛhyate sâṁnidhyât: asyâ 'nuvartanam evâ 'bhîshṭam atre 'ti pûrvasûtradvayasya*[4] *pṛthakkaraṇam.*

[1] W. ins. *saḥ*. [2] B. G. M. *vikâra*. [3] B. *-rva*; O. *-gha*. [4] G. M. *-trasya*.

cification of sequence by *a*, made in rule 7, is annulled by the word *tu*, and that an inferential sequence by a sonant consonant is assumed by vicinage [from rule 8]; and that the implication here of the latter only is the reason why rules 7 and 8 are given independently of one another. That is to say, such is the easiest way of arriving at the result desired, that the *ḥ* of *âḥ* and *âsh* is not directly dropped before *a*, but passes through the intermediate step of conversion into *y*, as before the other vowels.

अथ स्वरपरो यकारम् ॥ १० ॥

10. When followed by a vowel, it becomes *y*.

That is to say, *visarjanîya* does so, if preceded by an *a*-vowel (rule 9)—except in the case of *aḥ* followed by *a* (rule 7). And, as is intimated by the prefixion of *atha*, the specification "followed by a vowel" is of force also in the following rules (through chapter x.). I have remarked in the preceding note upon the anomalousness of this rule, as striving to fuse into one the winding-up of one subject and the introduction of another. It has not seemed possible to render the *atha* excepting by a longer and more tedious paraphrase than I was willing to introduce; accordingly, I have left it out in translating the precept.

The commentator's examples are *âpa undantu jîvase* (i.2.1[1]: G. M. O. omit *jîvase*), *tâ abruvan* (ii.3.5[2]; 5.1[5]), and *anvârabhyâ3 iti* (vi.3.8[1]; *anvârabhyâ3* for *anvârabhyâsh*, by protraction from *anvârabhyaḥ*); and he gives further, as counter-examples, *âpo varuṇasya* (v.5.4[1]: a not unexceptionably selected example, since *âpaḥ* even before a vowel might not follow the present rule), and *agnir ekâkshareṇa* (i.7.11[1]: a case under viii.6, as the preceding under ix.8).

This conversion of *visarjanîya* into *y* is only the preliminary step to its complete loss, by rule x.19. The same course of conversion is followed by the Âtharvan and Vâjasaneyi Prâtiçâkhyas (Ath. Pr. ii.41; Vâj. Pr. iv.36), but not by that of the Rik (ii.9,10).

एकारो ऽयम् ॥ ११ ॥

11. *E*, before a vowel, becomes *ay*.

---

10. [1]*athaçabdo 'dhikârârthaḥ*[1]*: svaraḥ paro yasmâd asâu*[2] *svaraparaḥ. ita uttaraṁ yad ucyate*[3] *svarapara ity evaṁ tatra nimittatvenâ 'dhikṛtaṁ veditavyam*[4]*. sâṁnidhyâd avarṇapûrva*[5] *iti labhyate: svaraparo visarjanîyo* [6]*'varṇapûrvo*[6] *yakâram*[7] *âpadyate. yathâ*[8]*: âpa---: tâ---: anvâ-----. svarapara iti kim: âpo----: avarṇapûrva iti kim: agnir----.*

(1) G. M. *athe 'ty ayam adhikâraḥ*; O. *-kâraḥ*. [2] O. *so 'yaṁ*. [3] G. M. *vakshyâmaḥ*. [4] G. M. O. *jñâtavyaṁ*. [5] O. om. *pûrva*. [6] G. M. put before *svaraparo*. [7] O. *yatvam*. [8] O. om.–

Of which, then, the *y* is lost by x.19, leaving only *a;* and this, by x.25, is not liable to further combination. The commentator's examples are *ima evâ 'smâi* (ii.4.10[3]), and *ta enam bhishajyanti* (ii.3.11[4]).

ओकारो ऽवम् ॥ १२ ॥

12. *O* becomes *av.*

The example is *vishṇav e 'hî 'dam* (ii.4.12[3]). For the further treatment of the *v* thus produced, see x.19 and the following rules.

नाकारपरौ ॥ १३ ॥

13. But not, in either case, when followed by *a.*

The dual number of the attribute in this rule, we are told, sufficiently shows that the two letters *e* and *o*, last mentioned, are its subject. There are two different rules in the treatise applying to the case of a final *e* or *o* coming to stand before initial *a*—namely rule 11, above [or rule 12], and rule xi.1, which directs that the latter shall be elided—and, since the rules of this chapter are of paramount force, as preceding the other, the present precept is required in order to annul them.

The commentator's examples are *mâ te asyâm* (i.6.12[5]), *samiddho añjan* (v.1.11[1]), and *te 'bruvan* (ii.5.1[3] et al.).

ऐकार आयम् ॥ १४ ॥

14. *Âi* becomes *ây.*

---

11. [1]*visṛshṭo visarjanîyaḥ*[1]. *idam*[2] *idanîm ucyate: svaraparaḥ padânta*[3] *ekaro 'yam iti vikâram âpadyate. ima----: ta----.*

[(1)] G. M. *visargo nivṛttaḥ;* O. *visargo vinirgataḥ.* [2] G. M. om. [3] W. *-taḥ;* B. *-te.*

12. *svaraparaḥ*[1] *padânta okaro 'vam iti*[2] *vikâram âpadyate. yathâ*[3]*: vish-----.*

[1] G. M. *svaraḥ.* [2] B. G. M. O. om. [3] W. B. G. M. om.

13. *dvivacanasâmarthyagṛhîtâv*[1] *ekârâukârâv akâraparâu*[2] *pûrvavidhiṁ*[3] *na prâpnutaḥ. yathâ*[4]*: mâ----: sam-----: te ----: ity âdâv ekâro 'yam* (ix.11) [5] *lupyate tv akâra ekârâukârapûrvaḥ* (xi.1) *iti* [6] *sûtradvayam prasaktam: tatrâ 'pi pûrvatvât prabalaṁ* [7] *yatvavidhiṁ nisheddhum ayam ârambhaḥ. akâraḥ paro yâbhyâṁ tâv akâraparâu.*

[1] B. G. M. O. *-thyât gṛ-;* and G. M. O. add *sannihitâv.* [2] G. M. O. om. [3] G. M. om. *pûrva.* [4] G. M. om. [5] G. M. ins. *iti ca;* O. ins. *iti.* [6] G. M. O. ins. *ca.* [7] O. ins. *ekârasya.*

The example is *âsâmahâ eve 'mâu dvâdaçâu mâsâu* (vii.5.2[1]: B. omits the last word, G. M. O. the last two).

To complete the *sandhi*, also, which is the subject of this rule and its successor, rule x.19 is needed.

औकार आवम् ॥ १५ ॥

15. *Âu* becomes *âv*.

The example is *ahâv anadatâ hate* (v.6.1[2]).

उकारो ऽपृक्तः प्रकृत्या वकारो ऽन्तरे ॥ १६ ॥

16. An *u*, uncombined with a consonant, remains unchanged, and *v* is inserted between it and the following vowel.

The definition of *apṛkta* was given above, at i.54, and such a word was directed to be treated both as initial and as final (i.55). This rule makes an exception for the particle *u*, which becomes *uv* before a vowel—which, moreover, never occurs after an *a*-vowel except as combined with it, forming part of the class of *pragrahas* in *o* which were treated above, in rules iv.6,7. The examples given are *sa uv ekaviñçavartaniḥ* (iv.3.3[2]), and *adanty uv evâ 'sya manushyâḥ* (ii.3.7[4]): I have noted further only iv.6.9[4], but am not sure that I have been careful to mark all the cases. As counter-examples, *svapatyâya deva* (v.5.4[4]; p. *su-apatyâya*) shows that the *u* must be *apṛkta*, and *bhakshe " 'hi* (iii.2.5[1]), that no other *apṛkta* vowel than *u* is thus treated.

न तत्तस्मात्सांहितः ॥ १७ ॥

17. But not in *sañhitâ*-text, after *tat* and *tasmât*.

The passages are *tad v âhur utsṛjyam* (vii.5.7[1]: O. omits after *âhuḥ*), and *tasmâd v âçyam* (vi.1.11[6]). So far as I have observed, these are the only instances which the text affords of *u* following

---

14. *svaraparaḥ padânta*[1] *âikâra âyaṁ vikâram âpadyate. yathâ*[2]*: âsâm-....*

[1] B. G. M. *-nte.* [2] G. M. O. om.

15. [2]*âukâraḥ padântaḥ*[1] *svarapara*[2] *âvaṁ vikâram âpadyate. yathâ*[3]*: ahâv....*

[1] B. *-nte.* [(2)] G. M. invert the order. [3] G. M. O. om.

16. *apṛktasaṁjñaka*[1] [2]*ukâraḥ svaraparaḥ*[2] *prakṛtyâ 'vatishṭhate: avikṛto*[3] *bhavatî 'ty arthaḥ: ukârasvarayor antare* [4]*vakâraç câ "gamo*[4] *bhavati. yathâ*[5]*: sa....: adanty.... apṛkta iti kim: sva-....: ukâra iti kim: bhak-....*

[1] G. M. *-jña.* [(2)] G. M. *ukârasvaḥ.* [3] G. M. *-kâro.* [(4)] O. *vakârâg-.* [5] W. B. G. M. om.

a consonant and preceding a vowel. Compare the similar rules in the other treatises (Rik Pr. ii.28; Vâj. Pr. iv.87; Ath. Pr. iii.36). The preceding precept being thus annulled with reference to these two cases, they fall under the general rule x.15, and the *u*, like any final, is converted into *v*. To show the bearing of the specification *sâṁhitaḥ*, 'in combined text,' the commentator gives us the two passages in *pada* and *krama* form: thus—*tat: u: âhuḥ: tad u: uv âhuḥ: âhur utsṛjyam* (but G. M. O. give simply the first two *krama-pada*'s), and *tasmât: u: âçyam: tasmâd u: uv âçyam* (here only W. has the statement in *pada*). It thus appears that the combination with the preceding consonant is indispensable to the treatment of the *u* as here prescribed; failing that, it falls under the preceding rule, and becomes *uv*.

ह्रस्वपूर्वो ङकारो द्विवर्णम् ॥ १८ ॥

18. A *ṅ*, when preceded by a short vowel, is doubled.

That is to say, when another vowel follows—the heading *atha svaraparaḥ* (ix.10) still continuing in force. The commentator adds also "when occurring at the end of a *pada*," as he has done in his paraphrase of the preceding rules: this is a matter of course, as we are dealing only with the conversion of *pada*-text into *saṁhitâ*. His illustrative examples are *nyaṅṅ agniḥ* (v.5.3²), and *tam u tvâ dadhyaṅṅ ṛshiḥ* (iv.1.3² and v.1.4⁴: only G. M. have the first two words). That the preceding vowel must be short, he shows by *parâṅ â vartate* (iii.2.9⁷ and vi.3.8³); that a vowel must follow, by *sadṛṅk samânâiḥ syât* (ii.2.8⁶: only O. has the last word; only B. G. M. have the inserted *k*, required by v.32, and G. M. convert it to *kh*, by xiv.12), and *pratyaṅk shadahaḥ* (vii.4.2⁵: here all have the *k*, but only G. M. make it *kh*).

---

17. *tat tasmâd ity*[1] *etâbhyâṁ sâṁhita ukâro 'pṛktaḥ pûrvavidhiṁ nâ "pnoti*[2]*: prakṛtyâvasthânaṁ vakâraç*[3] *ca na bhavatî 'ty arthaḥ. tad....: tasmâd..... ivarṇokârâu yavakârâv* (x.15) *iti daçame*[4] *'sya*[5] *vidhir vakshyate*[6]*. tat tasmât sâṅhita iti kim: tat....: tasm-.....*

[1] G. M. om. [2] G. M. "*padyate*; O. *prâpn-*. [3] G. M. O. *-râyamaç*. [4] O. *-ma*. [5] B. *tasya*. [6] O. ins. *tasya purastâdapavâdo 'yam*.

18. [1]*svaraparo ṅakâraḥ padântavartî hrasvapûrvo*[1] *dvivarṇam* [2]*bhajate. yathâ*[3]*: nyaṅṅ....: tam..... hrasvapûrva iti kim: par-....: svarapara iti kim: sad-....: praty-..... hrasvaḥ pûrvo yasmâd asâu hrasvapûrvaḥ: dvayor varṇayoḥ samâhâro dvivarṇam.*

(1) G. M. arrange *hr- sv- pad- ṅak-*. [2] G. M. O. ins. *dvitvaṁ*. [3] G. M. om.

नकारश्च ॥ १९ ॥

19. As does also a *n*.

The *a* in this rule brings down, we are told, the preceding cause of duplication and the duplication itself. The cited examples are *nir avapann' indrâya* (ii.4.2²), and *abruvann ṛdhnavat* (i.5.1²). The counter-examples, given for the same purposes as those under the preceding rule, are *niravapan yâny eva purastât* (ii.4.1²: O. omits the last two words), *omanvatî te 'smin* (ii.6.9⁵: O. omits the last word), *yân agnayo 'nvatapyanta* (iii.2.8³: O. omits the last word; G. M. omit the whole example), and *vidvân etam agniṁ cinute* (v.6.5³). The commentator does not give himself the trouble this time to inquire why two rules are furnished to prescribe a single process: the reason is, evidently, because continued implication of *n* only is desired in the rules that follow.

अनितिपरो ग्रहोख्ययाज्यापृष्ठ्यहिरण्यवर्णीयेष्वीकारोकारपूर्वो रेफमाकारपूर्वश्च यकारम् ॥ २० ॥

20. In *graha*, *ukhya*, *yâjyâ*, *pṛshṭhya*, and *hiraṇyavarṇîya* passages, a *n* preceded by *î* or *û* becomes *r*, preceded by *â* becomes *y*, except before *iti*.

The remainder of the chapter is occupied with rules respecting these conversions of a final *n* after *â*, *î*, and *û* before an initial vowel—conversions of which the original ground is the same with that which causes the combinations *ñçc*, *ñst* to result from the collision of *n* with *c* and *t* (v.20,vi.14), namely the partial retention of an original *s* which followed the *n* as part of the declensional termination of the word. See note to Âth. Pr. ii.27 for a full statement of the teachings of the other Prâtiçâkhyas respecting them. The conversion of *n* to *y* is equivalent to its omission, since the *y* is dropped by x.19. Rules xv.1–3 are also needed to complete the combinations intended, by the nasalization of the preceding vowel, or the insertion of *anusvâra* after it.

---

19. *cakâraḥ pûrvanimittaṁ*[1] *dvitvaṁ câ* "*nvâdiçati. hrasvapûrvo nakâro dvivarṇam*[2] *bhajate*[3] *svaraparaḥ. nir----: abr----. evampara iti kim: nir----: oman----: evampûrva iti kim: yân----: vid----.*

[1] G. M. *pûrvoktan-*. [2] G. M. O. *dvitvam.* [3] G. M. *âpadyate.*

20. *grahokhyâdishu*[1] *vishayeshv îkârapûrva ûkârapûrvo vâ cakârâkṛshṭo nakâro 'nitipara*[2] *itivyatiriktasvaraparo*[3] *repham âpadyate: âkârapûrvaç ced yakâram. graho nâma caturo 'nuvâ-*

As in other similar cases, the commentator, after his preliminary paraphrase of the rule, proceeds first to define the passages of the Sanhitâ designated by the titles it contains. By *graha* is meant the fourth chapter of the first book, excepting its last four sections—or i.4.1–42. By *ukhya*, the first two chapters of the "Agni" book (see iii.9), excepting their final sections (which are *yâjyâ*)—or iv.1.1–10; 2.1–10. The *yâjyâs* have been already defined (iii.9, note), as the concluding sections of all the chapters to book fourth, chapter third, together with ii.6.11. By *pṛshṭhya* are intended nine sections, pointed out by the citation of the first words of each: they are iv.4.12; 6.6–9; 7.15: v.1.11; 2.11; 2.12. *Hiraṇyavarṇîya* designates only a single section, v.6.1. Examples are then given from each set of passages. From *graha* passages, we have *jahi çatrûn̐r upa mṛdho nudasva* (i.iv.42), and *marutvân̐ indra vṛshabhaḥ* (i.4.19: G. M. O. omit the last word): there are four other cases, at i.4.20 twice, 21,41. From *ukhya* passages, *ye vâ vanaspatîn̐r anu* (iv.2.8^{3}), and *madhumân̐ astu sûryaḥ* (iv.2.9^{3}): there are ten others, at iv.1.3^{3} twice, 9^{2,3},10^{2,4}; 2.4^{2},5^{1}, 9^{5} twice. From *yâjyâ* passages, *ṛtûn̐r ṛtupate yaje 'ha* (iv.3.13^{4}: only O. has the last two words), to which W. B. O. add *amavân̐ ibhena* (i.2.14^{1}); but for this G. M. substitute *madhumân̐ indriyâvân* (iii.1.10^{2}), which is not in a *yâjyâ* passage at all, but falls under the next rule: I have noted more than thirty other cases, namely at i.1.14^{4}; 2.14^{2}; 3.14^{8}; 4.46^{2}; 5.11^{2}; 6.12^{4}; 7.13^{4,5}: ii.1.11^{5} thrice; 2.12^{3,8}; 3.14^{2,6}; 6.11^{1} thrice ^{4} twice, 12^{1,3}: iii.1.11^{1} thrice, ^{7}; 2.11^{3} twice; 4.11^{3}; 5.11^{2}: iv.2.11^{3}; 3.13^{2,3},^{4} twice. The same passages contain five exceptions, which are duly provided for in rules 23 and 24, below. From *pṛshṭhya* passages, the examples are *çatrûn̐r anapavyayantaḥ* (iv.6.6^{3}) and *jaghanân̐ upa jighnate* (iv.6.6^{5}): other cases at iv.6.7^{5},9^{4} twice; 7.15^{7}: v.1.11^{4}. Finally,

---

kân[4] *varjayitvâ "dade grâvâ*[5] (i.4.1^{1}) *iti praçnaḥ: agnikâṇḍasyâ "dyam praçnadvayam uttamânuvâkavarjam ukhyam*[6] *âkhyâyate: uktâ yâjyâḥ: samid diçâm* (iv.4.12^{1}) *jîmûtasya* (iv.6.6^{1}) *yad akrandaḥ* (iv.6.7^{1}) *mâ no mitraḥ* (iv.6.8^{1}) *ye vâjinam* (iv.6.9^{1}) *agner manve* (iv.7.15^{1}) *samiddho añjan* (v.1.11^{1}) *gâyatrî* (v.2.11^{1}) *kas tvâ* (v.2.12^{1}) *ity anuvâkanavakam*[7] *pṛshṭhyam iti paṭhyate*[8]*: hiraṇyavarṇâḥ* (v.6.1^{1}) *ity anuvâko hiraṇyavarṇîyaḥ.* [9]*grahe yathâ:*[9] *jahi----: mar-----. ukhye: ye----: madh-----. yâjyâsu: ṛtûn̐r----: ama-----. pṛshṭhye: çatr-----: jagh-----. hiraṇyavarṇîye: agnîn̐r----: sarv-----. anitipara iti kim: abhy-----: iḍâ-----. grahâdishv iti kim: trîn----: paçûn----: tân----.*

itiḥ paro yasmâd asâv itiparaḥ: ne 'tiparo 'nitiparaḥ.

[1] G. M. read *gṛh-* throughout. [2] B. om. [3] G. M. O. *ity etasmâd anyasvar-*; B. *iti 'ty etad asmâd anyas-*. [4] G. M. O. *'ntyânuv-*. [5] G. M. *-vâ 'si.* [6] G. M. O. ins. *ity.* [7] G. M. *anuvâkâḥ.* [8] W. O. *pachyate*; G. M. *paṭhyante.* [(9)] G. M. om.

from the *hiraṇyavarṇîya* section, *agnîn̆r apsushadaḥ* (v.6.1[2]), and *sarvân̆ agnîn* (v.6.1[2]), which are the only cases. Counter-examples, of *n* not converted as here prescribed, because occurring outside the passages specified, are *trîn imân̆ lokân iti* (vii.3.2[1]), *paçûn evâ 'va rundhe* (v.1.1[1] et al.), and *tân indro 'ntaryâmenâ 'ntar adhatta* (vi.4.6[1]: G. M. O. omit the last two words). And the bearing of the specification "except before *iti*" is illustrated by examples from the *krama* and *pada* texts, namely *abhyavartanta dasyûn: dasyûn iti dasyûn* (i.6.12[6]; *dasyûn* is thus repeated, as being the closing word of the *anuvâka:* but W. O. omit this repetition, which exhibits the very point requiring illustration, and B. adds only *iti dasyûn* to the first *dasyûn*), and *iḍâvân itî 'ḍâ-vân* (iii.1.11[1]; *saṁhitâ*-reading, *iḍâvân̆ eshaḥ*).

Any general examination of the aspect of this mode of combination in the Tâittirîya text I defer to the end of the chapter.

मर्त्यानुदयानमृतान्दुर्यानसोमपूर्वः सोअस्मानविमान्गोमान्मधुमान्हविष्मान्हूतमानार्षे चिकित्वानिडावान्कक्षीवान्बाणवान्हिपयस्वान्वशान्विदत्रानमित्रानरान्पोषान्महांश्च ॥ २१ ॥

21. Also in the words *martyân, ud ayân, amṛtân, duryân* not preceded by *soma, so asmân, avimân, gomân, madhumân, havishmân, hûtamân* before any vowel belonging to the text, *cikitvân, iḍâvân, kakshîvân, bâṇavân, hi payasvân, vaçân, vidatrân, amitrân, arân, poshân,* and *mahân.*

The *ca* in this rule, says the commentator, brings down from the preceding rule the specification "except before *iti;*" but we might fairly claim that it involves all the specifications there made excepting the restriction to certain passages: this exception the comment duly notes: "this and the rules that follow have a general application, without regard to special portions of the text."

The illustrative examples are: for *martyân, martyân̆ âviveça* (v.7.9[1]). For *ud ayân, ud ayân̆ ajasram* (iv.6.3[3]): with a counter-example, *vayobhir evâ 'yân ava rundhe* (v.2.10[7]), to show that

---

21. ----[1] ---- *eteshu*[2] *grahaṇeshu nakâro 'nitiparo* [3]*yakâram âpadyate*[3]. *anitiparatvâkarshako 'yaṁ*[4] *cakâraḥ. vishayân*[5] *anâdṛtya sarvârtho*[6] *'yaṃ itaḥ*[7] *param ârambhaḥ. yathâ: mart----: ud ay-----: ud iti kim: vayo-----: ud----: bhad-----: na somapûrvaḥ: duryân ity atra nakâraḥ somapûrvo yatvaṁ*[8] *nâ 'padyate: pra----: so----: so iti kim: indro----: avi-----: gom-----: madh-----: avigomadhv*[9] *iti kim: paçu-----: hav-----: hûtamân ârshe*[10]*: hûtamân ity atra nakâra* [11]*ârshe svare*

the *ut* before *ayân* needed to be quoted along with it. For *amṛtân*, *ud asthâm amṛtâñ anu* (i.2.8[1]). For *duryân*, *bhadrân duryâñ abhy e'hi mâm anuvratâ ny u* (i.6.3[1]: G. M. O. omit *mâm* etc.): there are two other cases, at i.2.13[1]: vi.2.9[1]; and a single exception, *pra carâ soma duryân adityâḥ* (i.2.10[1]), quoted by the commentator in justification of the restriction "not preceded by *soma.*" For *asmân*, *so asmâñ adhipatîn karotu* (i.6.6[4] and iii.2.7[2]): another example is at v.7.9[1]; and *asmân* becomes *asmâñ* also at i.6.12[4], but in virtue of the preceding rule. The counter-example, showing the necessity of prefixing *so* in the rule, is *indro asmân asmin dvitîye* (iii.1.9[2]: W. B. omit the last word). For *avimân*, *avimâñ açvî* (i.6.6[4]; 7.6[7]: iii.1.11[1]: but the last case falls under the preceding rule also). For *gomân*, *gomâñ agne* (i.6.6[4]; 7.6[7]: iii.1.11[1]—that is to say, in the same phrase with *avimân*). For *madhumân*, *madhumâñ indriyâvân* (iii.1.10[2]). Next follows a counter-example, intended to show why *mân* would not have been enough of itself to include the last three words, without the prefixed parts *avi*, *go*, and *madhu:* it is *paçumân eva bhavati* (vi.2.6[2] et al.). Then, for *havishmân*, *havishmâñ â vivâsati* (i.3.12): the word occurs a second time in the same section, and also at vi.4.2[4]. For *hûtamân*, *devahûtamâñ ity ukhâyâṁ juhoti* (v.5.3[1]: W. B. omit the last word): it is found again, in like form, in the succeeding division of the section. The specification "before any vowel belonging to the text (*ârshe*, 'coming from the *ṛshis*')," is declared to be meant as an annulment of the restriction, "except before *iti*," made in the preceding rule. And, to show that the *n* remains unchanged before a vowel not forming part of the fundamental text, is given the *pada*-reading *devahûtamân iti deva-hûtamân*. There is added further a remark which looks like a gloss that has worked its way into the text: "the specification 'before what comes from the *ṛshis*' has force in both directions, after the fashion of the crow's eye [Molesworth says, the crow is regarded as having a single eye, which shifts from one eye-

---

pare[11] *yatvam âpadyate*[12]*: dev-----: ârsha iti kim: dev-----:* [13] *ârshagrahaṇasâmarthyâd itiparatve*[14] *'pi* [15] *yatvam bhavati: ârsha iti kâkâkshivad*[16] *ubhayatra sambadhyate grahokhyâdimahânparyantam*[17]*: ârshasvayampâṭha*[18] *ity arthaḥ. cikit-----: iḍâv-----: kak-----: viç-----: iḍâkakshîbâṇe*[19] *'ti kim: ras------: sam-----: hî'ti kim: ûrj-----: ârsha itiparatvâd dev-----itivad yatvaprâptir higrahaṇena nishidhyate*[20]*. stuto-----: suvid-----: amit-----: arâñ-----: posh-----: agne-----.*

[1] For *asomapûrvaḥ*, G. M. read *ity esha nakâras somapûrvo 'nusvâran nâ "padyate;* B. O. *na som-*, as do T. G. M. in the rule itself. [2] G. M. O. *eshu.* [(3)] G. M. *yatvaṁ bhajate.* [4] G. M. om. *ayam.* [5] G. M. *vidhân.* [6] W. *sarvo 'rtho.* [7] W. B. *iti.* [8] G. M. *dvitvan.* [9] W. O. *avimâdhv.* [10] W. adds *cikitvân.* [(11)] G. M. O. *ârshasvaraparo.* [12] W. *nâjadyate;* B. *bhavati;* G. M. O. *bhajate.* [13] G. M. ins. *ity.* [14] G. M. *-pare.* [15] G. M. ins. *hûtamâṅ ity ukhâyâm ity atra.* [16] W. O. *kâksh-;* G. M. *-kshinyâyena.* [17] W. B. om. *mahân.* [18] B. *ârshaḥ sv-;* G. M. *ârshabhâvân.* [19] G. M. *iḍâdiviçesheṇa.* [20] G. M. O. *pratish-.*

ball to the other, as it is needed]—namely, from the beginning of the preceding rule to the end of the present one." This appears to mean that an *iti* belonging to the sacred text itself would admit the conversion of the *n* before it, in any case falling under these two rules. The opinion is doubtless a sound one; but, to prove its expression pertinent here, we require an example showing that there is a passage in the text requiring its application: and none such is furnished us; on the contrary, the addition of *ârshe* to *hûtamân* alone implies that none is to be found. The example for *cikitvân* is *cikitvẫn anu manyatâm* (iii.1.4[1]: O. omits the last word). For *iḍâvân*, *iḍâvẫn eshaḥ* (i.6.6[4]; also at iii.1.11[1], but this is a case falling under the preceding rule). For *kakshîvân*, *kakshîvẫn âuçijaḥ* (v.6.5[3]). For *bâṇavân*, *viçalyo bâṇavẫn uta* (iv.5.1[4]: O. omits the first word). Next we have again a counter-example, *rasavân eva bhavati* (ii.2.4[5]), showing that, of words ending in *vân*, only those preceded as here specified undergo the prescribed effect. For *hi payasvân*, *sam asṛkshmahi : payasvẫn agna â 'gamam* (i.4.45[3],46[2]: only O. has *sam*; and G. M. O. omit the last two words): the necessity of the prefixed *hi* is shown by the counter-example *ûrjasvân payasvân ity âha* (i.7.3[4]). Here, however, is a case of *payasvân* before an *iti* which comes from the *ṛshis*, and therefore might seem to require the reading *payasvẫn*, like *hûtamẫn* in the passage *devahûtamẫn ity ukhâyâm* (v.5.3[1])—according to the extension made above of the natural and obvious meaning of *ârshe;* but the commentator declares that the mention in the rule of *hi* as necessary preceding word prevents the conversion of *n* to *y* in the passage: it is, to be sure, a case of *payasvân* before *iti*, but not of *hi payasvân*. For *vaçân*, the example is *stuto yâsi vaçẫn anu* (i.8.5[1]). For *vidatrân*, W. O. give *suvidatrẫn apî 'ta* (i.8.5[2]), while G. M. have instead *suvidatrẫn avitsi* (ii.6.12[3]): B. is defective here, dropping out the last part of this quotation, and the first part of the next (reading *suvidatrẫn apabâdhamânaḥ*); G. M. are in the wrong this time, for the passage they quote falls under the preceding rule. For *amitrân*, *amitrẫn apabâdhamânaḥ* (iv.6.4[2]): an exception is provided for in the final rule of the chapter. For *arân*, *arẫn ivâ 'gne nemiḥ* (ii.5.9[3]: O. omits the last word). For *poshân*, *poshẫn apushyat* (vii.1.9). For *mahân*, *agne mahẫn asi* (ii.5.9[1]): another case at i.4.20.

इन्द्रोमेऽकऊढ्वमिहाप्येत्वगन्मेडेन्यानायजिष्ठआचर्त्वकुर्व-
ताऽदुहददितिरग्रेऽधरान्त्सपत्नानलंपरश्च ॥ २२ ॥

22. Also a *n* followed by *indro me*, *akaḥ*, *ûḍhvam*, *ihâ*, *apy etu*, *aganma*, *îḍenyân*, *âyajishṭhaḥ*, *â ca*, *ṛtu*, *akurvata*, *aduhat*, *aditiḥ*, *agre*, *adharânt sapatnàn*, and *alam*.

---

22. ------ *ity evamparo nakâra 'âkârapûrvo yatvam' âpadyate. cakâra' âkârapûrvatvâkarshakaḥ. yathâ: sap-----: ma iti kim: yush-----: nigr-----: yây----- agne-----: dîrgheṇa kim:*

The implication here, the commentator tells us, is of a *n* preceded by *â* only: he does not explain why, but would have a right to appeal to the mention of *ân* last in rule 20, and the exclusion of any other cases than those of a final *ân* in rule 21. His examples are as follows. For *indro me*, *sapatnâñ indro me* (i.1.13¹; 6.4²: iv.6.3⁴); with a counter-example, *yushmân indro 'vṛṇîta* (i.1.5¹), to illustrate the need of specifying *me.* For *akaḥ*, *nigrâbheṇâ 'dharâñ akaḥ* (i.1.13¹; 6.4²: iv.6.3⁴: that is to say, in the same passage as the preceding: O. omits the first word). For *ûdhvam*, *yûyaṁ devâñ ûdhvam* (i.3.8²: O. omits the first word). For *ihâ*, *agne devâñ ihâ" vaha* (i.3.14⁸; 5.5³: iv.6.1³); with a counter-example, *yajñiyân iha yân havâmahe* (i.5.10³: only W. has the last word), to show that the *nimitta* in this case is *ihâ*, not *iha.* For *apy etu*, *gharmo devâñ apy etu* (i.5.10⁴: B. omits *gharmaḥ:* again at i.6.3²); with the counter-example, *vidvân api janyeshu* (vi.1.6⁶), to show that *api* without *etu* does not cause the conversion. For *aganma*, *suvar devâñ aganma* (i.7.9²). For *îḍenyân*, *îḍâmahâi devâñ îḍenyân* (ii.5.9⁶). For *âyajishṭhaḥ*, *devâñ âyajishṭhaḥ svasti* (iv.3.13¹; 6.1⁵: O. omits the last word). For *â ca*, *devâñ â ca vakshat* (iv.6.3⁴ twice, and v.4.6⁶ twice); but this example is omitted by G. M., and they also omit the item *â ca* in the rule itself. A counter-example, *yân â vaha uçataḥ* (i.4.44²: G. M. omit the last word), is given by all but O.: in G. M., it should show that *â* causes *âñ* only when followed by *yajishṭhaḥ;* in W., only by *yajishṭhaḥ* and *ca;* but W. states the occasion for it in the same manner as G. M., and B. alone sets it in its proper relation to both the foregoing examples. For *ṛtu*, the example is, in W. B., *vâjo devâñ ṛtubhiḥ* (iv.7.12²), but G. M. O. give instead *yebhir devâñ ṛtubhiḥ* (i.1.14⁴): I have found no other case. For *akurvata*, *vittvâ kâmâñ akurvata* (i.5.9³). For *aduhat*, *yajño 'surâñ aduhat* (i.7.1¹). For *aditiḥ*, *vivasvâñ aditiḥ* (i.5.3³). For *agre*, *agnis tâñ agre* (iii.1.4²): we have also *vâyus tâñ agre* in the same division. For *adharân*, *anyâñ adharânt sapatnân* (iii.2.8⁵); with a counter-example, *bhrâtṛvyân adharân pâdayâmi* (iii.5.3¹). For *alam*, *puroḍâçâñ alaṁ kurv iti* (vi.3.1²). Finally, to show that the rule applies only to *ân*, *paridhîn akurvata* (vi.2.1⁵⁻⁶).

The comment closes with an exposition which I must confess that I do not fully understand. It is evidently intended to determine the readings which the words treated in these rules shall have in *jaṭâ*-text; and it furnishes abundant illustrations, in reference to the form of which, however, there is not a little difference between the different recensions: G. M. O. generally citing the passage first

---

yajñ-....: ghar-....: etv iti kim: vidvân....: suvar....: îḍâ-....: devâñ....: [3]*devâñ....:*[3] [4]*yajishṭhaç ce 'ti kim: yân ....:*[4] *vâjo....: vit-....: yajño....: vivas-....: agnis....: anyâñ....: sapatnân iti kim: bhrâ-....: puro-.... anvâdeçaḥ kimarthaḥ: pari-....: tattatpadagrahaṇe kartavye parapadagrahaṇam* [5]*anârshe 'pi*[5] *saṁhitâvidhâv*[6] *agrahaṇasya*[7] *ca*[8] *ya-*

in its *saṁhitâ*-form, and adding only a single *sandhi* from the *jaṭâ*-text, while W. B. give the complete *jaṭâ*-readings, and only those. The former quote first *amartyo martyâñ âviveça* (v.7.9[1]), and add *martyâñ amartyaḥ ;* W. gives *amartyo martyân martyâñ amartyo 'martyo martyân*, and *martyâñ âviveçâ "viveça martyân martyâñ âviveça ;* B. only the latter (and, blunderingly, treats it as *amartyâñ âviveça*, throughout); next, G. M. O. have *ud asthâm amṛtâñ anu: amṛtâñ asthâm* (i.2.8[1]); W. B., *amṛtâñ anv anv amṛtâñ amṛtâñ anu.* Then, in illustration of a second point, we receive two more examples: G. M. O. read *agne 'vimâñ açvî: avimâñ agne* (i.6.6[4] et al.), for which W. B. substitute *agne 'vimâñ avimâñ agne 'gne 'vimâñ ;* and G. M. O., again, *ud ayâñ ajasram* (iv.6.3[3]), O. this time adding the full *jaṭâ*-reading *ud ayâñ ayâñ ud ud ayân*, which G. M. also seem to mean to give (they actually have only *ayâñ ud ayân*); while W. B. set down the *jaṭâ*-form of the other pair of words: *ayâñ ajasram ajasram ayâñ ayâñ ajasram.* Yet once more, two examples for a third point close the tale: in G. M. O. *agnis tâñ agre: tâñ agniḥ* (iii.1.4[2]), in W. B. *tâñ agre 'gre tâñs tâñ agre ;* and, this time in all alike, *anyâñ adharân adharân anyâñ anyâñ adharân* (but G. M. have, doubtless by a copyist's blunder, *anyân* the second time, before *anyâñ*). It will be seen that the two versions are in part inconsistent with one another as regards the special points of combination to which they direct attention; and I am not able to make out what are the three classes of cases meant to be distinguished. The three points which one would most naturally think of as needing to be noticed are, perhaps, first, the occurrence of a word like *amṛtân* before itself—thus, *amṛtâñ amṛtân*—in the *jaṭâ* repetition; second, its occurrence before a preceding word (not its defined or natural *nimitta*) when that word begins with a vowel—thus, *amṛtâñ asthâm ;* and third, its occurrence in *jaṭâ* before the word which causes its alteration in *saṁhitâ*—thus, *amṛtâñ anu*—if, indeed, this last can be regarded as requiring any special prescription. Or, the second and third cases might be expected to concern the treatment respectively of a word, on the one hand, like *martyân*, which is itself quoted in the rule as suffering the prescribed change (which is at the same time *grahaṇa* and *nâimittika*, or *nâimittikaṁ grahaṇam*), and might therefore naturally be inferred to be liable to the change under all circumstances before a vowel; and one, on the other hand, like *anyân*, which is pointed

---

tvaṁ syâd iti nâimittikasya ca nimittâpekshatvât. grahaṇasya yathâ: amartyo....: ud..... evaṁ nâimittikagrahaṇasya: agne....: ud..... evaṁ grahaṇanâimittikasya[9]*: agnis....: anyâñ..... evaṁ sarvatra nakârasya yakârotpattir*[10] *drashṭavyâ.*

(1) B. om. [2] G. M. O. *yakâram.* (3) G. M. om. (4) O. om.; W. G. M. read *yajishṭha iti kim* etc. (5) G. M. *a.* [6] O. *-dhâne;* B. *-dhânasye.* [7] B. om. [8] G. M. O. om. [9] G. M. O: *-ṇasya nâi-.* [10] G. M. *ṅakâ-.*

out by means of the quotation of the following word *adharân* (which is itself, therefore, *nâimittika*, while *adharân* is *grahaṇa*; or which is *grahaṇanâimittika*, 'undergoing a prescribed effect under the influence of a quoted word'), and which one might suppose changeable only before that word. It is in accordance with this latter explanation that the last two pairs of examples are taken, the one from under rule 21, the other from under rule 22. At any rate, the general conclusion appears to be pretty well assured, that a word which shows a final *ṅ* in *saṁhitâ* shows it also in *jaṭâ* before a following vowel of whatever kind. This is markedly different from its treatment in *pada*, where, by the initial specification of rule 20, its power of conversion to *ṅ* is lost altogether: and even in *jaṭâ* (as was shown in the note to iii.1), an altered letter usually exhibits its *saṁhitâ* form only under the specific circumstances which condition that form in *saṁhitâ*-text.

न रश्मीञ्छ्रपयान्यमान्पतङ्गान्त्समानानर्चान्यज्ञीयान्॥२३॥

23. The *n* of *raçmîn*, *çrapayân*, *yamân*, *patañgân*, *samânân*, *arcân*, *yajîyân* remains unchanged.

All these are words occurring in the passages respecting which the comprehensive prescription of rule 20 was made; needing, therefore, to be specifically exempted from its action. The commentator quotes the phrases in which they occur, as follows: *purutrâ ca raçmîn anu* (iv.1.2³), *aditiḥ çrapayân iti* (iv.1.5⁴), *suyamân ûtaye* (iv.7.15⁴'⁵), *patañgân asaṁditaḥ* (i.2.14¹), *samanâ samânân uçann agne* (iv.3.13³: only G. M. have the first word), *arcân indra grâvâṇaḥ* (i.6.12⁶: G. M. have dropped out all but *arcâ*), and *yajîyân upasthe mâtuḥ* (i.3.14¹: O. omits the last word). The first two are from *ukhya* passages, the third from a *pṛshṭhya*, the rest from *yâjyâ*—as is noted also by the commentator (but G. M. omit these notices, save the first). Under the second, he further suggests the objection that, as the word following *çrapayân* is *iti*, the case might seem not to fall under the rule (since this expressly says "except before *iti*"); but he urges in reply that the word *ârshe* in rule 21 (that is to say, of course, according to his

---

23. [1]------ *eteshu*[1] *grahaṇeshu nakâraḥ svaraparo 'pi na khalu rephaṁ yakâraṁ*[2] *vâ bhajate. yathâ*[3]: *puru-----: adi-----: ukhyatvâd anayoḥ prâptiḥ*[4]. *nanv adi----- asye*[5] *'tiparatvâd eva nishedhe sati grahaṇam anartham*[6]: *iti cet: ârsha itiparatvât*[7] *punaḥ prâptiḥ: tan mâ bhûd iti brûmaḥ. suy-----:* [8]*pṛshṭhyatvât prâptiḥ:*[8] *patañ-----:* [9]*yâjyâtvât* [10] *prâptiḥ:*[9] *sama-----: arcân-----: yajî-----:* [11]*eshâm api sâi 'va prâptiḥ.*[11]

(1) G. M. *raçmîn ity âdishu*; O. *eshu* for *eteshu*. [2] G. M. *vâ yatvaṁ*. [3] B. *tathâ*; the rest om. [4] G. M. *-ptinishedhaḥ*. [5] G. M. *atra*. [6] G. M. O. *-thakam*. [7] O. om. *iti*. (8) G. M. om. (9) G. M. om. [10] O. ins. *asya*. (11) G. M. om.

"crow's eye" interpretation) gives the former precept authority over it, which requires to be annulled.

उदथापरश्चोदथापरश्च ॥ २४ ॥

24. Nor a *n* followed by *ut* or *athâ*.

The phrases to which this rule relates are, as quoted by the commentator, *amitrân un nayâmi* (iv.1.10³), and *vidvân athâ bhava* (iii.2.11²⁻³; our *saṁhitâ*-text has *atha*, because the word stands *vibhâge*, at the end of a division of the section: see rule iii.10 and note): I have noted no other cases. The commentator gives a counter-example to the former, showing why *ut* could not have been extended to *uta*, but needed to stop at the consonant (*hal*): it is *triñr uta dyûn* (ii.1.11⁵). Such a counter-example is quite out of the usual course, and very superfluous: the example itself would be counter-example enough; the substitution of *uta* for *ut* would have excluded the very passage aimed at. Of the two phrases, the one comes from an *ukhya*-passage, the other from a *yâjyâ:* the commentator might better have spent his spare energy in telling us this.

What remains of the comment to this rule is not altogether free from difficulties. First the statement is made that the word *athâ* in it implies also *atha*, with short *a;* in illustration, W. repeats, without change, *vidvân athâ bhava;* B. gives the same twice over; only O. has, in *krama*-text, *vidvân atha: athâ bhava*—which is doubtless correct, and shows the *krama*-reading (along, we may suppose, with the *jaṭâ*) to be the matter aimed at. That the now accepted *saṁhitâ*-reading—*vidvân atha: 2: bhava*—is contemplated, is not at all to be assumed. Both the statement and its illustration are wanting in G. M.: and this, although those manuscripts contain, under viii.34, the reference to it in advance there made. In regard to what follows, also, the recensions are considerably at variance. The *jaṭâ*-text is again under

---

24. *ut: athâ*[1]*: ity evamparo nakâro yathâvihitaṁ* [2]*rephaṁ yakâraṁ vâ*[2] *nâ "padyate.* [3] *yathâ*[4]*: amit-....: halmâtreṇa*[5] *kim: triñr-....: vidv-....:* [6]*dîrgho 'tra hrasvopalakshaṇam api: yathâ: vidv-....*[6] [7]*yathâsaṁhitâstham*[8] [9]*eva nimittaṁ*[10] *svakâryaṁ karoti*[9] [11]*nishedharûpam* [12] *yathâ: amit-.... vidhir apy*[13] [14]*evaṁ yathâsaṁhitâsthanimitta evaṁ sarvatra bhavaty*[11] *ato*[15] *'vocâma*[14]*:* [16] *so-....: asm-....: evamâdi veditavyam.*

iti tribhâshyaratne prâtiçâkhyavivaraṇe navamo 'dhyâyaḥ.

(1) W. B. O. *atha.* (2) G. M. O. put after *âpadyate;* G. M. *rephaṁ va yatvaṁ vâ.* 3 G. M. ins. *cakâro nishedhâkarshaḥ.* 4 G. M. O. om. 5 G. M. O. *ud iti.* (6) G. M. om.; B. om. *yathâ;* O. om. *api : yathâ.* 7 G. M. ins. *ity atra;* O. ins. *atra.* 8 G. M. O. *-stha.* (9) G. M. *nimittâir eva sambhavati;* O. *nimittâir eva sarvatra bhavati.* 10 W. B. *-tte.* (11) G. M. om. 12 O. ins. *vidhirûpaṁ vâ.* 13 W. *iti.* (14) O. only *yathâ.* 15 W. *atho.* 16 G. M. ins. *yathâ.*

treatment; and it appears to be laid down that any word has in that text the same form as under analogous circumstances in *saṁhitâ*, whether it fall under an exception or under a rule. Then, as example of an exceptional word, is given, as established by the present precept, *amitrân ud ud amitrân amitrân ut* (iv.1.10[3]), *amitrân* retaining its *n* throughout; and again, as examples falling under the more general rule, *so asmâñ asmânt sa so asmân: asmâñ avahâyâ 'vahâyâ 'smâñ asmâñ avahâya* (v.7.9[1]: under rule 21).

So far, now, as I have been able to discover, the teachings of the Prâtiçâkhya in rules 20–24 of this chapter precisely correspond with the conditions of the known Tâittirîya text: I have not found in the latter a single case of final *âñ*, *îñr*, *ûñr* which they do not duly notice, nor an exception to the more general rules which is not provided for. Of course, my observation is more to be trusted upon the former point than upon the latter.

The *sandhi* here treated of is comparatively unusual in our Sanhitâ, as it is in those of the other Vedas. According to my count, there are (including repetitions) 115 cases of *âñ* (including also one at iv.6.6[7], omitted above), 5 of *îñr*, and 4 of *ûñr*—in all, 124; while, of final *ân* remaining unchanged before a vowel, I have noted down over 450 instances (and probably not without overlooking a score or two), of *ûn*, about 150, of *în*, 16, and of *ṛ̂n*, 4—in all, about 620, or not less than five times as many. The numerical relation in the Atharva-Veda is probably nearly the same. See the end of the note to Ath. Pr. ii.27.

CHAPTER X.

CONTENTS: 1–9, combination of final and initial similar vowels, and of final *a* or *â* with initial vowels and diphthongs; 10–12, resulting accentuation and nasalization; 13, special cases of uncombinable final *â*; 14, of elision of final *a*, *â* before initial *e* and *o*; 15–17, combination of final *i* and *u* vowels, and resulting accentuation; 18, special cases of uncombinable final *î*; 19–23, elision of final *y* and *v*; 24–25, uncombinable final vowels.

अथैकमुभे ॥ १ ॥

1. Now for the coalescence of two vowels into one.

An introductory heading to the whole chapter. The commentator paraphrases: "both syllables become one form, of the same kind."

---

1. *athe 'ty ayam adhikâraḥ: ubhe akshare ekaṁ rûpaṁ sajâtîyam*[1] *âpadyete*[2] *ity etad adhikṛtaṁ veditavyam ita uttaraṁ yad vakshyâmaḥ.*

[1] O. puts before *rûpaṁ*. [2] MSS. *-yata.*

दीर्घं समानाक्षरे सवर्णपरे ॥ २ ॥

2. In the case of a simple vowel, followed by a similar vowel, the product is long.

For the terms *samânâkshara* and *savarṇa*, see rules i.2,3, where they are defined. The grammatical construction of the rule is not simple, or easily made homogeneous with that of its predecessor. The commentator brings it out thus: "there being a simple vowel, followed by one that is of like nature with itself, these two, being put in the relation of predecessor and successor, become a single long vowel." His examples are *tvacaṁ gṛhṇîshvâ 'ntaritañ rakshaḥ* (i.1.8: only O. has the first word; only G. M. the last), *râsnâ 'sî 'ndrâṇyâi* (i.1.2²), and *sûpasthâ devo vanaspatiḥ* (i.2.2³: only G. M. have the last word).

अथावर्णपूर्वे ॥ ३ ॥

3. Now for cases in which an *a*-vowel stands first.

A new sub-heading, having force as far as rule 9, inclusive. The word *avarṇapûrve* is explained by the commentator after the manner of a *karmadhâraya* compound, as meaning 'that which is both an *a*-vowel and first,' but I do not see how such a construction can be defended: we have, rather, to understand *akshare*, and make the meaning analogous with that of rule 2: "when there is a syllable that has an *a*-vowel before it."

इवर्णपर एकारम् ॥ ४ ॥

When an *i*-vowel follows, the product is *e*.

The commentator explains *ivarṇapare* in the same manner as *avarṇapûrve* in rule 3. The interpretations might hold good, if *pûrva* and *para* were taken substantively; but they are not so used anywhere in the treatise. His chosen example is *ne 'shṭir bhava-*

---

2. *samânâksnara âtmanaḥ savarṇapare sati pûrvâparîbhûte*[1] [2] *ete ubhe*[3] *dîrgham ekam*[4] *âpnutaḥ*[5]. *yathâ*[6]*: tvac-....: râs-....: sûp-....* *savarṇam paraṁ yasmât tat*[7] *savarṇaparam: tasmin*[8].

[1] G. M. *pûrvaḥ paraḥ te.* [2] W. O. ins. *saty.* [3] G. M. ins. *akshare.* [4] W. om.; G. M. *adhikam.* [5] B. *âpnoti.* [6] G. M. O. om. [7] W. om.; O. *tatrat.* [8] W. B. O. om.

3. [1]*athe 'ty ayam adhikâraḥ:*[1] *avarṇapûrve*[2] *satî 'ty*[3] *etad adhikṛtaṁ veditavyam ita uttaraṁ yad vakshyâmaḥ.* [4]*idam adhikârântaram*[4] *upasargapûrva âram* (x.9) *iti paryantam. avarṇaç câ 'sâu pûrvaç câ 'varṇapûrvaḥ: tasmin*[5].

(1) O. om. [2] O. *-vatve.* [3] W. om. *ity.* (4) G. M. *ayam adhikâra.* [5] O. adds *avarṇapûrve.*

ti (ii.5.5³: W. reads *neshṭu*); and O. alone adds *mahendrâya* (v.5.21; p. *mahâ-indrâya*).

उवर्णपर ओकारम् ॥ ५ ॥

5. When an *u*- vowel follows, the product is *o*.

The commentator's single illustrative example is *ishe tvo "rje tvâ* (i.1.1).

एकारैकारपर ऐकारम् ॥ ६ ॥

6. When *e* or *âi* follows, the product is *âi*.

The examples are *sam brahmaṇâ pṛcyasvâi 'katâya svâhâ* (i.1.8: O. omits the last word), and *somâindrâ babhrulalâmâḥ* (v.6.15; p. *soma-âindrâḥ*).

The commentator again very elaborately explains *ekârâikâra-pare* as a *karmadhâraya* compound, formed upon *ekârâikâra* as a *dvandva;* and remarks that the same explanation applies also in the following rule.

ओकारौकारपर औकारम् ॥ ७ ॥

7. When *o* or *âu* follows, the product is *âu*.

The examples are *brahmâudanam pacati* (not found in the Tâit-

---

4. *avarṇapûrva ivarṇapare ca sati* [1] *te*[2] *ubhe akshare ekâram âpnutaḥ. ne 'sh-....: mah-. ivarṇaç câ 'sâu* [3]*paraç ce 'varṇa-paraḥ*[3]*: tasmin.*

[1] G. M. ins. *ubhe akshare.* [2] O. om. [(3)] B. *pûrvaç ca avarṇapûrvaḥ.*

5. *avarṇapûrva uvarṇapare ca sati te*[1] *ubhe akshare*[2] *okâram âpnutaḥ. ishe....*

[1] G. M. O. om. [2] O. om.

6. *avarṇapûrva ekârâikârapare ca sati te*[1] *ubhe akshare*[2] [3]*pûr-vâparîbhûte*[3] *âikâram âpnutaḥ. sam....: som-..... ekâraç câi "kâraç câi 'kârâikârâu: tayoḥ samâhâra ekârâikâram*· [4]*sam-âhâre dvandvaḥ:*[4] *tac ca tatparaṁ câi 'kârâikâraparaṁ karma-dhârayaḥ: tasminn ekârâikârapare*[5]. *evam* [6]*uparitane 'pi sûtre*[6] *samâsaḥ.*

[1] G. M. om. [2] O. om. [3] G. M. *pûrvâpare,* and put before *akshare.* [(4)] G. M. om. [5] O. om. [(6)] O. *-tanasûtre 'pi.*

7. *avarṇapûrva okârâukârapare ca sati te*[1] *ubhe akshare*[2] *âukâ-ram âpnutaḥ. brah-....: dâm-....*[3]

[1] G. M. O. om. [2] G. M. O. om. [3] G. M. add *uktas samâsaḥ.*

tirîya Sanhitâ, although it is read at Tâittirîya Brâhmana i.1.9[3]: we have *brahmâudanam pacet* at v.7.3[4], and *brahmâudanam apacat* at vi.5.6[1]: O. omits *pacati*, leaving the citation such as might have come from either passage), and *dâmnâ 'pâu "mbhan* (ii.4.13)

अरमृकारपरे ॥ ८ ॥

8. When ṛ follows, the product is *ar*.

The examples are *ardharca ekâm* (i.6.10[5]), and *âgneyya rcâ "gnîdhram* (iii.1.6[1]; p. *âgneyyâ: ṛcâ*).

I have not noticed a single example in the Tâittirîya Sanhitâ of that retention of ṛ unchanged after *a* and *â*, only with correption of the latter, which is the rule in the Rik and Vâjasaneyi Sanhitâs, and which appears also in the Atharva-Veda, though against the authority of its Prâtiçâkhya (see Ath. Pr. iii.46 note)

उपसर्गपूर्वं आरम् ॥ ९ ॥

9. If a preposition precedes, the product is *âr*

The commentator points out that, as the implication "when an *a*-vowel stands first" is still in force from rule 3, this virtually means "if a preposition ending in *a* or *â* precedes;" ṛ, of course, is inferred from the preceding rule. According to the list of prepositions given at i.15, then, *â*, *pra*, *ava*, and *upa* would be the only words authorized to form with initial ṛ the *vṛddhi* vowel instead of the *guṇa*, *parâ* and *apa* being excluded. The commentator brings up but one example from the text, namely *upâ rchati* (i.5.9[6]: G. M. read *upâ rchaty askandâya*, which I do not find anywhere: we have *askandâya* after other words at i.5.8[5]: ii.5.8[6]: vi.3.8[1,3], the last time following *upâ 'syati;* possibly this text was in the mind of the scribe who added *askandâya* in the comment on the present rule); he gives another from the *jatâ*-text, *ṛtavyâ upo 'pâ rtavyâ ṛtavyâ upa* (v.3.1[1]; 4.2[1]), and, further, as counter-example, showing that only a preposition ending in *a* or *â* produces the prescribed effect, *vyṛddhaṁ vâ etat* (v.1.2[1] et al.: O. omits the last word). Additional cases of the same combination, with *â* and *ava*, are quoted under rule 10 (at the end); if the text affords yet others, I have failed to note them. Nor have I observed any cases of the different treatment of *parâ* and *apa* before ṛ; so that here also I do not discover any reason for the strange restriction of the class of prepositions made at i.15.

---

8. *avarṇapûrva ṛkârapare ca sati te*[1] *ubhe akshare*[2] *aram iti vikâram âpnutaḥ. ardh-....: âgn-....*

[1] O. om. [2] G. M. O. om.

9. *avarṇapûrva ity anuvartate*[1]*: tasmâd upasargapûrva ity aviçeshavarṇântoktâv*[2] *avarṇânto 'yam*[3] *upasargas tasyâi 'va grahaṇam: ṛkâraḥ sâṁnidhyâl labhyate. upasargapûrva ṛkârapare*

उदात्तमुदात्तवति ॥ १० ॥

10. When an acute enters into the combination, the result is acute.

That is to say, as the commentator points out, when the first constituent, or the second constituent, or both constituents, have the *udâtta* accent, their combination is *udâtta*. He gives a long list of examples in illustration of the working of the rule, promising that they shall exhibit the whole series of vowel-combinations just prescribed, from the second rule to the ninth, with all possible conditions of accentual combination. Thus, *savitâ' prâ' 'rpayatı* (i.1.1; p. *prá: arp-:* W. reads *-yati*) *bráhma yachâ' 'pâ 'gne* (i.1.7[1]; p. *yacha; âpa*), *yâjyâ'i " 'vâ'i 'nam* (ii.3.5[3]; p. *yâjyâ: â': evá: enam:* the pada-manuscripts have *é 'ti* for *â';* and so with the other prepositions), *pûshâ' " 'dhatta* (i.5.1[2]; p. *pûshâ': â': adhatta:* W. B. read *-tte*), *divī' 'va cákshuḥ* (i.3.6[2] and iv.2.9[4]; p. *diví: iva:* for this accent, which is opposed to the teachings of all the other Prâtiçâkhyas, see under rule 17 of the present chapter), *adyá vásu vasatī' 'tī' 'ndro hí devâ'nâm* (ii.5.3[7]; p. *vasati: íti: índraḥ:* O. reads at the end *'ndram eva*, which I do not find anywhere in the Sanhitâ), *mâitrâvaruṇī' 'ty âha* (ii.6.7[4]; p. *-ṇī': íti*). The question is then raised, whether the word *sû'nnīyam* (vi.2.4[1]) does not fall under this rule, since it exhibits a coalescence into one syllable of two vowels, whereof one is acute; but the reply is made, that a special rule in a later part of the chapter (r. 17) prescribes for it the circumflex. The examples are continued: *réto dadhâtû' 't sakthyòḥ* (vii.4.19[1]; p. *dadhâtu: út*), *vánaspátayò 'nû' 't tishṭhanti tâ'n* (vii.4.8[3]; p. *ánu: út:* only G. M. have *tân*), and *tâ' dīkshâ' 'pâ 'dadhata* (v.5.5[4]; p. *dīkshû: úpa:* G. M. omit *tâ*). So many are examples of the combination of two similar simple vowels into a long vowel: the rest illustrate the cases of coalescence in which *a* or *â* precedes. They are *sé 'mâ'ṁ no havyádâ-*

---

ca sati te[4] *ubhe akshare*[5] *âram iti vikâram âpnutaḥ. upâ-....: ṛt-..... avarṇântopasargaviçeshaṇena*[6] *kim: vyṛ-..... upasargaç câ 'sâu pûrvaç co 'pasargapûrvaḥ: tasminn*[7] *upasargapûrve*[8].

[1] G. M. O. om. *anu.* [2] W. *viçeshâvar-;* B. *viçeshoktâ yathâ;* G. M. *aviçeshokto 'pi;* O. *aviçeshâktâv api.* [3] O. om. *ayam.* [4] G. M. om. [5] B. G M. O. om. [6] G. M. O. *upas-;* G. M. B. *-sheṇa.* [7] B. om. [8] G. M. om.

10. *udâttadharmaviçishṭe varṇe pûrvataḥ parata ubhayato vâ sthite sati te ubhe apy ekâdeçam âpanne*[1] *udâttadharmakam*[2] *âpnutaḥ. udâtto 'syâ 'stî 'ty udâttavân: tasminn udâttavati. samânâksharam ârabhya sarvasmâd*[3] *ekībhâve 'yathâkramam udâttânudâttasvaritapûrva ubhayor udâtte vo*[4] *'dâharaṇâni darçayishyâmaḥ*[5]. *sav-....: brah-....: yâj-....: pûsh-....: div-....: adya....: mâit-..... nanu sûnnīyam ity atro 'dâttenâi 'kâdeçe sati kiṁ na syâd ayaṁ vidhiḥ: udâttapûrvâdhikâre*

tim (iv.6.6[6]; p. *sáḥ: imā́m:* compare rule v.17), *táṁ ghé 'd agnír vṛdhā́* (ii.6.11[3]; p. *gha: ít:* only G. M. have the last word), *savanamukhésavanamukhe kāryé 'ti* (vii.5.5[1]; p. *kāryā́: íti:* B. omits the first *savanamukhe*), *sé 'd u hótā*(i.1.14[4]; p. *sáḥ: ít:* compare rule v.17: W. B. omit the last word): so many are examples under rule 4. Now follow those under rule 5: *prókshitaṁ gopāyata* (vii.1.12; p. *prá-ukshitam:* G. M. omit this example), *ū́rja sthó "rjaṁ vo bhakshīya* (i.5.6[1]; p. *stha: ū́rjam:* O. omits the last word), *svāyúshó 'd óshadhīnām* (i.2.8[1]; p. *su-āyúshā: út:* G. M. omit this example also), and *imé evó 'pa dhatte* (v.2.7[3]; 5.3[3]: p. *evá: úpa*). The examples under rule 6 are *nā́'i 'nam pratyóshati* (i.5.9[7]; p. *ná: enam*), *éka evá yajetā́'i 'kaḥ* (vii.2.10[3]; p. *yajeta: ékaḥ*), *áthā́'i 'kam utthā́'nam* (vii.2.1[4]; p. *átha: ékam*), *yán nā́'i 'kāñ raçanā́'m* (vi.6.4[3]; p. *ná: ékām*), *indriyám evā́'i "ndréṇa* (vi.6.5[2]; p. *evá: āindréṇa*), *ví hí tád avā́'iryaté 'ti* (vii.1.5[4]; p. *ava-ā́'iryata*), and finally, from the *jaṭā*-text, *devébhya ā́'indhā́'i 'ndha devébhyo devébhya ā́'indha* (ii.5.9[1]: but G. M. give only the *saṁhitā*-reading, *devebhya āindha*). To illustrate rule 7, we have *kshatrásya cā́'u 'jase juhomi* (iii.3.1[1-2]; p. *ca: ójase:* B. O. omit the last word), *svā́'hā́'u 'shadhībhyaḥ* (i.8.13[3]; p. *svā́'hā: ósh-*), *sā́'u 'shadhīr ánu rudhyase* (iv.2.3[3],11[3]; p. *sáḥ: óshadhīḥ:* another case under rule v.17: G. M. omit the last word), *prā́'u "kshīḥ kénā 'pá íti* (ii.6.5[1]; p. *prá: āukshīḥ;* G. M. omit the last word), and *aruṇó ha smā "hā́'u "paveçiḥ* (vi.1.9[2]; p. *āha: ā́'upa-veçiḥ*). Under rule 8, again, fall *āgneyyá rcā́ "gnīdhram* (iii.1.6[1]; p. *āgneyyā́: ṛcā́*), *sā́'i 'vā́' 'syá' rddhiḥ* (vi.6.10[2]; p. *asya: ṛ'd-dhiḥ*), *ā́'indhá rshishṭutaḥ* (ii.5.9[1]; p. *ā́'indha: ṛ'shi-stutaḥ*), and *evá rshir asvadayat* (v.1.10[1]; p. *evá: ṛ'shiḥ*). Under rule 9, finally, we have *ā́'rtim ā́' 'rchati* (i.5.2[5] et al.; p. *ā́: ṛchati*), and *avā́'rchaty evám ávāram* (ii.6.3[4]; p. *ava-ṛ'chati*).

अनुनासिके ऽनुनासिकम् ॥ ११ ॥

11. When a nasal, the result is nasal.

" e commentator quotes rule xv.6, which declares it to be the

---

saty [6]*ūbhāve ça* (x.17) *iti*[6] *sūtreṇa svaritasya viçeshavidhānād*[7] *iti brūmaḥ. reto....: van-....: tā.... evaṁ samānākshara-saṁhitāyām ekībhāvo*[8] *'nyatrā*[9] *'pi drashṭavyaḥ*[10]. *evam avarṇa-pūrvatve*[11] *'pi vakshyate*[12]: *se....: taṁ....: sav-....: se 'd....: pro-....: ūrja....: svā....: ime....: nāi....: eka....: athāi....: yan....: indr-....: vi....: deve-....: ksha-....: svā-....: sāu....: prāu.... aru-....: āgn-....: sāi....: āindha....: eva....: ārt-....: avā.... evamādi*[13]

[1] W. *prāp-*. [2] B. G. M. *-rmam.*, [3] O. *-sminn;* G. M. *upasargāntam.* [(4)] G. M. *udāttānudāttasvaritānām pūrvatve ca paratve ca udāttayor udāttatve ca yathākramam.* [5] O. *prad-*. [(6)] G. M. *ubhāv eva sati.* [7] G. M. *-vidhinā.* [8] W. B. *-ve.* [9] G. M. *'trā.* [10] W. *-vyāḥ.* [11] G. M. *varṇ-.* [12] G. M. *-ti.* [13] G. M. *-dayaḥ.*

opinion of some authorities that nnal simple vowels, not *pragrahas*, are nasal; and he states that the present precept has reference to them: if such a nasal vowel, being acute, enters into a combination of the kind above described, the resulting single syllable is nasal. Examples, he says, are those already given. And he adds that the rule is not approved.

I cannot at all believe this to be the true interpretation. The rule seems, on the other hand, to belong to and represent the same view of the nature of a syllable ordinarily regarded as containing *anusvâra*, which appears so unequivocally at xv.1; and to mean that when such a syllable, being looked upon as one containing a nasal vowel, instead of a vowel with succeeding *anusvâra*, enters into combination with another vowel (of course, a preceding one), the result is also nasal. Thus, for example, *yaḥ* with *añçum* would make *yo 'ñçum*; *svâhâ* and *añsâbhyâm* (vii.3.16 1-2), *svâhâ 'ñsâbhyâm.*

स्वरितानुदात्तसंनिपाते स्वरितम् ॥ १२ ॥

12. When circumflex and grave are combined, the result is circumflex.

The examples of this accentual result of combination, as given by the commentator, are as follows: *kanyè 'va tunnâ'* (iii.1.11 8; p. *kanyâ`: iva*), *chavî'm chavyò 'pâ'kṛtâya svâ'hâ* (v.7.20; p. *chavyâ`: upa-â'kṛtaya:* G. M. O. omit *svâhâ*), *yâjyầi 'shâ' vâ'i saptápadâ çákvarî* (ii.6.2 6; p. *yâjyâ`: eshâ':* G. M. O. end with *'shâ'*), and *átha kvâ` 'syâ havanî'ya íti* (v.7.4 2; p. *kvà: asyâḥ:* O. omits the last two words). He then goes on to point out that the word *svarita*, 'circumflex,' being used in the rule without any distinctive sign, we are to understand the "constant" (*nitya*) or "independent" circumflex (see rule xx.2) to be intended. For this alone arises at the time of production of letters and syllables, elements of words; but the other kinds of circumflex arise after the time of origin of words, in connection with the euphonic combination of

---

11. *apragrahâḥ samânâksharâṇy anunâsikâny*[1] *ekeshâm*[2] (xv.6) *ity ekeshâm*[3] *matam: tân uddiçyâ 'yaṁ vidhiḥ. tasminn*[4] *udâttavaty anunâsike pûrvataḥ parata ubhayato vâ sthite saty*[5] *ubhe*[5] *akshare anunâsikadharmam ekam âpnutaḥ. uktâny evo 'dâharaṇâni.*

[7]etad anishṭam.[7]

[1] O. om. [2] B. G. M. O. om. [3] G. M. O. *yeshâṁ;* B. *eshṭâṁ.* [4] W. *tasmâd.* G. M. O: ins. *te.* [5] B. O. ins. *apy.* ([7]) G. M. om.; O. *ne 'daṁ sûtram ishṭam.*

12. *svaritânudâttayoḥ saṁnipâta ekâdeçe saty ubhâv api tâu svaritam âpadyete*[1]. *yathâ*[2]*: kan-....: chav-....: yâj-....: atha-.... iha svaritasyâ*[3] *'viçesheṇa*[4] *grahaṇe nityasvarita eva*[5] *gṛhyate: tasya svaritasya*[6] *vyañjanânâm aksharâṇâṁ ca*[7] *padâ-*

syllables and words, by the requirement of such rules as xiv.29 and xii.9; and therefore primary quality belongs only to the "constant" circumflex: whence, by the rule "when a general statement is made, that which is primary should be regarded as intended," it is proper that the constant circumflex should be here understood. In such cases, then, as *áthâ 'bravît* (iii.2.11[3]), where the long *â* resulting from the combination of the final *a* of *átha*, which has the enclitic circumflex (by xiv.29), with the initial *a* of *abravît*, which is grave, has itself the enclitic circumflex, this is not in virtue of the present rule, but falls under the same general rule (xiv.29) that prescribes the enclitic circumflex.

To this effect the commentator: and, whatever we may think of the argument by which he attempts to prove that *svarita* in the rule means only *nitya svarita*, we shall not question the soundness of his conclusions.

न धामापासिपरीबुध्नियाज्यापूषामिनन्तार्षे ॥ १३ ॥

13. Exceptions are *dhâ*, *mâ*, and *pâ*, when followed by *asi;* also *budhniyâ*, *jyâ*, *â pûshâ*, and *aminanta*—before a vowel belonging to the text.

That is to say, these words constitute exceptions, not to the last rules respecting accentuation, but to those which prescribe the combination of a final *a* or *â* with the following initial vowel. The commentator cites the passages in which the first three occur before *asi*, as follows: *svadhâ asy urvî* (i.1.9[3]), *sahasrasya pramâ asi* (iv.4.11[3]: O. omits the first word), and *dhanvann iva prapâ asi* (ii.5.12[4]: O. omits the first two words). I have also noted, for *dhâ*, *varcodhâ asi* (i.2.1[1]), *dhâ asi svadhâ asi* (ii.6.4[4]), and *abhidhâ asi* (vii.1.11[1]); for *mâ*, *pratimâ asi*, *vimâ asi*, and *unmâ asi*, all in the same section and division (iv.4.11[3]) with *pramâ*, as quoted; and, for *pâ*, *vratapâ asi* (i.1.14[4]; 2.3[1]: vi.1.4[6]) and *cakshushpâ asi* (i.2.1[2]). To explain the added specification "when followed by *asi*," the *pada*-readings are quoted for us, namely *svadhe*

---

vayavânâm utpattikâla eva sambhavât: anyeshâṁ tu[8] *padotpattikâlâd*[9] *ûrdhvam aksharâṇâm padânâṁ ca*[10] *saṁhitâyâm udâttât paro 'nudâttaḥ* (xiv.29) *iti vidhânât tasminn anudâtte pûrva "udâttaḥ svaritam*[11] (xii.9) *ity âdi*[12] *ca: tasmân nityasyâi 'va mukhyatvam: sâmânyoktâu ca*[13] *satyâm mukhye sampratyaya iti tasyâi 'va svîkâro yuktaḥ: athâ---- ity âdâv ekâdeçasyo 'dâttânantarabhâvitvâd*[14] *udâttât paro 'nudâttaḥ svaritam* (xiv. 29) *ity anenâi 'va svaritatvaṁ vijñeyam.*

[1] G. M. *ekam âpnutaḥ.* [2] G. M. om. [3] W. O. *-sya.* [4] B. *-shaṇa;* G. M. *-shaṇam eva.* [5] O. om. [6] B. *-ta;* G. M. *sa;* O. *sarva.* [7] W. om. [8] G. M. *ca.* [9] G. M. *paro-;* O. *aparo-.* [10] W. om.; G. M. O. *vâ.* [11] G. M. *udâttam.* [12] O. om. [13] W. om. [14] G. M. O. *-nânt-*

'ti sva-dhâ (only W. has *sva-dhâ* in the repetition), *prame 'ti pra-mâ*, *prape 'ti pra-pâ* (O. omits the readings of *pramâ* and *prapâ*). Further, to explain the final specification *ârshe*, 'before a vowel belonging to the text,' W. gives next the *jaṭâ* readings of *svadhâ asi* and *prapâ asi*, namely *svadhâ asy asi svadhâ svadhâ asi*, and *prapâ asy asi prapâ prapâ asi;* O. has only the former, and substitutes for the latter *dhruvâ 'si dharuṇâ* (iv.2.9[1]; 3.7[2]), which would be in place as a counter-example showing that other words than those specified in the rule are not treated as it prescribes before *asi*, but is not introduced as such, and does not make its appearance at all in the other versions; B. also has only the former (reading at the end *svadhâ 'si*), and adds *evam âdi*, 'and so on.' G. M. give no *jaṭâ*-readings at all here, but pass directly from the *pada*-readings to the quotations illustrating the remaining words of the rule, namely: *pra budhniyâ îrate* (iv.3.13[6]: G. M. omit *pra*); *dhanvaṅ jyâ iyam* (iv.6.6[1-2]: only G. M. have the first word); *â pûshâ etv â vasu* (ii.4.5[1]), with a counter-example, *tam pûshâ 'dhatta* (i.5.1[2]), to show that *pûshâ* after any other word than *â* is not uncombinable; and *â te suparṇâ aminanta evâiḥ* (iii.1.11[5]: G. M. omit the first two words, O. the first three). Now the question is asked again, "why is it said, 'when a vowel from the text follows?'" and W. B. O., having settled the point already so far as *dhâ*, *mâ*, and *pâ* were concerned, reply by quoting the *jaṭâ*-readings of the other four words, each with its successor, thus: *budhniyâ îrata îrate budhniyâ budhniyâ îrate* (but B. reads *budhniye "rate*, and O. *budhnye "rate*, the last time), *jyâ iyam iyaṁ jyâ jyâ iyam* (B. O. again have *jye 'yam* at the end), *pûshâ etv etu pûshâ pûshâ etu* (B. O. again *pûshâi 'tu* in the third repetition), and *aminanta evâir evâir aminantâ 'minanta evâiḥ* (B. O. once more *aminantâi 'vâiḥ* to close with). G. M., however, who have the application of *ârshe* in the first part of the rule still to illustrate, give us here a most liberal series of extracts from the *jaṭâ*-text: first, for *asi svadhâ* (i.1.9[3] or ii.6.4[4]), namely *asi svadhâ svadhâ asy asi svadhâ;* then for *svadhâ asi*, as set down above (with *svadhâ 'si* at the end, like B.; but it seems a merely accidental coincidence, for in all the other cases the third pair of words reads like the first, with the hiatus); for *iva prapâ*, *iva prapâ prapâ 've 'va prapâ;* for *prapâ asi*, as above reported from W.; for *pra budhniyâ;* for *budhniyâ îrate*, as in W.; for *dhanvaṅ jyâ;* for *jyâ iyam*, as in W.; for *â pushâ*, *â pûshâ pushâ " " pûshâ;* for *pûshâ etu*, as in W.; for *suparṇâ aminanta*, *suparṇâ aminantâ 'minanta suparṇâs suparṇâ aminanta;* and for *aminanta evâiḥ*, as in W. From all this illustration, we seem authorized to draw the inference that the words mentioned in the rule as having

---

13. *dhâ: mâ: pâ:* [1] *eteshv*[2] *antyasvara ârshe*[3] *pâṭhe*[4] *'siparaḥ: budhniyâ : jyâ : â pûshâ : aminanta : eteshv*[5] *antyasvara ârshe*[6] *svaraparaḥ pûrvavidhiṁ na prâpnoti. yathâ*[7]*: sva-....: sah-....: dhan-....: asipara iti kim: sva-....:* [8]*pra-....: pra-*

endings exceptionally uncombinable in *saṁhitâ* nevertheless combine with *iti* in *pada*-text, and also exhibit their uncombinable quality in *jaṭâ* only before the words whose sequence calls out that quality in *saṁhitâ—pûshâ*, for example, uniting with its predecessor *â* into *pûshâ*, and *aminanta* with itself into *aminantâ 'minanta* (only, if we may trust the example given, *svadhâ* being held apart from its predecessor *asi*, because this happens to be the same word with its successor: and it is by no means impossible that the manuscripts are in the wrong upon this point). But this would be quite sufficiently intimated by the single restriction *ârshe*, without adding *asi* also; and that the latter is specifically intended to apply to the *pada*-readings, and the former to the *jaṭâ*, is not easily to be believed. The *asi* would have best reason to be introduced because the words mentioned occur also before other vowels, with which they enter into combination—only, to be sure, I have not noted any cases in which they do so.

एष्टेतनेमन्नोद्मन्नोष्ठेवःपरो लुप्यते ॥ १४ ॥

14. When followed by *eshṭaḥ*, *etana*, *eman*, *odman*, *oshṭha*, or *evaḥ*, an *a*-vowel is elided.

That the elision mentioned in the rule is of an *a*-vowel is a consequence of the continued implication of the introductory rule x.3, above—although, as the commentator fails to point out, that implication was interrupted by rules 10-12, and was expressly stated at the outset to remain in force through rule 9. The passages contemplated are quoted by the commentator, as follows: *açîy' eshṭâ râyaḥ* (i.2.11[1]), *çamitâra upetana* (iii.1.4[3],5[2]), *apâṁ tv" emant sâdayâmi* (iv.3.1), *apâṁ tv" odmant sâdayâmi* (iv.3.1: G. M. O. omit *sâdayâmi* in both these citations), *svâh" oshṭhâbhyâm* (vii.3.16[1]), *upayâmam adharen' oshṭhena* (v.7.12: O. omits the first word), and *nir amimat' evaç chandaḥ* (v.3.5[4]: O. omits the last word). These are, so far as I have discovered, all the cases of application of the rule that the text contains. The commentator notes that rule i.22, which allows a theme ending in *a*, quoted in a rule, to stand for its various derivative forms, is the warrant for regarding *oshṭhâbhyâm* and *oshṭhena* as involved in *oshṭha*. The

---

----:[8] [9]*ârsha iti kim: sva-----:*[9] [10]*pra----:*[10] *dhan-----: â pû-----:* [11]*âkâraḥ kimarthaḥ:*[11] *tam----: â te----: ârshasvarapara*[12] *iti kim:* [13]*budh-----: jyâ----: pû-----: am-----*[13].

[1] O. ins. *ity.* [2] B. G. M. *eshv.* [3] B. G. M. *-sha.* [4] B. *pâṭhakâle.* [5] B. G. M. O. *eshv.* [6] G. M. *-shapâṭhe.* [7] B. G. M. O. om. [(8)] O. om. [(9)] G. M. om. [10] B. *evam âdi;* O. *dhru-----;* G. M. om. [(11)] G. M. *âkâreṇa kim.* [12] O. om. *para.* [(13)] See the note, above.

14. ------ *ity evamparo 'varṇo' lupyate: athâ 'varṇapûrve* (x.3) *ity anuvartanâd*[2] *avarṇa*[3] *iti labhyate. açî-----: çami-----: apâṁ----: apâṁ----: svâh-----: oshṭhaçabdasya sarvâvastha-*

same two cases were given by him in illustration of the previous rule (see note to i.22). As general counter-examples, to prove the implication of "an *a*-vowel," we have *çityoshṭhaḥ çitibhruḥ* (v.6.14), and *çityoshṭhâya svâhâ* (vii.3.17).

इवर्णोकारौ यवकारौ ॥ १५ ॥

15. An *i*-vowel and *u* become respectively *y* and *v*.

Here, the commentator tells us, the implication "preceded by an *a*-vowel" ceases, but the implication "followed by a vowel" has force—which implication comes all the way from rule 10 of the preceding chapter. The rule says *ukâra*, 'short *u*,' instead of *uvarṇa*, 'an *u*-vowel,' because long *û* has already (by iv 5) been declared *pragraha*, and protracted *û3* is made uncombinable below (by x.24). The examples are *abhy asthât* (iv.2.8[1]), *ûty açyâma* (i.3.14[3]), and *â pûshâ etv â vasu* (ii.4.5[1]).

उदात्तयोश्च परो ऽनुदात्तः स्वरितम् ॥ १६ ॥

16. And, when they are acute, a following grave becomes circumflex.

The word "and" (*ca*), we are told, brings down from the preceding rule the "*i*-vowel and *u*," there described as suffering a certain effect. The examples given of the production of this kind of circumflex accent, later (xx.1) described as the *kshâipra*, are *vy èvâ'i 'nena pári dhatte* (v.3.11[3]: only G. M. have the last two words), and *apsv àgne* (iv.2.11[3]). As counter-examples, we have first *nícâ' tám dhakshy atasám* (i.2.14[2]) and *mádhv agnâ'u juhóti* (ii.3.2[9]), to show that unless the converted vowels are acute, no circumflex appears; and then, to prove that the following vowel must also be grave, *tád yád ṛcy ádhy akshárâṇi* (ii.4.11[1]: G. M. omit the first word), *sá tv 'â'i yajeta* (ii.6.6[3] et al.: G. M. omit this whole example), and *ín nv 'â' úpastîrṇam ichánti* (i.6.7[3]):

---

sya grahaṇam bhavati grahaṇasya ca (i.22) *iti vacanât: upay-*----*: nir*----. [4]*avarṇo lupyata*[4] *iti kim: çity*-----*: çity*-----.

[1] G. M. *-ṇapûrvo.* [2] W. *-tamânînâd;* G. M. *-tamânaḥ.* [3] G. M. *avarṇapûrva.* (4) B. *-ṇapûrvo l-;* O. *-ṇalopa;* G. M. *-ṇapûrva.*

15. *avarṇapûrvâdhikâro nivṛttaḥ: svaraparâdhikâras tu vartate: atha svaraparo yakâram* (ix.10) *iti pûrvâdhyâye prakrântaḥ. ivarṇokârâu padântâu*[1] *svaraparâu yathâsaṁkhyena*[2] *yavakârâv âpadyete. abhy*----*: ûty*----*: â pû*-----. *dîrghasya pragrahavidhânât plutasya saṁdhinishedhâd ukârasya kârottaratvaṁ*[3] *kṛtam: ivarṇokârâu yavakârâv iti.*

[1] W. puts after the next word. [2] G. M. *-khyaṁ.* [3] G. M. *vakâr-.*

compare, for the peculiar *sandhi* in these last two examples, rule v.13.

ऊभावे च ॥१७॥

17. Also when *û* is the product of the combination.

The "also" (*ca*) of this rule is interpreted as implying that, as in the case of the combination last considered, the first element going to form the *û* must be acute, and the second grave. As examples of the combination and its accentual result are given *sû̀nnîyam iva* (vi.2.4[1]; p. *sú-unnîyam*), *sû̀dgâtâ* (vii.1.8[1]; p. *sú-udgâtâ*), and *mâsû̀ 'ttíshṭhan* (vii.5.2[2]; p. *mâsú: ut-*); to which G. M. add *dikshû̀ 'padâdhâti* (v.5.5[4]; p. *dikshú: upa-dá-*). The only other case of the kind which I have noted in the Sanhitâ is *sû̀pasadanaḥ* (vii.5.20; p. *sú-upasadanaḥ*). The commentator adds a couple of counter-examples: the first, *sûpasthâ' devấḥ* (i.2.2[3]; p. *su-upasthâ'h*), shows that the former *u* must be acute; the other, *tâ' dikshû' 'pâ 'dadhata* (v.5.5[4]), that the latter *u* must be grave.

A later rule (xx.5) gives this particular variety of the circumflex accent the name *praçlishṭa*.

None of the other Vedic texts has an accentual usage corresponding with this. Indeed, there is not in the Atharvan a single case of a combination of two *u*'s such as is here contemplated, nor has any from the other Vedas come to my notice; if such there be, they are left to follow the general analogy of combinations of acute and grave into one homogeneous vowel (as illustrated under rule 10, above), the acute element raising the other to its own pitch and making the result acute. On the other hand, an exception to this general analogy is made in the other Sanhitâs (and duly explained in their Prâtiçâkhyas: see Rik Pr. iii.7, Vâj. Pr. iv.132, Ath. Pr. iii.56) in favor of the coalescence of two short *i*'s into a long *î*; if the former be acute and the latter grave, they produce together a circumflex. Of such a combination, I have

---

16. *cakâraḥ pûrvasûtroktanimittinâv*[1] [2]*ivarṇokârâv anvâdiçati: udâttayor*[2] *ivarṇokârayoḥ paro 'nudâttaç ca*[3] *svaritam âpadyate. vy----: apsv----. udâttayor iti kim: nîcâ----: madhv-- paro 'nudâtta iti kim: tad----: sa----: in----.*

[1] G. M. *-ttino 'pi.* (2) G. M. om [3] O. om.

17. *çakâraḥ pûrvodâttatvânvâkarshakaḥ*[1]*:* [2]*parasyâ 'nudâttatvam anvâdiçati ca*[2]. *pûrveṇo 'dâttena parasyâ 'nudâttasyo "bhâve kriyamâṇe*[3] *svaritaṁ jânîyât. yathâ: sûn----: sûd---- : mâ-----: *[4]*dik----:*[4] *pûrveṇo 'dâttena kim: sûp----: parasyâ 'nudâttasye 'ti kim: tâ----.*

[1] B. O. *pûrvasyo 'd-*; O. *-tvânuk-*: G. M. *pûrvodâttaṁ paratvânudâttaṁ câ "karshati.* (2) G. M. om.; O. om. *ca.* [3] G. M. om. [4] W. B. O. om.

noted about thirty cases in the Tâittirîya text (examples, one in each book, are i.3.6²: ii.1.3¹: iii.5.5²: iv.1.6²: v.1.7²: vi.1.1⁶: vii.5.7⁴); the accentuation is throughout acute, as we should expect.

न श्येती मिथुनी ॥ १८ ॥

18. Exceptions are *çyetî* and *mithunî*.

That is to say, these words are exceptions to rule 15—and, being thus exempt from the conversion there prescribed, and there being no other rule requiring their alteration, they remain unchanged, as if they were *pragrahas*. The examples are *çyâitena çyetî akuruta* (v.5.8¹: O. omits the first word; *çyetî* occurs also in the next division of the same section, though not before a vowel), and *na mithunî abhavan* (v.3.6²: B. omits *na*). The latter word is found in two other places—at iii.4.9¹ and vi.5.8⁶—exhibiting the same uncombinable quality; and in the latter place it has been made (at iv.53) the subject of special exception as not a *pragraha*. The *pada*-text, in fact, writes both words as if no peculiar character belonged to them.

लुप्येते त्ववर्णपूर्वौ यवकारौ ॥ १९ ॥

19. But *y* and *v* are elided, when preceded by an *a*-vowel.

The word "but" (*tu*) in this rule, the commentator says, annuls the application of the rule to any other *y* and *v* than such as are the products of prescribed euphonic processes, and makes these alone the subjects of its action. As a *y* or *v* can never occur as final except by euphonic conversion, the particle has no very useful office to fill, according to the interpretation. Evidently enough, it is used here, as elsewhere in the treatise where a specific force is sought for it by the comment, simply as indicative of a sudden change of subject.

Vastly the largest class of cases falling under the rule is that in which, by ix.10, a *visarjanîya* has been converted into *y* after *a*, *â*, *â*3 before another vowel than *a*. In illustration of this class, the commentator quotes *âpa undantu* (i.2.1¹), *dhruvâ asmin gopatâu* (i.1.1: G. M. O. omit the last word), and *na vicityâ*3 *iti* (vi.1.9¹). The next class consists of cases of final *e* and *âi*, converted into *ay* and *ây* by ix.11,14: the examples are *ima evâ 'smâi* (ii.4.10³), and *âsâmahâ eve 'mâu* (vii.5.2¹). Yet another class embraces the endings in *ân* of which the *n* was turned to *y* (with nasalization of the *â*, or with *anusvâra* added, by xv.1–3) according to the rules at the end of the last chapter (ix.20–24): the selected example is *martyâñ âviveça* (v.7.9¹). But the rule teaches also the

---

18. *çyetî: mithunî: ity etayor antyasvaro yathâvihitaṁ*¹ *yatvaṁ nâ "padyate. yathâ*²*: çyâi-.....: na.....*

¹ O. om. ² W. G. M. O. om.

elision of final *v*; and O. boldly gives examples for this, as well: namely, *vâyav ishṭaye* (ii.2.12[8]: W. adds *duroṇe*), and *ahâv anadata* (v.6.1[2]), although the text, by a usage which the comment ratifies under the next rule but one (x.21), retains the *v* in such cases, and it is retained by O. in these very phrases given to illustrate its omission. W. has only the former of the two, foolishly prefixing to it *avarṇapûrva iti kim*, 'why is it said, "when an *a*-vowel precedes"?' The other manuscripts pass the point without notice here, leaving it to be settled under rule 21. The true counter-examples for this precept, showing that the elision takes place only after an *a*-vowel, are given by all alike: they are *abhy asthât* (iv.2.8[1]), and *hṛtsvasaḥ* (iv.2.11[3]).

नोख्यस्य ॥ २० ॥

20. Not so, according to Ukhya.

Ukhya denies that *y* and *v* are omitted in any case; and would therefore read *âpay undantu, imay eva, martyâñy â*, and so on.

वकारस्तु सांकृत्यस्य ॥ २१ ॥

21. Not *v*, according to Sâṁkṛtya.

The connection of this rule is somewhat anomalous, but its meaning is sufficienely evident. Sâṁkṛtya dissents from the principle laid down in rule 19, like Ukhya; "but" (*tu*) his dissent does not go the whole length of the latter's; according to him, only *v* is "not" elided. As the commentator has it, the fact that this rule teaches an exception is inferred, "by vicinage," from its predecessor: its *tu* is intended as an annulment of the opinion of former teachers. And he declares that it alone is approved, while the two that precede (the former of them, of course, only so far as it is inconsistent with this) and the two that follow (B. O. omit this) are rejected. The examples are those already given by a part of the MSS. under rule 19, namely *vâyav ishṭaye duroṇe* (ii.2.12[8]:

---

19. *avarṇapûrvâu svaraparâu yakâravakârâu*[1] *lupyete. yathâ: âpa----: dhru-----: na----: ima----: âsâ-----:* [2] *vây-----:* [3]*ahâv----:*[3] *mart-----. evampûrvâv*[4] *iti kim: abhy ----: hṛt-----. tuçabda itarâu yavakârâu nivartayann âdeçaprâptayor evâ 'nayor lopavishayatvaṁ dyotayati. avarṇaḥ pûrvo yâbhyâṁ tâv avarṇapûrvâu.*

[1] G. M. *yavak-*. [2] W. ins. *avarṇapûrva iti kim.* ([3]) Only in O. [4] G. M. *avarṇap-*.

20. *ukhyasya*[1] *çâkhinaḥ pakshe*[2] *'varṇapûrvâu*[3] *yavakârâu na*[4] *lupyete. uktâny evo 'dâharaṇâni.*

[1] G. M. ins. *mate.* [2] G. M. *mate.* [3] O. *'pûrvâu.* [4] B. om. G. M. have mixed together to some extent this and the following comment.

W. B. omit this example; O. puts it after the other one, and leaves off *durone*), and *ahâv anadatâ hate* (v.6.1[2]: O. omits *hate*).

This is rather the most striking example afforded us of the over-riding by the commentary of the obvious intent of the Prâtiçâkhya itself. The usage of the existing Tâittirîya text is on the side of the comment: we have a similar resolution of the final *a* of vocatives into *av*, with retention of the *v*, at i.2.13[2] twice; 4.39; 6.12[3]: ii.2.12[4,8]; 4.12[3]; 6.11[1]: iii.2.10[1]: vi.4.3[3]. Of *âv* as result of final *âu* before a vowel, I have failed to collect the examples; but had there been any cases of the omission of the *v*, I think I should not have omitted to observe and note them.

उकारौकारपरौ लुप्येते माचाकीयस्य ॥ २२ ॥

22. According to Mâcâkîya, both are omitted when followed by *u* or *o*.

Instead of Mâcâkîya, the southern manuscripts have, both in the rule and in the commentary, Mâyikâya.

All the manuscripts of the commentary declare that "respectively" (*yathâsaṁkhyam*) is to be understood in the rule—that is to say, that it directs us to drop *y* before *u*, and *v* before *o*; but their examples do not support this interpretation, and it is palpably a false one. It is difficult to believe that the rule itself is not corrupted, and that it ought not to read *ukârâukâraparo lupyate*, '*v* is dropped before *u* or *o*' (it does not occur in the text before *û*); for, while we can discover no phonetic reason for the omission of *y* before a labial vowel, there is a very obvious difficulty in the utterance of *v* (*w*) before *u* (no real Sanskrit word begins with *vu*, nor can I recall it in the interior of a word except as the rare result of *sandhi*); and, as thus amended, Mâcâkîya's view would accord with the accepted doctrine of the Rik Prât. (ii.9–11), and with one mentioned, though not adopted, by the Vâj. Pr. (iv.125).

The illustrative examples given are in part those which have appeared already, even more than once, under the preceding rules:

---

21. *sâṁnidhyân nishedho labhyate. sâṁkṛtyasya mate 'varṇapûrvo vakâro na lupyate: yakâras tu lupyata eve 'ty arthaḥ. 'vây-....:*[1] *ahâv..... pûrvâcâryamatanivartakas tuçabdaḥ. sûtram idam eve 'shṭaṁ: na tu pûrvadvayam*[2] *paradvayaṁ*[3] *ca.*

(1) W. B. om.; O. puts after the other example. [2] O. *pûrvasûtrad-*. [3] B. O. om.

22. *yakâravakârâv avarṇapûrvâv ukârâukâraparâu lupyete yathâsaṁkhyam*[1] *mâcâkîyasyâ*[2] *"câryasya mate*[3]*. âpa....: yâ ..... evamparâv iti kim: ta....: vây-..... lupyete iti 'ha punarârambhaḥ pûrvasûtradvayasthitanañaḥ*[4] *sambandhaçaṅkânirâkaraṇârthaḥ*[5].

[1] O. om.; G. M. after *mate.* [2] G. M. *mâyikâyasyâ*, as in the rule itself. [3] B. G. M. *matena.* [4] W. *-tajanana*; B. *-tajana*; O. *-tananabha.* [5] O. om. *çaṅkâ*; W. *-tham.*

âpa undantu (i.2.1[1]), and *yâ oshadhayaḥ* (iv.2.6[4-5]: so W. B.; but G. M. O. give instead *yâ jâtâ oshadhayâḥ*, iv.2.6[1]); to which O. adds an example for *v*, namely *çatakratav ut* (i.6.12[3]: it ought, in illustration of the rule, to read *çatakrata ut*), putting it between the other two. Counter-examples are *ta enam bhishajyanti* (ii.3.11[4]: we are to understand, apparently, that Mâcâkîya would read *tay enam*), and *vâyav ishṭaye* (ii.2.12[8]).

The commentator remarks in conclusion that the repetition of *lupyete* in the present rule (it was read above, in rule 19) is intended to remove all suspicion of the continued implication of the negative which forms a part of the two preceding rules.

लेशो वात्सप्रस्यैतयोः ॥ २३ ॥

23. According to Vâtsapra, they are imperceptibly uttered.

It might admit of question whether the "they" here spoken of are final *y* and *v* in general, or only *y* and *v* followed by *u* and *o*, as specified in the last rule. As things stand, the use of the demonstrative *etayoḥ* rather favors, though not unequivocally, the latter interpretation, and it is the one adopted by the commentator. But if the preceding rule be restored to what we have suggested above as its more probable original form, then the *etayoḥ* will be very well in place here as referring to *y* and *v* in general; and this interpretation is supported by the fact that the Ath. Pr. (ii.24) and Pâṇini (viii.3.18) ascribe a like opinion to another grammarian, Çâkaṭâyana, whose peculiar views upon the subject are likewise hinted at by the Vâj. Pr. (iv.126). As the meaning of *leça* is defined to be *luptavad uccâraṇam*, 'utterance as if omitted,' there is not much for the two opposing parties to contend about.

न प्लुतप्रग्रह्यौ ॥ २४ ॥

24. Exceptions are protracted and *pragraha* vowels.

Such, namely, are exempt from the rules of combination—and not merely those given in this chapter, but also such as are found elsewhere: for example, at ix.11,12. There is nothing about the

---

23. [1]*vâtsaprasya mata etayor*[2] *yakâravakârayor*[3] *avarṇapûrvayor leçaḥ syât*[1]. *leço nâma luptavad*[4] *uccâraṇam. etayor ity ukârâukâraparâu nirdiçati. uktâny evo 'dâharaṇâni.*

(1) B. om., along with the rule. [2] Only in W. [3] G. M. O. *yavak-*. [4] B. *-tam.*

24. [1]*na khalu plutaḥ pragrahaç ca*[1] *saṁdhividhim bhajete*[2]. *yathâ: astu....: te.... ityâdividhâu nishiddhe 'nyasmiṅç câ 'nârabhyamâṇe*[3] *prakṛtivad*[4] *bhavati.*

(1) G. M. *plutaç ca pragrahaç ca etâu na khalu.* [2] W. B. O. *-jate.* [3] G. M. *'rabh-.* O. *tyâ.*

rule pointing out that it has a bearing so extensive. Only one example is given for each class: *astu hî3 itu abrûtâm* (vii.1.6[1]), and *te enam abhi* (ii.5.6[5]).

The commentator points out, as he did not take the trouble to do under rule 18 of this chapter, that, the rules of combination being thus suspended with reference to these two classes, and no other rule being given about them, they remain in their natural condition.

All the Prâtiçâkhyas have rules equivalent to this (Rik Pr. ii.27; Vâj. Pr. iv.84; Ath. Pr. iii.33: in the note to Ath. Pr. i.73 I overlooked the present precept of the Tâittirîya-Prâtiçâkhya); none assumes that the pronouncing a vowel to be *pragraha* exempts it, *eo ipso*, from phonetic combination.

परश्च परश्च ॥ २५ ॥

25. Also the remaining vowel.

That is to say, the vowel remaining after the omission of the final *y* or *v* is, like those mentioned in the preceding rule, exempt from farther combination. According to the commentator, the "also" (*ca*) of the rule brings forward "*y* and *v*," the fact of their constituting an exception is inferred from the neighborhood of the preceding rule, and *paraḥ* means 'another,' and qualifies *saṁdhiḥ* understood: "no further combination takes place." This seems to me inadmissible, as there has been no suggestion of any such word as *saṁdhi*. Perhaps *para* may be better understood of the vowel "following" the *y* and *v* of which the chapter has been treating. It needs, at any rate, some violence to bring in the rule with the meaning which it is evidently intended to bear: no one would have any right to guess, from its form and position alone, at what it is aimed.

The commentator's examples are *âpa undantu* (i.2.1[1]) and *agra imam* (i.1.5[1]). In reply to the objection that it would be enough to state the implication of the rule as "where an omission has taken place" instead of "an omission of *y* or *v*," he brings up *se 'd u hotâ* (i.1.14[4]), *sâi 'nâ 'nîkena* (iv.3.13[2] et al.), and *sâu 'shadhîḥ* (iv.2.3[3]), as examples of an elision of a final which does not prevent the further combination of its predecessor and its successor under the rules of this chapter.

---

25. *cakârâkṛshṭayor yavakârayor lope sati paraḥ* [1]*saṁdhir na bhavati.*[1] *yathâ*[2]*: âpa....: agra.... sâṁnidhyân nishedho labhyate. nanu lope satî 'ty*[3] *etâvatâi 'vâ 'lam: yavakârayor iti kim. se 'd....:* [4]*sâi....:*[4] *sâu....: ity âdi.*

iti tribhâshyaratne prâtiçâkhyavivaraṇe[5] *daçamo 'dhyâyaḥ.*

(1) G. M. *sandhividhin na bhajate.* [2] G. M. om. [3] W. om. *iti.* (4) O. om. [5] O. adds *prathamapraçne.*

CHAPTER XI.

CONTENTS: 1, initial *a* elided after *e* or *o*; 2–18, exceptions, cases of retention of initial *a* after *e* or *o*; 19, dissident view as to the nature of the elision.

लुप्यते त्वकार एकारौकारपूर्वः ॥ १ ॥

1. But *a* is elided when preceded by *e* or *o*.

The subject of the omission or retention of initial *a* after final *e* or *o*, and of the accent thence arising, occupies the whole of this chapter and of the one next following, the cases of retention being mostly rehearsed in this. No attempt is made, here any more than in the treatment of other similar matters in the work, to effect a real classification—much less, an explanation—of the facts dealt with. Nor have I, on the other hand, drawn up such a classification, as I did for the Atharva-Veda (see Atharva-Prâtiçâkhya, under rule iii.54). Doubtless, if drawn up, it would show nearly the same state of things to prevail in the Tâittirîya as in the Atharvan text: namely, that the elision is the greatly prevailing, almost exclusive, usage in the prose passages; while, in the metrical passages, the *a* is more usually retained where the metre requires its retention, and omitted where the metre requires its omission—although with numerous exceptions, of which the most regular is that the *a* is dropped in writing at the beginning of a *pâda*, where, of course, it was always retained in metrical utterance. The general subject of the relation of the written and spoken texts to one another in regard to this special point is well worth an elaborate investigation, founded on all the Vedic texts.

For the word "but" (*tu*) in the rule is given an alternative explanation. Some, the commentator says, regard it as suspending the force of the exceptional rule x.24; others, as marking the discontinuance of the general direction "followed by a vowel," which has been in action since ix.10. As in other like cases heretofore, we have no good reason for applying it to any particular rule or phrase; it merely marks an abrupt transition to a new subject, somewhat exceptional in its relations to the principles already laid down. The subject was, however, anticipated and provided for in rule ix.13.

---

1. *ekârapûrva okârapûrvo vâ 'kâro*[1] *lupyate. yathâ*[2]*: te----:* [3]*so----.*[3] *tuçabdo na plutapragrahâv* (x.24) *iti nishedhasambandhavidhim*[4] *nivartayatî 'ti kecit: svaraparâdhikâram nivârayatî*[5] *'ty apare saṁgirante.* [6]*ekâraç câu 'kâraç câi 'kârâukârâu:*[6] *ekârâukârâu pûrvâu*[7] *yasmât*[8] *sa tathoktaḥ.*

[1] all the MSS. *akâro.* [2] G. M. om. (3) B. om. [4] G. M. *-bandhi*; O. *-bandham.* [5] G. M. *nivartayati.* (6) in W. only. [7] B. om. [8] G. M. *yasya.*

To illustrate the rule, only two phrases, both of frequent occurrence, are quoted: namely *te 'bruvan* (ii.5.1³ et al.) and *so 'bravît* (ii.1.2¹ et al.).

In the other Prâtiçâkhyas, the apparent loss of initial *a* after *e* or *o* is treated as an absorption of it into its predecessor, or a unification of the two. See Ath. Pr. iii.53 and note, and rule 19 of this chapter, where a somewhat similar view seems suggested.

All the MSS. excepting B. read in the rule *ekâraokârapûrvaḥ;* and, where the rule is quoted (i.61 and ix.13), we have six cases of this reading against three of *ekârâuk-*. But the former is simply an instance of the usage, so common in the commentary (see above, p. 4), of separating, for the sake of clearness, the elements of compound words, or otherwise disregarding the rules of *sandhi.*

अथालोपः ॥ २ ॥

2. Now follow cases of non-elision.

The rest of this chapter is occupied with an enumeration of the cases in which initial *a* is retained. First, in rule 3, a number of passages are specified in which non-elision is the rule, and elision (as determined by the rules of the next chapter) is exceptional; then, in the following rules, more isolated cases are disposed of.

धातारातिरूपवाजपेयजुष्टश्येनायोख्यध्रुवक्षितिरियमेव-सायाग्निर्मूर्धारुद्रप्रथमोपोत्तमविकर्षविहव्यहिरण्यवर्णी-ययाज्यामहापृष्ठ्ये ॥ ३ ॥

3. The *a* is not elided in the following sections: those beginning with *dhâtâ râtiḥ* and *upa;* those styled *vâjapeya;* those beginning with *jushṭa* and *çyenâya;* those styled *ukhya;* those beginning with *dhruvakshitiḥ*, *iyam eva sâ yâ*, and *agnir mûrdhâ;* the first and the next to the last of the *rudra* chapter; and those styled *vikarsha*, *vihavya*, *hiraṇyavarṇîya*, *yâjyâ*, and *mahâpṛshṭhya.*

Here are pointed out not less than seventy-three sections or *anuvâkas*, in which *a* is not elided (except in the cases specified in the rules of the next chapter). Those designated by the annotation of their first words are i.4.44; 5.5: iii.1.10; 2.8: iv.3.4,11; 4.4. The *vâjapeya* sections are six, namely i.7.7–12. The *ukhya* sections (as pointed out above, under ix.20) are twenty, namely iv.1.1–10; 2.1–10. The *rudra* chapter is iv.5, containing eleven sections;

---

2. ¹*athe 'ty ayam adhikâraḥ:*¹ *alopa ucyata ity etad adhikṛtaṁ veditavyaṁ ita uttaraṁ yad vakshyâmaḥ.* ²*na lopo 'lopaḥ:*² *lopâbhâva ity arthaḥ.*

(1) G. M. om. (2) all MSS. *na lopaḥ alopaḥ.*

those here referred to, then, are iv.5.1,10. The name *vikarsha* belongs to five sections, namely iv.6.1–5. Three sections, iv.7.12–14, are styled *vihavya.* The *hiraṇyavarṇîya* section (as shown under ix.20) is v.6.1. The *yâjyâs* have been repeatedly the subjects of prescription in earlier chapters (iii.9,11; ix.30); they are twenty-three sections, namely i.1.14; 2.14; 3.14; 4.46; 5.11; 6.12; 7.13; 8.22: ii.1.11; 2.12; 3.14; 4.14; 5.12; 6.11,12: iii.1.11; 2.11; 3.11; 4.11; 5.11: iv.1.11; 2.11; 3.13. The *mahâpṛshṭhya* sections, finally, are the first six of those which (as seen under ix.20) bear the name *pṛshṭhya;* they are iv.4.12; 6.6–9; 7.15.

Section i.4.44 is quoted by its two first words, instead of by *dhâtâ* only, according to the commentator, because of the occurrence in another *çâkhâ* of a section beginning *dhâtâ devebhyo 'surân* (G. M. omit *asurân*). Again, iv.3.4 is quoted by *dhruvakshitiḥ*, instead of by *dhruva* (the first *pada* of *dhruva-kshitiḥ*, i.48), because *dhruva* (by i.22) would include *dhruvaḥ*, and there is another section beginning with this word, and containing cases of elision, *dhruvo 'si dhruvo hañ sajâteshu bhûyâsam* (ii.3.9[1]: only G. M. have the last two words), which would otherwise be violations of the rule. Yet again, to quote iv.3.11 by *iyam* simply would not answer, because i.2.4 begins with *iyaṁ te çukra tanûr*, and contains a case of elision, *sagarbhyo 'nu sakhâ sayûthyaḥ* (i.2.4[2]: only O. has the last word; G. M. omit the example). But why quote by so long a phrase as *iyam eva sâ yâ*, of which the last two words are unnecessary? To this objection there is an alternative answer: some say that it is for the benefit of the dull-minded; others, that it is intended to include a verse which, though occurring in another place (at i.4.33), is a remainder to this, and which contains the case of non-elision *o te yanti ye aparîshu paçyân* (i.4.33: G. M. O. omit *paçyân*). Now it is true that the single verse constituting i.4.33 is of kindred subject with iv.3.11, and in the Rig-Veda forms part of the same hymn (i.113) with parts of the latter; and it is also true that the combination *ye aparîshu* is not otherwise authorized by the Prâtiçâkhya; but it is, of course, little less than absurd to assert that an excessive

---

3. [1]*dhâtârâtir ity*[1] *âdishv anuvâkeshv ekârapûrva okârapûrvo vâ 'kâro na lupyate.* [2]*dhâtâ râtir* (i.4.44) *ity atra yathâ:*[2] *nidh-....: râtir iti kim: dhâtâ devebhyo 'surân iti çâkhântare.* [3]*upaprayanto adhvaram* (i.5.5) *ity atra yathâ*[3]*: âre.... deva savitaḥ pra suva* (i.7.7) *ity* [4]*âdi shaḍanuvâkânâṁ*[4] *vâjapeyasaṁjñâ:* [5]*atra yathâ:*[5] *te no....: te agre.... jushṭo vâca* (iii.1.10) [6]*ity atra yathâ*[6]*: yas....:* [7]*yo....*[7] *çyenâya* [8]*patvane* (iii.2.8) *ity atra yathâ*[8]*: namaḥ....: viçve.... ukhye yathâ*[9]*: çṛṇv-....: namo.... dhruvakshitir* (iv.3.4) [10]*ity atra yathâ*[10]*: viçve....: ûrmir....:* [11]*kshitir iti kim: dhruve 'ty* [12]*akârântasya yadi*[12] *grahaṇaṁ syât*[11]*: dhruvo.... ity atra bhaved*[13] *iti.*[14] *iyam eva sâ yâ* (iv.3.11) [15]*ity atra*[15]*:*

quotation of the beginning of the one *anuvâka* has any right, or can have been intended, to include the other. The right of i.4.33, it may be remarked, to stand in the text to which our Prâtiçâkhya applies, is assured by the contemplation of others of its phonetic phenomena by rules found elsewhere (most unequivocally by vi.5); its case of non-elision would seem to have been overlooked by the makers of the treatise, but discovered by the commentators, some of whom have tried to force it violently within the ken of their rules. It is necessary to quote iv.4.4 by two words, because i.6.3 also begins with *agniḥ*, and in it we find *yo me 'nti dûre 'râtîyati* (i.6.3[1]: the example is wanting in G. M.). Finally, instead of *pṛshṭhya* passages, the *mahâpṛshṭhya* are specified, because of such cases as *pṛthivî te 'ntarikshena* (v.2.12[2]: the *anuvâka* is *pṛshṭhya*, but not *mahâpṛshṭhya*).

The commentator cites one or more examples from each of the sections or sets of sections which the rule specifies, as follows. From the section beginning *dhâtâ râtiḥ* is taken *nidhipatir no agniḥ* (i.4.44[1]); it contains three more cases, and one exception. From that beginning with *upa* comes *âre asme ca* (i.5.5[1]); it contains six other cases, and one exception. From the *vâjapeya* sections, *te no arvantaḥ* (i.7.8[2]) and *te agre açvam â 'yuñjan* (i.7.7[2]); they contain eleven examples, and eleven exceptions. The section beginning with *jushṭa* yields *yas te añçuḥ* (iii.1.10[1]), and O. alone adds *yo drapso añçuḥ* (iii.1.10[1]); there are two other cases, and no exception. From the *çyenâya* section, *namaḥ pitṛbhyo abhi* (iii.2.8[3]) and *viçve arapâ edhate* (iii.2.8[4]); there are four other cases, and two exceptions. From the *ukhya* sections, *çṛṇvanti viçve amṛtasya putrâḥ* (iv.1.1[2]: only W. has *putrâḥ*) and *namo astu sarpebhyaḥ* (iv.2.8[3]); they yield seventy-five cases, and forty-five exceptions. From the section *dhruvakshitiḥ* are cited the only two examples, *viçve abhi gṛṇantu* (iv.3.4[2]) and *ûrmir drapso apâm asi* (iv.3.4[3]: only G. M. have *asi*); there are no exceptions. From the section beginning *iyam* etc. are taken *ketum kṛṇvâne ajare* (iv.3.11[1]: G. M. omit *ketum*) and *trayo gharmâso anu* (iv.3.11[1]); there are three other cases, and one exception. The

---

ketum....: trayo....: iyam ity [16]*etâvatâi 'vâ 'lam:*[16] *iyaṁ te çukra tanûr* (i.2.4) *ity* [17]*atra sag-.... ity atra mâ bhûd iti: sâ ye 'ti padadvayam*[17] *mandadhiyâm pratipattyartham iti kecit: anye tu anyathâ kathayanti: asyâ 'nuvâkasya çeshabhûtâ* [18]*ya ṛg*[18] *anyatra sthitâ sâ 'pi* [19]*svîkartavye 'ti*[19]*: o te.... agnir mûrdhâ* [20]*diva* (iv.4.4) *ity atra yathâ*[20]*: sa....: enâ....: mûrdhe 'ti kim: agnir mâ durishṭâd* (i.6.3) *ity atra* [21]*yo me ....*[21] *rudrapraçnasya prathamopottamânuvâkayor yathâ*[22]*: namo....: drâpe....: uta....: uttamasya pûrvataḥ*[23] *saṁnikṛshṭa upottamaḥ. açmann ûrjam* (iv.6.1) [24]*ity atrâ 'nuvâkapañcasya*[24] *vikarshasaṁjñâ: tatrâ*[25] *'nyaṁ....: pâvako.... vâjo naḥ sapta pradiça*[26] (iv.7.12) *ity atrâ*[27] *"dyanuvâkatra-*

first example here is not well chosen, since the *e* of *kṛṇvâne* is *pragraha*, and *pragrahas* are not contemplated in the general rules for elision: see xii.8 and note. From the *agnir mûrdhâ* section, *sa yojate arushaḥ* (iv.4.4[4]) and *enâ vo agnim̐ namasâ* (iv.4.4[4]: O. omits *namasâ*); there are three other cases, and one exception. From the specified sections of the *rudra* chapter are taken *namo astu nîlagrîvâya* (iv.5.1[3]), *drâpe andhasas pate* (iv.5.10[1]), and *uta mâ no arbhakam* (iv.5.10[2]); they afford fourteen cases, and five exceptions. From the *vikarsha* sections, *anyam̐ te asmat tapantu* (iv.6.1[3,5]: only W. has *tapantu*) and *pâvako asmabhyam* (iv.6.1[1] etc.); there are thirty-three cases, and ten exceptions. From the *vihavya* sections, *viçve adya marutaḥ* (iv.7.12[1]: O. omits *marutaḥ*) and *viçve devâso adhi vocatâ me* (iv.7.14[2]: only O. has *viçve*); ten cases and five exceptions. The *hiraṇyavarṇîya* section affords three cases only, of which one is cited, *eko devo apy atishṭhat* (v.6.1[3]). The *yâjyâ* sections afford a hundred and twenty-nine cases, with thirty-eight exceptions; the selected examples are *supathâ râye asmân* (i.1.14[3]; repeated at i.4.43[1]) and *kâmena kṛto abhy ânaṭ* (i.1.14[2]: W. B. O. end with *abhi*). From the *mahâpṛshṭhyas*, finally, come *vivasvad vâte abhi naḥ* (iv.4.12[4]) and *somo adhi bravîtu* (iv.6.6[4]: O. adds *no dim̐*, doubtless for *no 'ditiḥ*, which follows in the text); they contain thirty-eight cases and nine exceptions.

This rule, accordingly, disposes at one stroke of three hundred and fifty-one cases of the retention of *a;* but it is at the cost of creating a formidable body of exceptions, a hundred and thirty-one in number, which have to be provided for by the counter-rules of the next chapter—while, once more, a considerable number of the cases falling under the rule have to be individually specified, partly in that chapter and partly in the two following rules of this, as exceptions under the counter rules. It is a complicated process, but it successfully attains at last its purpose.

---

yasya vihavyasam̐jñâ: tatra[28] *viçve----: viçve----. hiraṇyavarṇîye*[29] *yathâ*[30]*: eko----. yâjyâsu yathâ*[31]*: supathâ----: kâmena----. samid 'diçâm̐* (iv.4.12) *jîmûtasya* (iv.6.6) *yad akrando* (iv.6.7) *mâ no mitro* (iv.6.8) *ye vâjinam* (iv.6.9) *agner manve* (iv.7.15) *iti*[32] *shaṇṇâm eshâm*[33] *anuvâkânâm mahâpṛshṭhyasam̐jñâ: tatra*[34] *vivasvad----: somo ----: mahe 'ti kim: pṛthivî----.*

(1) W. B. *-râti 'ty.* (2) G. M. *krameṇo 'dâharaṇâni.* (3) G. M. *upa* only. (4) G. M. *âdinâm̐ shaṇṇâm an-.* (5) G. M. *tatra.* (6) G. M. om. (7) in O. only. (8) G. M. om.; W. omit *yathâ.* 9 G. M. om. (10) G. M. om. (11) G. M. *kshitigrahaṇam;* O. adds *tadâ* after *syât.* (12) O. *etâvanmâtrasya.* 13 G. M. *mâ bhûd;* O. *api bhavet.* 14 O. om. (15) G. M. om.; O. adds *yathâ.* (16) G. M. *ukte;* B. adds *kim anyâiḥ;* O. *etâvatâ 'lam̐ kim ebhi.* (17) G. M. *atrâ 'pi 'ty adhikopâdânam.* (18) W. O. *yâ ṛg;* G. M. *yâ ṛk;* B. *yâm ṛg.* (19) W. B. *svikaroti;* O. adds *yathâ.* (20) G. M. om. (21) G. M. *mâ bhûd iti.* 22 G. M. om. 23 W. *pûrvaḥ.* (24) G. M. *iti praçnasya âditaḥ pañcânuvâkânâm̐;* O. *âdi* for *atra.* 25 O. *tatra yathâ.* 26 G. M. om. 27 G. M. O. om. *atra.* 28 G. M. om.; O. *yathâ.* 29 G. M. *-rṇâḥ.* 30 G. M. om. 31 G. M. om. 32 B. om. 33 G. M. put before *shaṇṇâm.* 34 O. ins. *yathâ.*

अंहसोंऽहतिरनिष्टृतोऽवन्त्वस्मानवद्यादहनि च ॥४॥

4. Also in *an̐hasaḥ*, *an̐hatiḥ*, *anishṭṛtaḥ*, *avantv asmân*, *avadyât*, and *ahani*.

The cases of non-elision referred to are as follows: for *an̐hasaḥ*, *pramuñcanto no an̐hasaḥ* (iv.3.13[5]); for *an̐hatiḥ*, *pari dveshaso an̐hatiḥ* (ii.6.11[2]); for *anishṭṛtaḥ*, *vardhatâṁ te anishṭṛtaḥ* (iv.1.7[2]); for *avantv asmân*, *te avantv asmân* (ii.6.12[3]), with a counter-example, *te no 'vantu pitaro haveshu* (ii.6.12[4]: only G. M. have *haveshu*), to prove the necessity of giving *asmân* along with *avantu* in the rule; for *avadyât*, *mitramaho avadyât* (i.2.14[6]); and for *ahani*, *çuciḥ çukre ahany ojasînâ* (iv.4.12[1]: G. M. O. stop at *ahani*). All of them occur in passages which are the subject of the preceding rule, and the commentator points out that the "also" (*ca*) of the rule brings forward the implication of those passages, and that to any of the words specified, if occurring elsewhere in the text, the rule does not apply; citing as example *sa evâi 'nam pâpmano 'n̐haso muñcati* (ii.2.7[4]: all but G. M. stop at *an̐hasaḥ*). At first sight, then, the rule appears to be a superfluous repetition of part of the cases involved in the preceding one; in fact, however, its value is that of a rehearsal of exceptions under rule xii.4, which teaches that even in the sections above specified, an *a* before a *y*, *v*, *n*, or *h*, if those letters be followed by a vowel, is elided. The only thing calling for explanation about the matter is the connection in which the counter-exceptions are given, which is, to say the least, quite peculiar.

अनु घर्मासआपोमर्तोरथस्त्वोदत्तेवातःपूर्वः ॥५॥

5. Also in *anu*, when preceded by *gharmâsaḥ*, *âpaḥ*, *martaḥ*, *rathaḥ*, *tvaḥ*, *datte*, and *vâtaḥ*.

This rule belongs, in part, in the same category with the preceding, as pointing out cases in which the *a* of *anu* is retained according to rule 3 of this chapter, notwithstanding the prohibition of rule xii.4; but in part it is of a more general character, since the last two cases lie outside the sections specified in rule 3.

---

4. [1] *cakâro dhâtârâtir* (xi.3) *ityâdivishayânvâdeçakaḥ*[2]: *an̐hasaḥ*------ *ity eteshu grahaṇeshu dhâtârâtirityâdisthaleshv*[3] *ekârapûrvo vâu*[4] *'kârapûrvo vâ*[5] *'kâro na lupyate. yathâ*[6]: *pram*-----: *pari*-----: *vardh*-----: *te*-----: *asmân iti kim: te no*-----: *mitr*-----: *çuciḥ*----- *yavanahaparatvâd*[7] (xii.4) *eshu prâpyamâṇalopeshv*[8] *alopo 'yaṁ*[9] *vihitaḥ. anvâdeçaḥ kimarthaḥ: sa*-----.

[1] G. M. ins. *eteshu grahaṇeshu.* [2] G. M. *-disthalavish-.* [3] B. adds *antarvartishu;* G. M. *-lâpattishu;* O. *-lavartishu satsu.* [4] G. M. O. om. *vâ.* [5] O. om. [6] G. M. O. om. [7] W. *-ratv;* G. M. *-hasvarapar-.* [8] G. M. ins. *satsu.* [9] W. om.; B. *na.*

The commentator explains the phraseology used as signifying that the words rehearsed, having their final *visarga* [with the preceding *a*] converted to *o* [of course, excepting *datte*], have the office of preceding causes—that is, of producing an effect upon the word that follows them; but he gives no hint of the partial suspension of the implication made in the preceding rule; intimating rather, that the cases rehearsed are all of them exceptions under rule xii.4. He quotes the passages, as follows: *trayo gharmâso anu* (iv.3.11[1]), *tasmâd âpo anu sthana* (v.6.1[3]), *yadâ te marto anu* (iv.6.7[3]), *anu tvâ ratho anu* (iv.6.7[3]), *pîyati tvo anu tvaḥ* (iv.2.3[4]: only G. M. have the last word), *çukram â datte anuhâya jâryâi* (iii.2.2[2]: G. M. O. omit *jâryâi*), and *dhanus tad vâto anu vâtu te* (v.5.7[3,4]: O. ends with *anu*). To show that other words than *anu* are not relieved from the action of xii.4, he gives us *amushmiṅ loke vâto 'bhi pavate* (v.4.9[4]: all but G. M. begin at *vâto*); and further, to show that *anu* retains its *a* only after these words, *anu gâvo 'nu bhagaḥ kanînâm* (iv.6.7[2]: only G. M. O. have the last word).

I have noted ten cases in which the *a* of *anu* is elided under the operation of rule xii.4.

अभिवात्वपश्च ॥ ६ ॥

6. Also (after *vâtaḥ*) in *abhi vâtu* and *apaḥ*.

The *ca*, 'also,' here brings down as *pûrvanimitta* simply *vâtaḥ*, the word last specified in the preceding rule. The cases have nothing to do with xi.3: they are *mayobhûr vâto abhi vâtû 'srâḥ* (vii.4.17[1]: G. M. omit the first word, and they alone have the last), and *yad vâto apo agamat* (vii.4.20: O. omits *agamat*); and, as counter-examples, the commentator quotes *vâto 'bhi* (v.4.9[4]) to show the necessity of giving *vâtu* after *abhi* in the rule, and *ava rundhe 'po 'gre 'bhiryâharati* (vi.4.3[2]: G. M. omit the last two words) to attest the implication conveyed by the *ca*.

अन्वगमच्च ॥ ७ ॥

---

5. *atra visargântânâm otvam âpannânâm pûrvanimittatvam*[1] *iti*[2] *vijñeyam: gharmâsaḥ - - - - - - ity evampûrva anv ity atrâ 'kâro na lupyate. yathâ: trayo*[3] *- - - -: tasmâd - - - -: yadâ - - - -: anu - - - -: pîyati - - - -: çukram - - - -: dhanus*[3] *- - - -. anv iti kim: amushmiṅ - - - -: evampûrva iti kim: anu - - - -. yavanahaparatvanishedhârtho*[4] *'yam ârambhaḥ.*

[1] W. G. M. *-mittam.* [2] O. om. (3) a *lacuna* in B. [4] G. M. *yavanahasvarapa-*; O. *-shedhanisheçârtho.*

6. *cakâro vâta ity anvâdiçati: abhi vâtu: apaḥ: ity etayor akâro vâtaḥpûrvo na* [1]*lupyate. mayo- - - - -. vâtv iti kim: vâto - - - -* [2]*yad - - - -.*[2] *anvâdeçena kim: ava - - - -.*

[1] G. M. ins. *khalu.* (2) G. M. put before *vâtv* etc.

7. Also (after *apaḥ*) in *anu* and *agamat.*

Here, again, the *ca*, 'also,' brings forward only the last word in the preceding rule, namely *apaḥ*—and what is more, gives that word a new character, changing it from *nimittin* to *nimitta* or affecting cause. Of this the commentator takes no notice, and we are doubtless to regard it as quite in order, and as merely adding another to the formidable list of uncertainties involved in the curious system of *anuvṛtti* or continued implication. The passages had in view are *apo anv acârisham* (i.4.45[3],46[2]: B. reads *âpo adyâ 'nv*, which is the version of the Rig-Veda, i.23.23) and *apo agamad indrasya* (vii.4.20); as counter-example, is given *paçavo 'nû 'd âyan* (ii.1.5[1]), to prove the implication of *apaḥ*.

आपःपूर्वो ऽद्भिरपांनपादस्मान् ॥ ८ ॥

8. Also in *adbhiḥ*, *apâṁ napât*, and *asmân*, when preceded by *âpaḥ*.

The passages are *sam âpo adbhir agmata* (i.1.8), *devîr âpo apâṁ napât* (i.2.3[3]: vi.1.4[9]; 4.3[3]), and *âpo asmân mâtaraḥ çundhantu* (i.2.1[1]: O. omits *çundhantu*). The necessity of specifying *napât* after *apâm* is shown by *vâruṇîr âpo 'pâṁ ca* (ii.1.9[2]), and the restriction to preceding *âpaḥ* by *so 'smân pâtu* (v.5.5[1]).

रायेसइन्द्रःपूर्वश्चाकारपरे ॥ ९ ॥

9. In *asmân*, also, if followed by *a*, when *râye*, *saḥ*, and *indraḥ* precede.

The *ca*, 'also,' again brings down the word last mentioned in the preceding rule. The passages for *saḥ* and *indraḥ* are *mâ so asmâñ avahâya* (v.7.9[1]) and *indro asmân asmin dvitîye* (iii.1.9[2]: O. omits *dvitîye*): and other cases of *asmân* after *saḥ* are to be found at i.6.6[4] and iii.2.7[2]. As counter-examples, are given *so 'smân pâtu* (v.5.5[1]), to show that the *asmân* must be followed by *a;* and *smo 'smân amutra* (vi.6.1[4]: all the MSS. of the commentary have the false reading *so 'smân;* such a phrase would be precisely out of place here as illustration), to show that it is only

---

7. *apa iti cakâro 'nvâdiçati: anu: agamat: ity etayor akâro 'na khalv[1] apaḥpûrvo lupyate. apo anv....: apo ag-..... evampûrva iti kim: paçavo.....*

(1) G. M. O. om. *khalu*, and put *na* next before *lupyate*.

8. *adbhiḥ...... eteshv[1] akâra âpaḥpûrvo na lupyate. sam ....: devîr....: napâd iti kim: vâruṇîr....: âpo..... evampûrva iti kim: so.....*

[1] G. M. *eshv;* O. *eshu grahaṇeshv.*

after the words specified that *asmân*, even before *a*, remains unmutilated.

The other case, that of preceding *râye*, makes more difficulty, since the *saṁhitâ* contains no passage in which *asmân*, when itself followed by *a*, has *râye* before it. The commentator first declares the passage had in view to belong to another text (*çâkhâ*); but adds, as an alternative explanation, that the precept relates to the *jaṭâ*-text, where we read *râye asmân asmân râye râye asmân* (i.1.14³; 4.43¹). He proceeds further to say that, in case any one objects that in the *saṁhitâ* form of the passage the example does not hold good, since *asmân* is not there followed by *a* (it reads *râye asmân viçvâni*), he shall reply that the case is one falling under i.61. It is there taught, namely, that a passage of three words or more, if repeated in the text, reads as it read on its first occurrence: now the one in question first appears in i.1.14, which is a *yâjyâ* section, and hence the *a* of *asmân* is retained by xi.3; at i.4.43, then, its retention is assured. But then there ought to be no necessity for specially establishing its retention in *jaṭâ*, any more than in any other case where an *a* is retained in *saṁhitâ*. This difficulty the commentator evidently perceives, although he does not state it; for otherwise the *jaṭâ* explanation would have satisfied him, and he would never have thought of suggesting another *çâkhâ*. The difficulty really remains unsolved, and a serious one: either there was a blunder on the part of the makers of the treatise, or a passage not contained in the present Sanhitâ was contemplated by them: I incline to think the former more likely.

तेपूर्वो ऽद्यान्धोऽंशुरग्ने ॥ १० ॥

10. Also in *adya*, *andhaḥ*, *an̆çuḥ*, and *agne*, when *te* precedes.

The commentator quotes the passages, as follows: *paçum paçupate te adya* (iii.1.4¹: W. O. omit *paçum*), *upo te andhaḥ* (i.4.4 and iii.4.2¹), *an̆çunâ te an̆çuḥ* (i.2.6: B. omits the example), and *yat te agne tejas tena* (iii.5.3²: only B. has *tena*). Counter-examples are, first, to show that only these words keep their *a* after *te*, *te 'gnaye pravate* (ii.4.1²: B. has a corrupted reading, *te enam*, and W. a *lacuna* to the end of the comment, putting in place of it an example from under the next rule, *tena tvâ " dadhe 'gne an̆giraḥ*),

---

9. *cakârâkṛshṭe 'smâñgrahaṇe 'kârapare sati*[1] *vartamâno*[2] *'kâro râye sa indra ity*[3] *evampûrvo na lupyate. râyepûrvasyo 'dâharaṇaṁ çâkhântare:* [4]*atha vâ*[4] *jaṭâyâm bhavati: râye*____. *yathâsaṁhitâyâṁ* [5] *no 'dâharaṇam akâraparatvâbhâvât*[6] *tarhi*[7] *katham alopa*[8] *iti kecit*[9]*: tripadaprabhṛtipunaruktatvâd iti brûmaḥ. mâ*____*: indro*____. *akârapara iti kim: so*____. *evampûrva iti kim: smo*____. *akâraḥ paro yasmât* [10]*tad akâraparam*[10]*: tasmin.*

[1] in W. only. [2] G. M. put before *'kârapare*. [3] G. M. O. om. [(4)] O. om. [5] G. M. O. ins. *tu*. [6] W. O. *-patvâbh-*; G. M. *-parâbh-*. [7] O. *tathâ*; G. M. add *tadâ*. [8] G. M. *lopa*. [9] G. M. O. *cet*. [(10)] W. *tad akâṁ*; G. M. *akâraparaḥ*.

and second, to show that these words do so only after *te*, *prathamo 'ñçu skandati* (iii. .8³: only B. has *skandati*).

Of *agne* after *te*, the text presents eighteen other cases: namely i.2.11² twice; 4.43²; 5.2⁴,3²,4³; 6.6²; 7.6⁴: iii.4.10⁵; 5.3² (a second case): v.4.7⁵; 7.4¹,6³,8¹ three times: vi.2.2⁷; 6.1².

मेपूर्वश्च ॥ ११ ॥

11. In *agne*, also, when preceded by *me*.

Only *agne*, the last word of rule 10, is brought down into this. The commentator quotes *yan me agne asya* (i.6.2¹,10²: W. B. omit *asya*) and *imâ me agna ishṭakâḥ* (iv.4.11³,⁴ and v.4.2⁴); and there is another case in iv.4.11⁴. He adds, as usual, a number of counter-examples, of obvious intent: they are *tena tvâ " dadhe 'gne añgiraḥ* (i.2.12¹: O. omits *añgiraḥ*), *prâṇaç ca me 'pânaḥ* (iv.7.1¹), and *tad açakaṁ tan me 'râdhi* (i.6.6³).

अस्याश्विनापरा च ॥ १२ ॥

12. As also, in *asya*, *açvinâ*, and *aparâ*.

That is to say, when these words follow *me*. The passages are *viyantu devâ havisho me asya* (i.5.10³: O. begins at *devâ*), *punar me açvinâ yuvaṁ cakshuḥ* (iii.2.5⁴: W. B. omit the last word, O. the last two), and *yad vâ me aparâgatam* (vi.6.7²).

नःपूर्वो ऽसदग्निरघान्तमोऽभ्यस्मिन्नद्यपथि ॥ १३ ॥

13. Also in *asat*, *agniḥ*, *agha*, *antamaḥ*, *abhi*, *asmin*, and *adya pathi*, when preceded by *naḥ*.

The examples are *supârâ no asad vaçe* (i.2.3¹ and vi.1.4⁴), *ayaṁ no agnir varivaḥ* (i.3.4¹ and i.4.46³; there is another case of *no agniḥ* at v.7.9¹), *rakshâ mâkir no aghaçañsa îçata* (i.4.24 and

---

10. *adya...... eteshv*[1] *akâras ta ity evampûrvo na lupyate. yathâ*[2]*: paçum....: upo....: *[3]*añçunâ....:*[3] *yat.... eteshv iti kim: *[4]*te....: tepûrva iti kim: prathamo....*[4]

[1] O. *eshu.* [2] in W. only. (3) B. om. (4) W. om., and ins *tena tvâ* etc.

11. [1]*cakâro 'gna ity anvâdiçati: mepûrvo 'gna ity atrâ 'kâro*[1] *na lupyate. yathâ*[2]*: yan....: imâ.... mepûrva iti kim: tena....: anvâdeçena*[3] *kim: *[4]*prâṇaç....:*[4] *tad....*

(1) B. *cakârâkṛshte saty agna ity asminn akâro ma ity evampûrvo;* G. M. the same, omitting *sati;* O. the same, omitting *sati* and the second *iti.* [2] in W. only. [3] O. *-ça iti.* (4) O. om.

12. *mepûrva iti cakâro 'nvâdiçati: asya......* [1] *eteshv*[2] *akâro mepûrvo na lupyate. vi-....: punar....: yad....*

[1] G. M. ins. *iti.* [2] O. *eshv.*

iv.6.6[4]: G. M. O. omit *îçata*), *agne tvaṁ no antamaḥ* (i.5.6[3] and iv.4.4[8]), *svishṭiṁ no abhi vasîyaḥ* (iii.1.9[2]: G. M. O. omit *vasîyaḥ*), *çikshâ no asmin* (vii.5.7[4]), and *tebhir no adya pathibhiḥ sugebhî rakshâ ca naḥ* (vii.5.24: all but W. end with *pathibhiḥ*). The necessity of including *pathi* in the rule is shown by *no 'dya vasu vasatî 'ti* (ii.5.3[6-7]). Other counter-examples, of obvious intent, are *tasmâd açvâd gardabho 'sattaraḥ* (v.1.2[1]: G. M. omit the first two words), *so 'gnir jâtaḥ* (v.1.4[1]), *uttarato 'ghâyur abhidâsati* (v.7.3[1]: B. O. omit the last word), *te 'sminn âichanta* (vii.2.10[1]), *namo 'gnaye 'pratividdhâya* (i.5.10[1]: the example is found only in G. M.), and *te naḥ pântu te no 'vantu* (i.2.3[1]; 8.7[1]: iv.3.3[2]).

नमःपूर्वो ऽग्रेऽश्वेभ्योऽग्रियाय ॥ १४ ॥

14. Also in *agre*, *açvebhyaḥ*, and *agriyâya*, when preceded by *namaḥ*.

The passages are *namo agrevadhâya ca* (iv.5.8[1]), *namo açvebhyo 'çvapatibhyaḥ* (iv.5.3[2]: B. omits the last word; the whole example is wanting in W.), and *namo agriyâya ca* (iv.5.5[2]). Counter-examples are *apo 'gre 'bhivyâharati* (vi.4.3[2]) and *namo 'gnaye 'pratividdhâya* (i.5.10[1]).

आविन्नःसोमःपूर्वो ऽग्निपरः ॥ १५ ॥

15. Also when *âvinnaḥ* or *somaḥ* precedes and *agni* follows.

It may be made a question whether the rule should not read *gniparaḥ* (without sign of omission), and mean 'also an *a* preceded by *âvinnaḥ* or *somaḥ* and followed by *gni*.' But the authority of the comment (see below) is decidedly, though not unequivocally, in favor of what I have given, and the construction, though a peculiar one, has its analogies elsewhere in the treatise (compare x.4 etc.). The further difficulty remains, however, that the only passages in the text to which the rule can apply read *agniḥ*, in the nominative singular, after the two words specified, so that there appears to be no reason why we should not have simply *'gniḥ*, instead of *'gniparaḥ*. This the commentator does not fail to perceive;

---

13. *asat...... eteshv akâro na ity evampûrvo na lupyate. yathâ*[1]*: supârâ....: ayaṁ....: rakshâ....: agne....: svishṭiṁ....: çikshâ....: tebhir.... pathî 'ti kim: no.... naḥpûrva iti kim: tasmâd....: so....: uttarato....: te.... eteshv iti kim:* [2]*namo....:*[2] *te....*

[1] in W. only. [(2)] in G. M. only.

14. [1]*agre......*[1] *eteshv akâro namaḥpûrvo na lupyate. namo....:* [2]*namo açv-....:*[2] *namo agri-.... namaḥpûrva iti kim: apo....: eteshv iti kim: namo 'gn-....*

[(1)] O. om. [(2)] W. om.

and accordingly—resorting, as we cannot well help saying, to one of his usual subterfuges—he declares *agni* (or, according to W. B. O., *gni*) "a part of a word, intended to include a number of cases occurring in another *çâkhâ;*" not going so far, however, as to quote any of these cases. I suspect *'gniparaḥ* to be either a corruption of *'gniḥ*, or originally intended as equivalent with it.

The passages are *âvinno agnir gṛhapatiḥ* (i.8.12²) and *somo agnir upa devâḥ* (iii.2.4¹); and the commentator adds counter-examples, *so 'gnir jâtaḥ* (v.1.4¹) and *âvinno 'yam asâu* (i.8.12²).

धीरासोऽदब्धासएकादशासऋषीणांपुत्रःशार्यातेऽषाढःपितारःपृथिवीयज्ञआसतेयेगृह्णाम्यग्रेवाँएषजज्ञेसँस्फानोयुवयोर्यःपृष्ठेपतिर्वोगोशुष्मःपुवःसमिद्धऋषभःपाथोवचोवर्षिष्ठेजुषाणोयोरुद्रोवृष्णःपूर्वः ॥ १६ ॥

16. Also *a* is retained when preceded by *dhîrâsaḥ*, *adabdhâsaḥ*, *ekâdaçâsaḥ*, *ṛshîṇâm putraḥ*, *çâryâte*, *ashâḍhaḥ*, *pitâraḥ*, *pṛthivî yajñe*, *âsate ye*, *gṛhṇâmy agre*, *vâñ eshaḥ*, *jajñe*, *sañsphânaḥ*, *yuvayor yaḥ*, *pṛshṭhe*, *patir vaḥ*, *go*, *çushmaḥ*, *puvaḥ*, *samiddhaḥ*, *ṛshabhaḥ*, *'pâthaḥ*, *vacaḥ*, *varshishṭhe*, *jushâṇo*, *yo rudraḥ*, or *vṛshṇaḥ*.

The passages had in view are quoted as follows: *tâṁ dhîrâso anudṛçya yajante* (i.1.9³: G. M. O. omit the last word); *adabdhâso adâbhyam* (i.1.10² and iii.5.6¹); *ekâdaçâso apsushadaḥ* (i.4.11); *ṛshîṇâm putro adhirâja eshaḥ* (i.3.7²: G. M. O. omit the last word), with a counter-example, *yasya putro 'jâtaḥ* (i.5.8⁵; 7.6⁵), to show the need of including *ṛshîṇâm* in the *nimitta*; *yathâ çâryâte apibaḥ* (i.4.18: G. M. omit *yathâ*); *ashâḍho agniḥ* (i.5.10¹·²); *tvatpitâro agne devâḥ* (i.5.10²: G. M. O. omit *devâḥ*); *pṛthivî yajñe asmin* (i.6.5¹), with a counter-example, *te mâ 'smin yajñe* (iii.2.4¹), where, as only W. B. point out, the *jaṭâ*-text shows the mutilation of *asmin* after *yajñe* not preceded by *pṛthivî* (thus, *asmin yajñe yajñe 'sminn asmin yajñe*); *adhyâsate ye antarikshe* (iii.5.4³), with *ye pṛthivyâṁ ye 'ntarikshe* (iv.5.11²: only O. has the first *ye*) as counter-example; *mayi gṛhṇâmy agre agnim* (v.7.9¹·²), with *ashṭâu kṛtvo 'gre 'bhi shuṇoti* (vi.4.5¹: O. omits *shuṇoti*) as counter-example; *idâvâñ esho asura* (i.6.6⁴ and iii.1.11¹), with *çukra esho 'nto 'ntam manushyaḥ* (vii.2.7²: O. stops at

---

15. *âvinnaḥ: somaḥ:* [1] *evampûrvo* [2]*kâro 'gniparo*[2] *na lupyate: agnî*[3] *'ti padâikadeçaḥ çâkhântare bahûpâdânârthaḥ. âvinno ----: somo----. evampûrva iti kiṁ: so-----: evampara iti kiṁ: âvinno-----.*

[1] G. M. ins. *ity.* [(2)] G. M. *agni ity evamparaḥ akâro;* B. *akâraḥ agniparo.* [3] W. B. O. *gnî.*

'*ntam*) to show the need of *vân; itaḥ prathamaṁ jajñe agniḥ* (ii.2.4[8]: only G. M. have *itaḥ;* without it, also i.3.14[5]): see what is said of this passage, and of the rule as fixing its reading, under i.61; *sañsphâno abhi rakshatu* (iii.3.8[2]), as counter-example to which, to show that *sphânaḥ* in the rule would not have been enough, is given *gayasphâno 'gnishu* "from another *çâkhâ*," but the genuineness of the reason is open to doubt; *yuvayor yo asti* (iii.5.4[1]) with *yo 'psu bhasma praveçayati* (v.2.2[5]: only O. has the last word) to prove the need of *yuvayoḥ; nâkasya pṛshṭhe adhi rocane divaḥ* (iii.5.5[3]: G. M. O. omit *divaḥ;* another nearly identical case at iii.5.4[1]); *yajñapatir vo atra* (v.7.7[1]), with *na vo 'bhâgâni havyam* (v.1.1[1]: O. omits *havyam*) as counter-example; *goargham eva somaṁ karoti* (vi.1.10[1]: O. omits *-maṁ karoti; goargha* occurs twice more in this section, and at v.2.9[4] we have *goaçva* twice), to which, by rule i.52, *agoargham* (vi.1.10[1] three times) is to be added as further example; *uchushmo agne yajamânâyai 'dhi* (i.6.2[2]: only G. M. have *edhi*, and O. omits also the preceding word; there is a second case, of *niçushmaḥ*, in the same division); *agrepuvo agreguvaḥ* (i.1.5[1]); *samiddho añjan* (v.1.11[1]: and we have *samiddho agne* at i.6.6[2]; 7.6[4]: ii.5.8[6]), without any counter-example to show that *iddhaḥ* would not have been enough to answer the needs of the rule; *dyâm ṛshabho antariksham* (i.2.8[1]: O omits *dyâm*, and G. M. have, like the Calcutta edition, the false reading *yâm*); *priyam pâtho apî 'hi* (iii.3.3[3] three times); *ugraṁ vaco apâ 'vadhîm* (i.2.11[2]: another nearly identical case in the same division); *varshishṭhe adhi nâke* (i.1.8 and i.4.43[2]); *jushâṇo aptur âjyasya vetu* (i.3.4[1] and vi.3.2[2]: G. M. omit *vetu*); *yo rudro agnâu yaḥ* (v.5.9[3]: G. M. O. omit the last word), and, as counter-example, *yad upatṛñhyâd rudro 'sya* (vi.3.9[3]: but O. reads *açnîyâd* for *upatṛñhyâd*, which makes the reference to i.6.7[4]); and, finally, *vṛshṇo açvasya saṁdânam asi* (ii.4.7[2],9[4]: O. stops at *açvasya*, which would make the reference include also vii.4.18[2] twice; and there are further cases of retention after *vṛshṇaḥ* at i.4.2 and vi.4.5[3]).

---

16. *dhîrâsaḥ* ------ *evaṁpûrvo na*[1] *khalv*[2] *akâro lupyate. yathâ*[3]*: tâṁ*----*: adab-*----*: ekâd-*----*: ṛshîṇâm*----*: ṛshîṇâm iti kim: yasya*----*: yathâ*----*: ash-*----*: tvat-*----*: pṛthivî*----*: pṛthivî 'ti kim: te*---- [4]*ity atra jaṭâyâm*[4]*: adhy-*----*: âsatâ iti kim: ye*----*: mayi*----*: gṛhṇâmî 'ti kim: ashṭ-*----*: idâvâñ*----*: vân iti kim: çukra*----*: itaḥ*----*: sañs-*----*: sam iti kim: gayasphâno 'gnishv iti çâkhântare: yuvayor*----*: yuvayor iti kim: yo*----*: nâkasya*----*: yajña-*----*: patir iti kim: na*----*: go-*----*: apy akârâdi* (i.52) *vacanâd*[5] *agoargham* [6]*iti co 'dâharaṇam*[6]*: uchushmo*----*: agrepuvo*----*: samiddho*----*: dyâm*----*: priyam*----*: ugraṁ*----*: varsh-*----*: jushâṇo*----*: yo*----*: ya iti kim: yad*----*: vṛshṇo*----.

[1] O. puts next before *lupyate.* [2] O. om. [3] G. M. O. om. (4) G. M. O. om. [5] O. *iti prâptiḥ.* (6) O. om.

अरतिमस्ययज्ञस्यातिद्रुतोऽतियन्त्यनृणोऽविष्यन्ननमीवो-
ऽन्नेष्वर्चिरजीतानज्यानिमह्नियाअम्बाल्यर्वन्तमस्त्वकृणोद-
ङ्गिरोऽप्सुयोअस्कभायदच्युतोऽश्वसनिरस्थभिरशिश्रेदङ्गे-
ऽघ्निय ॥ १७ ॥

17. Also in *aratim*, *asya yajñasya*, *atidrutaḥ*, *ati yanti*, *anṛṇaḥ*, *avishyan*, *anamîvaḥ*, *anneshu*, *arciḥ*, *ajîtân*, *ajyânim*, *ahniyâḥ*, *ambâli*, *arvantam*, *astu*, *akṛṇot*, *angiraḥ*, *apsu yaḥ*, *askabhâyat*, *acyutaḥ*, *açvasaniḥ*, *asthabhiḥ*, *açiçret*, *ange*, and *aghniya*.

The passages had in view are quoted by the commentator as follows, with such counter-examples as are needed to justify the inclusion of more than one *pada* in any case: *mûrdhânam divo aratim pṛthivyâḥ* (i.4.13 and vi.5.2^{1}: O. begins at *divaḥ*, and it alone has *pṛthivyâḥ*); *yan me agne asya yajñasya* (i.6.2^{1},10^{2}), with the counter-example *ete 'syâ 'mushmin* (vi.1.10^{5}); *pratyank somo atidrutaḥ* (i.8.21: all the MSS. here insert the *k* before *somo*, as required by v.32, and G. M. even convert it to *kh*, according to xiv.12); *paçyanto ati yanti* (iii.2.2^{1}), and, as counter-example to both these last examples, *nai 'nan somo 'ti pavate* (vi.5.11^{4}: O. begins at *somo*); *tad agne anṛṇo bhavâmi* (iii.3.8^{2}: O. omits *bhavâmi*); *na yavase avishyan* (iv.4.3^{3}); *svâveço anamîvo bhavâ naḥ* (iii.4.10^{1}: B. O. omit *bhavâ naḥ*); *ye anneshu vividhyanti* (iv.5.11^{1}: O. omits the last word); *jâtavedo yo arciḥ* (v.7.8^{1}); *çarado ajîtân* (v.7.2^{3}); *teshâm yo ajyânim* (v.7.2^{3}); *tiroahniyâ mâ suhutâḥ* (vii.3.13: O. omits *suhutâḥ*); *ambe ambâli* (vii.4.19^{1,2} twice, ^{3} twice); *yo arvantam jighânsati* (vii.4.15: O. omits the last word); *bahis te astu bâl iti* (iii.3.10^{2}: O. stops at *astu*; the text furnishes eleven other cases of *astu* with *a* retained, at i.2.3^{3}; 4.45^{1}; 8.14^{2}: iii.1.1^{4}; 2.5^{7},8^{2}: v.5.9^{3} twice; 7.2^{4},4^{3,4}); *ita indro*

---

17. *aratim* ......[1] *eteshv akâro* [2]*na khalv*[2] *ekârapûrva okârapûrvo vâ lupyate. yathâ*[3]*: mûrdh*-....: *yan*....: *yajñasye 'ti kim: ete*....: *pratyan*....: *paçy*-....: *drutoyantî 'ty âbhyâm*[4] *kim: nâi*....: *tad*....: *na*....: *svâv*-....: *ye*....: *jâtavedo*....: *çarado*....: *teshâm*....: *tiro*-....: *ambe*....: *yo*....: *bahis*....: *ita*....: *agne*....: *yo*....: *ya iti kim: açvo*....: *yo*....: *madâya*....: *yo*....: *sanir iti kim: açvebhyo*....: *indro*....: *bhir*[5] *iti kim:* [6]*çam*.... *ity atra*[7] *jaṭâyâm*[6]*: asthabhyo*....: *varuṇo*....: *ange*-....: *aghniye 'ty akâragṛhîtaḥ padâikadeço bahûpâdânârthaḥ: etâni*....: *yad*....: *payo*....

[1] G. M. om. the enumeration, and ins. *iti.* [(2)] G. M. om. *khalu*, and put *na* next before *lupyate.* [3] G. M. O. om. [4] B. *tâbhyâm;* G. M. *etâbhyâm.* [5] B. G. M. *asthabhir.* [(6)] O. om. [7] B. om

akṛṇot (i.1.12); *agne añgiro yo 'syâm* (i.2.12[1]: there is another case in the same division, and one at vi.2.7[3]); *yo apsu ya oshadhîshu* (v.5.9[3]), with the counter-example *açvo 'psujo vetasaḥ* (v.3.12[2]: but O. gives instead *yo psu bhasma*, v.2.2[5]); *yo askabhâyad uttaram* (i.2.13[3]: G. M. O. omit *uttaram*); *madâya raso acyutaḥ* (i.2.6); *yo bhaksho açvasaniḥ* (iii.2.5[7]), and, as counter-example, *açvebhyo 'çvapatibhyaç ca* (iv.5.3[2]: only O. has *ca*); *indro dadhîco asthabhir iti* (v.6.6[3]: O. omits *iti*), and a counter-example from the *jaṭâ*-text of the passage *çam asthabhyo majjabhyaḥ* (v.2.12[2]: O. omits), namely *asthabhyo majjabhyo majjabhyo 'sthabhyo 'sthabhyo majjabhyaḥ* (G. M. give simply *majjabhyo 'sthabhyaḥ*); *varuṇo açiçret* (i.8.10[2]); *añge-añge ni dedhyat* (i.3.10[1] and vi.3.11[2]: it would have been better to include in the example the preceding word *prâṇo*, to show that the first *añge*, as well as the second, furnishes an example under the rule; there is another like pair of cases, after *apâno*, in i.3.10[1]); and finally, it is explained that the quotation of *aghniya* with final *a* makes it (by i.22) a part of a word, intended to include a variety of cases, and three such cases (being all that the text contains) are quoted: namely *etâni te aghniye nâmâni* (vii.1.6[8]), *yad âpo aghniyâ varuṇe 'ti çapâmahe* (i.3.11: B. omits the last word; G. M. O. the last three), and *payo aghniyâsu hṛtsu* (i.2.8[1]: O. omits *hṛtsu*, which would make the citation include also vi.1.11[3]). This exposition seems to prove that the proper reading at the end of the rule is *aghniya*, and I have ventured to adopt it, though all the MSS. (except T., which is ambiguous, running rules 17 and 18 together in *sandhi*) give *aghniyâ*. *Aghniyâ* would answer as including *aghniyâsu*, but it would not include also *aghniye*.

अध्वरे स्वरपरे ॥ १८ ॥

18. Also in *adhvara*, when a vowel follows [the *r*].

The examples given in illustration of the rule are *satyadharmâṇo adhvare* (i.2.1[2]), *havishmân devo adhvaraḥ* (i.3.12), and *upaprayanto adhvaram ity âha* (i.5.7[1]). In regard to the last of them, it is remarked that rule i.61 is not of force for it, since the conditions imposed by that rule do not arise in it. The rule, namely, directs that a passage of three words or more, being repeated in the text, is to be read as where it first occurred; now *upaprayanto adhvaram* was found at i.5.5[1], where the retention of the *a* comes under rule 3 of this chapter; but here only two

---

18. *adhvara ity asmin*[1] *grahaṇe svarapare*[2] *vartamâno 'kâro* [3]*na khalv*[3] *ekârâukârapûrvo*[4] *lupyate. satya-.....: havishmân .....: upa-.....: atra*[5] *tripadaprabhṛti* (i.61) *nyâye na prasarati*[6]*: tallakshaṇâsambhavât. svarapara iti kim: çug..:..: andho.....*

[1] G. M. *etasmin.* [2] O. ins. *sati.* (3) G. M. om. [4] G. M. O. *ekârapûrva okârapûrvo vâ;* G. M. adds *na;* B. adds *vâ.* [5] M. *tatra.* [6] B. *sarati.*

words, instead of three, are cited in the repetition. As counter-examples, showing the value of the restriction "when a vowel follows," are given *çug vâ agniḥ so 'dhvaryum* (v.6.2[4]) and *andho 'dhvaryuḥ syât* (v.1.3[1] and vi.1.8[3]: O. alone has *syât*, and, without that addition, the phrase is found also at v.1.3[2]). This proves that what is to be "followed by a vowel" is the *r* of *adhvara;* but how that meaning is conveyed by the terms of the rule is not easy to discover. The MSS. are at variance as to the reading of the first word of the rule, T. W. B. O. giving *adhvara*, and G. M. *adhvare*, between which I am at a loss to decide confidently, because neither of them appears to be what is wanted. But I prefer *adhvara*, both because it is better supported, and because it is not the usage of the treatise to put in a case-form the words or themes which it cites from the text.

An additional case falling under the rule is *ûrdhvo adhvaraḥ* (i.1.12); and yet others (as i.5.5[1] twice, and, doubtless, i.4.46[2-3]), to which it would else apply, are disposed of under the general rule xi.3.

स पूर्वस्यार्धसदृशमेकेषामर्धसदृशमेकेषाम् ॥ १९ ॥

19. In the opinion of some, it becomes half-similar with its predecessor.

This is a very blind precept, and we are permitted to doubt whether its purport is interpreted aright by the commentary; in which, moreover, there are peculiar and unintelligent variations of reading. What letter is the subject of the rule—the elided *a*, or the non-elided? The comment says the latter (although the majority of MSS. blunderingly say the "non-protracted" instead), and states that it acquires a quantity similar to half a *mora*, or becomes one and a half *moras* long. It is added, that no special examples are given, because such would not bring to light any difference (? only O. has the reading that means this: W. B. omit the "not;" G. M. are unintelligible). This appears to me quite unsatisfactory. The distinct demonstrative *sa* in the rule ought to point back to something distinctly stated above, and that is the

---

19. *yo 'yam akâro 'luptaḥ*[1] *sa pûrvasyâi* [2]*'kârasyâu 'kârasya*[2] *vâ 'rdhamâtrasadṛçaṁ*[3] *kâlam bhajata*[4] *ity ekeshâm ṛshîṇâm*[5] *matam*[6]*:* [7]*adhyardhamâtraḥ syâd*[7] *ity arthaḥ. uktâny evo 'dâharaṇâni viçeshâdarçanât*[8]*. ardhena sadṛço 'rdhasadṛçaḥ*[9]*: tam ardhasadṛçam*[10].

iti tribhâshyaratne prâtiçâkhyavivarana [11]
ekâdaço 'dhyâyaḥ. [12]

[1] W. B. O. *aplutaḥ.* [(2)] G. M. *ekâraokârapûrvasya.* [3] W. *-traṁ sad-;* G. M. *-trâsad-.* [4] G. M. *labhata.* [5] O. *âcâryâṇâm.* [6] O. om. [(7)] W. O. *-trasyâm;* B. G. M. *-tra syâd.* [8] W. B. *-shadar-;* G. M. *darçanât.* [9] G. M. *yaḥ.* [10] O. om. [11] O. ins. *prathamapraçne.* [12] G. M. add *çrîkṛshṇâya namaḥ.*

akâra which in rule 1 is said to be dropped after certain "predecessors." We have had no *akâra alupta* spoken of, but only cases of *alopa* of *akâra.* And it seems to be taught here, in accordance with the doctrines of all the other Prâtiçâkhyas (see note to Ath. Pr. iii.53), that some regard the *a* as (not elided, but) so absorbed into the preceding diphthong as to become assimilated to, or identified with, the latter half of that diphthong. We may with plausibility conjecture the rule to be a later addition to the original substance of the chapter.

CHAPTER XII.

CONTENTS: 1–8, elision and non-elision of initial *a* after final *e* or *o* in exceptional and special cases; 9–11, resulting accent.

अथ लोपः ॥ १ ॥

1. Now for cases of elision

This is a general heading to the chapter (that is to say, to its first eight rules); which, as the commentator points out, has for its sphere of action the passages specified in rule 3 of the preceding chapter. This is a matter of course: the general rule (by xi.1) being elision, there can be need of an additional authority for elision only where that rule is contravened by another of opposing character, and of wider application than to specific cases only.

असि ॥ २ ॥

2. The *a* of *asi* is elided.

The examples given are *suparṇo 'si garutmân* (iv.1.10⁵; 6.5³: v.1.10⁵: O. omits the last word) and *pratho 'si pṛthivy asi* (iv.2.9¹: O. stops at *'si*). The elision is not infrequent in this word, usually occurring in the little prose phrases which are inserted among the verses in the sections concerned; I have noted eighteen other cases: but they are hardly worth detailed reference.

न गर्भःसंनद्धोयमोभद्रःपूर्वः ॥ ३ ॥

---

1. *athe 'ty ayam adhikâraḥ: akârasya lopa ucyata ity etad adhikṛtaṁ veditavyam ita uttaraṁ yad vakshyâmaḥ. dhâtârâtir* (xi.3) *ityâdivishayo 'yam adhyâyârambhaḥ*[1].

[1] G. M. *etadadh-*.

2. *asî 'ty asminn akâro lupyata ekârâukârapûrvaḥ*[1]. *yathâ*[2]: *suparṇo....: pratho....*

[1] G. M. *-rvo vâ.* [2] in B. only.

3. But not when *garbhaḥ*, *saṁnaddhaḥ*, *yamaḥ*, or *bhadraḥ* precedes.

The examples quoted by the commentator are *garbho asy oshadhînâm* (iv.2.3^{3}), *saṁnaddho asi vîdayasva* (iv.6.6^{5}), *asi yamo asy âdityaḥ* (iv.6.7^{1}: G. M. O. omit the last word), and *tvam bhadro asi kratuḥ* (iv.3.13^{1}). There is another case of *asi* after *garbhaḥ* at iv.1.4^{2}, which is then repeated at v.1.5^{3}, the *a* standing this time unelided by rule i.61.

As usual, the commentator thinks it necessary to account for the inclusion of the double *pada sam-naddhaḥ*, instead of simply *naddhaḥ*, in the rule. Some, he says, quote as counter-example *upanaddho 'suraḥ* (iv.4.9); but its propriety is questionable, since the passage does not fall under xi.3, and moreover, there is no *asi* in it (O. has the good sense to pass without notice this most absurd suggestion); and the valid counter-example is to be sought in another *çâkhâ*. We have here an unusually clear example of the arbitrary way in which the plea *çâkhântare* is resorted to, in order to avoid the attribution of a slight inconsistency to the treatise-makers.

यवनहपरः स्वरपरेषु ॥ ४ ॥

4. *A* is elided before *y*, *v*, *n*, and *h*, when these are followed by a vowel.

The examples given are *hiraṇyaçṛṅgo 'yo asya pâdâḥ* (iv.6.7^{4}: O. omits *pâdâḥ*), *vanaspate 'va sṛjâ rarâṇaḥ* (iv.1.8^{3}: O. omits *rarâṇaḥ*), *vareṇyo 'nu prayâṇam* (iv.1.10^{4}), and *jambhayanto 'hiṁ vṛkam* (i.7.8^{2}: O. omits *vṛkam*). These are but specimens selected from among a considerable number of cases: namely, before *y*, two; before *v*, nineteen; before *o*, fourteen (all but three of them, cases of *anu*, the counter-exceptions to which form in part the subject of xi.5); before *h* (which, as the counter-exceptions noted in xi.4 show, includes also *ṅh*), five; in all, forty. To show the necessity of the restriction "when these are followed by a vowel," are cited *çukraṁ te anyat* (iv.1.11^{2}) and *agre ahnâṅ hitaḥ* (iv.1.3^{4}: O. omits *hitaḥ*).

There is a well-established difference of reading here in the rule itself: T. B. G. M. have *yavanaha svaraparesh u*, only W. and O. adding *para* (which I have amended to *paraḥ*) after *ha*. So also,

---

3. *garbhaḥ------* [1] *evampûrvaḥ sâṁnidhyât labdhe 'si* [2] *'ty asmin grahaṇe* [3] *'kâro* [4] *na* [5] *lupyate. garbho----: saṁnaddho ----:* [6]*sam iti kim: upan----- iti kecid udâharanti: tac cintyam: dhâtârâtir* (xi.3) *ityâdyantaḥpâtitvâbhâvâd asiçabdâdarçanâc* [7]*ca: mukhyaṁ tu* [7] *çâkhântare vijñeyaṁ pratyudâharaṇam* [6]. *asi----: tvaṁ----.*

[1] G. M. ins. *ity.* [2] W. *tasminn asi.* [3] B. O. om. [4] G. M. ins. *ekârapûrva okârapûrvo vâ.* [5] B. om. [(6)] O. simply *udâharaṇaṁ çâkhântare.* [(7)] W. *ca 'mukhyaṁ kiṁtu.*

where the rule is quoted under i.21, W. alone (there is no O. for that part of the work) introduces *para;* under xi.4 and 5, W. and B. alike have *yavanahaparatva* etc., but the testimony as to the rule is equivocal, since *para* might well have been added there by way of exposition instead of quotation. I have, as usual, followed W., although not without suspicion that the *para* is a gloss, introduced to help the otherwise blind and inaccurate phraseology of the rule—which latter, however, is not altogether discordant with the usage of the treatise elsewhere.

The exceptions under this rule, instead of being rehearsed after it, as is the general habit of the Prâtiçâkhya, are given in rules 4 and 5 of the preceding chapter, and, in the latter rule, mingled with instances of a wholly different character. Here, then, a particular specification of cases already included under a general rule is regarded as insuring against inclusion in a more general statement of exceptions under that rule. I believe that the treatise offers no other example of this canon of interpretation.

जकारग्नपर उदात्तः ॥ ५ ॥

5. Before *j* and *gn*, *a* is elided if acute.

The examples are *ojo 'jâyathâḥ* (i.6.12[4]) and *çuciḥ pâvaka vandyo 'gne* (i.3.14[5]); and the counter-examples, of *a* unaccented remaining unelided, are *ná tatṛshâṇó ajáraḥ* (iv.6.1[2]) and *nidhipátir no agníḥ* (i.4.44[1]). There is, as the examples show, a real reason in the accent: *ájâyathaḥ* and *ágne* are both words that are accented only at the beginning of a *pâda*, where (as remarked under xi.1) the elision of *a* is an almost universal rule. All the other cases of elision before *gn* (nine in number) are of the same kind; not, however, those before *j* (only two).

मोवचोदधानस्थेपूर्वश्च ॥ ६ ॥

6. Before *gn*, also when preceded by *maḥ*, *vacaḥ*, *dadhânaḥ*, and *sthe*.

The *ca*, 'also,' of this rule, brings down simply *gn* from its predecessor, the intent being to point out the cases where the *a* of *agni* is elided even when unaccented. *Maḥ*, it is stated, is a part

4. [1] *yakâravakâranakârahakâraparo 'kâro*[2] *lupyate teshu yakârâdishu svarapareshu satsu. hiraṇ-....: vanus-....: vareṇyo ....: jambh-..... svarapareshv*[3] *iti kim: çukraṁ....: agre ....*[4]

[1] G. M. ins. *ekâraokârapûrva akâraḥ.* [2] G. M. om. [3] O. *-para.* [4] G. M. add *evam âdi.*

5. *jakâraparo*[1] *gnaparaç ca 'kâra*[2] *udâtto lupyate. ojo....: çuciḥ..... udâtta iti kim: na....: nidhi-....*

[1] G. M. *jakâraç ca.* [2] O. puts after *udâtto.*

of a word, so given for the sake of conciseness, and including the two cases *áñgirasvad ache 'mo 'gnim* and *áñgirasvad bharishyâmo 'gnim* (both iv.1.2²: O. omits *áñgirasvad* in each). The other passages had in view by the rule are *vaco 'gnaye bharatâ bṛhat* (iii.2.11¹: O. omits the last two words), *dadhâno 'gnir hotâ* (iv.1.3⁴), and *sadhasthe 'gnim purîshyam* (iv.1.3¹: O. omits *purîshyam*). To prove the implication of *gn* only, is given *sadhasthe adhy uttarasmin* (iv.6.5³; 7.13⁴: v.7.7²: O. omits).

By xi.16, *vacaḥ* does not as a general thing elide the following *a;* but there is no clashing between the two rules, as they have reference to different parts of the text.

अभ्यावर्तिन्नपूपमपिदधाम्यद्यान्वदितिःशर्माग्नेर्जिह्वामग्न-
यःपप्रयोऽस्माकमस्मेधत्ताश्माश्वाश्रुतिरश्यामामार्यमन्नस्म-
त्पाशानस्मिन्यज्ञेऽस्ताव्यथमानाभिद्रोहमधाय्यदोऽथोऽदु-
ग्धाअरिष्टाअरथाअर्चन्त्यन्तरस्यामत्रस्थान्नायाङ्गिरस्वदकरम्

॥ ७ ॥

7. The *a* is elided in *abhyâvartin, apûpam, api dadhâmi, adyâ 'nu, aditiḥ çarma, agner jihvâm, agnayaḥ paprayaḥ, asmâkam, asme dhatta, açmâ, açvâ* wherever found, *açyâma, amâ, aryaman, asmatpâçân, asmin yajñe, astâ, avyathamânâ, abhidroham, adhâyi, adaḥ, atho, adugdhâḥ, arishṭâḥ, arathâḥ, arcanti, antar asyâm, atra stha, annâya, áñgirasvat*, and *akaram*.

The commentator gives an example for each specification of the rule, with counter-examples for every case in which more than one *pada* is taken, as follows: *agne 'bhyâvartin* (iv.2.1²), and, as counter-example, *kâmena kṛto abhy ânad arkam* (i.1.14²: G. M. omit the last word, O. the last two); *bhadraçoce 'pûpaṁ deva* (iv.2.2³: only W. has *deva*); *agne 'pi dadhâmy âsye* (iv.1.10²), and, as counter-example, *baddho apikaksha âsani* (i.7.8³: O. omits the last word); *anu no 'dyâ 'numatiḥ* (iii.3.11³: iv.4.12⁵; 7.15⁵), and, as counter-example, *pra tat te adya çipivishṭa nâma* (ii.2.12⁵: O. ends with *adya*, and G. M. substitute another passage,

---

6. *gnapara iti cakâro jñâpayati: maḥ...... ity evampûrvo gnaparo* [1]*'nudâtto 'py*[1] [2]*akâralopo bhavati.*[2] *yathâ*[3]*: añgi-....: ma ity* [4]*atra padâikadeçagrahaṇaṁ*[4] *saṁkshepârtham: añgir-....: vaco....: dadhâno....: sadhasthe.....* [5]*anvâdeçaḥ kimarthaḥ:*[5] *sadh-..... gnaparasyâ 'kârasyâ*[6] *'nudâttârtho 'yam ârambhaḥ.*

(1) in W. only. (2) G. M. O. *akâro lupyate.* [3] in W. only. (4) G. M. *apadagrahaṇam.* (5) G. M. *anvâdeçena kim;* O. om., along with the following example. [6] in W. only.

namely *viçve adya marutaḥ*, iv.7.12[1]); *adhi bravîtu no 'ditiḥ çarma yachatu* (iv.6.6[4]: G. M. O. omit the first two words), and, as counter-example, *yathâ no aditiḥ karati* (iii.4.11[2]: only O. has *karati* [reading it *karat*]; G. M. substitute a *jaṭâ* reading, *aditir no no aditir aditir naḥ*, without anything to show whether it is put forward as the *jaṭâ*-text of this passage, or of another, occurring at iv.6.9[4], where the *saṁhitâ* likewise reads *no aditiḥ*); *adhvaraṁ no 'gner jihvâm abhi gṛṇîtam* (iv.1.8[2]: B. omits the last word, O. the last two, G. M. the last and first), and, as counter-example, *vratâ dadante agneḥ* (iv.1.8[2]); *te no 'gnayaḥ paprayaḥ* (i.7.7[2]), and, as counter-example, *purishyâso agnayaḥ prâvaṇebhiḥ* (iv.2.4[3]: G. M. omit the last word); *naro 'smâkam indra* (iv.6.6[7]; there are two other cases, at iii.2.8[6] and iv.6.4[3]); *viçve 'sme dhatta* (i.4.44[2]), with the counter-example *draviṇaṁ vâjo asme : vâjasya mâ* (iv.7.12[1]: only B. has *mâ*, and G. M. O. end at *asme*); *pari vṛṅdhi no 'çmâ bharatu nas tanûḥ* (iv.6.6[4]: G. M. end with *'çmâ*, and only O. has the last two words); for the phonetic complex *açvâ*, however followed, *vṛshapâṇayo 'çvâ ratheebhiḥ* (iv.6.6[3]: O. omits after *'çvâ*), *pracetaso 'çvân* (iv.6.6[5]), and *bharanto 'çvâye 'va* (iv.1.10[1]: O. omits this example), with two counter-examples, *cashâlaṁ ye açvayûpâya takshati* (iv.6.8[2]: O. alone has the last word, and it omits the first) and *kshatraṁ no açvo vanatâm* (iv. 6.9[4]: O. omits *vanatâm*), to show that *açva* would not have answered the purpose instead of *açvâ*; *vâjayanto 'çyâma dyumnam* (i.3.14[3]: G. M. omit *dyumnam*); *punas te 'mâi 'shâm* (iv.7. 14[3]); *ye te 'ryaman* (ii.3.14[4]); *te 'smatpâçân* (iv.3.13[4]), with the counter-example *anyaṁ te asmat tapantu* (iv.6.1[3,5]: v.4.4[5]: only O. has *tapantu*); *yaḥ pitâ te 'smin yajñe* (ii.6.12[6]), with the counter-example *te asmin javam â 'dadhuḥ* (i.7.7[2]); *prasitiṁ drûṇâno 'stâ*

---

7. *abhyâvartin------ eteshv akâro lupyate ekârâukârapûrvaḥ*[1]. *yathâ*[2]: *agne----: âvartinn*[3] *iti kim: kâmena----: bhadraçoce----: agne----: dadhâmî 'ti kim: baddho----: anu----: anv iti kim: pra----: adhi----: çarme 'ti kim: yathâ----: adhv-----: jihvâm iti kim: vratâ----: te----: papraya iti kim: purîsh-----: naro----: viçve----: dhatte 'ti kim: drav------ pari----:* [4] *açve 'ty asya*[5] *yatrayatra çrutis*[6] *tatratatra lopaḥ: vṛsha-----: çrutir iti kim: prace-----: bhar-----: dîrghagrahaṇena* [7] *kim: cashâlaṁ----: kshatraṁ----: vâjay-----: punas----: ye----: te----: pâçân iti kim: anyaṁ----: yaḥ----: yajña iti kim: te----: prasitiṁ----: mâ----: jane----: droham iti kim: bṛhas-----: upa----: ye----: mahyam----: çûra----: pûrve----: ye----: gâya-----: abhi----: asyâm iti kim: rukmo----: ye----: sthe 'ti kim: tvashṭâ----: râyas----: pṛthivyâḥ----: ahaṁ----.*

[1] G. M. put before *lupyate*, and add *vâ*. [2] G. M. O. om. [3] W. *abhyâv-*. [4] O. ins. *açvâ çrutiḥ*. [5] G. M. O. om. [6] G. M. *çrûyate*. [7] G. M. ins. *iti*.

'si (i.2.14[1]: O. omits *prasitim*); *mâ suparṇo 'vyathamânâ* (iv.2.9[1]); *jane 'bhidroham manushyâḥ* (iii.4.11[6]: O. omits *manushyâḥ*), with a counter-example, *bṛhaspate abhiçaster amuñcaḥ* (iv.1.7[4]: only W. has *amuñcaḥ*); *upa prâ 'yât sumanme 'dhâyi manma* (iv.6.8[3]: all but O. begin at *sum-*, and G. M. end with *'dhâyi*); *ye 'do rocane divaḥ* (iv.2.8[3]: O. omits *divaḥ*); *mahyam agne 'tho sîda* (iv.1.9[3]; 2.1[5]); *çûra nonumo 'dugdhâḥ* (ii.4.14[2]); *pûrve 'rishṭâḥ syâma* (iv.7.14[2]: all the MSS. read *-shṭâ*); *ye pavayo 'rathâḥ* (i.6.12[6]: only G. M. have *ye*); *gâyatriṇo 'rcanty arkam* (i.6.12[2-3]: only G. M. have *arkam*); *abhi çûçuco 'ntar asyâm* (iv.1.9[3]; another case at iv.2.3[3]), with the counter-example *rukmo antar vi bhâti* (iv.1.10[4-5] et al.); *ye 'tra stha purâṇâḥ* (iv.2.4[1]), with the counter-example *tvashṭâ no atra varivaḥ* (i.4.44[1]); *râyas posho 'nnâya tvâ* (i.7.9[2]: O. omits *tvâ*); *pṛthivyâḥ sadhasthe 'ṅgirasvat* (iv.1.6[1,2] four times; other cases at iv.1.1[3,4] three times); and *ahaṁ tebhyo 'karaṁ namaḥ* (iv.5.1[3]).

गाह्मानोजायमानोहेतयोमन्यमानोवनस्पतिभ्यःपते-
स्रिधस्तपसःस्वधावोभामितोऽग्नयश्रायोऽध्वर्योक्रतोपूर्वः

॥ ८ ॥

8. An *a* is elided when preceded by *gâhamânaḥ*, *jâyamânaḥ*, *hetayaḥ*, *manyamânaḥ*, *vanaspatibhyaḥ*, *pate*, *sridhaḥ*, *tapasaḥ*, *svadhâvaḥ*, *bhâmitaḥ*, *agnayaḥ*, *âyo*, *adhvaryo*, and *krato*.

The quoted passages are *gâhamâno 'dâyaḥ* (iv.6.4[2]); *jâyamâno 'hnâṁ ketuḥ* (ii.4.14[1]); *hetayo 'nyam asmat* (iv.5.10[5]); *manyamâno 'martyam* (i.4.46[1]); *vanaspatibhyo 'dhi sambhṛtâm* (iv.6.1[1]: O. omits the last word), with the counter-example *namaḥ pitṛbhyo abhi* (iii.2.8[3]); *annapate 'nnasya* (iv.2.3[1] and [by i.61] v.2.2[1]); *niho ati sridho 'ty acittim* (iv.1.7[3]: O. omits the first two words); *tapaso 'dhi jâtaḥ* (iv.2.10[4]); *deva svadhâvo 'mṛtasya dhâma* (iii.1.11[6]: O. omits the first word and the last), with the counter-example *anyâ vo anyâm avatu* (iv.2.6[3]: O. omits the last word); *bhâmito 'mitrasyâ 'bhidâsataḥ* (i.6.12[5]: O. omits the last word); *yân agnayo 'nvatapyanta* (iii.2.8[3]: O. omits *yân*); *agne 'dabdhâyo 'çîtatano* (i.1.13[3]: O. omits *agne*); *adhvaryo 'ver apâḥ* (vi.4.3[4]: O. ends at *'veḥ*); and *çatakrato 'nu te dâyi* (ii.5.12[5]).

A special explanation is required for the passage in which *agnayaḥ* occurs, since the following *pada* is *anu*, which might seem to

---

8. *gâhamânaḥ ------ ity evampûrvo*[1] *'kâro lupyate. yathâ*[2]: *gâh-----: jây-----: hetayo ----: many-----: vanas-----: vanaspâtî 'ti kim: namaḥ : anna-----: niho ----: tapaso ----: deva ----: svadhe 'ti kim: anyâ ----: bhâmito ----: yân --- : ukârasya vakâravikriyâyâṁ vyañjanaparo nakâra*[3] *iti yavanaha* (xii.4) *nishedhâbhâvâd alope prâpte tadapavâdo*

fall under xii.4. Its inclusion here is necessary, because in *saṁhitâ* the word becomes *anv*, so that its *n* is no longer "followed by a vowel," as required by that rule. The question might arise, whether rule i.51 would not, at any rate, cause *anv* to be implied along with *anu;* but the commentator does not raise it, and the course taken by the treatise is evidently the more reasonable and safer one.

The last three cases which the rule deals with are of a peculiar character, and quite different from all the rest falling under this chapter, being those in which a final *pragraha* or uncombinable vowel elides an initial *a*, either in the passages specified in xi.3 (like the last of the three) or elsewhere (like the other two). This the commentator points out, and declares that in every other instance the *a* remains after a *pragraha*. I have already noticed (under iv.6,7) what the usage of the text is after *pragraha* in *o:* that, against the two cases here mentioned of *a* elided after a vocative in *o*, there are but two in which the *a* remains; but that after a final *o* containing the particle *u* we have twenty-one cases of *a* retained, and no case of its elision. The passages where *a* is retained after an *e* that is *pragraha*, I have omitted to note: but there is a considerable number of them, including many (e. g. i.4. 30 : ii.5.6[5] : vi.3.5[3] : vii.5.3[2] : the commentator cites a single one, *ime açvinâ saṁvatsaraḥ*, v.6.4[1]) where the retention is not otherwise authorized: so that inability to cause elision is unquestionably involved in the very character of a *pragraha* vowel, according to the view of the treatise, and needs not to be expressly stated. At this we have a right to be surprised, especially for two reasons: first, that it is thought necessary to teach (see x.24) that *pragrahas* are not liable in general to combination with the initial vowels that follow them; and secondly, that according to this treatise there is no combination of the initial *a* with the preceding *e* or *o*, but an actual loss of it, leaving the *e* or *o* unaffected (except sometimes as to accent). But the essential character of the *pragraha* vowels, the reason of their peculiar treatment, and the proper significance of the term by which they are called, are obscure points as yet in Hindu phonetics and nomenclature.

It remains to inquire how complete and accurate is the enumeration by the Prâtiçâkhya of the cases of elision or non-elision of *a* occurring in the Tâittirîya Sanhitâ. I have, in looking through the Sanhitâ, carefully considered every case with reference to the rules of the treatise, and the result is that, apart from *ye aparishu*

'yam. agne----*: adhvaryo*----*: çatakrato*----*: atra yavanâ ha* (xii.4) *ityâdinâi 'va lope siddhe punar asya grahaṇam niyamârtham: âyo 'dhvaryo*[4] *krato ity etatpadatrayapûrvasyâi 'vâ*[5] *'kârasya*[6] *lopo na tv itarapragrahapûrvasye*[7] *'ti: yathâ: ime*----.

[1] G. M. *-vas tv.* [2] G. M. O. om. [3] B. *-rapara.* [4] O. *âdh-.* [5] B. om. [6] O. *kâra.* [7] B. *itaratra pr-.*

(i.4.33) already treated of under xi.3 (p. 244), I have found only two cases of *a* retained which are not accounted for: namely *ūrdhvo asthât* (v.2.1[5]; R-V. x.1.1) and *so agniḥ* (v.2.3[3]; R-V. vii. 1.16); and both these I suspect to fall under i.61, I having failed to note the previous occurrence of the passages. Of cases explained by i.61 there is a considerable number; only, as was remarked under that rule (see p. 47), there are three among them to which, if the commentator's forçed interpretation of its terms be admitted, it cannot be made to apply. Of cases of elision of *a* unaccounted for, I have found none. Of course, my examination of the Sanhitâ, having been made by the help of a single *saṁhitâ* manuscript, is not to be credited as absolutely accurate: yet I have a good deal of faith in the trustworthiness of its result.

तस्मिन्ननुदात्ते पूर्व उदात्तः स्वरितम् ॥ ९ ॥

9. When the elided *a* is grave, the preceding diphthong, if acute, becomes circumflex.

All the Prâtiçâkhyas, and the usage of the known Vedic texts, are in accord upon this point (see note to Ath. Pr. iii.55). To the particular circumflex hence resulting, the treatise gives later (xx.4) the name *abhinihata;* the others call it *abhinihita.* The examples given are *tè 'bruvan* (ii.5.1[3] et al.) and *sò 'bravīt* (ii.1.2[1] et al.). The representation of the tone of the elided *a* in the resulting accent of the eliding diphthong, of course, favors the view that regards it as absorbed into the latter, rather than elided.

उदात्ते चानुदात्त उदात्तम् ॥ १० ॥

10. When it is acute, the preceding diphthong, if grave, becomes acute.

This, also, is a universal usage. The commentator quotes two examples: *áva rundhaté 'satram vâ'i* (vii.3.8[1]: O. omits *ava*) and *ánnapaté 'nnasya* (iv.2.3[1] and v.2.2[1]).

स्वरितश्च सर्वत्र स्वरितश्च सर्वत्र ॥ ११ ॥

11. As also, in every case, if circumflex.

The commentator explains *ca*, 'also,' as bringing down *udâtte*,

---

9. *yam*[1] *adhikṛtyâ 'yam prabandha uktas tasminn*[2] *akâre 'nudâtte lupte sati pûrva ekâra okâro vo 'dâttaḥ*[3] *svaritam âpadyate. yathâ*[4]*: tè....: sò....*

[1] G. M. *ayam.* [2] G. M. *asm-.* [3] G M. put next after *pûrva.* [4] in B. only.

10. *tasminn*[1] *evâ 'kâra udâtte*[2] *lupte sati*[3] *pûrva ekâra okâro vâ 'nudâtta udâttam âpadyate. yathâ*[4]*: ava....: anna-....*

[1] O. *asm-.* [2] O. puts next after *eva.* [3] O. om. [4] in O. only.

'when the elided *a* is acute,' from the preceding rule, and *sarvatra*, 'in every case,' as signifying 'whether the circumflex be independent or enclitic.' His examples are *bheshajáṁ gávè 'çvâya* (i.8.6[1]) and *ójó 'jâyathâḥ* (i.6.12[4]), where the final syllables of *gáve* and *ójaḥ* have the enclitic circumflex by xiv.29, and *átho 'kthyó 'thâ 'tirâtrâḥ* (vii.1.5[4]: G. M. O. omit the first word), where the final syllable of *ukthyàḥ* has the independent circumflex before the elision.

We might perhaps also fairly conclude that *sarvatra* implies an inclusion of the case treated of in rule 9, and virtually teaches that a final circumflex, eliding an initial grave, is still circumflex.

With this chapter ends the first *praçna*, or section, of the treatise. The division into *praçnas* is a purely external and formal one, and (as I gave notice would be the case, in the Introductory Note to the Atharva Prâtiçâkhya) is made no account of in this edition. References made to the succeeding chapters by section and chapter will easily be found by adding twelve to the number of the chapter as given.

CHAPTER XIII.

CONTENTS: 1–3, loss of *m*, before semivowels and spirants; 4, its retention before *râjan* etc.; 5–15, details of the occurrence of *ṇ*, otherwise than as the result of *sandhi*; 16, interchange of *ḍ* and *l*.

अथ मकारलोपः ॥ १ ॥

1. Now for the omission of *m*.

---

11. *udâtta iti caçabdo jñâpayati: tasminn*[1] *akâra udâtte*[2] *sati sarva*[3] *ekâra okâro vâ svarita udâttam âpadyate. bheshajaṁ ----: ojo -----. sarvatre 'ti vacanân nityasvarito*[4] *'pi tathâi 'va tad vidhânaṁ syât: atho -----.*

iti tribhâshyaratne prâtiçâkhyavivaraṇe dvâdaço 'dhyâyaḥ.
[5]*iti prathamaḥ praçnaḥ.*[5]

[1] O. *asm-*. [2] G. M. ins. *lupte;* O. ins. *ca lupte.* [3] O. *sarvatra;* G. M. *sarvatra-sthita.* [4] O. *-ritasyâ.* [(5)] O. om.; G. M. *prathamapraçnas samâptaḥ. hariḥ om: çubham astu om;* W. adds 1 *hari hi om*, and, as prelude to the next section, *çrîgaṇeçâya namaḥ. hariḥ om;* B. adds *hariḥ om.*

1. *athe 'ty ayam adhikâraḥ: makâralopa*[1] *ucyata ity etad adhikṛtaṁ veditavyam* [2]*ita uttaraṁ yad vakshyâmaḥ*[2]. *makârasya lopo makâralopaḥ*[3].

[1] O. *-rasya l-*. [(2)] W. B. om. [3] B. om.

A general heading, of which, however, the force extends but a very little way (through rule 4). The subject is a supplement to that treated at v.27–31, where we are told what is done with *m* before a mute, or before any other semivowel than *r*.

रेफोष्मपरः ॥ २ ॥

2. A *m* is omitted, when followed by *r* or a spirant.

This omission of *m* is accompanied, according to xv.1–3, by the nasalization of the preceding vowel, or else the insertion of *anusvâra* after it. Respecting the relation of these alternative views to one another, see the note to ii.30. The definition of the *m* as lost or omitted accords best with the former view: it is sufficiently logical and consistent to say that the consonant is lost and the vowel nasalized; if, however, an *anusvâra*, as a separate vocal element, is to take the place of *m* after the vowel, the only acceptable form of statement must be that the *m* is directly converted into *anusvâra*. This form of statement is in fact adopted by the Rik (iv.5) and Vâj. (iv.1) Prâtiçâkhyas, which acknowledge an *anusvâra*, while the other is rightly preferred by the Ath. Prât. (ii.32, i.67), which holds the theory of the nasalized vowel: our own treatise, as was pointed out above (p. 68), trims between the two views.

The commentator's examples are *pratyushṭañ rakshaḥ* (i.1.2[1] et al.), *sañçitam me brahma* (iv.1.10[3]: v.1.10[2]), *tañ shaḍ ahâni* (v.5.2[6]), *sañ-sam id yuvase vṛshan* (ii.6.11[4]: iv.4.4[4]: only G. M. have *vṛshan*), and *tvañ ha yad yavishṭhya* (ii.6.11[1]). Counter-examples are given: to show that *m* before other letters is not dropped, *idaṁ vâm âsye* (iii.3.11[1]); to show that the dropped *m* must be a final, *tasmât tâmrâ âpaḥ* (vi.4.2[4]). The commentator, namely, has quietly introduced the limitation *padântaḥ*, 'when final,' into his explanation of the rule, without pointing out whence he derives it: it comes, in fact, only from the general scope of the treatise, which thus far, having the relation of *pada* and *saṁhitâ* texts under treatment, has dealt almost exclusively with final and initial letters.

यवकारपरश्चैकेषामाचार्याणाम् ॥ ३ ॥

3. As also, according to some teachers, when followed by *y* or *v*.

---

2. *rephaparaç*[1] *co*[2] *''shmaparaç ca padânto*[3] *makâro lupyate. yathâ*[4]*: praty-....: sañ-....: tañ....: sañ-....: tvañ....* [5]*evampara iti kim: idaṁ....: padânta iti kim: tasmât....:*[5] *rephaç co ''shmâṇaç*[6] *ca* [7]*rephoshmâṇaḥ: te pare*[7] *yasmât sa tathoktaḥ.*

[1] W. *rephaç.* [2] O. om. *ca.* [3] B. *-nte.* [4] G. M. om. (5) O. om. [6] G. M. O. *-mâ.* (7) B. G. M. O. *rephoshmâṇâu tâu parâu.*

The authorities here quoted are, as the commentator does not fail to point out, the same with those referred to above, in v.30, where we were taught that some teachers hold *m* not to be assimilated to a following *y* or *v*, any more than to *r*. The accepted teaching of the treatise, however, is (v.28–9) that *m* before *y*, *l*, and *v* becomes a nasal counterpart to those letters respectively: whence the present rule is pronounced unapproved. For the bearings of the discordant doctrine, see note to v.30.

The examples are *tvaṅ yajñeshv îḍyaḥ* (i.1.14[4]; 2.3[1-2]: O. omits *îḍyaḥ*) and *taṅ vâ etaṅ yajamânaḥ* (v.6.9[3]: O. omits the last word): the ordinary and approved reading would be *tvaṁ*, *taṁ*, and *etaṁ*—as all the MSS. in fact read, neglecting the illustration of the opinion set forth in the rule. A counter-example is given, *yaṁ kâmayeta* (i.6.10[4] et al.).

न सम्̐साम् इति रापरः ॥ ४ ॥

4. But not the *m* of *sam* and *sâm*, when followed by *râ*.

This is a precept applying only to the two words *samrâj* and *sâmrâjya*, and in the other Prâtiçâkhyas (see note to Ath. Pr. ii.36) these words or the root *râj* are particularly specified; since, however, the syllable *râ* does not chance to occur in the Tâittirîya Sanhitâ except in these words after *sam* or *sâm*, there is no inaccuracy in the more general statement as here made. The examples of the occurrence of the words in question selected by the commentator as illustrations are *pra samrâjam* (i.6.12[3]) and *sâmrâjyâya sukratuḥ* (i.8.16[1]: O. omits *sukratuḥ*). As counter-examples, we have *çaṅ râjann oshadhîbhyaḥ* (iii.2.3[1]) to show that no other words

---

3. *yakâraparo* [1] *vakâraparo vâ makâro lupyata ity ekeshâm* [2] *matam: ya evâ 'sya pañcamâdhyâye*[3] *savarṇâpattim*[4] *pratishedhayanti*[5] *teshâm evâi 'sha lopavidhir iti tân anvâdiçati cakâraḥ siṅhâvalokanena*[6]. *yathâ: tvaṁ----: taṁ----: evampara iti kim: yaṁ----. yakâraç ca vakâraç ca yavakârâu: tâu parâu yasmât sa tathoktaḥ.*

[7]*etat sûtram anishṭam.*[7]

[1] G. M. ins. *vâ*. [2] G. M. O. ins. *âcâryâṇâm*. [3] B. G. M. *-mânuvâke*. [4] B. *savarṇam agre vartinaḥ*; G. M. *-ṇapratip-*. [5] W. B. *-dhanti*. [6] O. *-kaṁnyâyena*. [(7)] G. M. O. *nâi 'tat sûtram ishṭam*.

4. [1]*re 'ty*[1] *evamparaḥ* [2]*saṁsâm ity etayor grahaṇayor*[2] *makâro na lupyate. yathâ*[3]: *pra----: sâmr-----. saṁ sâm iti kim: çañ----: râpara iti kim: sañrarâṇaḥ. padântaç ca vyañjanaparaḥ prâkṛta* (xiv.28) *iti*[4] *vakshyamâṇaṁ*[5] *dvitvanishedham itiçabdo*[6] *nivârayati: tasmâd atra dvitvasiddhiḥ.* [7]

[(1)] the MSS., as usual in such a case, *râ ity*. [(2)] G. M. put at beginning; O. om. *grahaṇayor*. [3] in G. M. only. [4] O. om. [5] G. M. *-ṇa*. [6] G. M. *tuç-*. [7] G. M. add *itiçabdas saṁ sâm ity anayor eve 'ti samarthayati.*

retain an unchanged *m* before *râ*, and *sam̃rarâṇaḥ* (i.4.44[1]) to show that only *râ*, not *ra*, effects the retention.

According to W. B. O., the particle *iti* in the rule is intended to deny the application to the word here had in view of rule xiv.28, respecting duplication, and to assure the duplication of the *m* before the *r*. But G. M. insert *tu*, 'but,' in the rule after *iti*, ascribing to it the effect just defined, and making the *iti* simply signify that the words mentioned, and no others, are the subjects of the rule. And G. (not M.) writes the examples accordingly, *sammrâjam* and *sâmmrâjyâya*. That this bit of constructive interpretation is a pure figment of the commentators does not need to be pointed out; respecting its occasion and bearing, see the note to xiv.28. I have adopted the reading of W. etc., which is presumably the older and more genuine: in the comment on xiv.28, even G. M. agree with the others in making *iti* the bond of connection between the two rules.

अथ वर्णानाम् ॥ ५ ॥

5. Now of individual sounds.

According to the comment on rule xxiv.2 (see the note to that rule), we have here one of the main division lines of the treatise. Thus far, from the beginning of the fifth chapter, we have had to do chiefly with the combination of separate words or *padas* into connected text; now we turn to the determination of individual letters, which are read alike in both forms of text. That the intention of the treatise-makers recognized so grand a transition here may be doubted; but that the change is one of some importance is not questionable.

ऋकारर्कारेरषपूर्वो नकारो णकारꣳ समानपदे ॥ ६ ॥

6. Within the same word, a *n* preceded by *ṛ*, *ṝ*, *r*, or *sh*, becomes *ṇ*.

---

5. *athe 'ty ayam adhikâraḥ: varṇânâm̃ sam̃hitâ vakshyata*[1] *ity etad adhikṛtam̃ veditavyam:* [2]*atha vâ:*[2] *athaçabdaḥ*[3] *padasam̃hitânishedhakaḥ.*[4]

[1] O. *ucyata.* [(2)] G. M. om. [3] B. *çabdaḥ.* [4] B. *-tâyâm̃ nish-.*

6. *samânapada ekapada ṛkârarkârarephashakârapûrvo*[1] *nakâro ṇakâram*[2] *âpadyate*[3]. *tribhir....: tvam̃....: esha....: kṛshṇo....* [4]*evampûrva iti kim: devânâm̃....:*[4] *samânapada iti kim: ebhir.... samânam̃ ca tat padam̃ ca samânapadam: tasmin.*

O. has a *lacuna*, beginning with *-napade* at the end of the rule, and ending with *tribhir ṛ-* in the first example. [1] G. M. *ṛṝkârareph-.* [2] G. M. *ṇatvam.* [3] B. G. M. *âpnoti.* [(4)] O. om.

Already, in a previous chapter (vii.1–12,15,16), we have had detailed all the cases in which a *n* is changed to *ṇ* in the course of the combination of words into phrases, in the conversion of *pada* into *saṁhitâ;* now, the treatise sets out to account for every single *ṇ* occurring in the whole text. And the present is the leading general rule, involving, with the extensions and restrictions imposed later, by far the greater number of cases.

The commentator's examples are *tribhir ṛṇavâ jâyate* (vi.3.10^{5}: O. has a *lacuna*, involving the beginning of this citation), *tvañ hotṝṇâm* (iv.3.13^{4}), *esha vâ ṛco varṇaḥ* (vi.1.3^{1}: but W. has instead *esha vâ ahno varṇaḥ*, vi.1.3$^{1\cdot2}$), and *kṛshṇo 'si* (i.1.11^{1}); his counter-examples are *devânâṁ vâ antaṁ jagmushâm* (vii.5.8^{1}: but G. M. have only *devânâm*, which of course is found in various places; and O. omits altogether), where none of the lingual letters specified comes before a *n*, and *ebhir no arkâiḥ* (iv.4.4^{7}: O. omits *arkâiḥ*), where the *r* is in another word than the *n*. All these are cases in which the alterant letter immediately precedes the altered.

व्यवेतो ऽपि ॥ ७ ॥

7. Even though other sounds are interposed.

Rule 15, below, puts a restriction upon this, pointing out what letters may not intervene between the affecting and the affected letter. The examples are *aparaçurṛkṇaṁ dahati* (v.1.10^{1}: W. B. omit *dahati;* O. inserts *ha* between the other two words), *âtmann evâ "ramaṇaṁ kurute* (vi.5.11^{4}: only O. has the first two words, and it omits the last), *adhishavaṇam* (i.1.5^{2}: but G. M. O. have *adhishavaṇe*, iv.7.8 or vi.2.11^{4}), and *kṛshamâṇaḥ pratishṭhâkâmaḥ* (iii.4.3^{3}).

हिरण्मयम् ॥ ८ ॥

8. Also in *hiraṇmayam.*

The only passage in which the word occurs is quoted by the commentator: *hiraṇmayaṁ dâma dakshiṇâ* (ii.4.13: O. omits *dakshiṇâ*). The intent of the rule is to establish in advance a counter-exception to the exception "not when followed by a mute," made in rule 15, below.

---

7. *uktanimittapûrvo nakâro 'nyena* [1] [2]*vyaveto 'pi*[2] [3]*vyavahito 'pi*[3] *ṇatvam âpnoti. yathâ*[4]*: ap-....: âtmann-....: adhi-....: kṛsh-.....*

[1] G. M. ins. *varṇena.* (2) W. O. om. (3) G. M. om. [4] in O. only.

8. *hiraṇmayam ity asmin grahaṇe nakâro* [1]*ṇatvam âpnoti*[1]*. yathâ*[2]*: hiraṇ-..... sparçapara* (xiii.15) *iti*[3] *vakshyamâṇa-pratishedhasya*[4] *pratiprasavârtham idaṁ sûtram.*

(1) G. M. *nakâram âpadyate.* [2] in B. only. [3] O. om. [4] O. *-ṇasya pr-.*

पाणिगणपुण्यकण्वकाणगाणबाणवेणुगुणमणिप्रवादेषु पूर्वः ॥ ९ ॥

9. Also, in the inflectional and derivative forms of *pâṇi*, *gaṇa*, *puṇya*, *kaṇva*, *kâṇa*, *gâṇa*, *bâṇa*, *veṇu*, *guṇa*, and *maṇi*, the first nasal is *ṇ*.

The word *pravâda* is not found elsewhere in our treatise or its commentary. From the latter's explanation and use of it we derive for it a meaning somewhat different from that which, according to Regnier (note to Rik Pr. ii.39), it bears in the Rik Prâtiçâkhya. The latter makes it mean 'theme:' in our comment, on the other hand, it evidently signifies a derived form of a theme, in any gender or case, in composition, or in extension by secondary suffix; and I have translated it accordingly. So far as I can see, however, the same signification belongs to it in most of the passages of the Rik Pr. also, and Regnier's exposition of its use calls for revision.

There is an abrupt change of implication here, without any intimation of it in the terms of the precept itself; it is only at the end of rule 14, below, that we find the word *prâkṛtâḥ*, which we must understand as applying to rules 9–14—a kind of footing instead of heading (*adhikâra*): see another like case in the third chapter, rules 2–7 (note on iii.2). In this connected paragraph of rules we have an enumeration of the words in which a *ṇ* is "original," and hence found equally in all the forms of the text.

The examples are *supâṇiḥ svaṅguriḥ* (iii.1.11⁴: iv.1.6³: O., in this and the two following examples, has only the first word), *vṛshapâṇayo 'çvâḥ* (iv.6.6³), and *hiraṇyapâṇim ûtaye* (i.4.25: ii.2.12²): the text contains half a dozen other examples of the *pravâdas* of *pâṇi*;—*gaṇânâṁ tvâ gaṇapatiṅ havâmahe* (ii.3.14³: O. omits the last word), *gaṇâ me mâ vi tṛshan* (iii.1.8²), *gaṇena gaṇam* (v.4.7⁷), and *dûreämitraç ca gaṇaḥ* (iv.6.5⁶): the cases,

---

9. *pâṇî 'tyâdiçabdânâm*[1] *pravâdeshu pûrvaḥ prathamo ṇakâraḥ prakṛtyâi 'va veditavyaḥ. prakarsheṇa vâdaḥ*[2] *pravâdaḥ*[3]*: liṅga-vibhaktibhedasamâsataddhitâdibhir*[4] *nirdeça*[5] *ity arthaḥ. yathâ*[6]*: sup-----: vṛshap-----: hiraṇ-----: gaṇânâṁ-----: gaṇâ-----: gaṇena-----: dûre-----: puṇyo-----: sâ-----: kaṇvâ-----: tasyâi-----: akarṇayâ-----: gâṇap-----: viçalyo-----: veṇur-----: veṇunâ-----: yad-----: yathâ-----: maṇinâ-----.* [7]*nanu gaṇaçabdapravâdatvâd gâṇagrahaṇam ayuktam:* [8]*mâi 'vam:*[8] *gaṇapravâdatve sati tad bhavet: kiṁtu gaṇapatiçabda-pravâdo 'yam. pûrva iti kim: gaṇ-----: veṇ-----: maṇ-----:*[7] *ityâdishû 'ttarasya*[9] *ṇatvam mâ bhûd iti.*

[1] G. M. *-âdinâṁ grahaṇânâm.* [2] W. *-dâḥ.* [3] W. *-vadâḥ;* G. M. om. [4] W. om. *bheda.* [5] W. *nirdishṭâ.* [6] G. M. om. [(7)] G. M. om. [(8)] W. *ivam.* [9] G. M. O. *-ra-nakârasya.*

compounds, and derivatives of *gaṇa* are found by dozens in the Sanhitâ;—*puṇyo bhavati vasantam* (i.6.11[4]: O. omits the last word) and *sâ mâ sarvân puṇyân* (vii.1.7[1]): *puṇya* occurs in five other passages, once (iii.3.8[5]) in composition;—*kaṇvâ abhi pra gâyata* (iv.3.13[7]: O. ends with *abhi*): there are two other cases of declensional forms;—*tasyâi kâṇo yâ datah* (ii.5.1[7]: O. alone has the last word, and it omits the first; G. M. end with *kâṇaḥ*) and *akarṇayâ 'kâṇayâ 'çloṇayâ* (vi.1.6[7]: only W. has the last word): there is no other case;—*gâṇapatyân mayobhûr e 'hi* (iv.1.2[2]: O. has only the first word; only G. M. have the last two): I have noted but one other case;—*viçalyo bâṇavân̐ uta* (iv.5.1[4]: O. omits the first word): we have a declensional case of *bâṇa* at iv.6.4[5];—*veṇur vâiṇavî bharati* (v.1.1[4]: O. omits the last word), *veṇunâ vi mimîte* (v.2.5[2]), and *yad veṇoḥ sushiram* (v.1.1[4]): there are a couple more of cases;—*yathâ guṇe guṇam* (vii.2.4[2]): we have elsewhere only *driguṇa*, at v.2.5[2,3];—and *maṇinâ rûpâṇi* (vii.3.14): elsewhere only *maṇivâla*, at v.6.13. To explain the limitation *pûrvaḥ*, 'the first nasal,' in the rule, the commentator quotes parts of passages already given—namely *gaṇânâm tvâ*, *veṇunâ vi*, and *maṇinâ rûpâṇi* (but O. omits the second example, and the second word of the third)—in which the *pravâdas* exhibit a second nasal which is dental. He raises the objection, moreover, that the mention of *gaṇa* in the rule is unnecessary, since the word is a *pravâda* of *gaṇa*; but replies that the word (*gâṇapatya*) aimed at is a *pravâda* of *gaṇapati*, not of *gaṇa*. It is true, now, that *gâṇapatyât* stands one degree farther removed from *gaṇa* than does, for instance, *gaṇapatibhyaḥ*, or than would *gâṇikaḥ* if it occurred in the text; yet we should hardly have expected it on that account to receive a different treatment.

पणिपणिंवीयमाणाऊण्योः ॥ १० ॥

10. Also in *paṇi*, *paṇim*, *vîyamâṇaḥ*, and *ûṇyoḥ*.

The passages are *agne deva paṇibhir vîyamâṇaḥ* (i.1.13[2]: only G. M. have the last word), *paṇim goshu starâmahe* (ii.6.11[2]: O. omits the last word), *vîyamâṇaḥ : tam tu etam* (i.1.13[2]: O. has only the first word; G. M. read *-nas tam* etc., neglecting the pause of division between the two words), and *ûṇyoḥ kavikratum* (i.2.6[1]). These words are said to be made a separate rule of because there is no longer any inclusion of *pravâdas* or derived forms.

टवर्गपरः ॥ ११ ॥

11. Also before a lingual mute.

---

10. [1] *paṇi 'tyâdigrahaṇeshu*[2] *ṇakâraḥ prakṛtyâi 'va veditavyaḥ. apravâdârtho 'yam ârambhaḥ. agne----: paṇim----: vîy----: ûṇyoḥ----.*

[1] O. prefixes the whole series of words. [2] O. *-âdishu*; G. M. *-âdishu gr-*.

The examples are *çitikaṇṭhâya ca* (iv.5.5¹: but G. M. have instead *çitikaṇṭhâya svâhâ*, which I do not find in the text, not even at vii.3.17, where a number of similar expressions are read) and *kaṇḍûyeta pâmanambhâvukâḥ* (vi.1.3⁸: O. has the first word only). The combinations *ṇṭ* and *ṇḍh* do not occur in the Sanhitâ.

चङ्कुणफणात्स्थूणौहिणुयाद्धिणोतिकौणेयोऽणिष्ठाउल्बणमुगणाश्रुतिश्चुपुणीकाबाणिजायाणवश्चात्णारस्थाणुंतूणवेवीणायामश्लोणायापणेतवाणीःकल्याणीकुणपंवाणःशतशोणाश्रुतिर्धाणिकामेणी ॥ १२ ॥

12. Also in *cañkuṇa*, *phaṇat*, *sthûṇâu*, *hiṇuyât*, *hiṇoti*, *kâuṇeyaḥ*, *aṇishṭhâḥ*, *ulbaṇam*, *ugaṇâ* wherever found, *cupuṇîkâ*, *bâṇijâya*, *aṇavaç ca*, *âtṇâraḥ*, *sthâṇum*, *tûṇave*, *vîṇâyâm*, *açloṇayâ*, *paṇeta*, *vâṇîḥ*, *kalyâṇî*, *kuṇapam*, *vâṇaḥ çata*. *çoṇâ* wherever found, *dhâṇikâ*, and *m eṇî*.

The passages aimed at are quoted by the commentator as follows: *avabhṛtha nicañkuṇa niceruḥ* (i.4.45²: all but O. omit *niceruḥ*, which would allow the passage to be found also at vi.6.3⁴; O. omits *avabhṛtha*): *nicañkuṇa* occurs a second time in i.4.45²; *anvâpaníphaṇat* (i.7.8³); *ayâsthûṇâv uditâu* (i.8.12³); *bhrâtṛvyâya pra hiṇuyât* (ii.2.6⁵: O. begins with *pra*); *evâ 'smâi pra hiṇoti* (ii.2.6⁵); *rajano vâi kâuṇeyaḥ* (ii.3.8¹); *ye 'ṇishṭhâs tân* (ii.5.5²); *yajña ulbaṇaṁ kriyate* (iii.4.3⁷), and also, by i.53, *anulbaṇam* (at iii.4.3⁶); *âvyâdhinîr ugaṇâ uta* (iv.1.10²: the example is wanting in W.) and *ugaṇâbhyas tṛñhatîbhyaḥ* (iv.5.4¹: O. omits the last word); *varshayantî cupuṇîkâ nâmâ 'si* (iv.4.5¹: only W. has the first word, and it omits the last); *mantriṇe bâṇijâya kakshâṇâm pataye* (iv.5.2²: B. G. M. omit the first word, G.

---

11. ¹*ṭavarge pare*¹ *ṇakâraḥ*² *prakṛtyâi 'va veditavyaḥ. çiti-____: kaṇḍ-____. ṭavargaḥ paro yasmât sa tathoktaḥ.*

(¹) B. G. M. *-rgaparaḥ*; O. *-rgaparo vâ.* ² G. M. put after *'va*

12. *cañkuṇa______ eshu ṇakâraḥ prakṛtyâi 'va veditavyaḥ. avabh-____: anv-____: aya-____: bhrât-____: evâ____: rajano____: ye____: yajña____: yatrayatra çrutir ugaṇâgrahaṇasya*¹ *tatratatra ṇatvaṁ karaṇîyam:* ²*âvyâ-____:*² *ugaṇ-____: varsh-____: mantriṇe____: priy-____: ce 'ti kim: anavas____: etaṁ____: ya____: yâ____: açloṇayâ____: paṇe-____: indraṁ____: kalyâṇî____: purushak-____: vâṇaḥ____: çate 'ti kim:* ³*ṛtâv-____:*³ *çoṇâ____:* ⁴*çrutir iti kim: çoṇâya____:*⁴ *ni____: vanas-____: makâreṇa kim: ubhay-____.*

¹ G. M. O. put before *yatra-* (²) W. om. (³) O. om. (⁴) O. om.

M. the last, W. O. the last two); *priyaṁgavaç ca me 'ṇavaç ca me* (iv.7.4^{2}: G. M. omit the first word, O. the first three), with a counter-example, *anavas te ratham* (i.6.12^{6}), to prove the need of *ca* in the citation; *etaṁ vâi para âṭṇâraḥ* (v.6.5^{3}); *ya sthâṇuñ hanti* (vii.3.1^{1}): we have *yajñasthâṇu* twice at vi.1.2^{4}; *yâ tûṇave yâ vîṇâyâm* (vi.1.4^{1}); *açlonayâ 'saptaçaphayâ krîṇâti* (vi.1.6^{7}: only O. has *krîṇâti*); *paṇetâ 'goargham* (vi.1.10^{1}); *indraṁ vâṇîr anûshata* (i.6.12^{2}); *kalyâṇî rûpasamṛddhâ sâ syât* (vii.1.6^{6}: only O. has the last two words): *kalyâṇî* occurs in one or two other passages; *purushakuṇapam açvakuṇapaṁ gâuḥ* (vii.2.10^{2}: only O. has *gâuḥ*): we have *kuṇapam* as independent word at vii.2. 10^{2}; *vâṇaḥ çatatantur bhavati* (vii.5.9^{2}), with a counter-example, to show the necessity of adding *çata* in the rule, *ṛtâvânaç cayamânâ ṛṇâni* (ii.1.11^{5}: only G. M. have *ṛṇâni*; O. omits the example: *vânaḥ* is a *pada* in the word as divided, *ṛta-vânaḥ*); *çoṇâ dhṛshṇû nṛvâhasâ* (vii.4.20: W. B. end with *dhṛshṇû*) and *çoṇâya svâhâ* (vii.3.18: O. omits the example, along with the specification of the point it illustrates), the only examples of *çoṇa* that the text contains; *ni jalgulîti dhâṇikâ* (vii.4.19^{3}); and *vanaspatînâm eṇî* (v.5.15: O. reads *eṇya*), with a counter-example, to show that the word only occurs after a *m*, *ubhayata enî syât tad âhuḥ* (vii.1.6^{5}: G. M. O. end with *syât*).

अवग्रहो वृषणशीर्षणब्रह्मणक्षणचर्मणचर्षण् ॥ १३ ॥

13. As final of the former member of a compound, *ṇ* is found in *vṛshaṇ*, *çîrshaṇ*, *brahmaṇ*, *akshaṇ*, *carmaṇ*, and *carshaṇ*.

The term *avagraha*, we are told, is here taken in the sense of *avagrahastha.* The same interpretation has been given before (under vi.9); and the whole use of *avagraha* in the treatise verges toward an equivalence with its derivative. Only T. O. change the *ç* of *çîrshaṇ* to *ch* after *ṇ*; but, as this is in accordance with the teaching of the Prâtiçâkhya (v.34), I have adopted it.

The examples quoted by the commentator are *vâto apâṁ vṛshaṇvân* (ii.1.11^{1}: O. omits *vâto*), *çîrshaṇvân medhyo bhavati* (vii.5.25^{1}), *brahmaṇvanto devâ âsan* (vi.4.10^{1}: W. B. omit *âsan*), *akshaṇvate svâhâ* (vii.5.12^{1}), and *carmaṇvate svâhâ* (vii.5.12^{2}): we have *vṛshaṇ-* also at ii.5.8^{4}: iv.1.2^{1}: vii.5.5^{1}; *çîrshaṇ-* at vii.5.12^{1}; and *brahmaṇ-* at v.7.8^{3} and vi.4.10^{1} (a second time). As counter-examples, to show that the *ṇ* occurs in these words only before a

---

13. *vṛshaṇṇ ityâdigrahaṇeshv*[1] *avagraho ṇakâraḥ prakṛtyâi 'va veditavyaḥ. vâto----: çîrsh-----: brahm-----: aksh-----:* [2]*carm-----.*[2] [3]*carshaṇgrahaṇasya*[4] *çâkhântare* [5]*vijñeyam udâharaṇam*[5]*: mitrasya---- iti kecid udâharanti*[6,3]*: tan na sâdhu: anto 'lopâd* (xiii.15) *iti vakshyamâṇapratishedhapratiprasavârtham uktatvâd eshâṁ grahaṇânâṁ carshaṇîdhṛta ity atra*[7] *ṇakârasya padântatvâbhâvât. athavâ: ṛkârarkârarashâ*[8] (xiii.6)

pause of division, he gives (the whole subject is omitted in O.) *vṛshann agne viçvâny arya â* (iv.4.4^4), *tasmât saptaçîrshan* (v.1.7^1), *brahman viçaṁ vi* (ii.3.3^5: G. M. omit *vi*), *akshann amîmadanta* (i.8.5^2), and *paçûnâṁ carman* (vi.1.9^2).

This disposes of all the *avagrahas* cited in the rule save *carshaṇ*. No such *pada* as *carshaṇ* is to be found in the Tâittirîya-Sanhitâ, nor, so far as has yet come to light, in any other Vedic text; nor does the word seem like one that could anywhere occur. One cannot help surmising that its presence in the rule may be by a blunder merely, it being, perhaps, an unintelligent repetition of *carmaṇ*. But, by whatever hap or mishap it found its way in, it is now an accepted part of the text, and has to be dealt with. And the commentator first creeps out of the difficulty through the hole to which he usually betakes himself in a like case, asserting that the passage aimed at is read in another text (*çâkhâ*). He then proceeds to state that "some quote as here referred to the passage *mitrasya carshaṇîdhṛtaḥ çravaḥ* (iii.4.11^5 and iv.1.6^3: O. omits *çravaḥ*): this is not good, since the words are quoted in the rule by way of antecedent exception to an exception [to rule 6] which is to be made farther on, by the words 'nor when final, nor by the omission of *a*' (rule 15); and in *carshaṇîdhṛtaḥ* the *ṇ* is not final. Or: others are of opinion that the words in question are specified for the sake of removing any doubt which might arise as to whether the *ṇ* in them were a product of alteration under rule 6 of this chapter; and, in this aspect, the citation of *mitrasya carshaṇîdhṛtaḥ* is to be approved." The logic of this final conclusion I entirely fail to see: for no question can possibly arise as to whether the *ṇ* of *carshaṇîdhṛtaḥ* falls under rule 6; that it does so is palpable and undeniable.

As we should expect, considering the way in which the Prâtiçâkhya treats the cases, these words are read with *ṇ* in the *pada*-text also: namely *vṛshaṇ-vân*, *brahmaṇ-vantaḥ*, and so on. The same is the case in the *pada*-texts of the Rik and the Atharvan (see Ath. Pr. iv.99).

ऋण्णषण्णष्णम्णराव्णा चेति प्राकृताः ॥ १४ ॥

14. Also in *ṛṇṇ*, *shaṇṇ*, *shṇ*, *mṇ*, and *râvṇ*—these are original.

The application of the term *prâkṛtâḥ*, 'original,' in this rule is, as was pointed out above (under rule 9), to all the cases rehearsed in rules 9–14.

"*diprâpter atra ṇakâro vâikṛta iti çaṅkânirâkaraṇârtham etâni grahaṇânî 'ty anye*[9] *manyante: tathâ sati mitrasya carshaṇîdhṛta ity udâharaṇaṁ ramaṇîyam.* [10]*avagruha*[11] *iti kim: vrshann ----: tasmât ----: brahman ----: akshann ----: paçûnâṁ ----. avagrahastho*[12] *'vagraha iti lakshyate.*[10]

[1] W. *-ṇe; G. M. -dishu gr-.* (2) O. om. (3) B. om. [4] W. *-shaṇh-.* (5) G. M. om. [6] W. *-haraṇaṁ.* [7] G. M. om. [8] G. M. *ṛkârâ.* [9] B. *anena.* (10) O. om. [11] W. *-hasthâ.* [12] G. M. put next before *lakshyate.*

The commentary, after pronouncing the citations of the rule parts of words, intended to include a number of cases," quotes examples, as follows: *svayamâtṛṇṇâm upa* (v.2.8[1]; 3.2[1],7[4]; 5.4[3]: O. omits *upa*), *asaṁtṛṇṇe hi hanû* (vi.2.11[3]: O. omits *hanû*), and *svayamâtṛṇṇâ jyotiḥ* (v.7.6[2]): I have noted *ṛṇṇ* elsewhere only in *anâchṛṇṇam* (v.1.7[4]); *abhishaṇṇo yasmât* (ii.4.2[3]), *nishaṇṇâya svâhâ* (vii.1.19[1]: only G. M. have this example), and *daçamâsâ nishaṇṇâ âsan* (vii.5.1[1],2[1]: O. omits the first word); *pûshṇo rañhyâi* (i.3.10[2]), *pûshṇâ sayujâ saha* (iv.1.2[2] and v.1.2[4]: only G. M. have *saha*), and *pûshṇe prapathyâya svâhâ* (vii.3.15: G. M. O. omit *svâhâ*): I have noted further only *pâushṇa* (i.8.9[2] et al.); *aryamṇe caruṁ nir vapet* (ii.3.4[1] twice, [2]: G. M. O. stop at *caruṁ*): I find besides *sutrâmṇe* (i.8.9[2] et al.) and *nṛmṇa* (i.7.13[2]), which last, however, the rule was not specially intended for; finally, *dadhikrâvṇo akârisham* (i.5.11[4] and vii.4.19[4]: O. omits *akârisham*) and *â grâvṇaḥ* (vi.3.2[3]: O. omits this example): further cases of *dadhikrâvan* and *grâvan* are met with in the text showing the combination *vṇ;* I have noted no other words in which it occurs. Counter-examples, showing that *vṇ* follows *râ* only, would have been easy to furnish: thus, *râyasposhadâvne*, at i.2.10[1].

Cases of quite various and discordant nature are here thrown together. Most unequivocally calling for treatment in the Prâtiçâkhya, in order to determine their reading, are the three passages in which *sanna* is altered to *shaṇṇa* after *abhi* and *ni*, since (as quoted by the commentator below) the *pada*-text restores the original form of the word, reading *abhishaṇṇa ity abhi-sannaḥ* etc. Its *s* is converted to *sh* according to vi.2, but there is no authority excepting here for the change of *nn* to *ṇṇ;* chapter vii. does not deal with this, because it takes up only those cases in which the alterant cause and the altered nasal are found in different *padas;* and rule 6 of the present chapter does not apply to it because its first *n* is protected (according to xiii.15) by being "followed by a mute," and its second *n* by "having a lingual mute interposed." The case of *tṛṇṇa* is akin with this, only with the important difference that the alteration of its nasals lies beyond the ken of the Prâtiçâkhya, the *ṇṇ* being read in every text. The remaining three all fall under rule 6 of this chapter, but they require specification because they are also covered by one of the exceptions in rule 16; for they exhibit, as compared with their

---

14. *atrâ*[1] *sûtre padâikadeçâ ete*[2] *bahûpâdânârtham uktâḥ: ṛṇṇâdishv eshu*[3] *ca*[4] *ṇakârâḥ prâkṛtâ eva vijñeyâḥ. svay-....: asaṁ-....: svay-....: abhish-....:* [5]*nish-....:*[5] *daça-....: pûshṇo....: pûshṇâ....: pûshṇe....: aryamṇe....: dadhi-....: â....*

prâkṛtaçabdo 'yam paṇyâdishv eva carshaṇparyanteshu mukhyaḥ: catasṛshu saṁhitâsu ṇatvasadbhâvât[6]*: ṛṇṇe*[7] *'ty âdishu tu*[8] *na mukhyaḥ: kiṁtu prâptyabhâve 'pi*[9] *ṇatvaprâpaṇârthaḥ. tathâ hi: ṛṇṇâdâu pûrvaṇakârasya*[10] *sparçaparatvân nishedhaḥ:*

themes (*aryaman*, *-krâvan*, *grâvan*), a "loss of *a*" (*alopa*): compare what is said of this *alopa* below.

As regards the application of the term *prâkṛta*, 'original,' their discordance is more essential, and, indeed, irreconcilable. In *tṛṇṇa*, to be sure, the cerebral *ṇ*'s are as original as in the words specified by rule 13, since, in all alike, the alteration is an accomplished fact in all the forms of text, although ultimately referable to the cause laid down in rule 6. But the last three cases, although also read alike in all texts, are introduced here as counter-exceptions to rule 15, and their *ṇ* is no more original than is that of any other of the words falling under rule 6. And finally, there is no sense whatever in which the lingual nasals of *-shaṇṇa* are "original." To call them all original, then, seems even more than a looseness or inaccuracy in the use of that term: it is a blunder.

The commentator perceives the difficulty, and attempts to remove it by a lengthy passage of special pleading. The term *prâkṛta*, he says, is *mukhya*, 'of primary value' or 'of full force,' as applied to the words beginning with *pâṇi* (rule 9) and ending with *carshaṇ* (rule 13), since in them the lingualized nasal is found in all the four *saṁhitâs;* but in *ṛṇṇ* and the rest it is not *mukhya*, but is simply intended to authorize the nasalization even in the absence of a rule prescribing it. Thus, namely: in *ṛṇṇ* etc. (i. e. in *ṛṇṇ* and *shaṇṇ*), the first nasal constitutes an exception (under rule 6) as being followed by a mute (rule 15); the other nasal, as having a *ṭ*-mute between it and the altering cause (rule 15). In *shṇ* and *mṇ*, again [why not in *râvṇ?*], the nasal falls under the exception touching the loss of *a* (rule 15). And if it be objected that the lingualization is assured by the competency of the citation—still [it is answered], the implication is avoided that the occasion of the citation is the originality of the *ṇ* [?]. Moreover, the word *ca*, 'also,' in the rule, being used in the sense of subsidiary adjunction (*anvâcaya*), shows the lingualization to be not of primary value; if it were primary, it would be found in all the four kinds of text; but it is not so found; for we read in *pada*-text *abhishaṇṇa ity abhi-sannaḥ* and *nishaṇṇâye 'ti ni-sannâya.* And since, from the words *pûshan* and *aryaman*, which end in *n*, such forms as *pûshṇo rañhyâi* and *aryamṇe carum* are read in the *varṇa*-text, therefore the conversion into *ṇ* (all but O. say "non-conversion into *ṇ*") in

---

[11]*itarasyo 'ttamasya*[11] *ṭavargîyavyavahitatvât*[12]*: shṇamṇagrahaṇayos tv alopâd iti nishedhaḥ. grahaṇasâmarthyâd eva*[13] *ṇatvaṁ sidhyatî 'ti cet: evaṁ svabhâvatvam eva grahaṇasyâ 'pi*[14] *mûlam iti parihâraḥ. kiṁ ca: anvâcaye*[15] *vartamânaç cakâro 'py eteshu ṇatvam amukhyaṁ*[16] *iti dyotayati: mukhyaṁ*[17] *cet: catasṛshu saṁhitâsu vidyeta*[18]*: na câ 'tra vidyate: tathâ hi: abhishaṇṇa ity abhi-sannaḥ: nishaṇṇâye 'ti ni-sannâya: ity atra*[19] *padasaṁhitâyâm: pûshann aryamann iti nakârântaçabdayoḥ: pûshṇo rañhyâi: aryamṇe carum: ity âdi siddharûpatvâd*[20] *atra varṇasaṁhitâyâm etatsâhacaryâd ekasûtrasthayor*[21]

varṇa-text is to be inferred also for *ṛṇṇ* and *shaṇṇ* (O. says *râvṇ*) in virtue of association with the others, they being found in the same rule with them; for all who understand the rules of affairs hold that the determination of equivocal classes is made by mention in connection with words unequivocal. Therefore the meaning of *prâkṛta* (all but O. say *prakṛti*) as defined by us is alone acceptable.

By comparison with the explanations given above, it may readily be seen how much of reason there is in all this talk. The commentator raises an obscuring dust about the difficulty, but does not at all remove it. The *mukhyatvam* of the term *prâkṛta* as here applied is more easily disproved than its *mûrkhatvam*.

न षुम्नो ऽग्निर्युष्मानीतो ऽन्तो ऽलोपात्स्पर्शपरो व्यवायेषु शसचटतवर्गीयेषु ॥ १५ ॥

15. But not in *shumna*, *agni*, and *yushmâṇîta*; nor when final; nor after the omission of an *a*; nor when followed by a mute; nor when *ç*, *s*, or a palatal, lingual, or labial mute intervenes.

It would be rather more in accordance with the ordinary usage of the treatise to make five distinct rules of the five independent and unconnected specifications which are here crowded together into a single precept: in fact, we should be guilty of no great violence if we were to divide it into five, affixing to each its own (independently constructed, as if for an independent rule) portion of the comment. But in that case, at any rate, the first rule should read *na shumno'gniyushmâṇîtaḥ* (not *'gnir*). It is not unobjectionable as it stands, since we should expect the first and third complete *padas* to be quoted as they stand in the text, and the second, which is only a fragment of a *pada*, to be distinguished as such from a possible *agniḥ*. As to the first, moreover, there is a difference of reading among the MSS. of the text: only T. W. have *shumno;* B. O. have *sumno;* G. M. have *sushumno;* and, as is seen below, even W. has *sumnaḥ* in the reiteration of the rule by the comment. G. M., it may be added, read *vyavâyishu* for *-yeshu* in the last specification.

---

apy[22] *ṛṇṇashaṇṇayor*[23]. *varṇasaṁhitâyâṁ ṇatvabhâvo*[24] *mantavyaḥ: prasiddhapadasamabhivyâhâreṇâ*[25] *'prasiddhapadârthasamarthanam*[26] *arthaçâstravidaḥ*[27] *sarve khalu svîkurvate. tasmâd asmadukta eva yuktaḥ prâkṛtaçabdârthaḥ*[28].

[1] G. M. om.; O. *asmin*. [2] O. om. [3] B. *eteshu*. [4] O. om. (5) in G. M. only. [6] G. M. *-saṁbhavât*. [7] O. *ṛṇṇ i*. [8] G. M. put after *na*. [9] G. M. O. om. [10] O. *-vanakâra*. (11) G. M. O. *uttarasya*. [12] W. B. *savarg-*; G. M. *tavarg-* (?). [13] O. *evâ*. [14] W. om. *api*. [15] G. M. *atra yo*. [16] B. G. M. *mukh-*; O. *anumu-*. [17] G. M. *-yaç*. [18] B. G. M. *vidyate*. [19] O. om. [20] O. om. *rûpa*. [21] W. *-yo*; B. *-trayor*; G. M. *-trasthitayor*. [22] W. om. [23] O. *ṛṇeṇardvuṇaṇayor*. [24] W. B. G. M. *-tvâbh-*; O. *eva ṇatvasadbhâ-*. [25] W. G. M. *-ṇa*, but W. inserts a sign of omission before the following *pr-*. [26] B. *-dârthaṁ*; G. M. *-dârthaṇ na bhavati*. [27] B. *sarvaçâ-*; G. M. *niyamaṁ çâ-*. [28] W. B. G. M. *prakṛtiç-*.

Under the first part of the rule, the passages aimed at are quoted as follows: *sushumnaḥ sûryaraçmiḥ* (iii.4.7[1]), *indrâgnibhyâṁ tvâ sayujâ* (iv.4.5[1]: G. M. omit *sayujâ;* the *pada*-reading is doubtless *indrâgni-bhyâm*, so that the *r* and *n* are *samânapade*, as required by rule 6), and *yushmânîto abhayaṁ jyotiḥ* (ii.1.11[6]: only O. has *jyotiḥ;* from its inclusion here, the word must remain undivided in *pada*-text, though in that of the Rig-Veda [ii.27.11] it is read *yushmâ-nîtaḥ*).

Examples of final *n* not lingualized are *pitṝn havishe attave* (i. 6.12[1]) and *pra mṛṇîhi çatrûn* (i.2.14[2]).

The precept touching the omission of an *a* has reference, so far as I can discover, only to the oblique cases of *vṛtrahan*, of which two (and I have failed to note any others) are cited, namely *vṛtraghna indrâya tvâ* (i.4.1[1]: O. omits the example) and *vṛtraghna stomâḥ* (iv.7.15[1])—for the derivative adjective *vârtraghna* (ii.5.2[5] et al.) can hardly be aimed at; and yet, the authority of this rule is needed to establish the dental *n* in this word also, which would otherwise fall under rule xiii.6. The mode of definition of the cases here intended is in very remarkable contrast with the usage elsewhere of the treatise, which, as has been repeatedly pointed out, differs from the other Prâtiçâkhyas especially in avoiding all reference to grammatical categories, forms, and derivations, and defining the words to which its rules relate simply by external circumstances of position and surroundings in the text. And this departure from its custom is a quite unfortunate and ill-judged one: for, in the first place, it renders necessary a part of the specifications of the preceding rule (namely *shn*, *mn*, and *râvn*), which really lie outside the province of the treatise, and have no good reason to be mentioned; and, in the second place, as the commentator points out, it involves an inconsistency with the general subject of the chapter, which has to do with conversions arising *samânapade*, 'within the limits of the same *pada*,' while in *vṛtra-ghnaḥ* etc. the affecting cause is in one *pada* and the nasal to be affected in another. The commentator explains that the intent is, by a far-reaching glance backward (literally, 'a lion's look'), to lay down a further example to a rule in the seventh chapter, where the restriction *samânapade* is not in force: *ghnaḥ* etc., namely, are altered forms of *han*, whose

---

15. *shumnaḥ*[1]: *agniḥ*[2]: *yushmânîtaḥ: eteshu*[3] *nakâro ṇatvaṁ nâ "padyate: sush-.....: indrâ-.....: yushm-.....* *antaḥ*[4] *padânto nakâro ṇatvaṁ nâ "padyate: pitṝn-....: pra-....* *alopâd akâralopât*[5] *paro 'pi nakâro ṇatvaṁ nâ "padyate:* [6]*vṛtra-....:*[6] *vṛtra-.....* *nanv atra nimittanimittinor bhinnapadasthatvâd vishamo dṛshṭântaḥ: satyam: siṅhâvalokananyâyena*[7] *prathamapraçne*[8] *saptamâdhyâye*[9] *çeshodâharaṇarûpeṇa*[10] *ghaṭate: tatra ca samânapadaniyamo*[11] *nâ 'sti: ghna ity asya hançabdavikṛtatvâd*[12] [13]*rashaḥpûrvo havanî*[13] (vii.11) *'ti prâptiḥ.* [14] *sparçaparo nakâraç ca*[15] *ṇatvaṁ nâ "pnoti*[16]*: saṁkr-....: ava-....*

nasal, by vii.11, is liable to lingualization. But *han*, by the usage of the treatise, signifies 'the syllable or audible complex of sounds *han*,' not 'the theme *han* and its derivatives;' and, as the text contains no example of the combination *ghn*, it would have been easy to exempt *n* from lingualization *ghakârât*, 'after *gh*.'

The cited examples of *n* remaining unchanged when followed by a mute are *saṁkrandano 'nimishaḥ* (iv.6.4[1]: O. has the first word only), *ava rundhe târpyam* (ii.4.11[6]: O. omits the last word), and *nakhanirbhinnam* (i.8.9[1]).

The commentator then proceeds to enter into a long discussion of more than usual subtilty and obscurity, of which I am by no means confident that I apprehend the meaning. The point aimed at, indeed, seems quite clear: by xiv.4, the *ṇ* of such a word as *pûrṇa* is to be doubled, making *pûrṇṇa;* here, then, is a case where the first *ṇ* is "followed by a *mute*" (*sparçaparaḥ*), and so would seem to have its lingual character forbidden by the present rule. The reasonable reply to so hair-splitting and impertinent an objection would appear to be that, a duplication being ordered by the treatise, the product can be nothing but *ṇṇ*, since *nṇ* would be no duplication at all. The commentator, however, prefers to get around the difficulty by limiting the word *sparça*, 'mute,' as here used, to one which is not the product of express prescription (?). For in *pûrṇâ paçcât* (iii.5.1[1] et al.) there is duplication, making *pûrṇṇâ* (not one of the MSS. writes the duplication), the one *ṇ* being prescribed by xiv.4, the other being its occasion or root (*mûla*). With this, O. prudently ends; the other MSS. go on to explain "express" (? *prasiddha*) by referring to the word *nakha-nirbhinnam*, already quoted above, as, with its like, also exhibiting an instance of occasion of prescription. This word, namely, falls under rules xiv.4,5 (becoming thereby *nakhanirbbhinna*); and in rule 5 the term "succeeded by a consonant" (*vyañjanottara*) is used in a different sense from "followed by a consonant" (*vyañjana-para*); the meaning of which will be there explained at full length (as we shall find to our cost, in one of the obscurest discussions of the entire treatise). The appositeness of the whole reference I do not understand.

Finally, examples are quoted of the suspension of nasalization by

---

nakha-..... *sparço 'trâ*[17] *'prasiddhalakshaṇavishayo*[18] *vivakshyate*[19]*: anyathâ*[20] *pûrṇâ paçcâd ity âdâu ṇatvaṁ na syât: rephât paraṁ ca* (xiv.4) *iti hi prasiddhaṁ*[21] *lakshaṇaṁ tanmûlaṁ ca*[22] *pûrṇṇe 'ty atra dvitvam.* [23]*prasiddhapadena kim*[24]*: nakhanirbhinnam ity âdâv api kathaṁ cil*[25] *lakshaṇamûlatvaṁ sambhavati. kiṁ tal lakshaṇam iti cet: dvitîyacaturthayor* (xiv.5) *ity atra sûtroktavyañjanottarayor*[26] (xiv.5) *iti vâco yuktyantaram iti brûmaḥ: tasya lakshaṇaṁ tatrâi 'va sphuṭîkarishyate*[27] *mahatâ prabandhena*[23]. *sp·rçaḥ paro*[28] *yasmâd asâu sparçaparaḥ.* [29] *çasacaṭatavargîyeshu* [30] *vyavadhâyikeshu*[31]

an intervening *ç* or *s*, or a palatal, lingual, or dental mute: namely *raçanâm â datte* (vi.3.6[3]), *agne rasena tejasâ* (i.4.46[2]: only G. M. have *tejasâ*), *rocante rocanâ divi* (vii.4.20: O. omits *rocante*), *somañ râjânam* (i.7.10[1] et al.), *prakrîḍinaḥ payodhâḥ* (iv.3.13[7]), *pṛtanâ jayâmi* (iii.5.3[1,2]), and *janaprathanâya svâhâ* (iii.2.8[1]: only O. has *svâhâ;* G. M. have the false reading *-pradha-*, and O. has dropped out a part of the word, giving *janandya*).

In the note to Âth. Pr. iii.94, I have pointed out the physical reason why these sounds, by their interposition, prevent the lingualization of the nasal: they are, all of them, such as call into action for their utterance the tip of the tongue, throwing it out of adjustment for the lingual contact. The tendency which the history of Aryan language in India exhibits toward the conversion of dentals into linguals shows itself most actively in the case of the nasal: the tongue, being rolled back into the position of lingual articulation by the utterance of *ṛ*, *ṝ*, *r*, or *sh*, hangs suspended there, as it were, and makes the next nasal contact lingual, unless the tendency is satisfied by the intermediate production of such a contact, or frustrated by the transfer elsewhither of the articulating organ.

The Prâtiçâkhya's enumeration of the cases of occurrence of the lingual nasal is, so far as I have been able to determine, complete. No one of the other treatises undertakes such an enumeration.

पृक्तस्वरात्परो लो डं पौष्करसादेः पौष्करसादेः ॥ १६ ॥

16. In the opinion of Pâushkarasâdi, *l* after a mixed vowel becomes *ḍ*.

The mention of Pâushkarasâdi (O. has everywhere Pâuskarasâdi), the commentator says, is out of respect, and not because the rule is not a peremptory one. "Mixed vowel" is a term which is not elsewhere employed by the treatise, nor does the latter contain anything that should intimate an explanation of its meaning. The comment glosses it by 'the sound *ṛ*:' it appears, then, that *ṛ* is thus styled, from having its vocalic quality "mixed" with consonantal, namely, with the *ṛ*-sound. The other Prâtiçâkhyas (see

---

satsu nakâro ṇatvaṁ nâ padyate: yathâ[32]*: raçanâm----: agne----: rocante----: somañ----: prakrî----: pṛtanâ ----: jana-----. ṛkârarkârâ* (xiii.5) "*diprâpteḥ*[33] *pratishedho*[34] '*yaṁ vihitaḥ.*

[1] W. B. O. *sumnaḥ;* G. M. *sushumnaḥ.* [2] W. O. *agni.* [3] O. *eshu;* G. M. *eshu grahaṇeshu.* [4] W. B. *tataḥ.* [5] W. B. O. om. [(6)] O. om. [7] G. M. *-kanena.* [8] O. om. [9] G. M. *-yâya.* [10] W. O. *viçesh-.* [11] G. M. O. *-datvani-.* [12] G. M. *-bdâdhikṛ-.* [(13)] G. M. *dṛshṭaḥ púrvo bhavati.* [14] G. M. ins. *sparçaparaḥ.* [15] G. M. om. [16] G. M. "*padyate.* [17] B. G. M. *tra.* [18] B. *-viçeshayor.* [19] O. *vikshyate;* G. M. *pi vâ yujyate.* [20] W. B. *yathâ;* G. M. *athâ 'pi.* [21] O. *-ddha;* W. *pratisiddha.* [22] W. *ce 'ti;* O. om. [(23)] O. om. [24] W. B. O. ins. *ca.* [25] W. O. *etal.* [26] B. *sûtravy-;* G. M. *sûtre vy-.* [27] G. M. *spashṭik-.* [28] W. *pûrvo.* [29] G. M. ins. *vyavâyishu.* [30] B. ins. *vyavâyeshu.* [31] G. M. O. om. [32] in W. only. [33] G. M. *-tiḥ.* [34] W. O. *pratinish-.*

note to Ath. Pr. i.37) directly define it as so composed. The *l* liable to the change into *ḍ* is called in the comment *duḥçlishṭa*, 'ill joined;' i. e., I presume, 'of difficult articulation' (G. M., to be sure, seem to apply this title the first time to the *ḍ* instead of *l*, and only O. attaches it the second time clearly to the *l*, the others' readings being corrupt; yet there can hardly arise a doubt as to its true connection); it is, of course, the lingual *l* which forms an acknowledged part of the alphabet of the Rig-Veda (Rik Pr. i.11–2, r. 52 etc.). But no such articulation belongs to the alphabet accepted by this treatise—although, on the strength of the present rule alone, it is crowded into that alphabet by the commentator under rule i.1. Nor does the edition of the Sanhitâ, nor do the MSS., so far as known to me, make any use of a lingual *l*. As for the MSS. of the Prâtiçâkhya and its comment on this rule, B. O. write the ordinary *l* throughout; W. alternates irregularly between the two; G. M. and T. have the lingual letter only. As regards the binding force of the rule, the commentator is right so far as this—that a *ḍ*, not *l*, is read of necessity in the words to which it relates; but that this is, to the makers of the Prâtiçâkhya, the result of alteration of an original *l* there is no reason to believe; the euphonic exchange of the two letters is not less strange to the Tâittirîya text than to the Vâjasaneyi (of the Mâdhyandina *çâkhâ*: see Vâj. Pr. iv.143, viii.45) and Atharvan; and the rule is really *pûjârtham* only, and an intrusion into our treatise of something foreign to its system.

The commentator first gives his own explanation and illustration of the precept. As example of the operation of the rule, he cites *mṛḍâtî* "*dṛçe* (i.1.14^{3}); and, as counter-example, to show that the change is made only after a "mixed vowel," he has nothing better to offer than an alleged passage "from another text," *nalam plavam.* For, in such words as *îḍitaḥ* (i.1.11^{1}), *pravoḍhum* (i.1.14^{3}), *iḍâyâḥ* (i.2.5^{1}), *ayâḍ* (i.4.45^{2}), *heḍaḥ* (i.5.11^{3}), *çrâushaḍ* (i.6.11^{1}), where the Rig-Veda reads regularly the lingual *l* and its aspirate, the Tâittirîya-Sanhitâ maintains the *ḍ*, not less firmly than after *ṛ*. This, the commentator goes on to say, is an interpretation (but the term he uses is *pâṭha*, properly 'reading' or 'ver-

---

16. *pṛktasvarâd ṛkârât*[1] *paro*[2] *lakâro duḥçlishṭasaṁjñiko*[3] *ḍakâram âpadyate: pâushkarasâder*[4] *mate*[5]. *mṛḍâtî*.... *pṛktasvarâd iti kim: nalam plavam*[6] *iti*[7] *çâkhântare. pâushkarasâder*[8] *grahaṇam pûjârthaṁ* [9]*na tu vikalpârtham*[9]. *mûrdhasthânatayâ duḥçlishṭalaḍakârayoḥ*[10] *sâdṛçyam*[11] *astî 'ti vyâkaraṇânusârî*[12] *sûtrapâṭho 'yam: katham anusâritvam iti cet:* [13]*tathâ hi*[13]*: sthâne 'ntaratamaḥ: sthâne prâpyamâṇânâm* [14] *antaratama*[15] *âdeço bhavatî 'ti.*

sûtrasya[16] *pâṭhântaram api*[17] *vyâkhyâyate: pṛktasvarât paro lo ḍam* [18] *pâushkarasâdeḥ*[19]*: atra samânapada*[20] *ity asyâ 'nuvartanaṁ vijñeyam: pâushkarasâdeḥ çâkhinaḥ* [21] *samânapade pṛkta-*

sion') of the rule founded on the authority of the grammarians, who assert a homogeneousness of the *duḥçlishṭa l* and of the *ḍ*, as being both produced in the lingual position: and if the question is raised as to how it is so founded, reference is made to a rule of Pâṇini (i.1.50), which prescribes that, in case of substitution, the most nearly related letter is to be taken. I do not see that this exposition and reference have any pertinence whatever.

Then, the commentator adds yet another interpretation, which, he remarks, is also highly esteemed. It differs from the one already given only in implying (apparently, from xiii.6) *samâna-pade*, 'within the limits of a single *pada*;' taking, then, a different example, *te no mṛḍayantu* (iv.4.3² et al.), with the counter-example *ilâṅḍam bhavati* (vii.5.9¹)—which, in view of the frequent occurrence in the Sanhitâ of *iḍâ*, *iḍâvant*, and their like, is not much to the point—and finally, as further counter-example, to justify the restriction *samânapade*, the phrase *pitṛlokañ somena* (ii.6.2¹; p. *pitṛ-lokam*), where the *l* does not become *ḍ* after *ṛ*. But in this last case is involved an additional difficulty; namely, that in the compound *pitṛlokakâmasya* (vi.6.4¹; p. *pitṛloka-kâmasya*) the *ṛ* and *l* do meet *samânapade*, and yet the *l* maintains itself: over this, the commentator hobbles as best he may, with the plea that, prohibition having been made in the case of *pitṛloka*, it is extended by association to the further compound.

The groundlessness and unintelligence of all this special pleading, resorted to for the purpose of forcing in as an integral part of the Prâtiçâkhya a precept altogether foreign to it, is palpable enough; and one grudges the time and words spent in its exposure.

---

svarâd ṛkârât[22] *paro lakâro ḍakâram âpadyate. yathâ*[23]*: te----. pṛktasvarâd iti kim: ilâṅ-----: samânapada iti kim: pitṛl------. sahacâritvâd*[24] *ekasya*[25] *nishiddha*[26] *itarasyâ 'pi pitṛloka-kâmasye*[27] *'ty asyâ 'pi*[28] *samânapadatve saty api nishedho bhavati. idam api pâṭhântaram bahvâdṛtam.*

iti tribhâshyaratne prâtiçâkhyavivaraṇe
trayodaço[29] *'dhyâyaḥ.*

¹ W. B. om. ² B. om.; G. M *lo ḍam.* ³ all but B. *duçl-*; B. *-jñako*; O. *-jño*; G. M. *-jñakam.* ⁴ O. everywhere *pauska-.* ⁵ W. *-tena*; B. *-tam.* ⁶ B *-vad.* ⁷ B. *iti 'ti.* ⁸ G. M. O. *-di.* ⁽⁹⁾ W. om. ¹⁰ all but B. *duçl-*; W. B. *-shṭaḍalak-*; O. *-lakâra-ḍak-*; G. M. *-ṭaḍakâr-.* ¹¹ O. *sadṛçyasamjño ḍakâram.* ¹² W. *-sârât*; G. M. *-sâra.* ⁽¹³⁾ G. M. *ucyate.* ¹⁴ G. M. ins. *varṇânâm.* ¹⁵ G. M. O. *-mas sadṛçatama.* ¹⁶ W. *asya*; O. *sûtra.* ¹⁷ B. *iti.* ¹⁸ B. ins. *iti.* ¹⁹ O. *-sâda ity*; G. M. *ity* only. ²⁰ G. M. *-dasya*, and om. *ity asya.* ²¹ G. M. ins. *pakshe.* ²² W. om. ²³ O. om. ²⁴ W. B. O. *-caritatv-.* ²⁵ O. *-smin.* ²⁶ B. *nishedha.* ²⁷ W. B. *-kasye*; G. M. *-lokamasye.* ²⁸ G. M. O. om. *api.* ²⁹ G. M. O. *dvitiye praçne prathamo.*

CHAPTER XIV

CONTENTS: 1–7, duplication of one of the members of a group of consonants; 8, duplication of *ch*, *kh*, and *bh*, in certain cases; 9–11, insertion between a surd spirant and mute; 12–13, aspiration of a surd mute before a spirant; 14–28, exceptions to the rules for duplication, and discordant views of certain authorities respecting them; 29–33, occurrence of the enclitic circumflex.

स्वरपूर्वं व्यञ्जनं द्विवर्णं व्यञ्जनपरम् ॥ १ ॥

1. A consonant preceded by a vowel is doubled, if followed by a consonant.

The intricate and obscure subject of duplication in consonant-groups is treated at more length in this than in the other Prâtiçâkhyas (compare R. Pr. vi.1–3; V. Pr. iv.97–114; A. Pr. iii.26–32; also Pâṇini viii.4.46–52), but chiefly on account of the liberal citation here made of the discordant views of various teachers respecting it. The doctrines of the treatise itself are mainly in accordance with those of the rest. This first and leading principle, that the first consonant of a group is doubled, is stated in equivalent terms by all. The principal restrictions to its application are, as stated below, that *r*, *ḥ*, *χ*, *φ* (rule 15), and a letter doubled, or a mute followed by another of the same series (rule 23), are exempted from duplication. For the details, see the following rules.

Of course, in applying the rules for duplication, we have to assume the form of the consonant-groups as determined by the other precepts of the Prâtiçâkhya—treating *visarjanîya*, for example, as is prescribed in the ninth chapter, and making the insertions pointed out in the fifth (v.32,33 etc.). And further, to finish the matter, the rules for *yama*, *nâsikya*, and *svarabhakti* (xxi.12–16) must be duly taken into account.

In an additional note to the Atharva Prâtiçâkhya, I gave a complete list of the consonant-groups of the Atharva-Sanhitâ, with the forms which they come finally to assume under the laws of combination. It has been necessary to prepare a similar one for the Tâittirîya-Sanhitâ, in testing the reach and bearing of the rules of the present treatise: but the scheme is hardly worth giving in full.

---

1. *svarapûrvaṁ vyañjanaṁ*[1] *vyañjanaparaṁ*[2] *dvivarṇam âpadyate. yathâ*[3]*: uru*_ _ _ _ . *evampûrva iti kim: tat*_ _ _ _ . *evampara iti kim: uru-*_ _ _ _ . *vyañjanam iti kim: pra-*_ _ _ _ . *svaraḥ pûrvo yasmât*[4] *tat*[5] *svarapûrvam: vyañjanam asmât param iti vyañjanaparam: dvayor varṇayoḥ samâhâro dvivarṇam.*[6]

[1] G. M. put next before *dvivarṇam.* [2] O. *param.* [3] G. M. om. [4] W. ins. *asâu.* [5] B. om. [6] O. adds *svarapûrvam iti kiṁ: prajananaṁ: padbhyâṁ*_ _ _ _*: vyañjanaparam iti kiṁ: ugaṇâ uta: vyañjana iti kiṁ: praügaṁ.*

The commentator offers a single example, *uru prathasva*, i. e. *uru ppratthassva* (i.1.8 et al.: the MSS. of the comment only very rarely and irregularly write the groups in their duplicated form, so as to illustrate the rules of the chapter), and adds counter-examples: first, to show that the consonant is liable to duplication only after a vowel, *tat pravâte* (vi.4.7[2]: hardly a well-chosen example, since, though the *p* of *pra* is this time unchanged, the *t* before it must be doubled, *tatt pr-;* a *pra* after a pause would have answered better); second, that the duplication takes place only before a consonant, *urukṛd uru ṇaḥ* (ii.6.11[3]); third, that only a consonant, not a vowel, in the defined position, is duplicated, *praügam uktham* (iv.4.2[1]). O. appends a new set of counter-examples, as if a part of a new exposition; namely *prajananam* (i.5.9[1]), *padbhyâṁ dve savane* (vi.1.6[4]: an ill-chosen example, containing cases of duplication as well as of its omission), and *ugaṇâ uta* (iv.1.10[2]).

लवकारपूर्वं स्पर्शश्च पौष्करसादेः ॥ २ ॥

2. Likewise, according to Pâushkarasâdi, a mute preceded by *l* or *v*.

The commentator declares that the *ca*, 'likewise,' in this rule brings down from the one preceding the being preceded by a vowel, and duplication. The former part of the defined implication is at least otiose, since *l* and *v* never occur in the Sanhitâ before a mute, except as themselves preceded by a vowel: *v*, indeed, is found in combination only with the nasal mutes, *ṇ* and *n;* *l*, in the groups *lk*, *lg*, *lp*, *lb*, *lbh*, *lm*, and *lpy*. The examples quoted are *kalpâṅ juhoti* (v.4.8[5]) and *vibhûdâvne* (iii.5.8[1],9[2]: all save B. actually read this time *-dâvnne*, with doubled *n*). According to the interpretation given to the next rule, the worthy Pâushkarasâdi does not regard the duplication of the mute after the semivowel as suspending the duplication of its predecessor also, by rule 1; and he would accordingly read *kallppâṅ* and *-dâvvnne;* and this part of his doctrine is, as we shall see, declared unapproved.

Counter-examples are given: *kalyâṇî rûpasamṛddhâ* (vii.1.6[6]: to be pronounced *kallyâṇî*, or, by rule 21, *kalyâṇî*) and *vâyavyam* (i.8.7[1] et al.: to be made *vâyavvyam*), to show that no other letter than a mute is thus doubled; and *kûçmâṅ chakabhiḥ* (v.7.23) and *tasmâd etat* (vi.3.11[6]), instancing other consonants than *l* and *v*, with the following mute not doubled: in these words, the sibilant

---

2. *pâushkarasâder*[1] *mate lakarapûrvo* [2] *vakârapûrvo vâ sparço* [3]*dvivarṇam âpadyate*[3]. *kalpâṅ-...: vibh-.....* *svarapûrvatvaṁ dvitvaṁ câ 'nvâdiçati cakâraḥ*[4]. [5]*sparça*[6] *iti kim: kaly-....: vây-.....* *evampûrva iti kim: kûç-....: tasm-.....*[5] *lakâraç ca vakâraç ca lavakârâu*[7]*: tâu pûrvâu yasmât sa tathoktaḥ.*

[1] O. *pauskar-*, as also in the rule. [2] B. G. M. ins. *vâ*. [(3)] O. *dvitvam âpnoti.* [4] G. M. put at beginning of clause. [(5)] O. om. [6] G. M. *sparçapara.* [7] W. O. *lakâ·avak-.*

is itself doubled (except by Hârîta, rule 18), a first mute of the same series with the nasal is inserted before the latter (rule 9), and between the two mutes a *yama* (xxi.12); so that we have as final result the formidable combinations *ççpp̄m* and *ssppm*.

The Rik Pr. (vi.2) also requires a double mute after *l*, and the Vâj. Pr. (iv.99) after any semivowel—which last is equivalent with our rule, since *y* is never followed by a mute.

We have a right to be surprised at the introduction of this and the rule next following before rule 4, since the duplication they teach is analogous to that after *r*, and of secondary importance to it.

स्पर्श एवैकेषामाचार्याणाम् ॥ ३ ॥

3. According to some teachers, the mute only.

That is to say, in the combinations just treated of, the mute is duplicated, but not the preceding semivowel also; and we are to read *kalppân* and *ribhûdâvnne.*

According to the commentator, this rule represents the approved usage in the *çâkhâ.* It seems very strange to find such approved usage laid down in the Prâtiçâkhya merely as the *dictum* of certain authorities. But a rule (xiv.7) is given below, without any restriction, which plainly implies the validity of the present one.

रेफात्परं च ॥ ४ ॥

4. Also a consonant that follows *r*.

The *r* itself being, by rule 15, not liable to duplication. This is the rule second in importance in the whole system, and is found in all the Prâtiçâkhyas and in Pâṇini. The Ath. Prât. (iii.31), the Vâj. Prât. (iv.98), and Pâṇini (viii.4.46) ascribe the same effect to *h* as to *r:* and it is strange that our treatise, which is so liberal in its citation of discordant opinions, makes no reference to one so well supported as this. After *h* we find in the Sanhitâ only the three nasals specified in rule xxi.14 as requiring the insertion of a *nâsikya*, and the three semivowels *y, r, v*; *r*, on the other hand, forms numerous groups as first member: I have noted twenty-four of two consonants, forty-three of three consonants, and five of four consonants; a few of them are exempted from duplication by rules 16, 20–23. The cited examples are *arcanty arkam arkinaḥ* (i.6.12[3]:

---

3. *ekeshâm* [1] *mate lavakârapûrva*[2] *sparça*[3] *eva dvivarṇam*[4] *âpnoti*[5]: [6]*anenâ 'vadhâraṇena sûtrântarârambhaṇena ca pâushkarasâdimate lavakârayoç ca dvitvam astî 'ti gamyate*[6].

idam eva sûtram ishṭam na tu pûrvam[7]. *pûrvoktâny*[8] *evo 'dâharaṇâni.*

[1] G. M. O. ins. *âcâryâṇâm.* [2] B. *-rvaç ca;* G. M. put after *eva.* [3] G. M. *-çapara,* as also in the rule. [4] O. *dvitvam.* [5] G. M. O. *âpadyate.* (6) O. om. [7] O. *sûtram.* [8] O. *ukt-.*

i. e. *arccanty arkkam arkkinaḥ*), *arkyeṇa vâi* (vii.5.9[1]: i. e. *arkkyeṇa:* wanting in O.), and *ûrg vâ udumbaraḥ* (v.1.10[1] et al.: i. e. *ûrgg vâi*).

The *ca*, 'also,' of the rule, according to the commentator, implies duplication, and precedence of the *r* by a vowel (bringing down *svarapûrva* from rule 1). The question is raised by an objector whether sequence of the consonant following the *r* by another consonant (in virtue of *vyañjanaparam* in rule 1) is not also implied: but such sequence is declared not obligatory; and it is pointed out that later rules (15,16), exempting a consonant *in pausâ*, and a spirant before a vowel, from duplication after *r*, prove that the present rule prescribes duplication also where no consonant follows, and where a vowel follows; since there would be no propriety in denying by a special rule what had not been already enjoined by a general rule. In support of his assertion that the *r* must be preceded by a vowel, the commentator cites the word *tryambakam* (i.8.6[2]), in which he says that the *y* must not be doubled: and he fortifies his claim by appealing to Pâṇini's rule (viii.4.46), which expressly restricts duplication after *r* and *h* to cases in which these letters follow a vowel (G. M. add the remark that in Pâṇini also no implication of *vyañjanaparam*, 'followed by a consonant,' is found). The Vâj. Pr. (iv.102) makes an equivalent restriction explicitly. The groups are not numerous in the Tâittirîya-Sanhitâ in which a *r* that does not stand first is followed by a consonant, and the only consonant so following is *y:* the combinations are *jry*, *try*, *ṅtry*, *ttry*, *ntry*, *stry*, and *tstry*.

This finishes the proper exposition and illustration of the rule; but the commentator suffers himself to be enticed into a lengthy and tedious refutation of a trivial suggestion which some one has been impertinent enough to make. There are those, he says, who

---

4. *rephât paraṁ* [1] *vyañjanaṁ* [2]*dvivarṇam âpadyate*[2]: [3] *yathâ*[4]: *arc-....:* [5]*arky-....:*[5] *ûry-....* [6]*svarapûrvadvitvayor âkarshakaç cakâraḥ. nanu*[6] *vyañjanaparatvâkarshakaḥ kiṁ na syât: ne 'ti brûmaḥ: niyamâbhâvât: tathâ hi: avasâne*[7] (xiv.15) *ûshmâ svarapara* (xiv.16) *ity etannishedhadvayena rephât parasya*[8] *vyañjanasya*[9] *vyañjanaparatvâbhâve*[10] *svarapûrvatve*[11] *'pi dvitvam astî 'ti niçcîyate*[12]*: aprasaktapratishedhânupapatteḥ*[13]. *svarapûrvatvânuvâdeçena*[14] *kim: tryambakam ity âdâu mâ bhûd iti: kiṁ ca:* [15]*aco rahâbhyâṁ dve iti*[15] *pâṇinîyasûtreṇâ 'pi svarapûrvatve saty eva*[16] *dvitvaṁ vidhîyate:* [17] *tasyâ*[18] *'yam arthaḥ: aca uttarâu yâu rephahakârâu tâbhyâm uttarasya yaro dve bhavata*[19] *iti.* [20]

kecid evam ûcuḥ[21]*: svarapûrvâdiçabdavad rephapûrvam iti vâcye*[22] *vâco*[23] *yuktyantaram arthântaram samarthayati*[24]*: ahar .... ity âdâu*[25] *vâikṛtarephâd*[26] *uttarasya* [27]*na syâd dvitvam*[27] *iti. tad etadadhyayanaviruddhapaddhatim adhyâste*[28]*: vayaṁ tu va-*

maintain that the analogy of *svarapûrvam* in rule 1 would require *rephapûrvam*, 'preceded by *r*,' to be employed here (instead of *rephât param*, 'following *r*'), and that the difference of phraseology intimates a difference of meaning—namely, that a consonant coming after a *r* which is the product of euphonic alteration, as in *ahar devânâm âsît* (i.5.9²: only W. B. have *âsît*), is not doubled. But this, he replies, enters upon a path which is at variance with the reading of this *çâkhâ;* and he proposes himself to set forth the true ground of the different term employed. If *rephapûrva*, namely, were used, the rule would be liable to the suspicion of meaning the direct opposite of its real intent, since *rephapûrvam* admits of being understood as *rephât pûrvam*, 'preceding *r*.' And if it be retorted that this false implication is of no account, since the case it would involve is already provided for in the first rule of the chapter, and the present rule would be a mere useless repetition, and that the avoidance of such repetition is of itself enough to refute the implication—then the farther reply is made, that that is not sound doctrine, in view of the principle stated in the verse "non-contact with mud is far preferable to the washing of it off;" and the teacher uttered the rule in its form as given, with the intent that not even a particle of suspicion of wrong meaning should find occasion from it.

There is no good reason to suppose that the author of the treatise, in saying *rephât param*, intended to do anything more than use a lawful discretion in the selection of his phraseology. The ambiguity which the commentator ascribes to the other reading is suffered to pass in numberless other cases. The more desirable cleanliness of him who has incurred no need of ablution has been referred to once before (under iv.23), in a case somewhat similar.

---

dâmo vâco yuktyantaraprayojanam: rephapûrvam ity ukte viruddhavigrahena[29] *sûtram saṁdigdhaṁ syât: rephât pûrvaṁ rephapûrvam*[30] *iti: bhavatv*[31] *esha*[32] *vigraha iti cet: adhyâyâdisûtreṇâi 'tad gatam iti*[33] *pâunaruktyam asya sûtrasyâ "padyate: nanu pâunaruktyabhayâd eva viruddhavigrahaṁ nivârayâmaḥ*[34]*: ne 'yaṁ saralâ vṛttiḥ: prakshâlanâd dhi* [35]*pañkasya dûrâd asparçanaṁ varam iti*[35] *nyâyâd*[36] *atra viruddhaçañkâleço 'pi nâ 'vakâçaṁ labhatâm iti vâco yuktyantareṇa sûtram âcâryaḥ provâca.*

[1] G. M. ins. *ca.* [(2)] O. *dvitram âpnoti.* [3] G. M. ins. *svarapûrvatvadvitvayor âkarshakaç cakâraḥ na tu vyañjanaparatvâkarshakaḥ.* [4] in G. M. only. [(5)] O. om. [(6)] G. M. *cakâro* only. [7] G. M. *atha na* (xiv.14) *ity uttaranishedhâdhikâre avasânavisarjanîyajihvâmûlîyopadhmânîyâḥ* (xiv.15). [8] W. O. *paraç ça.* [9] W. B. om. [10] W. B. *-vena;* O. *-bhâne;* G. M. om. [11] G. M. *-raparatve;* O. om. [12] O. *gamyate;* G. M. *niçcaye katham.* [13] G. M. *-ktasya pra-.* [14] O. *-rvânv-.* [(15)] G. M. om. [16] W. O. *evaṁ.* [17] G. M. ins. *tat kathaṁ: aco rahâbhyân dve.* [18] G. M. *asy-.* [19] G. M. *sta.* [20] G. M. add *tatrâ 'pi vyañjanaparatvaprasaktir na dṛçyate.* [21] O. *âhuḥ.* [22] B. om. [23] W. om.; G. M. *rephât param iti vâco.* [24] G. M. *-yati 'ti arthântarasyâ 'dâharaṇam ucyate.* [25] G. M. *atra.* [26] W. om. *vâikṛta.* [(27)] G. M. *vyañjanasya dvitvan na syâd.* [28] O. *-âsita.* [29] W. *viruddhâv iti grahaṇena;* G. M. O. *-haṇe.* [30] W. B. *pûrvam;* O. corrupt. [31] W. B. *bhavaty.* [32] G. M. *eshu.* [33] G. M. *tataḥ.* [34] O. *-ma iti cet.* [(35)] G. *pañke 'ti;* B. om. *varam.* [36] G. M. *-yenâ.*

द्वितीयचतुर्थयोस्तु व्यञ्जनोत्तरयोः पूर्वः ॥५॥

5. In place, however, of second and fourth mutes, when followed by consonants, is put the preceding mute.

That is to say, when an aspirate occurs between a preceding vowel (as the commentator specifies in his paraphrase of the rule) and a following consonant, or in such circumstances that by rule 1 it would be doubled, it receives instead an increment (*âgama*) of the mute next preceding it in its own series, or of its corresponding non-aspirate. Examples are *vikhyâya* (i. e. *vikkhyâya*) *cakshushâ tvam* (iv.1.2³: only G. M. have the last two words) and *meghyâ* (i. e. *megghyâ*) *vidyuto vâcaḥ* (v.2.11¹: only G. M. have *vâcaḥ*); to which W. B. add *tat savituḥ* (i.5.6⁴ et al.; the *t* is converted to *th* by xiv.12, and to the *th* is then prefixed *t*, making *tatth savituḥ*) and *sâdhyâ* (i. e. *sâddhyâ*) *vâi devâḥ* (vi.3.4⁸ et al.). To show that only the aspirates are thus treated, is quoted *âdyam* (i. e. *âddyam*) *asyâ 'nnam* (ii.2.5⁶: O. omits *annam*); to show that a vowel must precede, *vashaṭ svâhâ* (vii.3.12; by v.33, *t* is inserted between *ṭ* and *s*, and the inserted letter is made *th* by xiv.12; then, by this rule, no farther change of the *th* occurs, and we read *vashaṭṭth*, not *vashaṭṭṭth*; W. goes so far on this road as to read *vashaṭh svâhâ*) and *padbhyâṁ* (i. e. *paddbhyâṁ*, not *paddbbhyâṁ*) *dve savane* (vi.1.6⁴)—but G. M. O. substitute for the former another similar case, *vaṭ svayamabhigûrtâya* (iii.2.8¹ seven times: i. e. *vaṭṭth sv-*; O. writes *vaṭth sv-*)—; to show that a consonant must follow, *ukhâyâi sadane sve* (iv.1.9³ et al.: W. B. omit *sve*) and *meghâyate svâhâ* (vii.5.11¹). The word *tu*, 'however,' in the rule, the commentator (with more than his usual success in dealing with this particle) explains as intimating the denial of duplication, enjoined by rule 1. He adds that some give the particle a different interpretation, as

---

5. *dvitîyacaturthayoḥ*[1] *svarapûrvayor vyañjanottarayoḥ pûrvâgamo bhavati: yathâkrameṇa dvitîyasya prathamaç caturthasya tṛtîyaḥ. yathâ*[2]*: vi-....: me-....:* [3]*tat....: sâ-....*[3] *dvitîyacaturthayor iti kim: âdyam..... evampûrva*[4] *iti kim: vashaṭ....: pad-....: evamparayor*[5] *iti kim: ukh-....: megh-.... prathamasûtreṇa prasaktaṁ dvitvaṁ nivartayati tuçabdaḥ. anye tv anyathâ manyante: pûrvâgamasya dvitvaṁ nivartayatî 'ti. nâi 'tat sâram: savarṇasavargîyapara* (xiv.23) *ity uttaranishedhâd*[6] *eva tasya tannivṛttiḥ*[7].

atra kecid âhuḥ: vyañjanaparayor iti vâcye[8] *vâco yuktyantaram arthântaraṁ sûcayati*[9]*: sâṁhitâsâṁhitasâdhâraṇam*[10] *paranimittam*[11] *uktam*[12]*: tata*[13] *ihâ 'nyatarastha*[14] *âgamanimittatve prâpte 'sâṁhitapadânâṁ nityatvât tadgrahaṇam*[15] *eva*[16] *nyâyyam iti kṛtvâ vâikṛtavyañjanaparatve sati nâi 'tad vidhânam bhavati*[17]*: yathâ: abhy asthâd ity âdi. nâ 'yam pakshaḥ: adhyayana-*

signifying that the increment-consonant is not itself to be doubled; but justly pronounces this to be inappropriate, as such duplication is forbidden by rule 23 of this chapter.

In this and the three following rules is contained, for all the cases which come within the purview of the Prâtiçâkhya, the explicit prohibition of a double aspirate. Such double aspirates are, however, sometimes written by the Hindu scribes, both in situations where the authority of the phonetic treatises directly forbids them, and elsewhere. Thus, my manuscript of the Tâittirîya-Sanhitâ has, three times, *ḍh ḍh* instead of *ḍ ḍh* as the result of combination of *ṭ* and *h* (at ii.6.12⁵ : iii.4.1⁴ : v.3.12²), and the Calcutta edition, so far as printed, gives, unadvisedly, the same. Both authorities agree in reading *dididhdhi* at iii.1.11⁴. The edition, absurdly enough, gives *adhaththâḥ* at i.1.13², where my manuscript has *adhatthâḥ*. And I find a few cases of *khkh* and *chch*, which will be noted under rule 8, below.

As under the preceding rule, the commentator here also enters into a tedious and useless discussion of a verbal question; namely, why 'followed by consonants' is represented by *vyañjanottarayoḥ* instead of *vyañjanaparayoḥ*. Some, he says, have maintained that a difference of meaning is intended by the difference of phraseology; that it is desired, namely, to except cases like *abhy asthât* (iv.2.8¹), where the following consonant is the product of euphonic alteration. The ground alleged for this claim is not entirely clear to me: it seems to be that a specified following cause (one that produces an effect in something that precedes it) is common to the *saṁhitâ*-text and that which is not *saṁhitâ*; hence, a cause of increment occurring in either kind of text being in question, a citation of words from outside the *saṁhitâ* is alone suitable, on account of their constancy—that is, *abhi : asthât* not being citable as an example under the rule in its *pada*-form, it must not be so treated in its *saṁhitâ*-form, as well. But the claim is disallowed, as being opposed to the actual reading, and also to the fundamental

---

virodhân mûlasûtravirodhâc[18] *ca: tathâ hi: mûlasûtre svarapûrvatve vyañjanaparatve*[19] *ca sati vihitaṁ*[20] *dvitvam atra nishpâdyate*[21]*: na tu*[22] *tatra vyañjanaṁ viçeshitam: tadapavâdakatvâd atrâ*[23] *'pi tadviçesho vaktum ayuktaḥ*[24]. *çikshâdiparîkshaṇâd*[25] *adhyayanânurodhâc ca vâco yuktyantarâbhiprâyo 'smâbhir abhidhîyate*[26]. *apavâdyâpavâdakayor*[27] *anayor* [28]*niyamo nâ 'sti: kim iti:*[28] *svarapûrvatve sati vyañjanaparam eva vyañjanaṁ*[29] *dvitvam*[30] *bhajate:* [31] *dvitîyacaturthâu ca*[32] *vyañjanaparâv*[33] *eva pûrvâgamam*[34] *bhajata iti: kiṁ tu prâcuryâbhiprâyeṇe 'daṁ sûtradvayam pravṛttam. katham niyamâbhâvaḥ: anyathâ* [35] *kutracit kâryadvayadarçanât.* [36] *attâ----: annapata ityâdâu dvitvam: pra----: addhi---- ityâdâu pûrvâgamaḥ*[37]*: tâñ hasta ity atra tu*[38] *prâptâu satyâm api ne 'dam kâryaṁ dṛçyata iti ca*[39] *niyamâbhâvaḥ. çikshâ câi 'vaṁ vakshyati:*

rule. For, the intent is to cast out or deny a duplication established by the fundamental rule (xiv.1), where the being preceded by a vowel and followed by a consonant was implied; and there no limitation was laid down for the following consonant; hence, it is improper to lay one down here, where an exception is prescribed.

The commentator then goes on to say that he will set forth the real intent of the difference of phraseology, with due regard to the Çikshâ, and in accordance with the accepted reading of the text. But I am compelled to confess myself incapable of extracting a satisfactory meaning from his exposition and argument. The point of it is an asserted absence of *niyama* in the two rules (1 and 5), as of one suffering and the other prescribing exception. *Niyama*, 'obligatory force,' appears to signify here joint application, and so a mutual or reciprocal influence. When a vowel precedes, he continues, a consonant is doubled only when followed by a consonant; and second and fourth mutes take increment of the mute that stands before them in the alphabet only when followed by a consonant. But the pair of rules in question is constructed with the intent of multiplicity ('diversity' or 'independence?' *prâcurya* is not found elsewhere). How does an absence of *niyama* appear? Why, from the fact that otherwise a twofold effect would in some cases come to light. In *attâ havīn̄shi* (ii.6.12²) and in *annapate* (iv.2.3¹ et al.), and so on, there is duplication; in *pracchac chandaḥ* (iv.3.12³: G. M. have instead *acchâvâkaḥ*, the reference for which I have failed to note) and *addhi tvaṁ deva prayatâ* (ii.6.12⁵: G. M. O. omit *prayatâ*), and so on, there is increment of a preceding mute; but in *tân̄ haste* (vi.1.3⁷: W. has *tân̄s te* [iv.1.10³], but doubtless by accidental omission of *ha*), even though it falls under the rule, the same effect is not seen: hence, there is

---

svarât[40] *pûrvasya*[11] *varṇasya kvacid dvitvaṁ ca kathyate*[42]:
na ca vargadvitîyasya na caturthe kadâ[43] *cana.*
vyâkhyâtaṁ ca vacanam etadvidvadbhiḥ:
kutracit svarayor madhye dvitvaṁ lakshyânusâratah:
pûrvâgamas tathâ tatra jñeyo varṇavicakshaṇâiḥ.

[44] *evaṁrûpam aniyamaṁ sûcayituṁ vyañjanottarayor*[45] *ity antarasvîkâraḥ*[46].

vyañjanam uttaraṁ yâbhyâṁ tâu[47] *vyañjanottarâu*[48]: *tayoḥ.*

¹ G. M. O. put next before *pûrv-*, O. adding *tu.* ² in O. only (3) G. M. O. om. ⁴ G. M. O. *svarapûrvayor.* ⁵ G. M. *vyañjanottarayor.* ⁶ B. *utaratrani-*; G. M. *uttarasûtrani-.* ⁷ G. M. O. *-tteḥ-*; O. om. *tan.* ⁸ B. om. ⁹ G. M. O. *-ti 'ti*; G. M. add *tatra.* ¹⁰ G. M. *saṁhitâsaṁh-.* ¹¹ G. M. *paramani-*; O. *uktani-.* ¹² O. om. ¹³ O. *tatra.* ¹⁴ G. M. *-rasya.* ¹⁵ W. O. om. *tad*; B. *guṇam.* ¹⁶ W. O. *evam*; M. exchanges the places of *eva* and *iti.* ¹⁷ O. *-ti 'ti.* ¹⁸ O. om. *sûtra.* ¹⁹ O. *-namâtrapar-.* ²⁰ G. M. *-ta*; O. puts after *dvitvam*, and adds *ity.* ²¹ G. M. *nishidhyate*; O. *viçishyate.* ²² W. B. O. *nu.* ²³ W. B. *tatr-.* ²⁴ G. M. *yuktaḥ.* ²⁵ W. *-dipavâcaksh-*; G. M. *-ṇa.* ²⁶ O. *abhikshi-.* ²⁷ W. B. *apavâdâp-.* (28) G. M. *nâ 'sti virodha iti.* ²⁹ O. *paramaṁ.* ³⁰ W. om. ³¹ O. ins. *svarapûrvo.* ³² B. *tu*; O. om. ³³ O. *parâv.* ³⁴ W. *-me*; G. M. *-mâu.* ³⁵ B. G. M. ins. *'pi.* ³⁶ G. M. ins. *katham.* ³⁷ W. B. *-maṁ.* ³⁸ O. om. ³⁹ W. om. ⁴⁰ O. *-ra.* ⁴¹ W. *sa-vasya.* ⁴² G. M. *vakshyate.* ⁴³ G. M. *kathaṁ.* ⁴⁴ O. ins. *ity.* ⁴⁵ O. *-janayor.* ⁴⁶ G. M. O. *uttarasv-.* ⁴⁷ G. M. *tad.* ⁴⁸ G. M. *-raṁ.*

absence of *niyama*. The examples here furnished, which ought to give us the clue to the commentator's meaning, seem to leave us wholly in the dark, since not one of them falls under either of the rules in question: the first, second, and fourth are by rule 23, below, exempt from duplication; the third is a case under rule 8; and the combination *n̄h* is (see under rule 15) treated as a simple *h*. Next, the Çikshâ is quoted, to the effect that "in some cases, also, duplication of the first consonant of a group after a vowel is prescribed; not, however, of a second mute, nor of a fourth, under any circumstances;" and, by those versed in the subject, the statement is explained [in conformity with what follows]: "in some cases, there is duplication of a consonant between two vowels, in accordance with rule; so there also is to be understood prefixion of the preceding mute, by those skilled in alphabetic sounds" (in the known Çikshâ, it may be remarked, no such verses as these are to be found). And the final conclusion is, that the different term in *vyañjanottarayoḥ* is intended to signify an absence of *niyama* of this sort. That is to say, perhaps, the real independence of the two rules is intimated by the choice of a different term in expressing the common factor which they contain.

रेफपूर्वयोश्च नित्यम् ॥ ६ ॥

6. As also, in all cases, when they follow *r*.

This, it is pointed out, has the value of an exception under rule 4. The dual number of *rephapûrvayoḥ* shows that the pair, "second and fourth mutes," spoken of just above, is intended. "Also" (*ca*) implies the increment by prefixion of the next preceding mute. And the meaning is, that second and fourth mutes, with the limitations prescribed, as preceded by *r*, take always their respective predecessors as increment. Thus, *ûrdhvo* (i. e. *ûrddhvo*) *bhava* (i.2.14²), and *ardhyavâñ* (i. e. *arddhy-*) *prâṇaḥ* (vi.5.2²: only G. M. have *prâṇaḥ*). *Nityam*, 'in all cases,' implies that the increment is made after *r* when the mute to be increased is followed by a vowel also (not alone when it is *vyañjanottara*, as specified in rule 5). Thus, in *artheta* (i. e. *artth-*) *sthâ 'pâm* (i.8.11: only B. has *apâm*), *mûrkhâm̐* (i. e. *mûrkkhâm̐*) *tajjaghanyâm* (vii.1.6⁴), and *goargham* (i. e. *goargghum*) *eva* (vi.1.10¹).

लकारपूर्वे च ॥ ७ ॥

---

6. *rephât param̐ ca* (xiv.4) *ity asyâ 'pavâdakam etat*¹*: dvivacanena dvitîyacaturthâu gṛhyete: saviçeshaṇayo*² *rephapûrvayor anayor*³ *nityam pûrvâgamo bhavati*⁴*: âgamânvâdeçakaç cakâraḥ. yathâ*⁵*: ûrdh-....: ardhy-..... nityam iti kim: svaraparatve 'pi bhavatv*⁶ *etad iti: arthe....: mûrkhâm̐....: go-.....*

¹ W. *avadat.* ² W. B. *navi-;* G M. O. *-shaṇâu.* ³ O. *tayor.* ⁴ O. *syât.* ⁵ in G. M. only. ⁶ G. M. *-ty.*

7. And when *l* precedes.

The *ca*, 'and,' here brings down from rule 5 only the fourth mute [the last of the two there mentioned] and the increment. The second mute is not also included, because (see note to rule 2) no second mute occurs after *l* in the Sanhitâ. The examples are *pragalbho* (i. e. *-galbbho*) *'sya jâyate* (ii.5.5[3]: only G. M. have *jâyate*) and *namo madhyamâya câ 'pagalbhâya* (i. e. *-galbbh-*) *ca* (iv.5.6[1])—but, in place of the latter, G. M. give *apagalbho jâyate* (ii.5.5[3]: O. reads *agagalya* simply, which doubtless means the first word of this).

As was remarked above (under rule 3), the laying down of the present precept without any limitation appears to confirm the commentator's interpretation of rules 2 and 3, as teaching the accepted doctrine of the *çâkhâ*. It would, to be sure, be not impossible to understand *lbbh* for *lbh* as required here, without any reference to the other groups—*lk*, *lg* etc.—in which the duplication after *l* depends upon the earlier rules; but that seems quite unlikely.

उपसर्गपाथएषोऽत्यातिधामपरमभूतेपूर्वेषु छखिभुजेषु च ॥ ८ ॥

8. Also the preceding mute is inserted before *ch*, *khi*, and *bhuja*, when these follow either a preposition, *pâtha eshaḥ*, *ati*, *âti*, *dhâma*, *parâma*, or *bhûte*.

The examples after a preposition (in which situation alone the increment of *khi* and *bhuja* is made) are first given by the commentator: they are *â cchṛṇatti* (v.1.7[4]: the preceding word, *anâcchṛṇṇam*, might well have been included, as an additional instance; my MS. has simple *ch* in both cases); *nama âkkhidate ca prakkhidate ca* (iv.5.9[2]: G. M. omit the first word, G. M. O. the last two); *ayakshmayâ paribbhujâ* (iv.5.1[4]), with *vibhu ca me prabhu ca me* (iv.7.4[1-2]: O. stops at the first *me*) as counter-example, to show the necessity of saying *bhuja*, instead of *bhu* simply, in the rule; and *yâ ca vicchandâḥ* (v.2.11[1]). Then follow counter-examples: first, to show that *kh* is increased only when followed by *i*, *nikhâtam manushyâṇâm* (vi.3.4[6]) and *datsv adhi khâdati* (vi.2.11[4]: only G. M. have *datsv*); next, to show that the increment takes place only after a preposition, *sachandâ yâ* (v.2.11[1]). The examples after the remaining words, as particularly specified in the rule, are *priyam apy etu pâthaḥ : esha cchâgaḥ* (iv.6.8[1]: only O. has *priyam*), with *ṛtubhir vâ esha chandobhiḥ* (vii.5.15[2]), to prove the need of quoting *pâthaḥ* along with *esha* in the rule; *aticchan-*

---

7. *cakâraç caturthâgamayor*[1] *âkarshakaḥ : caturthasparçe*[2] *lakârapûrve sati pûrvâgamo bhavati. prag-.... : namo.... lakâraḥ pûrvo yasmâd asâu*[3] *lakârapûrvaḥ : tasmin.*

[1] G. M. *-gam.* [2] G. M. *-the sp-* [3] G. M. O. *sa.*

dasam upa dadhâti (v.3.8³), *savitra âticchandasâya* (vii.5.14), *dhâmacchad iva khalu vâi* (ii.4.10²: B. O. omit *vâi*), *paramacchado vare* (iv.6.2¹), and *yad bhûtecchadâñ sâmâni* (vii.5.9⁴).

Further examples of the increment of *ch*, falling under this rule, are *âcchad* and *pracchad* (at iv.3.12²,³) and *âcchettâ* (i.1.2¹): if there are others, I have omitted to note them. The usage in the manuscripts, of our commentary and of the Sanhitâ, is quite irregular, varying between *ch* simply, *cch*, and *chch*, without much regard to whether the case is one to which this rule applies or not. I have collected the cases in which my manuscript of the Sanhitâ has *chch:* they are *dhâmachchad* (ii.4.10²; but *dhâmachad* in the same division), *prachchach chandaḥ* (iv.3.12³), and *âyachchadbhyaḥ* (iv.5.3²); and, in the combination of separate words (besides the case just quoted), *âcchach chandaḥ* (iv.3.12²), *kakuch chandaḥ* (iii.1.6³), and *yach chreshthaḥ* (iii.4.8¹). In every one of these instances, the Calcutta edition, so far as it yet reaches, reads correctly *cch*.

I have found no other cases of the increment of *khi* under the rule; but my manuscript has (without authority) *udakhkhidat* (ii.1.1⁴,5¹), *sam akhkhidat* (vi.6.11¹), and *akhkhidrâh* (iii.5.8), while (along with the MSS. of the comment) it reads *khkh* instead of *kkh* in the example (iv.5.9²) cited above. The edition reads *kkh* at ii.1.1⁴,5¹, remarking at the latter place that its manuscript authorities have *khkh*. Of course, the doubled aspirate is to be rejected, here as elsewhere, in obedience to sound phonetic theory as well as to the concordant authority of the Prâtiçâkhyas.

अघोषादूष्मणः परः प्रथमो ऽभिनिधान स्पर्शपरात्तस्य सस्थानः ॥ ९ ॥

9. After a surd spirant followed by a mute is inserted a first mute of the same position with the latter, as *abhinidhâna*.

The surd spirants are (see i.9,12,13) five, namely χ (*jihvâmûlîya*), *ç*, *sh*, *s*, and φ (*upadhmânîya*). The rule is to be paralleled with those in the Vâj. Pr. (iv.99,100), which direct that a mute be doubled after a spirant, and after *jihvâmûlîya* and *upadhmânîya* (which in that treatise are not reckoned as spirants); also with

---

8. *upasargapûrveshu pâtha ...... evampûrveshu ca*[1] *satsu cha khi bhuje 'ty eteshu pûrvâgamo bhavati*[2]. *cakâra âgamânvâdeçakaḥ. yathâ*[3]: *â ....: nama ....: ayak- ....: je 'ti kim: vibhu .... yâ ....: 'khî 'ti kim: nikh- ....: datsv ....: upasarga*[5] *iti kim: sa- ....:*[4] *etâny upasargapûrvâṇi. anyâny*[6] *ucyante: priyam ....: pâtha iti kim: ṛtubhir ....: ati- ....: savitra ....: dhâma- ....: parama- ....: yad ....*

[1] G. M. om. [2] O. *syât.* [3] G. M. O. om. (4) O. om. [5] ... M. *-rgapûrva.* [6] G. M. O. ins. *apy.*

that in the Rik Pr. (vi.2) which allows, but does not require, duplication of a mute after the spirants (namely *ç*, *sh*, *s*, *ḥ*, *χ*, *φ*, *ñ*). The Ath. Pr. (unless such a precept is lost by the *lacuna* occurring in the treatment of this subject: see note to Ath. Pr. iii. 28) and Pâṇini have nothing similar. Our rule, however, is quite alone so far as the treatment of a nasal after a spirant is concerned, making an insertion of a surd non-aspirate, instead of a nasal: and, as will be seen, the next rule quotes an opinion which would bring the Tâittirîya usage more nearly into accordance with that of the Rik and Vâjasaneyi Sanhitâs; but the commentator pronounces that opinion unapproved.

The examples quoted are as follows: *yaḥ kâmayeta* (i. e. *yaχ kkâm-*: ii.1.2[3] et al.); *açmann* (i. e. *açpman*, or, after all rules are applied, *aççppman*) *ûrjam* (iv.6.1[1]: O. omits the example and puts here, instead of below, that for *φ*); *grîshme* (i. e. *grîshpme* or *grîshshppme*) *madhyandine* (ii.1.2[5]); *ayasmayam* (i. e. *ayaspmayam* or *ayassppmayam*) *vi cṛtâ bandham* (iv.2.5[3]: only W. has *bandham*); *yaḥ pâpmanâ* (i. e. *yaφ ppâ-*: ii.3.13[2]): O. adds to this last *tasmin* (vii.1.5[1] et al.: to be treated like *ayasmayam*, above), and, after *madhyandine*, *prâ 'çnâti* (*prâççtînâti*: I have overlooked this citation in searching out the references). As counter-examples, we have first *çarady aparâhṇe* (ii.1.2[5]: but O. substitutes *brahmavâdino vadanti*, i.7.1[4] et al.), to show that the sonant spirant, *h*, does not require a like insertion (the case is one of *nâsikya*, xxi. 14); then *rukmam upa dadhâti* (v.2.7[1,2]; the case is one for *yama*, xxi.12), to show that a mute receives the increment only after a spirant; and lastly *ishvâ ca vajreṇa ca* (v.7.3[1]), to show that a mute only is increased after a spirant. For the second of these counter-examples, O. substitutes two of the same character, namely *yam apnavânaḥ* (i.5.5[1]) and *sa pratnavat* (ii.2.12[1] et al.); for the last, it gives (in a passage which has strayed out of place, and got inserted near the end of the comment to rule 10) *agnaye svâhâ* (i.2.2[1] et al.).

In all these combinations, *χ* and *φ* are exempt from duplication by xiv.15, but the sibilants are doubled, except as some authorities (xiv.17,18) would leave them unchanged.

---

9. *sparçaparâd aghoshâd ûshmaṇaḥ paraḥ*[1] *prathama*[2] *âgamas*[3] *tasya sparçasya sasthânaḥ*[4] *samânasthâno 'bhinidhâno bhavati. abhinidhîyata*[5] *ity abhinidhânaḥ: âropaṇîya ity arthaḥ:* [6]*vedântare tasyâ*[6] *'bhâvâd atrâ "ropaṇîyatvam. yathâ*[7]*: yaḥ ----:* [8]*açm- ----:*[8] *grîsh- ----: ayasm- ----: yaḥ ---- aghoshâd iti kim: çarady ---- ûshmaṇa iti kim:* [9]*rukmam ----*[9] *sparçaparâd iti kim: ishvâ ----.*

sûtram idam eve 'shṭam: na tatparadrayam[10].

[1] G. M. om. [2] B. O. *pratham.* [3] G. M. *-mo bhavati.* [4] B. om. [5] W. O. *-dhîyata*; B. *-niyata.* [(6)] G. M. *vedântarasyâ*; O. *-reṇa tad a.* [7] G. M. O. om. [(8)] O. om. [(9)] O. *yam apnavânaḥ: sa pratnavat*, and om. all that follows (but see various readings to next rule). [10] G. M. *tu par-*.

The commentator illustrates with groups of two consonants only (of which the Sanhitâ presents twenty-three that would come under the action of the rule); the question arises, then, whether in groups of three or more consonants (of which there are over fifty)—where the mute is followed by another consonant (as *χkl*, *çny*, *shky*, *stm*, *stry*, *φpr*), or where the spirant stands second (as *rçm*, *kshṇ*, *rshṇy*, *tsk*, *tsphy*), or where each is the case (as *tstr*, *tstry*, *ntstr*), or where there are two spirants followed by mutes in the same group (as *χkshṇ*)—the rule is to be relentlessly applied. It can admit of little doubt that the sequence of another consonant would not affect the case; whether a preceding consonant would do so is more doubtful. Such resultant groups as *nthsttr*, *tthspphy*, *kkhshṭṭṇy*, and *χkkhshṭṭṇ*, have a tolerably frightful appearance; but whether they would stagger the heroic soul of a Hindu *çâkhin*, is another matter.

To the inserted mute is applied the name *abhinidhâna*, which the commentator explains by *abhinidhîyate*, 'it is set down against;' giving as its synonym *âropaṇîya*, (I presume, simply) 'to be inserted;' and adding the remark, "owing to the absence of this in any other Veda, there is here insertibility" (?). He takes no notice of the doctrine of *abhinidhâna* as a peculiar and imperfect utterance of certain letters in certain situations, which plays so formidable a part in the phonetic systems of the Rik and Ath. Prâtiçâkhyas (see especially the note to Ath. Pr. i.43): we, however, bearing that doctrine in mind, may conjecture with plausibility that the word here not merely signifies an insertion, but designates also a peculiar quality of the inserted letter.

अघोषे प्लाक्षेः ॥१०॥

10. According to Plâkshi, when the following mute is surd.

That is to say, not when it is a nasal: Plâkshi would ratify *χkk*, *χkkh*, *shṭṭ*, *shṭṭh*, and so on, but would make no insertion in *çm*, *shṇ*, and their like. This, as was remarked under the last rule, would correspond more nearly with the teachings of the Rik and Vâj. Prâtiçâkhyas. The commentator illustrates with *nishkevalyam* (iv.4.2[2]), *yaḥ kâmayeta* (ii.1.2[3] et al.), *paçcât prâcîm* (v.3.7[3]: B. reads *prâcî*, which is found in the same division; W. has *prâñcam*, which does not occur in the Sanhitâ after *paçcât*), *nish ṭapâmi* (i.1.10[1]), *doshâvastaḥ* (i.2.14[4] et al.), *yaḥ pâpmanâ* (ii.3.

---

10. [1] *aghosha eva sparçe*[2] *pare* [3]*saty aghoshâd ûshmaṇaḥ* [4] *prathamâgamo*[3] *bhavati:* [5]*plâksheḥ pakshaḥ*[5]. *yathâ*[6]: *nish-* - - - -: [6]*yaḥ* - - - -: *paçc-* - - - -: *nish* - - - -: [7]*aksh-* - - - -:[7] *dosh-* - - - -: *yaḥ* - - - -: *âsp-* - - - - -.[8] *aghosha eve 'ti kim: kûçmâñ* - - - - -.[9]

[1] O. ins. *plâksheç çâkhino mate.* [2] W. B. G. M. *-ça*; O. *-çe 'pi.* [(3)] O. *prathamo 'bhinidhâno.* [4] G. M. ins. *paraḥ.* [(5)] O. om. [6] G. M. O. om.; W. puts out of place, before *aksh-.* [(7)] G. M. om. [(8)] O. substitutes *suçcandra* - - -: *sparçaparâd iti kim: agn-* - - - -. *sûtram idam eve 'shṭaṁ na tu paradvayaṁ.* 95. *aghosha eva sparçapare prathamâ yaç chandasâm: naç cid ati: syâtram: bṛhaspatisûrapate.* [8] O. adds *abhinidhânaniyamo nâ 'sti.*

13[2]), and *âspâtram juhûr devânâm* (ii.5.9[3]: G. M. have only the first word). All these are examples quite needless to be given, as they are read by Plâkshi precisely as prescribed by the preceding rule. Counter-examples,[1] exhibiting his discordant view, are *kûçmâñ chakabhih* (v.7.23: W. G. M. have *kûçmân* only, and B. reads *kûshmândân*, which I have not found in the Sanhitâ, although *kûçmânda* occurs in the Tâitt. Âranyaka, at ii.7,8) and *akshnayâ vyâghârayati* (v.2.7[5] et al.: given only by W. B., and introduced out of place, between *nish tapâmi* and *doshâvastah*, above).

O. follows an independent course in the interpretation and illustration of this rule. It calls the insertion an *abhinidhâna* (though adding at the end "there is no obligation of *abhinidhâna*") and, for the examples *yah kâmayeta* to *âspâtram*, it substitutes *suçcandra dasma viçpate havyavât* (iv.4.4[6]: the MS. omits *dasma*), *yaç chandasâm* (the thing nearest to this that I have found in the text is *prajâpatiç chandasâm*, iii.3.7[1]), *naç cid ati* (this I have overlooked in searching out the references), *syâtram* (doubtless meant for *âspâtram*), and *brhaspatisûrapate* (probably *brhaspatisutasya te*, i.4.27).

The present precept was pronounced unapproved in the comment to rule 9.

उत्तमपरात्तु प्लाक्षायणस्य ॥ ११ ॥

11. But according to Plâkshâyana, on the contrary,[1] when the following mute is a nasal.

This can only mean to teach the precise opposite of the preceding rule; or, that there is no insertion when a surd mute follows the spirant, but only when a nasal follows. And it is first so explained by the commentator, who gives as examples *akshnayâ vyâghârayati* (v.2.7[5] et al.), *açnâti* (i.6.7[3] et al.), and *tîrthe snâti*

---

11. [1]*plâkshâyanasya tu paksha uttamaparâd aghoshâd ûshmanah parah*[1] *prathamâgamo bhavati. yathâ*[2]: *akshn-....: açnâti: tîrthe..... uttamaparâd iti kim: nish-....:* [3]*yah k-....:*[3] [4]*yah p-....:*[4] *paçcât. tuçabdah plâksheh paksham prakshipati*[5].

kecid evam ûcuh: aghoshatvam ûshmanas tuçabdo nivartayatî 'ti[6]. *tatrâ 'yam sûtrârthah: uttamaparât tu*[7] *ghoshavata*[8] *ûshmanah parah prathamâgamo bhavati. ahnâm-....: çarady-....: brahm-..... ghoshavata*[9] *iti kim: açmâ-....: grîsh-....: ayas-.....*

(1) G. M. om. [2] G. M. om. (3) B. om. (4) G. M. om. [5] W. *apakshiyati*; B. *-kshîyati.* [6] G. M. om. *iti.* [7] in W. only. [8] G. M. *ghoshâd.* [9] G. M. *agh-*.

O. substitutes for the whole comment *aghoshaprakrtam tuçabde nirayati: plâkshâyanasya çâkhino mate aghoshâd ûshmanah uttamasparçaparât: sasthânaprathamahgamo bhavati: aksh-....: grî-....: çnâti: ayas-.....*

(vi.1.1²); and, as counter-examples, *nishkevalyam* (iv.4.2²), *yaḥ kâmayeta* (ii.1.2³ et al.: B. omits), *yaḥ pâpmanâ* (ii.3.13²: G. M. omit), and *paçcât* (v.2.9⁴ et al.). Plâkshâyaṇa would read the first class as rule 9 requires, but would leave the mute without increment in the second class.

Then a second and wholly different interpretation is set forth as taught by certain authorities: namely, that *tu*, 'but,' in the rule, instead of negativing Plâkshi's opinion, reverses the quality of the spirant as prescribed in rule 9, changing it from surd to sonant—that is to say, admitting the increment only after *h*. The examples given are *ahnâṁ ketuḥ* (ii.4.14¹), *çarady aparâhṇe* (ii.1.2⁵: only W. has *çarady*), and *brahmavâdino vadanti* (i.7.1⁴ et al.: W. B. omit *vadanti*); the counter-examples, illustrating omission of the increment after a surd spirant, are *açmâ ca me* (iv.7.5¹), *grîshmo hemantaḥ* (v.7.2⁴), and *ayasmayaṁ vi cṛta* (iv.2.5³: W. B. omit *cṛta*). This, which is in itself forced and inadmissible, would also be equivalent to limiting the insertion to the little class of cases in which a later rule (xxi.14) requires the interposition of a *nâsikya*.

In the exposition of this rule, O. goes its own peculiar way, and takes no notice of the second interpretation which the other manuscripts report. It furnishes no counter-examples, and its examples agree only in part with those already given: they are (corrected) *akshṇayâ vyâghârayati*, *grîshme madhyandine* (ii.1.2⁵), *açnâti* (or *snâti*), and *ayasmayaṁ vi cṛta*.

The rule was pronounced unapproved by the commentator under rule 9.

प्रथम ऊष्मपरो द्वितीयम् ॥ १२ ॥

12. A first mute followed by a spirant is changed into its corresponding aspirate.

Literally, becomes a second mute—of course, of its own series. The examples given are as follows: *visṛpo virapçinn* (i. e. *viraphçin;* or, by xiv.1, *virapphçin*) *udâdâya* (i.1.9³: only O. has the first word, and it omits the last; W. reads *vâratrivadâya*, which is evidently merely a corruption); *tat shodaçy* (i. e. *-tth sh-*) *abhavat* (vi.6.11¹: only G. M. have *abhavat*); *pratyaṅ somaḥ* (i.8.21: i. e. *pratyaṅk s-* by v.32; then *pratyaṅkh s-*); and *tat* (i. e. *tatth*)

---

12. *ûshmaparaḥ prathama sparçaḥ*¹ *savargîyaṁ dvitîyam âpadyate. vis-....: tat....: praty-....: tat....* ²*prathama iti kim:* ³*tâḥ....*² *ûshmapara iti kim*³*: vâk....* ⁴*arvâg.... ity atra prathamapûrvo hakâraç caturthaṁ tasya sasthânam* (v.38) *iti hakârasya caturthâpattir viçeshavihitatvât: tatas tṛtîyañ svaraghoshavatparas* (viii.3) *tṛtîyatvam.*

*idam eva sûtram ishṭam*⁴.

*ûshmâ paro yasmâd asâv*⁵ *ûshmaparaḥ.*

¹ O. *âtmana.* ⁽²⁾ O. om. ⁽³⁾ W. B. om. ⁽⁴⁾ in O. only. ⁵ G. M. *sa.*

savituḥ (i.5.6[4] et al.). As counter-examples, we have *tâḥ* (i. e. *tâs*, ix.2) *sanrohaḥ* (v.3.6[3]: omitted by O.; dropped out in W. B.) and *vâk ta â pyâyatâm* (i.3.9[1]: only O. has the last two words), in which no aspiration takes place.

A possible difficulty in the application of this rule is noticed and removed by O. alone. Such a case as *arvâk : hi : enam : parâiḥ* (vi.3.3[1]) might seem to fall under its action, the spirant *h* following a surd mute. But it is pointed out that, in virtue of v.38, *h* becomes a fourth mute by special prescription; and hence that rule viii.3 alone applies to the preceding surd, changing it to a sonant.

The place of introduction of this precept and the following—coming in, as they do, right in the midst of the rules respecting duplication, with which they stand in no relation—is quite surprising and objectionable. The commentator, however, passes the matter without notice.

I have not noted any case in which my manuscript of the Sanhitâ attempts the aspiration of a mute before a sibilant, as here required. The manuscripts of the commentary, however, which almost never heed the rules for duplication, even in illustrating those rules themselves, often (as we have repeatedly had occasion to notice) observe this one in their citations, although they yet more often neglect it (thus, in the examples here given, G. M. O. aspirate the mutes, and W. B. leave them unchanged). Being taught in company with the duplication, as part of the *varṇa-krama*, it has no claim to be taken account of in the construction of an ordinary Tâittirîya text. Respecting the teachings of the other Prâtiçâkhyas upon the subject, see the note to Âth. Pr. ii.6.

बाडभीकारस्यासस्थानपरः ॥ १३ ॥

13. According to Bâḍabhîkâra, when the following spirant is not of the same position with it.

Rule ii.44 teaches the accordance of the several (surd) spirants, in their order, with the series of mutes, in point of position—more literally, of place of production.

T. calls the individual here referred to Bâḍavîkâra, and W. O. have in the rule *vâḍabhîkâra*, but in the comment *bâḍabh-;* the rest have uniformly *b* as initial letter, which I have therefore adopted, as being decidedly better supported than *v*. Weber gives the two forms *vâḍabh-* (V. Pr. p. 250) and *vâṭabh-* (ib., p. 78).

---

13. *bâḍabhîkârasya* [1] *mata âtmano*[2] *'sasthânoshmaparaḥ prathamaḥ savargîyam*[3] *dvitîyam âpadyate.* [4]*samânam sthânam yasyâ 'sâu sasthânaḥ: na sasthâno 'sasthânaḥ: sa paro yasmât sa tatho 'ktaḥ. yathâ*[5]*: vis-.....: tat.....*[4] *asasthâna iti kim: tat.....* [6]

ne 'daṁ sûtram ishṭam.

[1] O. ins. *çâkhino.* [2] G. M. O. om. (and begin the next word *as-*). [3] O. om. [(4)] O. om. [5] B. om. [6] O. ins. *idarâ(?)sthâno yaṁ sakâraḥ.*

The commentary (except in O.) is at the pains to repeat a couple of the examples of aspiration already given, namely *visṛpo virapçin* (i.1.9[3]: W. omits *visṛpo*) and *tat shoḍaçî* (vi.6.11[1]): and it adds, in illustration of the peculiar view of the quoted authority, *tat savituḥ* (i.5.6[4] et al.), where the dental mute, being followed by the dental sibilant, remains unchanged.

This rule is pronounced unapproved.

अथ न ॥ १४ ॥

14. Now for exceptions.

A heading, introducing the detail of exceptions to the rules as already given, and continuing in force through rule 28.

अवसाने रविसर्जनीयजिह्वामूलीयोपध्मानीयाः ॥ १५ ॥

15. A consonant before a pause is not doubled; nor *r*, *visarjanîya*, *jihvâmûlîya*, or *upadhmânîya*.

As example of a consonant before a pause, is given *ûrk* (iv.7.4[1] et al.: W. has instead *so 'rkaḥ* [v.4.3[3]], but it is not an illustration of the rule, and is evidently here only a corrupted reading of *ûrk*), of which the *k* would otherwise be doubled by xiv.4. Of course, it is only a final after *r* that would fall under the rules of duplication before a pause. The text affords, I believe, no instance of a consonant occurring in this position in *saṁhitâ*, but such words as *ûrk* and *amârt* (vii.1.1[2] et al.) need to have their reading in the other forms of text determined by a rule like this. The commentator quotes *ûrk ca* (i. e. *ûrkk ca*) *me sûnṛtâ ca me* (iv.7.4[1]: B. omits the last two words, G. M. O. the last three), as showing that the *k* is doubled when in *sandhi* with a following letter. To illustrate the exemption from duplication of the other letters specified, are given *nâ "rtim â rchati* (ii.2.4[7]), *manaḥ ksheme* (v.2.1[7]), *yaḥ* (i. e. *yaχ*) *kâmayeta* (ii.1.2[3] et al.), and *yaḥ* (i. e. *yaφ*) *pâpmanâ* (ii.3.13[2]). According to the approved usage of this *çâkhâ* (see ix. 2,3), *visarjanîya* comes within the ken of this rule only when it

---

14. *athe 'ty ayam adhikâraḥ:* [1] *uktasya dvitvavidher*[2] *yathâsambhavaṁ nishedho 'dhikriyata*[3] *ity* [4]*etad adhikṛtaṁ*[4] *veditavyam ita* [5]*uttaraṁ yad vakshyâmaḥ*[5].

[1] G. M. ins. *atha.* [2] W. G. M. *-dhe;* O. *vidh-*. [3] W. *-kṛta.* [(4)] B. G. M. om. [(5)] B. *no varṇaḥ.*

15. *padâvasâne*[1] *vartamâno varṇo* [2]*repho visarjanîyo jihvâmûlîya upadhmânîyaç*[2] *ce*[3] *'ty ete varṇâ dvitvaṁ nâ "padyante*[4]. *ûrk: rephât paraṁ ca* (xiv.4) *iti prâptiḥ. avasânavacanaṁ*[5] *virâmâbhiprâyam: tasmân na saṁdhâne nishedhaḥ: yathâ*[6]: *ûrk ca----. nâ----: man----: yaḥ----: yaḥ----: svarapûrvam* (xiv.1) *ity anenâi 'shâm prâptiḥ.*

precedes *ksh*, since elsewhere it can stand only *in pausâ*. *Jihvâmûlîya* occurs (by the conversion of final *ḥ* according to ix.2) in the groups *χk*, *χkl*, *χkr*, *χksh*, *χkshṇ*, *χkshv*, and *χkh*; *upadhmânîya*, in like manner, in *φp*, *φpy*, *φpr*, *φpl*, and *φph*: the combinations of *r* have been enumerated above (under rule 4).

The other Prâtiçâkhyas have rules equivalent with this, into the variety of expression of which we do not need to enter.

It is to be accounted as a reprehensible omission on the part of our treatise, that it gives no direction as to the treatment of a group beginning with *anusvâra*. The Vâj. Prât. (iv.107) expressly exempts *anusvâra* from duplication; and, in the Rik Prât., in the fundamental rule (vi.1), *anusvâra* is ruled out of account in the estimation of consonant groups, it being taught that a consonant is doubled after it in the same manner as after a vowel. There is no good reason to doubt that the same is to be understood as the doctrine of the present work, and that it would have *anusvâra*, so far as duplication is concerned, deemed and taken as merely an affection of the vowel to which it is attached. That this is not explicitly stated, stands in connection with the equivocal position of the Tâitt. Prât. in reference to the nature of *anusvâra* (see p. 68): according to the view taken at the beginning of the next chapter (xv.1), rules respecting it are no more required than in the Ath. Prât., where they are equally wanting.

The commentator notices that some would read the rule now under discussion as two, cutting off *avasâne* from the rest; and for the reason that otherwise, as the rule stands, it seems natural to understand that "*r*, *ḥ*, *χ*, and *φ*, when standing before a pause," are not doubled; as a similar construction was made in rule 10 of the fifth chapter. But he denies the validity of the objection, since duplication of *r* and the rest before a pause is not in the remotest

---

[7]*avasâna iti:* [8]*caturṇâṁ varṇânâm*[8] *pṛthag eva sûtraṁ* [9]*kecid ûcuḥ:*[7] *ekîkaraṇe*[9] *doshadarçanât: asâu*[10] *doshaḥ: avasâne vartamânâ rephavisarjanîyâdaya*[11] *ity anvayasampâdanam*[12]*: avagraha âçîr dhûḥ suvar* (v.10) *itivad iti cet*[13]*: nâi 'sha doshaḥ: ravisarjanîyâdînâm*[14] *padâvasâne* [15]*dvitvaprâptir*[16] *dûrotsârite*[17] *'ti ne 'yam atra çankâ 'sti*[18]*: avasânepṛthakkaraṇe*[19] *saty*[20] *avasâne*[15] *kiṁ vâ bhavatî 'ti sâkâṅkshatayâ*[21] *vacanam anarthakaṁ*[22] *syât: ekîkaraṇe tu ravisarjanîyetivarṇasâhacaryâd*[23] *avasâne vartamâno varṇa iti*[24] *labhyate: tasmâd ekîkaraṇam eva ramaṇîyam.*

[1] W. B. *yad-*. [(2)] W. B. combine, as in rule. [3] O. om. *ca*. [4] G. M. *-dyeran*. [5] G. M. *-âna iti v-*. [6] O. om. [(7)] G. M. *kecid idaṁ sûtraṁ pṛthag evo "cuḥ : avasâna iti ca : ravisarjaniyajihvâmûliyopadhmâniyâ iti ca : kathaṁ pṛthakkaraṇam.* [(8)] W. *caturvarṇâḥ*; B. om. *varṇânâm*. [(9)] W. corrupt. [10] G. M. O. *ko 'sâu*. [11] G. M. O. *ravi-*; B. *-niyâ*. [12] G. M. *avayavasaṁbhâvanam*; O. *asya dvitvaṁ samp-*. [13] O. om. [14] O *avasânevyatiriktasthale vis-*. [(15)] B. om. [16] W. *rephaprâptiḥ*. [17] W. *tatsâ-*; O. *dûratot-*. [18] G. M. *kiṁ cit*; O. *kiṁ ca*. [19] G. M. O. *pṛth-*. [20] W. *sti*; G. M. *nâsti*. [21] G. M. *-kshâ tathâ*; O. *-kshayâ*. [22] B. *arth-*. [23] W. *savis-*; B. *vis-*; O. om. *varṇa*. [24] O. om.

manner suggested by the rules (literally, 'is expelled to a distance'), and consequently cannot be suspected of being taught here. If, on the other hand, *avasâne*, 'before a pause,' were set by itself, the inquiry would be "what under the sun is it that happens before a pause?" and the expression would appear meaningless. When, however, it is combined with the names of letters that follow, we naturally infer from the association that 'a letter *in pausâ*' is intended. Hence, the inclusion of the two precepts in one rule is alone to be approved.

This defense of the unity of the rule is evidently of the most trifling and futile character, and the objectors are in the right—not, indeed, as the separation into two rules is absolutely necessary, but as it is decidedly preferable, and more in accordance with the general usage of the treatise elsewhere.

ऊष्मा स्वरपरः ॥ १६ ॥

16. Nor a spirant, when followed by a vowel.

It is only, of course, after *r* (xiv.4) that a spirant can be liable to duplication before a vowel, so that the combinations to which the rule applies are *rç*, *rsh*, *rs*, and *rh*. All the other treatises excepting the Vâj. Prât. have the same rule (R. Pr. vi.2; A. Pr. iii.32; Pâṇ. viii.4.49).

The commentator's examples are *darçapûrṇamâsâu* (ii.2.5[4] et al.), *varshâbhyaḥ* (vii.4.13: I presume; my MS. of the Sanhitâ has *varshyâbhyaḥ* twice instead of *varshyâbhyaḥ* and *varshâbhyaḥ*: O. gives instead *suvarshâṁ*, iv.4.4[1]), *barsaṁ nahyati* (ii.5.7[1-2]), and *barhishâ* (i.7.4[1] et al.: G. M. have instead *barhisho 'ham*, also i.7.4[1]). To illustrate the limitation to a spirant, he gives *ebhir no arkâiḥ* (i. e. *arkkâiḥ*; iv.4.4[7]: O. omits); to show that a vowel must follow, *pârçve* (i. e. *pârççve*; vii.3.10[3]), *varshyâbhyaḥ svâhâ* (i. e. *varshshy-*; vii.4.13: G. M. omit *svâhâ*), *barsvebhiḥ* (i. e. *barssv-*; v.7.11), and *agnir hy asya* (i. e. *hhy*; v.1.5[5])—but O. has a different series, namely *dârçyaṁ yajñam* (iii.2.2[3]), *varshyebhiḥ* (the MS. has *varshebhiḥ*; I have not succeeded in finding either word in the Sanhitâ), and *agner hy etat purîsham* (vi.2.8[6]).

The combinations in which the spirant after *r* is doubled, being followed by another consonant, are *rçm*, *rçy*, *rçv*, *rshṭ*, *rshṇ*, *rshm*, *rshy*, *rsv*, and *rhy*. To complete the *sandhi*, either with or without duplication, the rules for insertion of *svarabhakti* (xxi.15,16) have to be further applied.

---

16. *svarapara ûshmâ dvitvaṁ nâ "padyate. svaraḥ paro yasmâd asâu svaraparaḥ. yathâ*[1]*: darç-....: varsh-....: barsaṁ....: barh-.....* [2]*rephât paraṁ ca* (xiv.4) *iti prâptiḥ. ûshme 'ti kim: ebhir....*[2] *svarapara iti kim:* [3]*pârçve: varsh-....: barsvebhiḥ: agnir....*[3]

[1] G. M. O. om. (2) O. om. (3) O. *dâ-....: varshebhiḥ: agner....*

प्रथमपरश्च प्लाक्षिप्लाक्षायणयोः ॥ १७ ॥

17. Or, according to Plâkshi and Plâkshâyaṇa, when followed by a first mute.

That is to say, these two *çâkhinâu* would leave a spirant free from duplication before an unaspirated surd mute, contrary to the first rule of the chapter. The groups which would be thus affected are *çc* and *çcy*, *çp*, *shk* and *shky* and *shkr*, *shṭ* and its further combinations (*shṭy*, *shṭr*, *shṭv*), *shp*, *sk*, *st* and its further combinations (*stm*, *sty*, *str* and *stry*, *stv*), and *sp*. One hardly sees why combinations with a second mute (namely *çch* and *çchy*, *shkh*, *shṭh* and *shṭhy*, *sth* and *sthn*, *sph* and *sphy*) should not be subject to the same rule—but then, one must not expect to see the reason of anything whatever, general rule or particular exception, in this doctrine of duplications. It may be made a question whether the single case, *rshṭ*, falling under rule 4 is not also here aimed at; if the pair of kinsmen did not overlook it, it is doubtless included with the rest.

The examples (which are lost in W.) are *suçcandra dasma* (iv. 4.4[6]: O. omits *dasma*) and *ashṭâu kṛtvaḥ* (vi.4.5[1]); a counter-example, with a last mute after the spirant, is *tasmâd evâṁ vidushâ* (vi.4.9[2]: O. omits *vidushâ*); but O. has, with B., omitted to point out that this is a counter-example, and gives further, as such, *ishvâ ca vajreṇa* (v.7.3[1]).

The commentator then goes on to say that although the word *ca*, 'or,' in the rule brings down by implication a spirant pure and simple (without exclusion of any sound belonging to that class), yet the real application is only to *ç*, *sh*, *s*, and *h*, since otherwise the mention of χ and φ in rule 15 would be without meaning, their exception being assured by the present precept. The interpretation is doubtless true, but the reason given for it is only acceptable on the supposition that what is here put forward as the view of two individual authorities is in fact the accepted doctrine of the Prâtiçâkhya; in any other case, there is no inconsistency or interference between rules 15 and 17, and the commentator should rather have said that, as the pair of dissidents doubtless accepted

---

17. *plâkshiplâkshâyaṇayoḥ pakshe*[1] [2]*prathamapara ûshmâ dvitvaṁ nâ "padyate. cakâra ûshmâṇam anvâdiçati. suçc-....: ashṭau-....* [3]*prathamapara iti kim:*[3] *tasmâd-....*[2] *prathamaḥ paro yasmâd asâu prathamaparaḥ.* [4]

cakâro 'tra[5] *yady apy*[6] *ûshmamâtrâkarshakas*[7] *tathâ 'pi*[8] *çashasaheshv eva sampratyayaḥ: anyathâ*[9] *'vasâne ravisarjanîya* (xiv.15) *iti*[10] *sûtre jihvâmûlîyopadhmânîyayor grahaṇaṁ vyarthaṁ: anenâi*[11] *'va nishedhasiddheḥ*[12].

[1] O. *mate.* (2) W. om. [3] B. O. om. [4] O. ins. *prathamapara iti kim: ishvâ-....* [5] G. M. O. om. [6] W. om. [7] G. M. *ûshmak-.* [8] W. O. *hi.* [9] G. M. om. [10] W. O. om. [11] O. ins. *shâi.* [12] W. O. *-shedhe s-.*

rule 15, it was not necessary to regard the present statement of their views as having any reference to χ and φ. That the rule is accepted in the *çâkhâ* represented by the commentator may be inferred also from the fact that (under rule 22) he pronounces the five that follow unapproved, but says nothing of this.

ऊष्माघोषो हारीतस्य ॥ १८ ॥

18. According to Hârîta, a surd spirant is not doubled.

There is unusual variety and inaccuracy of reading among the different manuscripts of the commentary of this rule, and O. goes off upon a course of its own: yet the aim of all is the same, and not difficult to discover. The word *ûshmâ* (which was present or implied in the two preceding rules, and therefore might naturally enough come down into this by continued implication) is here expressly repeated, for the purpose of breaking connection with what goes before. If *aghosha*, 'surd,' only were specified, and *ûshmâ*, 'spirant,' implied, the latter would have to be implied along with the attributes attached to it above, namely "followed by a vowel," or "followed by a first mute," and to such a spirant the further qualification of "surd" would be given; while the meaning intended is that Hârîta would forbid the duplication of a surd spirant altogether, in any situation.

O. alone gives as first example *dârçyaṁ yajñam* (iii.2.2^{3}); all have *vâiçyo manushyâṇâm* (vii.1.1^{5}); to which W. B. add *pushyati prajayâ paçubhiḥ* (ii.4.6^{2}) and *vâiçvânarasya rûpam* (v.2.3^{2} et al.), which O. omits, while G. M. substitute the single passage *asyâ 'parûpam* (iii.5.7^{3}). As counter-example, showing the limitation to a surd spirant, W. B. give *tiroahniyâ mâ* (vii.3.13: B. omits *mâ*); but G. M. give instead *mahyam imân* (iii.1.9^{6}), and O. *sapta jihvâḥ sapta* (i.5.3^{2}).

---

18. [1] *hâritasya* [2] *mate* [3]*'ghosha ûshmâ dvitvaṁ nâ*[3] *'padyate.* [4]*dârç-....:*[4] *vâiçyo....:* [5]*pushy-....: vâiçv-....*[5] *aghosha iti kim:* [6]*tiro-....* *ûshmagrahaṇam*[7] *pûrvasûtrânapekshârtham*[8]*: atra yady apy ûshmagrahaṇaṁ na kriyata ûshme 'ty etat svaraparatvena* [9] *sambaddham*[10]*: tasmâd ihâ 'pi tatsambandhasyâi 'vâ*[11] *'ghoshavattvaviçeshaḥ*[12] [13] *syât: atas tannivṛttyartham ûshmagrahaṇam*[14] *atra kṛtam: ataḥ sarvâvastha ûshmâ 'tra dvitvanishedhabhâk*[15]. [6]

[1] O. begins *ûshmagrahaṇaṁ pûrvâsûtrânapekshâthaṁ : pûrvasûtre svaraparatvena prathamaparatvena ca saṁbandha iti aghoshagrahaṇaṁ tasyâi 'va viçeshaṇaṁ syât: atas tannivṛtayeshu punar ushmagrahaṇaṁ hâri-* etc. [2] O. ins. *çâkhino.* [(3)] O. *sarvâvasthâ eva ûshmâ 'ghosho nyo na dvivarṇam â.* [(4)] in O. only. [(5)] O. om.; G. M. *asyâ....* [(6)] O. simply *sapta....* [7] W. *çûshmayâg-;* G. M. *-mâg-.* [8] W. B. *pûrvatrân-.* [9] G. M. ins. *ca.* [10] W. *-bandham;* B. *-bandhaḥ.* [11] W. B. *va.* [12] W. *-vatve vi-;* B. *-vatve 'ti vi-;* G. M. *'ghoshatvaviçeshaṇaṁ.* [13] W. B. ins. *na.* [14] G. M. *ûshme 'ti gr-.* [15] W. *nishedhâyât;* B. *nishedhâya,* and adds, out of place, the first part of the comment to the next rule (to *rephaparo,* excl.).

Rules 18–22 are pronounced unapproved under rule 22.

रेफपरश्च हकारः ॥१९॥

19. Nor *h*, when followed by *r*.

The word *ca* in the rule is declared to continue the implication of "according to Hârîta." This individual having in the former rule limited his denial of duplication to a surd spirant, and so left the sonant spirant *h* (? the MSS. say "a surd spirant") liable to be always doubled, it is now taught that *h* with the distinctive mark of a following *r* remains single. The example given, alike in all MSS., is *duduhre ahrayah* (i.5.5[1]); counter-examples are *juhve* (i. e. *juhhve*) *hy agnis tvâ "hvayati* (i.1.12: G. M. end with *agniḥ;* W. B. omit altogether, along with the introductory explanation to the next citation), to show that *h* would be doubled by Hârîta before any other letter than *r;* and *çukraṁ* (i. e. *çukkraṁ*) *te anyat* (iv.1.11[2]: O. omits), to show that any other letter than *h* would be doubled before *r*.

O., though using two of the citations given by the other MSS., has a wholly independent exposition of this rule.

टवर्गश्च तवर्गपरः ॥२०॥

20. Nor a lingual mute, when followed by a dental.

That is to say, in the opinion of Hârîta. Thus, in *vashaṭ te vishṇo* (ii.2.12[4]: O. has *vishaṭ te vikshaṇe*, but it is doubtless only a corrupt reading) and *viḍ draviṇam* (i.8.13[1] et al.), Hârîta would leave the groups *ṭt* and *ḍdr* untouched, while the rules of the treatise would require *ṭṭt* and *ḍḍdr*. The other groups in which he would teach the simpler combination are *ṭtr*, *ḍd*, *ḍdhr*, and *rṭt;* and *ṭs*, *ṭsv* and *rṭs* would fall indirectly under the same exception, since, by v.33, *t* (converted to *ṭh* by xiv.12) must be inserted between *ṭ* and *s: ṭs*, then, would in Hârîta's hands become *ṭṭhs;* in those of the regular adherents of this school, *ṭṭṭhs*. Counter-examples, of obvious application, are *vâk te* (i. e. *vâkk te;* i.3.9[1]: wanting in B. O.), *tat te* (i.3.9[1] et al.: found in W. only, and of no

---

19. [1]*pûrvam ûshmâ 'ghosha ity ukte*[1] *'ghoshoshmaṇo nityaṁ dvitve prâpte* [2]*viçishṭa idânîṁ*[2] *rephaparo hakâraç*[3] *cakârâkṛshṭa-hâritamate dvitvaṁ nâ "padyate. yathâ*[4]*: dud-.... rephapara iti kim:* [5]*juhve.... hakâra iti kim*[5]*: çukraṁ.... rephaḥ paro yasmâd asâu rephaparaḥ.*

(1) G. M. *a.* (2) W. *viçeshṭâdinâm;* B. *viçishṭâçivadanam;* G. M. *viçinashṭi id-.* [3] W. *-re.* [4] G. M. om. (5) W. B. om.

O. substitutes *caçabdo hâritasyâ 'nvâdeçakaḥ : hâritasya çâkhino mate rephaparo hakâro dvivarṇam âpadyate. dud-.... rephapara iti kim: juhve....*

20. *cakâro*[1] *hârîtânvâdeçakaḥ*[2]*:* [3] *ṭavargas tavargaparo na dvitvam âpadyate. yathâ*[4]*:* [5]*vashaṭ....:*[5] *viḍ....* [6]*tavargaḥ paro*

account, since exempt from duplication by xiv.23), *shaṭkapâlaṁ niḥ* (i. e. *shaṭṭk-;* i.8.5[1]: wanting in O.), and *viḍ vâi marutaḥ* (i.e. *viḍḍ vâi;* vi.6.5[3]).

लतवर्गौ यवकारपरौ ॥ २१ ॥

21. Nor *l* nor a dental mute, when followed by *y* or *v*.

Hârîta is this time implied "by vicinage" merely, there being no word in the rule to which his memory can be directly fastened. Examples of *l* before *y* and *v* are *kalyâṇî* (vii.1.6[6]) and *bâilvo yûpo bhavati* (ii.1.8[1]: G. M. omit *bhavati*); of a dental mute in like situation, *kanye 'va tunnâ* (iii.1.11[8]) and *ishe tvâ* (i.1.1 et al.). The accepted usage of the school requires *lly*, *llv*, *nny*, *ttv*, while Hârîta would leave the groups as in the ordinary text.

Combinations of a dental mute with a following *y* or *v* are quite numerous (I have noted about twenty in the Sanhitâ).

परश्च ॥ २२ ॥

22. Nor the following.

This rule completely puzzles the native comment, which has nothing of any value to say about it. Two explanations are suggested, evidently on the barest conjecture only, and it would be hard to say which of them is the more senseless. In the first place, it is said that *paraḥ*, being singular, implies the sound *v* (as being the one last mentioned in the preceding rule); it, namely, of the two affecting causes (*y* and *v*) specified in rule 21, does not suffer duplication: examples are *vibhûdâvne* (iii.5.8 et al.) and *â grâvṇaḥ* (vi.3.2[3]: W. B. omit *â*); and a counter-example, showing the limitation to *v*, is *kalpân juhoti* (v.4.8[5]). And the intent of the rule is to remove a restriction imposed in rule 3 of this chapter—that is to say, to allow the duplication of *l* before a mute, which is there forbidden. In the second place, *paraḥ* is said to be equivalent to *dvitîya*, 'second,' and to signify that, when the

---

yasmâd asâu tavargaparaḥ. ṭavarga[7] *iti kim:* [8]*vâk----:* [9]*tat ----.*[9] *evaṁpara*[6] *iti kim*[8]*:* [10]*shaṭ----:*[10] *viḍ----.*

[1] O. *caçubâo.* [2] O. *-tasyâ 'nv-.* [3] O. ins. *hâritasya çâkhino mate.* [4] G. M. O. om. [(5)] G. M. om. [(6)] O. *tavargapara.* [7] W. *-gapara.* [(8)] B. om. [(9)] G. M. om. [(10)] O. om.

21. *hâritaḥ sâṁnidhyâl labhyate: tanmate latavargâu na khalu yavakâraparâu dvitvam âpnutaḥ.* [1]*yathâ: lakâraḥ:*[1] *kalyâṇî: bâilvo----:* [2]*tavarge 'pi:*[2] *kanye----: ishe----. yavakârâu*[3] *parâu yâbhyâṁ tâu tathoktâu*[4].

[(1)] G. M. om. [(2)] G. M. om. [3] W. B. *-ra.* [4] G. M. *yavakâraparâu.*

My collation of O. gives nothing whatever upon rules 21 and 22 and their comment, and I do not know whether there is a *lacuna* in the MS., or whether the collator has overlooked the passage.

duplication has been once performed, it is not done over again, as otherwise the process would go on *ad infinitum.* And if it be objected that rule 23 sufficiently forbids this repeated duplication, and that this one would therefore be an unnecessary repetition, the answer is made that that is no fault, since the matter in hand is a division of opinions—that is to say, doubtless, that here Hârîta's view only is concerned, and so there is no necessary connection between the two rules.

Fortunately, the commentator is able to add that the present precept, along with its four predecessors, is to be ruled out of account as unapproved, so that what it means is of very little consequence.

सवर्णसवर्गीयपरः ॥ २३ ॥

23. A letter followed by one homogeneous with itself, or one of the same mute-series, is not duplicated.

By *savarṇa*, 'of like color or sound,' we are told, is signified identity of form, not merely correspondence as regards place and organ of production. The difference is, that the latter description would apply to the spirants, in their relation to the series of mutes (ii.44,45), and it is not the usage of this school to exempt the spirants (except χ and φ, rule 15) from duplication, even before a mute with which they are akin. The Ath. Pr. (iii.30) does so exempt them. The epithet *savarṇa*, then, applies only to an identical letter and to the nasal semivowels into which (by v.26,28) *n* and *m* are converted before *y*, *l*, and *v*.

The cited examples of the application of the rule to homogeneous sounds are *âtvakkâya* (vii.5.12²), *attâ havîn̈shi* (ii.6.12²), *pippakâ te çaravyâyâi* (v.5.19: only O. has the last word), *saṁyattâḥ*

---

22. *cakâro hârîtâkarshakaḥ*[1]*: para ity ekavacanena*[2] *vakâro*[3] *gṛhyate: pûrvasûtrasthanimittayoḥ* [4] *so 'pi* [5] *na dvitvam âpadyate. yathâ: vi-....: â.... vakâra iti kim: kalpân̈.... sparça*[6] *evâi 'keshâm âcâryâṇâm* (xiv.3) *ity 'atrâ 'vadhâraṇanirâkaraṇâyâ 'yam*[7] *ârambhaḥ. athavâ*[8]*: taddvitve*[9] *kṛte paro dvitîyaparyâyo*[10] [11]*dvitvavidhir nâ 'sti*[11]*: anavasthâprasan̄gât. nanu savarṇasavargîyapara* (xiv.23) *iti parasûtreṇâ*[12] *'pi punardvitvanishedhaḥ:* [13] [14]*pâunaruktyam mâ bhûd iti*[14]*: matabhedân nâi 'sha*[15] *dosha iti brûmaḥ.*

hârîtamatâd[16] *ûshmâ 'ghosha* (xiv.18) *ityâdisûtrapañcakam*[17] *anishṭam.*

[1] G. M. *-tamatâk-.* [2] W. *eva v-.* [3] W. *sav-*, and puts after *gṛhyate.* [4] G. M. ins. *paraḥ.* [5] G. M. ins. *hâritamate.* [6] G. M. *-çapara.* (7) G. M. *evandhâ- . . . -ṇâyâyâ 'yam.* [8] W. B. *yathâ.* [9] G. M. om. *tad.* [10] G. M. *-âyeṇa.* (11) G. M. *-dhin na prâpnoti.* [12] W. om. *para.* [13] G. M. ins. *tasmât.* (14) W. *-ktyo mâ bhavati*; G. M. *-ktyam âvahati.* [15] W. *va.* [16] G. M. *-mate.* [17] G. M. *ityâdi paraç ce 'tyantaṁ sû-.* O. wanting (see above).

(i.5.1[1] et al.: wanting in W. B.), *yal lohitam* (ii.1.7[2]), and *tvaṁ vâtâir aruṇâiḥ* (i.3.14[1]: only O. has *aruṇâiḥ*). Those which illustrate absence of duplication of a mute before another of the same series are *añkâu nyañkâu* (i.7.7[2]), *prâñcam upa* (v.2.7[3]: O. omits *upa*), *kâṇḍât-kâṇḍât* (iv.2.9[2] et al.), *taṁ te duçcakshâḥ* (iii.2.10[2]), and *ambha stha* (i.5.6[1] et al.). Then the commentator quotes from some unnamed authority a verse prescribing that "when a nasal precedes, a *k* or *g* is inserted before *t* or *dh* respectively," and claims that, in virtue of it, there fall under the rule also such cases as *pañkto yajñah pâñktâḥ* (i.5.2[1] et al.: G. M. O. omit the last word) and *tân brûyâd yuñgdhvam iti* (iii.4.8[2]: O. omits the first two words). From this we should draw the inference that, in forms like those here quoted, the omission of the non-nasal mute (specially prescribed by the Ath. Pr., at ii.20) is the regular and proper reading of the *çâkhâ*, its presence, when found, being regarded as an irregular insertion, or a process forming part of the *varṇakrama*—which is just the opposite of the etymologically correct view. I have not collected all the passages illustrating the point, but the omission is certainly the prevailing, though not exclusive, reading in my manuscript of the Sanhitâ, as also in the Calcutta edition. That the verse quoted is from some treatise dealing specifically with the Tâittirîya text may be inferred (not too confidently) from its making no mention of *th* as requiring the insertion of *k*; it being the fact that no example of *th* in such a situation is to be found in the Sanhitâ.

Finally, as counter-examples, where the two mutes are of different classes, we receive (except in O.) *vâñ ma âsan* (v.5.9[2]: G. M. end with *me*), *shaṇ mâsaḥ* (vi.5.3[4]), *vidathâni manmahe* (iv.7.15[3]), and *dâmnâ 'pâu "mbhan* (ii.4.13: W. B. have *dâmnâ* only): here the combinations are to be made *ñṅm*, *ṇṇm*, *nnm*, and *mmn*. The illustrations are quite one-sided, both for and against the rule, being only groups containing a nasal.

This rule furnishes the most important of all the prescribed

---

23. *savarṇaparaḥ savargîyaparaç ca dvitvaṁ nâ "padyate: savarṇatvaṁ nâma sârûpyam[1] ucyate: na tulyasthânakaraṇatâmâtram: savargîyaḥ samânavargasambandhî. yathâ: atvakkâya: attâ----: pipp----: saṁyattâḥ[2]: yal----: tvaṁ ----. savarṇaparâṇy evamâdîni: savargîyaparâṇy[3] api[4] vadâmaḥ: añkâu----: prâñcam----: kâṇḍât----: taṁ----: ambha----.*

anunâsikapûrvas[5] tu kakâro madhya[6] âgamaḥ:
gakâraç ca takâre[7] ca [8]dhakâra ca[8] yathâkramam.

itivacanâd idaṁ apy udâharaṇam: pañkto----: tân----. [9]evampara iti kim: vâñ----: shaṇ----: vida----: dâmnâ ----.[9]

[1] B. *-pyatvam.* [2] W. B. om. [3] W. *savarṇap-.* [4] W. *eva.* [5] W. *anusvârap-.* [6] W. *-dhyamâ.* [7] O. *-raç.* (8) W. om.; G. M. *yak-.* (9) O. om.

restrictions to the sphere of duplication, as there are somewhat over a hundred consonant groups to which it applies.

नानुत्तम उत्तमपरः ॥ २४ ॥

24. Unless, indeed, it be a non-nasal followed by a nasal.

This is a precept of counter-exception, contravening in part the exceptions established by the foregoing rule. Examples are *yâcñâ* (i.5.7[4]: the only example of this combination which the text affords), *yajñe-yajñe* (iii.1.11[2]: but O. has *yajñena*, vi.5.3[1] et al.), *âtnârah* (v.6.5[3]: also the sole instance), *sa pratnavat* (ii.2.12[1] et al.: in O. only), and *pâpmânam* (i.4.41 et al.): a counter-example is *tam mâ devâḥ* (iii.3.2[2]: wanting in O.).

The cases here denied exemption from duplication are those in which, according to xxi.12, *yama* is introduced between the two mutes. According to the Vâj. Prât. (iv.111), *yama* suspends duplication.

अथैकेषामाचार्याणाम् ॥ २५ ॥

25. Now for the views of certain teachers.

A simple heading for the rules that follow, in force as far as rule 28 inclusive—or, according to the commentator's interpretation of rule 28, through 27 only.

लकारो हशवकारपरः ॥ २६ ॥

26. A *l* is not doubled when followed by *h*, *ç*, or *v*.

The commentator's examples are *malhâ â 'labhanta* (ii.1.2[4]: but B. O. have *-bheta*, which is found in the same division, and G. M. read *-bhate*, which is doubtless a corruption of the same), *çatavalço vi roha* (i.3.5 and vi.3.3[3]: O. omits *vi roha*), and *tato bilvaḥ* (ii.1.8[2]: O. substitutes *bâilvo yûpaḥ*, ii.1.8[1]); his counter-examples (omitted in O.) are *kalmâshî* (v.1.1[4]) and *kalyâṇî* (vii.1.6[6]).

This rule, we are told, determines the usage of the school so far as the combinations *lh* and *lç* are concerned, but not in the case of

---

24. *nakâro 'yam pratiprasavârthaḥ*[1]: [2]*uttamaparo 'nuttamo dvitvam âpadyate. yathâ*[3]: *yâcñâ: yaj-....: âtṇâraḥ:* [4]*sa....:*[4] *pâpmânam.* [5]*anuttama uttamapara iti kim: tam....*[5] *uttamaḥ paro yasmâd asâv*[2] *uttamaparaḥ. savarṇasavargîyapara*[6] (xiv.23) *iti pratishedhaprâptâv ayam ârambhaḥ.*

[1] O. *pravârtha.* (2) G. M. om. [3] O. om. (4) in O. only. (5) O. om.; B. om. *anuttama;* W. om. *uttama.* [6] G. M. om. *para.*

25. *athe 'ty ayam adhikâraḥ: ekeshâm* [1] *mate*[2] *kriyata*[3] *ity etad adhikṛtaṁ veditavyam ita uttaraṁ yad vakshyâmaḥ.*

[1] G. M. ins. *âcâryâṇâm.* [2] G. M. *matam;* O. *maçcitam.* [3] G. M. O. *adhikri-.*

lv. But O. has an inserted passage, so corrupted as to be hardly intelligible, which quotes a verse (easily made such by a little emendation) from some authority unspecified, making a distinction between *lv* as occurring in a circumflexed syllable or otherwise—that is to say, between *bilvàḥ* and *bâilváḥ*.

All the groups here treated of are quite rare, *lç* occurring, I believe, only in *valça* (vii.3.19) and its compounds, and *lh* only in *malha; lv* is sometimes found also as the result of *sandhi* (as at i.5.9[6] : ii.5.1[6]).

The commentator adds, finally, that the next rule also is not approved.

स्पर्शे स्पर्शपरः ॥२७॥

27. Nor a mute that is followed by a mute.

This is a view of certain authorities merely, and unapproved. The examples are *vâg devî* (i.7.10[2]), *apâm ojmânam* (iv.6.6[6]), *âṭnâraḥ* (v.6.5[3]), *sa pratnavat* (ii.2.12[1] et al.), and *ya..ı apnavânaḥ* (i.5.5[1]): O. has only the first two of them.

पदान्तश्च व्यञ्जनपरः प्राकृतः ॥२८॥

28. Nor an original final that is followed by a consonant.

The natural meaning of this rule would appear to be simply that, in the opinion of some authorities, a final mute which is not the product of euphonic alteration is exempted from duplication before any initial consonant whatever (not before a mute only, as in the preceding rule). The commentator, however, manages to extract from it a very different value: namely, that *n* final is not liable to duplication before a semivowel or spirant (i. e. *h*); and he regards

---

26. [1] *ekeshâm* [2] *mate haçavakâraparo lakâro*[3] *dvitvaṁ nâ "padyate. malhâ....: çata-....: tato....* [4]*evampara iti kim: kalmâshî:* [5]*kalyâṇî*[4]. *hakâraç ca çakâraç ca vakâraç ca haçavakârâḥ: te*[6] *pare yasmât sa tathoktaḥ.*

atra[7] *haçapare kâryam ishṭam*[6] *na tu vakârapare:* [8] *nâ 'pi parasûtram*[9] *ishṭam.*

[1] G. M. ins. *sa.* [2] G. M. O. ins. *âcâryâṇâṁ.* [3] G. M. *lavakâro.* [(4)] O. om. [(5)] W. om. [6] O. *ete.* [7] G. M. O. om. [8] O. ins. *lakârasya haçavakârapara iti sûtre sthitaḥ kiṁ kâraṇaṁ nanu vakâra iti prayojanam asti : lakâravakârasya saṁyoga svarito yadi : tadâ saṁyukta eva syâd asaṁyuktas tadanyathâ : iti vacanâm asti tasmât kâraṇât : yadâ lakâravakâraparu iti: tato bilvaḥ.* [9] O. *sûtram.*

27. *ekeshâm* [1] *mate sparçapara sparço*[2] [3]*dvitvaṁ nâ "padyate*[3]. *vâg....: apâm....:* [4]*âṭnâraḥ: sa....: yam....*[4] *sparçaḥ paro yasmâd asâu sparçaparaḥ.*

[1] O. ins. *âcâryâṇâm.* [2] O. puts next after *mate.* [(3)] O. *na dvitvam âpnoti.* [(4)] O. om.

this as the accepted doctrine of the school, and as determining the reading in this *çâkhâ*. How this strange result is arrived at, we have to follow through his lengthy exposition closely enough to discover.

In the first place, *vyañjanapara*, 'followed by a consonant,' is declared to mean 'followed by any other consonant than a mute,' because otherwise, as we have read 'followed by a mute' in the preceding rule, the treatise would be guilty of a needless repetition so far as sequence by a mute is concerned. To this the natural answer would be that the two rules do not come into collision, since they do not occupy the same ground: the former relates to any mute in any situation, the latter only to an unaltered mute at the end of a word; and if the one is declared to have a single pronunciation before a mute only, the other before any consonant whatever, what objection can possibly be taken? Moreover, we are stating here the views of certain authorities, of whom one set might hold rule 27, and the other rule 28: and even if they partly covered one another, there would be nothing wrong about it. Once more, *sparcapara* is claimed to be implied here merely for the purpose of denying it, the commentator's conclusion being that there *is* duplication of *n* before a mute, though not before a semivowel; and that is certainly a very remarkable kind of *anuvṛtti* which should work thus by contraries. Of the last two considerations, the commentator takes no notice (although he has once appealed to the former of them in a somewhat similar case above, under rule 22): the first he states and replies to. It may be objected, he says, that there is a difference of affecting cause laid down in consequence of the difference of the affected letter; the latter is here qualified as final and as original; and the former as being any consonant whatever. Nevertheless, he claims, there would be meaninglessness of the qualification of the affecting cause,

---

28. *vyañjanapara iti sparçavyatiriktavyañjanapara ity arthaḥ: anyathâ sparçânâm api grahaṇe pûrvasûtre 'pi sparça*[1] *ity uktatvât pâunaruktyaṁ syât. nanu nimittiviçeshân*[2] *nimittaviçesho*[3] *'sti: padântatvam prâkṛtatvaṁ ca nimittino*[4] *viçeshâ*[5] *nimittasya tu sarvavyañjanâtmakatvam*[6]*: iti cet: tathâ 'pi sparçabhâge*[7] *nimittaviçeshasya*[8] *vâiyarthyam*[9]*: sparçapara ity* [10]*atra sâmânyenâ 'pi*[10] *nimittaviçeshasya*[11] *vigatatvât*[12]*: tasmâd*[13] *antasthâdaya evâ 'tra vyañjanaçabdeno 'cyante.* [14]*cakâro yady api sparçamâtrâkarshakas tathâ 'pi pâriçeshyân*[14] [15]*nakârasyâ 'nukarshaṇam:*[15] *tathâ hi: antasthâdivyañjanaparatve 'nyasparçânâm*[16] *avikṛtânâm padânte sthitir nâ 'sti: samrâḍ ity atrâ 'stî 'ti cet: mâi 'vam: na sañ sâm iti* [17] *râpara* (xiii.4) *ity atra vâiyarthyât*[18]*: itiçabdo makârasya dvitvasadbhâvam bodhayatî 'ty*[19] *adhyayanânurodhâd upapâditam: tasmân nâi 'sha nishedhavishayaḥ.* [20]*nâ 'pi brahmaṇvantaḥ: nyañ---- ityâdivishayaḥ:*[20] *kutaḥ: iha*

so far as mutes were concerned: the reason he gives is of course a mere quibble, and the point of it is so fine that I am not confident of seeing it rightly: it seems to be, that there is an absence of such qualification in the implied term *sparçapara*. At any rate, the comfortable conclusion is, that only the semivowels etc. are intended by the term "consonant" as employed in the rule. The next step is, to declare that *ca*, 'nor,' although it strictly brings forward 'a mute,' without qualification, yet really amounts, on the principle of exclusion, to an implication of *n* only. Namely, thus: no other consonant remains unchanged at the end of a word before a semivowel or spirant. It may be objected that *m* also does so before *r* (by xiii.4) in such words as *samrâj*: but this is of no account; for, if admitted as a reproach to the interpretation now under treatment, it would convict of superfluousness a part of rule xiii.4: namely, the *iti*, which was shown, in accordance with the received reading of the *çâkhâ*, to teach the duplication of the *m*. We see now why that atrociously forced and groundless construction of the meaning of rule xiii.4 was made; it was needed to bolster up in advance the forced and groundless construction to be put upon the present precept. As the *m*, then, constitutes no ground of exception, so neither do the nasals *ṇ* and *ṅ* in such cases as *brahmaṇvantaḥ* (vi.4.10[1]) and *nyaṅ raçmibhiḥ* (ii.4.10[2]). For why? the qualification *prâkṛta*, 'original,' in the rule involves [as belonging to the letter to which it is applied] the quality of being alterable, since it would otherwise be meaningless; and there is no case to be found where either *ṇ* or *ṅ* is altered bfore a semivowel or spirant. If, then, the term *prâkṛta* is to be allowed its proper force, the implication of any other mute than *n* must be excluded. Here is another most arbitrary act of construction—as if *prâkṛta* meant necessarily '(an alterable mute) *when* it retains its original form,' instead of simply '(a mute) that retains its original form.'

---

prâkṛta iti viçeshaṇaṁ vikṛtasadbhâvaṁ[21] *kalpayati:* [22]*anyathâ svasya*[23] *vâiyarthyât: tac ca vikṛtatvaṁ ṇakârasya*[24] *ṅakârasya*[25] *vâ 'ntasthâdiparatve*[26] *sati kvacid api padânte na dṛçyate: tasmât prâkṛta iti*[22] *prayogasâphalyâya*[27] *nakârasyâi 'vâ 'nukarshaṇaṁ yuktam iti pâriçeshyam.*

kiṁ ca: mâhisheye 'pi nakârasyâi 'vâ 'nukarshaṇaṁ sidanavatkṛtyo[28] *'ktam:* [29]*tatre 'yaṁ sûtrayojanâ*[29]*: ekeshâm* [30] *mate padântaḥ prâkṛto nakâro 'ntasthâdivyañjanaparo*[31] *na dvitvam âpadyate. yathâ: mitro----: om-----: etân----. padânta iti kim: anyâ----: anv----. antasthâdipara iti kim: tân----: imân----. prâkṛta iti kim: tân----:* [32]*vâish-----.*[32] *nanu katham atra*[33] *vikṛtatvam:*

> *rephâd ṛvarṇât*[34] *pûrvaç ca ṭavargâc*[35] *ca paraç ca naḥ*[36]*:*
> *ṭavargasthâna*[37] *ity âhur atatsthâno*[38] *'nya*[39] *ucyate.*

iti vacanâd asti sthânabhede[40] *kṛtaṁ*[41] *vikṛtatvam* [42] *iti brûmaḥ.*

The authority of Mâhisheya (see note to the introductory verses, p. 7) is further appealed to as making the same restriction of implication. His explanation is that, in the view of some teachers, a final unaltered *n* followed by a semivowel or spirant is not doubled. Examples are *mitro janân yâtayati* (iii.4.11[5]: only G. M. have *mitro*), *omanvatî te* (ii.6.9[5]; p. *oman-vatî*), and *etân homân* (i.5.4[4]); in all which we are to understand that the *n* remains single. On the other hand, there is duplication in *anyâ* (i. e. *annyâ*) *yanti* (ii. 5.12[2]) and *anv* (i. e. *annv*) *aha mâsâḥ* (i.7.13[1]), where the *n* is not final; in *tân* (i. e. *tânn*) *kalpayati* (v.3.1[2]) and *imân* (i. e. *imânn*) *bhadrân* (i.6.3[1]), where the *n* is followed by a mute; and also in *tân rakshadhvam* (i.2.7) and *vâishṇavân rakshohaṇaḥ* (i.3.2[2]), where, it is asserted, the *n* does not maintain its original form. Since, however, there is no rule in the Prâtiçâkhya for altering a *n* in this last pair of cases, the commentator quotes (from the same authority, we may conjecture, which has been recently twice appealed to, under rules 23 and 26) a prescription to the effect that *n* when preceding a *r* or an *ṛ*-vowel, or when following a lingual (the MSS. say, a dental) mute, is uttered in the lingual position: thus, he says, in virtue of its change of position, the *n* is phonetically altered. Finally, he makes an alleged citation from the Çikshâ (not found in the version known to us), which teaches that a final *n* preceding *r* exhibits a peculiarity, and is liable to duplication. Such a modification of the utterance of *n* forms no part of the phonetic system of any of the Prâtiçâkhyas.

Thus is brought to an end the tedious subject of duplication, the physical foundation of which is of the obscurest, although the pains with which the Hindu *çâkhinaḥ* have elaborated it, and the earnestness with which they assert their discordant views respecting it, prove that it had for them a real, or what seemed like a real, value.

çikshâ câi 'vaṁ vakshyati:

[43]*rephât pûrvo*[43] *nakâro yaḥ padânte*[44] *yatra*[45] *dṛçyate:*

viçeshaṁ tatra jânîyâd dvitvam ity[46] *abhidhîyate.*

[47] *vyañjanam asmât* [48]*param iti*[48] *vyañjanaparaḥ: prakṛtiḥ*[49] *svabhâvaḥ: tatsambandhî prâkṛtaḥ.*

[1] O. *-çapara.* [2] G. M. *-ttavaçân;* O. *-ttanimittav-.* [3] G. M. *-viçishṭo 'py artho;* O. *nâimittikaviçesho 'py a.* [4] G. M. *-tto.* [5] G. M. O. *-shaḥ.* [6] G. M. *-kam.* [7] G. M. *-çavibh-.* [8] G. M. *-çishṭe 'sya.* [9] O. *-rthye.* [(10)] O. *avyañjanasâmânye;* G. M. om. *api.* [11] G. M. *-syâ;* O. *-sha.* [12] G. M *'pi g-;* O. *pag-.* [13] O. om. [(14)] W. B. *cakâra sparçâksharapâri-;* G. M. *cakârasthânisparçâkarshakaḥ pariçeshyan.* [(15)] B. *takârâkarshaṇaṁ.* [16] G. M. O. *saty any-.* [17] G. M. ins. *tu.* [18] G. M. om. [19] W. om. *iti.* [(20)] W. om. [21] W. *-âve.* [22] G. M. om. [23] B. *svarasya.* [24] W. B. *nak-.* [25] W. *dak-;* B. om. [26] O. *-divyañjanap-.* [27] W. *-sâkal-.* [28] O. *-ddhev-.* [(29)] O. om.; B. G. M. *tatrâi 'vaṁ s-;* G. M. *-tre yo-.* [30] O. ins. *âcâryâṇâm.* [31] W. *-sthâvy-.* [(32)] O. om. [33] W. *a.* [34] W. O. *av-;* B. *v-;* G. M. *rav-.* [35] all the MSS. *tav-.* [36] G. M. *na.* [37] W. B. O. *tav-.* [38] W. O. *ata sth-;* G. M. *asthâne.* [39] G. M. om. [40] O. *-da;* G. M. *-dât.* [41] G. M. om. [42] O. ins. *asti.* [(43)] all but O. *rephap-.* [44] W. G. *-to.* [45] G. M. *yadi.* [46] B. om. [47] O. ins. *cakâro kanasyarçakarshakaḥ.* [(48)] W. *paro.* [49] G. M. O. *-tir iti.*

उदात्तात्परो ऽनुदात्तः स्वरितम् ॥ २९ ॥

29. A grave following an acute becomes circumflex.

The following rule shows that the substantive here to be understood is *svarah*, 'vowel.' All the other Prâtiçâkhyas, in their corresponding rules (R. Pr. iii.9, V. Pr. iv.134, A. Pr. iii.67), state the principle as applying to an *aksharam*, 'syllable.' In his explanation and illustration, however, the commentator is not careful to bear this in mind. He states the sphere of the rule to be all the three kinds of enclitic circumflex, the *prâtihata* (xx.3), *pâdavṛtta* (xx.6), and *tâirovyañjana* (xx.7), although these in part include cases to which only the next rule attributes the circumflexed quality. And his examples are *sá idhânáḥ* (iv.4.4[5]), *áthâ 'bravît* (iii.2.11[3]), *vásvy asi* (i.2.5[1] et al.), *práügam* (iv.4.2[1]), and *táyâ devátayâ* (iv. 2.9[2] et al.): of which only the first and fourth show the circumflex vowel following the acute without an intervening consonant (rule 30). Nor are all the examples unexceptionable in other respects: for though the *i* of *idhânáḥ* and the *a* of *asi* are really *anudâtta*, 'grave,' in the *pada*-text, and so show an actual conversion into circumflex, the other exhibited cases of enclitic circumflex are circumflexed in the *pada*-text as well, and undergo no alteration in consequence of their change to *saṁhitâ*. It is at this that the commentator aims, when he adds that, "there being grave quality in the condition of separation of letters, then, when these are combined together, circumflex quality appears in accordance with the present precept." That is to say, it is the natural unaccented quality of the syllable that is here implied in *anudâtta*, not its being technically grave, and marked as such. This understanding is also needed in order to make good rule 31, where we are not taught that the enclitically circumflexed final of *átha*, for example, becomes grave before an acute or circumflex (as in *átha tvám*, *átha kvâ*), but that the unaccented final *a*, which was made circumflex by rules 29 and 30 after *á*, is exempted from the change when so followed, and remains unaccented.

The enclitic circumflex is written in the recorded Tâittirîya text in the same manner as in the Rik and Atharvan; namely, by the perpendicular stroke above the syllable, the same that is used for the independent circumflex. The method is so familiar to all students of the Veda that it does not need to be illustrated here. Certain specialties of Tâittirîya usage will come up for notice under later rules (xix.3, xxi.10,11).

---

29. *prâtihatapâdavṛttatâirovyañjanavishayam*[1] *etat: udâttât paro 'nudâttaḥ svaritam âpadyate. yathâ: sa----: athâ----: vasvy----: pra-----: tayâ-----. varṇavibhâgâvasthâyâm anudâttatve saty* [2]*eva punas tatsaṁhitâyâm*[2] *eva*[3] *tallakshaṇasvaritatvam*[4] *praügam ityâdâu vijñeyam.*

[1] O. om. *pâdavṛtta*, and ins. *prâvṛtta* before *-vish-*. [(2)] W. *evâ 'dhastât saṁ-*. [3] G. M. O. om. [4] G. M. O. *etallakshaṇât sv-*.

For an exposition of the place and value of the enclitic circumflex in the Hindu accentual system, see the note to Ath. Pr. iii.65. It may doubtless admit of question whether the Hindu phonetists, in noting the syllable naturally grave as being otherwise than grave when immediately preceded by an acute, would not have apprehended it better, and described it more truly, as a middle tone between acute and grave, rather than a combination (i.40) of acute and grave. Arguments drawn from the analogies of the Greek and Latin accentual systems (see F. Misteli, in Kuhn's Zeitschrift, vol. xvii., 1868; also Prof. J. Hadley, in the Proceedings of the Am. Oriental Society for Oct. 1869 [Journal, vol. ix., pp. lxii.–lxiii.]) may press upon us this latter view as the more plausible. But that any one having access to the sources of knowledge upon the subject should dispute the substantial identity in physical character of the Greek circumflex and the Sanskrit independent *svarita*, and should set down the latter as a "middle tone," in the face of all authority and of all sound phonetic theory, savors of inexcusable carelessness or prejudice.

व्यञ्जनान्तर्हितोऽपि ॥ ३० ॥

30. Even when consonants intervene.

For the necessity of this explicit statement, see the note on the preceding rule. The commentator, having already given under the latter several cases in which the affected and the affecting vowel were separated by one or more consonants, has nothing that is new to offer; but he quotes, nevertheless, *tád agne anṛṇó bhavâmi* (iii. 3.8[2]: B. O. omit *bhavâmi*) and *yás tvâ hṛdâ'* (i.4.46[1]): in the first case, *ag-* and *bha-* are circumflexed; in the second, *tvâ*.

नोदात्तस्वरितपरः ॥ ३१ ॥

31. Not, however, when an acute or circumflex follows.

That is to say, the syllable naturally unaccented or grave—but which, coming next after an acute, would usually take, by rule 29, the tone of transition from higher to lower pitch—retains its low or grave tone if immediately followed by an acute, or by a (*nitya* or independent, of course) circumflex, of which the first element is acute: the pitch of voice is governed by the following tone in preference to the preceding, and sinks at once, without perceptible movement of transfer, to the level of *anudâtta*, as a vantage-ground from which to rise to the immediately succeeding high point.

In this rule, as well as that to which it constitutes an exception,

---

30. *vyañjanântarhito*[1] *'py udâttât paro 'nudâttaḥ svaritam*[2] *âpadyate. yathâ*[3]*: tad....: yas....* [4]*ity âdi*[4]. *antarhito vyavahita ity arthaḥ.*

[1] O. *ant-*. [2] B. *-tatvam*. [3] G. M. om. [(4)] O. om.

all authorities are agreed (see note to Ath. Pr. iii.70); although we should not less naturally expect the double attraction, of a high tone on either hand, to exercise at least as much assimilating effect upon the pitch of an intermediate syllable as a preceding high tone alone exerts.

The commentato 's examples are *sá imáṁ lokám* (i.5.9⁴: but G. M. add *ajayan*, which doubtless means *tá imáṁ lokám ajayan*, vii.1.5³), *tásmât tá âdyâ' annadhâ'nât* (vii.1.1⁵: only O. has the first word and the last), *kīrinâ mányamânaḥ* (i.4.46¹), and *tásyâi vy'ṛddham âṇḍám ajâyata* (vi.5.6¹: only G. M. have the last two words): the vowels between acute and acute, or between acute and circumflex, in these examples, are *anudâtta*, and written, as such, with the horizontal stroke beneath.

The three rules here given only apply, in strictness, to a single unaccented syllable following an acute; where there is more than one such, the rules for *pracaya* (xxi.10,11) come into force.

नाग्निवेश्यायनस्य ॥ ३२ ॥

32. Not so, according to Âgniveçyâyana.

The significance of this rule (which is declared unapproved, in the comment to its successor) is more clearly stated by O., in an independent exposition, than by the other four versions of the comment. It is meant to exhibit an opinion contravening the doctrine laid down by its predecessor, and allowing the circumflex accent to stand, even when the following syllable has, or begins with, the high tone. No examples are given, except by O., which has *vóḍhavê* (i.6.2¹ et al.) and *tásya kvà suvargáḥ* (ii.6.5⁵).

G. M. read, in rule and comment, Âgnivâiçyâyana.

सर्वो नेत्येके सर्वो नेत्येके ॥ ३३ ॥

33. Some say not, in all cases.

---

31. *udâttasvaritapara*[1] *udâttât paro 'nudâtto na*[2] *svaritam âpadyate*[3]. *yathâ*[4]: *sa----: tas-----: kīr-----: tasyâi-----. udâttaç ca svaritaç co 'dâttasvaritâu: tâu parâu yasmât sa tatho 'ktaḥ.*

[1] W. *-paro nân;* B. *svaritaparo vâ;* G. M. *udâttapara svaritaparo vâ;* O. do., except *vâ.* [2] G. M. O. put after *svaritam.* [3] B. *âpnoti;* O. *prâpnoti.* [4] G. M. om.

32. *pûrvasûtrapratiprasavârtho*[1] *'yaṁ nakâraḥ: udâttât paro 'nudâttaḥ svaritam*[2] *âgniveçyâyanasya*[3] *mata udâttaparo*[4] *vâ*[5] *svaritaparo vâ* [6] *nâ ''padyata iti na*[7]. *pûrvoktâny evo 'dâharaṇâni.*

[1] B. *-trasya prati-.* [2] G. M. om. [3] G. M. *-yana.* [4] W. B. G. M. *-ttât pa-.* [5] B. *'nudâtta;* G. M. om. [6] B. G. M. ins. *svaritam.* [7] B. om.

O. substitutes *âgniveçyâyanasya çâkhino mate udâttarapara svaritaparo vâ udâttât paro 'nudâtta svaritam âpadyate na pratishedhaḥ. yathâ: vo-----: tas-----.*

According to the majority of MSS. of the comment, the denial of these skeptical people is not limited to the enclitic *svarita*, but extends to the whole accent, in all its seven forms (xx.1–8). Thus, namely; in the *brâhmaṇa* of the Vâjasaneyins (that is to say, the Çatapatha-Brâhmaṇa) there are only two accents, the acute and the grave. But O. has once more a version of its own, stating that the authorities here referred to would not, like Âgniveçyâyana, annul rule 31 simply, but would also deny the rules in general for the enclitic circumflex, as in *sá idhânâḥ* (iv.4.4[5]) and *prapâ'* (? MS. *prathâ*) *asi* (ii.5.12[4]). We cannot well hesitate to prefer the latter interpretation; there has been no question here of the independent circumflex, and a denial of its existence would be altogether out of place and impertinent. Nor is the reference to the Çatapatha-Brâhmaṇa one at all likely to have been intended by the Prâtiçâkhya. And it is not true, except so far as the mode of designating the accents is concerned, that that treatise has no circumflex accent: it writes, to be sure, only the *anudâtta* sign, so that, if the value of this were the same as in the other usual systems of designation, all its syllables would be either grave or acute: and on this foundation, later Hindu systematists have declared them such, and painfully elaborated an exposition of them (see Weber's Ind. Studien, x. 397 ff.).

Rules 32 and 33 are, naturally enough, declared unapproved; but to us it is both interesting and important to find that there were Hindu phonetists in the ancient time who did not admit such an element of utterance as the enclitic circumflex.

CHAPTER XV.

CONTENTS: 1–3. nasalization of vowels, or insertion of *anusvâra*, in cases of the loss or alteration of *n* or *m*; 4–5, the same, in the cases detailed in the next chapter; 6–8, the same, in the case of certain finals; 9, utterance in monotone.

---

33. *na kevalam udâttât paraḥ: kiṁ tu sarva eva saptavidhasvarito nâ 'stî 'ty eke çâkhino manyante. tathâ hi: vâjasaneyibrâhmaṇe*[1] *dvâv eva svarâu: udâttaç câ 'nudâttaç ca.*

ne 'daṁ sûtradvayam[2] *ishṭam.*

O. substitutes *eke çâkhino manyante na kevalânudâttaḥ udâttassaritaparaḥ : pratishidhyati kiṁ tarhi udâttakapûrvakaç ca : sa....: prathâ....* *ne 'daṁ* etc.

iti tribhâshyaratne prâtiçâkhyavivaraṇe caturdaço[3] *'dhyâyaḥ.*

[1] W. *vâjanepibrâ-*; B. *-nehibr-*; G. M. *-neyabr-*. [2] W. *-tram.* [3] G. M. O. *dvitiye praçne dvitiyo.*

नकारस्य रेफोष्मयकारभावाल्लुप्ते च मलोपाच्च पू-
र्वस्वरो ऽनुनासिकः ॥ १ ॥

1. In case of the conversion of *n* into *r*, a spirant, or *y*—also when the *y* is omitted—or in case of the omission of *m*, the preceding vowel becomes nasal.

That this Prâtiçâkhya takes no distinct and consistent ground upon the question whether the so-called *anusvâra* consists in a nasalization of the vowel or in a nasal consonantal element following the vowel, has been already pointed out (note to ii.30); as also, that the present rule is the one where the former view is most unequivocally taken. As the school to which the commentator belongs has adopted the other view, he declares (under rule 2) that the doctrine here laid down is unapproved.

The "conversion of *n* into *r* or a spirant" is, of course, the retention of a historical final *s* after *n* unchanged before *t* (vi.14), or changed to *ç* before *c* (v.20), or to *r* before a vowel (ix.20 etc.); its "conversion into *y*," with the (invariably) consequent "loss of the *y*" (ix.20 etc., x.19), goes back to the same cause. The commentator's illustrative examples are *agnîn̐r apsushadaḥ* (v.6.1²), *sa trîn̐r ekâdaçân̐ iha* (iii.2.11³: found in O. only), *karṇân̐ç câ 'karṇân̐ç ca* (i.8.9³), *trîn̐s tṛcân* (ii.5.10¹), and *mahân̐ indraḥ* (i.4.20 et al.); of which the last is by part of the MSS., rather needlessly quoted twice, once for the conversion of the *n* into *y* (for which it should be written *mahân̐y indraḥ*), and again for the loss of the *y*. For the loss of *m* (by xiii.2), the examples are *pratyushṭan̐ rakshaḥ* (i.1.2¹ et al.) and *san̐çitam me* (iv.1.10³ et al.).

The commentator explains *anunâsika* by *sânunâsika*, as if the word were properly a noun, and needed reduction to adjective form: in this treatise, however, it is always and only an adjective, meaning 'nasal' (see note to ii.30).

नैकेषाम् ॥ २ ॥

2. Some deny this.

---

1. [1]*nakârasya rephabhâvâd ûshmabhâvâd yakârabhâvâc cakârâkṛshṭayakâre lupte ca*[2] *sati* [3]*makâralopâc ca*[3] *pûrvasvaro 'nunâsiko*[1] *bhavati: sânunâsiko bhavatî 'ty arthaḥ.* [4]*yathâ: rephabhâvât*[4]*: agn-....:* [5]*sa....*[5] [6]*atho "shmabhâvât:*[6] *karṇ-....: trîn̐s....* [7]*yakârabhâvâd yathâ*[7]*: mahân̐....* [8]*yakâre lupte yathâ*[9]*: mahân̐....*[8] [10]*atha makâralopât:*[10] *praty-....: san̐-....:* [11]*ity âdi*[11]. *makârasya lopo makâralopaḥ*[12]*: tasmât.*

(1) wanting in B. [2] O. om. (3) W. om. (4) O. om. (5) in O. only. (6) O. om.; G. M. om. *atha.* (7) O. om.; G. M. om. *yathâ.* (8) W. O. om. [9] G. M. om. (10) O. om.; G. M. om. *atha.* (11) O. om. [12] B. *malo-*.

This is a mere introduction to the next rule, which informs us what the doctrine is which these dissidents hold instead. The commentator pronounces it the approved doctrine for this *çâkhâ*.

ततस्त्वनुस्वारः ॥ ३ ॥

3. And claim that, on the contrary, *anusvâra* is inserted after the vowel.

The *anusvâra* here prescribed is called by the commentator an *âgama*, 'increment.' Its insertion is the alternative view to the nasalization of the vowel, and, as is pointed out, is held where that nasalization is denied—of which denial, the *tu*, 'on the contrary,' is the sign in the rule. There is one example given: *sa trîn̐r ekâdaçân̐ iha* (iii.2.11³: W. B. omit *sa*).

The approval of this rule is, of course, involved in that of its predecessor; and the usage of the recorded Tâittirîya text corresponds.

स्रादिषु चैकपद ऊष्मपरः ॥ ४ ॥

4. *Anusvâra* is also inserted in the case of *sra* etc., in a single word, before a spirant.

"Also" (*ca*) in the rule, we are told, brings down the implication of the above specified increment. The *srâdayas*, '*sra* etc.,' are the whole detail, given in the next chapter, of the occurrence of *anusvâra* in the Tâittirîya-Sanhitâ otherwise than as the result of the rules of combination, implied in rules 1–3 of this chapter. The precept, then, is introductory to the detail referred to, and also lays down some general limitations affecting it. The commentator quotes a single case, *çon̐sâ moda ive 'ti* (iii.2.9⁵: it falls under xvi.2); and then gives counter-examples, establishing the restrictions made: *tâsâṁ trîṇi ca* (ii.5.8³) shows that the insertion is made only under the circumstances defined in chapter xvi.; *tam mâ san̐ srja varcasâ* (i.4.45³ et al.: only G. M. have *varcasâ*) and *prastaram â hi sîda* (ii.6.12⁶: found in O. only) show that it is to

---

2. *ekeshâm mate pûrvasûtrokteshu* [1] *sânunâsikyaṁ*[2] *na*[3] *bhavati. uktâny evo 'dâharaṇâni.*

idam [4]*eve 'shṭaṁ*[4] *na tu pûrvam.*

[1] O. ins. *sthâneshu.* [2] G. M. *nâ 'nu-.* [3] W. G. M. O. om. [(4)] O. *eva sûtram ish-.*

3. *tata iti sarvanâmnâ parâmṛshṭât*[1] *svarât*[2] *paro 'nusvâra*[3] *'gamo bhavati. yathâ*[4]*: sa . . . . . parâmṛshṭasvarasyâ*[5] *'nunâsikaṁ*[6] *guṇaṁ tuçabdo nivartayatî*[7] *'ti*[8]*: tasmâd anunâsikapratishedhapaksha*[9] *evâ 'yam anusvârâgamaḥ syât.*

[1] G. M. *-shṭa.* [2] G. M. *-ra.* [3] B. G. M. *-svâr.* [4] G. M. om. [5] O. *-shṭât svarâ.* [6] G. M. *-ka.* [7] O. *-vâray-.* [8] G. M. O. om. *iti.* [9] W. B. *-dhât p-;* G. M. *-dhaḥ vakshyamâṇa.*

be made only in a single word—that is to say, if I understand the meaning, that if *mā sám* and *hi sīda* were single words, they would fall respectively under rules 8 and 13 of the next chapter, and have the increment—; and *māyā māyinām* (iii.1.11⁷) shows that a spirant must follow (*māyinām* otherwise falling under xvi.8). To the specification *ekapade*, 'in a single word,' the commentator adds in his paraphrase the explanation *akhaṇḍapade*, 'in an undivided word;' and then, in his illustration, he treats this as a restriction or limitation, and establishes it by an example, *trishāhasro vāi* (v.6.8³; p. *tri-sāhasraḥ*); rule xvi.25 would otherwise require the increment after *tri.*

नान्तविकारात्पूर्वः ॥ ५ ॥

5. Not before an altered final.

The illustrative example is *bahis te astu bāl iti* (iii.3.10²: G. M. omit the last two words): we have in it a *s* following *hi* in a single undivided word; and hence, by xvi.13, should have to read *bahiṅs*, but for this restriction. The alteration is from *ḥ* to *s*, according to ix.2. As counter-example is given *mā hiṅsīr dvipādam* (iv.2.10¹: G. M. O. omit the last word), a case falling under the rule already referred to.

अप्रग्रहाः समानाक्षराण्यनुनासिकान्येकेषाम् ॥ ६ ॥

6. According to some authorities, the simple vowels, except the *pragrahas*, are nasalized.

This and the remaining rules of the chapter have the aspect of an intrusion, as they interrupt the natural connection of what precedes and what follows, and merely give the view of certain authorities on points which the Prātiçākhyas in general leave untouched. They are brought in here as having to do with nasalized vowels, which are the subject of this chapter and its successor.

With the nasalization thus taught is to be compared that noticed in the Rik Prât. (at i.16, r. 63, lxiv), which teaches that the first

---

4. [1]*āgamānvādeçakaç cakāraḥ: srādishv ekapade 'khaṇḍapada*[2] *ūshmaparo*[1] *'nusvārāgamo bhavati. yathā*[3]*: çoṅsā.... srādishv iti kim: tāsām.... ekapada iti kim: tam....:* [4]*prast-....*[4] *akhaṇḍaviçeshaṇena*[5] *kim: trish-.... ūshmapara iti kim: māyā....*

(1) wanting in B. [2] O. *pada.* [3] G. M. O. om. (4) in O. only. [5] O. *-sheṇa.*

5. *na khalu padāntavikārāt*[1] *pūrvasminn anusvārāgamo bhavati. yathā*[2]*: bahis....: hipujigā* (xvi.13) *iti prāptiḥ. antavikārād iti kim: mā.... antasya vikāro 'ntavikāraḥ: tasmād antavikārāt.*[3]

[1] W. *vik-.* [2] G. M. O. om. [3] G. M. om.

eight vowels (namely *a*, *á*, *i*, *í*, *u*, *ú*, *ṛ*, *ṝ*) are by [some?] teachers declared nasal when they are not *pragṛhya*, and stand as finals before a pause. This is different, first, in including *ṛ* and *ṝ* (which are not *samânâksharâṇi* according to our treatise: compare i.2; but the difference amounts to nothing, as the vowels in question never occur *avasâne*, but only *avagrahe*); and secondly, in limiting the nasalization to finals, before a pause. But it is perf ctly evident that our rule also applies to finals only, and, as we shall see, the commentator resorts to great violence to bring in the implication of "final" in rule 8, below. Again, the specification "in *saṁhitâ* also," in rule 8, and the interpretation of *padam* in rule 7 as signifying *padakâle*, 'in *pada*-text,' sufficiently prove that the present precept does not apply in *saṁhitâ*—that is, that *avasâne*, '*in pausâ*,' is implied here. And the absence of statement or *anuvṛtti* of these two essential implications is strong additional evidence that the rules are interpolated.

By most of the MSS., only one example is given, namely *kulâyinî vasumatî* (iv.3.4[1]), which, if our understanding, as above explained, is correct, is to be read, in *pada*-text, *kulâyinîň : vasumatîň*. O. adds *aminanta evâiḥ* (iii.1.11[5]), one of the cases of suspended combination falling under x.13, and (by R. Pr. ii.31,32) in the Rig-Veda requiring nasalization of the uncombined final: its citation seems to indicate that O. would not limit the operation of the rule to the *pada*-text. To show that the nasalization does not take place in uncombinable vowels, or *pragrahas*, are quoted, in *pada*-form, *amî iti* (iii.3.7[1] et al.) and *tanû iti* (ii.2.7[5]: omitted in O.). To illustrate the limitation to simple vowels, we find in most MSS. *so evâi 'shâi 'tasya* (ii.2.9[7]); but O. gives instead *agnaye 'nîkavate* (i.8.4[1] et al.), *'vishṇav e 'hî 'dam* (ii.4.12[3]), and *vâyav ishṭaye* (ii.2.12[8]).

The commentator, as he has done repeatedly before (under i.49, ii.7, v.2), notices the apposition in the rule of *apragrahâḥ* and *samânâksharâṇi*, two words of different gender. He signifies, further, under the next rule, that both that and this are unapproved.

पदं च प्लुतं शाङ्खायनकाण्डमायनयोः ॥ ७ ॥

7. As is also, according to Çânkhâyana and Kâṇḍamâyana, a protracted *pada*.

By *pada* is here signified, according to the commentator, a word

---

6. [1] *yâni samânâksharâṇy apragrahasaṁjñâni tâny [2]ekeshâm mate bhavanty[2] anunâsikâni[3]. [4] kul-.... apragrahâ iti kim: amî iti: [5]tanû iti.[5] samânâksharâṇî 'ti kim: [6]so.... pragrahâksharaçabdayor niyataliṅgatayâ[7] parasparânvayo ghaṭate. na pragrahâ apragrahâḥ[6].*

[1] O. ins. *ekeshâm âcâryâṇâm mate.* [(2)] O. om. [3] O. *-kaguṇâni paṭashaṅte.* [4] O. ins. *am-.....* [(5)] O. om. [(6)] O. *agn-....: vish-....: vây-.....* [7] W. *niyamal-.*

in the *pada*-text; and the interpretation, as was remarked above, is fully supported by the specification of *saṁhitâ* in the next rule.

As examples of nasalized protracted vowels, are given *tvî3 ity abravît* (ii.4.12[6]) and *astu hî3 ity abrûtâm* (vii.1.6[1]), both in *saṁhitâ*-form, although it is again expressly pointed out that the nasalization is not made in *saṁhitâ:* the two worthies referred to would read *tvîñ3:* and *hîñ3.* It is added that *ca*, 'also,' in this rule effects its connection with what is prescribed in the preceding one—or, as O., in more customary phrase, expresses it, brings forward by implication the preceding rule.

Some, we are further informed, restrict the application of the precept to words which contain a single vowel protracted, and would not regard it as authorizing nasalization in *na chinattî3 iti* (i.7.2[1,4]) or *na vicityâ3 iti* (vi.1.9[1]: G. M. omit *iti*).

The rule is declared to be of no binding force.

अकारस्तु संहितायामपि ॥ ८ ॥

8. An *a*, however, is nasalized in *saṁhitâ* also.

The commentator's explanation is that nasality and protraction are here implied (from the preceding rule) by vicinage; and that *tu*, 'however,' is intended to annul the implication that only the opinion of the two authorities specified in rule 7 is reported. And though the comprehensive statement "an *a*" is made in the rule, nevertheless, in virtue of rule i.58, "continued implication is of that which is last (or final)," the "also" (*api*) really brings down only a final *a* as suffering a prescribed effect by the attribution of nasal quality. The sense, then, is that a protracted final *a* is nasalized, both in *saṁhitâ* and elsewhere. Examples are *suçlokâñ3 sumañgalâñ3* (i.8.16[2]), *upahûtâñ3* (ii.6.7[3]), *yaço mamâñ3* (vii.4.20); these are, in fact, all the cases of protraction of simple final *a* which the text contains; and the edition (so far as it goes) and my MS. nasalize the *â*, as required by the interpretation of the rule here given. The cases are much more numerous in which a final *aḥ* exhibits *â3* as the ultimate result of protraction, the *ḥ* being lost before a following vowel or sonant consonant: namely, at i.5.9[6]: v.5.1[3],3[2] twice: vi.1.9[1] twice; 3.8[1]; 4.3[4]; 6.2[3]; and in one place, vi.5.8[4], the same final *â3* comes from a protracted *e:* the question might possibly arise whether these do not also fall under

---

7. *yat*[1] *plutavat padaṁ*[2] [3]*tuc ca*[3] *padakâle* [4]*çâñkhâyanakâṇḍamâyanayor mate*[4] *'nunâsikam bhavati. yathâ*[5]*: tvî3....: astu ..... padam iti kim: saṁhitâyâm mâ bhût. cakâraḥ*[6] *pûrvasûtroktavidheyasamuccayaṁ*[7] *karoti*[8]*. apara âhuḥ:* [9]*plutâikasvaram padam iti: anyam mâ bhût:*[9] *na....: na....*

ne 'daṁ sûtradvayam[10] *ishṭam.*

[1] W. *yatra.* [2] O. om. [(3)] W. *tatra.* [(4)] O. puts after *bhavati.* [5] G. M. om. [6] G. M. O. *caçabdaḥ.* [7] O. *-vidhim.* [8] O. *anvâdiçati.* [(9)] O. *plutevarṇapadam iti 'ha mâ bhût.* [10] W. *sûtram.*

the rule, but it would have to be answered in the negative (see the counter-examples below); and the text reads accordingly. The manuscripts of the commentary give as found "in another *çâkhâ*," one example, read *brahmâ3n* in W. B. (O. is wanting), and *yadghrâ* in G. M.: I do not quite know what to make of this, as there se ms to be no call for quoting from another text examples of wha is capable of being fully illustrated from the received Veda of the school; *brahmâ3n* is found at i.8.16^{1} twice, ^{2} twice, but would be a counter-example to this rule, its *a* not being final; it is, in fact, of the same character with the first of the counter-examples given. These are *satyarâjâ3n* (i.8.16^{2}), *agnâ3 ity âha* (vi.5.8^{4}: W. has dropped out *agnâ3*), and *vicityaḥ somâ3 na vicityâ3 iti* (vi.1.9^{1}: O. has only this).

Finally, the commentator remarks that Çânkhâyana and Kâṇḍamâyana also accept this principle. He may well say this, for the natural interpretation of the rule is to make it represent simply the view of those authorities; and the action of the comment, in cutting it loose from its predecessors, and declaring it alone to express the approved doctrine of the treatise, is in a high degree forced and arbitrary. It was noticed under i.58 what an unjustifiable act of violent interpretation was there committed, by way of preparation for this one. The implication of "final" is not needed in rule 8 any more than in rules 6 and 7, and is clearly enough made in them all; whence it comes, it would be the business of those who put the passage in to tell, if they could.

The Ath. Prât. gives (at i.105) an enumeration of the protracted vowels occurring in the text to which it relates. This our treatise omits to do, and it may be well to repair the omission in this place. A final *a* is protracted to *âñ3* at i.8.16^{2} twice: ii.6.7^{3}: vii.4.20: ——*aḥ* to *â3ḥ* at i.4.27: v.5.1^{3}; and to *â3* (the *ḥ* being lost) at i.5.9^{6}: v.5.1^{3},3^{2} twice: vi.1.9^{1} twice; 3.8^{1}; 4.3^{4}; 6.2^{3}:——*an* to *â3n* at i.8.16^{1} twice, 16^{2} thrice: ii.6.5^{6}:——*am* to *â3m* at vi.1.4^{5}; 5.9^{1}: vii.1.7^{4}; 5.7^{1} twice:——*i* to *î3* at i.7.2^{1,4}: ii.4.12^{6}: vi.5.9^{1}: vii.1.6^{1},7^{4}: ——*iḥ* to *î3ḥ* or *î3r* at i.5.9^{6}: vi.3.10^{1}:——*in* to *î3n* at vii.4.20 twice:——*uḥ* to *û3r* at vi.3.8^{1}:——*e* to *â3i* at i.4.27: vi.1.4^{5}; and

---

8. *sâṁnidhyâd anunâsikaplutâu*[1] *gṛhyete: tuçabdaḥ prakṛtâcâryamatanivartakaḥ*[2]*: ata*[3] *eva*[4] *saṁhitâyâm asaṁhitâyâṁ*[5] *câ 'kâraḥ padântaḥ pluto 'nunâsiko bhavati: yady apy akâra iti*[6] *sâmânyeno 'ktaḥ: tathâ 'py anvâdeço 'ntyasya* (i.58) *iti vacanâd apiçabdo 'nunâsikadharmatayâ nimittinam padântam evâ 'kâram anvâdiçati. yathâ*[7]*: suçl-....: upa-....:* [8]*yaço....: brahmâ3n*[9] *ity anyasyâṁ*[10] *çâkhâyâm*[8]. *apiçabdaḥ kimarthaḥ:* [11]*saty-....: agn-....:*[11] *vicityaḥ.....* *çânkhâyanakâṇḍamâyanayor apy ayaṁ vidhir* [12]*akâre plute sammataḥ*[12].

[1] G. M. *-plute.* [2] O. *pûrvâcâry-.* [3] W. *eta;* M. *tata.* [4] O. om. [5] W. O. om. [6] O. om. [7] B. O. om. (8) O. om. [9] G. M. *yadghrâ.* [10] G. M. *asya.* (11) O. om (12) G. M. *-raplutas sammataṁ.*

to *â* (see i.4) at vi.5.8[4]:——*âu* to *â3v* at vi.6.2[3]. The protracted syllable has always the acute accent.

सर्वमेकयमं पूर्वेषाꣳ सर्वमेकयमं पूर्वेषाम् ॥ ९ ॥

9. According to the former ones, all is of one pitch.

The comment is completely at a loss as to how this rule is to be understood, and gives three more or less discordant interpretations of it, the first of which we are probably to regard as the preferred one, if there be a preference. "All" means 'every kind of articulate sound;' "of one pitch" is equivalent to *ekaçruti*, *yama* denoting the tone of an acute syllable; "the former ones" are 'the sacrificers;' the meaning is, then, that in the sacrificial usage of the sacrificers everything is uttered in acute monotone. O. has an exposition of its own, which is in great part too corrupt to be read without considerable emendation, and which conducts to the same conclusion: it quotes, *apropos* of *pûrve*, a *pada* of a *trishṭubh* verse from some sacred text, "the former ones spoke those words to the former ones."

The second interpretation differs from the first only in declaring *pûrve*, 'the former ones,' to designate certain *çâkhinaḥ*, or 'holders of a Vedic text.'

The third is of quite another character; it makes *yama* to be equivalent to *svara* in the sense of 'vowel,' and explains 'every monosyllable is nasalized'—the intent being to annul the restriction to simple vowels only (as made in rule 6). Who the *pûrve* are, is not told us this time.

The commentator consoles himself at the end by declaring the rule not approved. We may fairly extend the same condemnation

---

9. [1]*sarvaṁ*[2] *varṇajâtam*[3] *ekayamam ekaçrutî 'ti pûrveshâm*[4] *matam. yamo nâma svara*[5] *udâtta ity arthaḥ: pûrve nâma yâjñikâḥ*[6]*: teshâṁ yajñakarmaṇi sarvam*[7] *ekaçruti*[8] *bhavati.*[1]

anye manyante[9]*: pûrve nâma kecic châkhinaḥ: teshâṁ sarvam*[10] [11]*ekaçrutî 'ti*[11].

athâ[12] *'pare kathayanti*[13]*: sarvam ekasvaram anunâsikam bhavatî 'ti*[14]*:* [15]*samânâksharamâtrâpekshâm adhikshepturn*[15].

ne 'daṁ sûtram ishṭam.

iti tribhâshyaratne prâtiçâkhyavivaraṇe pañcadaço[16] *'dhyâyaḥ.*

(1) O. substitutes *sarvam iti lakshyaṁ lakshaṇavishayaṁ gṛhṇâti : ekayam ekaçrutiḥ : yamaçrutisvara ity athântarâ pûrveshâ pûrvâi nâma yâjñikâ pûrve pûrvebhyo vaca etad ucur iti darçanât : yâjñikânâṁ yajñakarmaṇi sarvam ekaçrutir bhavati.* [2] W. B. *sarva.* [3] B. *varṇam ajñâtam*; G. M. *-tayamam.* [4] W. *sarv-.* [5] G. M. put after *udâtta.* [6] W. *-ñiyâḥ.* [7] W. puts after *bhavati.* [8] B. *-tir.* [9] O. *âhuḥ.* [10] O. om. (11) W. *-çrutâni*; O. *-çrutir bhavati.* [12] G. M. om. *atha.* [13] O. *vyâcakshatè.* [14] O. om. *iti.* [15] O. *sarvam iti samânâksharâṇâm apekshâ grahavyudâsa sarvaṁ tathâ vidhiyate*; W. *-ramatrâpekshâm apikshiptaṁ*; B. *-ksham adh-*; G. M. *-mâtrapaksham âksheptum.* [16] G. M. O. *dvitiyapraçne tṛtîyo.*

to his treatment of it, and conjecture that, if he could only have told us what it meant, we might have found in it something to approve. We are tempted to seek in it some statement as to the accent of the protracted syllable, or *pada;* and, if it were allowed to amend *pûrveshâm* to *ekeshâm*, we might translate, 'some hold that the whole word in which protraction occurs is to be uttered in the same tone'—only then, to be sure, we should look for a statement of the usage actually followed in the text.

CHAPTER XVI.

CONTENTS: 1–31, detail of the cases of occurrence, in the Sanhitâ, of *ṅ* in the interior of a word, before a spirant.

अथ सकारपराः ॥ १ ॥

1. Now for cases in which *s* follows.

A simple heading, of force through a considerable part of the chapter (i. e. through rule 13). The essential item of the precept laid down was given above, in xv.4, which directed that in all the cases to be specified in this chapter is to be assumed the presence of *anusvâra* following a vowel and followed by a spirant. Words in which that spirant is *s* form by far the most numerous class, and until rule 14 they alone are treated.

The Rik Pr. is the only one of the other treatises which offers anything at all analogous with this enumeration; it (at xiii.7–10) gives rules for the occurrence of *anusvâra* after long vowels only.

स्रशोह्पाश पदादयः स्वरपरे ॥ २ ॥

2. *Sra*, *ço*, *ha*, *pâ*, and *ça*, at the beginning of a *pada*, take *anusvâra* before a *s* that is followed by a vowel.

The commentator cites examples, as follows. For *sra*, *visrañsayed amehenâ 'dhvaryuḥ* (vi.2.9[4],10[7]: G. M. O. have only the first word); we have other cases at ii.5.7[2]: v.1.6[1]: vii.3.10[3], all from the same root, *sras.*; For *ço*, *çoñsâ moda ive 'ti* (iii.2.9[5]: G. M. omit the last word, O. the last two); I have noted no other case: as counter-example, to show that only *o* after *ç* takes the increment, is given *âçâsânâ sâumanasam* (i.1.10[1]: O. alone has the latter

---

1. *athe 'ty ayam adhikâraḥ: itâ uttare grahaṇaviçeshâḥ*[1] *sakâraparâ*[2] *ity etad adhikṛtaṁ veditavyam. sakâraḥ paro 'yebhyas te sakâraparâḥ*[3].

[1] B. *-shoḥ.* [2] B. *-para.* (3) G. M. *yasmât sa tathoktaḥ* (and *-paraḥ* in the rule).

word). For *ha*, *hañsaḥ çucishad* (i.8.15²: iv.2.1⁵); various other cases of *hañsa* are found in the text, and *hañsi:* that *hâ* is not treated in the same way is shown by *prajâ mâ mâ hâsît* (v.6.8¹: O. omits). For *pâ*, *pâñsura irâvatî* (i.2.13²); other cases are *pâñsûn* and *pâñsavyâya*, at ii.6.10² and iv.5.9¹ respectively: that *pa* would not have been correct is shown by *âhataṁ gabhe pasaḥ* (vii.4.19³: O. omits *âhataṁ*); *pâsi*, which would seem to fall under the rule, is excepted by rule 17, below. For *ça*, *yad âsînaḥ çañsati tasmât* (iii.2.9⁷: W. B. G. M. omit *tasmât*, thus allowing the citation to be found also at iii.2.9⁶); cases of this combination, all of them coming from the root *çañs*, are not infrequent in the Sanhitâ. As general counter-examples, we have, to establish the necessity of the restriction "at the beginning of a *pada*," *agnir ukthena vâhasâ* (i.5.11¹), *somam pipâset* (ii.1.10¹), and *dahâ* "*çasaḥ* (i.2.14⁶: O. omits); while *tasmât sa visrasyaḥ* (vi.2.9⁴,10⁷: only O. has the first two words), *hastayoḥ* (iv.1.5³ et al.: G. M. O. omit), and *kaviçastâḥ* (ii.6.12⁶: all the MSS. have *-çastaḥ*, which I have not found in the text, but probably by my own fault) do the same service for the specification "when a vowel follows."

The commentator goes on to say that some authorities accept *hi* as a part of this rule: which is not to be approved, since "at the beginning of a word" is here implied, and so *ahiñsâyâi* (v.2.8⁷) would be left without the increment. And if it be pleaded that *hiñsîḥ parame* (iv.2.10¹⁻² et al.) should be an example here, the reply is made, that the *anusvâra* is assured to it by rule 13, below, where there is no restriction to the beginning of a word; and that to repeat here the specification of *hi* would be useless. The only criticism to be offered upon this is that the objection has too little reason to be really worthy of notice.

---

2. *sra: ço: ha: pâ: ça: ity ete grahaṇaviçeshâḥ*[1] *padâdayaḥ sakâraparâs tasmint sakâre svarapare saty anusvârâgamam*[2] *bhajante*[3]. *yathâ*[4]*: vi-....: çoñsâ-....: okâreṇa kim: âçâ-....: hañsaḥ-....:* [5]*hrasva iti kim: prajâ-....:*[5] *pâñsura-....: dîrghena*[6] *kim: âh-....: yad-.... padâdaya iti kim: agnir-....: somam-....:* [7]*dahâ-....*[7]. *svarapara iti kim: tasmât-....:* [8]*has-....:*[8] *kav-.....*

kecid atra sûtre [9]*higrahaṇam*[10] *aṅgîkurvate*[11]*: tad anupapannam padâdaya iti niyamât: ahiñsâyâ ity atrâ 'nusvârâbhâvaprasaṅgât*[12]. *nanu hiñsîḥ.... ity etad atro 'dâharaṇam iti cet: mâi 'vam:* [13]*hipujigâ* (xvi.13) *ity atra niyamâbhâvât padâdâv apadâdâu ca*[9] *higrahaṇasya kâryasiddheḥ punar atra grahaṇaṁ vyartham.*[13]

svaraḥ paro yasmâd asâu svaraparaḥ: tasmin.

[1] G. M. *-ṇaparâḥ viç-*. [2] O. *-ma.* [3] O. *syât.* [4] G. M. O. om. (5) O. om.; G. M. *hrasvena kim* etc. [6] O. *-ghe.* (7) O. om. (8) G. M. O. om. (9) W. om. [10] G. M. *him.* [11] G. M. *aṅgiṁk-* [12] G. M. *-raḅhâ-*; O. *-râbodhapra-*. (13) B. om.

विकृते ऽपि ॥ ३ ॥

3. Even when the vowel is altered.

That is to say, even when the vowel that is by the last rule required to follow the *s* has undergone euphonic alteration, so as to become a consonant. A single example is cited, *apahañsy agne* (iv.7.13[1]; p. *apa-hañsi*); if the text contains any others, they have escaped my notice.

रापूर्वश्च ॥ ४ ॥

4. As also, when they are preceded by *ra*.

This rule is made for the purpose of establishing a single additional case under the general rule given above (xvi.2), namely, the word *nârâçañsíbhyaḥ* (vii.5.11[2]); the case being one, as the comment points out, where the *ça* is not at the beginning of a *pada*. The *ca*, 'also,' brings down only *ça;* and we are assured that this is the reason why *ça* was mentioned last in rule 2, even at the cost of a violation of the natural order of the vowels. Of this point we need not make much, since the rule contains other and unexplained violations of alphabetic order.

शंस्तानन्तोदात्ते ॥ ५ ॥

5. Also in *çañstâ*, except when it is accented on the final syllable.

Here is another single case, falling under rule 2 by the suspension of one of the restrictions laid down in that rule—namely, that the *s* be followed by a vowel. The passage is *utá çáñstâ súvipraḥ* (iv.6.8[2]: O. omits *suvipraḥ*). The restriction as to accent

---

3. *apiçabdaḥ svarânvâdeçakaḥ*[1]*: sakârât pare tasmint svare vikṛtam âpanne 'pi vyañjanatâm upagate 'pi syâd*[2] *anusvâravidhiḥ*[3]*. yathâ: apa-* - - - - -

[1] B. *sakârân-.* [2] W. and O.(?) *svârad.* [3] *lacuna* in O., from (*anusvâra-*) *vidhiḥ* to *svara* under the next rule.

4. [1]*caçabdaḥ srâdishu*[1] *çakâram anvâdiçati*[2]*: etadartham eva svaravyatyaye*[3] *'pi çakâragrahaṇaṁ tatrâ 'nte kṛtam. râ: ity evampûrvaḥ çakâraḥ sakâraparo 'nusvârâgamam bhajate. yathâ*[4]*: nâr-* - - - - - *apadâdyartho*[5] *'yam ârambhaḥ.*

(1) W. *çabdasyâdishu;* B. *sacaçabdâdishu.* [2] W. B. ins. *cakâraḥ.* [3] G. M. *vyaktaye;* O. begins again with *vyatyaye.* [4] G. M. O. om. [5] W. O. *apadârtho.*

5. *çañstâ: ity etasmin*[1] *grahaṇe 'nantodâtte*[2] *sakârapare bhavaty*[3] *anusvârâgamaḥ. uta* - - - - - *anantodâtta*[4] *iti kim: açv-* - - - - - *sraçoha* (xvi.2) *iti prâptâu satyâṁ*[5] *sakârasya*[6] *svaraparatvâ-*

is intended to exclude *áçvasyá viçastá'* (iv.6.9[3]: O. adds *dvá yaṁ-*).

अशंसन् ॥ ६ ॥

6. Also in *açan̆san.*

Yet another case belonging with those disposed of by rule 2, but requiring special treatment because the *ça* in it does not stand "at the beginning of a *pada.*" The passage is *abhi vy açan̆san* (vi.6.11[5]).

O., in an added paragraph, brings forward the objection that, in virtue of rule i.52 (which makes the citation of any word include also the same word with *a* prefixed), *açan̆san* has its *n̆* already assured by rule 2; but refutes it by pointing out that the principle appealed to has to do only with a *pada* or word, not with a mere fragment of one, like *ça* (compare rule 10, below). It adds that "another reading is *çan̆sán.*"

न शसनं विशसनेन ॥ ७ ॥

7. But not in *çasanam* and *viçasanena.*

These are exceptions, the only ones the Sanhitâ affords, under rule 2. The passages are *çasanaṁ vájy arvá* (iv.6.7[5]: O. ends with *vájî*) and *çuno viçasanena* (v.7.23).

T. and O. have the simple *pada çasanena*, instead of *viçasanena* (p. *vi-çasanena*) in the rule, and O. reads the same in its comment. This is doubtless an emendation, and makes a reading more strictly in accordance with the approved usage of the treatise. The comment has (especially in the fourth chapter) explained away many a like inaccuracy by the allegation of a phrase "in another *çákhá:*" and we might expect to find added here *ví 'ti kim: áçan̆sanene 'ti çákhántare.*

---

bháve 'pi ná 'yaṁ vidhir nishidhyatám [7] *iti grahaṇam*[8]. *anta*[9] *udátto yasya tad antodáttam:* [10]*ná 'ntodáttam*[10] *anantodáttam: tasmin.*[11]

[1] O. *asmin.* [2] W. B. O. *antod-.* [3] O. *syád.* [4] W. *antod-.* [5] G. M. om. [6] W. B. *çak-.* [7] G. M. ins. *eva.* [8] B. *padagr-.* [9] W. O. *ante.* [(10)] O. om. [11] O. adds *apadádyartho . . . . ity anetanái* (which belongs at the end of the comment on rule 6).

6. *açan̆sann ity asmin grahaṇe syád anusváráqamaḥ. abhi* ---- [1]*apadádyartho 'yam árambhaḥ*[1].

[1] O. puts at end of comment on rule 5, and adds, partly there and partly here (a little amended), *kimartham idam. sraçohapáça* (xvi.2) *ity anenái 'va tatsiddháu: apy akárádi* (i.52) *'ti vacanát: mái 'vam: apy akaradi 'ti vacanaṁ padasya padávayavaḥ çaçabdaḥ: çan̆sánn iti páṭhántaram.*

7. *çasanam: viçasanena*[1]*: ity etayor grahaṇayor*[2] *anusvárágamo na syát. ças-*----*: çuno*---- *sraçoha* (xvi.2) *iti práptiḥ.*

[1] O. *ças-*, as also (with T.) in the rule itself. [2] O. om.

मा पदादिरनुदात्तः ॥ ८ ॥

8. *Mâ* takes *anusvâra* when beginning a *pada* and unaccented.

All the implications of rule 2 are here cut off (as is distinctly enough intimated by the express repetition of one of them, *padâdi*), and hence it is to be understood that the increment takes place before a *s* whether this be or be not followed by a vowel. The examples are *áhar mâñséna* (v.7.20) and *mâñspácanyâḥ* (iv.6.9[1]). The restriction to the beginning of a *pada* is established by quoting *sílikamadhyamâsaḥ* (iv.6.7[4]); that as to the accent, by *mấ saṁ dîkshitâḥ syât* (v.6.7[3]: only O. has *syât*).

So far as I have discovered, this rule applies only to forms and combinations of *mâñsa*, which are not infrequent in the Sanhitâ. The four following rules give it certain extensions and limitations.

पुमीपूर्वश्च नित्यम् ॥ ९ ॥

9. As also when preceded by *pu* or *mî*, under all circumstances.

The closing specification of the rule amounts to a removal of the restriction as to accent, imposed in rule 8—that as to initial position being virtually removed by the prescribed prefixion of *pu* or *mî*. The examples quoted are *ut pumâñsañ haranti* (vi.5.10[3]: O. omits *haranti*, and B. runs the two citations together, having dropped out a part of each) and *mîmâñsante kârye* (vi.2.6[4]). We have *pumâñsam* again at iv.6.6[5], and other forms of *mîmâñs* at vi.2.6[4] and vii.5.7[1]: I have noted no other words as falling under the rule.

सकायपरश्च ॥ १० ॥

10. And when followed by *sakâya*.

The *ca*, 'and,' we are told, here brings down *mâ;* and G. M. add that the intent of the rule is to establish an exception under

---

8. *mâ: ity evaṁ*[1] *varṇaḥ padâdir anudâttaḥ sakâraparo 'nusvârâgamam bhajate. atra niyamâbhâvât sakârasya svaraparatvâbhâve 'pi nimittatvam bhavaty eva. yathâ*[2]*: ahar----: mâñs-----. padâdir iti kim: sili-----. anudâtta iti kim: mâsaṁ -----*

[1] G. M. O. *ayaṁ.* [2] O. om.

9. *caçabdo me 'ti jñâpayati: pu: mî: ity evampûrvo me 'ti*[1] *varṇaḥ sakâraparo nityam anusvârâgamam bhajate. ut-----: mîm-----. anudâttatvanivartako*[2] *nityaçabdaḥ.*

[1] G. M. O. ins. *ayaṁ.* [2] O. *-niyamavyâvar-.*

rule 8—that is to say, to bring under that rule a word which would otherwise be excluded in virtue of the requisition "when beginning a *pada.*" The case is similar to that about which O. raises a question under rule 6. The passage is *amâñsakâya svâhâ* (vii.5.12²).

नावग्रहपूर्वः ॥ ११ ॥

11. But not when preceded by a former member of a compound.

Or, 'by a pause of division (between the two members of a compound),' taking *avagraha* in its more original sense. W. B. O. define the rule as establishing exceptions under rule 8; G. M., which have taken in this notification (less correctly) as part of the preceding comment, say simply that *mâ* is to be understood as implied here by vicinage. The examples given are *pûrṇámâse vâ'i* (ii.5.5⁴: O. omits *vâi*) and *ardhamâsé devâ'ḥ* (ii.5.6⁶ twice). The words would satisfy all the conditions of rule 8, the separated element *-mâse* or *-mâsé* being itself (by i.48) a *pada.* Since *mâñsa* nowhere appears as the latter member of a compound, this rule exempts from the increment of *anusvâra* all the cases in which forms of *mâs* or *mâsa* are found in such a situation; others are the subject of the next following precept.

मासिमासुमासोमासामिति च ॥ १२ ॥

12. Nor in *mâsi, mâsu, mâsaḥ,* or *mâsâm.*

These are words which, without special exception, would fall under rule 8. The examples for the last three are *daçásu masû' 'ttíshṭhan* (vii.5.2²), *shấn mâsó dákshiṇena* (vi.5.3⁴: only O. has the last word), and *mâsâ'm prátishṭhityâi* (vii.5.1⁶): we have *mâsấḥ* also at vii.5.7¹, and *mâsâ'm* at v.7.18. The first, *mâsi,* raises a difficulty. Some, the commentator says, cite in illustration of it *prathamé mâsí pṛshṭhâ'ni* (vii.5.3¹: O. omits the last word); but this is wrong; for the exemption of *mâsi* in that passage is assured by rule 17, below: we are to assume, then, the occurrence in another text of some word of more than two syllables beginning

---

10. *caçabdo me 'ti jñâpayati: me 'ty evaṁ*¹ *varṇaḥ sakâyaparo*² *'nusvârâgamam*³ *bhajate. am-.....* ⁴

¹ B. G. M. O. *ayaṁ.* ² W. B. *sakârap-.* ³ G. M. *nityam anu-.* ⁴ G. M. add *mâ padâdir anudâtta* (xvi.8) *ity asyâ 'yam apavâdaḥ.*

11. *'mâ padâdir anudâtta* (xvi.8) *ity asyâ 'yam apavâdaḥ:*¹ *avagrahapûrvo me 'ty evaṁ*² *varṇo nâ*³ *'nusvârâgamam bhajate. yathâ*⁴*: pûrṇ-.....: ardha-.....* *avagrahaḥ pûrvo yasmâd* ⁵*asâv avagrahapûrvaḥ.*⁵

⁽¹⁾ G. M. have this as part of the comment on the preceding rule, and substitute here *sânnidhyân mâ iti labhyate.* ² B. G. M. O. *ayam.* ³ B. om. *na.* ⁴ G. M. O om. ⁽⁵⁾ G. M. *sa tathoktaḥ;* W. om. *asâv.*

with *mâsi.* This interpretation is, of course, forced and false: *mâsí* is included with the rest here because it is an example of the same class with them; and the makers of the treatise, when they put it in, either overlooked or neglected the fact that it falls technically under rule 14, and so also under rule 17, establishing exceptions to 14. We have also *masí-mâsi*, more than once, at vii.5.1[6].

हिपुजिगाजिघाछꣳसिनेऽतꣳसयदाताꣳसीत्कनीयाज्याया-
द्राघीयारघीयाश्रेयाह्रसीयावसीयाभूयाꣳसोजक्षिवाजघ्निवा-
जिगिवाजीगिवातस्थिवादाश्वादीदिवापपिवापीपिवावि-
द्वाविविशिवाशुश्रुवाससृवा ॥ १३ ॥

13. The following words have *anusvâra* before *s: hi, pu, jigâ, jighâ, chan̈sine, atan̈sayat, âtân̈sît, kanîyâ, jyâyâ, drâghîyâ, raghîyâ, çreyâ, hrasîyâ, vasîyâ, bhûyân̈sah̤, jakshivâ, jaghnivâ, jigivâ, jîgivâ, tasthivâ, dâçvâ, dîdivâ, papivâ, pîpivâ, vidvâ, viviçivâ, çuçruvâ, sasr̤vâ.*

The commentator's examples are as follows: *hin̈sîh̤ parame vyoman* (iv.2.10[1,2,3]: O. omits *vyoman*, and G. M. substitute *mâ hin̈sîs tanuvâ*, iv.2.3[1] et al.) and *cinute 'hin̈sâyâi* (v.2.8[7]: O. omits *cinute*); respecting this first specification, see further below;——*tena pun̈svatîh̤* (ii.5.8[5]) and *pun̈sah̤ putrân* (iv.6.9[4]): I have only noted farther two cases of *pun̈sah̤*, at ii.6.5[5] and vi.5.8[2];——*lokam ajigân̈san* (v.5.5[4]: vi.5.8[2]: O. omits *lokam*): elsewhere only at iii.2.2[3];——*tvashṭâram ajighân̈san* (vi.5.8[4]): the text presents fourteen other cases of *jighân̈s;*——*brâhmaṇâchan̈sine* (i.8.18): the only case: a counter-example (but O. omits all the counter-examples), *pra yuchasy ubhe ni pâsi* (i.4.22), shows the necessity of including in the citation the *ne* of *chan̈sine;*——*gabhe mushṭim atan̈sayat* (vii.4.19[4]), with a counter-example, *atasaṁ na çushkam* (i.2.14[2]), to explain the citation of the whole word *atan̈sayat;*——*anvâtân̈sît tvayi* (iv.7.13[5]: O. omits *tvayi*), with *anu vrâtâsas tava* (iv.6.7[3]), to prove the need of the final *ît;*——*kanîyân̈so devâh̤* (v.3.11[1]): the text offers half-a-dozen cases of this comparative, and about the same number of the next;——*jyâyân̈so bhrâtarah̤*

---

12. [1]*cakâro nishedhâkarshakah̤*[1]*: mâsi...... ity eteshu grahaṇeshu na syâd anusvârâgamah̤. eshâm api mâ padâdir* (xvi.8) *iti prâptih̤. kecid atra prath-.... ity udâharanti*[2]*: tad asâdhu: na pade dvisvare nityam*[3] (xvi.17) *ity anenâi 'va nishedhasiddheh̤*[4]*: tasmâd anyaçâkhâyâm*[5] *bahusvaram aparam*[6] *udâharaṇam avadhâraṇîyam. daçasu....: shaṇ....: mâsâm....*

(1) O. om. [2] W. *-raṇaṁ.* [3] W. O. *n;* G. M. om. [4] W. *-dhaṁ siddhah̤;* B. *-dhah̤ siddhah̤.* [5] G. M. *anyasyâṁ ç-.* [6] B. G. M. *param;* O. om.

(ii.6.6[1] et al.);——*drâghîyâṅsâu bhavataḥ* (v.2.5[1]): the only case;——*atho raghîyâṅsaḥ* (vii.4.9): also the only case;——*pra çreyâṅsam* (ii.4.1[4]: but O. substitutes the only other case, *çreyâṅsam pâpîyân*, v.1.2[3]);——*atha hrasîyâṅsam âkramaṇam* (vi.6.4[2]: but G. M. O. omit the last word, thus allowing the citation to include also the only other case, found in the same division);——*vasîyâṅsam bhâgadheyena* (v.4.10[5]): there are two or three further cases;——*bhûyâṅso 'nyebhyaḥ* (vii.1.1[5]), with *annâdo bhûyâsam* (i.6.2[3] et al.) as counter-example, proving that the final *ḥ* had to be cited with the rest of the word: there are seven other cases of *bhûyâṅs* in the text;——*jakshivâṅsaḥ papivâṅsaḥ* (i.4.44[2]: O. omits the last word): the only case;——*vṛtraṁ jaghnivâṅsam mṛdho 'bhi* (ii.5.3[1]: W. B. omit the first word, O. the first and last; G. M. have only the first two, which are read also at ii.5.4[5]): I have noted the word besides only at ii.1.10[2] three times, with the negative prefix;——*vâjaṁ jigivâṅsaḥ* (i.7.8[4]): the only case;——for *jîgivâ* is found only a case "in another *çâkhâ*," namely *jîgivâṅsasya* (so W. G. M., though the word is not grammatically admissible; O. has *jîgivâṅsamyâmâ* [i. e. *-ṅsaḥ syâma?*]; B. is corrupt, running the previous citation and this together into *vâjaṁ jigivâṅsam iti çâkhântare*);——*dyumnâ tasthivâṅso janânâm* (i.2.14[4]: O. alone has the last word): there is one other case, at iv.2.2[2];——*dâçvâṅso dâçushaḥ sutam* (i.4.16: O. alone has *sutam*): another case at ii.2.12[8];——*çucayo dîdivâṅsam* (ii.5.12[2]): another case at i.2.14[4];——*papivâṅsaç ca viçve* (i.4.44[2]): the only case;——*pîpivâṅsaṅ sarasvataḥ* (iii.1.11[2]: O. has *-tas trayaḥ*, probably corrupt for *-ta stanam*, as the text reads): the only case;—*vidvâṅso vâi purâ hotâraḥ* (ii.5.11[1-2]: only O. has the last two words) and *avidvâṅsaç çakṛma* (iv.7.15[6]: O. begins *vishṭâvid-*, by mutilation of the preceding word in the passage): the Sanhitâ has over thirty cases of *vidvâṅs*;——*praviviçivâṅsam îmahe* (iv.7.15[1]);——*yac chuçruvâṅsaḥ* (ii.5.9[2] twice): there is another case at v.3.4[1];——and, finally, *vâjaṅ sasṛvâṅsaḥ* (i.7.8[4]).

After the second example (*ahiṅsâyâi*), G. M. insert the remark that it is brought under the present rule by the principle of "prefixion of *a*" (i.52). This is wrong, being inconsistent with the

---

13. [1]*hi* ------[1] *ity evampûrvaḥ sakâraparo 'nusvârâgamo*[2] *bhavati*[3]. *yathâ*[4]: *hiṅsîḥ* ----: *cin-* ----: [5] *tena* ----: *puṅsaḥ* ----: *lokam* ----: *tvasht-* ----: *brâhm-* ----: [6]*na iti kim: pra* ----:[6] *gabhe* ----: [7]*yad iti kim: atasaṁ* ----:[7] *anv-* ----: [8]*îd iti kim: anu* ----:[8] *kan-* ----: *jyây-* ----: *drâgh-* ----: *atho* ----: *pra* ----: *atha* ----: *vasî-* ----: *bhûy-* ----: [9]*visargeṇa kim: ann-* ----:[9] *jaksh-* ----: *vṛtraṁ* ----: *vâjaṁ* ----: *jîgivâṅsasye 'ti çâkhântare: dyum-* ----: [10]*dâçv-* ----: *çucayo* ----: *papiv-* ----: *pîpiv-* ----:[10] *vidv-* ----: *avid-* ----: *pravi-* ----: *yac* ----: *vâjaṅ* ----. [11] *dâçvâviviçivâçuçruve*[12] *'ty atra srâdishu câi 'kapada* (xv.4) *iti prâptyâ çakâraparo 'nusvârâgamaḥ kiṁ*

exposition given under rule 2 (see note on that rule) of the reason why *hi* was not there included: *hi* here is meant not as initial only, but wherever found in a word. Since, however, it is only in this one word that *hiṅs-* occurs otherwise than as initial, it would seem better to have disposed of the single case as of those which form the subject of rules 6 and 10, and to put *hi* into 2, where it would look much more at home than here at the head of a troop of perfect participles and comparatives. And why *pu* was not put into rule 2 without any ceremony, I cannot see at all; unless I have overlooked some case or cases of its occurrence, *puṅs* is invariably initial.

The commentator raises the question why rule xv.4 does not require us to insert an *anusvâra* before the *ç* of *dâçvâ*, *viviçivâ*, and *çuçruvâ*, since these too are *srâdayaḥ;* and he makes answer that it is because the restriction conveyed in xvi.1 is still in force. But in that case, he goes on to say, is there not a nasal increment before the *s* of *hrasîyâ*, *vasîyâ*, *tasthivâ*, and *sasṛvâ?* The answer to this objection is twofold. First, the competency of the citation is pleaded—that is to say, the words being read in the rule itself without nasal, that is to be understood as their authoritative form (compare under rule 19, where this plea leads to a further discussion). Secondly, the words in question being found associated with *âtâṅsît*, *kanîyâ*, *jyâyâ*, and so on, all of which show the *anusvâra* to follow a long vowel, we are to infer that in the others also it does not follow a short vowel. The first of these answers is not such as is wont to be pleaded in this treatise, and the second is evidently very weak: I should almost prefer to assume that the difficulty was not remarked by the authors of the treatise, and that the commentators who have discovered it have been forced to make the best excuse they could for it.

A more serious objection to the rule, it seems to me, is that it mixes together cases of two different classes—those in which (*chaṅsine* etc.) the nasal appears in the word itself as cited, and those in which it is to be added before a following *s*. Of this, however, the comment takes no notice.

---

na syât. atha sakâraparâ[13] (xvi.1) *ity ûshmaviçeshasya*[14] *sakârasyâ 'nuvṛttir*[15] *iti vadâmaḥ. tarhi hrasîyâvasîyâtasthivâsasṛve 'ty atra* [16]*sakârapara evâ ''gamaḥ*[16] *kiṁ na syât. uccâraṇasâmarthyâd eve 'ty prathamaḥ*[17] *parihâraḥ. atha vâ: âtâṅsîtkanîyâjyâye 'tyâdishu sarvatra dîrghânantaram evâ 'nusvârasthânam*[18] *iti sâhacaryâd*[19] *atrâ 'pi na syâd anusvârasya hrasvânantaraṁ*[20] *sthânam ity*[21] *aparaḥ parihâraḥ.*

(1) B. om. 2 O. *-maṁ.* 3 G. M. *syât;* O. *bhajate.* 4 O. om. 5 G. M. ins. *apy akârâdi* (i.52) *prâptiḥ.* (6) O. om. (7) O. om. (8) O. om. (9) O. om. (10) G. M. om. 11 G. M. ins. *nanu.* 12 O. *vidvâviviçivâsuçrushâsasṛve.* 13 W. om. *parâ;* G. M. *-para.* 14 G. M. *-shaṇasya.* 15 G. M. O. *-tter.* (16) W. *makârasyâ ''gamaḥ;* O. . . . *evâ 'nusvârâg-.* 17 G. M. *-ma.* 18 W. *-svâraḥ.* 19 G. M. O. *tatsâh-.* 20 W. G. M. *hrasvânt-.* 21 W. *iti 'ty.*

आकारेकारोकाराः सिषिपराः पदान्तयोः ॥ १४ ॥

14. The vowels *â*, *î*, and *û* have *anusvâra*, when they are followed by *si* or *shi* final.

This rule, of course, applies to the nominative, accusative, and vocative plural of neuters in *as*, *is*, and *us*. The illustrative examples are *vayâñsi pakvagandhena* (v.7.23), *tamâñsi gûhatâm ajushtâ* (i.8.22[5]: only O. has *ajushṭâ*), *daça havîñshi* (vii.5.14[2]), *jyotîñshi kurute* (v.4.1[4]: O. omits), *agna âyûñshi* (i.3.14[7] et al.), and *avabhṛthayajûñshi juhoti* (vi.6.3[1]: G. M. omit *juhoti*). To show that the *si* or *shi* must be final, are quoted *tasmâd vâsishṭho brahmâ* (iii.5.2[1]: only G. M. have *brahmâ*), and *manîshiṇo manasâ* (iv.6.2[5]: O. omits *manasâ*). To show that the preceding vowel must be long, we have *yathâ 'nasi yukta âdhîyate* (v.4.10[2]: only G. M. have the last word), *jyotis tvâ jyotishi* (i.1.10[3]), and *âyushi durone* (i.2.14[3]); and, finally, to show that no other vowel than *i* after the *s* or *sh* calls out the increment, *prajâsv eva prajâtâsu* (vi.4.1[3]), *oshadhîshu* (iii.5.5[2] et al.), and *tanûshu baddham* (i.8.22[5]).

The last six counter-examples are omitted in O., which adds at the end the obvious remark that, as *si* and *shi* are here indicated as occasions of the preceding *anusvâra*, that value no longer belongs to *s* merely—that is to say, the force of the heading given in rule 1 is henceforth at an end.

विकृते ऽपि ॥ १५ ॥

15. Even when the *i* is altered

That the *i* of the ending *si* or *shi* is here aimed at is in the nature of the case obvious enough, but not at all distinctly intimated by the terms of the rule. The commentator quotes in illustration *chandâñsy upa dadhâti* (v.3.8[1,2]), *havîñshy â sâdayet* (i.6.10[3]), and *tapûñshy agne juhvâ* (i.2.14[1]: G. M. omit *juhvâ*).

---

14. *sishiparâ âkârekârokârâs tayoḥ sishyoḥ padântayoḥ sator anusvârâgamam bhajante*[1]. *yathâ*[2]*: vay-....: tam-....: daça ....:* [3]*jyot-....:*[3] *agna....: avabh-..... padântayor*[4] *iti kim: tasmâd....: manî-.....* [5]*âkârekârokârâ iti dîrgheṇa*[5] *kim: yathâ....: jyotis....: âyushi..... sishî 'ty*[6] *atre 'kâreṇa kim: praj-....: osh-....: tan-.....*[7]

[1] MSS. *-jate.* [2] O. om. (3) O. om. [4] O. *-ta.* (5) G. M. *dirghaiḥ;* O. om., with all that follows. [6] W. B. *ity.* [7] O. adds *sishiparanimittayor nideçât sakârasya paranimittatva bhati.*

15. *apiçabdânvâdishṭe*[1] *sishyor ikâre vikṛte 'pi yakâram âpanne 'pi bhavaty anusvârâgamaḥ. yathâ*[2]*: chand-....: hav-....: tap-.....*

[1] W. B. O. *-bdonv-;* G. M. *-bdenâ 'nv-.* [2] G. M. O. om.

अनाकारो ह्रस्वः सांकृत्यस्य ॥ १६ ॥

16. According to Sâṁkṛtya, the vowel, except *â*, is short.

That is to say, the two vowels *î* and *û*, to which alone reference has been made above, become short in the cases here referred to: for example, in *havîn̄shi bhavanti* (v.5.1[7] et al.: O. omits *bhavanti*) and *samishṭayajûn̄shi juhoti* (vi.6.2[1]: G. M. O. omit *juhoti*), where Sâṁkṛtya would read *havin̄shi* and *yajun̄shi*, while in *vayân̄si* (v. 7.23 et al.: O. omits) he would admit the long vowel.

A curious case of dissent upon a point in grammar which we have not been accustomed to regard as open to any difference of opinion. The rule is, naturally enough, pronounced unapproved.

G. M. add *ca* to the rule, after *sâṁkṛtyasya.*

न पदे द्विस्वरे नित्यम् ॥ १७ ॥

17. Not, under any circumstances, in a dissyllabic word.

This is a rule prescribing exceptions under rule 14; the addition *nityam*, 'under any circumstances,' confirms its application to words ending in *si* or *shi* after *â*, *î*, or *û* which would otherwise fall under any other rule prescribing the increment.

Examples under rule 14 alone are first quoted, namely *stuto yâsi vaçân̄ anu* (i.8.5[1]: G. M. O. end with *yâsi*) and *yâsi dûtaḥ* (iii.5. 5[3]: G. M. have dropped out *yâsi*). Then, as a case also under rule 2, we have *vidhataḥ pâsi nu tmanâ* (i.3.14[1]); and, as one under rule 8, *prathame mâsi pṛshṭhâni* (vii.5.3[1]: G. M. omit the last word), which has been already made the subject of discussion under rule 12, above. The force of the *nityam* does not go so far as to prohibit an *anusvâra* in every dissyllabic word before *si*, what-

---

16. *âkârâd anyo 'nâkâraḥ: îkâra ûkâraç ce 'ty arthaḥ: tayor eva prakṛtatvât. sâṁkṛtyasya mata îkâra ûkâraç ca hrasvam âpadyate. yathâ*[1]*: hav-....: sam-.....* [2]*anâkâra iti kim: vayân̄si.*[2]

ne 'daṁ sûtram ishṭam.

[1] O. om. [(2)] O. om.

17. *dvisvare*[1] *pade vartamânâ*[2] *âkârekârokârâḥ*[3] *padântasishiparâ*[4] *nâ*[5] *'nusvârâgamam* [6] *bhajante. yathâ*[7]*: stuto....:* [8]*yâsi ..... nityaçabdaḥ prâptyantarapratishedhârthaḥ: vidhataḥ ....:*[8] [9]*sraçoha*[10] (xvi.2) *iti prâptiḥ: prathame....: mâ padâdir*[11] (xvi.8) *iti prâptiḥ. dvâu svarâu yasmin* [12] *vidyete tad dvisvaram: tasmin.*[9]

[1] O. *dvitvasv-.* [2] G. M. *-na.* [3] G M. *âkâraḥ îkâraḥ*; O. *âkâraûkârâḥ.* [4] G. M. *-ntas sishiparo;* O. *-ntâ si-.* [5] B. om.; G. M. *nityan nâ.* [6] B. ins. *na;* O. ins. *nityam.* [7] G. M. O. om. [(8)] W. om. [(9)] B. om. [10] O. *-hapâça padâdaya.* [11] O. *-dir ijâs.* [12] G. M. ins. *pade.*

ever vowel precedes, or it would include *hañsi* also, and possibly other cases.

ऋजीषिजिगासिजिघास्यजासियजासिददासिदधासिवर्तयासि च ॥ १८ ॥

18. Nor in *ṛjîshi*, *jigâsi*, *jighâsi*, *ajâsi*, *yajâsi*, *dadâsi*, *dadhâsi*, and *vartayâsi*.

These are verbal forms which need to be excepted under rule 14, and which, as containing more than two syllables, are not reached by rule 17. The passages in which they occur are quoted by the commentary, as follows: *tena ṛjîshi sarvâṇi* (iii.2.2[1]: only O. has *sarvâṇi*), *achâ jigâsi* (iv.2.4[2]), *â tvam ajâsi garbhadham* (vii.4.19[1]), *havishâ yajâsy agne bṛhat* (iii.5.11[2] et al.: O. omits the last two words), *yâbhir dadâsi dâçushe* (iii.3.11[5]: G. M. omit *dâçushe*), *dadhâsi dâçushe kave* (iv.2.7[2]), and *açvam â vartayâsi naḥ* (vii.4.20). *Yajâsi* I have noted in two or three other passages; if the rest occur elsewhere, I have overlooked them. This leaves unaccounted for *jighâsi*, which is declared to occur "in another text," in the passage *prathame jighâsi*.

दंसनाभ्योदंसोभिर्दंसंवृषदंशोदंशुकादंष्ट्राभ्यां परः ॥ १९ ॥

19. In *dañsanâbhyaḥ*, *dañsobhiḥ*, *dañsam*, *vṛshadañçaḥ*, *dañçukâ*, and *dañshṭrâbhyâm*, *anusvâra* is taken in the latter place.

The commentator's citations are *vâiçvânarasya dañsanâbhyaḥ* (i.5.11[1]); *sajoshâv açvinâ dañsobhiḥ* (v.6.4[1]), to which is added as counter-example, proving the need of the *-bhiḥ*, *yushmâko 'tî riçâdasaḥ* (iv.3.13[3]: O. has only the last word, and G. M. begin

---

18. [1] *cakâro nishedhâkarshakaḥ: ṛjîshiprabhṛtishu*[2] *grahaṇeshu*[3] *nâ 'nusvârâgamaḥ syât: âkârekârokârâ* (xvi.14) *iti prâptiḥ. bahusvaratvâd*[4] *eshu*[5] *pûrvasûtranishedo*[6] *na sidhyatî 'ty atrâ*[7] *'yam ârambhaḥ. yathâ*[8]*: tena....: achâ....: jighâsî*[9] *'ti çâkhântare:* [10]*prathame jighâsî 'ti*[10]*: â....: havishâ ....: yâbhir....: dadhâsi....: açvam....*

[1] O. ins. an enumeration of the words in the rule. [2] G. M. *-ṛti.* [3] O. om. [4] G. M. *-râdi.* [5] B. *esha;* G. M. om. [6] G. M. *-tre ni-;* W. B. *-dhân.* [7] O. om. *atra.* [8] G. M. O. om. [9] G. M. *-âṅsi.* [(10)] O. om.; W. *prathame* — — — (as being illegible in the MS. from which the copy was made); B. *-ghâsati.*

19. [1] *dañsanâbhya ityâdishu*[2] *grahaṇeshu para evâ 'nusvârâgamo bhavati*[3]*. yathâ*[4]*: vâiçv-....: saj-....: bhir iti kim: yushm-....:* [5] *purud-....: vṛsh-....: paçûn....: dañsh-.... dañse 'ty etâvatâi 'vâ 'lam: kim akhilapadapâṭhena*[6]*. kur-*

with *ûtî*); *purudañsañ sanim* (iv.2.4[3]); *vṛshadañças te dhâtuḥ* (v.5.12): there is another case at v.5.21; *paçûn dañçukâḥ syur yad vishûcînam* (v.2.9[6]: O. omits the first word, and it alone has the last two); and *dañshṭrâbhyâm malimlûn* (iv.1.10[2]): there is another case at v.7.11. To the objection that the citation in the rule of *dañsa* simply might have saved the rehearsal of whole words [in a part of the cases given], the commentator replies by quoting *kurvato me mo 'pa dasat* (i.6.3[3] et al.) as an example of cases which need to be excluded. The addition of *paraḥ*, 'in the latter place,' is because *vṛshadañçaḥ* contains two places at which, by xv.4, the *anusvâra* would otherwise require to be inserted.

This last point, however, does not pass (except in O.) without farther question and discussion. The objection is raised that the mere citation of *vṛshadañça* without *anusvâra* before the former sibilant is enough to settle its reading, according to the same principle that was appealed to under rule 13, for *hrasîyâ*, *vasîyâ*, and so on. This is undeniable; and the only real answer to be made is that there was no harm in adding *para* here, to make the matter sure, while it could not have been employed in rule 13 without occasioning a great deal of additional trouble. The commentator, however, prefers to have recourse to a plea of exceptionally puerile character. In xv.4 (the rule here in force), he says, the spirants in general are implied, but in xvi.1 (in force at rule 13) a special spirant, *s*; and it is an acknowledged principle that, as between a generality and a specification, the specification is the more powerful. That being the case, the putting down of that

---

vato.... ityâdâu mâ bhûd iti. 'para iti kim: vṛshadañça ity atra[8] *sthânadvaye 'pi srâdishu câi 'kapada* (xv.4) *iti prâptâu satyâm pûrvatra*[9] *mâ bhûd iti. nanu grahaṇasâmarthyâd evâ 'nusvâraḥ*[10] *pûrvatra na bhavati: yathâ hrasîyâvasîyâ* (xvi. 13) *ityâdâu grahaṇasâmarthyâd*[11] *upapâditam. nâi 'sha doshaḥ: srâdishu câi 'kapada* (xv.4) *ity atro "shmasâmânyam uktam: atha sakâraparâ* (xvi.1) *ity atra tu tadviçesha uktaḥ: sâmânyaviçeshayor viçesho balavân iti nyâyaḥ: tathâ sati* [12]*balavadbâdhanam*[13] *eva bhûshaṇam* [14]*na tu*[14] *durbalabâdhanam*[15] *iti*[12] *tatrâi 'va grahaṇasâmarthyaṁ*[16] *samarthanîyam: na tv atra*[17] *durbalasthâne: tathâ 'pi*[18]: [19] *adhikaḥ*[20] *purusho virodhinam*[21] *adhikam eva bâdhate bhûshaṇatvât: na tu kadâcid alpabalam*[22]: *iti*[23] *paraçabdaprayoga*[24] *upapadyate.'*

[1] O. prefixes a separate rehearsal of the words in the rule. [2] G. M. *-di.* [3] G. M. *syât.* [4] in W. only. [5] O. ins. *ity atrâ 'py akârâdi* (i.52) *iti vacanâd anusvârâgamaḥ syât: tan mâ bhûd iti.* [6] G. M. *-ṭhanena.* [(7)] O. om. [8] W. *ava.* [9] W. *-rva.* [10] B. *-râgamaḥ.* [11] W. *sâmarthyâgrahaṇam.* [(12)] W. *balavatiyam eva bhûshaṇaṁ: vâdhanam eva bhûshaṇaṁ na tu durbalam iti bâdhana.* [13] G. M. *-vatsâdh-*; B. *-dham.* [(14)] G. M. om. [15] G. M. *-lasâdhanaṁ na sâdhv.* [16] W. *-ṇam eva sâmarthyaṁ*; B. *-rthya.* [17] B. *artha.* [18] G. M. *hi.* [19] G. M. ins. *loke.* [20] W. *âdh-*; G. M. *-ka.* [21] W. *-dhanam.* [22] W. B. *apy alpam.* [23] B. *iti 'ti.* [24] W. B. *atra çabd-.*

which is powerful, not of that which is weak, is honorific; hence, the competency of the citation was to be insisted on in the former rule, but not here, in a weak position. Moreover, a superior man puts down, for honor's sake, a mighty opponent, but never a weak one. Therefore, the use of the word *para* here is right and proper!

All the MSS. except B. (and G. M., which have a slight *lacuna*, involving the word) read *dan̆san* instead of *dan̆saṁ* in the rule.

मंस्येमंसतैयंसद्यंसन्वंसतेवंसगः ॥ २० ॥

20. Also in *man̆sye*, *man̆satâi*, *yan̆sad*, *yan̆san*, *van̆sate*, and *van̆sagaḥ*.

The commentator quotes as follows: *paçûn nâ 'bhi man̆sya iti* (iii.1.9[6]), *anu nâu çûra man̆satâi bhadrâ indrasya râtayaḥ* (vii.4.15: O. alone has the first two words, B. alone the last one), *çocishâ yan̆sad viçvaṁ ny atriṇam* (iv.6.1[5]: G. M. O. omit *çocishâ*), *ishavaḥ çarma yan̆san* (iv.6.6[4]), *agnir no van̆sate rayim* (iv.6.1[5]), and *tigmaçṛn̂go na van̆sagaḥ* (ii.6.11[4]). The words here dealt with occur only in the passages quoted, except *yan̆sat*, which is found also at iv.1.11[2]; 7.14[3]. To the objection that it would have been enough to give *man̆s*, *yan̆s*, and *van̆s* (the MSS. leave it doubtful whether these are the precise forms suggested) in the rule, instead of citing whole words, the commentator replies by giving the counter-examples *uttamasyâ 'va dyati* (vi.3.10[4]), *yasya bhûyân̆so yajñakrataraḥ* (iii.1.7[3]), and *adya vasu vasati* (ii.5.3[7]).

उन्न वंशम् ॥ २१ ॥

21. Also in *van̆çam*, after *ut* or *na*.

The passages are *ud van̆çam iva yemire* (i.6.12[3]: W. has dropped out *yemire*, along with all the rest of the comment) and *prâcînavan̆çaṁ karoti* (vi.1.1[1] twice). A counter-example, with a different preceding word, is *brahmavarcasy eva bhavati vaçaṁ vâ esha carati* (ii.1.7[7]: only O. has the first two words, and it omits the last two).

---

20. [1] *man̆sya ityâdishu*[2] *syâd anusvârâgamaḥ. yathâ*[3]*: paçûn ----: anu----: çoc-----: ishavaḥ----: agnir----: tigm-----.* [4]*man̆s: yan̆s: van̆s:*[4] *ity etâvatâi 'vâ 'lam: kim akhila-padapâṭhena: utt-----: yasya----: adya---- ityâdâu mâ bhûd iti.*

[1] O. prefixes a separate rehearsal of the words in the rule. [2] B. *-di.* [3] G. M. O. om. [(4)] W. *bhadrayan̆;* B. *saṁsûr yaṁs vaṁs;* G. M. *maṁsa : yaṁsa : vaṁsa;* O. *man̆se : yan̆se : van̆se.*

21. *ut*[1]*: na: ity evampûrve*[2] *van̆çam ity asmin grahaṇe syâd anusvârâgamaḥ. ud----:* [3]*prâ-----.* [4]*evampûrva iti*[4] *kim: brahm-----.*[3]

[1] O. *un̆syatebhrat.* [2] W. *-rvo;* B. *-rva.* [(3)] W. om. [(4)] O. *unne 'ti.*

अक्रंस्तक्रंस्यतेरंस्यतेभ्रंशते ॥ २२ ॥

22. Also in *akrañsta, krañsyate, rañsyate,* and *bhrañçate.*

The passages are *dyâm vâjy â 'krañsta* (vii.5.19¹), *utkrañsyate svâhâ* (vii.1.19³), *uparañsyate svâhâ* (vii.1.19¹: B. O. omit), and *nâ 'smâd râshtram bhrañçate* (v.7.4⁴: O. omits the first two words); *bhrañçate* occurs also at i.6.11¹ twice.

G. M. read *utkrañsyate* for *krañsyate* in the rule.

रंह्यै च ॥ २३ ॥

23. And also in *rañhyâi.*

The only passage is *pûshṇo rañhyâi* (i.3.10²). The significance of the *ca,* 'and,' which is here out of its proper place, will be given, we are told, under the next rule.

ऐकार उख्यस्य नितान्तः ॥ २४ ॥

24. The *âi,* according to Ukhya, is excessive.

That is to say, according to the commentator, the *âi* of the word *rañhyâi,* here brought forward by the *ca,* 'and,' which is read in the preceding rule. *Nitânta,* 'excessive,' is explained as signifying 'uttered with more violent effort.' The whole business is a very queer one—Ukhya's opinion itself, its introduction here at a place where it is entirely impertinent, and the bit of interpretation whereby it is worked into the connection.

विरित्रि संख्यासु ॥ २५ ॥

25. Also in *vi, ri,* and *tri,* in numerals, except in *su.*

---

22. [1]*akrañste 'tyâdishu syâd anusvârâgamaḥ*[1]. *dyâm....: utkr-....:* [2]*upa-....:*[2] *nâ....*

(1) O. substitutes a separate rehearsal of the words in the rule (except the last), and *eteshu grahaṇeshv anusvârâgamo bhavati.* (2) B. O. om.

23. *rañhyâ ity asmin grahaṇe syâd anusvârâgamaḥ. pûshṇo .... cakârasya* [1]*vyatihâreṇa 'nvaya*[1] *uttarasûtre prayojanam ucyate.*

(1) G. M. *vyavahârâd anvayâd.*

24. *rañhyâ ity asmin*[1] *grahaṇe pûrvasûtrasthacakârasamarpita*[2] *âikâro nitânto bhavatî 'ty*[3] *ukhyasya*[4] *mate*[5]. *nitântas tîvrataraprayatna ity arthaḥ.*

nâi 'tan matam ishṭam.

[1] G. M. om. [2] B. *-trasya cak-;* O. *-treprayosthacak-;* G. M. *-pite.* [3] G. M. om. *iti.* [4] W. *ukhya;* O. *ukhyasyâ "câryasya.* [5] O. *-tam.*

The syllable *su* is here, the commentator tells us, the ending of the locative case, just as *aḥ* (at i.23) is used as representing the nominative case. This remark is called for, because (see the example below) the actual form in which the syllable appears in the cases aimed at is *shu.* We have a right to be surprised at finding it given as *su* in the rule; and perhaps, also, to conjecture that *saṁkhyâsu* was originally simply the locative plural of *saṁkhyâ*, and that the other value was interpreted into it when the cases calling for exception were noticed.

The quoted examples are *viñçatyâi svâhâ* (vii.2.13 et al.: O. omits), *yad viñçatir dve tenu virâjâu* (v.3.3³: G. M. omit the last two words, O. the last three), *catvâriñçate svâhâ* (vii.2.17: G. M. O. omit *svâhâ;* B. has dropped out *-te svâhâ*, the next example, and the first word of the next but one), *triñçate svâhâ* (vii.2.17: O. omits *svâhâ*), and *triñçat trayaç ca* (i.4.11¹); there are other cases, which I have not taken the trouble to collect. The inclusion of *tri* in the rule, the commentator says, is for the sake of greater plainness, since *ri*, of course, involves *tri* also; it is to be compared with the inclusion of the *v* of *vâghâ* in rule vii.13. Begging the commentator's pardon, however, the two cases are not at all analogous; and the citation of *tri* and *ri* together must be esteemed an oversight, and an offense against the law of economy of expression, obligatory in the *sûtra*-style. The need of restriction to numerals is illustrated by *viçe janâya* (ii.5.12³), *sa rishaḥ pâtu naktam* (i.2.14⁷ et al.: G. M. O. omit *naktam*), and *trishṭubhâi 'vâ 'smâi* (ii.5.10¹ et al.). Finally, the specification "not before *su*" is established by *trishv â rocane divaḥ* (iv.2.4⁴ et al.: O. omits *divaḥ*); if there is another case of this kind, I have failed to note it.

There is yet another word, *trishâhasraḥ* (v.6.8³; p. *tri-sâhasraḥ*), which would properly fall under this rule, but is exempted by a pregnant interpretation of the word *ekapade* in xv.4 (see the note to that rule).

शिंशुमारः शिंषत्सं श्वासं स्वासं सृष्टसं स्कृत्यसं स्कृ-
तसं शितसं शिताकिं शिलकिं शिला ॥ २६ ॥

---

25. *vi. ri: tri:* [1] *evampûrva ûshmaparo*[2] *'nusvârâgamaḥ*[3] *syât: ebhir yadi*[4] *saṁkhyo 'cyate*[5]*: asu*[6] *suçabdaṁ varjayitvâ. su*[7] *saptamî vibhaktir uktâ: yathâ 'ḥkâraḥ*[8] *prathamâvibhaktyupalakshaṇam*[9]*: viñ-....: yad....: catv-....:*[10] *triñ-....:*[10] *triñçat.... trigrahaṇaṁ vispashṭârtham: yato*[11] *viri saṁkhyâ 'sv ity*[12] *etâvatâi 'vâ 'lam: yathâ vâghâshapurva* (vii.13) *ity atra vakâro vispashṭârthaḥ. saṁkhye 'ti kim: viçe....: sa....: trishṭ-..... asv iti kim: trishv....*

[1] G. M. O. ins. *ity.* [2] B. *úkárap-.* [3] G. M. *-ra ág-.* [4] G. M. *yadá.* [5] O. *'cyeta.* [6] W. *a.* [7] G. M. *sv iti;* O. *su iti.* [8] B. *ak-;* G. M. *âk-.* [9] O. *-kler up-.* [10] B. om. [11] G. M. om. [12] O. om.

26. Also in *çiñçumâraḥ, çiñshat, sañçvâ, sañsrâ, sañsṛshṭa, sañskṛtya, sañskṛta, sañçita, sañçitâ, kiñçila,* and *kiñçilâ.*

The passages, as quoted, are *sindhoḥ çiñçumâro himavataḥ* (v. 5.11: only O. has the last word); *kiṁ tata uc chiñshatî 'ti yad dhiranyeshṭakâḥ* (v.5.5[2]: only O. has the last two words, and it omits the first two); *ubhayataḥsañçvâyi kuryâd avadâyâ 'bhi* (ii. 6.8[4]: only O. has the last two words, and it leaves off *ubhayataḥ*); *sañsrâvabhâgâ stha* (i.1.13[2]); *sañsṛshṭajit somapâḥ* (iv.6.4[1]: W. B. put this after the next following example; see farther on); *çarîram eva sañskṛtyâ 'bhyârohati* (v.6.6[3-4]: O. omits the first two words; and all but O. omit the last one, thus making a citation which is also found again in v.6.6[4]); *tan naḥ sañskṛtam* (i.4.43[2]); *brahmasañçito hy esha ghṛtâhavanaḥ* (ii.5.9[2]: only O. has the last word); *çaravye brahmasañçitâ* (iv.6.4[4]); *kiñçila vanya yâ ta ishuḥ* (v.5.9[1]: all but G. M. end with *te*); and *kiñçilaç caturtho vanyaḥ* (v.5.9[2]: G. M. alone have *vanyaḥ*) and *kiñçilâya ca kshayaṇâya ca* (iv.5.9[1]: O. ends with the first *ca*). The commentary prefaces the last two passages with the remark that the second citation of *kiñçila* is that of a part of a word, including a variety of cases. But this, in the first place, would imply that the reading of the rule at the end was *kiñçilakiñçila*, which is the case only in T.; and, in the second place, even were that the reading, the explanation would be a bad one, and the repeated *kiñçila* should be defined as a theme ending in *a*, and so including the declensional forms of that theme, by i.22: in fact, it was expressly cited under that rule, as an example of its application. If *kiñçilâ* is the true reading (as I presume to be the case), then we must suppose that the makers of the rule intended both words as *padâikadeça*'s, the one involving the first two examples quoted, the other the third, and the case being quite parallel with that of *sañçita* and *sañçitâ*, just preceding: but the comment has discovered a difficulty, namely, that *kiñçila* is actually a *pada* in the text (v.5.9[1]), and therefore cannot be quoted without ceremony as a *padâikadeça* (see under rule 29, where this is more distinctly brought out); and hence its efforts to amend the reading and interpretation—efforts in which it is too intent upon the end to be gained to be mindful of consistency in the means employed. In short, here as in many other places, the Prâtiçâkhya is less minutely accurate in its modes of statement than the commentator would fain have it, and he undertakes to make it what it should be by forced interpretation.

---

26. [1] *çiñçumâra ityâdigrahaṇeshu*[2] *syâd anusvârâgamaḥ. yathâ*[3]*: sindhoḥ....: kiṁ....: ubhay-....: sañsr-....: sañsṛ-....: çarî-....: tan....: brahm-....:* [4] *çar-....: kiñç-.... parakiñçilagrahaṇam*[5] *padâikadeçatayâ bahûpadânârtham: kiñçilaç...: kiñçilâya.... nanu*[6] *sañsṛshṭe 'ty atra shakâraparo 'nusvârâgamaḥ kiṁ na syât. mâi 'vam: atra sûtre sarvatra*[7] *padâdivarṇânantaram*[8] *evâ 'nusvâradarçanât: tatsâha-*

Cases of various character are here intermingled. The first two and the last are indivisible words, of which the *anusvâra* forms an essential part, as of those cited in rules 19 and 20, or 29 and 30. The others come from combinations with the preposition *sam*, and are of two classes: *saňskṛtya* and *saňskṛta* the *pada*-text does not attempt to analyze, although (see v.6,7) it divides *saňskurute* and *samaskurvata*, ejecting the intrusive sibilant: those remaining are compounds with *sam* which enter into further composition, so that their compound character does not appear in the *pada*-text. And one or two cases of this last class seem to have been overlooked by the makers of the treatise: they are *svâdushaňsadaḥ* (iv.6.6[3]; p. *svâdu-saňsadaḥ*) and *strîshaňsâdam* (ii.5.1[5]; p. *strî-saňsâdam*). The former of them, indeed, is noticed in G. M., which introduce *saňsadaḥ* into the rule, after *saňskṛta*, and quote the compound in the comment—seeming to betray their consciousness that the word is not a part of the ordinary reading of the rule by saying "when *saňsadaḥ* is read, the instance is *svâdushaňsadaḥ*."

There are further varieties of reading in the rule: G. M. have *çiňshati*; W. B. put *saňsṛshta* between *saňskṛtya* and *saňskṛta*, and give its example a corresponding place among the examples; T. B. G. M. read *saňskṛtaň*, which is perhaps to be preferred; other differences are mere copyists' errors, and not worth reporting.

So far as I have discovered, *saňskṛtam* (i.2.9) and *saňçita* (iv.6.4[4] a second time) are the only words included in this rule which occur further in the Sanhitâ.

The commentator raises the question whether we must not suppose that an *anusvâra* is also to be inserted before the spirant *sh* in *saňsṛshṭa*; but, without this time appealing to the "competency of the citation" to settle the reading, replies that, the word being associated here with others all of which have *anusvâra* only after the first vowel, we must assume the same to be the case with it also; all but O. adding that "there is no reason for inconsistency" in this respect.

सितृदृ हकारपरः ॥ २७ ॥

27. Also after *si*, *tṛ*, or *dṛ*, when *h* follows.

The quoted examples are *siňho vayaḥ* (iv.3.5), *çatatarhâňs tṛňhanti* (i.5.7[6] et al.), and *dṛňhasva mâ hvâḥ* (i.1.3 et al.). Of the

---

caryâd[9] *atrâ 'pi tathâi 'va*[10] *vijňeyam*: [11]*na vâiparîtye kâraṇam asti*[11].

[1] O. prefixes a separate rehearsal of the words cited in the rule. [2] G. M. *-dishu gr-*; O. *-dishu*. [3] G. M. O. om. [4] G. M. ins. *saňsada iti pâṭhe svâdushaňsadaḥ.* [5] W. *paraṁ ki-*. [6] G. M. om. [7] W. G. M. *sarva.* [8] W. *varṇ-*; G. M. *-ṇâñcaram.* [9] O. *sâh-*. [10] B. *'vâ 'pi.* [(11)] O. om.; W. om. *na.*

27. *si: tṛ: dṛ: ity evampûrvo hakâraparaḥ*[1] *syâd anusvârâgamaḥ*[2]. *yathâ*[3]: *siňho....: çatat-....: dṛňh-....* [4]*evam-*

noun *siṅha*, and of forms from the roots *tṛṅh* and *dṛṅh*, which alone come under the action of the rule, there are other cases in the Sanhitâ. Counter-examples are given (excepting in O.): to show that no other syllables take the increment before *h*, *sapatnasâhî 'svâhâ* (i.2.12[2]: but G. M. substitute *saputnasâhîṅ sam mârjmi*, i.1.10[1]) and *anatidâhâyo 'vâca* (v.2.10[3]); that *ṛ* takes the increment only when preceded by *t* or *d*, *gṛhâṇâm asamartyâi* (iii.3.8[2]); that the increment is taken only before *h*, *sishâsantîḥ* (vii.5.2[1]: G. M. read *sishâsaḥ*, but doubtless by a blunder only), *tṛshvîm anu* (i.2.14[1]), and *naktaṁ dṛçe dîpyate* (v.6.4[4])

मꣳहिष्ठस्य च ॥ २८ ॥

28. As also, in *maṅhishṭhasya.*

That is to say, before the *h*, which is brought down from the preeding rule by *ca*, expressly in order to exclude the assumption of *anusvâra* before the *sh* and *s* in the same word. The passage is *maṅhishṭhasya prabhṛtasya* (iv.2.3[4]), and there is no other.

आदिरꣳहतिरꣳहोऽꣳहोरꣳहोमुगत्यꣳहाꣳहसोऽꣳह-
साꣳशमꣳशुभिरꣳशभुवाꣳश्वꣳशूꣳशवोऽꣳशुरꣳशुमꣳशू-
नꣳशुनाꣳशोरꣳशायोपाꣳश्वꣳशौ ॥ २९ ॥

29. Also, after the first vowel, in *aṅhatiḥ*, *aṅhaḥ*, *aṅhoḥ*, *aṅhomuc*, *atyaṅhâḥ*, *aṅhasaḥ*, *aṅhasâ*, *aṅçam*, *aṅçubhiḥ*, *aṅçabhuvâ*, *aṅçu*, *aṅçû*, *aṅçavaḥ*, *aṅçuḥ*, *aṅçum*, *aṅçûn*, *aṅçunâ*, *aṅçoḥ*, *aṅçâya*, *upâṅçu*, and *aṅçâu.*

We have here a detailed list of complete *padas* (or, in one or two instances, more than a whole *pada*), in which *anusvâra* is found. The illustrative examples are as follows. For *aṅhatiḥ*, *pari dveshaso aṅhatiḥ* (ii.6.11[2]): the only case. For *aṅhaḥ*, *aṅhomucaṁ vṛshabhaṁ yajñiyânâm* (i.6.12[4]; p. *aṅhaḥ-mucam:* G. M. O. omit the last word); *aṅhaḥ* is found four or five times in the Sanhitâ as an independent word, and about fifteen times in the

---

pûrva iti kim: sap-....: anati-..... ṛkâreṇâi 'vâ[5] *'lam: kiṁ takâradakârâbhyâm: gṛh-..... evampara iti kim: sish-....: tṛshvîm....: naktaṁ....*[4] *hakâraḥ paro yasmâd* [6]*asâu hakâraparaḥ.*[6]

[1] G. M. *-raç ca.* [2] O. *asâu hekâraparaḥ.* [3] B. G. M. O. om. [(4)] O. om. [5] G. M. om. *eva.* [6] G. M. *sa tathoktaḥ.*

28. *maṅhishṭhasye 'ty asmin grahaṇe cakârâkṛshṭahakâraparo 'nusvârâgamo bhavati*[1]. *yathâ*[2]*: maṅh-.....* [3]*cakâraḥ kimarthaḥ: atrâi 'va grahaṇe sashakâraparo mâ bhûd iti.*[3]

[1] G. M. O. *syât.* [2] G. M. O. om. [(3)] O. om.

compound *aṅhomuc*—one of the forms of which, as we shall see farther on, has to be made separate account of. For *aṅhoḥ*, *aṅhoç cid yâ* (i.4.22 and ii.1.11[4]): there is no other case. For *aṅhomuk*, *aṅhomugbhyâṁ dvikapâlaḥ* (vii.5.22: O. omits *dvikapâlaḥ*, and W. B. put it in out of place); of all the forms of *aṅhomuc*, this is the only one in which *aṅhaḥ* does not form a *pada* (it is divided, of course, *aṅhomuk-bhyâm*), and which therefore is not disposed of by the citation of *aṅhaḥ*. For *atyaṅhâḥ*, *ṛtapâç câ 'tyaṅhâḥ* (i.8. 13[2-3]): the word is found again at iv.6.5[5]; it is more than a simple *pada* (p. *ati-aṅhâḥ*), and the *ati* is included in the citation, we are told, to prevent confusion of *aṅhâḥ* with *ahâḥ* in such phrases as *shaḍahâ bhavanti* (vii.5.1[4]; *shaṭ-ahâḥ*). For *aṅhasaḥ*, *te no muñcatam aṅhasaḥ* (iv.7.15[6]: all except B. read *muñcantv*, which does not occur before *aṅhasaḥ*): of this case of *aṅhas* I have noted about twenty instances. For *aṅhasâ*, the only example is the one quoted, *aṅhasâ vâ esha gṛhîtaḥ* (ii.4.2[3]: O. ends with *vâi*). The commentator next raises the question why whole *padas* should have been cited, when *aṅha* (as part of a word) would have been sufficient to assure the reading, and replies by quoting *sa rasam aha vasantâya* (vii.2.10[1]: O. begins with *aha*), as an example of cases that required to be excluded. For *aṅçam*, *pari paçyâmo 'ṅçam â* (vii.1.6[2]: O. omits *â*): the form is found again in the same division. For *aṅçubhiḥ*, *shaḍbhir aṅçubhiḥ pavayati* (vi.4.5[7]: O. omits *yavayati*; W. B. put this example off until after that for *aṅçu*, which would be, to be sure, a more suitable place for it, if the same order were followed in the rule; but there all authorities agree: see further on). For *aṅçabhuvâ*, *tvayâ 'ṅçabhuvâ somam* (vi.4.8[2]: G. M. O. omit *somam*): the word is found again at vi.4.8[3]. For *aṅçu*, *tenâ 'ṅçumat* (iii.2.2[1]); and it is pointed out that, by rule i.53 (the comment blunderingly quotes i.52 instead), *anaṅçu kurvantaḥ* (iii.2.2[1]) is involved with *aṅçu* (O. has lost, of this, all but the example *anaṅçu ku*). For *aṅçû*, *vṛshṇo hy etâv aṅçû* (vi.4.5[3]). For *aṅçavaḥ*, *prâṇâ vâ aṅçavaḥ* (vi.4.4[4]). For *aṅçuḥ*, *aṅçur aṅçus te* (i.2.11[1] et al.): the word is found in eight other passages. For *aṅçum*, *yam âdityâ aṅçum âpyâyayanti* (ii.3.5[3] et al.: only W. has the last word): there are five other instances. For *aṅçûn*, *aṅçûn apa gṛhṇâti* (vi.4.4[4]: lost in W.): it occurs further in the

---

29. [1] *aṅhatiḥ ...... eteshv âdir*[2] *anusvârâgamo*[3] *bhavati*[4]. *yathâ*[5]: *pari ....: aṅho- ....:* [6]*sûtre saṁhitâyâm otvavidhânâd*[7] *ahar .... ityâdâu na syâd ayaṁ vidhiḥ: kiṁtu yasmin visarjanîyo rephaṁ nâ 'padyate tasyâi 'vo 'pâdânam:*[6] *aṅhoç ....:* [8] [9]*nanv ayaṁ*[10] *câi*[11] *'kabandhaḥ: rephaprâptasyâ*[12] *'yaṁ vidhiḥ: vihitânusvârasyâi 'va*[13] *rephanishedhate*[14] *'ti: nâ 'yaṁ doshaḥ: siddhasyâi 'vâ* [15]*'nusvârasya bodhanaṁ*[16] *na tu vidhir iti*[17]: *aṅhom- ....*[15,9] *ṛtap- ... . atî 'ti kim: shaḍ- ....: te ....: aṅhasâ ....:* [18]*aṅhe 'ty*[18] *etâvatâ*[19] *siddhe*[20] *sakalapadapâṭhaḥ kimarthaḥ*[21]: *sa rasam .... iti*[22] *nishedhârthaḥ: pari ....:* [23]*shaḍ-*

same division, and in no other. For *añçunâ, añçunâ te añçuḥ* (i.2.6: G. M. O. end with *te*). For *añçoḥ, yo vâ añçor âyatanam veda* (vi.6.10²: O. omits the last two words, and B. has lost the whole example, with most of the preceding one). For *añçâya, añçâya svâhâ bhagâya* (i.8.13³: G. M. omit *bhagâya*). For *upâñçu, upâñçusavano yad upâñçusavanam* (vi.4.4¹: O. omits the first two words). The word *upâñçu*, when not further compounded, is separated in *pada*-text into *upa-añçu*, and so most of its forms come under the various citations of the cases of *añçu* already illustrated (thus, it furnishes additional instances, not counted above, to *añçu, añçuḥ, añçum*, and *añçoḥ*, twenty in all); but in its compounds it makes, of course, a single *pada* of itself (thus, *upâñçu-savanaḥ*), and so has to be cited in the rule as such (we have other combinations, namely, with *pâtra, yâja*, and *antaryâma*); and, moreover, we have one case, *upâñçâu*, showing a form of *añçu* which does not appear independently, and so furnishing the final citation, for which the example is *tam upâñçâu sam asthâpayan* (vi.4.6¹): there is another in the same division.

The restriction *âdiḥ*, 'after the first vowel,' is intended to guard against any one's imagining that the *s* of *añhasaḥ* and so on is to be preceded by *anusvâra*.

What has thus been given represents the whole comment as found in O.; the other MSS. make two or three troublesome additions, to which it is necessary to return. The last of them regards the citation of *añçu* and its inflectional forms (namely, those that contain *añçu* as a part, or *añçubhiḥ, añçuḥ, añçum, añçunâ*); and, if I understand it aright, it asserts that, if *añçu* alone were cited, the other forms would not be included, because *añçu* itself occurs as a *pada* (and would therefore have to be taken as such, and not as a part of a word, *padâikadeça*); and if it be proposed to cite it with each value, as was done with *kiñçila* (in rule 26: see note to that rule), there remains the difficulty that, as a phonetic complex only, it would involve such cases as *paçum paçupate te adya* (iii.1.4¹: W. omits *paçum*)—where, namely, we have the same elements in combination, only without the *anusvâra*. With regard to *añça*, a somewhat similar statement appears to be made: namely, that if *añça* simply were quoted, it would be understood as a *pada* (being such in *añça-bhuvâ*), and hence *añçam* would

----:[23] *tvayâ----: [24]bhuve 'ti kim: añçe 'ty etâvatâ[25] grahaṇe tathâvidhapadasadbhâvâd añçam[26] ity atra na[27] syât:[24] tenâ ----: [28]apy akârâdi* (i.52) *iti vacanâd anañçu---- ity apy[29] udâharaṇam:[28] vṛshṇo----: prâṇâ----: [30]añçur----:[30] yam ----: [31]añçûn----:[31] añçunâ----: yo----: añçâya----: upâñçu-----: tam----: [32]añçv[33] ity[34] etâvati[35] gṛhîta itareshâm aparigrahaḥ[36] syât [37] tathâvidhapadasadbhâvât: atho 'bhayaṁ gṛhyate padam ekadeçaç[38] ca kiñçilavat: tathâ sati padâikadeçeshu paçum---- ityâdishu prâpnuyâd anusvâraḥ[39]: tac câ 'nish-*

not be included. The comment, however, puts this forward as a reason for including the *bhuvâ* of *añçabhuvâ*, which, according to the interpretation here offered, it would not be; and perhaps my comprehension of the argument is insufficient. I do not see any reason why, if the *pada*-text divides *añça-bhuvâ*, the *bhuvâ* should be given in the rule. Equally unexplainable to me is the special citation of *añçubhiḥ*, which, being divided in *pada* into *añçu-bhiḥ*, falls under *añçu:* we have also in the Sanhitâ *añçubhyâm* (i.4.2 and vi.4.5[3]), which is a case analogous with the other, and ought to be treated like it. Possibly we may infer from the unsuitable position of *añçubhiḥ* in the rule, and from the place of its example as given in W. B., next after that containing *añçu-mat* (as if it were, like the latter, a case of *añçu*), that it has been interpolated, by an awkward and blundering hand; but the conjecture is a more daring one than I venture seriously to make.

The first *excursus* of the comment is in connection with the second citation, *añhaḥ*. Since the *saṁhitâ*-form of this word, we are told, appears by the rule itself to be *añho*, the rule does not apply to *ahaḥ*, which shows a different result of combination in *ahar devânâm* (i.5.9[2]: G. M. read *aharahar*, which is not found in the Sanhitâ before *devânâm*), but only to a word the *visarjanîya* of which does not become *r*. This seems plausible enough; but what shall we say of the *ahaḥ* which appears in *saṁhitâ* as *aho* in *ahobhyâm*, *ahobhiḥ*, and *ahorâtre* (p. *ahaḥ-râtre*)? Either the makers of the treatise overlooked these words, or they did not attribute to the form *añho* in the rule the significance which is here claimed for it.

The remaining passage is more obscure to me than any of the others. In G. M., it is both preceded and followed by the examples for *añhoḥ* and *añhomuk;* in W. B., these examples precede it, excepting the last word of the second, which comes after it. I imagine that its true place is between the two, and that its intent is to turn against the rule the argument just pleaded respecting *añhaḥ*, pointing out that, as *añhoḥ* becomes *añhor* in the rule, it ought not to exhibit *anusvâra* except when occurring in that phonetic form: the objection being then evaded by the plea that the form is given merely as it happens to occur, and not with any

---

ṭam[32]. *âdir iti kim: sarveshu sthâneshu mâ bhûd iti: yathâ*[40] *'ñhasa ityâdi.*

[1] O. ins. *âdiḥ*. [2] G. M. *svarâd-*. [3] G. M. *-gamaṁ*. [4] G. M. *bhajate*. [5] O. om. [(6)] O. om. [7] G. M. *otvasya*. [8] MSS. ins. *añhomugbhyâm*. [(9)] O. om. [10] W. *aya*. [11] G. M. *ca*. [12] W. B. *ekapr-*. [13] G. M. om. *eva*. [14] W. B. *-phaṁ ni-*. [(15)] W. *'nusvâraḥ syât : nodhyayana syât : tu vidhir iti dvikapâlaḥ*; B. *'nusvâra syât : bodhyatâ nanu vidhir iti : dvikapâlaḥ*. [16] G. M. *udbodhanam*. [17] G. M. *ity añhoç cid yâ*. [(18)] W. *añh*; B. *aty*. [19] G. M. *-atâi 'va*. [20] O. *-dheḥ*; B. *dheḥ kutaḥ*. [21] W. *kiṁ*; B. om. [22] B. *ity atrâ 'pi*; G. M. *ityâdi*; O. *ityâdâu*. [(23)] W. B. put next before *apy akârâdi*. [(24)] O. om. [25] G. M. *-vad*. [26] W. B. *açam*. [27] W. B. om. [(28)] O. *anañçu ku* simply. [29] W. om. [(30)] G. M. put before *vṛshṇo*.... [(31)] W. om. [(32)] O. om. [33,34] W. *añça 'ty*; G. M. *añçe 'ty*. [35] B. *-vatâ*. [36] B. *uparigṛha*; G. M. *api grahaṇaṁ*. [37] G. M. ins. *kathaṁ*. [38] G. M. *-devaṁ*. [39] G. M. *-râgamaḥ*. [40] W. O. *a*.

intent of prescription. But I have too little confidence in the correctness of this conjecture to be led to attempt amending the text into giving it consistent expression.

अवग्रह उदात्तो ऽंसेऽंसायाऽंसाभ्यामंसाविति ॥ ३० ॥

30. Also in *añse*, *añsâya*, *añsâbhyâm*, and *añsâu*, when accented on the first syllable.

The term *avagraha* is declared by the commentator to be equivalent here to *âdi* or *padâdi*, 'beginning of the word.' This is, of course, wholly and entirely inadmissible, except as we are driven by the irresistible force of circumstances to give it that meaning or none. There has evidently been some blunder committed, but we can hardly venture to attempt its rectification. Not one of the words here cited occurs, or could occur, as *avagraha*, 'former member of a compound.' The restriction is made with reference to *áñsâu* alone, in order to distinguish it from *asâ'u*. The examples are *dakshiṇe 'ñsa upa dadhâti* (v.3.1[5]: O omits *dadhâti;* W. has lost the whole), *çityañsâya* (vii.3.17: W. has lost *çity*), *añsabhyâñ svâhâ* (vii.3.16[2]), and *uttare 'ñsâv eva prati dadhâti* (v.3.1[5]: O. reads *tishṭhati* for *dadhâti*, but doubtless by a copyist's error only); the counter-example is *asâv alravîc citravihitâ* (ii.5.2[5]: O. omits the last word); *añsâbhyâm* alone is found more than once in the text (namely, again at v.7.13).

नासावा नासावा ॥ ३१ ॥

31. But not in *asâv â*.

There is a single passage where the pronoun *asâu*, in the vocative case, stands at the beginning of a clause, and is, accordingly, accented on the first syllable; hence the necessity of the present rule, establishing an exception under its predecessor. The passage is *brûyâ'd ásâv é 'hî 'ty evám evá* (ii.4.9[3]: O. alone has *eva;* G. M. omit also *evam*, and B. blunderingly reads instead of it *atra*).

The Prâtiçâkhya's rehearsal of the cases of interior *anusvâra* is,

---

30. *avagraha âdir ity arthaḥ: yadi*[1] *padâdir udâttaḥ syât tarhy añse* [2]------ *ity eteshu*[3] *syâd anusvârâgamaḥ. itiçabdaḥ svarûpavâcî. dakshiṇe*----:[2] *çity*----: *añsâ*----: *uttare*---- *âdir udâtta iti kim: asâv*----

[1] B. *pari.* [(2)] W. om. [3] G. M. *-shaṁ.*

31. *âdyudâtte*[1] *saty apy*[2] [3]*asâv e 'ty*[3] *asmin* [4]*grahaṇe na khalu*[4] *syâd anusvârâgamaḥ. brûyâd*----

iti tribhâshyaratne[5] *prâtiçâkhyavivaraṇe*
shoḍaço[6] *'dhyâyaḥ.*

[1] W. *yady ud-;* B. *yady udâttatve.* [2] B. O. om. [(3)] W. *asâv ii ty;* B. *asâu;* G M. O. *asâv ity.* [(4)] O. om. [5] B. *çritri-.* [6] G. M. O. *dvitîyapraçne caturtho.*

so far as I have been able to discover, complete for the present Tâittirîya-Sanhitâ, with the exception of the two compounds (*strîshañsâda* and *svâdushañsad*) noticed under rule 26. Whether its rules are so drawn as to involve no cases that require to be excluded, is a much more difficult question, and one which my examination of the text has not been close enough to enable me to determine; but I have noted no instances of inaccuracy, unless the possible confusion of *añhaḥ* and *ahaḥ*, pointed out under rule 29, is to be so considered.

CHAPTER XVII.

CONTENTS: 1–4, opinions of various authorities, as to the degree of nasality in different nasal letters; 5, as to increase of quantity in connection with *anusvâra;* 6, as to increased effort required by certain accents; 7–8, as to other more general matters of utterance.

तीव्रतरमानुनासिक्यमनुस्वारोत्तमेष्विति शैत्यायनः ॥ १ ॥

1. Çâityâyana says that the nasal quality is stronger in *anusvâra* and the nasal mutes.

We have here a chapter entirely composed of the cited opinions of certain specified authorities, and none of them of any definite value or importance in themselves, though interesting as affording us a glimpse of subjects to which the attention of the old Hindu phonetists was drawn, and to their hair-splitting and discordant speculations respecting them.

The commentator's exposition adds nothing to our comprehension of the rule. It quotes the rule at the end of the second chapter (ii.52) as to the cause of nasal quality, and tries (without good reason) to connect with it the present one. Examples of the stronger nasal utterance are given, as follows: *agnîñr apsushadaḥ*

---

1. [1]*anusvâraç co 'ttamâç*[2] *câ 'nusvârottamâḥ: teshu tîvrataram bhavaty ânunâsikyam iti çâityâyano nâma munir manyate*[1]. *tîvrâd adhikaṁ tîvrataram: anunâsikatâ*[3] *'nunâsikyam: nâsikâvivaraṇâd ânunâsikyam* (ii.52) *ity asya vidheḥ prayatnadârḍhyam*[4] *upadiçyate.* [5] *yathâ*[6]*: agnîñr....:* [7]*tâñs....: martyâñ....*[7]*: yaṁ....:* [8]*vañcate....: maṇinâ....*[8] *eteshv*[9] *iti kim: rukmam....: tigmam....:* [10]*suçl-....*[10]

(1) O. om. [2] W. *-maç.* [3] W. *-sikâ;* B. *-sikânâṁ bhâvaḥ.* [4] W. O. *-dirgham;* B. *-dârbyûm;* G. M. *prâyadârthyam.* [5] O. ins. *anusvârottamâ anunâsikâ ity etâny anunâsikasthânâni. anusvârottameshu titrataram ânunâsikyaṁ bhavati çâityâyano nâma manyate.* [6] G. M. O. om. (7) in O. only. (8) O. *prâṅ....* [9] O. *anusvârottameshv.* (10) O. *sa....: eteshu câi 'va tivrataram.*

(v.6.1[2]), *yam kâmam kâmayate* (vii.1.1[2]: G. M. O. substitute *yam kâmayeta*, i.6.10[4] et al.), *vañcate parivañcate* (iv.5.3[1]), and *maninâ rûpâṇî 'ndreṇa* (vii.3.14); but O. introduces after the first *tâñs te dadhâmi* (iv.1.10[3]) and *martyâñ âviveça* (v.7.9[1]), and substitutes for the last two *prâń prâ 'dravat* (v.7.10[1]). Counter-examples, of the weaker utterance, are *rukmam upa dadhâti* (v.2.7[2]: but W. substitutes, by an evident blunder, *kûrmam upadadhâti*, v.2.8[5]), *tigmam âyudham* (iv.7.15[4]), and *suçlokâñ3 sumańgalâñ3* (i.8.16[2]); O. giving instead of the last *sa imam lokam* (i.5.9[4]), and spoiling the whole illustration by adding, "in these likewise it is stronger." The first two counter-examples are evidently given for the *yama* which, by xxi.12, is to be inserted between the mute and nasal in each: the last is a case falling under xv.8, which prescribes nasalization of a protracted final *a*. The other nasal sounds are the *nâsikya* (xxi.14), and the nasal semivowels into which *m* and *n* are to be converted (v.26,28) before *l*, *y*, and *v*: these last are instanced by the phrase quoted in O. alone.

The manuscript O. follows an independent course in the exposition of this rule, as of the rest composing the chapter.

समꣳ सर्वत्रेति कौहलीपुत्रः ॥ २ ॥

2. Kâuhalîputra says that it is the same everywhere.

The comment interprets *samam*, 'same,' as signifying here *tîvrataram*, which it had explained above as an absolute rather than a relative comparative—'very excessive,' rather than 'more excessive.' That does not seem likely to be the real meaning. As examples, are cited, rather needlessly, *sañrarâṇâḥ* (iv.6.1[1] et al.), *saṁyattâḥ* (i.5.1[1] et al.), *nyańń agniç cetavyaḥ* (v.5.3[2]: only O. has *cetavyaḥ*), and *upahûtâñ3 ho* (ii.6.7[3]). O. gives an entirely different, though equivalent, exposition, and only the last two of these examples, with two others, namely *sarvâñ agnîñr apsushadaḥ* (v.6.1[2]) and *imâń lokâń* (ii.1.3[1]).

The name of the authority quoted is given by G. M. as Kâuhalîyaputra, and by O. as Kohalîputra, in both the text and commentary.

अनुस्वारेऽण्विति भारद्वाजः ॥ ३ ॥

3. Bhâradvâja says it is faint in *anusvâra*.

---

2. *sarvatrâ 'nunâsikavarṇeshu*[1] *tîvrataratvaṁ* [2]*samam iti*[2] *kâuhalîputro*[3] *manyate. saṁr-....: saṁy-....: nyańń-....: upa-....: ityâdi.*

[1] W. B. *-sikyav-*; G. M. *-sikyaṁ v-*. [(2)] W. *sarvatve 'ti*. [3] G. M. (as also in the rule) *-liyap-*.

O. substitutes for the whole *anusvârottamâdishu sarveshu samaviçesheṇâ 'nunâsikyaṁ syâd iti kohalıputra âcâryo manyate sma: tivrataram ity arthaḥ: nyańń ....: sarvâñ....: imâń....: upa-....*

The term *aṇu*, 'faint,' is explained by *sûkshmatamam* (or, in G. M. O., *sûkshmataram*), 'exceedingly gentle.' In other nasals than *anusvâra*, we are told, Bhâradvâja accepts Çâityâyana's rule, that the nasal quality is extra-strong in the nasal mutes, and simply strong in the *yamas* etc. Most of the MSS. quote only *tanuvâ jaya tvañ satvâ* (iv.6.6[1]: B. has dropped out all but the beginning, *nanu*, and O. has lost *tanuvâ ja* from the beginning); but O. adds counter-examples, *brahmaṇvanto devâ âsan* (vi.4.10[1]), *rukmam upa dadhâti* (v.2.7[2]), and *tat saṁyatâñ saṁyatvam* (v.2.10[6]).

नकारस्य रेफोष्मयकारभावाल्लुप्ते च मलोपाच्चोत्तरमुत्तरं तीव्रतरमिति स्थविरः कौण्डिन्यः ॥ ४ ॥

4. Old Kâuṇḍinya says that when *n* is converted into *r*, or into a spirant, or into *y̆* (with loss of the *y*), or when *m* is lost, it is stronger in each case successively.

The alterations of an original nasal mute are here rehearsed in the same order, and in the same terms, as in a previous rule (xv.1). The comment gives an example for each case: namely *trîñr ekâdaçâñ iha* (iii.2.11[3]: G. M. have lost *iha*, along with all that follows, to the last example; O. substitutes *trîñr uta dyûn*, ii.1.11[5]), *çuklâñç ca kṛshṇâñç ca* (ii.3.1[3]: O. substitutes *ṛtûñs tanvate*, iv.3.11[3]), *mahâñ indraḥ* (i.4.20 et al.: O. substitutes *svarâñ indro asme*, i.7.13[5]), and *sañçitam* (iv.1.10[3] et al.: O. substitutes *viharyañ çasyam*, vii.5.5[2]). The first combination is styled *saṁyo-*

---

3. *'aṇu sûkshmatamam*[1] *ânunâsikyam anusvâre syâd iti bhâradvâjo manyate. yathâ*[2]*: tanuvâ----. anusvârâd anyatra çâityâyanavidhiḥ: uttameshu tîvrataratvaṁ yamâdishu tîvramâtram iti.*

[1] G. M. *anusûkshmataram.* [2] G. M. om.

O. substitutes for the whole *bhâradvâjasya ''câryasya mate 'nusvâre 'ṇur bharaty ânunâsikyaṁ : sûkshmataram ity arthaḥ: ya tvañ----: anusvâra iti kiṁ : ato 'nyatra çâityâyanavidhiḥ: brahm-----: ruk-----: tat----*

4. *nakârasya rephoshmayakârabhâvâc*[1] *cakârâkṛshṭayakâre*[2] *lupte* [3] *sati malopâc co 'ttaram uttaram*[4] *ânunâsikyam*[5] *ânupûrvyeṇa tîvrataraṁ syâd*[6] *iti sthaviraḥ kâuṇḍinyo manyate. yathâ*[7]*:* [8]*trîñr----* [2]*ity atrâ ''nunâsikyaṁ saṁyogamâtravat: çukl----- ity* [10]*atra saṁçlishṭam*[10]*: mahâñ----: ity atra tîvrataram:*[9] *sañ----- ity atra tîvrataram: ity ânupûrvyaṁ vijñeyam*[8]*:* [11]*ato 'nyatra*[11] *çâityâyanavidhiḥ.*

[1] O. *rephabhâvâd ûshmabhâvâd yak-.* [2] O. *-shṭe ya-.* [3] G. M. ins. *ca.* [4] G. M. om. (and read *'ttamam* for *'ttaram uttaram* in rule). [5] O. om. [6] O. *anunâsikyam bharati.* [7] G. M. om.; O. *sma.* [(8)] O. substitutes *trîñr--- : ṛt-----: sva-----: â viveça: vih-----: trîñr---- ity atra tîvrata saṁyogamâtraṁ : ṛt----- ity atra saṁçlishṭaṁ: sva----- ityatra tîvrataraṁ: vih---- itra tîvrataraṁ.* [(9)] G. M. om. [(10)] W. *atra tu çl-;* B. *atrânunâ saṁçl-.* [(11)] W. B. G. M. *atra.*

samatravat, 'simple conjunction;' the second, *sañçlishṭa*, 'fused together;' the third and fourth, only *tivratara*, 'more excessive.' And it is added at the end (only O. making the statement intelligibly) that in other cases Çâityâyana's rule (xvii.1) applies.

व्यञ्जनकालश्च स्वरस्यात्राधिकः ॥ ५ ॥

5. And to the vowel is added, in this case, the time of a consonant.

The "and" (*ca*) in the rule is declared to continue the implication of Old Kâuṇḍinya's opinion: according to this authority, here, in the prescription of *anusvâra*, the time of a consonant, half a *mora* (i.37), is to be added to the vowel that is accompanied by *anusvâra*; an example is *yuñjâthâñ râsabhaṁ yuvam* (iv.1.2[1] et al.). And "in this case" (*atra*, literally 'here') is added in the rule because the prescription of increased quantity is not of force in the cases detailed in the sixteenth chapter, in nasal mutes, nor where *n* or *m* is converted into *l* (v.25,26,28).

O. states the same thing in other language, giving two additional examples, *çatrûñr anapavyayantaḥ* (iv.6.6[3]) and *añhomuce* (i.6.12[3] et al.)—of which the latter, being one of those established in the sixteenth chapter (xvi.29), ought to be a counter-example—and remarking further that in the opinion of other teachers the *anusvâra* merely was added to the vowel. *Anusvâra*, namely, was declared by i.34 to have the quantity of a short vowel; and we should be grateful if the commentator had pointed out in what relation this rule really stands to that; if, indeed, there is any connection between them, and if this does not belong properly to a doctrine that regards the *anusvâra* as an affection of the vowel merely; causing the latter's prolongation, to be sure, but not adding an element with independent quantity to it. O. appends the further restriction that the vowel undergoing prolongation is to be a simple one (not a diphthong). And it mentions another interpretation, as put forward by some authorities: that *atra* signifies wherever *anusvâra* is prescribed: and that where there is *anusvâra*, there the quantity of the vowel is to be short in every case.

---

5. *cakâra sthavirakâuṇḍinyam*[1] *anvâdiçati: atrâ 'nusvâravidhâne sânunâsikasvarasya vyañjanakâlo hrasvârdhakâlo 'dhikaḥ syâd iti sthaviraḥ kâuṇḍinyo manyate: yuñj---- ityâdi. atrâi 'va svarasye 'ti kim: svâdishû 'ttameshû 'ttamalabhâve*[2] *câi*[3] *'tad adhikakâlavidhânam*[4] *mâ bhûd iti.*

[1] W. B. *-raḥ kâu-*; G. M. *-nyamatam.* [2] W. B. *-mâbhâ-.* [3] B. *nâi*; G. M. *vâi.* [4] W. *adhikâl-*; G. M. *adhitakâl-.*

O. substitutes for the whole *atrâ 'nusvâre vyañjanakâlo hrasvârddhakâlamâtraḥ svarasyâ 'dhiko bhavati svarakâlât: çatr----: añh----: yuñj----. caçabda sthaviraḥkâuṇḍinyamatanvâdiçati: itarâcâryamate 'nusvâra eva svarasyâ 'dhika syât: atre 'ti kim: svâdishu 'ttameshu uttamalabhâve samânâksharâshu câi 'tad adhikâlavidhâna mâ bhût teshu svarakâlâdhiko 'nusvâra syât: apara âhuḥ atre 'tyanunâsikavidhâna ity arthaḥ: anusvârabhâve 'pi vyañjanakâlo hrasvakâlo bhavati yadâ 'nusvâras tadâ sarvatra hrasvakâla eva syât.*

The Rik (xiii.13) and Vâjasaneyi (iv.147–8) Prâtiçâkhyas also concern themselves with the respective length of a vowel and of *anusvâra* as constituents of a syllable, but their rules stand in no definable relation to the one here given.

स्वारविक्रमयोर्दृढप्रयत्नतरः पौष्करसादेः ॥ ६ ॥

6. Pâushkarasâdi says the utterance of *svâra* and *vikrama* is attended with firmer effort.

Most of the manuscripts supply in the comment *prayoga*, 'use, application,' as the subject involved in this rule; O. supplies simply *varṇa*, 'alphabetic sound.' *Svâra*, we are told, means *svarita*, 'circumflex;' O. signifying the same thing by pointing out that the *svâras* are enumerated in the twentieth chapter (xx.1–8). *Vikrama* is a particular kind of *anudâtta*, 'grave;' or, O. says, is explained in the nineteenth chapter (xix.1,2). As examples are given *yò 'syá svò 'gnís tám ápi* (v.7.9[1]: G. M. O. omit the last two words) and *ásyè havíḥ priyám* (iii.3.11[1]), for the latter of which O. substitutes *çikyàm abhy úpa dadhâti* (v.2.4[3]): we have here two kinds of *svâra* or *svarita*, namely *abhinihata* (xx.4) and *nitya* (xx.2), and one or more cases of *vikrama* (the grave syllable standing directly between two that are either acute or circumflex) in each example. A counter-example is *gá'm̐ vá'vá tá'u tát páry avadatâm* (i.7.2[2]: only O. has the last two words), which contains (except in O.'s addition) neither *svâra* nor *vikrama*.

प्रयत्नविशेषात्सर्ववर्णानामिति शैत्यायनः ॥ ७ ॥

7. Çâityâyana says, of all the letters, according to their difference of effort.

The comment (except in O.) supplies the same subject as in the preceding rule, namely *prayoga;* and also continues the predicate of that rule, *dṛḍhaprayatnataraḥ.* The latter we can hardly approve, since to assert a specially firm effort of all alphabetic sounds without exception is little better than nonsense. Çâityâyana may rather be credited with meaning that each constituent of the alphabet has its own proper (*svocita*) degree of articulative effort—which is more true than edifying.

---

6. *svâre vikrame ca prayogaḥ pâushkarasâder mate*[1] *dṛḍhaprayatnataro bhavati. svâraḥ svarita ity arthaḥ: vikramo nâmâ 'nudâttaviçeshaḥ. yathâ*[2]*: yo....: âsye..... svâravikramayor iti kim: gâm̐..... dṛḍhaḥ*[3] *prayatno* [4]*yasyâ 'sâu*[4] *dṛḍhaprayatnaḥ: atiçayena dṛḍhaprayatno dṛḍhaprayatnataraḥ.*

[1] B. *-tam̐.* [2] G. M. om. [3] W. B. *-ḍha;* G. M. *-ḍha eva.* (4) G. M. om.

O. substitutes for the whole *svârâ vinçadanuvâke gâṇyante : ekâttavinçadanuvâke vikramâḥ svâreshu vikrameshu ca dṛdhaprayatnataro vaṇo bhavati páuskarasádar mate çikyam ... yo....: svâravikramayor iti kim : gá m̐ ....*

As example, is cited the first phrase of the Sanhitâ, *ishe tvo "rje tvâ* (i.1.1: only O. has the last two words).

The manuscripts of the commentary leave us quite in a quandary as to the value of these seven rules, W. B. calling them approved, but G. M. O. unapproved.

नातिव्यक्तं न चाव्यक्तमेवं वर्णानुदिङ्गयेत् ।
पयःपूर्णमिवामत्रं हरन्धीरो यथामति ॥

इत्यात्रेय आत्रेयः ॥ ८ ॥

8. Âtreya says, one must utter the sounds not over-distinctly and not indistinctly; taking, as it were, a vessel filled with drink, steady, according to the sense.

The commentator gives only a simple paraphrase of this verse, and casts no real light upon its meaning, even as regards the naïve and not very instructive comparison in the second line.

CHAPTER XVIII.

CONTENTS: 1–7, opinions of various authorities as to the mode of utterance of the auspicious syllable *om.*

---

7. *sarvavarṇânâm prayogaḥ*[1] *svocitaprayatnaviçeshâd*[2] *dṛḍhaprayatnataro*[3] *bhavatî 'ti çâityâyano manyate. yathâ*[4]*: ishe---- ityâdi.*

[5]*nâi 'tâni*[5] *sapta sûtrâṇî 'shṭâni.*

[1] B. *-ga.* [2] B. *syoc-;* W. B. *-shâ;* G. M. *-shât.* [3] W. *-tnaḥ prayatnatamo;* B. *-tnaḥ prayatnataro.* [4] G. M. om. [(5)] W. B. *etâni.*

O. substitutes for the whole *çâityâyanasyâ "câryasya mate svaprayatnaviçeshâtth sarvavarṇânâṁ vâiçeshyâd dṛḍhaprayatnataraḥ evaṁ varṇeshu bhavati : na svâsvâravikramayor eve 'ti : yathâ : ishe---- nâi 'tâni* etc.

8. *ativyaktam*[1] *atispashṭam avyaktam aspashṭaṁ ca*[2] *yathâ na bhavaty evaṁ varṇân udiṅgayed uccârayed* [3]*ity arthaḥ*[3]*: payaḥpûrṇam ivâ*[4] *'matraṁ kshîrapûritam*[5] *bhâjanaṁ*[6] [7]*harann iva*[7] *yathâmati matim*[8] *anatikramya* [9]*dhîro 'dhyetâ*[9] *bhaved*[10] *ity âtreyo manyate.*

iti tribhâshyaratne prâtiçâkhyavivaraṇe
saptadaço[11] *'dhyâyaḥ.*

[1] W. *nâ 'tiv-.* [2] O. om. [(3)] G. M. om. [4] O. om. *iva.* [5] W. *kshîram apû-;* B. *-îraparipû-;* O. *-îraṁ pû-* [6] G. M. *amatram.* [(7)] O. *pâratniva.* [8] W. O. *m.* [(9)] W. O. om. *dhîro;* G. M. *adhyatâ yathâ dhîro.* [10] G. M. *-vet tathe.* [11] G. M. O. *dvitiyapraçne pañcamo.*

ओकारं तु प्रणव एके ऽर्धतृतीयमात्रं ब्रुवते ॥ १ ॥

1. As *praṇava*, some utter *o* with two and a half *moras*.

In the text of this rule, T. reads *oṅkâram*, and B. *oṁkâram;* in the comment, at the beginning, W. B. have *oṁkâram*. Doubtless the unnasalized form is the true reading; that *oṅ* or *oṁ* should be uttered with more than the quantity of a long syllable would not be worth the trouble of specifying, in view of rules i.34 and xvii.5, which would require either three or two and a half *moras* for the combination. Whether we are to infer that this holy exclamation was not yet uttered with a nasal ending at the time when the Prâtiçâkhya was made, is a more doubtful question; the whole matter lies, at any rate, outside the proper province of a Prâtiçâkhya. By way of examples, the comment appears to intend to quote the first and last words of the Sanhitâ and of the Brâhmaṇa: namely *oṁ ishe tvâ* (i.1.1), *samudro bandhuḥ oṁ* (vii.5.25²? see below: B. omits the *oṁ*), *oṁ brahma saṁdhattam* (Tâitt. Brâh. i.1.1), and *yebhyaç câi 'nat prâhuḥ oṁ* (B. omits the *oṁ*. the Calcutta edition of the Tâittirîya-Brâhmaṇa being incomplete, I can only presume that these are the concluding words of that treatise). The manuscripts G. M. O. put these extracts in a different order, giving the two conclusions first, and then the two beginnings; G. M. add *oṁ* at the end of each, while O. gives no *oṁ* at all. G. M. further append two more citations, *bhadraṁ karṇebhiḥ : oṁ*, and *âi 'va tapati : oṁ*, of which the former is the beginning, and the latter, I presume, the end, of the Tâittirîya-Âraṇyaka. With regard to the phrase *samudro bandhuḥ*, it is to be observed that the Sanhitâ as found in my manuscript (or rather, manuscripts, for mine contains the last leaf of another and entirely independent one, which has the same reading), and in those to which Prof. Weber has access, ends with *samudraḥ* simply; but another word like this is evidently wanting to complete the sense (the concluding sentence is *samudro vâ açvasya yoniḥ samudraḥ*), and is not less needed to make up the tale of words as enumerated in the ending, which counts "twelve" after *avahat*, while without *bandhuḥ* there are

---

1. *praṇava*[1] *okâram*[2] [3]*ardhatṛtîyamâtrạm eke bruvate*[3]*:* [4]*eka âcâryâ ardhatṛtîyamâtram* [5] *âhur ity arthaḥ*[4]*.* [6]*ardhaṁ*[7] *tṛtîyaṁ yayos te ardhatṛtîye: ardhatṛtîyamâtre*[8] *yasyâ 'sâv*[6] *ardhatṛtîyamâtraḥ*[9]*. yathâ*[10]*:* [11]*om ishe tvâ: samudro bandhuḥ: oṁ: oṁ brahma saṁdhattam: yebhyaç câi 'nat prâhuḥ: oṁ*[11]*. kâlanirṇaye 'py evaṁ* [12] *varṇitam:*

svâdhyâyârambhaçeshasya [13]*praṇavasya svarasya ca*[13]*:*
adhyâyasyâ[14] [15]*'nuvâkasyâ 'nte syâd ardhatṛtîyatâ*[15]*.*

tuçabdasya[16] *prayojanam ucyate: saṁdhyaksharâṇâṁ vedapraṇavaṁ*[17] *câ 'ntarâ tathe 'ti kâlanirṇaye: saṁdhyaksharâṇâṁ* [18]*hrasvâ na santî*[18] *'ti*[19] *pâṇinîye 'py okâramâtrasya*[20] *dîrghakâlo*[21]

only eleven. This is a very strange fact, and calls for a wider examination of Tâittirîya manuscripts, to see if any of them have saved the lost final word.

Then is quoted a verse "from the Kâlanirṇaya," to the effect that "the quantity of two and a half *moras* belongs to the *praṇava* and to a vowel forming the beginning or end (?) of a passage that one reads in the Veda, also at the end of a chapter or section." The Kâlanirṇaya quoted here and below must, of course, be a very different work from that of Mâdhava bearing the same title (Weber's Catalogue of the Berlin Sanskrit MSS., No. 1166).

In explanation of the word *tu* in the rule, another half-verse, from which I extract no suitable meaning, is quoted from the Kâlanirṇaya, and the authority of Pâṇini is further appealed to to prove that among the diphthongs there is no short quantity: hence for simple *o* long quantity is determined: here, "however" (*tu*), when the diphthong stands in *praṇava*, that quantity is negatived; and (quoting, apparently, another half-verse) for the *praṇava*, as occurring in the Veda, is prescribed long quantity along with [the quantity of?] a *m*. That is to say, the *tu* intimates a denial of the ordinary quantity of the diphthong *o*. And the remark is finally added that a difference of quantity is to be recognized in the different *praṇavas*.

उदात्तानुदात्तस्वरितानां कस्मिंश्चिदिति शैत्यायनः ॥ २ ॥

2. Çâityâyana says it is to be uttered with either one of acute, grave, or circumflex.

The comment simply paraphrases the rule, adding nothing in its explanation—not even telling us in what relation it stands to rule 7, and whether Çâityâyana would let us give the word, in any given case of its use, whatever accent we chose, or would have us governed by reasons in our choice between the three accents.

---

nirûpitaḥ[22]*: iha tu*[23] *praṇavasthatvaviçesheṇâ*[24] *'sâu kâlo nishidhyate: vedasthapraṇave*[25] *tu syât* [26]*samakâradvimâtrate*[26] *'ti.* [27]*praṇavaviçeshe kâlaviçeshaḥ*[27] *pratyetavyaḥ.*

[1] W. B. *-vc*; G. M. *-vena.* [2] W. B. *oṁkâ-.* (3) O. *-tiyamâvate.* (4) G. M. O. om. [5] B. ins. *iti.* (6) W. *ardhatṛtiyamâtraṁ bruvate : praṇave okâram.* [7] B. O. *ardha.* [8] G. M. O. *mâtre.* [9] G. M. *-tiyas tam*; O. *tiyamâs tam : sârdhadvimâtra ity arthaḥ.* [10] W. B. O. om. (11) G. M. *sam-....: oṁ: ye-....: oṁ: ish-....: oṁ: brah-.... : oṁ: bhad-....: oṁ: âi....: oṁ*; O. *sam-....: ye-....: ish-....: brah-....* [12] B. ins. *ca.* (13) B. *praṇavasvaratasya* [14] B. *adhyâyaç câ.* (15) G. M. *-kasya tv ante 'to 'rdhatṛ-*; O. *-tiye tâ.* [16] B. *nuç-*; G. M. *antaç-.* [17] G. M. *-dañ ca pr-*; O. *-daṁ ca prâṇavâṁ.* (18) O. *-svo nâ 'sti.* [19] W. om. *iti.* [20] O. *okârasya.* [21] W. G. M. *-le.* [22] G. M. *-te.* [23] B. om. [24] O. *-shâd*; G. M. *-shaṇâd.* [25] W. B. O. *-sya pr-.* (26) B. *-kâlo dv-*; G. M. *-kâle dv-*; O *-kâre dvimâtrete.* (27) G. M. *praṇavasya viçeshaḥ.*

2. *udâttânudâttasvaritânâm madhye kasminç cit svare praṇavaḥ prayoktavya iti çâityâyano brûte. yathâ: oṁ.*

O. substitutes *utte anudâtte svarite vâ eshâ madhyaṭamena svareṇa prayoktavya syâd i çâityâyanamaḥ âcâryo manyate : os os.*

धृतप्रचयः कौण्डिन्यस्य ॥ ३ ॥

3. According to Kâuṇḍinya, it is a sustained *pracaya.*

I have ventured to translate the word *dhṛta* in *dhṛtapracaya* by 'sustained,' but without feeling sure that it might not have been better to follow the lead of the commentator, who treats *dhṛtapracaya* as equivalent to simple *pracaya.* He brings up, it is true, the objection that in xix.2 the use of the term *pracaya* itself is attributed to this same Kâuṇḍinya, and that hence it should have been used here; but replies "not so; by this pair of words, even, an appellation is given: thus, namely: on the principle that even where there is no difference of meaning there may be a difference of application, the teacher exhibits a nicety of application: other examples of the principle are the names [of the second Pâṇḍava] Bhîmasena and Bhîma, [of one of Çiva's wives] Bhâmâ [G. M. say Satyâ] and Satyabhâmâ, *pidhâna* and *apidhâna*, *dîpa* and *pradîpa.*" The *pracaya* is defined as the fourth accent; and O. adds that it is to be explained in the twenty-first chapter (namely, at xxi.10,11): it is there said to be of the same tone as *udâtta*, 'acute;' so that, unless *dhṛta* is to be regarded as signifying a modification, one does not see in what respect Kâuṇḍinya's opinion differs from that of Vâlmîki, given in rule 6 of this chapter.

मध्यमेन स वाक्प्रयोगः ॥ ४ ॥

4. That application of the voice is with middle tone.

The meaning of this precept is very obscure, and the commentator's exposition does not give the impression that he comprehended it. According to him, the *sa*, 'that,' points us back to the utterance as prescribed by Kâuṇḍinya in the preceding rule: in whatever pitch of voice the application is made, the *praṇava* is to be used with medial effort, or with one that takes into account the

---

3. *kâuṇḍinyasya*[1] *mate praṇavo dhṛtapracayo bhavati: caturthaḥ*[2] *svaro dhṛtapracaya iti kathyate. nanu pracayapûrvaç ca kâuṇḍinyasya* (xix.2) *itivat pracaya ity etâvatâi 'vâ 'lam:* [3]*kiṁ dhṛtaçabdena. mâi 'vam:*[3] *padadvayenâ 'py anena nâmadheyam abhidhîyate*[4]*: tathâ hi: arthabhedâbhâve*[5] *'pi prayogabhedo*[6] *'stî 'ti prayogacâturyam*[7] *âcâryaḥ prakaṭayati: yathâ: bhîmaseno*[8] *bhîmaḥ: bhâmâ*[9] *satyabhâmâ* [10]*: pidhânam apidhânam: dîpaḥ pradîpa ityâdi.*

[1] W. *-nya.* [2] B. G. M. *-tha.* (3) G. M. *dhṛtaçabdo nâma : evaṁ.* [4] G. M. *evá 'bh-.* [5] B. *ardhabh-;* G. M. *itthaṁ bhe-.* [6] B. *-gaprabh-.* [7] W *-gântaracâ-.* [8] W. *-ne;* B. *-na.* [9] G. M. om. [10] G. M. ins. *satyâ.*

O. substitutes *dhṛtaḥpracayo nâma turiyasvaraḥ sa evâi 'kar[illegible]se 'nuvâke vakshyate dhṛtapracaya iti nâmadheyaṁ prayâṇâm api vyapadiçyate iti kauṅḍinya âcâryo manyate dhṛtapracayaḥ praṇavo bhavati yathâ om iti: udâttapracayo çrutyabhedaṁ tat svaravijñânukṛtaṁ phalam anutiyate.*

combination of high and low tone. The relation of *vâk* in the compound is described as that of a locative case, and the word is paraphrased by *vâcaḥ sthâne*, 'in position (i. e., I presume, 'quality' or 'temperament:' compare xxii.11, xxiii.4,5) of voice.'

स्वरितः प्लाक्षिप्लाक्षायणयोः ॥ ५ ॥

5. According to Plâkshi and Plâkshâyaṇa, it is circumflexed.

This rule is, along with its three predecessors, pronounced by the commentator unapproved.

उदात्तो वाल्मीकेः ॥ ६ ॥

6. According to Vâlmîki, it is acute.

This is the only rule in the chapter, except the first, which the commentator allows to stand as approved. In his school, then, the vowel part of the sacred exclamation is to be two and a half *moras* long, and of acute tone. This agrees with the teaching of the Vâj. (ii.51) and Rik (xv.3) Prâtiçâkhyas, save that these give (what is really equivalent to the same thing) three *moras* to the whole word *om;* and the Rik Pr. mentions other opinions both as to its quantity and its accent.

यथाप्रयोगं वा सर्वेषां यथाप्रयोगं वा सर्वेषाम् ॥ ७ ॥

7. All allow that it may also be according to the application.

The commentator first quotes an absurd opinion of Mâhisheya's, to the effect that *yathâprayogam*, 'according to the application,' here means *udâtta*, 'acute;' but then goes on to set forth, as given by Vararuci, what appears to be the real meaning of the rule: namely, that with whatever tone the passage to be read [i. e. its beginning] is used, that tone is to be given also to the introductory exclamation. Thus, before *ishé tvâ* (i.1.1 et al.), which begins with

---

4. *prayujyata iti prayogaḥ: madhyameno 'ccanîcasamâhâravicakshaṇena prayatnena praṇavaḥ*[1]*: yatra*[2] *kvacana vâca sthâne*[3] *prayogo bhavati. sa*[4] *iti kâuṇḍinyâbhimataḥ pûrvokto gṛhyate. vâci prayogo vâkprayogaḥ.*

[1] W. *-vi;* G. M. *-vaḥ prayoktavyaḥ.* [2] W. *anya-.* [3] W. B. *-na.* [4] B. om. O. substitutes *ko 'yaṁ praṇavo nâma câvaprayogaḥ* [i. e. *vâkpr-*] *kâudinyamatam âdiçya yatra kvacana sthâne dıyate : tena madhyamena svareṇa prayoktavyaḥ.*

5. *plâkshiplâkshâyaṇayoḥ* [1] *pakshe*[2] *svarito bhavati. nâi 'tat sûtracatushṭayam ishṭam.*

[1] O. ins. *âcâryayor.* [2] O. *mate;* G. M. O. add *praṇava.*

6. *vâlmîker mate praṇava udâtto bhavati.*[1]

[1] O. adds *yathâ.*

grave, the *om* is to be grave; before *ấpa undantu* (i.2.1[1]: wanting in W. B.), acute; before *vy'ṛddham* (v.1.2[1]: W. B. have instead, evidently as a corrupt reading only, *vyûdhaḥ*, with which word no *anuvâka* in the Sanhitâ begins), circumflex.

The rule is declared unapproved—rather hard treatment for one which professes to lay down a principle accepted by all authorities.

CHAPTER XIX.

CONTENTS: 1–2, occurrence of *vikrama*, between syllables of high tone; 3–5, of *kampa*, in a circumflex followed by a circumflex.

स्वरितयोर्मध्ये यत्र नीचं स्यादुदात्तयोर्वान्यतरतो वोदात्तस्वरितयोः स विक्रमः ॥ १ ॥

1. Where a syllable of low tone occurs between two circumflex syllables, or two acute, or two of which either one is acute and the other circumflex, that is *vikrama*.

The commentator paraphrases the rule as if *anyataratah* meant 'between a preceding circumflex and a following acute,' and the following *udâttasvaritayoḥ* 'between a preceding acute and a fol-

---

7. *yathâprayogaçabdeno*[1] *'dâtto 'bhidhîyata iti mâhisheyapakshaḥ: praṇave*[2] *yathâprayogaṁ vâ kuryâd iti sarveshâm ṛshîṇâm matam. vararucipakshas tu vakshyate: adhyeshyamâṇaṁ*[3] *yathâprayogaṁ yathâvidhasvaraṁ 'tathâvidhena vâ*[4] *svareṇa praṇavaḥ prayoktavya iti sarveshâm matam iti. yathâ*[5]*: ishe tve 'ty anenâ 'dhyeshyamâṇenâ*[6] *'nudâttena prâṇavo 'py anudâttaḥ: 'âpa undantv ity udâtteno 'dâttaḥ*[7]*: vyṛddham iti*[8] *svaritena svaritaḥ.*

ne 'daṁ sûtraṁ ishṭam.

O. (corrected a little) substitutes *yathâvidhena svareṇá 'dhyeshyamâṇo bhavati: tathâvidhena svareṇâi 'va praṇavaḥ prayoktavyaḥ: esho vá sarveshâm âcâryâṇâṁ sâdhâraṇapraṇavavidhir bhavet: ishe tve 'ty etad adhyeshyamânena udâttaḥ praṇavo vaktavyaḥ: âpa...., ity udâttaḥ: vyṛddham iti svaritaḥ: âcâryagrahaṇaṁ teshâṁ kîrtyarthaṁ: pakshaparigrahavijñânasadṛshṭaḥ parikalpanâ: ne 'daṁ sûtram ishṭaṁ.*

iti tribhâshyaratne prâtiçâkhyavivaraṇe ashṭâdaço[9] *'dhyâyaḥ.*

[1] W. *-gasaç-*. [2] G. M. *-vaṁ.* [3] W. *adhyeprathamâṇaṁ*. [4] G. M. *-vidha*. [5] W. B. om. [6] W. *'dhyayamâṇâ*; B. *-mâṇâ*. [7] W. B. om. [8] W. B. om. [9] G. M. O. *dvitiyapraçne shashṭho*.

lowing circumflex.' He adds examples of a *vikrama* syllable in each of the four defined positions: namely *yò 'sya svò 'gnís tám ápi* (v.7.9[1]: G. M. O. omit the last two words), *vóḍhavé* (i.6.2[1] et al.), *dhánvanā gā́'ḥ* (iv.6.6[1]), and *tásya kvà suvargó lokáḥ* (ii.6.5[5]: O. omits the last word, G. M. the last two). In the third example, the circumflex by which the *vikrama* syllable is preceded is the enclitic; this shows us (what we should have inferred without it) that, as regards the application of the present precept, no distinction is made between the independent and the enclitic circumflex. As an example of the use of the term, and showing the necessity of its definition here, is quoted rule xvii.6, where we are told that Pâushkarasâdi asserts the utterance of *svâra* ('circumflex') and *vikrama* with a firmer effort. The word occurs elsewhere only at xxiii.20 and xxiv.5, where we have no assurance that it signifies the same thing as here. It is found, among the other Prâtiçâkhyas, in that to the Rig-Veda only, and has there no such meaning.

The *vikrama* is marked by the usual sign of low tone, the horizontal stroke beneath. The following rule, as we shall see, extends its definition so as to include nearly all the syllables so marked.

The construction of *sa* in the rule, as agreeing in gender with *vikramaḥ*, though referring to *nīcam* (*aksharam*), was alluded to above, under v.2.

प्रचयपूर्वश्च कौण्डिन्यस्य ॥ २ ॥

2. As also, according to Kâuṇḍinya, when a *pracaya* precedes.

The *pracaya* (see xxi.10,11) is the series of unaccented syllables following a circumflex (enclitic or independent) in connected discourse, and uttered, save the one next preceding another following circumflex or an acute, in the tone of acute. This last one of the

---

1. [1]*yatra* [2] *svaritayor*[1] *madhya* [3] *udâttayor vâ*[4] *'nyatarato ve 'ti svaritodâttayor ve*[5] *'ty arthaḥ:* [6] *udâttasvaritayor vâ*[7] *madhye nīcaṁ yad aksharaṁ sa vikramo*[8] *bhavati. svaritayor*[9] *madhye yathâ: yo.....* [10]*udâttayor yathâ*[10]*: voḍhave. svaritodâttayor yathâ: dhanv-..... udâttasvaritayor yathâ: tasya..... vikramasaṁjñâyâḥ prayojanam: svâravikramayor dṛḍhaprayatnatara* (xvii.6) *iti.*

(1) O. *yad dvayor.* [2] B. G. M. ins. *sthale.* [3] G. M. ins. *vâ.* [4] G. M. om. [5] G. M om. *vâ.* [6] G. M. ins. *iti vâ.* [7] O. om.; G. M. put after *madhye.* [8] G. M. *-masaṁ jño.* [9] O. *tayor.* (10) O. om.

2. *cakâro*[1] *vikrama iti jñâpayati:* [2]*kâuṇḍinyasya mata udâttaparaḥ svaritaparo vâ pracayapûrvaç ca vikramo vijñeyaḥ. udâttaparo yathâ: pary.....*[2] *svaritaparo yathâ: upar-..... pracayaḥ pûrvo yasmâd* [3]*asâu pracayapûrvaḥ.*[3]

[1] G. M. O. *caçabdo.* (2) W. om. (3) G. M. *sa tathoktaḥ.*

series, which retains its grave tone, is here declared to be, on Kâuṇḍinya's authority, likewise entitled to the appellation *vikrama.* This makes the term apply to all syllables in the *saṁhitâ* that are marked by the horizontal stroke below, excepting those which, after a pause, precede the first accented syllable. The commentator cites two examples: *páry avadatâṁ yâ' yajñè dîyáte* (i.7.2[2]: lost in W.; only O. has the last two words) and *upárishṭâllakshmâ yâjyâ'* (ii.6.2[3-4] et al.), in the first of which the *pracaya* is followed by an acute, in the second by a circumflex.

It is to be observed that the *vikrama* appears, so far as this treatise is concerned, to be a mere name; no peculiarity of tone is claimed to belong to it: the other treatises offer nothing analogous.

As nothing is said of the non-approval of the rule, we may regard it as accepted in the school represented by the commentator.

द्वियम एके द्वियमपरे ता अणुमात्राः ॥ ३ ॥

3. According to some, in a circumflex syllable that is followed by a circumflex, quarter-*moras* are so.

I have rendered this rule according to my own persuasion of its true meaning, and not at all in conformity with the interpretation of the commentator, who says "*yama* [W. alone says *dviyama*] is a synonym of *svarita;* where there are two such *yamas,* without intervention of anything, that is a *dviyama;* what is followed by such a *dviyama,* that is *dviyamapara:* in the former, and also in the latter, where there is a third *yama* [so in G. M., which is the best reading: the others perhaps mean *triyame*], whatever circumflexed materials there are, all those are depressed at the end to the extent of a quarter-*mora:* so some think. An example of a *dviyama* is *tè 'nyò 'nyásmâi* (ii.2.11[5]: but B. G. M. have instead *tè 'nyò 'nyám,* vi.1.5[1]); of a *dviyamapara, sò 'pò 'bhy àmriyata* (vi.1.1[7]; 4.2[3]). Whence do we derive the implication 'at the end?' from the precept 'and likewise, at the end of a word are *kampas,* quarter-*moras* depressed at the end.' And the implication of

3. *yamaçabdaḥ*[1] *svaritaparyâyaḥ: dvâu yamâu yatra deçe nâirantaryeṇa*[2] *vartete sa dviyamaḥ: tasmin: dviyamaḥ paro yasmâd asâu dviyamaparaḥ: tasmiṅç ca dviyame*[3] *sati yâḥ*[4] *svaritaprakṛtayas tâḥ sarvâ antato 'ṇumâtrâ*[5] *nihatâ*[6] *bhavantî 'ty eke manyante. dviyamo yathâ: te.....:* [7]*dviyamaparo yathâ*[7]*: so..... antata*[8] *iti katham pratîyate: padânte ca*[9] *tathâ*[10] *kampâ antata nihatâṇukâ*[11] *iti vacanâd iti brûmaḥ: nihataṁ*[12] *tu svaritayor madhye yatra nîcam* (xix.1) *ity*[13] *etatsâṁnidhyâl labhyate. çikshâ câi 'vaṁ vakshyati*[14]*:*

nityo 'bhinihataç[15] *câi 'va kshâipraḥ praçlishṭa eva ca:*
ete svârâḥ[16] *prakampante yatro 'ccasvaritodayâ*[17] *iti*[18]*:*
çeshasyo 'dâttatâ vâ syât svâratâ[19] *vâ vyavasthaye 'ti:*

depression comes by vicinage from rule 1, above, where a syllable of low tone between two that are circumflexed is spoken of. This seems to me entirely inadmissible. In *yama* as a synonym of *svarita*, and meaning 'circumflex,' I cannot in the least believe; and the designation of a case of three successive circumflexes as *dviyamapara* would be excessively awkward, even without the omission of the *ca*, 'and,' which would be needed to connect it, in that signification, with *dviyama*. On the other hand, *dviyama*, 'of double pitch,' is an entirely natural and acceptable synonym for *svarita*, 'circumflex,' the essential characteristic of which is that it combines the high and the low tone within the limits of the same syllable; and "a circumflex followed by a circumflex" includes every possible case. The limitation "at the end" is properly enough left to be understood from the nature of the case; but that the predicate "depressed," the most important part of the precept, should remain to be inferred by vicinage only, and from the subject, not the predicate, of the two preceding rules, is not to be tolerated. And I have no doubt that the *tâḥ* in the rule is the predicate, and represents *vikrama*, its gender and number being adapted to those of *aṇumâtrâḥ* by the grammatical figure *anyonyânvaya*, to which the commentator (see under ii.7, v.2) has several times appealed in other like cases. There remains, as the only difficulty, the plural number of both words: we should certainly expect rather *sâ 'ṇumâtrâ;* but even if we have to let this pass unexplained, it is vastly more easy to get along with than the difficulties which beset the other interpretation. One hardly dares presume to suggest that the present reading is the result of an alteration, made after the meaning given in the comment was ascribed to the rule.

The commentator goes on to quote a verse from the Çikshâ, to the effect that the four kinds of independent circumflex (see xx.1, 2,4,5) suffer *kampa* when they precede either an acute or a circumflex. This verse is (save that it gives the Tâittirîya instead of the Rik names to the accents) the same with that which is interpolated in the Rik Pr., at the end of the third chapter (iii.19). He adds further, in another half-verse, doubtless from the same authority, that "of the remainder, there may either be the quality of acute or of circumflex, respectively;" and explains this "respectively" as

---

vyavasthâçabdenâ 'nena[20] *dvividhaḥ kampa uktaḥ: saṁhitâyâṁ svaritakampa*[21] *itaravedabhâga*[22] *udâttakampa*[23] *iti ye*[24] *kampâḥ prasiddhâs*[25] *teshv* [26] *etal lakshaṇaṁ na tu kampavidhâyakam: anyathâ yo.... ityâdâu kampaḥ prasajyeta.*

ne 'daṁ sûtram ishṭam.

[1] W. *dviy-.* [2] W. *noraṅ-;* O. *noraṅtatory-.* [3] G. M. *tṛtiyayame.* [4] W. *yaṁ;* M. *vâ.* [5] O. *-tra.* [6] W. *niyatâ;* B. *abhihatâ;* G. M. *'bhihitâ.* (7) O. om. [8] O. *anta.* [9] O. *ka.* [10] W. B. *yâthâ.* [11] O. *hi hat-.* [12] G. *nihit-;* O. *-tatvaṁ.* [13] B. om. [14] O. *-te.* [15] B. *-hitaç.* [16] G. M. *svar-.* [17] W. *trasv-;* M. *ccâccasv-;* O. *ccasyasv-;* G. M. *-yâd;* O. *-ye.* [18] O. om. [19] B. *-tor;* G. M. *svarito.* [20] W. *ṅte;* O. om. *anena.* [21] W. *-taḥ k-;* B. *-ta uktaḥ k-.* [22] G. M. *-re ve-.* [23] W. *-ttah k-.* [24] W. B. O. om. [25] G. M. om. [26] B. O. ins. *eva.*

implying that there are two kinds of *kampa:* in the Sanhitâ, that before a circumflex; in other parts of the Veda, that before an acute; and concludes the exposition with pointing out (if I understand him) that this is a definition applying to those cases of *kampa* which are otherwise established; but that it is not a precept requiring *kampa*, since this would otherwise have to appear in such passages as *yò 'pầ'm púshpaṁ véda* (only G. M. have *veda:* the passage is not to be found in the Sanhitâ, and possibly is intended to be quoted from one of those "other parts of the Veda," referred to above). Finally, he remarks that the rule is unapproved.

The term *kampa* is not found anywhere in the text of our Prâtiçâkhya, or of that of the Rig-Veda, although the commentary to the latter (under iii.3,4), like our own, employs it to signify the peculiar modification undergone by the circumflex, when immediately followed by a high tone. The Atharva-Prâtiçâkhya (iii.65) gives to the same modification the kindred name of *vikampita.* It is signified, in the Rik and Atharvan texts (as is fully explained and illustrated in the note to Ath. Pr. iii.65), by appending to the vowel of the circumflex syllable a figure, either 1 or 3, and applying to the figure the signs of both circumflex and grave accentuation. The theory of this mode of designation is obscure, and no account of it is given in any Prâtiçâkhya, nor, so far as I am aware, in any other Hindu authority that has yet come to light. We should imagine the figure to be a mere *point d'appui* for an added sign of grave tone, but that there appears in a part of the Vedic texts an accompanying prolongation of the *vikampita* vowel (if the vowel be short), of which the figure, therefore, appears to be the sign: of this prolongation the Prâtiçâkhyas give no hint.

This accent wears a quite peculiar aspect in the Tâittirîya text, as compared with those to which reference has been made. In the first place, being limited to the case of a circumflex before a circumflex, it is relatively of rare occurrence, there being fewer examples of it in the whole Tâittirîya-Sanhitâ than in the first book alone of the Atharvan (it occurs in the former, if I have overlooked nothing, only at ii.1.6⁵; 2.11⁵: v.4.3³: vi.1.1⁷,5¹,11²,⁵; 2.2¹,²; 3.2⁵, 4²; 4.2³,9²,10¹; 6.8¹: and in the ending to v.2.1). Secondly, it is always intimated by an appended figure 1, with simply the mark of *anudâtta* tone, or of *vikrama*, written beneath, while the circumflex vowel retains the mark of circumflex accent*—and this is clearly the method most easily defensible on theoretic grounds:

* That is to say, this is uniformly the case in my manuscript, which, for example, writes the commentator's quoted instances as follows:

ते॑१॒ न्योन्यस्मै॒ सो॑१॒ पो॑१॒ भ्यं॑म्रियत॒

and the MSS. of the comment all add the figure 1, although, as everywhere else, they omit the accent signs. In the two cases that occur in the part of the Calcutta edition thus far printed, it seems to be by mere unintelligent blundering that the above method is departed from, a 3 being added in the one (ii.1.6⁵), without any sign of *vikrama* beneath it, and no designation being attempted in the other (ii.2.11⁵).

the figure represents the quantity that is added to the syllable to make room for the *vikrama* tone at the end, and it gets, therefore, the *vikrama* sign. Thirdly, in the only two passages (vi.3.4[2]; 6.8[1]) in which the vowel of the circumflexed syllable is short, it is made long.

What the commentator means by declaring the rule of no force, it is not easy to say. It can hardly be that his school acknowledged no *kampa* at all; and we should have expected him rather to interpret into his text the usage which he and his fellow-*çâkhinaḥ* accepted as proper—as he has done in so many other cases. There appears to be no discordance between the teachings of the Prâtiçâkhya in this chapter and the practice in the known Tâittirîya text (but see the note on the next rule); the former, to be sure, do not fully explain the latter; but this is the case also with the other Vedas.

The denial of *kampa* in a circumflex syllable before an acute constitutes the most important and conspicuous peculiarity in the Tâittirîya system of accentuation as compared with that of the Rik and Atharvan, and also puts the former at a disadvantage in respect to clearness. Its effect is to deprive us of any constant means of distinguishing whether the syllable following a circumflex is an acute, or a grave with *pracaya* tone (xxi.10); and whether that distinction shall be shown at all depends upon mere accident. For example, *sò 'smā́'t* and *sò 'smât* would be accented before a pause precisely alike; and so with any number of acutes or graves following a circumflex before a pause: e. g. *sò 'smâd abhavat* and *sò 'smā́'d yó vā́'i tát.** And even if, instead of a pause, other syllables follow, there must be at least two grave syllables in succession to bring out the true condition of things: we see that the syllable after the circumflex is acute in *hy èshá pṛthivyā́'ḥ*, but not in *hy ètád devā́'ḥ*, and the *saṁhitâ* does not tell us whether in *so 'smâd etarhi* the *asmât* is accented or toneless.† And so often does this ambiguity arise, that in the first chapter of the third book there are not less than twenty cases of *pracayas*, all whose syllables except the last admit of being understood as true acutes.‡ Other possible cases of ambiguity, of less frequency and importance, I pass without notice.

This same peculiarity belongs also to the existing Tâittirîya-Brâhmaṇa and Âraṇyaka, so that the commentator's allusion to "other parts of the Veda" as differing from the Sanhitâ in respect to *kampa* is of doubtful meaning.

---

* Thus. सो ऽस्मादभवत् । and सो ऽस्माद्यो वै तत् ।

† Thus, ह्येष पृथिव्याः and ह्येतद्देवाः and सो ऽस्मादेतर्हि

‡ Thus, सो ऽकामयत प्रजाः may be either *sò 'kâmayata prajā́'ḥ* or *sò 'kā́'máyátá prajā́'ḥ*.

तस्यामेव प्रकृतौ ॥ ४ ॥

4. In that very material.

The commentator's interpretation of this rule is just as violent and unsatisfactory as is that which he gave of its predecessor, and with which he forces it into strange connection. He says, "in a *dviyama* passage there is depression to the extent of a quarter-*mora* only in that—namely, the former—circumflex material; but, in a passage where a *dviyama* follows, there is depression to the extent of a quarter-*mora* of the two former materials; but they do not all share in the quarter-*mora* effect: that is what the *eva* means. And Kâuhaleya says thus: 'of two, the former is *aṇumâtrika;* of three, the two former are *aṇumâtrika;* beyond that, the natural condition holds.'"

I think we can have no hesitation whatever as to rejecting this: if the treatise had been intending to say what is here claimed, it would have said it in a very different manner. What is really meant, may be much more doubtful; but I imagine that we are directed to find our quarter-*mora* of *vikrama* in the very substance of the circumflex syllable itself; that is to say, not in any protraction of it; and so, that that treatment of the case which is signified by the insertion of a figure after the circumflex vowel is rejected. This, if established, would make the doctrine of the authorities (*eke*, rule 3) here reported in fact discordant with the practice followed in the recorded text.

न पूर्वशास्त्रे न पूर्वशास्त्रे ॥ ५ ॥

5. Not in the former teaching.

A rule of very obscure import, and respecting which the commentator has only his guesses to give us. He ventures two: first, that *pûrvaçâstra* signifies the rule respecting *vikrama*, and that in it this affection of the quarter-*mora* finds no place; second, that *pûrvaçâstra* means the first rule of the chapter (which amounts, so far, to the same thing with the other), and that the name of

---

4. *dviyamasthale pûrvasyâm* [1]*eva tasyâm*[1] *sva* '*taprakṛtâv aṇumâtrayâ*[2] *'pi*[3] *nihatatvam*[4] *bhavati: dviyamapare tu*[5] *sthale pûrvayor eva prakṛtyor*[6] *aṇumâtrayâ*[7] *nihatatvam*[8] *bhavati: na tu*[9] *tâḥ sarvâ aṇukâryabhâja*[10] *ity evakâro bodhayati. evam eva kâuhaleya*[11] *âha: dvayoḥ pûrvo*[12] *'ṇumâtrikas*[13] *trishu* [14] *pûrvâv*[15] *aṇumâtrikâv*[16] *uttaraḥ*[17] *prakṛtye 'ti.*

(1) W. *aparasyâṁ.* [2] B. *-trayo;* G. M. *anumâtram a.* [3] O. om. [4] B. *-hit-.* [5] G. M. *tat.* [6] B. *-tyâyo.* [7] B. *ṇumâtrayor;* G. M. *anumâtrâyâ.* [8] B. *-hit-.* [9] W. O. *nu.* [10] G. M. *anuk-;* O. *aṇumâtraṁ bhajate.* [11] W. *-liya.* [12] W. *-rva;* B. O. *-rvaḥ.* [13] W. B. O. *aṇu-;* M. O. *-trakas.* [14] W. ins. *ca.* [15] O. *pûrvo vâ;* G. M. *pûrvo yathâ uparishṭ-* etc. (end of comment to rule 2, above). [16] W. *-kâ;* M. *-trakâv;* O. *-trako 'py.* [17] W. *-rataḥ.*

vikrama, there given, does not apply here in the rule for *kampa*, since, by xvii.6, *vikrama* is uttered with a firmer effort of the organs, while that is not the case with *kampa*. There is nothing in either of these proposals to commend it to our acceptance. If we were ourselves to guess, we should perhaps say that the reference was to rule 4 only, which teaches *kampa* without any protraction, and that this was confessed to be a doctrine not before authoritatively taught. But we should not presume to put the conjecture forward with any confidence.

CHAPTER XX.

CONTENTS: 1–8, names of the different kinds of circumflex, independent and enclitic; 9--12, different degrees of force of their utterance.

इवर्णोकारयोर्यवकारभावे क्षैप्र उदात्तयोः ॥ १ ॥

1. When *i*, *î*, and *u* are converted into *y* or *v*, the accent is *kshâipra*, if they were acute.

The conversion of *i*, *î*, and *u* into *y* or *v* is by rule x.15; *û* does not fall under such a rule on account of its being always *pragraha* (iv.5). Rule x.16 prescribes the conditions under which a circumflex accent is the result of such a conversion; and the addition of *udâttayoḥ* to the present rule is wholly unnecessary—a case to exercise the ingenuity of the commentator in defending the treatise from the charge of *pâunaruktya*: but either it escapes his notice, or he declines to touch it, as beyond his powers. Of course, if it be necessary to explain here that the altered vowel is acute, it needs to be added that the following vowel is grave

---

5. [1]*pûrvaçâstraṁ nâma vikramavidhiḥ*[1]*: tasminn etad anukâryaṁ na bhavati. evaṁ vâ sûtrârthaḥ: pûrvaçâstre*[2] *'dhyâyaprathamasûtre yâ vikramasaṁjño 'ktâ* [3]*sâ kampavidhâv atra*[3] *na bhavati: vikramasya dṛḍhaprayatnatvât*[4] *kampasya tadabhâvâd iti.* [5]

iti tribhâshyaratne prâtiçâkhyavivaraṇe ekonaviṅço[6] *'dhyâyaḥ.*

(1) W. *-strâṇâm api kram-*; B. *-stre 'pi yo vikr-*; O. *-dhiva.* [2] O. *-rvasûtre.* (3) W. *-dhâu yatra*; G. M. *sâ 'tra pracayavidhâu*; O. *sâ kampavidhâyakatvaṁ.* [4] G. M. *-tnatara syât.* [5] G. M. add *dvâv arthâu.* [6] G. M. O. *dvitiyapraçne saptamo.*

1. *udâttayor ivarṇokârayor yathopadeçaṁ*[1] *yavakârabhâve sati yaḥ svarito vihitaḥ sa kshâipra iti saṁjñâyate*[2]. *yathâ*[3]: *vy----: kṛdhî----. udâttayor*[4] *iti kim: vas----: anv----.*

[1] W *-çâir*; O. *-çe.* [2] G. M. *-jñâ jâyate.* [3] G. M. om. [4] W. *-tta.*

The examples are *vy èvá'i 'nena* (v.3.11[3]) and *kr̥dhí' sv àsmá'n* (iv.7.15[7]); counter-examples, where the altered vowel was not acute, are *vásvy asi* (i.2.5[1] et al.) and *ánv enam mâtá'*, which is not, I believe, to be found in the Sanhitâ; the nearest thing to it is *ánv enaṁ víprâḥ* (iv.6.8[3]); *ánu tvâ mâtá'* occurs several times (i.3.10[1] et al.).

All the Prâtiçâkhyas agree in calling this particular kind of circumflex by the name *kshâipra* (see note to Ath. Pr. iii.58).

सयकारवकारं वाक्षरं यत्र स्वर्यते स्थिते पदे ऽनुदात्तपूर्वे ऽपूर्वे वा नित्य इत्येव जानीयात् ॥ २ ॥

2. But where a syllable containing a *y* or *v* is circumflexed in a fixed word, being preceded by a grave syllable, or not preceded by anything, that is to be known as *nitya*.

This definition of the original circumflex accent, which belongs to the word in which it occurs, and does not merely arise as a consequence of the combination of words into phrases (although ultimately of the same nature with the *kshâipra*, just described), is a long and awkward one, but fairly attains its purpose: only we do not see why the reading is not *anudâttapûrvam apûrvaṁ vâ*, qualifying *aksharam* formally, as it does logically. A syllable that has the circumflex in *pada*-text (to which *sthite pade* is explained as equivalent), otherwise than enclitically after an acute, is an original (*nitya*, 'constant, invariable') circumflex. The other Prâtiçâkhyas (see note to Ath. Pr. iii.57) call it *jâtya*, 'natural.'

The commentator defines *aksharam*, 'syllable,' in the rule as meaning *svaraḥ*, 'vowel;' and, in fact, the use of *aksharam* here is somewhat at variance with the general custom of the treatise, which elsewhere talks of the vowel, not the syllable, as having tone (compare i.43, xiv.29). He inserts *sarvatra*, 'everywhere,' in his paraphrase, and then explains it, as if it were a part of the rule, to signify that the accent holds in *saṁhitâ*, *pada*, and *jaṭâ* text. His examples are *vâyavyàm* (i.8.7[1] et al.), *kanyè 'va tunná'* (iii.1.11[8]: O. omits *tunnâ*), *táto bilvàḥ* (ii.1.8[2]), *nyàñcaṁ cinuyá't* (v.5.3[2]: W. B. add, after a pause, as if a new example, *anyañcaṁ* [B.

---

2. *sayakâraṁ vâ savakâraṁ vâ 'ksharaṁ*[1] *svara ity arthaḥ: sthite pade padakâla ity arthaḥ: yatra sthale svaryate: anudâttapûrve*[2] *'pûrve*[3] *vâ pûrvâbhâve*[4] *sati*[5]*: nitya eve 'ti sarvatra jânîyât: sarvatre 'ti*[5] *saṁhitâpadajaṭâsv ity arthaḥ. yathâ: vây----: kanye----: tato----: nyañ-----:*[7] *kva----: kvâ---- iti jaṭâyâm. tuçabdo nityâdâv uccodayavishaye*[8] *no 'dâttasvaritapara* (xiv.31) *iti nishedhaṁ nivârayati. nanu*[9] *nityaḥ katham etannishedhavishayaḥ*[10]*: udâttât paro 'nudâtta*[11] (xiv.29) *itilakshaṇâsambhavât*[12]*. atro 'cyate: varṇavibhâgavelâyâm*[13] *udâttapûrvatvam*[14] *asti: samâhâraḥ svarita* (i.40) *ity ucca-*

reads *-câṁ*], but no such word is to be found in the Sanhitâ, and it is probably only a blundering repetition of *nyañcam*), and *kvà jágatî ca* (vii.1.4[3]); and, from the *jaṭâ*-text, *kvầ 'syâ 'sya kvầ* 1 *kvầ 'sya* (v.7.4[2]: B. has lost a part; it involves a case of *kampa*, with resulting prolongation, and use of the sign 1: see xix.3). Counter-examples are given in O. only: namely, of a circumflex not found in *pada*-text, *vy èvấi 'nena* (v.3.11[3]: the MS. has *vevyâi*), *drvànnaḥ sarpíḥ* (iv.1.9[2]; p. *drú-annaḥ*); of one which has an acute before it, *mártyâñ âvivéça* (v.7.9[1]) and *sárvâñ agnî́n* (v.6.1[2]). We have also one of the common attempts to give a profound significance to the word *tu*, 'but,' in the rule; and, as usual, it is abortive, involving difficulties which the commentator only pretends to get rid of. He says the *tu* signifies that, so far as the *nitya* circumflex etc. (i. e. and the other varieties of the independent circumflex) are concerned, the exception laid down in rule xiv.31—namely, that the circumflex character is not retained before a following acute or circumflex—has no force. But it is objected, with entire reason, that rule xiv.31 has nothing to do with the *nitya* at all, but only with the enclitic accent prescribed in rule xiv.29. His reply is, that in the condition of complete separation of sounds, there is, after all, a grave element preceded by an acute, as required in rule xiv.29, the combination of the two, by i.40, giving the circumflex character. Whether this implies his recognition of the fact that the semivowel in every *nitya* syllable really represents an acute vowel, pronounced as such in an earlier stage of the language—*kvà* being equivalent to *kúa*, and *kanyầ* to *kaníâ*—admits of question. He expounds *anudâttapurve* as a descriptive instead of a possessive compound, and *apûrve* as a substantive of the same character, as if the construction were 'there being a preceding grave, or there being no preceding accent;' it is doubtless better to supply in idea *tasminn akshare*, and to render 'when that syllable is' etc. The remaining bit of exposition is much corrupted in its readings, and the drift of it is not clear to me. O. brings it in very differently from the rest, and makes it involve an additional example, *yâjyấi " 'vấi 'nam* (ii.3.5[3]; p. *yâjyầ : ấ : evá : enam*).

---

pûrvatvât[15] *svaritasye 'ti nishedhavishayatvam. anudâttaç câ 'sâu pûrvaç câ 'nudâttapûrvaḥ:* [16] *tasmin:* [17]*pûrvâbhâvo 'pûrvaḥ: tasmin*[17]. [18]*çûnye tu sarvatrapûrvatvât*[18] *pûrvatvaviçeshaṇadvayasyâ*[19] *'nyathâ*[20] *vâiyarthyât*[21]*: tasmât tatra*[22] *nityasvaritatvam*[23] *eva na*[24] *saṁjñântaram iti vijñeyam.*

[1] W. B. om.; G. M. add *yatra svaryate.* [2] O. ins. *vâ.* [3] B. om. [4] G. M. ins. *vâ.* [5] G. om. [6] O. *pi.* [7] W. B. ins.: *anyañcaṁ* [8] G. M. O. *-darkav-*; O. *-shayo.* [9] G. M. *na tu.* [10] O. *nish-.* [11] G. M. ins. *svaritam.* [12] O. *laksh-.* [13] all MSS. have the lingual *l.* [14] W. *-rvam.* [15] W. B. *ucyate pû-.* [16] W. ins. *tasmât.* (17) G. M. om. (18) O. *na çunya ity arthaḥ : sthite pada iti kim: vy----: drv-----: anudâttapûrva iti kim: mart-----: sar-----. kicid evam úcuḥ: yâj----- ity âdi: prâtihaṁniça-karoty evakâraḥ : pada samuccaye anudâttapûrvatvât*; G. M. *çûnyapûrvasapûrvatvât*; W. . . . . *sarvatrâ*; B. *bhûnye* etc. [19] W. *pûrvaviçeshadv-*; B. *pûrvatraviçeshaṇâd-*; O. *pûrvaviç-.* [20] O. *ntathâ.* [21] W. *-thyaṁ*; G. M. *-thyaṁ syât.* [22] W. *aṁ*; B. *tat*; O. *tra.* [23] W. O. *nityatvam*; B. *svaritatvaṁ nityatvam.* [24] B. *ca.*

अपि चेन्नानापदस्थमुदात्तमथ चेत्साꣳहितेन स्वर्यते स प्रातिहतः ॥ ३ ॥

3. If, moreover, there is an açute standing in another word, then, if there be a circumflex resulting from a rule of combination, it is *prâtihata.*

The phraseology of this rule is very peculiar indeed, and its peculiarity hard to account for. The Rik and Atharva Prâtiçâkhyas distinguish only two kinds of enclitic circumflex: the *pâdavṛtta*, in which a hiatus intervenes between the acute and its successor, and the *tâirovyañjana*, in which the two are separated by consonants. According to the explanation, now, of our commentator, the present treatise sets off from the latter, as a separate class, a circumflexed syllable at the beginning of a word, following an acute at the end of the preceding word. He gives us four examples (of which, however, W. B. omit the first two, and O. the last two): *mâ' te asyâ'm* (i.6.12⁵), *yás tvâ hṛdâ' kîriṇâ* (i.4.46¹: only O. has *kîriṇâ*), *ishé tvâ* (i.1.1 et al.), and *tám te duçcákshâḥ* (iii.2.10²): the second word in each has the *prâtihata* circumflex. As counter-examples, we have *yán nyàñcam* (v.5.3²: W. gives instead *yán návam* [ii.3.10¹ et al.], but it does not illustrate the point arrived at, and so is doubtless a corruption of the other), to show that the following circumflex must be a result of a rule of combination, and *táyâ devátayâ* (iv.2.9² et al.: O. substitutes *tasmâd varupam*, which is corrupt; I have overlooked it in searching out the references, and do not know how, if it in fact represents a real citation, it ought to be amended), to show that the acute must stand in another word.

In working out this meaning for the rule, the commentator declares *api*, 'moreover,' to have the office merely of bringing down from the preceding rule the quality of going before (*pûrvatva*); *atha*, 'then,' according to him, either cuts off the continued implication of *nitya* (that is to say, means nothing at all), or else gives the value of a heading to "the being preceded by an acute standing in another word"—which is wholly to be rejected; in the first place because unnecessary (*tasmât* in the next rule having just that purpose), and in the second place because the word could at any rate make a heading only of what followed it in the rule, not of what went before.

---

3. *apiçabdaḥ* [1]*pûrvatvamâtrâkarshakaḥ*[2]*: athaçabdo nityasaṁjñâvyavachedakaḥ: nânâpadasthodâttapûrvatvâdhikârako*[3] *vâ: nânâpadastham aksharam udâttapûrvaṁ*[1] *cet parato nîcaṁ sâṁhitena vidhinâ svaryate cet sa prâtihato 'tra*[4] *veditavyaḥ.* [5]*yathâ: mâ....: yas....:*[5] [6]*ishe....: taṁ....*[6] *sâṁhitene 'ti kim:* [7]*yan..... nânâpadastham iti kim: tayâ....*[7]

(1) W. *pûrvaç* simply. [2] G. M. om. *-tva-*; O. om. *-âtr-*. [3] O. *-kâro.* [4] G. M. om. (5) W. B. om.; G. M. om. *yathâ.* (6) O. om. (7) O. *tasmâdvarupaṁ.*

If this be indeed the original intent of the rule, it would seem that, to the apprehension of the Hindu phonetists, there was difference enough between the enclitic circumflex which *te* in *táṁ te* assumes in *saṁhitâ*, having been grave in *pada*-text, and that which the *shâḥ* of *duçcákshâḥ* has in *saṁhitâ* as well as in *pada*, to furnish ground for a difference of classification and nomenclature.* But there are various obstacles in the way of our accepting the interpretation as satisfactory. In the first place, why ought not the same distinction to apply where the acute and circumflex are separated by a hiatus, as well as by consonants? or why, when a circumflex after an acute in the same word is called *tâirovyañjana*, alike whether a hiatus or consonants intervene, should a circumflex after an acute in another word have a different name according as it is preceded by a consonant or not? In the second place, why should the rule be thrust in here, wholly out of connection with the others respecting the enclitic circumflex, and with such a frightful sacrifice of that economy of expression which the *sûtrakâra* proverbially rates so highly? for, following rule 7, a simple *nânâpadasthât tu prâtihataḥ* would have done the whole business, and much more unequivocally. Not one of the other treatises mixes together thus the enclitic and independent *svaritas*, when they come to be defined and named. Nor, again, does any other authority found a separate species of accent upon the basis here laid down. I have been inclined, therefore, to conjecture that the rule ought to be rendered 'when there is besides (*api*) a [preceding] acute in another word, then, provided a circumflex arises as the result of a rule of combination, it is *prâtihata*:' understanding an independent *svarita* (except a *nitya*) to be intended, whenever that *svarita* was preceded by an acute, and so held a position which would make it an enclitic *svarita* as well; and the reason for thus calling attention to it being that, as written, it is not distinguished from a mere enclitic accent.† But there are too many difficulties connected with this interpretation also to allow of its being accepted as at all satisfactory.

The Vâjasaneyi-Prâtiçâkhya (i.118) gives a special name, *tâirovirâma*, to the enclitic circumflex which falls in the *pada*-text upon the first syllable of the second member of a compound, under

* And this difference, it should be noted, applies in the same manner where division is made between the two parts of a compound word; for the extant Tâittirîya *pada*-text, in marked contrast with those of the other Vedas, regards the *avagraha* pause as suspending, like the *avasâna*, all accentual influence, and writes *çukrá-vati*, for example, in the same fashion as it writes *çukrám : asti*—that is to say,

शुक्रऽवती । instead of शुक्रऽवती. as the rest would read.

† For example, *ghṛtâír vy ùdyate* (iii.1.11[4]) and *ánaçânā́ḥ svìshṭim* (iii.1.9[2]) are written precisely as if they were *ghṛtâír vy udyate* and *ánaçânā́ḥ svishṭim*; namely,

घृतैर्व्युद्यते and आनशानाः स्विष्टिम्: this is an ambiguity which is common to all the Vedic texts.

the influence of an acute on the final of the first member, and which is therefore 'separated by an intervening pause' from the tone which calls it forth. Thus, the *va* of *çukrá-vatî* (as written the second time in the first marginal note on p. 369) has a *tâirovirâma svarita*, being marked by the ordinary *svarita*-sign. Now the *vatî*, as well as the *çukra*, in this word, is to the apprehension of the present treatise (i.48) a *pada;* and hence its syllable *va* appears to fulfil all the conditions laid down in rule 2, just above, as determining a *jâtya:* it is circumflexed in the *pada*-text; it is *apûrva*, or preceded by no other accent in the same *pada;* and it is *savakâra*, or contains a *v*. Here, now, as it appears to me, we have the best explanation of the value, and at the same time of the position, and also, at least in part, of the phraseology, of the rule under discussion. This accent needs definition, though enclitic, immediately after the *nitya*, lest it be confounded with the latter: "even if all the conditions of the previous rule are fulfilled, if there is likewise an acute [preceding the syllable] in another word, and the accent is one which is produced by a rule of combination, this accent is not *nitya*, but *prâtihata*."

The most conspicuous difficulty in the way of accepting this interpretation is the fact, already referred to, that in the extant *pada*-text of the Tâittirîya-Sanhitâ there is no such circumflex as is here assumed; the *va* of *çukrá-vatî*, and all other syllables in like position, being grave, and marked as such. But the difficulty is more apparent than real, since we have no right to assume that this *pada*-text is precisely the same with that held by the school from which the Prâtiçâkhya, or this particular rule, emanated: they may have accented their *iñgyas*, or separable words, after the same fashion which prevails in the *pada*-texts of the other Vedas. Of more account is the awkwardness of the whole expression, and especially the use of *nânâpadastham* instead of *avagrahastham*, which would be the proper term to use in this treatise (compare i.49) in the sense here indicated. But, if not completely acceptable, the interpretation has more for it and less against it, in my opinion, than either of those given above.

Professor Roth, in his early digest of the teachings of the Prâtiçâkhyas respecting accent (introduction to the Nirukta, p. lvii. etc.), identified the *prâtihata* accent with the *tâirovirâma*, but only in consequence of a misunderstanding of the character of the latter, which he supposed (ibid., p. lxv.) to designate an enclitic circumflex separated by consonants from its occasioning acute in a preceding word, thus giving it the same meaning which is attributed by our commentator to the *prâtihata* in the present rule. And Weber (under Vâj. Pr. i.118), while defining the *tâirovirâma* correctly, repeats the same identification; I do not know whether as taking it incautiously from Roth, or as having arrived by conjecture at an independent interpretation of our present rule. He does not allude to any difficulties as connected with the latter, nor state his identification to rest upon a different basis from that of Roth.

तस्मादकारलोपे ऽभिनिहतः ॥ ४ ॥

4. After such a one, in case of the loss of an *a*, it is *abhinihata*.

The word *tasmât* the comment explains as bringing down *nânâpadastham udâttam* from the preceding rule: 'after an acute occurring in another word.' But the specification (like that of *udâttayoḥ* in rule 1) is wholly unnecessary: rule xii.9 prescribes the circumflex and defines its conditions: here we need only to have given us the name by which it is to be called.

O. has an independent exposition, but of equivalent meaning.

The examples are *sò 'bravît* (ii.1.2[1] et al.) and *tè 'bruvan* (ii.5.1[3] et al.); and a counter-example, where, as the eliding diphthong is not acute, no circumflex results, is *bhrâ'jo 'si devâ'nâm* (ii.4.3[2]).

All the other treatises (see note to Ath. Pr. iii.55) give to this circumflex the name *abhinihita*, of which our own term has the aspect of being an artificial variation.

ऊभावे प्रश्लिष्टः ॥ ५ ॥

5. Where an *û* results, it is *praçlishṭa*.

Rule x.17 prescribes the circumflex to which the name of *praçlishṭa* is here assigned; and the examples given are to be found there also, being all the instances save one which the Sanhitâ affords. They read in this place *sû'nniyam iva* (vi 2.4[1]), *sû'dgâtâ* (vii.1.8[1]), *mâsû' 'ttishṭhan* (vii.5.2[2]: G. M. omit *mâ*), and *dikshû' 'padâdhâti* (v.5.5[4]: G. M. O. omit).

The same name (or, in the Ath. Pr., *prâçlishṭa*) is given by the other treatises to the circumflex which results from the fusion of two short *i*'s, the first acute and the other circumflex (see note to Ath. Pr. iii.56).

पदविवृत्त्यां पादवृत्तः ॥ ६ ॥

6. Where there is a hiatus between two words, it is *pâdavṛtta*.

Here there is abrupt change, without notice, from the independent to the enclitic circumflex. The examples given are *tâ' asmât sṛshṭâ'ḥ* (ii.1.2[1]: B. omits *sṛshṭâ'ḥ*), *sá idhânâ'ḥ* (iv.4.4[5]), and *yá*

---

4. [1]*tasmân nânâpadasthodâttât parabhûtânudâttâkârasya*[2] *lope sati yaḥ svaritaḥ so 'bhinihato veditavyaḥ*[1]. *yathâ: so----: te ----. tasmâd iti kim: bhrâjo----.*

(1) O. substitutes *tasmât sañhitâyâm na svaryamâṇârddhe te: sadakâle asvarita ity arthaḥ: akâralupte ya svara âdiçyate so 'bhinihato nâma svarito bhavati.* [2] W. B. *-dâttasya*; G. M. *parabhûtâd anudâttasya akârasya.*

5. *ûbhâve yatra svaryate sa praçlishṭo veditavyaḥ. sûn----: sûd----: mâsû----:* [1]*dikshû----.*[1]

(1) G. M. O. om.

upasádaḥ (vi.2.4[1]); while, as counter-example, to show that the hiatus must be between two *padas*, not two parts of the same *pada*, we have *práügam ukthám* (iv.4.2[1]: this implies, of course, that the *pada*-text does not treat the word as a separable one).

The Rik Pr. (iii.9,10) calls this accent *vâivṛtta*, and there is nothing in its definition or in that of the Vâj. Prât. (i.119) which should limit the accent to the case of a hiatus between two *padas*, or deprive the *u* of such a word as *praüga* of its right to rank as a *pâdavṛtta*. See the note to the next rule.

उदात्तपूर्वस्तैरोव्यञ्जनः ॥ ७ ॥

7. Where an acute precedes, it is *tâirovyañjana*.

The form of this rule, again, is almost unaccountably peculiar. The term *tâirovyañjana* means 'with consonant-intervention,' and all the other treatises (see note to Ath. Pr. iii.62) define the accent in accordance with this, as being one in which the circumflex is separated by intervening consonants from the occasioning acute. Here, to be sure, such a definition would hardly answer, as there is a single word in the Sanhitâ, *praügam*, in which a vowel is regarded as having *tâirovyañjana*, although there is no consonant between it and the acute. But why specify *udâttapûrva*, 'preceded by an acute,' in this rule, when it was just as necessary in rule 6? The commentator says that, as the implication has been made all along, its repetition here is for the purpose of signifying that the acute is now to be understood to be in the same word with the circumflex. That may satisfy him, but is not calculated to content us. If *nânâpadastham udâttam* was implied in rule 6 from above, then *padavivṛttyâm* should have been simply *vivṛttyâm*. Things would be made much better by putting rule 6 after rule 7: then we should be able to give *udâttapûrva* in rule 7 a meaning, as recalling to mind the actual cause of these two accents; and rule 6 would stand as an exception to the other and more general statement, pointing out a class of cases in which, though depending on a preceding acute, another name was applied to the accent.

The commentator's examples are *yuñjánty asya* (vii.4.20), *vásvy*

---

6. *padayor vivṛttiḥ padavivṛttiḥ*[1]*: tasyâm yaḥ svaryate sa pâdavṛtto veditavyaḥ.*[2] *yathâ*[3]*: tâ----: sa----: ya----. vivṛttir vyaktir*[4] *ity arthaḥ. padayor iti kim: pra-----.*

[1] W. B. O. om. [2] B. *bhavati.* [3] in O. only. [4] B. *vyâptatirikta.*

7. *udâttapûrvâdhikâre sati punar atra tatkathanâd*[1] *ekapadasthodâttaviçesha*[2] *'vagamyate*[3]*: tasmâd ekapadasthodâttapûrvo yaḥ svaritaḥ sa*[4] *tâirovyañjano veditavyaḥ. yathâ*[5]*: yuñj----: vas-----: sa----: tad----: pra----: taṁ----.*

[1] G. M. *kath-*; O. *tu k-*. [2] G. M. *-sthityavi-*; O. *-sthatvavi-*. [3] O. *gam-*. [4] O. *asâu.* [5] in O. only.

asi (i.2.5[2] et al.), *sá indro 'manyata* (vii.1.5[5]: G. M. omit *sa*), *tád áçvo 'bhavat* (v.3.12[1]), *práügam* (iv.4.2[1]), and *tám tváshṭâ' " 'dhatta* (i.5.1[3]: G. M. omit the last word). It is very odd—but, I presume, merely accidental—that in every one of these cases (except *praügam*) the vowel which finally shows the circumflex is not of the same word with the acute, but belongs to another word which has been combined with its predecessor, and, after the combination, gets the circumflex by the general rules xiv.29,30 (for the commentator has expressly denied under rule x.12 that the initial grave *a* of *asya*, for example, receives the circumflex in virtue of its combination with the enclitic circumflex *ti* of *yuñjáhti*). I do not see why, in the first two cases, at any rate, the circumflex is not *prâtihata*, according to the commentator's explanation of the meaning of that term; and should even incline to conjecture that these are the examples selected and current for the present rule before the erroneous interpretation of rule 3 was established.

No one of the other Prâtiçâkhyas limits *tâirovyañjana* to an enclitic circumflex following its acute in the same word (see note to Ath. Pr. iii.62); it is quite an oversight, therefore, that the St. Petersburg lexicon gives the term only this restricted meaning (perpetuating Roth's original error, referred to above, in the note to rule 3).

इति स्वारनामधेयानि ॥ ८ ॥

8. These are the names of the circumflex accents.

The commentator simply gives examples for each accent, in part new, in part the same with those furnished under the rules defining each: namely, for the *kshâipra* (omitted in G. M.), *abhy àsthât* (iv.2.8[1]) and *ádhvaryó 'veḥ*, (vi.4.3[4]: this is a blunder, there being no *kshâipra* in the phrase; B. O. read instead *adhvaryúḥ* [vi.2.9[4] et al.], which does not mend the matter); for the *nitya*, *vâyavyàm* (i.8.7[1] et al.] and *kvà' 'sya* (v.7.4[2]: G. M. have *kva* simply); for the *prâtihata*, *sá te lokáḥ* (v.7.26: G. M. omit *lokaḥ*) and *yát tvâ kruddháḥ* (i.5.4[2]: G. M. omit *kruddhaḥ*); for the *abhinihata*, *sò 'bravît* (ii.1.2[1] et al.); for the *praçlishṭa*, *sû'dgâtâ* (vii.1.8[1]); for the *pâdavṛtta*, *tá enam* (ii.3.11[4]: W. reads, blunderingly, *tám nemím* [ii.6.11[1]], and B. substitutes *sá idhânáḥ*, iv.4.4[5]); and for the *tâirovyañjana*, *máma nâ'ma* (i.5.10[1]).

क्षैप्रनित्ययोर्दृढतरः ॥ ९ ॥

---

8. *ity etâni sapta svaritanâmadheyâny*[1] *âkhyâtâni*[2]. *yathâ:* [3]*abhy....: adhv-.... iti kshâipraḥ*[3]. *vây-....: kvâ.... iti nityaḥ. sa....: yat.... iti prâtihataḥ. so.... ity abhinihataḥ. sûd-.... iti praçlishṭaḥ. ta.... iti pâdavṛttaḥ. mama.... iti tâirovyañjanaḥ.*

[1] W. *-mâny;* B. *-yâni svaritanâm.* [2] O. *vyâkh-.* [(3)] G. M. om.

9. In the *kshâipra* and *nitya*, the effort is firmer.

The commentator makes very short work of the remaining rules of the chapter, and we can afford to do the same, as they teach us nothing of value.

अभिनिहते च ॥१०॥

10. As also in the *abhinihata*.

The commentator says that *ca* in this rule is used in the sense of secondary adjunction (*anvâcaya*), and so signifies that the effort of utterance in the *abhinihata* is *dṛḍha*, 'firm,' merely—a less degree than the *dṛḍhatara*, 'firmer,' or 'quite firm,' of the preceding rule. The same may be also inferred, he adds, from the fact that the *abhinihata* is made the subject of a separate rule, instead of being included in rule 9, with the other two.

प्रश्लिष्टप्रातिहतयोर्मृदुतरः ॥११॥

11. In the *praçlishṭa* and *prâtihata*, it is gentler.

Nothing is to be inferred from its association here as to the real character of the *prâtihata*. This rule and its successor were referred to under i.46, but for no intelligibly useful purpose.

तैरोव्यञ्जनपादवृत्तयोरल्पतरो ऽल्पतरः ॥१२॥

12. In the *tâirovyañjana* and *pâdavṛtta*, it is feebler.

---

9. *kshâipre nitye ca prayatno*[1] *dṛḍhataraḥ kâryaḥ*[2].

[1] W. *-tna;* B. *-tni;* O. *yatno.* [2] W. B. om.

10. *anvâcaye vartamânaç cakâro dṛḍhamâtram bodhayati: abhinihate*[1] *ca*[2] *prayatno* [3] *dṛḍhaḥ*[4] *syât: na tu dṛḍhataraḥ: iti pṛthaksûtrârambhâd api*[5] *pratîyate.*

[1] B. *-hite* (as also in the rule). [2] O. om. [3] G. M. insert *mṛdutaraḥ*, and rule 12. [4] O. *-ḍhataraṁ.* [5] W. *abhi;* B. om.

11. *praçlishṭe prâtihate ca prayatno mṛdutaraḥ kâryaḥ.*

12. *tâirovyañjane pâdavṛtte* [1]*ca prayatno 'lpataraḥ syât*[1]. [2]*yady apy*[3] *alpamṛdudṛḍhabhâvas* [4] *tatro 'ktas tathâ 'pi*[5] *dîpavad veṇupatravad iti çikshânurodhât*[6] *komalaçiraskatvaṁ*[7] *sarvatra vijñeyam*[8].[2]

iti tribhâshyaratne prâtiçâkhyavivaraṇe
viñço[9] *'dhyâyaḥ.*

[1] O. *cá 'lpataraṁ karaṇam bhavati.* [2] W. om. [3] G. M. O. om. [4] G. M. ins. *tatra.* [5] M. *'pi 'ti.* [6] B. *kshithânurodhoktâu.* [7] B. *âlpaçisk-;* G. M. *kâivalyaçirastv-.* [8] O. *jñeyam : yathâ: yuvâ kavi.* [9] G. M. O. *dvitiyapraçne ashṭamo.*

Alpatara, 'feebler,' is doubtless meant to signify a still less degree of force of utterance than *mṛdutara*, 'gentler.'

To the commentator, his Çikshâ appears to be a higher authority than the Prâtiçâkhya, at least in this part; and he adds that, although the qualifications 'feeble, gentle, firm' are here attributed to the accents in question, yet, in accordance with what the Çikshâ says, "like a candle, like a rush-leaf" (? unintelligible without the context), it is to be understood that there is softheadedness (?) in them all alike. And O. adds an example, *yúvā kavíḥ* (i.3.14[1]).

CHAPTER XXI.

CONTENTS: 1–9, division of consonants in syllabication; 10–11, *pracaya* accent; 12–13, *yamas* or nasal counterparts; 14, *nâsikya*; 15–16, *svarabhakti*.

व्यञ्जनं स्वराङ्गम् ॥ १ ॥

1. The consonant is adjunct of a vowel.

This brief principle calls forth a long discussion. Reference is first made (except in G. M.) to rule xxiv.5, as, by its requirement of a comprehension of *añga*, 'adjunct' (literally 'limb, member'), creating a necessity for the present precept (and for those that are to follow). Objection is then at once taken to the principle: if, in such cases as *kûpa* and *yûpa* (and G. M. add yet other words as illustrations), it is the consonant that indicates the difference of meaning, ought not the vowel, rather, to be considered as adjunct

1. [1] [2]*vyañjanaṁ svarâñgam bhavati: çvâso nâdo 'ñgam eva ca* (xxiv.5) *iti vijñeyatvena*[2] *vidhânâd ayam ârambhaḥ. nanu*[3] *kûpo yûpa*[4] *ityâdâu vyañjanam evâ 'rthaviçeshabodhakam*[5] *iti svaro vyañjanâñgaṁ kiṁ na*[6] *syât. ucyate: vyañjanaṁ kevalam avasthâtuṁ na çaknoti: kiṁ tu sâpeksham*[7]*: svaras tu nirapekshaḥ*[8]*: sâpekshanirapekshayor nirapeksham eva viçishṭam âcakshate prekshâvantaḥ: viçishṭapratyañgatvam*[9] *aviçishṭasyâi*[10] *'va. kiṁ ca: svaravâiçishṭyabodhakam anyad api vidyate*[11]*.*

durbalasya yathâ râshṭraṁ harate[12] *balavân nṛpaḥ:*
durbalaṁ vyañjanaṁ tadvad dharate[13] *balavânt svaraḥ.*[14]

[15]*kiṁ ca: çikshâvyâkhyâne*

yaḥ svayaṁ râjate taṁ tu svaram âha patañjaliḥ:
uparisthâyinâ tena vyañgaṁ vyañjanam ucyate.[15]

svarâs tu[16] *brâhmaṇâ jñeyâ ityâdi.*

udâttaç câ 'nudâttaç ca[17] *svaritaç ca svarâs trayaḥ*[18]*:*
[19]*hrasvo dîrghaḥ pluta iti*[19] *kâlato*[20] *niyamâ*[21] *aci*[22] *'ti*[23]

of the consonant? The answer given is, that a consonant is incapable of standing alone, and so is dependent, while a vowel is independent; and that, as between a dependent and an independent, the enlightened regard the independent as superior; and it belongs to the inferior to be adjunct to the superior. Moreover, there is found also another proof of the superiority of the vowel, in the verse "as a mighty monarch takes possession of the realm of a weak one, so the mighty vowel takes possession of the weak consonant." The beginning of another verse is added: "the vowels are to be known as belonging to *brahman*." But between this part of a verse and the whole verse that precedes, G. M. insert another, which is asserted to come from "the exposition of the Çikshâ," and which gives a highly imaginative derivation for *svara*, 'vowel,' and *vyañjana*, 'consonant:' "Patanjali styled that a vowel which *shines* by *itself* [*sva-ra* from SVA-*yam* RÂ-*jate*]: the consonant is so called as being imperfect [*vyañjana* from *vyañga*, literally 'limbless'] without [? the expression needs mending, to bring out a desirable sense] the other following it." Then all start together upon a new argument for the superiority of the vowel with yet another verse, which is actually found in the known *pâninîya* Çikshâ (verse 23; see Weber's Indische Studien, iv.353): "acute, grave, and circumflex, the three accents, and short, long, and protracted, these, in regard to quantity, are the necessary characteristics of the vowels;" which shows that acute tone and so on are attributes of vowels only, and of consonants in virtue of their being adjuncts of vowels.

---

svarâṇâm evo 'dâttâdayo dharmâḥ: [24] *vyañjanânâṁ*[25] *tu*[26] *tadaṅgatayâ*[27]. *vyañjanam ardhamâtram*[28]*: svaraç ca mâtrâkâlaḥ: tayoḥ saṁdhir*[29] *adhyardhamâtraḥ*[30]*: ity evaṁ dîrghakâlaḥ prasaktaḥ: tatpratishedhârthaṁ vyañjanaṁ svarâṅgam ity uktam: svarasaṁsṛshṭasya*[31] *vyañjanasya svarakâla eva kâlo drutavṛttâu*[32] *na tu* [33]*svarasyâi 'va*[33] *sarvatre*[34] *'ty arthaḥ.* [35]*drutavṛttâv iti kim:*[35] *hrasvârdhakâlaṁ vyañjanam* (i.37) *iti*[36] *vyarthaṁ syâd iti brûmaḥ. yathâ*[37] *kshîrodakasampa.ke*[38] *kshîrasyâi 'vo 'palabdhir no 'dakasya tathâ svaravyañjanasamparke*[39] *svarasyâi*[40] *'vo 'palabdhir*[41] *vâiçishṭyam.*[42]

[1] O. ins. *svarasyâ 'ṅgaṁ svarâṅgaṁ.* [(2)] G. M. *svara.* [3] G. M. *na.* [4] G. M. *-pas sûpaḥ kâlaḥ vâlaḥ bâlaḥ: phâla.* [5] O. *-sha iti bo-.* [6] O. om. [7] W. B. *-kshâ:* O. *sâksheyaṁ.* [8] O. *-kshakah.* [9] G. M. *-shṭaṁ svaraṁ prat-;* O. *-shṭaṁ prat-.* [10] G. M. *-sya vyañjanasyâi.* [11] G. M. *asti.* [12,13] G. M. *hareta.* [14] G. M. *-ra iti.* [(15)] in G. M. only [16] G. M. *ca.* [17] B. om. [18] G. M. put before *svarâs.* [(19)] G. M. O. *hrasvadîrghaplutâç câi 'va.* [20] G. M. *-lako.* [21] G. M. *-yatâ;* O. *-yatâs.* [22] W. *çrayi;* G. M. *api;* O. *tate.* [23] G. M. ins. *vacanât.* [24] G. M. ins. *na tu.* [25] O. *-janaṁ.* [26] W. *tu daṁ;* G. M. om. [27] O. *tadharmatayâ.* [28] G. M. *-trakaṁ.* [29] O. *sam* [30] B. G. M. O. *ardham-;* G. *-trika;* M. *-traka.* [31] W. *-rasamashṭi.* [32] W. *dut-;* B. *dût-;* O. *dṛgatatâu.* [(33)] W. *svâruḥ sparçasyâi 'va;* O. om. [34] B. *-vasye.* [(35)] B. om.; W. *dût-;* O. *dṛṭav-.* [36] G. M. om. [37] G. M. om. [38] G. M. *-rkâiḥ;* O. *kshirâudakesaṁpa.* [39] G. M. *-rkâis.* [40] W. *sparçasyâi.* [41] W. O. *-bdhir;* B. *-bdhâir.* [42] B. *vaçishṭaya;* G. M. *-shyam.*

Next we pass to the consideration of another reason why the principle stated in the rule needed to be laid down. The consonant (by i.37) has half a *mora* of quantity; and a vowel has [for example] a *mora:* their combination, then, would seem to have a *mora* and a half, and so would be liable to be understood as of long quantity: this untoward conclusion is avoided by the present rule, which implies that in fluent utterance the quantity of the vowel belongs in all cases to the combination of consonant and vowel, and not to the vowel alone. The specification "in fluent utterance" (literally, 'in running action') is made in order to save the significance of rule i.37.

Finally, the superiority of the vowel is once more inferred from the fact that, when it is combined with a consonant, it alone is perceptible; just as, when milk and water are mingled, the milk alone is perceived, and not the water.

तत्परस्वरम् ॥ २ ॥

2. And it belongs to the following vowel.

The commentator explains *parasvaram* as a descriptive compound (*karmadhâraya*), governed by *bhajate* understood; such an ellipsis, however, is so violent as to be hardly admissible, and the word is perhaps better taken as a possessive (*bahuvrîhi*), somewhat anomalously used. The occasion of the rule, we are told, is the doubt which is liable to arise as to when the consonant—which, owing to its having the vowel as a superior, is unable to stand by itself—is an adjunct of the preceding, and when of the following vowel. A single phrase is quoted as example, namely *imân eva lokân upadhâya* (v.5.5[3]: O. omits the last word).

This is the leading and introductory principle in all the Prâtiçâkhyas (see note to Ath. Pr. i.55); it is greatly restricted in its application by the following rules.

अवसितं पूर्वस्य ॥ ३ ॥

3. A consonant *in pausâ* belongs to the preceding vowel.

The commentator explains *avasitam* as meaning 'standing at the end of a *pada*,' and gives as examples *ârk* (i.2.2[2] et al.: W. has instead *ṛk* [iv.7.9[1] et al.], and O. has *vâk* [i.3.9[1] et al.]), *vashaṭ*

---

2. *svarapradhânatayâ kevalam avasthâtum asahamânaṁ*[1] [2]*vyañjanaṁ kadâ pûrvasyâ 'ṅgaṁ*[2] [3]*kadâ parasyâ 'ṅgam*[3] *iti saṁdehe*[4] *vyavasthâpayati: tad aṅgabhûtaṁ*[5] *vyañjanam parasvaram bhajate. yathâ*[6]*: imân..... paraç câ 'sâu svaraç ca parasvaraḥ:* [7] *taṁ*[8] *svaraparam*[9].

[1] O. om. [(2)] G. M. om. [(3)] W. O. om.; G. M. *kadácid apar-*. [4] G. M. *-haṁ.* [5] W. *aṅçabh-;* O. *egasûtrataṁ.* [6] B. om. [7] W. ins. *paraṁ svari.* [8] O. om. [9] G M. O. om.

(ii.2.12[4] et al.), *tat* (*passim:* given by G. M. only), and *haviḥ* (i.2.4[1] et al.)

This principle, of course, is without exception in its application. It is either stated or implied in the rules of the other treatises (see note to Ath. Pr. i.57).

संयोगादि ॥ ४ ॥

4. Also the first consonant of a group.

That is to say, as the commentator points out, of a group consisting of either two consonants or more than two. The "also" (*ca*) expressed in the next rule is declared to be implied here also, and to prescribe adjunction to the preceding vowel. The examples given are *yajñân vyâdiçat* (vi.6.11[1]) and *apsv antaḥ* (i.4.45[2] et al.: but G. M. substitute *apsv agne* [iv.2.11[3]], and W. has the corrupt reading *açvataḥ*). If, now, we had only to take the groups of consonants as they stand in the ordinary text, and divide them, the application of this and of the remaining rules for syllabication would be simple enough; but we are required to apply also the rules for duplication etc. as found in chapter xiv., and to make the insertions required by the rules of the fifth (v.32,33) and the present chapter (12–16), which puts quite a different face upon the matter. In fact, in the examples furnished, *nt* is the only group which is divided *n-t* without farther ceremony; *gr* becomes and is divided *g-gr; nvy*, in like manner, *n-nvy; psv* is expanded into *p-phsv;* and *jñ* into *j̄j-jñ* (writing the *yama*, as I have done elsewhere, with a straight line above the letter), where, by the action of the next rule, two consonants go to the preceding vowel. The class of groups consisting of two consonants only, and such consonants as (by xiv.23) are not liable to duplication, is the only one of which the division is settled by the present rule alone: it contains (in the Tâittirîya-Sanhitâ) thirty-nine groups, such as *nt, tth, pp, yy, ṅy, çç.*

The other treatises hold this same principle, and teach it in an equivalent manner (see Ath. Pr. i.56 and note)—save that the Rik Pr. (i.5, xviii.18) allows the letter to be adjoined to either the preceding or the following syllable.

---

3. *avasitam padântavarti*[1] *vyañjanam* [2]*pûrvasya svarasyâ 'ṅgaṁ*[2] [3]*syât. yathâ*[4]*: ârk: vashaṭ: tat*[5]*: haviḥ.*[3]

[1] G. M. *antarv-.* [(2)] G. M. *pûrvasvarâṅgaṁ.* [(3)] B. om. [4] O. om. [5] W. O. om.

4. [1]*dvayor*[2] *bahûnâṁ*[3] *vâ saṁyogo bhavati*[4]*: tasya saṁyogasyâ "di*[5] *vyañjanam*[6] *pûrvasvarasyâ*[7] *'ṅgaṁ*[1] *bhavati.* [8]*yathâ*[9]*: yajñân..... apsv..... parasûtre cakâraḥ*[8] [10]*pûrvasvarâṅgatvabodhaka*[11] *ity atrâ 'pi tal*[12] *labhyate*[10].

[(1)] B. om. [2] G. M. om. [3] W. *varṇânâṁ;* G. M. *saṁyogânâṁ.* [4] G. M. ins. *yadi.* [5] G. M. ins. *yad.* [6] G. M. ins. *tat.* [7] W. *pûrvasyâ;* O. *-svarâ.* [(8)] O. om. [9] G. M. om. [(10)] W. O. om. [11] G. M. *svarasyâ 'ṅg-;* B. *-ṅgaṁ bo-.* [12] G. M. om.

The manuscripts of the commentary are more than usually defective in this neighborhood: B. has lost the present rule, with something of what precedes and follows it; O. omits the next rule, with passages before and after; W. has done the same, to a somewhat less extent; but rule 5 and the lacking part of its comment were apparently restored on the margin of W.'s original, and its copyist has put them in in the wrong place, next before rule 6.

परेण चासंहितम् ॥ ५ ॥

5. And one that is not combined with the following vowel.

The comment supplies the word *svareṇa*, 'vowel,' as that with which *pareṇa* here agrees, and the whole interpretation is constructed accordingly. The meaning is, then, that (with the exceptions to be further specified in the following rules) only the final member of a group of consonants is to be adjoined to the following vowel, the rest belonging to that which precedes. By way of illustration is given merely *tat savituḥ* (i.5.6[4] et al.): a most insufficient and ill-chosen example; since, in the final form of the group *ts*, only one consonant goes with the preceding syllable: thus, *t-ths.* But the commentator is obliged to spend his strength, and vainly, in endeavoring to refute an obvious objection to the rule itself, which he thus states: "well, but then the foregoing rule is meaningless, since by this one also the quality of adjunction to the preceding vowel is assured to the consonant that begins a group." And he replies, "you must not think that: for, in such cases as *maryaçrîḥ* (iv.1.2[5] et al.) and *arvâ 'si* (i.7.8[1] et al.), in which the *y* and *v* are doubled after *r* by rule xiv.4, the former *y* or *v* is by the present rule made an adjunct of the preceding vowel, but the *r*, by rule 7 below, would become an adjunct of the following vowel: and that is impossible, since no such pronunciation ever takes place. So, as one or the other must needs be annulled, the question arises which is to be annulled; and here rule 4 comes in to settle the question."

This is not a very acceptable exposition, although it in a manner involves the true relations. Rule 4 is not meant as a safeguard against the misapplication of following precepts, but as a fundamental principle, with reference to which the present rule stands in a subordinate position; and the two must be understood as if they read "the first member of a group belongs to the preceding vowel; and, along with it, such other members as are not immediately combined with the following vowel." The former principle obtains everywhere, without exception; to the latter, rules 7–9

---

5. [1]*pareṇa*[2] *svareṇâ 'saṁhitam*[3] *asaṁyuktaṁ*[4] *vyañjanam*[5] *pûrvasvarâñgam bhavati*[1]. *yathâ*[6]: *tat*---- *nanu tarhi pûrvasûtram anarthakam: saṁyogâdibhûtasyâ*[7] *'pi vyañjanasyâ 'nenâi 'va*[7] *pûrvasvarâñgatvasiddheḥ. mâi 'vam mañsthâḥ*[8]: *maryaçrîḥ: arvâ 'si: ity atra yavakârayo rephât paraṁ ca* (xiv.

establish very important and extensive classes of exceptions. If the mode of statement adopted in the treatise is open to some objection, we cannot help it; the slight inaccuracy is perhaps a consequence of the general prevalence of the doctrine of rule 4, to which its successor is added as an extension peculiar to this school.

No one of the other Prâtiçâkhyas recognizes any such principle as this: those of the Rik (i.5, xviii.18) and Atharvan (i.58) add to the initial consonant of a group only the first of a following pair which is the result of duplication, that of the White Yajus including further (i.104,105) the other one of the pair, provided a mute follows. Its sway is, as already remarked, much more limited than would be thought at first sight, because rule 7 establishes a different usage for the immense class of groups of which a semivowel stands as final member, and rule 9 for the much smaller but yet important class in which a spirant stands last, or followed by a semivowel. Its general effect is to attach to the following vowel only such consonants or groups as could begin a word, leaving the rest to belong to the foregoing syllable. There seems to be need of illustrating, more fully than the commentator has deigned to do, the sphere of its application.

This is, in consonant-groups originally of two members, to

1. Groups in which a mute is doubled (or its corresponding non-aspirate prefixed to it, as will be understood hereafter without special remark) after a surd spirant (*χ* or *φ*, xiv.9,15), *l* (xiv.2,3), or *r* (xiv.4,15), the first member of the group remaining unchanged: thus, *χk-k*, *lk-k*, *rk-k*. These are twenty-seven in number; and to them may be added *ry-y*, *rl-l*, *rv-v*, which, by the final specification of rule 7, follow the same mode of division. In regard to these, the usage as fixed by our treatise is the same with that sanctioned by the rest, as already mentioned.

2. Groups in which a mute, or *v*, is doubled before a mute of another series: thus, *kk-c*, *vv-ṇ*. Of these there are fifty-one in the Sanhitâ.

3. The same, but with the addition (by xxi.12) of *yama* before the final member: thus, *gg-ḡn*. Twenty-three groups.

4. Groups in which the initial spirant (sibilant) is doubled, and also the following mute (by xiv.9), only the last of all going to the following syllable: thus, *çç c-c*. Thirteen groups.

5. The same, but with *yama:* thus, *ççp-p̄m* (*çm*). Six groups.

6. Groups in which *h* is doubled before a nasal, with *nâsikya* (by xxi.14: but see the note to that rule, for a different interpretation): thus, *hh-ⁿn*. Three groups only.

Against these one hundred and twenty-six groups, growing out

---

4) *iti dvitve ⁹ kṛte prathamayavakârayoḥ pareṇa câ 'sañhitam*[10] *ity anena pûrvasvarâñgatvam*[11] *prâptam*[12]*: rephasya tu*[13] *nâ 'ntasthâparam asavarṇam* (xxi.7) *ity anena parasvarâñgatvam*[14] *prâptam*[15]*: tac câ 'çakyam: tathoccâraṇâsambhavât: anyatarabâdhe*[16] *kartavye sati kiṁ vâ bâdhyam*[17] *iti saṁdehaḥ*[18]*:*

of original simple pairs, there are eighty like *k-ky* (from *ky*) and *k-khsh* (from *ksh*), in which, by rules 7 and 9, only the initial consonant of the finally resulting group goes with the preceding vowel.

When, now, the pairs here rehearsed come to be extended to triplets by the addition of a third member, if that member be a semivowel, or a spirant (sibilant) following a mute, the point of division remains just where it was before. And so also, of course, in the like extension of the groups mentioned under rule 4, above, as undergoing no change in the *varṇakrama*. Thus, *ggr* (*g-gr*) is divided like *gg* (*g-g*); *çcy* (*çç-cy*) like *çc* (*çç-c*); *ṅksh* (*ṅ-khsh*) like *ṅk* (*ṅ-k*); and *rks* (*rk-khs*) like *rk* (*rk-k*). And the very great majority (one hundred and fifty-four) of the groups of three consonants occurring in the Sanhitâ have a semivowel as their final member; with final sibilant there are only seven.

If, on the other hand, double groups are extended to triplets by appending a mute, either non-nasal or nasal (which happens in thirty-one cases), the point of division is, by the operation of the present rule, shifted toward the end of the group. Thus, we have

1. *ṅ-k*, but *ṅk-t*, two groups; and *ñ-ch*, but *ñj-jñ*, two groups;
2. *rk-k*, but *rkk-c*, five groups; and *rj-j*, but *rjj-jm*, five groups;
3. *dd-gh*, but *ddgh-g̅hn*, two groups;
4. *sst-t*, but *sstt-t̅n*, two groups;

which are extensions of the groups of two members already treated of, and advance the division only one point. But further, groups ending in a sibilant, and falling under rule 9, below, and those which by rule 15 have *svarabhakti*, exhibit, when a mute is added, a still greater transference forward of the point of division, and we have

5. *k-khs* (*ks*), but *kkhst-t* (*kst*), four groups; and *k-khsh* (*ksh*), but *kkhshp-p̅m* (*kshm*), five groups; and, finally,
6. *r^r-sh* (*rsh*), but *rshsht̩-t̩* (*rsht̩*); and *r^r-ç*, but *rççp-p̅m* (*rçm*), three groups.

In the yet further extension to groups of four members, the same principles prevail. There are found nineteen such groups in which the additional letter, being a semivowel, has no effect upon the division; and only three in which the division is altered by an added mute. These last are: *ṅkhsht̩-t̩n* (*ṅkshn*), from *ṅkhsh*; *ḥkhsht̩-t̩n* (*ḥkshn*), from *ḥ-khsh* (*ḥksh*); and *nthst-t* (*ntst*), from *n-ths* (*nts*).

Finally, the only two groups of five consonants occurring in the

---

tatra niçcâyakatvena[19] *saṁyogâdi*[20] (xxi.4) *sûtram upatishṭhate*.[21]

[1] O. om., with the rule; W. puts, with the rule, at the end of the comment, having here also *pûrvasvarâṅgam bhavati*. [2] B. *svar-*; W. adds *svareṇa*. [3] G. M. *'sâṁh-* (as also in the rule). [4] W. ins. *ca*; G. M. ins. *yad*. [5] G. M. ins. *tat*. [6] B. G. M. om. [7] W. *-dibh-*. [8] G. M. om. [9] G. M. ins. *ca*. [10] G. M. *'sâṁh-*. [11] O. *-tva*. [12] O. *-tiḥ*. [13] W. B. om. [14] O. *-tva*. [15] O. *-tiḥ*. [16] W. B. *anyadbâ-*. [17] O. *câryam*. [18] G. M. *-ha syât*. [19] W. *niyatatv-*; B. *niçcayatv-*. [20] G. M. *-di 'ti*. [21] O. *iva ti-*.

Sanhitâ (*ntstr* and *tstry*) are formed by added semivowels, and so do not come under the further action of the present rule.

G. M. read *asân̆hitam* instead of *asan̆hitam* in the rule.

अनुस्वारः स्वरभक्तिश्च ॥ ६ ॥

6. Also *anusvâra* and *svarabhakti*.

By G. M., this rule is divided into two, *anusvâraḥ* and *svarabhaktiç ca* (while, on the other hand, T. reads *anusvârasvarabhaktyoç ca*); and such a division is noted, if not accepted, in the comment, by all the manuscripts, which say "of this rule (*svarabhaktiç ca*) is made a setting-apart, although the prescription is identical (with that made in the other rule, *anusvâraḥ*)." And the object of thus separating what is confessed properly to belong together is stated to be "to bring about the adjunction of *svarabhakti*, in some cases, to the following vowel," on the authority of a verse which is quoted, to the effect that "the knowing man should connect with its predecessor (?) the *bhakti* that follows a short vowel; and in *ṛtasya dhûrshadam* the *bhakti* is said to do as it pleases;" but G. M. substitute for the latter half of the verse "to it should be assigned one *mora*, also before a pause and in cases of hiatus." The whole matter is exceedingly obscure, or quite unintelligible, without aid from the context of the quoted verse. The words cited as examples are not found in the Sanhitâ; but they occur in the Rig-Veda (at i.143.7), and also in the Tâittirîya-Brâhmaṇa (i.2.1[12]), where the *svarabhakti* has assumed the form of a full vowel, and the word reads *dhûrushadam*. It looks as if the commentators had set out to divide into two rules what they nevertheless have to acknowledge to be really only one, for the purpose of interpreting into the latter half of it, when set by itself, a license to the element in question to be treated either way; but, as they have not fully carried out their intention, I have preferred to retain the unity of the rule. It is quoted, we may further remark, under rule i.34, in all the manuscripts of the comment, apparently without any thought of a division.

---

6. *cakâraḥ samuccayakathanadvârâ*[1] *pûrvasvarâṅgatvâkarshakaḥ.* [2]*anusvâraḥ*[3] *pûrvasvaram*[4] *bhajate*[5]. *yathâ*[6]: *an̆ç-----.*[2] *svarabhaktiç ca pûrvasvaram*[7] *bhajate. yathâ*[8]: *gârh-----. vidhâu*[2] *samâne*[10] *sûtrasyâ 'sya pṛthakkaraṇam*[11]: *kvacit svarabhakteḥ*[12] *parâṅgatvam*[13] *âpâdayitum*[14]. *tathâ hi:*

[15]*svarâd dhrasvât*[15] *parâṁ bhaktim pracayatvaṁ nayed*[16] *budhaḥ:*
[17]*ṛtasya dhûrshadaṁ ce 'ti svatantrâ bhaktir ucyate*[17].

[1] B. *-ra;* G. M. *-thanâd vâ;* O. *-dvât.* [(2)] G. M. put after *anusvâraḥ*, as its comment, giving all the rest as comment to *svarabhaktiç ca* as a separate rule. [3] O. om. [4] W. G. M. O. *-svarâṅgaṁ.* [5] G. M. *syât.* [6] G. M. O. om. [7] O. *svar-.* [8] G. M. O. om. [9] O. *samavi-.* [10] O. *-na;* G. M. add *anusvâra svarabhaktiç ce 'ti.* [11] B. *-kkâr-.* [12] O. *pṛthagnaktâuḥ.* [13] W. B. G. M. *padâ-.* [14] W. B. *-ditum.* [(15)] B. *svarâṅga hr-.* [16] G. M. *na ced.* [(17)] G. M. substitute *tasyâ mâtrâ bhaved ekâ virâme ca vivṛttishu;* O. adds [(2)] from comment to next rule.

Anusvâra appears here once more with the distinct value of a consonantal element following the vowel—and yet not as a full consonant, else it would fall under rule 4 above, and would require no separate treatment. The treatise is not so explicit as were to be desired in defining what is to be done with it in syllabication; but I presume we may infer that it does not count as *saṁyogâdi* at all, but only as if an affection of the preceding vowel; and hence, that all the groups which it introduces are to be divided as if it were not there; that *n̄çc*, for example, is to be made into *n̄çç-c*, *n̄sm* into *n̄ssp-p̄m*, and *n̄str* into *n̄sst-tr*. The example given by the commentator is *an̄çunâ te* (i.2.6); but it is an ill-chosen one, and quite worthless, as, in any view of the nature and treatment of *anusvâra*, no question could arise as to the division *an̄-çunâ*.

For *svarabhakti*, see the concluding rules of this chapter (xxi. 15,16). The example given is *gârhapatyaḥ* (i.6.7[1] et al.), which we are to read and divide *gâr^r-ha-pat-tyaḥ*.

नान्तस्थापरमसवर्णम् ॥ ७ ॥

7. But not a consonant that is followed by a semivowel, if dissimilar with it.

The negative here signifies a direct reversal of the implication, as it denotes a denial of adjunction to the preceding vowel, and hence necessarily involves adjunction to the one that follows, since the consonant cannot stand by itself. "Dissimilar" is simply explained by *vilakshaṇa*, 'of diverse characteristics, different;' it excludes from the operation of the rule the doubled semivowel itself, and would also exclude the nasal semivowel into which *n* and *m* are converted before *l*, and *m* before *y* and *v* (v.26,28), if these occurred where the rule could apply, which is not the case.

The examples quoted by the commentator are *adhyavasâya diçaḥ* (vi.1.5[1]; i. e. *ad-dhya-*), *madhumiçreṇa* (v.2.8[6] et al.; i. e. *miç-çre-*), *açlonayâ* (vi.1.6[7]; i. e. *aç-çlo-*), and *ishe tvâ* (i.1.1 et al.; i. e. *i-shet-tvâ*): they are not to be commended as at all fully illustrating the wide range of application of the rule. This has been sufficiently set forth above, under rule 5. It helps to determine the division of one-third of the groups of two consonants, of four-fifths of those of three, of six-sevenths of those of four, and of all those of five—or of four-sevenths of the whole number of consonant

---

7. *nakâraḥ pûrvasvarâṅgatvavyâvartakaḥ: antasthâparaṁ vyañjanaṁ tasyâ antasthâyâ asavarṇaṁ vilakshaṇam pûrvasvarâṅgaṁ na bhavati: arthât parasvarâṅgaṁ* [1]*tad iti veditavyam*[1]: [2]*svata sthâtum açakyatvât*[2]. *yathâ*[3]: *adhy-....: madh-....: açl-....: ishe.....* *antasthâ parâ yasmât tad antasthâparam. asavarṇam iti kim: pari-....*

(1) G. M. *iti vijñeyam*; O. om. (2) O. puts at end of comment on preceding rule; B. *svaraṁ vinâ sthâ-*. [3] O. om.

groups. By way of further examples, we may cite the two groups of five; they are *vi-yu-yâtthst-tryas-sya* (ii.6.5[4-5]) and *ab-bru-vanthst-trî-kâ-mâ* (vi.1.6[5]).

But if the commentator's direct illustration of the rule is scanty, his counter-illustration is yet less satisfactory. To establish the necessity of the specification *asavarṇam*, 'dissimilar,' he cites only *paricâyyaṁ cinvîta* (v.4.11[3]). Such cases as this, however, are rather covered by the fundamental rule *saṁyogâdi* (xxi.4), and the application of the present one is to the groups in which a semi-vowel is doubled after *r*, and which we are to read *ry-y*, *rl-l*, *rv-v*; while, on the other hand, in the half-dozen groups in which two different semi-vowels follow a mute, both of them, along with the preceding mute, go to the succeeding vowel: thus, *vish-shvañ-ñvyârc-chat* (ii.3.2[6]), *a-vit-trya-va-tu* (i.8.22[1]), and *gṛ-hâd-dvrî-hîn* (ii.3.1[3]).

नासिक्याः ॥ ८ ॥

8. Nor the nose-sounds.

The "nose-sounds" are here again (as under ii.49) defined as the *yamas* (xxi.12,13) only; but there is no reason why we should not regard the *nâsikya* (xxi.14) as likewise included (see the note on rule 14). The examples given are also of *yamas* only: *rukmam upa dadhâti* (v.2.7[1] et al.: O. has *rukmam* only) and *râjñe sûkaraḥ* (v.5.11: O. substitutes *svarâjñe*, v.6.21). The groups, in their full form, are read and divided *kk-km* and *jj-jñ*. An example of the *nâsikya* would be *vahh-"ni-ta-mam* (i.1.4[1]).

The Vâj. Pr. (i.103) reckons the *yama* to the preceding vowel; neither of the other treatises says anything about it.

स्पर्शश्चोष्मपर ऊष्मा चेत्परश्च ॥ ९ ॥

9. Nor a mute that is followed by a spirant—provided the following spirant is likewise in the same case.

The first *ca* (translated 'nor' here), the commentator says, effects the connection of the rule with its predecessor; the second (rendered 'likewise') implies adjunction to the following vowel. This is not very lucid, for the two things are really equivalent to one another. And in the further exposition, the *paraḥ* appears (the readings are not consistent or clear) to be taken as signifying *parasvarâñgam*; but this cannot well be correct. The phrase-ology of the rule, indeed, is very peculiar, and I do not see how it is to be accounted for unless we may conjecture that the proviso *ûshmâ cet paraç ca* is a later addition, made after it had been noticed that the more general statement *sparçaç co "shmaparaḥ*

---

8. *nâsikyâ*[1] *yamâḥ*[2] *parasvaram*[3] *bhajante. yathâ*[4]: *rukmam ---: râjñe ---*

[1] B. om. [2] G. M. *yaḥ*. [3] W. *svaraparam*. [4] G. M. O. om.

included too much. The meaning is clear: that a spirant which itself belongs to the following syllable, as being either directly combined with the vowel of the latter (xxi.5) or followed only by a semivowel before that vowel (xxi.7), carries with it a preceding mute; but if, on the other hand, it be cut off from the succeeding vowel by a mute, so as itself to belong to the antecedent syllable, a mute before it goes, of course, to the same syllable. The examples given in the comment are this time well selected, and illustrate the three cases involved: they are *shaṭt sam padyante* (v.4.3[4] et al.) and *vashaṭt svâhâ* (vii.3.12); in both of them a *t* is inserted, by rule v.33, between the *ṭ* and *s*, and the final reading and division is *ṭt-ths* and *ṭt-thsv*. As counter-example we have *akshṇayâ vyâghârayati* (v.2.7[5] et al.), where, after all rules are satisfied, we have *kkhshṭ-ṭṇ*.

As compared with those to which rule 7 applies, the consonant groups falling under this rule are few, only forty-six in all; in thirty of which the spirant carries the mute before it to the following vowel, while in the remaining sixteen both go together to the one that precedes. The detail is as follows.

Of double groups, composed of a single mute and spirant, there are seven: for example, *k-khsh* (*ksh*).

Of groups containing three consonants, the largest class is that formed by the addition of a semivowel to the preceding: for example, *k-khshy* (*kshy*): it contains ten groups. Then there are two like *ń-khsh* (*ńksh*), three like *tt-khsh* (*tksh*), and the isolated *rk-khs* (*rks*).

Of groups of four consonants there are seven on this side, all but one (*rṭt-ths=rṭts*) like those of three, but with an added semivowel, which does not (xxi.7) change the division.

On the other side, where the spirant goes back to the vowel of the antecedent syllable, there are, of course, no groups of two consonants. Of groups of three we have nine, four with following non-nasal mute (as *kkhst-t=kst*), and five with following nasal (as *kkhshṭ-ṭṇ=kshṇ*). Of groups of four, there are two (as *tthst-tr=tstr*) formed from the foregoing with added semivowel, and three from triplets ending in a sibilant increased by a mute, either non-nasal (namely *nthst-t=ntst*) or nasal (as *ńkhshṭ-ṭṇ=ńkshṇ*). The two groups of five consonants, which also belong here, have been given above, under rule 7.

This finishes the subject of the division of consonant-groups in syllabication, the special elaborateness and intricacy of whose treat-

---

9. *pûrvaç cakâro nâsikyó* (xxi.8) *ity anena samuccayavâcakaḥ: uttaras tu[1] parasvarâńgatvâkarshakaḥ: ûshmapara sparçaç ca parasvarâńgam bhavati: asâv[2] ûshmâ[3] paraç cet[4] parasvarâńgam[5] ced ity arthaḥ. shaṭ----: vashaṭ----. ûshmaparaç ced iti kim: aksh-----. ûshmâ paro yasmâd asâv ûshmaparaḥ.*

[1] G. M. *cakâro 'pi.* [2] B *asâ.* [3] MSS. *-ma.* [4] W. *cen na*; O. *cen : sha.* [5] W. B. *-gaç*; O. *-ga.*

ment in this Prâtiçâkhya has rendered necessary a fuller illustration than was thought worth while in connection with the others, in order to render apprehensible the views held regarding it by the authors of the treatise.

स्वरितात्सꣳहितायामनुदात्तानां प्रचय उदात्तश्रुतिः ॥ १० ॥

10. Of grave syllables following a circumflex in *saṁhitâ* there is *pracaya*, having the tone of acute.

The theory of the *pracaya* accent has been so fully set forth in the note to Ath. Pr. iii.65 that I do not need to spend many words upon it here. Its effect is, as there pointed out, to give to all the syllables which are left in the written text without any accent-mark the same high tone, whether they be *udâtta*, 'acute,' or *anudâtta*, 'grave.' Thus, in the example given by the commentator, *ágne dudhra gahya kiñçila vanya yâ' te* (v.5.9[1]: G. M. omit *yâ te*), which is written in *pada*-text

अग्ने । दुध्र । गह्य । किंशिल । वन्य । या । ते ।,

the *saṁhitâ*-reading is

अग्ने दुध्र गह्य किंशिल वन्य या ते;

the grave syllables *dudhra gahya kiñçila van-* being without written designation of accent, like the two acute syllables *ág-* and *yâ'*, and being by this rule uttered upon the same pitch with them. It makes no difference whether the circumflex which precedes the *pracaya* is enclitic (as in the illustration given) or independent; and I have pointed out above (under xix.3) that, owing to the absence of *kampa* in the Tâittirîya-Sanhitâ where a circumflex precedes an acute, there are very numerous cases in the text where the *saṁhitâ* alone does not show us whether the unmarked syllables following a circumflex are *udâtta* or *pracaya*—whether, for example,

ह्येतद्देवाः, सो ऽस्मादेतर्हि, and सो ऽकामयत प्रजाः,

are to be read *hy ètád devâ'h* or *hy ètad devâ'h, sò 'smâ'd etárhi* or *sò 'smâd etárhi, sò 'kâ'máyátá prajâ'h* or *sò 'kâmayata prajâ'h*.

In the note referred to, I ventured the conjecture that the mode

---

10. *svaritât pareshâm anudâttânâm anudâttayor anudâttasya vâ saṁhitâyâm* [1] *pracayo nâma dharmo*[2] *bhavati. yathâ: agne* .... *anudâttânâm iti kim: agnaye*.... *saṁhitâyâm iti kim: agne*.... *udâttasya çrutir iva çrutir yasyâ 'sâv*[3] *udâttaçrutir iti*[4] *pracayasvarûpanirûpaṇam*[5]*: ato na punaruktiçaṅkâ*[6].

[1] B. ins. *ca*. [2] G. M. *dheyo*. [3] G. M. *sa* for *asâu*. [4] W. om. [5] B. *-svarûpaṇam*. [6] W. *-ktikâṅkâ*.

of writing the accent might not have been without influence on the theory as to its character—that is is to say, that the Vedic phonetists may have come by an afterthought to declare the *pracaya* syllables of acute tone, and to pronounce them so, *because* they agreed with the acute in being without a sign of accent, while originally no such correspondence in character was perceived or intended to be signified. The conjecture will doubtless have appeared to many somewhat wild, but I think that in studying the development of the Hindu theory respecting accent it at any rate deserves to be taken fully into account and carefully considered. I am far from regarding it at present as anything more than a conjecture; yet one or two matters have come to light since it was put forth which at least add to its plausibility. Haug, namely, in a valuable and interesting communication from India to the Journal of the German Oriental Society (vol. xvii., 1863, p. 799 ff.), shows that the modern Hindu reciters of the Veda give tonic distinction only to the syllables that have the accent-signs, the *svarita* and *anudâtta*, so that the *udâtta* appears to be no accent at all, and is entirely confounded with the toneless *pracaya* —thus, under the influence of the mode of written designation, turning topsy-turvy, as it were, the whole system of spoken accent. And again, the peculiar system of writing the accent practised in the Çatapatha-Brâhmaṇa (which uses only one sign, the horizontal stroke beneath the syllable, applied in all the other known systems to mark the *anudâtta* tone), has been turned in later times into a peculiar system of accenting, and treatises have been written to explain and teach it as such (see Kielhorn and Weber, in Weber's Indische Studien, x. 397 ff.*).

The commentator points out that two grave syllables, or even one, following the circumflex, receive the character of *pracaya* (of course, with the restriction made in the next rule), and not more than two only, as is literally signified by the plural *anudâttânâm* in the rule. To show that the conversion into *pracaya* is limited to grave syllables, he quotes *agnáye právate* (ii.4.1[2] et al.); to show that the conversion is made only in *saṁhitâ*, he gives part of the other passage in *pada*-form, namely *agne : dudhra : gahya : kiñçila : vanya* (O. adds *yâ*). We might naturally infer from this that the *pracaya* accent does not occur at all in *pada*-text; but the inference is not a necessary one (since the rule only says that syllables which are *anudâtta* in their *pada*-form become *pracaya* in *saṁhitâ*, without implying that there may not be *pracayas* in *pada*-text which remain such in *saṁhitâ*), and would doubtless be erroneous; for at least the extant *pada*-text of the Tâittirîya-Sanhitâ agrees in this respect with those of the other Vedas, and writes *gírvaṇase*, *antárikṣham*, and *samágachanta*, for example,

* It ought to be added, that Haug and Kielhorn do not look at the matter in the same light in which I have placed it, but incline to believe in the reality and antiquity of what I have called the modern and artificially substituted systems: this is no place to discuss the subject; but I feel confident that the view I have taken will prove the only one tenable.

गिर्॑वणसे । अ॒न्तरि॑क्षं । and स॒मगं॑स्ते॒ति सं॒ऽअगं॑स्त ।,

not गिर्॑वण॒से॒ । अ॒न्तरि॑क्षं॒ ।----सं॒ऽअगं॑स्त॒.

The peculiarity of this *pada*-text in treating the *avagraha* as a full *avasâna* in regard to the designation of accent (as shown in the third of the examples), has been already spoken of above (under rule xx.3).

The terms of the rule would justify us in understanding *pracaya* to have its etymological meaning of 'accumulation, continued series,' and translating 'a series of grave syllables following a circumflex in *saṁhitâ* is of acute tone;' and perhaps this was actually the intent of the rule-makers; but I have preferred, as the safer course, to follow the authority of the commentator in translating. To him, indeed, the term is so distinctly a technical one, implying utterance with acute tone, that he thinks it necessary to explain that *udâttaçrutiḥ* is added by way of definition of the peculiar character of the *pracaya*, and therefore is not open to the reproach of *punarukti*, or superfluous repetition.

नोदात्तस्वरितपरः ॥ ११ ॥

11. But not when an acute or circumflex follows.

That is to say, when such a series or *pracaya* of grave syllables is followed by an acute or a circumflex syllable, the one next preceding the latter is not made to be of acute tone, but retains its proper grave character, and is marked with the *anudâtta* sign. The commentator offers as examples *táyâ devấḥ sutám* (iv.1.2[1]: W. B. omit *sutam*, without which the passage is found elsewhere; G. M. substitute *táyâ devátayâ*, iv.2.9[2] et al.) and *tád âhuḥ kvà jágatî* (vii.1.4[3]: G. M. omit *jagatî*). These illustrations are wanting in variety, inasmuch as they show between the two independent accents only two original grave syllables, whereof one becomes an enclitic circumflex and the other remains grave; we may take the first example under the preceding rule as showing how an actual *pracaya* ends with a grave before the following original accent.

The subject to be supplied with the predicate in this rule is *svaraḥ*, of course. There is an objectionable ambiguity in the form of the rule, inasmuch as there might most naturally seem to be *anuvṛtti* of *pracayaḥ*, and so a denial of that accent anywhere excepting before a pause.

We have seen at xix.2 that the name *vikrama* is given to the

---

11. *udâttaparaḥ*[1] *svaritaparo vâ 'nudâttaḥ pracayo na bhavati. yathâ*[2]*: tayâ----: tad----. udâttaç ca*[3] *svaritaç co 'dâttasvaritâu: tâu parâu yasmât sa tatho 'ktaḥ.*

[1] O. *-ro vâ.* [2] G. M. O. om. [3] B. om.

grave following a *pracaya*, as well as to one that comes immediately after a circumflex.

स्पर्शादनुत्तमादुत्तमपरादानुपूर्व्यान्नासिक्याः ॥ १२ ॥

12. After a non-nasal mute, when it is followed by a nasal, are inserted, in their order, nose-sounds.

Which nose-sounds, as we are told in the next rule, some call *yamas;* and by this familiar name, which the other Prâtiçâkhyas apply to them directly, we shall here, as we have done elsewhere, know them. The treatise teaches us nothing more about them, except (ii.49–51) that their place of production is either the nose or the mouth and nose, and that the producing organ is as in the series of mutes; and farther (xxi.8), that in syllabication they are to be reckoned with the following vowel.

The theory of these curious and equivocal constituents of the ancient Hindu alphabet I have discussed pretty fully in the note to Ath. Pr. i.99, and I have no new light to throw upon the subject here. They are transition-sounds, assumed to intervene between non-nasal and following nasal, as a kind of nasal counterpart to the non-nasal, and therefore called its *yama* or 'twin.'

The meaning of *ânupûrvyât*, 'in their order,' is ambiguous, as it might be understood to refer to the order either of the twenty non-nasal mutes or of the five nasals; or, of the four kinds of non-nasal mutes in each series—in which last sense the comment understands it, declaring that the first *yama* follows a first mute, the second a second, and so on; and he has before (under i.1) reckoned the *yamas* as four in the catalogue of alphabetic sounds. I have pointed out under ii.51 how difficult it is to reconcile this view with that of a variation of their organ of production as in the five series of mutes.

The commentator's examples are *tam pratnathâ* (i.4.9), *vimathnânâḥ* (iii.5.4^{3}), *vidmâ te agne* (iv.2.2^{1}: O. omits *agne*), and *dârûṇi dadhmasi* (iv.1.10^{1})—one, namely, for each of the four classes of mutes. As rule xiv.24 expressly enjoins duplication of the non-nasal mute in these combinations, we are to read and divide *pratt-tnathâ*, *vidd-dma*, and so on. The counter-examples (of which all but the last are lost in W.) are as follows: to show that the insertion is made only after a mute, *kalmâshî bhavati* (v.1.1^{4}: O. substitutes *brahmavâdinaḥ*, i.7.1^{4} etc.); that this mute must be a

12. *uttamaparâd anuttamât sparçâd* [1] *ânupûrvyâd yathâkramam nâsikyâ âgamâ bhavanti: prathamasparçât prathamanâsikyaḥ*[2]*: dvitîyâd*[3] *dvitîyaḥ*[4]*: evam* [5]*anyatrâ 'pi.*[5] *yathâ*[6]*: tam* ....: *vim*-....: *vidmâ*....: *dâr*-....: *ityâdi. sparçâd iti kim:* [7]*kalm*-..... *anuttamâd iti kim: sumn*-..... *uttamaparâd iti kim:*[7] *sabdaḥ*.....

[1] G. M. ins. *parata;* O. ins. *paraḥ.* [2] G. M. O. *-kyâḥ.* [3] O. *-yasparçâd.* [4] G. M. *-yâḥ.* (5) G. M. *anye.* [6] O, om. (7) W. om.

non-nasal, *sumnaya sumninî* (i.1.13[3] et al.: O. substitutes *sushumnaḥ*, iii.4.7[1]); and that it must be followed by a nasal, *sabdaḥ sagaraḥ sumekaḥ* (iv.4.7[2]: G. M. omit *sumekaḥ;* O. substitutes *vashaṭt svâhâ*, vii.3.12).

These examples are one-sided, in that they only exhibit the simplest form of group in which the *yama* is taken as increment. Of such simplest groups there are twenty-three met with in the Sanhitâ: namely, after first mutes, *kṇ*, *kn*, *km*, *cñ*, *cm*, *ṭṇ*, *tn*, *tm*, *pṇ*, *pn*, *pm;* after second mutes, *chm*, *thn;* after third mutes, *gn*, *gm*, *jñ*, *jm*, *dn*, *dm;* after fourth mutes, *ghn*, *dhn*, *dhm*, *bhṇ*. Then, of groups of three consonants involving such combinations: *jñy* (*jj̄-jñy*), *tny;* *ñchm*, *ñjñ* (*ñj-jñ*); *dghn* (*ddgh-gh̄n*), *nghn;* *rjm* (*rjj̄-jm*), *rtn*, *rtm*, *rdhn*, *rdhm;* *stm* (*sst-t̄m*), *sthn*. And of groups of four consonants, *rjmy* (*rjj̄-jmy*).

According to the phonetic systems of the other Prâtiçâkhyas, this would finish the tale of *yamas*. But, by the peculiar rule (xiv.9) which here requires a surd mute to be everywhere inserted between a sibilant and a following nasal, is brought forth a new and numerous brood of these curious twins. Thus, in double groups, *çn* (*çct-t̄n*), *çm*, *shṇ*, *shm*, *sn*, *sm*. Of groups of three containing these: *çny*, *shṇv;* *kshm* (*kkhshp-p̄m*), *kshṇ*, *tsn*, *tsm*, *psn;* *rçm* (*rççp-p̄m*), *rshṇ*, *rshm;* *ssm*. Of groups of four, *ṅkshṇ*, *ḥkshṇ*, *ççny*. In all, of both classes, fifty-seven groups.

तान्यमानेके ॥ १३ ॥

13. Some call these *yamas.*

The commentator adds nothing of value.

हकारान्नणमपरान्नासिक्यम् ॥ १४ ॥

14. After *h*, when followed by *n*, *ṇ*, or *m*, is inserted *nâsikya.*

I have translated this rule according to its obvious and incontrovertible meaning, which, if it needed any external support, would find it in the almost precisely accordant rule of the Ath. Pr. (i.100: the teachings of the other treatises upon the subject are much less distinct: see the note on the Atharvan rule). But the commentator gives it an entirely different interpretation. The ablative *hakârân*, he says, is here used in the sense of an accusative (his addition, "in the absence of *lyap* [the suffix *ya*]," I do

---

13. *tân nâsikyân eke çâkhino yamân bruvate*[1]. *uktâny evo 'dâharaṇâni.*

[1] G. M. *iti vadanti.*

14. *hakârâd iti karmaṇi*[1] *lyablope*[2] *pañcamî. tasmân naṇamaparaṁ hakâram âruhya nâsikyam bhavati*[3]: *s[..]unâsikyo hakâraḥ syâd ity arthaḥ. ahnâṁ----: apar-----: brahm-----.*

[1] W. *-ṇu.* [2] W. *lyapûlope;* B. *lyaplope;* O. *lyaçlope.* [3] B. *-ed iti.*

not understand); and the sense is, that a nose-sound is imposed upon the *h* itself, or that the latter becomes nasal. It is not difficult to see on what this theory of the quality of a *h* preceding a nasal is founded—namely, a recognition of the fact that such a *h* is really an expiration of breath through the nose: it being not less true of *h* before a semivowel or nasal than before a vowel, that it is (borrowing the phraseology of an earlier rule, ii.47) *udayavarṇâdisasthâna*, 'produced in the position of the succeeding letter.' The commentator's exposition might have come from the "some authorities" to whom the doctrine of that rule is attributed.

The examples given are *ahnâṁ ketuḥ* (ii.4.14[1]), *aparâhṇe* (ii. 1.2[5]), and *brahmavâdinaḥ* (i.7.1[4] et al.). Giving to the rule its real meaning, and applying the principle laid down at xxi.8 for the syllabic division, we should read *ahh-ⁿnâm:* and so with the rest. As was suggested under Ath. Pr. i.100, it is probably this separation of the *h* from the nasal in syllabication that has led to the division of the two in point of utterance, and then to the thrusting in between them of a transition-sound.

G. M. have adapted the reading of the rule to the new interpretation, and give *hakâran naṇamaparan nâsikyam* (the writing of *n* instead of *ṁ* before *n* is frequent with these MSS.).

रेफोष्मसंयोगे रेफस्वरभक्तिः ॥ १५ ॥

15. In the combination of *r* and a spirant, there is a *svarabhakti* of *r*.

The doctrine of our Prâtiçâkhya respecting the *svarabhakti* is less detailed, and less distinctly expressed, than that of the other treatises (for which, see the note to Ath. Prât. i.101–2); from the statement here made, we should not even understand that this "vowel-fragment" is to be an insertion between the *r* and the spirant, although that is doubtless intended to be signified. The commentator enters into a long exposition of the subject; by no means, however, limiting himself to explaining and illustrating his text. The two South-Indian manuscripts (G. M.) are in some parts of this exposition fuller than the rest, and will be followed

---

15. [1]*rephasya co "shmaṇaç ca saṁyoge sati*[1] *rephasvarabhaktir iti jânîyât:* [2]*svarasya bhaktiḥ svarabhaktiḥ*[2]*: yo 'sya rephasya samânasvaras*[3] *tadbhaktiḥ syât: ṛkâraç câ 'sya jihvâgrakaraṇatvena*[4] *raçrutyâ*[5] *ca*[6] *samânadharmaḥ:* [7]*bhaktir avayava ekadeça iti yâvat*[7]*: etad uktam bhavati: ṛkârâvayavo*[8] *bhavatî 'ty arthaḥ. sûtreṇâ 'nena svarabhaktir eva*[9] *vihitâ: svarabhaktisvarûpaṁ tu*[10] *vispashṭaṁ*[11] *vyâcashṭe vararuciḥ:* [12]*ṛkârâdir aṇumâtrâ*[13] *repho 'rdhamâtrâ madhye çeshâ*[14] *svarabhaktir iti*[15]*. asyâ 'yam arthaḥ*[12]*:*

indriyavishayo[16] *yo*[17] *'sâv aṇur ity ucyate budhâiḥ:*
caturbhir[18] *aṇubhir mâtrâparimâṇam*[19] *iti smṛtam.* [20]

in the abstract of it here given: the version of W. B. O., indeed, has rather the aspect of being an abbreviation of the other, and one not everywhere skilfully made.

At the outset, G. M. alone specify that the *svarabhakti* is combined with the spirant (and yet, by xxi.6, it is to be separated from the spirant in syllabication, going with the *r* to the preceding vowel). The term *svarabhakti* means 'a fragment, piece, or part of a vowel;' and a *rephasvarabhakti*, '*r*-vowel-fragment,' means a bit of the vowel that is akin, or has the same mode of utterance with, the *r*. Now the *ṛ* is of like quality with *r*, in being produced with the tip of the tongue and in having the sound of *r:* and it is a part of *ṛ* that is intended. The rule merely prescribes the insertion; the nature of the latter is clearly set forth by Vararuci (one of the three principal sources of the present comment: see note to the introductory verses, pp. 6,7). The vowels are defined at i.5, and since among them only *ṛ* agrees in place and organ with *r*, the "fragment" is of *ṛ*. The *ṛ* is by i.31 declared to be short, or of one *mora;* and Vararuci defines the short *ṛ* as composed of a quarter-*mora* of vowel at the beginning, a half-*mora* of *r* in the middle, and a quarter-*mora* of vowel (W. B. O. say, of vowel-fragment) at the end. Then a verse is quoted describing the word *aṇu* as signifying a quarter-*mora.* This half-*mora* of *r*, now, found in the middle of *ṛ*, being divided, its two parts, each combined with the quarter-*mora* of vowel, severally receive the name of *svarabhakti.* Hence there are two *svarabhakti*'s. And in answer to the question where this *svarabhakti* of half a *mora* occurs, the makers of the Çikshâ have declared that the one ending with the vowel element occurs before *ç*, *sh*, and *s*, and the one ending with the consonant element before *h;* the former, moreover, being open, and the latter close. And it is added that in *yo vâi çraddhâm* (i.6.8[1]) there is no *svarabhabkti*, on account of absence of the order prescribed in the rule.

---

mâtrikasya rkârasyâ "dir aṇumatrâ[21] *svarabhâgo madhye repho 'rdhamâtrâ*[22] *çesho*[23] *'py aṇumâtrâ*[24] *svarabhâgaḥ: etad ṛkârasvarûpam. atra*[25] *rephe 'rdhamâtre bhajyamâne*[26] *sati*[27] *tâu bhâgâu pûrvottarâv*[28] *aṇusahitâu*[29] *pratyekaṁ svarabhaktinâmadheyam bhajete*[30]*:* [31]*sâ ca svarabhaktir ardhamâtrâ. kutra*[32] *vâ*[33] *svarabhaktir*[31] *ity âçaṅkya çikshâkârâir*[34] *uktam:*

çashaseshu svarodayâṁ[35] *hakâre vyañjanodayâm*[36]*:*
çashaseshu tu[37] *vivṛtâṁ*[38] *hakâre saṁvṛtâṁ*[39] *vidur* *iti*[40].

yo ---- ityâdâu [41]*sûtroktakramâbhâvân na svarabhaktiḥ.*[41]

svarabhaktyantaraṁ[42] *çikshâyâm uktam:*

[43]*kareṇuḥ karviṇî câi 'va hariṇî hârite*[44] *'ti ca:*
haṅsapade[45] *'ti vijñeyâḥ pañcâi 'tâḥ svarabhaktayaḥ.*[43]
[46] *kareṇû*[47] *rahayor*[48] *yoge*[49] *karviṇî lahakârayoḥ:*
hariṇî [50]*raçasânâṁ ca*[50] *hâritâ*[51] *laçakârayoḥ.*

So much by way of (would-be) explanation of the rule. But the commentator goes on to say that the Çikshâ teaches other *svarabhakti*'s, to the number of five: namely, the *kareṇu*, between *r* and *h*, as in *barhiḥ* (i.1.2[1] et al.); the *karviṇî*, between *l* and *h*, as in *malhâḥ* (ii.1.2[4]); the *hariṇî*, between *r* and *ç* or *s*, as in *darçapûrṇamâsâu* (ii.2.5[4] et al.) and *barsam* (ii.5.7[1]); the *hâritâ* (or *haritâ*), between *l* and *ç*, as in *sahasravalçâḥ* (vi.3.3[3]); and the *hañsapadâ* (or *hañsapâdâ*), between *r* and *sh*, as in *varshâhvâm* (ii.4.10[3])—and he who wants to go to heaven (on the score, no doubt, of patience, faith, and punctiliousness) must utter the five kinds of *bhakti*, as thus laid down. It appears, then, that the commentator's Çikshâ, like the Vâj. Pr. (iv.16), regards *l*, not less than *r*, as followed by *svarabhakti* before a spirant.

न क्रमे प्रथमपरे प्रथमपरे ॥ १६ ॥

16. But not in case of *krama*, when a first mute follows the spirant.

The commentator defines *krama* as the equivalent of *dvitva*, 'duplication,' and refers as authority to rule xxiv.5, where the word occurs again without, according to him, admitting any other meaning; whence, he infers, it must signify the same thing here also. We should rather turn the argument the other way, and say that, as *krama* can have no other meaning here, it may be conjectured to signify the same thing at xxiv.5. He further coolly

---

[52]"*yâ tu hañsapadâ nâma sâ tu*[52] *rephashakârayoḥ:*
[53]"*evam pañcavidhâm bhaktim uccaret svargakâmukaḥ.*"[53]

(1) G. M. *reph-shmaṇos sayyoge sati tatra ûshmasayyukto.* (2) G. M. *svarabhaktir iti kim: idṛçı svarasya bhakti svarabhaktiḥ bhaktir bhâgaḥ: avayava iti ekadeça iti yâvat;* B. O. om. *svarabhaktiḥ.* [3] G. M. O. *-nakaraṇasv-.* [4] O. *-ṇena.* [5] G. M. *çrutyâ.* [6] W. *yana.* (7) G. M. om.; O. *-ça ity arthaḥ.* [8] W. O. *ṛkâra eva ya-;* G. M. *ṛkârasya 'vay-.* [9] G. M. *evaṁ.* [10] B. om. [11] O. *spa-.* (12) G. M. *svaras tâvat kiṁviçishṭa iti cet shoḍaçâ "ditaḥ svarâḥ* (i.5) *iti svarasañjñoktaṁ teshu ṛkârarephayos samânasthânakaraṇatvâd ṛkârasvarasyâi 'va bhaktiḥ ṛkâras tâvat kiṁviçishṭa iti cet ṛkâralkârâu hrasvâu* (i.31) *iti hrasvatvâd ekamâtro bhaved dhrasva iti ekamâtraka ṛkâraḥ vararucinâi 'vam uktaṁ mâtrikasya rkârasyâ "dâu svarasyâ 'ṇumâtraḥ rephasyâ 'rdhamâtro madhye 'nta svarasyâ 'ṇumâtra iti: aṇumâtra iti kiṁ.* [13] B. *-tratâm api.* [14] O. *çesha.* [15] B. om.; O. *aṇumâtrâ.* [16] W. *nish-;* G. M. *-driyâv-.* [17] B. O. om. [18] W. O. *-tur.* [19] W. *mâtrâprayâṇam;* B. *-trâpramâṇam;* G. M. *-ṇa.* [20] G. M. ins. *asyâ 'yam arthaḥ.* [21] B. G. M. *-tra.* [22] G. M. *-traḥ.* [23] G. M. *ante.* [24] W. *-traḥ;* G. M. *-tra.* [25] G. M. ins. *ṛkâramadhyavartini.* [26] G. M. *vibh-.* [27] O. om. [28] G. M. *-râ.* [29] W. B. O. *-saṁh-.* [30] W. B. *bhajyate;* G. M. O. *bhajate.* (31) G. M. *tato dve svarabhakti vidyete ardhamâtrikasvarabhaktiḥ kutra vâ tishṭhati.* [32] W. *atra.* [33] W. om.; B. *kâ.* [34] G. M. ins. *evam.* [35] W. B. *-yâ.* [36] W. B. *-yâ.* [37] B. O. *ca.* [38] W. *-tâ.* [39] W. *-tâ.* [40] O. om. (41) G. M. *sûtreṇo 'ktakrameṇa syât svarabhaktiḥ.* [42] G. M. O. ins. *api.* (43) O. om. [44] G. M. *har-.* [45] G. M. *-pâde.* [46] G. M. ins. *kidṛçya etâ iti cet.* [47] W. B. *-ṇu;* G. M. *-ṇuṁ.* [48] B. *hayor;* G. M. *harayor.* [49] W. B. G. M. *vidyât.* (50) W. B. *raçayor yoge;* G. *çasurâṁ jñeyâ;* M. *çasâṁ jñeyâ.* [51] G. M. *har-.* (52) G. M. *svarabhaktiṁ hañsapâdâṁ vidyâd.* (53) O. om.; G. M. *-muka iti: yathâ: kareṇuḥ: barhiḥ: yathâ karviṇi: malhâḥ: hariṇi: darçapûrṇamâsâu: barsaṁ: haritâ: sahasravalçâḥ: hañsapâdâ: varshâhvâm ityâdi.*

inserts an "or" in the rule, and declares it to mean 'either when the spirant is doubled or when it is followed by a first mute.' This must evidently be condemned: for, in the first place, the text contains no "or;" and, in the second place, if that were the meaning, the specification would be superfluous, since the spirant is always doubled before a first mute, and so *krame* would include all the cases—except, indeed, according to the doctrine of Plâkshi and Plâkshâyaṇa, who (xiv.17) deny the duplication of the spirant in such a situation; and we are perhaps to connect his interpretation of the present rule with his apparent acceptance of the doctrine referred to, and suppose that he would read *rsh-ṭ*, and *rçp-p̄m* etc. (namely, for *rçm*, *rshṇ*, and *rshm*), while the reading actually approved by the treatise is *rshsh-ṭ*, *rççp-p̄m* etc. There are five groups—namely *rçy*, *rçv*, *rshy*, *rsv*, and *rhy*—in which the difference of interpretation would make a difference as regards the presence or absence of *svarabhakti;* if the "or" is implied, they will be read and divided *rç-çy* etc.; if not, they will be *r*ʳ*ç-çy* etc.

The commentator's examples are *dârçyaṁ yajñam* (iii.2.2[3]: only O. has *yajñam;* G. M. read *dârçyaṁ hi*, which, if it be an actual passage, I have overlooked in searching out the references), *varshyâbhyaḥ* (vii.4.13: W. B. O. read *varshâbhyaḥ*), *barsvebhiḥ* (v.7.11), and *etarhy ârûdhaḥ* (v.1.5[5]: found in O. only), illustrating four of the five cases in which his interpretation would exclude the *svarabhakti;* and further, for cases in which a first mute follows, *adarçma jyotiḥ* (iii.2.5[4]: omitted in O.), *kârshṇî upânahâu* (v.4.4[4] et al.), and *varshṭâ parjanyaḥ* (vii.5.20: found in G. M. only).

CHAPTER XXII.

CONTENTS: 1–2, formation of articulate sounds in general; 3–8, definition of terms used in the treatise; 9–10, mode of production of high and low tone; 11–12, established tone and pitch; 13, length of pauses in the text; 14–15, heavy and light syllables.

---

16. [1]*kramaçabdo dvitvaparyâyaḥ: katham etat: prakṛtir vikramaḥ krama* (xxiv.5) *ity atra dvitvasyâi*[2] *'va*[3] *kramaçabdenâ*[4] *'bhidhânâd atrâ 'pi sa evâ*[4] [5]*'rtha iti niçcinumaḥ.*[5] *ûshmaṇaḥ krame sati*[6] *tasminn ûshmaṇi prathamapare vâ*[7] *sati na svarabhaktir bhavati.*[8] [9]*krame yathâ*[9]*: dârç-....: varsh-....: bars-....* [10]*prathamapare yathâ: ad-....:*[10] *kâr-....* [11] *prathamaḥ paro yasmâd asâu prathamaparaḥ.*

iti tribhâshyaratne prâtiçâkhyavivaraṇe ekaviṅço[12] *'dhyâyaḥ.*

(1) O. om. [2] G. M. *-tvam asty e.* [3] W. *-bdo nâmâ.* [4] W. *rvâ.* (5) G. M. *'rtho niçcitaḥ.* [6] O. om.; G. M. add *vâ.* [7] G. M. put after *sati.* [8] W. *-vet.* (9) O. om. (10) O. *etar-....*; G. M. *etasya prathamaparo y-.* [11] G. M. add *varshṭâ....* [12] G. M. O. *dvitiyapraçne navamo.*

शब्दः प्रकृतिः सर्ववर्णानाम् ॥ १ ॥

1. Tone is the material of all articulate sounds.

The putting-together, as well as the material, of this and the following chapter is rather peculiar, and makes the impression of a supplement to the Prâtiçâkhya proper. This present rule and its successor are akin with the first two of the next chapter, and all these with the rules of the second chapter. As under ii.1, the commentator explains *çabda* by *dhvani*; for *prakṛti* he gives as synonym *mûlakâraṇam*, 'radical cause;' and *varṇa* he declares to designate the whole congeries of vowels and consonants.[1]

तस्य रूपान्यत्वे वर्णान्यत्वम् ॥ २ ॥

2. In the difference of form of the former consists the difference of the latter.

That is to say, in the difference resulting from the variety of positions giving audible quality: compare ii.3.

तत्र शब्दद्रव्याण्युदाहरिष्यामः ॥ ३ ॥

3. Here we will instance the offices of terms.

A complete and violent change of subject is introduced by this rule, continuing to rule 9; which last, again, attaches itself closely enough to the beginning of the chapter to have been its natural continuation. The intervening batch of rules looks like an interpolation, thrust in at this point *apropos* of *çabda* in rule 1; the word being taken here, however, in an entirely different sense. The commentator tries to smooth over the transition by pronouncing *çabda* a synonym of *çâstra*, 'text-book, body of doctrine;' which latter is formed by the putting to use of combinations of the alphabetic sounds just above spoken of. He distinctly ascribes to *dravya* the sense of 'office, aim,' as the connection also requires,

---

1. *sarvavarṇânâṁ*[1] *çabdo* [2] *dhvaniḥ prakṛtir mûlakâraṇam bhavati: varṇaçabdena svaravyañjanâtmako râçir ucyate. sarve ca te varṇâç ca sarvavarṇâḥ*[3]*: teshâṁ*[4].

[1] G. M. om. [2] G. M. ins. *nâma*. [3] O. om. [4] G. M. add *sarvavarṇânâm*.

2. *prâtiçrutkasthânabhedât*[1] *tasya* [2] *prakṛtibhûtasya*[3] *rûpânyatve sati varṇânyatvaṁ syât*[4]. *yathâ: a: i: u: ityâdi.*

[1] B. *prat-*; G. M. *-nâd bhe-*. [2] G. M. ins. *çabdasya*. [3] W. *pratibh-*. [4] O. om.

3. *teshâṁ varṇânâṁ sarvatra*[1] *saṁghâtaprayoge* [2] *çâstram*[3] *ity*[4] *ucyate: ' tasya çabda*[5] *iti paryâyanâma: tatra tasmiñ châstre yâni dravyâṇi bhavanti tâny udâharishyâmaḥ. yat karma yena kriyate*[8] *tat*[9] *tasya dravyaṁ*[10] *sâdhanam iti yâvat*[11]*: yathâ gha-*

giving *sâdhana*, 'efficiency,' as its equivalent. As clay to a vessel, we are told, so are alphabetic sounds to a text-book.

वर्णकारौ निर्देशकौ ॥ ४ ॥

4. *Varṇa* and *kâra* are indicatory.

These two terms have already formed the subject of rules i.16–20. Rules vi.1,7 are cited as examples of their use.

चापीत्यन्वादेशकौ ॥ ५ ॥

5. *Ca* and *api* are implicative.

Rules vi.3 and iv.4 are cited as containing examples of the use of these signs of continued implication from something that has gone before.

त्वथैवेति विनिवर्तकाधिकारकावधारकाः ॥ ६ ॥

6. *Tu*, *atha*, and *eva* are exceptional, introductory, and restrictive, respectively.

The use of these connectives is instanced by quoting rules i.19, v.1, and xiv.3 (G. M. substitute vii.1 for the second).

These rules are too trivial and superficial to make it worth while to enter, in connection with them, into any discussion of the use of the particles in the text of the Prâtiçâkhya. The index, and the notes on each rule, will give the means of investigating the matter. We have often had occasion to animadvert upon the commentator's

---

ṭasya mṛd ity evaṁ çâstrasya varṇâḥ[12]*: yâni dravyâni saṁvyavahârârthâni kartavyâni tâni vyâkhyâsyâmaḥ. çabdasya dravyâṇi çabdadravyâṇi : tâni.*

[1] O. *-ta.* [2] O. ins. *vâ.* [3] W. *-tre.* [4] W. B. *katham;* O. om. [5] W. B. ins. *tasya rûpâṇi.* [6] W. O. *-bdâ.* [7] O. *pradarçayishy-.* [8] O. *karmayate.* [9] W. *tatra;* B. *na.* [10] B. *-ya;* M. om. [11] O. om. [12] W. *-ṇa;* G. M. *-ṇânâṁ;* O. *savarṇaḥ.*

4. *varṇaçabdaḥ kâraçabdaç ca nirdeçakâu*[1] *nirdeçavâcakâu*[2] *syâtâm. yathâ: avarṇavyañjanaçakuni* (vi.7) *iti: atha shakârañ sakâravisarjanîyâv* (vi.1) *iti. varṇaç ca kâraç ca varṇakârâu.*

[1] G. M. om. [2] W. B. *-deçakâu vâc-;* O. om.

5. *ca: api: ity etâv* [1] *anvâdeçakâu syâtâm. pûrvâpekshayâ*[2] *'nvâdeça ity ucyate. yathâ: asadâmâsiñcañç ca* (vi.3)*: itiparo 'pi* (iv.4).

[1] G. M. ins. *çabdâu.* [2] W. B. *pûrvapaksho;* O. *pûrvo paksho.*

6. *tu: atha: eva: ity ete çabdâ yathâkrameṇa*[1] *vinivartakâdhikârakâvadhârakâ bhavanti: yatra tuçabdaḥ çrûyate tatra*

tendency to put into them (especially into *tu*) a meaning which they were never intended to bear.

वेति वैभाषिकः ॥ ७ ॥

7. *Vâ* is alternative.

Rule ii.50 is quoted as example.

नेति प्रतिषेधकः ॥ ८ ॥

8. *Na* is prohibitive.

The example this time is xiii.15 (G. M. substituting xiv.14); and in it appear again some of the differences of reading which were noted in the rule itself where it occurred.

आयामो दारुण्यमणुता खस्येत्युच्चैःकराणि शब्दस्य ॥ ९ ॥

9. Tension, hardness, smallness of aperture, are producers of high tone.

Reference is made to rule i.38, in which the acute accent is defined as consisting in high tone; and the present precept is declared to be given for the sake of that, and in order to prohibit that slack or indifferent utterance which prevails in common life. *Âyâma*, 'tension,' is explained as meaning rather 'extension (literally 'longness') of the members;' *dâruṇya*, as 'severity of the vowel;' and *aṇutâ khasya*, as 'closure of the orifice of the throat:' this is what one who would utter a sound in high tone must do.

There is evidently much more guess-work than true observation in this rule and the one next following: if they had been given as definitions of sonant and surd utterance, instead of high and low

---

nivṛttiḥ: yatrâ 'thaçabdas tatrâ 'dhikâraḥ: yatrâi 'vaçabdas tatrâ 'vadhâraṇam[1] *veditavyam. yathâ: ephas tu rasya* (i.19): [3]*atha sañhitâyâm ekaprâṇabhâve*[4] (v.1).[3] *sparça*[5] *evâi 'keshâm âcâryâṇâm* (xiv.3). *viçesheṇa nivartayatî 'ti vinivartakaḥ: adhikarotî 'ty adhikârakaḥ*[6]*: avadhârayatî 'ty avadhârakaḥ.*

[1] G. M. *-mam.* [2] G. M. O. ins. *ce 'ti.* [(3)] G. M. *atha nakâro ṇakâram* (vii. 1). [4] O. om. [5] G. M. *-çapara.* [6] W. O. G. M. *-raḥ.*

7. *ve 'ty esha çabdo vâibhâshiko*[1] *vâikalpiko bhavati. yathâ: mukhanâsikyâ vâ* (ii.50).

[1] G. M. *-shako* (as also in the rule).

8. *ne 'ty esha çabdaḥ pratishedhako bhavati*[1]*: yathâ:* [2]*na shumnognir* (xiii.15) *iti.*[2]

[1] G. M. O. *syât.* [(2)] G. M. *atha na* (xiv.14): B. *na sushu-;* O. *-na sum-;* W. B. *-gni 'ti.*

tone, they might more easily have been regarded as describing real processes of articulation.

अन्ववसर्गो मार्दवमुरुता खस्येति नीचैःकराणि ॥ १० ॥

10. Relaxation, softness, wideness of aperture, are producers of low tone.

The exposition of this rule runs quite parallel with that of the preceding (only O., however, referring to the definition of *anudâtta*, 'grave,' as of low tone, at i.39). To *anvavasarga* is given *vinatatâ*, 'drooping condition,' as synonym; to *mârdava*, *snigdhatâ*, 'smoothness;' and to *urutâ*, *sthûlatâ*, 'bigness.' There is nothing at all to commend in such a description of the way in which low tone is produced.

मन्द्रमध्यमताराणि स्थानानि भवन्ति ॥ ११ ॥

11. Soft, middle, and loud are the three qualities.

Their use, we are told, will be explained farther on—namely, in rules 4–10 of the next chapter. I have ventured to render *sthâna*, literally 'place' or 'position,' by 'quality,' as better expressing the nature of the distinctions implied. The name apparently comes from such theories as that laid down in rule xxiii.10 as to the "place" of production of the different qualities of tone.

In answer, we are told, to the suggested inquiry, "of what are

---

9. *uccâir udâtta* (i.38) *ity uktam: tadartham idam ârabhyate: lokavad yâdṛchikoccâraṇapratishedhârtham*[1]*: âyâmo gâtrâṇâṁ dâirghyam: dâruṇyaṁ svarasya kaṭhinatâ:* [2]*aṇutâ khasya galavivarasya*[3] *saṁvṛtatâ:*[2] *etâni sâdhanâni*[4] *çabdasyo 'ccâiḥkarâṇi*[5] [6]*çabdam uccâir udâttaṁ kurvantî 'ty arthaḥ. uccaçabdam uccârayatâi 'tat kartavyam iti vidhiḥ.*[6] [7]*uccâiḥ kurvantî 'ty uccâiḥkarâṇi*[7].

[1] W. *yâvach-;* B. *hâdach-;* W. B. O. *-rthaḥ.* (2) W. om. [3] B. *-viraraṇasya;* G. M. *-viralasya*, and put after *saṁvṛtatâ* (B. O. *-vṛtâ*). [4] G. M. *nâmadheyâni.* [5] W. *'ccak-.* (6) G. M. om. (7) W. G. M. om.; B. adds *kapaṇini*, and om. the following rule.

10. [1] *anvavasargo gâtrâṇâṁ vinatatâ*[2]*: mârdavaṁ svarasya snigdhatâ: khasyo 'rutâ kaṇṭhasya sthûlate 'ty*[3] *etâni sâdhanâni çabdasya nîçâiḥkarâṇi çabdaṁ nîcam anudâttaṁ*[4] *kurvantî 'ty arthaḥ: nîcaçabdam uccârayatâi*[5] *'tat kartavyam iti vidhiḥ: nîcâiḥ kurvantî 'ti nîcâiḥkarâṇi.*

(1) O. ins. *nicâir anudâtta* (i.39) *ity uktam.* [2] G. M. O. *vistṛtatâ.* [3] G. M. om. *iti.* [4] G. M. *ud-.* [5] W. *uddhârayanû;* B. *-yan;* G. M. *-raṇıyatâ;* O. *-raṇatâ.*

11. [1]*mandram madhyamaṁ târaṁ ce 'ti*[2] *sthânâni bhavanti:*[1] *mandram iti prathamam: madhyamam iti dvitîyam: târam iti*

these positions or qualities?" the subject is continued in the next rule.

तत्रैकविंशतिर्यमाः ॥ १२ ॥

12. In them are twenty-one tones.

For the application of these tones or keys, also, we are referred to a later passage (xxiii.11 etc.). As synonym of *yama* is given *svara*, 'tone.'

The commentator chooses to connect these rules with those that follow in the next chapter, and to overlook the obvious fact that in the two chapters we have separate and independent statements upon the same subject, which cannot have come from the same hand, and of which the second renders the first wholly superfluous.

ऋग्विरामः पदविरामो विवृत्तिविरामः समानपदविवृत्तिविरामस्त्रिमात्रो द्विमात्र एकमात्रोऽर्धमात्र इत्यानुपूर्व्येण ॥ १३ ॥

13. The verse-pause, *pada*-pause, pause for hiatus, and pause for hiatus in the interior of a word, are respectively of three *moras*, two *moras*, one *mora*, and a half-*mora*.

As example of the pause of three *moras* at the end of a verse is quoted *ubhâ vâjasya sâtaye huve vâm:* (i.5.5[2]: O. omits the first two words); of the pause of two *moras*, in *pada*-text, between the *padas*, *ishe : tvâ : ûrje : tvâ* (i.1.1 et al.): and, for all that the Prâtiçâkhya tells us, we are to regard the *avagraha* pause, dividing the two parts of a compound word, as of the same length (the Rik [i.6, r. 29] and Vâjasaneyi [v.1] Prâtiçâkhyas give it only one *mora*); of the hiatus-pause, *sa idhânaḥ* (iv.4.4[5]), *ta enam* (ii.3.11[4]), and *tâ asmât* (ii.4.4[1]: W. prefixes *â*, but doubtless only by

---

tṛtîyam: eteshâṁ[3] *sthânânâm prayojanam uttaratra*[4] *vakshyate.* [5]*etâni sthânâni keshâm ityapekshâyâm âha parasûtram*[5].

(1) G. M. om. [2] O. 'ty etâni. [3] G. M. O. esh-. [4] B. iturtra. (5) O. om.

12. *teshu*[1] *sthâneshv ekaviñçatir yamâḥ svarâ bhavanti: teshâṁ yamânâm uttaratra prayojanaṁ vakshyate.*

[1] O. *tatra trishu;* B. adds *trishu.*

13. *ṛgvirâmâdayas trimâtrâdikâlâ*[1] *yathâkramam*[2] *bhavanti. yathâ*[3]*: ubhâ----: ity ṛgvirâmaḥ: ishe----: iti padavirâmaḥ: sa----: ta----: tâ----: iti vivṛttivirâmaḥ: praügam iti samânapadavivṛttivirâmaḥ.* [4]*ṛci*[4] *virâma ṛgvirâmaḥ: padasya virâmaḥ padavirâmaḥ: padadvayavivṛttâu*[5] *virâmo vivṛttivirâmaḥ*[7][4]. *çikshâyâm* [6] *asya viçesha uktaḥ:*

a copyist's blunder); of the pause of interior hiatus, *praügam* (iv. 4.2[1]), which is, I believe, the only case. The commentator also quotes a couple of verses from his Çikshâ, laying down four subdivisions of the pause of hiatus, and assigning them different quantities: that between a short and long vowel is *vatsânusṛti*, and is one *mora* long; that between a long and following short is *vatsânusâriṇî*, of the same length; between two short vowels, *pâkavatî*, three quarters of a *mora;* between two long vowels, *pipîlikâ*, a quarter-*mora* only (Uvaṭa's comment on the Rik Prât. [ii.1] states the intervals quite differently). In W. there are two verses which are not found in the rest; as they stand, their meaning is in great part obscure to me, and I prefer to leave them unamended and untranslated.

यद्व्यञ्जनान्तं यदु चापि दीर्घं
संयोगपूर्वं च तथानुनासिकम् ॥
एतानि सर्वाणि गुरूणि विद्याच्
छेषाण्यतो ऽन्यानि ततो लघूनि ॥ १४ ॥

14. A syllable that ends with a consonant, one that has a long vowel, one that precedes a conjunction of consonants, one that is nasal—all these are to be accounted heavy; the rest, other than these, are light.

---

[9]*pipîlikâ dîrghasame ca madhye*
savarṇatâ pâkavatî padâikye:
dṛshṭvâ ca vatsânusṛjas tv asâmye
*tv atho 'ci mukhyas tu virâmakâlaḥ.*1.
svarodaye tv anusvâro bhaved adhyaṇumâtrikaḥ:
*virâmaç ca tayor madhye vâiçeshikâc ca dîrghayoḥ.*2.[9]
hrasvâdir vatsânusṛtir[10] *ante vatsânusâriṇî:*
pâkavaty ubhayahrasvâ[11] *dîrghobhayâ*[12] *pipîlikâ.*
[13]*mâtrâ*[14] *ca*[15] *vatsânusṛtis*[16] *tathâ vatsânusâriṇî:*
pâdonâ syât pâkavatî pâdamâtrâ pipîlikâ.[13]

[17]*samânaṁ ca tat padaṁ ca samânapadam: ekapadam ity arthaḥ*[17]*:* [18] *samânapade vivṛttiḥ samânapadavivṛttiḥ: tasyâṁ*[19] *virâmaḥ*[20] *samânapadavivṛttivirâmaḥ.* [21] *tisro mâtrâ yasyâ 'sâu trimâtraḥ:* [22]*dve mâtre yasyâ 'sâu dvimâtraḥ: ekâ mâtrâ yasyâ 'sâv ekamâtraḥ: ardhâ mâtrâ yasyâ 'sâv ardhamâtraḥ*[22].

[1] W. *-trak-*. [2] O. *-meṇa*. [3] G. M. om. [(4)] O. puts below, at [18]. [5] W. *ṛg;* G M. *ṛco*. [6] B. *padavi-;* O. *-yamadhye vivṛtti*. [7] W. B. om.; O. *padaviv-*. [8] G. M. ins. *apy*. [(9)] in W. only. [10] W. *-tsânujasṛtimadhyer;* G. M. *-nusûtir*. [11] B. *-yoh-;* G. M. *-yeh-*. [12] G. M. *-ghayos tu*. [(13)] O. om. [14] G. M. *-trikâ*. [15] G. M. om. [16] W. *-nusṛjanti;* G. M. *-nukṛtis*. [(17)] O. puts below, at [21]. [18] O. puts [(4)] here. [19] W. om.; B. *-smâ;* O. *-sya*. [20] W. om. [21] O. puts [(17)] here. [(22)] in G. M. only.

The commentator instances the different kinds of "heavy" syllable, as follows: one ending with a consonant, *mâte 'va putram* (iv.2.3² et al.: G. M. omit); one long by its vowel, *te te 'dhipatayaḥ* (iv.4.11³: G. M. omit the last word); one followed by a consonant-group, *açmâ ca me* (iv.7.5¹: W. has *ânmâyinâ*, which appears to be merely a corrupt reading; I have found nothing at all like it in the Sanhitâ); one that is nasal, *viñçatyâi* (vii.2.13 et al.).

The distinction of the syllable as "heavy" or "light" has value only in a metrical point of view, and does not make its appearance elsewhere in our treatise (except as it is referred to in rule xxiv.5—which rule we might have expected the commentator to quote here, as the occasion of this one). The quality of "long" or "short" belongs to the vowel alone, and (see xxi.1 and its comment) the consonants accompanying the latter are regarded as absorbed into it, and forming part of its natural quantity. This separation of "heavy" and "long," or of weight and quantity, is practically convenient, perhaps, but theoretically indefensible; and we have reason to be surprised that phonetic observers so acute as the Hindus had not worked the theory of syllabic quantity into a more consistent shape. The other treatises agree with this: see Ath. Pr. i.51–54, and notes.

The use of the word *anunâsika* in describing a syllable containing *anusvâra* is (as already noted, under ii.30) one more sign of a theory which regards the *anusvâra* as a quality and not an element. The Ath. Prât., which holds this theory, uses the same term in its definition (i.53). It deserves to be noted, however, that to read *anusvâram* instead of *anunâsikam* in the verse would help the metre, making the four *pâdas* similar.

This rule is enough by itself to determine the weight of any syllable whatever: but, as the commentator points out, the one following is added to resolve any doubts which might after all arise as to what syllables were light.

---

14. *vyañjanântaṁ yad aksharam: [1]vyañjanam ante[2] yasya tad vyañjanântam:[1] yad u câ 'pi dîrgham [3] aksharam: [4] saṁyogapûrvaṁ ca yad aksharam: [5]saṁyogât pûrvaṁ[6] saṁyogapûrvam[6]: tathâ 'nunâsikam: sânunâsikaṁ[7] yad aksharam: uktâny etâni sarvâṇy aksharâṇi gurûṇi vidyât: jânîyât. yathâ [8]vyañjanântam: mâte.....[8] yathâ dîrgham: te..... yathâ[9] sâṁyogapûrvam: açmâ..... yathâ 'nunâsikam[10]: viñçatyâi. [11] çeshâṇy ato 'nyâni [12] : ata[13] ebhyo gurubhyaḥ çeshâṇy anyâny aksharâṇi [14]tato 'nantaraṁ[14] laghûni vijânîyât[15]. çeshâṇi[16] kânî 'ty âçañkyo 'ttaraçlokena[17] vivṛṇoti.*

(1) G. M. put at beginning. 2 G. M. *-taṁ.* 3 G. M. ins. *yad.* 4 G. M. ins. *yogât pûrvaṁ.* (5) G. M. om. 6 B. G. M. om.; O. *-gaṁ.* 7 O. om.; G. M. *anu-.* (8) G. M. *vyañjanânâṁ ity atra.* 9 G. M. om. 10 O. puts before *yathâ.* 11 B. omits from here to the middle of rule 15 (beginning again with *saṁyogaparaṁ*). 12 G. M. O. ins. *tato laghûni.* 13 W. *eta.* (14) G. M. om. 15 G. M. *jân-.* 16 W. *-ṇî 'ti.* 17 W. *-ke.*

अव्यञ्जनान्तं यद्ध्रस्वमसंयोगपरं च यत् ।
अननुस्वारसंयुक्तमेतल्लघु निबोधत
तल्लघु निबोधत ॥ १५ ॥

15. A syllable that does not end with a consonant, that has a short vowel, and that is not followed by a conjunction of consonants, and one that is not combined with *anusvâra*—know that to be light.

This is a mere negative to the preceding rule, and a wholly superfluous addition to it—and an addition made, we may conjecture, by a different and later hand: the use of the term *anusvâra* distinctly suggests this.

The commentator quotes, by way of example of light syllables, simply *madudayanâ asan* (vi.1.5[1]: B. O. omit the last word).

CHAPTER XXIII.

CONTENTS: 1–3, causes of the differences of articulated sounds; 4–10, qualities or temperaments of voice; 11–19, tone or pitch of utterance; 20, general mode of correct utterance.

अथ वर्णविशेषोत्पत्तिः ॥ १ ॥

1. Now for the origin of the differences of articulate sounds.

---

15. [1]*avyañjanântaṁ yad aksharaṁ yac ca hrasvaṁ yac* [2]*câ 'saṁyogaparaṁ*[2] *yac câ 'nanusvârasaṁyuktam etat sarvam aksharaṁ laghu*[3] *nibodhata*[1] *jânîdhvam. yathâ*[4]*: mad- - - - ityâdi. vyañjanam ante*[5] *yasya tad vyañjanântam:* [6]*na vyañjanântam avyañjanântam:*[6] *saṁyogaḥ paro yasmât tat saṁyogaparam:* [7]*na saṁyogaparam*[7] *asaṁyogaparam:* [8]*anusvâreṇa saṁyuktam*[8] *anusvârasaṁyuktam:* [9]*nâ 'nusvârasaṁyuktam*[9] *ananusvârasaṁyuktam.*

iti tribhâshyaratne prâtiçâkhyavivaraṇe
dvâviṅço[10] *'dhyâyaḥ.*

(1) G. M. om. (2) W. *ca saṁyogapûrveraṁ.* 3 W. B. *laghû.* 4 W. om. 5 G. M. *antaṁ.* (6) W. om. (7) G. M. *tadbhinnam.* (8) O. om.; W. *yuktam* only. (9) B. om.; G. M. *anusvârayogavirahitam.* 10 G. M. O. *dvitîyapraçne daçamo.*

1. *athe 'ty ayam adhikâraḥ: varṇânâṁ viçeshotpattir ucyata ity etad adhikṛtaṁ veditavyam ita uttaraṁ yad vakshyâmaḥ. varṇânâṁ viçesho varṇaviçeshaḥ: tasyo 'tpattiḥ sâ tatho 'ktâ.*

It was hardly worth while to give a rule introductory to so very brief a treatment of the subject as is here to follow.

अनुप्रदानात्संसर्गात्स्थानात्करणविन्ययात् ।
जायते वर्णविशेष्यं परिमाणाच्च पञ्चमाद् इति ॥ २ ॥

2. The differentiation of articulate sounds arises from emission, closure, position, disposition of producing organ, and, fifthly, from quantity.

That is to say, according as any sound is different from another in respect to one or more of these five constituent or determining elements, so its nature or quality is different. The *anupradâna* is the emitted material, whether tone, breath, or the intermediate *h*-sound (ii.8–10); by *sañsarga* (a term not elsewhere used) is doubtless intended the degree of approximation of the articulating organs, as contact (*sparçana*, ii.33), approach (*upasañhâra*, ii.31), and the like (ii.14,16,45 etc.); *sthâna*, 'place, position,' and *karaṇa*, 'producing organ,' are the familiar names given respectively to the more passive and the more active of the two parts of the mouth by whose contact or approach the sound receives its articulate character (*vinyaya*, which the commentator explains by *vinyâsa* [B. reads this in the rule itself], seems to be added more to make up the verse than for the sake of its meaning); *parimâṇa*, 'measure' (used only here), is synonymous with *kâla*, 'time, quantity' (see i.31–37). The commentator takes *a* as an example, and says of it that its "emitted material" is tone; its "closure," in the throat; its "position," the two jaws; and its "disposition of producing organ," the two lips. Excepting in the first item, this is blundering work: *a* is, of all the alphabetic sounds, the one least easy to try by the tests laid down in this rule; and the commentator would have done well to choose some more manageable illustration.

वर्णपृक्तः शब्दो वाच उत्पत्तिः ॥ ३ ॥

3. Sound combined with articulation is the origin of voice.

The commentator defines *pṛkta* by *miçra*, 'mixed,' and *utpatti*

---

2. *anupradânâdibhiḥ pañcabhiḥ*[1] *karaṇâir varṇavâiçeshyaṁ*[2] *jâyate. akârasya tâvad anupradânaṁ nâdaḥ: saṁsargaḥ kaṇṭhe: sthânaṁ hanû: karaṇavinyaya*[3] *oshṭhâu: vinyayo nâma vinyâsaḥ: parimâṇam*[4] *mâtrâkâlaḥ: evaṁ sarvavarṇânâm boddhavyam. viçeshabhâvo*[5] *vâiçeshyam: varṇânâṁ vâiçeshyaṁ varṇavâiçeshyam*[6].

[1] G. M. om. [2] G. M. O. *-ṇânâṁ v-*. [3] O. *-nyâsa*. [4] W. O. *parim-*, as also (with T.) in the rule. [5] G. M. O. *-shasya bh-*. [6] W. O. om.; G. M. *tathâ*.

3. *pṛkto miçra ity arthaḥ: varṇamiçraḥ*[1] *çabdo vâco vâkyasyo*

by *upâdâna* and *kârana*, 'cause.' This combination denies the quality of voice to the mere "sound" of drums and the like.

सप्त वाच स्थानानि भवन्ति ॥ ४ ॥

4. Of voice, there are seven qualities.

Here is a different and expanded version of the doctrine of three qualities, as laid down above, in rule xxii.11. The following rules give the details. The commentator gives of *sthâna* the lucid definition "those whereby the voice is put to use, and that wherein it stands—that is *sthâna*."

उपांशुध्वाननिमदोपब्दिमन्मन्द्रमध्यमताराणि ॥ ५ ॥

5. Namely, inaudible, murmur, whisper, mumbling, soft, middle, and loud.

The rules that follow define the senses in which we are to understand the terms here given. They indicate plainly enough a continual progression, from inaudible and merely mental utterance up to loud and distinct speaking; but it is not easy to find words which shall represent them closely.

करणवदशब्दममनःप्रयोगमुपांशु ॥ ६ ॥

6. "Inaudible" is without sound, without application of mind, but with articulating action.

The commentator explains *karaṇavat* by *prayatnavat*, 'with effort,' and states its object to be to deny absolute silence to the *upâñçu*. "Without sound" signifies the exceeding littleness of

---

'tpattir upâdânaṁ[2] *kâraṇam bhavati. varṇapṛkta iti kim: dundubhyâdiçabdânâṁ vâkyatâ*[3] *mâ bhûd iti.*

[1] MSS. *-çra.* [2] B. G. M. O. *-na.* [3] B. *-tvaṁ.*

4. *'vacaḥ sapta sthânâni bhavanti:*[1] *tâny uttarasûtre vakshyante. yâir vâk*[2] *prayujyate*[3] *yasminç ca tishṭhati tat*[4] *sthânam: tâni yathâkramam udâharishyâmaḥ.*

(1) G. M. om. [2] B. *-kyaṁ.* [3]B. *yuj-;* W. O. add *se.* [4] O. om.

5. *upâñçv iti prathamaṁ vâca sthânam: dhvâna*[1] *iti dvitîyam: nimada*[2] *iti tṛtîyam: evam itarâṇy api nâmataḥ saptâi 'tâni sthânâni jânîyât. uparitanaṁ*[3] *sûtram ârabhya pratyekam eshâṁ lakshaṇaṁ*[4] *vakshyate*[5].

[1] O. *-nam;* G. M. *-naṁ.* [2] O. *-dam.* [3] B. O. *-na.* [4] G. M. *sthânânâṁ.* [5] G. M. *lak-.*

6. *karaṇavat prayatnavad ity arthaḥ: nâ 'sti çabdo dhvanir asminn ity*[1] *açabdam*[2]*: manasâ prayogo manaḥprayogaḥ*[3]*: nâ 'sti*

sound in this mode of utterance. "Without application of mind" excludes any intentional use of *udâtta* etc. This last is not very satisfactory; and, indeed, we should as soon expect the contrary term, *manaḥprayoga*, 'with application of mind,' to be read, as indicating an utterance in which the mind does its full part, though not the voice also (G. M., in fact, read it in the rule).

अक्षरव्यञ्जनानामनुपलब्धिर्ध्वानः ॥ ७ ॥

7. "Murmur" is inaudibleness of syllables and consonants.

The commentator explains *akshara*, 'syllables,' as meaning here 'vowels,' but there seems no need of refusing the word its ordinary signification. Inaudibleness, we are further told, being a characteristic of *upâñçu* also, it is here again specified in order to teach that there is no actual sound heard. Of what follows, a great part has dropped out in B. G. M., and is much corrupted in the other two manuscripts, so as to be very obscure. The separate mention of syllables and consonants is for the sake of clearness (?), and indicates exceeding inaudibleness: and there is added a comparison with tame and wild cattle, of which I fail to make any sense. Others say that the inaudibleness is of *s*, *ḥ*, and so on. All of which is very trivial and unedifying.

उपलब्धिर्निमदः ॥ ८ ॥

8. "Whisper" is their audibleness.

---

manaḥprayogo yasminn[4] *ity amanaḥprayogam*[5]. [6]*vâca sthânam îdṛçam*[6] *upâñçv ity upadiçyate. tatra karaṇavad iti tûshṇîmbhâvanivṛttyartham*[7]*: açabdam iti çabdasyâ 'tyantâlpatârtham*[8]*: amanaḥprayogam ity udâttâdînâṁ sâṁkalpikaprayogapratishedhârtham*[9].

[1] W. B. put before *asmin*. [2] G. M. *-daḥ*. [3] W. *manaḥ*; B. *-gaḥ stvam*; O. *manasaḥ pr-*. [4] G. M. O. *'sminn*. [5] G. M. *-gaḥ*. [(6)] W. *sthânaṁ vâca ichvâṁ*. [7] G. M. *-thaḥ*. [8] G. M. *-thaḥ*. [9] G. M. *saṁkalpakaprati-*; B. G. M. *-thaḥ*.

7. *aksharâṇi svarâḥ: aksharâṇâṁ vyañjanânâṁ*[1] *câ 'nupalabdhir dhvâno nâma dvitîyaṁ vâca sthânam. upâñçulakshaṇe 'py anupalabdhâu satyâṁ punarvacanam*[2] *açabdopalabdhividhânârtham*[3]*:* [4]*aksharavyañjanânâm bhedagrahaṇam*[5] *abhikhyârtham*[6]*: atyantânupalabdhir*[7] *ity arthaḥ.* [8] *anye tv*[9] *âhuḥ:*[4] *aksharavyañjanânâṁ savisarjanîyâdînâm*[10] *anupalabdhir iti.*

[1] G. M. *svarâṇâṁ*. [2] W. B. *-cana*; O. *-canaṁ*. [3] W. B. O. *çabd-*; G. M. *-rthaḥ*. [(4)] B. G. M. om. [5] O. *bhedena gr-*. [6] W. *âbhâkshayyayârthaṁ*; O. *âbh-*. [7] O. *-ntâpal-*. [8] W. ins. *yâmaṇyasya paçor araraṇyasya pi tûcyam iti*; O. ins. *yathâ na grâmyasya paçor aṅte nâraṇyasâdhyetacyam iti*. [9] O. om. *tu*. [10] G. M. *vis-*.

8. *aksharavyañjanânâm upalabdhir nimado nâma tṛtîyaṁ vâça sthânam bhavati.*

I have rendered *nimada* by 'whisper' rather at a venture: whether the word accurately represents it or not is at any rate of very small consequence.

सशब्दमुपब्दिमत् ॥ ९ ॥

9. "Mumbling" is the same, with sound.

Çabda would seem to be used here in the sense of *nâda*, 'tone,' if the definition is to be made anything of; the term *upabdimat* is found in the Tâittirîya-Sanhitâ (at iii.1.9[1]), used in antithesis to *upâṅçu.*

उरसि मन्द्रं कण्ठे मध्यमं शिरसि तारम् ॥ १० ॥

10. "Soft" is in the chest, "middle" in the throat, "loud" in the head.

The South-Indian manuscripts (G. M.) divide this rule into three, and break up the comment into three corresponding parts, without other change. I presume that the treatment of the whole as one rule is more original; the subject joins on, as it were, to rule xxii. 11, and gives the received doctrine as to the mode of production of the three qualities of voice there laid down. And the distinction of the four other qualities by which "soft" shades off into utter inaudibility is a later addition to the doctrine—one of those pieces of useless over-refinement which are thoroughly characteristic of the Hindu mode of working.

The commentator points out that the first four of the seven *sthânas* described in this chapter are used "in sacrifices etc.;" and the last three, at the morning, noon, and evening *savanas*, or soma-libations, respectively. And he quotes "from the Çikshâ" a pair of verses which are found in the Rik-version of the *pâṇinîya* Çikshâ (verses 36,37; see Weber's Indische Studien, iv.363–4), to the effect that "in early morning, one must always read with chest-tone, resembling the growl of the tiger; at noon, with throat-tone,

---

9. [1] *aksharavyañjanânâṁ saçabdam upalabdhir*[2] *upabdiman*[3] *nâma caturthaṁ vâca sthânam bhavati*[4].

[1] G. M. ins. *çabdena saha vartata iti saçabdam.* [2] W. O. om.; B. *-bdhiman.* [3] B. om. [4] W. B. O. om.

10. *yatro 'rasi sthâne prayoga upalabhyate tan mandraṁ nâma*[1] *vâcaḥ pañcamaṁ*[2] *sthânam* [3]. *yatra kaṇṭhe sthâne prayoga upalabhyate tan madhyamaṁ nâma shashṭhaṁ vâca sthânam* [4] *yatra çirasi sthâne prayoga upalabhyate tat târaṁ nâma saptamaṁ vâca sthânam* [5]. *eteshv âditaç caturṇâṁ*[6] *'yajñâdishu prayogaḥ*[7]*: mandram* [8]*prâtaḥsavana upayujyate*[8]*: madhyamam mâdhyandine savane*[9]*: târaṁ tṛtîyasavane. çikshâ câi vaṁ vakshyati:*

like the warble of the *cakravâka;* the third soma-libation is known as accompanied with loud tone, and this is always to be employed as head-tone, with sound proceeding from the head, and resembling the cries of the peacock, *hańsa* and *kokila.*"

The Rik Pr. (xiii.17) teaches the same three *sthânas*, but calls the third *uttama* instead of *târa.* The Vâj. Pr. (i.10,30) lays down their number and their place of production (assigning to the third the *bhrûmadhya*, 'middle of the brows,' instead of *çiras*, 'head'), but gives them no specific names. We cannot well avoid regarding them as involving a difference of pitch, as well as of force or loudness of utterance; the first is low, the third high and shrill, the other intermediate between them, or at the ordinary natural pitch of the voice. They answer to the lower, middle, and upper "registers" of a voice; and our modern musical theory recognizes an analogous distinction of chest-tone and head-tone. Each register, as the following rules go on to explain, is divided into seven tones or pitches.

मन्द्रादिषु त्रिषुं स्थानेषु सप्तसप्त यमाः ॥ ११ ॥

11. In the three qualities beginning with "soft," there are seven tones each.

As synonym of *yama*, the commentator gives *svara*, doubtless here to be understood as 'musical note, tone of the gamut;' he adds 'acute, and so on,' which might be said blunderingly, as if the word he had just given meant 'accent' instead of 'musical tone,' or also intelligently, as implying the identity of accent with

---

prâtaḥ pathen[10] *nityam urasthitena*[11]
svareṇa çârdûlarutopamena[12]*:*
madhyandine kaṇṭhagatena câi 'va
cakrâhvasaṁkûjitasaṁnibhena.
târaṁ tu vidyât savanaṁ[13] *tṛtîyaṁ*[14]
çirogataṁ[15] *tac ca sadâ*[16] *prayojyam:*
mayûrahańsânyabhṛtasvanânâṁ
tulyena nâdena çirasthitena[17]*.*

[1] B. om. [2] G. M. O. put before *vâcaḥ.* [3] G. M. ins. *bhavati. kaṇṭhe madhyamam.* [4] G. M. ins. *bhavati. çirasi târam.* [5] G. M. ins. *bhavati.* [6] B. *caturvarṇânâṁ.* [(7)] G. M. ins. *'pay-.* [(8)] W. *-nam up-;* G. M. *-ne urasi prayu-.* [9] B. G. M. om. [10] W. *ka-;* G. M. *-ṭhan.* [11] G. M. *-sthalena* [12] G. M. *-rato-.* [13] G. M. *-ne.* [14] G. M. *-ye.* [15] G. M. *-otthitaṁ.* [16] G. M. *tathâ.* [17] G. M. *çirogatena.*

11. *trishu mandrâdishu sthâneshv ekâikasmint saptasapta yamâ bhavanti: yamâḥ 'svarâḥ: udâttâdaya*[1] *iti yâvat. saptasapte 'ti vîpsâyâ*[2] *ekâikasminn iti labhyate. ke te*[3] *yamâ ity âçańkyo 'ttarasûtreṇo*[4] *'ttaram âha.*

[(1)] G M. *svarâdaya.* [2] W. B. *-yâḥ;* O. *-yâm.* [3] W. O. *ne;* G. M. O. put before *ke.* [4] W. *-tro.*

musical pitch—an identity which is the ground of their common appellation.

The same statement, as to the seven *yamas* or 'tones' in each *sthâna*, 'register' or 'scale,' and the same identification with the *svaras*, are made in the Rik Prât. (xiii.17). We are to assume, without much question, that the scales pass into one another by a constant ascending series, like the bass and soprano scales in our own system of musical notation.

कृष्टप्रथमद्वितीयतृतीयचतुर्थमन्द्रातिस्वार्याः ॥ १२ ॥

12. Namely *kṛshṭa*, first, second, third. fourth, *mandra*, and *atisvârya*.

These are not the ordinary names of the seven notes of the Hindu scale, or *svaras* (for which, see Jones "on the Musical Modes of the Hindus," As. Res., vol. iii.; Weber's Indische Studien, viii.259 ff.); but they are, apparently, alternative appellations for the same thing; they are given by Uvaṭa, in his comment on Rik Prât. xiii.17, as used *sâmasu*, 'in the *sâmans*,' or 'in the Sâma-Veda' (Müller's Rik Pr., p. cclxxii.). Uvaṭa calls the first *krushṭa*, instead of *kṛshṭa*, and the same is the reading of G. M. in our rules and their commentary, as also of T. in rule 14 only (Müller, l. c., p. cclxxiii., marginal note, states *krushṭa* or *kushṭa* to be the reading of O. also, but the maker of my collation does not note the fact, except once, under rule 14, in putting in on the margin a passage inserted out of place).

तेषां दीप्तिजोपलब्धिः ॥ १३ ॥

13. Of these, the perception is born of brightness.

I have simply translated the problematical word *dîptijâ* literally, without claiming to understand what it signifies. The comment throws no light upon it, nor do I get any from any other quarter. The former says merely that the perception of each preceding one is "born from the brightness" of its successor; namely, the per-

---

12. *kṛshṭaç*[1] *ca*[2] *prathamaç ca*[3] *dvitîyaç ca tṛtîyaç ca caturthaç 'ca mandraç*[4] *câ 'tisvâryaç ca kṛshṭaprathamadvitîyatṛtîyacaturthamandrâtisvâryâḥ*[5]*: te tatho 'ktâḥ:* [6]*ete khalu*[6] *yamâ nâma.*

[1] G. M. *krushṭaç* (as also in the rule). [2] O. om. *ca.* [3] O m. *ca.* [(4)] B. O. om. [5] G. M. O. om. [(6)] B. *kṛshtâdayo.*

13. *teshâṁ* [1]*khalu saptayamânâm*[2] *uttarottaradîptijâ*[3] *pûrvapûrvopalabdhiḥ*[4,1] *syât. tat*[5] *katham: atisvâryadîptijâ mandropalabdhiḥ*[6]*: mandrâc caturthopalabdhiḥ: caturthât tṛtîyaḥ: tṛtîyâd dvitîyaḥ: dvitîyât prathamaḥ: prathamât kṛshṭa*[7] *upalabhyate.*

[(1)] W. *diptijopalabdhiḥ.* [2] G. M. O. *saptasvarâṇâm.* [3] B. *-râd-;* G. M. *-ran d-.* [4] O. *pûrvop-.* [5] G. M. om. [6] W. B. *mantr-;* G. M. *nimadop-.* [7] G. M. *krushṭaḥ;* O. *kṛshṭaḥ ity.*

ception of *mandra* from that of *atisvârya;* that of the fourth, from *mandra;* and so on through the series. Perhaps the expression is nothing more than one violently figurative, signifying that each tone receives light from, or is set in its true light by, the rest, or the ones or one nearest it: only, in that case, we should look for some word combined with *dîpti* to indicate the source of the light.

Müller (under Rik Prât. xiii.17, r. dccli.) surmises that the present rule may mean the same thing with the rule of the Rik Prât. *anantaraç câ 'tra yamo 'viçeshaḥ*, which he translates 'in these three places (*sthâna*) a *yama* without another *yama* is undistinguishable.' It is very doubtful, however, whether he is justified in rendering *anantara* by 'not having another,' and whether his rule is not rather intended to signify that the three scales pass directly into one another, the first note of the second being equivalent to an eighth of the first, and so on.

द्वितीयप्रथमकृष्टास्त्रय आह्वारकस्वराः ॥ १४ ॥

14. "Second," "first," and *kṛshṭa* are the three tones of the Âhvârakas.

This rule makes a *çloka* with the one that follows: which is, of course, a marked indication that both are interpolated here. The same thing may be inferred from the fact that rule 15 teaches nothing which is not found also in 16.

The comment adds nothing whatever to our understanding of the rule.

The Âhvârakas are mentioned in the Caraṇavyûha (paragraph 12: see Weber's Indische Studien, iii.257) as holders of one *çâkhâ* of the Yajur-Veda.

मन्द्रादयो द्वितीयान्ताश्चत्वारस्तैत्तिरीयकाः ॥ १५ ॥

15. The four beginning with *mandra* and ending with "second" are those of the Tâittirîyas.

This second half-verse, as already pointed out, is superfluous in view of the next rule, which treats the same subject, and much more explicitly.

---

14. *dvitîyaç ca prathamaç ca kṛshṭaç*[1] *ca te tatho 'ktâḥ*[2]*: ete traya âhvârakasvarâḥ*[3] *syuḥ:* [4]*eshâṁ*[5] *tâir eva prayogo veditavyaḥ*[4]*.* [6]*âhvârakâṇâṁ svarâ*[6] *âhvârakasvarâḥ.*

O. inserts the whole comment out of place, after that to the next rule. [1] G. M. *krush-* (as also, with T., in the rule); O. *kush-*. [2] B. ins. *dvitiyâdayaḥ*. [3] W. *-kâsv-*; O. *-kârâ*. (4) O. om. [5] G. M. *te-*. (6) B. *-kashṭâsvarâṇâm*; G. M. *-kasvarâ*.

15. *mandrâdayaç catvâro*[1] *dvitîyântâḥ svarâ*[2] *mandracaturthatṛtîyadvitîyâs tâittirîyakâḥ syuḥ*[3]*.*

[1] G. M. O. *-ra svarâ*. [2] G. M. O. om. [3] O. *teshâṁ tittirîyake prayogo veditavyaḥ*.

द्वितीयान्मन्द्रस्तैत्तिरीयाणां तृतीयचतुर्थावनन्तरं तच्चतुर्यममित्याचक्षते ॥ १६ ॥

16. According to the Tâittirîyas, the *mandra* proceeds from the "second," and the "third" and "fourth" come next after: this they style the tone-quaternion.

The order of the four tones is not made entirely clear by this rule, nor by the commentator's explanation of it. The latter says that "the *mandra* of the Tâittirîyas is born or produced from the 'second;'" and, if the expression be used in a manner akin with those under rule 13, this would imply that the *mandra* came first, and the "second" after—which would, of course, accord best with the value of the two names: *mandra* would thus be the lowest of the four *yamas*, as it is the lowest of the three *sthânas*. But the commentator then goes on to say that the series of *yamas* thus "beginning with 'second'" is styled tone-quaternion: and this would imply that the order is second, *mandra*, third, fourth. Yet further, he adds that "second" is *udâtta*, *mandra* is *anudâtta*, and "third" and "fourth" are *svarita* and *pracaya*. This makes the impression of a purely formal and unintelligent identification, or a forcing through of a parallelism between the four tones and the four accepted accents (which, however, are in respect to tone only three, since the *pracaya* is "of *udâtta* tone," xxi.10), without the slightest regard to the already defined tonic quality of the accents. The comment, in truth, through this whole subject, seems to be written with a very insufficient comprehension of the meaning of the text: see especially the rules that follow.

Our attention is called to the fact that the preceding rule laid down the number of the Tâittirîya *yamas*, the present one undertaking nothing more than to describe their order; and that the intention of the last words of the rule is therefore simply to give a name to the series. I have pointed out above, however, that rules 14 and 15 seem to have been put in by themselves, without any regard to 16.

---

16. [1]*tâittirîyâṇâṁ dvitîyât khalu mandro jâyate: tadanantaraṁ*[1] [2]*tṛtîyacaturthâu syâtâm:*[2] *etad eva dvitîyâdi*[3] *svaramaṇḍalaṁ*[4] *caturyamam*[5] *ity âcakshate. yo* [6]*dvitîyaḥ sa udâttaḥ:* [7]*yo*[6] *mandraḥ so 'nudâttaḥ:*[7] *yâu tṛtîyacaturthâu*[8] *tâu svaritapracayâv* [9]*ity arthaḥ*[9]*. anena sûtreṇa pûrveshâṁ*[10] *eva caturṇâṁ svarâṇâṁ kramaniyamaḥ kriyate: catuḥsaṁkhyâ tu pûrvasûtreṇâi 'vo*[11] *'ktâ: tasmâd atra caturyamam ity etat saṁjñâvidhiparam*[12] *iti pratîyate.*

(1) B. om. (along with all the rule save the first three words). (2) G. om. [3] W. B. O. *-âdiḥ.* [4] W. B. *-ṅḍanaṁ.* [5] G. M. *-yam.* (6) B. *dvitiyo udâttayor.* (7) G. M. O. om. [8] W. *dviti-.* (9) G. M. om. [10] W. *sarv-;* G. M. O. *pûrvoktânâm.* [11] O. om. *eva.* [12] W. O. *-dhindparamam;* G. M. *-dhânap-*

The mention of the Tâittirîyas here, and in this manner, seems to indicate that the Prâtiçâkhya does not belong to their school, or concern itself with their *çâkhâ;* although, perhaps, both stand in an especially near relation to it. See what is said upon this point in the concluding note.

तस्मिन्द्वियमान्तरा वृत्तिः ॥ १७ ॥

17. In it, progression is by intervals of two tones.

I have rendered this rule according to what seems to me most likely to be its real meaning—although, at the same time, I do not feel by any means confident that I understand it correctly. If the Tâittirîyas acknowledge only four notes in the scale or octave, it seems natural that they should fix these at wider intervals from one another; and the phraseology of the rule is well enough calculated to express this. The verification or rejection of my version may be left till we shall better comprehend the Hindu musical system, and its modification or adaptation as here presented. I am, at any rate, persuaded that my guess is more likely to be right than either of the two which the commentator ventures. Of these, the first is nothing less than absurd: it makes *tasmin* refer to *anudâtta*, although such an antecedent can only have tumbled in out of the clouds, there having been nothing whatever to suggest it in the preceding rules; and renders 'in this *anudâtta* there is a being-within of two *yamas;* that is to say, in *anudâtta* inheres the quality of *svarita* and also that of *pracaya*'! And, as examples of this wonderful *anudâtta*, are quoted *sá naḥ parshat* (not found in the Tâittirîya-Sanhitâ, but occurs Rig-Veda i.99.1; x.187.1–5; and Atharva-Veda vii.63.1), and *páry avadatâm* (i.7.2[2]).

The commentator's second guess is so far better than his first that he gives the obviously correct interpretation of *tasmin*, as referring to *caturyamam* in the preceding rule; but he makes out the meaning to be that, in this series of *svaras*, two are contained in the interior, or are included between the other two. And he

---

17. *dvâu ca tâu yamâu ca*[1] *dviyamâu*[2]*: dviyamayor*[3] *antarâvṛttir madhyavṛttis*[4] *tasminn anudâtte 'bhavati: svaritatvam pracayatvaṁ câ 'nudâtte*[5] *bhavatî 'ty arthaḥ. yathâ: sa----: pary----.*

kecid anyathâ kathayanti: tasmiṅ[6] *caturyame*[7] *svaramaṇḍale dviyamântarâ*[8] *vṛttiḥ: svaradvayasya*[9] *madhye vartamânaṁ syât*[10]*.*

anudâtto hṛdi jñeyo mûrdhny udâtta udâhṛtaḥ:
svaritaḥ karṇamûlîyaḥ[11] *sarvâṅge*[12] *pracayaḥ smṛtaḥ.*

[13]*asyâ 'yaṁ arthaḥ:*[13] *udâttânudâttayor*[14] [15]*madhye svaritapracayayor*[15] *antarâvṛttir bhavati.* [16]*tathâ kâuhaleyahastavinyâsasamaye 'pi*[16] *svaritapracayayor antarâvṛttir upadiçyate:*

cites a verse: "*anudâtta* is to be known as in the heart; *udâtta* is uttered in the head; *svarita* is at the root of the ears (or of the throat, as G. M. have it); *pracaya* is declared to be in the whole member (or to belong to the whole mouth, W. says);" the meaning of which he states to be that *svarita* and *pracaya* are found between *udâtta* and *anudâtta*—forgetting that under the previous rule he had assigned them a different position. Further, he says that the interior position of *svarita* and *pracaya* is shown in Kâuhaleya's system of motions of the hand, as appears from the verse "the chief of the digits (i. e. the thumb) points out *udâtta* when its apex is applied to the root of the forefinger; when to the last but one (i. e. the ring-finger) and to the middle finger, it points out the *svarita* and the *dhṛta;* when to the little finger, the *anudâtta.*" This verse occurs in the Rik-version of the *pâṇinîya* Çikshâ (as verse 43: see Weber's Indische Studien, iv.365): the commentator does not regard it as a Çikshâ verse, but adds yet another which he claims to take from his Çikshâ, although it is not found in either version of the known treatise of that name (but compare verse 44, l. c., p. 366): "the little finger, the ring-finger, the middle finger, and the forefinger—these, along with the tip of the thumb, severally point out the grave, circumflex, *dhṛta*, and acute accents." The *pracaya* is here twice called *dhṛta*, and it again, apparently, receives the same name in the last rule of the chapter (unfortunately, I overlooked these passages when commenting on the term *dhṛtapracaya* in rule xviii.3): "sustained" or "continued" is a sufficiently natural substitute for *pracaya*, as appellation of the accent in question.

I do not understand precisely what and how much credit the commentator intends to claim for these two explanations in calling them (in his final remark) *mukhya:* if he means that they are the best among a number which had been suggested and might have been reported, it is so much the worse for the rest.

---

[17]*udâttam âkhyâti vṛsho 'ṅgulînâm*
pradeçinîmûlanivishṭamûrdhâ:
upântamadhye[18] *svaritaṁ dhṛtaṁ ca*
kanishṭhikâyâm anudâttam eve 'ti[17].

[19]*çikshâvacanam api*[19] *câi 'vaṁ vakshyati:*
kanishṭhikâ[20] *'nâmikâ ca*[21] *madhyamâ ca pradeçinî:*
nîcasvâradhṛtodâttân aṅgushṭhâgreṇa[22] *nirdiçet.*
mukhyam eva[23] *vyâkhyânadvayam*[24] *etat.*

[1] MSS. om. [2] W. O. om. [3] W. B. O. *-mor.* [4] G. M om.; B. *medhyev-*; O. *madhyev-.* [(5)] O. om. [6] G. M. *-iṅç.* [7] W. B. O. *ma.* [8] W. B. O. *dvitiy-.* [9] G. M. *-dviyamasya.* [10] G. M. O. ins. *tathâ hi.* [11] G. M. *kaṇṭham-.* [12] W. *sarvâsyaḥ*; O. *sayâsye.* [(13)] W. om.; B. om. *asya.* [14] G. M. *udâttânudâttasvarita.* [(15)] W. om. [(16)] O. om.; G. M. *-leye hast-.* [(17)] O. om.; G. M. *âkhyâti yathâ : pradeçinîmûla udâttam upântamadhyayor madhye svaritaṅ ca kanishṭhikâyâm anudâttam iti.* [18] W. *atecam-.* [(19)] O. *çikshâ.* [20] O. *-shṭhâ.* [21] G. M. *câ 'pi*; O. *câ 'tha.* [22] O. *âṅgushṭhayena.* [23] G. M. *evaṁ.* [24] W. O. *-naṁ dv-.*

तामुपदेक्ष्यामः ॥ १८ ॥

18. That progression we will set forth.

The commentator declares *tâm* here to bring forward solely the word *vṛttim* from the preceding rule (not that word with its qualifications), and the *vṛtti* aimed at to be the fourfold progression of the *caturyama* taught in rules 16 and 19. This is, of course, forced and unacceptable. I imagine that, on the contrary, in the oral tradition of the Prâtiçâkhya, an uttered illustration of the four tones, separated by double intervals and so covering the whole octave, was given—which illustration, of course, could not be set down in the written text.

तच्चतुर्यममित्युक्तम् ॥ १९ ॥

19. That is what is called the quaternion of tones.

This is naturally enough explainable as a winding-up remark, after the exemplification of the four Tâittirîya tones notified in the preceding rule has been duly given. To the commentator, it is a mere repetition of what had been already stated above, in rules 15 and 16; and he excuses it as being intended, under the guise of a summing-up, to confirm the view laid down, and repel other opinions inconsistent with it. For, he adds, some people hold the doctrine that there are three *svaras* only, as appears from the half-verse "acute, grave, and circumflex are the three accents." This verse (from the *pâṇinîya* Çikshâ) was quoted in full above, under rule xxi.1; and W. adds the second half of it here also.

The futility of this exposition, as well as of much that precedes it, will, I think, be obvious to any one. Instead of tracing and pointing out the relation which actually exists between the accents and the *yamas*, and letting us see what musical intervals are re-

---

18. *yad etad âcâryâiç caturyamam ity uktaṁ tasya caturbhedabhinnâ*[1] *vṛttir*[2] *nâma: tâm upadekshyâma ity ucyate.* [3]*tâm iti tachabdena*[3] *pûrvoktavṛttimâtram anukṛshyate*[4].

[1] G. M. *-âṁ.* [2] G. M. *-iṁ.* [(3)] W. O. *tânimittaçabd-*; B. *tâm iti labdhena.* [4] W. *-kathy-.*

19. *ity anena prakâreṇa caturyamam ity*[1] *uktam. yady api mandrâdayo dvitîyântâ* (xxiii.15) *ityâdisûtradvayena yamacatushṭayatvaṁ*[2] *siddhaṁ tathâ 'py upasaṁhâramisheṇa*[3] *matântaranivṛttyarthaṁ*[4] *dṛḍhayati. yataḥ kâraṇâd evam anye manyante svaratrayamâtram:*

udâttaç câ 'nudâttaç ca svaritaç ca [5]*svarâs trayaḥ:*[5]
[6]*hrasvo dîrghaḥ pluta iti kâlato niyamâ aci.*[6]

[1] O. om. [2] W. *caturyayamacatushṭayaṁ pra*; B. *-ṭayaṁ na*; O. *cat-.* [3] W. *-shṭena*; G. M. *-hâreṇa mi-.* [4] G. M. ins. *imam artham.* [(5)] B. O. *-ya iti*; G. M. *trayasvarâ iti manyante.* [(6)] in W. only.

garded as separating the different accentual pitches from one another, the commentator simply confuses the two together, and regards as said of the one what has reference only to the other.

क्रमविक्रमसंपन्नामद्रुतामविलम्बिताम् ।
नीचोच्चस्वारसंपन्नां वदेद्धृतवतीꣳ समां
वदेद्धृतवतीꣳ समामिति ॥२०॥

20. It must be uttered with *krama* and *vikrama*, not hurried, not delayed, with grave, acute, and circumflex accent, with *pracaya*, and even.

The commentator supplies *vṛttim* as the subject of all these attributes, accounting for it as derived from rule 17, above. This is hardly admissible; but what is to be understood instead is doubtful, depending upon the connection in which this verse may have stood in the text from which it was taken. The same connection would perhaps explain what *krama* and *vikrama* are to be regarded as meaning: the commentator defines *krama* by *dvitva*, 'duplication' (taught in chapter xiv.), and *vikrama* as the accent of that name prescribed at xix.1,2; but it seems very unlikely that two things so dissimilar would be thus combined, or that a detail of accent would not be put in the second line, with the rest of its kind (compare rule xxiv.6, where *krama* and *vikrama* are found again in conjunction). *Dhṛta* is defined as synonymous with *pracaya:* compare the note to rule 17, above. *Samâm* means, we are told, 'free from the faults of deficiency and excess in the matter of *udâtta* and the other accents.'

There are slight variations of reading in the rule, T. giving *adhrutâm* in *pâda b;* B. *svara* for *svâra* in *c;* W. G. M. having *vade* for *vaded*, and W. *drutavatîñ* and T. *dratav-* after it; but they are mere errors of scribes, as the comment plainly shows.

---

20. *tâittirîyâhvârakamatanirûpako*[1] *'yaṁ çlokaḥ: kramavikramâbhyâṁ*[2] *sampannâm: kramo nâma*[3] *dvitvam*[4]*: vikramas tu svaritayor madhye yatra nîcam*[5] (xix.1) *ityuktalakshaṇaḥ: adrutâm atvaritâm: avilambitâm amandâm: nîcoccasvârasampannâm anudâttodâttasvaritasahitâṁ*[6] *dhṛtavatîm pracayavatîm: samâm udâttâdibhir nyûnâtirekâdidosharahitâm*[7]*: vaded brûyât:* [8] *vṛttim*[9] *ity arthaḥ: vṛttim iti kathaṁ labhyate: tasmin dviyamântarâ vṛttir*[10] (xxiii.17) *itiprakṛtatvâd*[11] *iti brûmaḥ.*

iti tribhâshyaratne prâtiçâkhyavivaraṇe trayoviṅço[12] *'dhyâyaḥ.*

[1] W. B. *-rakam etan nir-;* O. *-rakâmatan nir.* [2] W. *-vikrama.* [3] G. M. O. om. [4] G. M. *dvitvaparyâyaḥ.* [5] O. *-cañ syâd.* [6] B. *-ritapracayasaṁh-.* [7] B. *nyûnâtiriktâdi-;* O. *nyûnâdirek-.* [8] G. M. ins. *imâṁ.* [9] B. om. [10] O. *v.* [11] O. *-kṛtitv-.* [12] G. M. O. *dvitîyapraçne ekâdaço.*

CHAPTER XXIV.

CONTENTS: 1-4, the four *saṁhitâs* or texts; 5-6, qualifications of a Veda-reader and teacher.

अथ चतस्रः संहिताः ॥ १ ॥

1. Now for the four texts.

A simple heading to the following rules.

पदसंहिताक्षरसंहिता वर्णसंहिताङ्गसंहिता चेति ॥ २ ॥

2. Word-text, syllable-text, letter-text, and member-text, namely.

Here is a very curious and problematical enumeration and designation of *saṁhitâs*. The commentator divides up among them the teachings of the Prâtiçâkhya. To the "word-text" he assigns chapters v.–ix., xi., xii., and xiii.1–4—that is to say, the great body of rules for the combination of *pada*-text into *saṁhitâ*. To the "syllable-text" he assigns chapter x., which has to do chiefly with such euphonic combinations of vowels as make one syllable out of two. With the "letter-text" are concerned chapters xiii. (i. e. except rules 1–4), xiv., and xvi., mainly occupied with the subjects of duplication and of the occurrence in the Sanhitâ of *ṇ* and *n̐*, otherwise than as these are results of the rules of euphonic combination. And the "member-text" is said to be taught in chapter

---

1. *athe 'ty ayam adhikâraḥ: catasraḥ saṁhitâ* [1] *ucyanta*[2] *ity etad adhikṛtaṁ veditavyam ita uttaraṁ yad vakshyâmaḥ*[3].

[1] G. M. ins. *ity.* [2] O. om. [3] O. *-yate.*

2. *padâksharavarṇâṅgâçrayâç*[1] *catasraḥ saṁhitâḥ krameṇa boddhavyâḥ. pañcamâdhyâyam* [2]*ârabhyâ " navamâd ekâdaça-dvâdaçâu*[2] *trayodaçasyâ*[3] *"dâu sûtracatushṭayaṁ ca padasaṁhitâ. daçamo 'ksharasaṁhitâ. trayodaçacaturdaçâu*[4] *shoḍaçaç ca varṇasaṁhitâ.* [5]*vyañjanan̐ svarâṅgam* (xxi.1) *ity eshâ*[5] *'ṅga-saṁhitâ. etâç*[6] *catasraḥ saṁhitâḥ. eteshv anyatra* [7] *vihitaṁ nishiddhaṁ*[8] *ca kâryaṁ sarvasaṁhitâsu*[9] *kuryât*[10]*: yatrâ*[11] *"rsha-grahaṇâdiko viçesho 'sti* [12].

[1] W. *-gâ ayâç*; O. *-gâyâç.* (2) W. B. O. *ârabhya â nav-*; G. M. *ârabhya ûnapadâikâdaç-*; W. O. *-dvâdaça.* [3] O. *-çâ.* [4] W. *-rdaça.* (5) B. G. M. *ekaviñço.* [6] G. M. om. [7] O. ins. *ca.* [8] G. M. *nishidhyakañ.* [9] B. *-tâ*; G. M. *sarvatra saṁh-*; O. *sahit-.* [10] G. M. *syât.* [11] W. B. O. *atrâ.* [12] G. M. add *tatra kuryât.*

xxi. (rules 1–9), which prescribes of what vowel each consonant shall be regarded as "member" or adjunct, or lays down the rules of syllabication. And it is added that whatever is prescribed or forbidden elsewhere than in [the rules belonging to each of] these is of force in all the different texts, unless there be some special restriction, as by the use of the word *ârsha* (ix.21; x.13) or the like.

It is unnecessary to point out that the Prâtiçâkhya contemplates no such division of its rules and restriction of their application as is here made, and that, unless the distinction of texts laid down in the rule means something different from what the commentato explains it to be, it is trivial and worthless.

नानापदसंधानसंयोगः पदसंहितेत्यभिधीयते ॥ ३ ॥

3. Conjunction of independent words by euphonic combination is called word-text.

The commentator first explains *saṁdhâna* as modifying *saṁyoga* in quality of a locative, and then declares the use of the two equivalent terms to be for the purpose of signifying the exceeding closeness of the combination (if, as I presume to be the case, the reading of B. is here the correct one). And he quotes the rule of Pâṇini (i.4.109) as what "the grammarians" say upon the subject, giving the definition of *saṁhitâ* or combined text. As example of word-text, he gives *agne dudhra gahya kiñçila vanya yâ ta ishuḥ* (v.5.9[1]: only G. M. have *ishuḥ*).

This interpretation makes *padasaṁhitâ* signify what we are wont to call *saṁhitâ* simply, in distinction from *padapâṭha*, or *padasaṁhitâ* as usually employed, '*pada*-text.'

यथास्वमक्षरसंहितादीनामप्येवम् ॥ ४ ॥

4. And in like manner with the syllable-text and the rest, in accordance with their several names.

The commentator explains *yathâsvam* as signifying 'it goes on without exceeding that which is its own,' and pronounces it a 'distinction of office or use;' thus, namely, the peculiar form of all the other specified texts is to be determined; the combination of inde-

---

3. *nânâbhûtayoḥ padayoḥ saṁdhâne yaḥ saṁyogaḥ sa padasaṁhite 'ty abhidhîyata ucyata ity arthaḥ. yathâ: agne..... ekârthayoḥ saṁdhânasaṁyogaçabdayoḥ*[1] *prayogaḥ saṁdhânâdhikyârthaḥ*[2]. *tathâ ca vâiyâkaraṇâḥ*[3] *paṭhanti*[4]*: paraḥ saṁnikarshaḥ saṁhite 'ti.*

[1] G. M. *-yogayoḥ;* O. *saṁyogesaṁbadhânaç-.* [2] W. *-nâdikyâdityarthaḥ;* G. M. *sambandhikârthaḥ;* O. *sambandhikthâdhârthaḥ.* [3] G. M. O. *-nâ.* [4] G. M. *bhaṇanti;* O. *api.*

4. *svaṁsvam*[1] *anatikramya vartata iti yathâsvam: kriyâviçeshaṇam* [2]*evâi 'tat*[2]*; evam aksharasaṁhitâdînâm api yathâsvam*[3]

pendent syllables is syllable-text—and so on. And he quotes three passages from the text, by way of illustration: *athâ 'bravît* (iii.2.11[3]), *adhishavanam asi* (i.1.5[2]), and *akshṇayâ vyâghârayati* (v.2.7[5] et al.). Of these, the first is an example of the combination of two separate syllables (vowels) into one syllable, by a rule (2) of the tenth chapter; the second, of the occurrence of *ṇ* after *sh*, by rule xiii.6,7; the third offers (like almost any other pair of words in the Sanhitâ) cases of the division of consonant-groups, *akkhsht-ṭna-yâv-vyâ-* etc. Or, by a different treatment of the successive distinctions, it is said that the combination of two vowels alone is "syllable-text;" that of a vowel and consonant in one word is "letter-text;" that of consonants alone in one word (consonants being "members" or adjuncts of vowels, xxi.1) is "member-text;" anything else than these is "word-text."

It appears from all this that *saṁhitâ* is here used nearly in the sense of *saṁdhi*, 'euphonic combination,' and that these four rules have no significance whatever, being a mere bit of outside classification, in which some one has amused himself by indulging.

गुरुत्वं लघुता साम्यं ह्रस्वदीर्घप्लुतानि च ।
लोपागमविकाराश्च प्रकृतिर्विक्रमः क्रमः ॥
स्वरितोदात्तनीचत्वं श्वासो नादो ऽङ्गमेव च ।
एतत्सर्वं तु विज्ञेयं छन्दोभाषामधीयता ॥ ५ ॥

5. Heaviness, lightness, evenness; short, long, and protracted quantity; elision, increment, and euphonic alteration; natural state, *vikrama*, *krama*; circumflex, acute, and grave quality; breath, tone, and adjunction—all this must be understood by him who reads the Veda language.

---

svarûpaṁ nirûpaṇîyam. nânâksharasaṁyogo 'ksharasaṁhitâ: [1]nânâvarṇasaṁyogo varṇasaṁhitâ: nânâṅgasaṁyogo 'ṅgasaṁhitâ[1]. [5]krameṇo 'dâharaṇâni bhaṇâmaḥ[6]: yathâ[7]: athâ----: adhi-----: akshṇ-----. kevalasvarayoḥ saṁyogo 'ksharasaṁhitâ:[8] [8]ekapade svaravyañjanasaṁyogo varṇasaṁhitâ: ekapade kevalavyañjanasaṁyogo 'ṅgasaṁhitâ:[8] anyatra padasaṁhitâ: ity avântarabhedo vijñeyaḥ.

[1] W. B. *svam.* (2) G. M. om.; O. om. *eva.* [3] O. *-sva.* (4) G. M. put also after rule 4 in the text of the Prâtiçâkhya, as if rules 5 and 6. (5) O. om. [6] W. om.; G. M. *vyâharâmaḥ.* [7] G. M. om. [8] B. om.

5. *yad gurutvâdyashṭâdaçavidham etat sarvaṁ chandobhâshâṁ vedarûpâṁ[1] vâcam adhîyatâ paṭhatâ vijñeyam. atha vâ chandobhâshâṁ[2] vedalakshaṇam[3] ity arthaḥ. tuçabdo 'dhyetṛvyatiriktanishedhârthaḥ[4]: anena[5] tu sarvathâ vijñeyam ity arthaḥ.*

The commentator explains *vedabhâshâm* as meaning either 'voice having the form of Veda,' i. e. the uttered material of the Veda, or (according to another sense of *bhâshâ*) 'explanation of the Veda.' The particle *tu* in the last half-verse (which I have omitted in translating, as being a mere expletive or *pâdapûraṇa*), he states to mean that the reader referred to must by all means understand all this, but not any one besides. And he adds at the end that *vijñeya* indicates the peremptoriness of the rule, there being risk of harm in the absence of the required knowledge, as is shown by the verse "a *mantra* deficient in respect to accent or to letters" etc. This is the familiar verse, found in the *pâṇinîya* Çikshâ (verse 52: see Weber's Indische Studien, iv.367–8), and quoted times innumerable in Hindu works, where the present subject is under consideration: O. alone adds the second *pâda*, "being falsely applied, does not express the intended sense;" the rest is, "it, an uttered thunderbolt, harms the sacrificer, like the word *indraçatru* [when used by Tvashṭar] with false accent."

The rest of the comment is occupied with illustration of the points referred to in the rule, along with now and then a few words of explanation. For "heavy" quality (see xxii.14) is cited *vashaṭ svâhâ* (vii.3.12); for "light" (see xxii.15), *akuruta* (v.5.8¹ et al.: W. B. give instead *akurvata* [i.7.3³ et al.], which is less acceptable, as containing also a heavy syllable). *Sâmya*, 'evenness, sameness,' is defined as implying that, of two elements compared, there is—in respect to place and organ of articulation, quantity, etc.—sameness (so G. M., but B. O. read 'bigness' instead, and W. has 'steadiness'): what is really meant, is obscure; we may compare the use of the adjective *sama* in xxiii.20. The examples for short, long, and protracted, respectively, are *gamayati* (i.7.3⁴ et al.), *vâyâv evâ 'sya* (vi.3.7⁴), and *astu hî3 iti* (vii.1.6¹: G. M. omit *iti*). Elision is instanced by *îm 'andrâsu* (iv.1.8²: see above, v.12); increment, by *trapuç ca me* (iv.7.5¹: see above, v.4); euphonic conversion, by *sam indra no manasâ* (i.4.44¹: only O. has *manâsa:* a case under vii.2). To illustrate *prakṛti*, 'original condition,' are given three phrases, *agne dudhra gahya kiñcila vanya yâ te* (v.5.9¹: W. B. end with *kiñcila*, and G. M. with *vanya;* and G. M. O. omit *agne*), *prapâ asi* (ii.5.12⁴), and *na mi-*

---

gurutvaṁ yathâ: vashaṭ..... laghutâ yathâ: akuruta. sâmyaṁ yathâ: sthânakaraṇakâlâdibhir[6] *anayor asti sthâuryam*[7] *iti. hrasvadîrghaplutâni ca*[8] *yathâ: gamayati: vâyâv.....: astu ..... lopo yathâ:* [9] *îm..... âgamo yathâ: trapuç.....* [10]*vikâro yathâ: sam..... prakṛtir yathâ: agne.....: prapâ.....: na.....*[10] *vikramo yathâ: voḍhave. kramo nâma dvitvam* [11] *yathâ: yad.....:* [12]*yad.....*[12] *svaritodâttanîcânâm bhâvaḥ svaritodâttanîcatvam:* [13]*tad yathâkramaṁ*[13] *nirdiçyate*[14]*: nyañcam: gâṁ.....: avadatâm. vivṛte çvâsa* (ii.5) *ity uktaḥ*[15] *çvâso yathâ: pâ-..... saṁvṛte*[16] *kaṇṭhe nâdaḥ kriyata* (ii.4) *ity*

thunî abhavan (v.3.6²: G. M. omit *na*). Of these, the second is a case under x.13; the third, under x.18: both exhibiting a vowel which irregularly remains *prakṛtyâ*, or exempt from alteration. But the particular bearing of the first example on the point of *prakṛti* is more obscure: the phrase is one in which the *saṁhitâ*-reading is (except in respect to accent) the same with the *pada*; and this, probably, is the reason why it is taken. Compare the comment and note to v.2, where this part of the rule now in hand is quoted. For *vikrama* is given the word *vóḍhavé* (i.6.2¹ et al.), of which the second syllable has the accent called *vikrama*, by xix. 1. *Krama* is again (as under xxiii.20) defined as 'duplication,' and a phrase is quoted containing a case that calls for duplicated utterance, *yad vâi hotâ* (iii.2.9¹: i. e. *yad drâi*, by xiv.1): O. adds another of like character, *yad venoḥ* (v.1.1⁴). We are permitted to doubt, however, here as at xxiii.20, whether these terms were intended by the maker of the rule in the sense which the commentator assigns to them. The three accents are instanced, in their order as mentioned, by *nyàñcam* (v.5.3²), *gâ'ṁ vâ'vá tâ'u tát* (i.7.2²), and *avadatâm* (i.7.2²). Reference is made to rule ii.5 as defining "breath," and as example of breath-sounds, or surd consonants, is cited *pûshâ te* (i.1.2²: B. has instead *pûte*, and W. *pûrte*, which occurs at iv.7.13⁵). Rule ii.4, again, is referred to as defining "tone" or sonant utterance, and the example is *bhâgadhe bhâgadhâh* (ii.5.6⁶). Finally, *añgam*, which I have rendered 'adjunction,' is interpreted as alluding to the subject of syllabication (xix.1 etc.), and a phrase is quoted, *tam matsyaḥ prâ 'bravît* (ii.6.6¹), which we are to divide *tam-mat-thsyaç-prâb-bra-vît*.

The verses composing this rule are found in a passage prefixed to the proper text of the Rik Prât. (see Müller's edition, p. viii.).

पदक्रमविशेषज्ञो वर्णक्रमविचक्षणः ।
स्वरमात्राविभागज्ञो गच्छेदाचार्यसंसदं
गच्छेदाचार्यसंसदमिति ॥ ६ ॥

6. He who understands the distinctions of the *pada-krama*, who is versed in the *varṇa-krama*, and knows the divisions of accent and quantity, may go and sit with the teachers.

---

ukto nâdo yathâ: bhâg-.... vyañjanañ svarâñgam (xxi.1) *ity uktam añgaṁ yathâ: tam.... vijñeyatvam*[17] *iti*[18] *nityavidhiḥ: vipakshe bâdhât: mantro hînaḥ svarato varṇato re*[19] *'tyâdi*[20].

[1] G. M. *-dasvar-*. [2] O. *-shá*. [3] W. O. *-ṇát*; G. M. *-ṇáṁ*. [4] W. *-kta iti nish-* [5] G. M. *anená 'dhíyatá*. [6] G. M. *sthánakâl-*. [7] B. O. *stháulyam*; G. M. *ti sámyam*. [8] G. M. O. om. [9] W. ins. *etat sarvaṁ tu vijñeyaṁ chandobhávádháyatá*. [10] B. om. [11] G. M. ins. *tad*. [12] in O. only. [13] W. *padakr-*; O. *tad yathá*. [14] O. om. [15] MSS. *-taṁ*. [16] W. om. [17] G. M. O. *-yam*. [18] G. M. *ita*. [19] O. *vá*. [20] W. *-diná*; B. *-diná náma*; O. *mithyá prayukto na tam artham áha tyádináṁ*.

This verse also is prefixed to the Rik Prât. (Müller, p. viii.).

The commentator gives a merely mechanical explanation of the two terms composing the first half-verse, without telling us what he understands them really to mean. Doubtless the *pada-krama* is that which is commonly known as the "*krama*-text," and for the construction of which the other Prâtiçâkhyas (Rik Pr. x., xi.; Vâj. Pr. iv.179–194; Ath. Pr. iv.101–126) give full directions; and the *varṇa-krama* is the text with duplicated consonants, according to the rules of our fourteenth chapter. The compound *svaramâtrâvibhâga* we are taught to treat as a dependent one; we might also be tempted to regard it as copulative, and to understand *vibhâga* in the sense of 'separation' (as in *pada*-text etc.), as in the only other place where it occurs in the treatise (iii.1). "Going to the assembly of teachers" is interpreted to signify not merely the sitting with them on earth, but the enjoyment with them of the abode of felicity, the *brahmaloka*—it being explained (except in G. M.) that "the teachers" are Vyâsa and his like. Then, *apropos* of this promise of heaven to those versed in the class of subjects of which the Prâtiçâkhya treats, the commentator proceeds to quote from various *purâṇas* and kindred works the praises and promises there given to those who teach the Veda

Thus, from the Garuḍa-purâṇa: "Of all kinds of knowledge, that of the Veda is called highest; hence, he who communicates that wins heaven and final beatitude. As chief of all sciences has been produced the *brahma*-science; hence, he who is devoted to giving it will receive the whole recompense of giving." From the Devî-purâṇa: "To those twice born, the Veda is the chief means

---

6. [1]*padânâṁ kramaḥ padakramaḥ*[2]*: tasya viçeshaḥ: taṁ jânâtî 'ti padakramaviçeshajñaḥ. varṇânâṁ kramo varṇakramaḥ*[3]*: tasmin vicakshaṇo nipuṇo varṇakramavicakshaṇaḥ*[4]*. svarâç ca* [5]*mâtrâç ca*[5] *svaramâtrâḥ: tâsâṁ vibhâgaḥ: taṁ jânâtî 'ti svaramâtrâvibhâgajñaḥ*[1]*. mâtrâçabdena kâlaviçeshaḥ kaçcid ucyate: so*[6] *'pi caturaṇur*[7] *ityâdishu*[8]*. evaṁvidhaḥ purusha âcâryasaṁsadaṁ* [9] *gachet:* [10]*âcâryâ*[11] *vyâsâdayaḥ*[10]*: teshâm* [12] *brahmaloke*[13] *sthânam:* [14]*yaç ce 'daṁ*[14] *çâstraṁ jânîte so*[15] *'py âcâryatvât teshâṁ sadṛçam*[16] *brahmalokaṁ gachati*[17].

tathâ ca[18] *paurâṇikâ bhaṇanti*[19]*. gâruḍapurâṇe*[20]*:*

âhuḥ samastavidyânâṁ vedavidyâm anuttamâm[21]*:*
atas taddâtur asty eva lâbhaḥ svargâpavargayoḥ.
vidyânâm paramâ[22] *vidyâ brahmavidyâ*[23] *samîritâ:*
atas [24]*taddânaçîlaç ca*[24] *sarvaṁ*[25] *dânaphalaṁ labhet*[26].

devîpurâṇe[27]*:*

veda eva dvijâtînâṁ sâdhanaṁ [28]*yaçasaḥ phalam*[28]*:*
ato[29] *svâdhyayanâbhyâsât*[30] *paraṁ brahmâ 'dhigachati.*
[31]*tam eva çîlayet prâjñaḥ çishyebhyas tam pradâpayet:*
tadabhyâsapradânâbhyâm [32]*etat kiṁ nâ*[32] *'dhigachati*[31]

of obtaining good things; hence, by application to the reading of the Veda one attains the highest *brahma.* To that let him who is wise especially devote himself; that let him deliver over to pupils; by application to that and communication of it what is there that one does not attain?" From Yâjñavalkya: "Above all sacrifices, and ascetic practices, and pure works, the Veda is the highest means of felicity to the twice-born ones. The Brahman who, not reading the Vedas, expends his labor in other directions—he quickly falls, while living, into the condition of a Çûdra, and his posterity with him" (the latter of these two verses, which is not given by W. B., is found in Manu, at ii.168). From the Mahâbhârata: "Whoever shall repeat to pupils the religious, sacred Sarasvatî, he shall gain a reward equal to that from the giving of land and kine." From the Vishṇudharmottara-purâṇa: "By imparting the Veda, a man attains all the fruits of sacrifices; by imparting an *upaveda*, he shares in the bliss of the Gandharvas." From the Brahma-purâṇa: "That reward cannot be told in a thousand æons, which, oh sage! one obtains by even a very little teaching of the Veda." And from the Bhavishyat-purâṇa: "The sonless obtains sons; the poor becomes rich; but he who is ever devoted to the study of the Veda is dissolved in the highest *brahma.*"

Next we are told the characteristic form of the Veda: "The Yajur-Veda is brown-eyed, slim-waisted, big-throated, big-cheeked, black-footed, dusky, born of the family of Kaçyapa." If there is (as may be the case) real meaning hidden under these apparently senseless epithets, it escapes my discovery

---

tathâ ca yâjñavalkyaḥ:
yajñânâṁ tapasâṁ câi 'va çubhânâṁ[33] *câi 'va karmaṇâm:*
veda eva dvijâtînâṁ niḥçreyasakaraḥ paraḥ.
[34]*yo 'nadhîtya*[35] *dvijo vedân anyatra kurute çramam:*
sa jîvann eva çûdratvam âçu gachati sânvayaḥ[34].
mahâbhârate[36]:
yo brûyâc câ 'pi çishyebhyo[37] *dharmyâm brâhmîṁ sarasvatîm:*
pṛthivîgopradânâbhyâṁ sa tulyaphalam açnute.
vishṇudharmottare 'pi[38]:
vedadânâd avâpnoti sarvaṁ yajñaphalaṁ naraḥ:
upavedapradânena gandharvâiḥ saha modate.
brahmapurâṇe 'pi[39]:
na tat[40] *kalpasahasreṇa gadituṁ*[41] *çakyate phalam:*
yad vedadânâd âpnoti[42] *svalpâd*[43] *api mahâmate.*
bhavishyatpurâṇe 'pi[44]:
aputro labhate putrân adhano dhanavân bhavet:
sadâdhyayanayuktas tu [45]*pare brahmaṇi*[45] *lîyate.*
vedasvarûpam ucyate:
yajurvedaḥ piñgalâkshaḥ kṛçamadhyo bṛhadgalaḥ.
bṛhatkapolah krshnâñghris[46] *tâmrah kaçyapagotrajaḥ*[47].

Once more, the *vedâṅgas* and *upâṅgas* are rehearsed: the former, in the usual number and with the usual names: the latter, as *anupada*, *ânupada* (?), *chandobhâshâ*, *mîmâṅsâ*, *nyâya*, and *tarka*—the first two of these last are elsewhere called *pratipada* and *anupada* (see Weber's Indische Studien, iii.260–261, and the St. Petersburg Lexicon).

With this, in W. B., the Tribhâshyaratna ends; but G. M. O. have an added passage, the bearing of which is not in all points quite clear to me. It begins with stating that he who reads the Veda thus accompanied by the *aṅgas* and *upâṅgas*, and with knowledge of the characteristic form and family, becomes purified. A verse then follows, in which it appears to be laid down how far the rules of the Prâtiçâkhya have force: namely, as regards other texts, and passages which are not the subject of *sûtras* and are of human authorship (?). By way of illustration, nine passages are quoted, not one of which is to be found in the Sanhitâ proper, although five are from its endings of sections, or the summaries of words with which the divisions of sections (half-centuries, *kaṇḍikâs*) conclude: they are *pra nakshatrâya devyâya* (G. M. omit *devyâya*, and O. begins *anaksh-*), *sa îm mamâda mahi karma kartave* (O. omits *karma*: Tâittirîya-Brâhmaṇa ii.5.8[9]; Rig-Veda ii.22.1), *mahi-saptadaçenâ-'vasyuvâtâḥ* (from the ending of iv.4.12), *api-sîda-mithuny ashṭâu ca* (from the ending of vi.5.8), and *asmiṅs-tanuva-stuhi-pinâkam* (from the ending to iv.5.10): in these the rules are said not to hold good; and *siṅhe vyâghra uta yâ pṛdâkâu* (Tâittirîya-Brâhmaṇa ii.7.7[1]; Atharva-Veda vi.38.1; Kâṭhaka xxxvi.15), *dvâdaçâ 'gnishṭomasya stotrâṇi* (O. *stotroṇi*), *âtmanâparâ-nish-pra-çukraçocishâ* (from the ending of vi.4.10: G. M. stops at *pra*), and *uçmasî-posham ekânnaviṅçatiç ca* (ending of i.3.6: G. M. stop at *posham*), in which the rules are said to hold good. So much as this, now, seems clear: that the first two quotations in each class are given as coming from some other Vedic text than the Tâittirîya-

---

vedâṅgâny ucyante:

çikshâ kalpo vyâkaraṇaṁ niruktaṁ jyotishaṁ tathâ:
chandasâṁ[48] *lakshaṇaṁ ce 'ti shaḍ aṅgâni vidur budhâḥ*[49].
anupadaṁ[50] *câ*[51] *''nupadaṁ chandobhâshâsamanvitam:*
mîmâṅsânyâyatarkaṁ[52] *ca upâṅgâni vidur budhâḥ*[53].
[54]*evaṁ sâṅgopâṅgavedasya lakshaṇaṁ sampûrṇam.*[54]

iti tribhâshyaratne prâtiçâkhyavivaraṇe
çaturviṅço[55] *'dhyâyaḥ.*
iti dvitîyapraçnaḥ samâptaḥ.

(1) G. M. om. [2] W. B. om. [3] W. B. om. [4] O. om. (5) O. om. [6] O. *sá.* [7] W. *caraṇ-*; O. *-ṇuka.* [8] G. M. *ity avadishma*; O. *ity avâdishma.* [9] O. ins. *sthânaṁ.* (10) G. M. *saṁsadaṁ sthânaṁ âcâryasya saṁsadam.* [11] W. B. O. *-ryah.* [12] O. ins. *ca.* [13] W. *-kaṁ*; G. M. *-ko hi.* (14) B. *pada.* [15] B. om. [16] G. M. *sadanaṁ*; O. *saṁsadaṁ sthâna.* [17] O. *gachet.* [18] W. om. [19] W. B. *bhavanti*; O. *vadanti.* [20] B. *gar-*; G. M. *-de p-.* [21] W. B. *-maṁ.* [22] G. M. *ca parâ.* [23] W. om. (24) G. M. O. *-nato râjan.* [25] B. G. M. *-rva.* [26] W. B. *bhavet*; O. *bhet.* [27] O. *tathâ ca dev-.*

Sanhitâ (I should guess that they would all prove to occur in the Brâhmaṇa or Âraṇyaka), and that the first class are offered as containing cases of combination at variance with the rules of the Prâtiçâkhya, while in the second class these rules are observed throughout. Thus, in the first example, vii.4 would require *ṇaksh-* after *pra;* in the second, v.12 would require *îm 'amâda;* in the third, the *s* of *sapta* should be *sh* by vi.2; in the fourth, the *î* of *mithunî* should remain unchanged by x.18; in the fifth, *asmin* is not included among the words which by vi.14 have an increment of *s* before *t*. In the other class, on the contrary, *agnishṭomasya* follows vi.2, *nish pra* is by viii.24 and 35 (see the comment to viii. 35, where the passage is quoted as illustration), and *uçmasî* by iii. 13; the first example has nothing but cases under the general laws of euphony. I conjecture, then, that the *na* in the second line of the introductory verse is to be amended to *ca;* and that we are instructed that the rules of the treatise are followed, outside the Sanhitâ proper, only according to the nature of each particular case, or even by arbitrary choice. If there is any definite system according to which the phonetic peculiarities of the Sanhitâ are observed or neglected in putting together the endings of sections and other divisions, I, at any rate, have not been at the pains to study it out, and the work belongs rather to an editor of the Sanhitâ than to an editor of the Prâtiçâkhya: it seems somewhat strange to find the prolonged *î* of *uçmasî* retained in the ending, while the uncombinable character of the final of *mithunî* is neglected.

There can be little question that the passage here treated is an appendage to the proper text of the Tribhâshyaratna, which, with the Prâtiçâkhya, takes in general (the only exception is at viii.35) no account of the subdivisions of *anuvâkas.*

By way of conclusion, the remark is added that the repetition of the final words of the rule indicates the end of the treatise. This is not to be approved, for the repetition is simply that which is made at the end of every chapter, and so shows nothing more than the conclusion of the chapter.

---

(28) W. *yasasaḥ ph-;* G. M. *çreyasâṁ paraṁ;* O. *çreyasaḥ param.* 29 G. M. O. *tato.* 30 G. M. *-dhyâyaniratât.* (31) W. B. om. (32) O. *tat ki yajñâ.* 33 O. *çucinâṁ.* (34) W. B. om. 35 O. *nadhitva.* 36 G. M. O. *-te 'pi.* 37 G. M. *çishyâya.* 38 G. M. O. om. 39 G. M. O. om. 40 W. O. *tulya.* 41 O. *gaṇi-.* 42 W. B. *avâp-.* 43 W. O. *svâtmâd.* 44 G. M. O. om. (45) O. *parabrahmaṇi.* 46 W. *-ṇâdhriḥ;* O. *-shṭaṇâṅdhi.* 47 G. M. *kâç-.* 48 W. *-dâṅsi.* 49 W. *-dhâiḥ.* 50 O. *-prad-.* 51 G. M. *nâ.* 52 W. B. O. *-rkaç.* 53 W. *-dhâiḥ.* (54) B. *sâṅgopâṅgavedasvalakshaṇam,* and put below, after *-varaṇe;* G. M. O. substitute *evaṁ sâṅgopâṅgaṁ vedaṁ gotrasvarûpâdijñânena* (G. M. *-di vijânann*) *adhiyânaḥ pûto bhavati.* [*yadṛchayâ:*
granthântare yathâtattvam (O. *yathâ tadvad*) *idaṁ çastraṁ* (G. M. ins. *yathâvidhi*) *asûtriteshu* (O. *sûcakeshu*) *sthâneshu pâurusheshu na* (O. om.) *vartate.*
tathâ hi: pra----: sa----: mahi----: api----: asmiṅs----: ityâdâu na (O. om. *na*) *vartate* (G. *prav-*)*: siṅhe----: dvâd-----: âtm-----: uçmasi----: ityâdâu tu vartate. gached âcâryasaṁsadaṁ iti vîpsâ çâstrasamâptiṁ* (O. *-traparisam-*) *dyotayati.* 55 B. *-ṅçatimo;* G. M. O. *dvitiyapraçne dvâdaço.*

Concluding Note.

It seems desirable to present here, at the end of the work, a discussion and exposition of certain points which could not be connectedly or fully treated in the notes upon the rules.

A first important question is that of the relation of the Prâtiçâkhya to the known text of the Black Yajur-Veda, or to the Tâittirîya-Sanhitâ.

In considering this question, it is impossible to separate entirely the Prâtiçâkhya itself from its commentary. The former does not quote passages in its rules, but defines situations or specifies words, singly or in combination. Sometimes, indeed, either of these virtually amounts to the citation of a passage; but, in the great majority of cases, only the commentator can inform us what are the passages had in view. For example, we may regard *eshtaḥ* (viii.18) as in effect a reference to i.2.11[1] and vi.2.2[6]; but the words cited in viii.8 (as *abibhar*, *akar*, *punar*, *pitar*) are indefinite in their indications, and it would be impossible to say that any given passage in the Sanhitâ in which one of these words occurs either was or was not contemplated by the makers of the rule. I shall therefore present in connection with one another the evidence derivable from the text itself and that from the comment.

There are four words or parts of words specified in the Prâtiçâkhya-text which are not to be found in the Tâittirîya-Sanhitâ: they are *stanutar* (viii.8), *carshan* (xiii.13), *jîgivâ* (xvi.13), and *jighâsi* (xvi.18). It is very remarkable, however, that each of these is a kind of reflex or varied repetition of another word preceding it in the same rule: thus, we have *sanuta stanutaḥ*, *carman carshan*, *jigivâ jîgivâ*, and *jigâsi jighâsi*. And this, taken in connection with the fact that all of them appear to be in themselves ungenuine, never having been found, so far as I am aware, in any Vedic text, and being, at least in part, impossible or highly implausible forms, is sufficient to stamp them as probable corruptions, blundering intrusions into the Prâtiçâkhya, and of no force to prove that the latter was made for a text that contained them.

The cases are much more numerous in which the commentator declares the Prâtiçâkhya to have in contemplation phrases not to be found in the Sanhitâ. They are nearly all of this kind: in iv. 11, *viçâkhe* is declared *pragraha;* now the word is divided in *pada*-text, *vi-çâkhe*, and *çâkhe* is by itself a *pada* (according to i. 48); and therefore, unless there were some other *çâkhe* not a *pragraha* in the Sanhitâ, it would be enough to cite *çâkhe* alone in the rule; hence, as the citation of *bhâgadhe* (p. *bhâga-dhe*) just before implies that the maker of the rule had in view such a word as *uda-dhe*, whose *dhe* was not *pragraha*, so the citation of *viçâkhe* is declared to have in view such a word as *sahasra-çâkhe*, not a *pragraha*, "in another text." The phrases thus quoted from outside the Sanhitâ by the commentator are as follows: under iv.11, *tas-*

mint sahasraçâkhe, *ûrdhve çastre pratishṭhite*, *brahmasâme pratishṭhite*, *agnidhṛte*, and *prathamaje;* under iv.12, *paçuçrapaṇî* (or *bhasmaçrapaṇî*); under iv.15, *tam* (or *tâm*) *âhurî hvayante* (or *vâcayati*), *hûti punar* (or *manur*) *juhoti*, and *hutî tasmâd vivâḥ* (or *evâḥ*); under iv.37, *indrâgnî havâmahe;* under vi.5, *pramatis te devânâm;* under xi.3, as beginning of an *anuvâka*, *dhâtâ devebhyo 'surân;* under xi.16, *gayasphâno 'gnishu.* All this, in my view, is false and arbitrary interpretation; the Prâtiçâkhya is less careful to limit itself to the *minimum citabile* than the commentator would fain have it, and it quotes, for example, the whole word *viçâkhe* instead of *-çâkhe* alone, simply because *çâkhe* occurs as *pragraha* only in that word.* The same implication is appealed to by the commentator under xi.9,15, xii.3, xvi.12 (though without actual citation of phrases), to explain away what would otherwise be inaccuracies in the Prâtiçâkhya; *nalam plavam* is given under xiii.16, in the course of the unjustifiable exposition of that rule; and *brahmâsn*, though found in the Sanhitâ, is credited under xv. 8 to another *çâkhâ.* I do not regard anything in this whole class of cases as authorizing us to suppose that the Prâtiçâkhya had in view a text including anything not found in the Tâittirîya-Sanhitâ.

Next, as to citations made in the commentary as if from the text to which the Prâtiçâkhya relates, but not found in the Sanhitâ. And here I have first to report a few phrases which are among those occurring only in the manuscripts that came last to my hands, and which escaped my notice when preparing for my last search through the Sanhitâ, so that I have not looked for them (not having had the courage to undertake the long and tedious quest through the Sanhitâ a fourth time for so little). They are *achâvâkah* (xiv.5), *uccâ ratnam ayajanta* (ii.49), *tasmâd varûpam* (xx.3), *dârçyañ hi* (xxi.16), *naç cid ati* (xiv.10), *prâçnâti* (xiv.9), and *bṛhaspati sûrapate* (xiv.10). Respecting several of these, it is doubtful whether they are not mere corruptions of phrases actually found and referred. Then there is *kaviçastaḥ* (xvi.2), instead of which, by an error, I sought and found *kaviçastâḥ.* There remain, of quotations hunted for but not discovered, the following: *adya vasu vasatî 'tî 'ndram eva* (x.10: O. only), *anv enam mâtâ* (xx.1: Weber refers me for this to Çânkh. vi.17.2 [?], Âcval. iii.3; also Âit. Brâh. ii.6), *ahorâtre pârçve* (viii.7: only W. and [?] O.: found in Tâitt. Âr. iii.13.2), *uta çravasâ pṛthivîm mitrasya* (v.12: only G. M.), *upârchaty uskandâya* (x.9: only G. M.), *caturhotâ* (ii.25: Tâitt. Br. ii.2.3[2]), *brahmâudanam pacati* (x.7: Tâitt. Br. i.1.9[3]), *yaç chandasâm* (xiv.10: O. only), *yâ prâcî dik* (iv.33: W. B. O.), *varshâbhyaḥ* (xiv.16: but I am not certain that I did not satisfy myself with *varshyâbhyaḥ* and omit to search for this), *varshyebhiḥ* (xiv.16: O. only, and it reads *varshebhiḥ*),

* The quotation of *dhâtâ râtiḥ* (xi.3), to be sure, is more out of the way, and only to be explained as irregularly pleonastic, like that of *iyam eva sâ yâ* (xi.3), into which the commentator, with equal arbitrariness, tries to interpret a very different meaning.

çitikanṭhâya svâhâ (xiii.11: only G. M.), and *sa naḥ parshat* (xxiii.17: Rig-V. i.99.1 et al.).

Along with these may properly be reported the few phrases which are quoted by the comment, confessedly or impliedly from outside the text contemplated by the Prâtiçâkhya. Thus, we have under xviii.1 the beginning and concluding words of the Tâittirîya-Brâhmaṇa and the Tâittirîya-Âraṇyaka (that is to say, of the latter, the concluding words, *âi 'va tapati*, of the fifth *prapâṭhaka*, with which, accordingly, to the apprehension of our commentator, the whole treatise appears to have ended); under xxiv.6 are given (by G. M. O.) *dvâdaçâ 'gnishṭomasya stotrâṇi*, *pra nakshatrâya devâya*, *sa îm mamâda mahi karma kartave* (Tâitt. Br. ii.5.8[9] etc.), and *sin̄he vyâghra uta yâ pṛdâkâu* (Tâitt. Br. ii.7.7[1] etc.); in a quoted verse under xxi.6 is read *ṛtasya dhûrshadam* (Tâitt. Br. i.2.1[12] etc.); and the comment to xix.3 has *yo 'pâm pushpaṁ veda.*

Finally, we note that the comment gives, under xviii.1, a word, *bandhuḥ*, which ought to form the conclusion of the Sanhitâ, by its own count, but which is lost in the known manuscripts.

In all this, again, there is no satisfactory evidence that the Sanhitâ of the Prâtiçâkhya or its commentators was other than the one we know. The missing citations are in part found in a minority of the MSS.; in part, they are perhaps corruptions; in part, they are likely to have been taken by an error of the quoter's recollection from some other Tâittirîya-text—and the remainder, if there be a remainder, is too scanty to prove anything.

When we come farther to inquire whether any part of the Tâittirîya-Sanhitâ as it exists was not before the authors of the Prâtiçâkhya, we seem to be brought to the same negative result. There are, to be sure, here and there points in the text which the rules do not cover, but we have reason only to wonder that in executing so immense and intricate a task as that undertaken by the Prâtiçâkhya there should have been so few oversights. These, so far as they have been discovered, have been pointed out in the notes; I recapitulate them here. The word *rakshâ* (p. *rakshâḥ*), at i.4.24, should have been exempted in some way from the operation of rule iii.8, which requires its *â* to be shortened when separated from the following word. *Devî*, at vi.1.7[7], is made *pragraha* by the strict letter of rule i.61 (see under i.59), though the passage in which it occurs is not one to which that rule was meant to apply. In the rehearsal of cases of elision or non-elision of initial *a* (chapters xi. and xii.), there are a couple of cases which the commentator is driven into attempting to provide for by forced and false interpretations of the rules (see under i.61 for *ye 'ntarikshe* at iv.5.11[2], and under xi.3 for *ye aparîshu* at i.4.33); and I have noted beside (under xii.8, at the end) only *so agniḥ* at v.2.3[3] as unaccounted for thus far (its companion case, *ûrdhvo asthât*, is read first in an *ukhya*-passage, at iv.2.1[4], as Prof. Weber has pointed out to me; and *so agniḥ* may yet find a like solution). And in the enumeration of cases of interior *n̄* (see under xvi.26), two compound words appear to have been overlooked, *svâdushan̄sadaḥ* (iv.6.6[3]) and *strîshan̄sâdam* (ii.5.1[5]).

I would repeat here, what I have already said, that my testing of the precise adaptation of the Prâtiçâkhya to the Sanhitâ is not absolute, since I possess neither an *index verborum* to the latter nor a *pada*-manuscript, and my results will probably admit of rectification in some points—but I trust not to any such extent as should invalidate the general conclusion.

This conclusion is, that the Prâtiçâkhya probably contemplates the same text, neither more nor less, as that which constitutes the Tâittirîya-Sanhitâ, the only *çâkhâ* left us (unless the Kâṭhaka be regarded as another) of the many which formerly represented the Black Yajur-Veda. The name Tâittirîya-Prâtiçâkhya, then, is both a convenient and a suitable one to be applied to the treatise.

If, however, this name be understood as implying that the text-book emanates directly from the Tâittirîya school, its propriety is much more questionable. Besides the numerous teachers and "holders of *çâkhâs*" referred to in the rules, whose names in some cases are related with those of traditional schools of the Black Yajus (see Weber's notes to the Caraṇavyûha, in his Indische Studien, iii.256 ff.), three schools are mentioned by name, those of the Mîmâṅsakas (v.41), Âhvârakas (xxiii.14), and Tâittirîyas (xxiii.15, 16). Now we do not expect the text-book of a school to name that school; its rules are those which apply "here," "with us," and only outsiders need specification; besides, the Tâittirîyas are represented as holding a doctrine which is not that of the treatise itself, although it is deemed of consequence enough to be set forth with a detail elsewhere unknown. We are far from fully comprehending as yet the origin, nature, and relations of the "schools" of Vedic study and their accepted texts or *çâkhâs*, or the causes which have preserved to us so few of the latter, and of the school-treatises or *prâtiçâkhyas;* but we must of course assume that there were various degrees of difference among the *çâkhâs*, and that some were only infinitesimally unlike some others. And it is perhaps possible to point out certain minor points, in which the orthoepical form of the Tâittirîya-text as recorded differs from that to be inferred from the Prâtiçâkhya.

Among these points we are not allowed to reckon the retention of *h* before surd gutturals and labials and before sibilants (against ix.2), nor of *n* before palatals (against v.24) and *l* (against v.25), nor the omission of *t* (required by v.33) between *ṭ* and *s*, nor of the various duplications and insertions and aspirations taught in chapter xiv., since these are matters on which we are to expect discordance between theory and practice. Nor would it be safe to make anything of the consistent and emphatic acceptance in the Sanhitâ of *anusvâra* as an alphabetic element, while the Prâtiçâkhya wavers (see under ii.30) between regarding it as such and as a mere affection of the preceding vowel. Of more consequence is the division of the sections or *anuvâkas* in the recorded text into fifties of words, or *kaṇḍikâs*, which causes the disappearance of more than one specialty of reading expressly prescribed in the treatise (e. g., of the *î* of *uçmasî*, at the end of i.3.6[1]: see under iii.

13). The retention of the final *v* of *av* and *âv* (from *o* and *âu*) before a vowel is also against the letter of rule x.19, and in accordance with a dissident opinion quoted in x.21. The *kampa* of a circumflex accent followed by a circumflex, consistently made in the Sanhitâ, is only mentioned in the Prâtiçâkhya (at xix.3) as taught by some authorities, nor is the form of the doctrine taught in full and clear accordance with the practice followed. And it is very questionable whether the prescription of nasalization of a final protracted *a* (xv.8) is not merely reported by the treatise as made by certain specified teachers. These are small matters, and few, and a degree of doubt, perhaps, hangs over them all; but they are worthy of notice, as being all that we have on which to found any discordance between the Sanhitâ of the manuscripts and that of the Prâtiçâkhya. While, on the other hand, the points of accordance, even in matters which are most specially characteristic of the Tâittirîya-text, are very numerous and important.*

Of course, the existence of other forms of the text besides the ordinary *saṁhitâ* is assumed by the Prâtiçâkhya. Such a work without a *pada*-text at least as its foundation would be a thing inconceivable. Our treatise does not give, as the others do (see add. note 1 to the Ath. Prât.), formal rules for the construction of any of the other texts; its nearest approach to doing so is in the third chapter, where (see note to iii.1) it teaches us what final or initial vowels, long in *saṁhitâ*, are to be shortened whenever the word in which they occur is thrown out of *sandhi* with its next neighbor—a form of statement which applies to *krama* and *jaṭâ* text as well as *pada*. The occurrence of such terms as *pada*, *nânâpada*, *iṅgya*, *avagraha*, implies also the familiar usages of the *pada*-text; and the employment of *iti* is directly alluded to in iv.4 and ix.20, and indirectly assumed in the use of *ârsha* in ix.21 and x.13. What were the limits to the use of *iti* in the *pada*-text held by the school from which the Prâtiçâkhya proceeded does not appear: its combination in the extant *pada* with the prepositions (thus *pré 'ti* for *pra*, *vî́ 'ti* for *vi*, and so on—and without restriction to the ten words which alone are allowed by the Prâtiçâkhya, at i.15, to count as prepositions) does not come to light anywhere either in the text or commentary. Nor does the treatise chance to show whether its *pada* treated the *iṅgyas* or separable compounds after the same manner as the extant Rik and Atharvan texts—writing simply *upa-âyavah*, for example—or as the extant *padas* of the Yajur-Veda (including that to the Tâittirîya-Sanhitâ) and the one assumed by the Atharva-Prâtiçâkhya (see note to Ath. Prât. iv.74)—writing *upâyava ity upa-âyavaḥ*. The commentator, however, accepts and follows the latter method. Reason has been

* I have pointed out under rule ii.25 that the peculiar Tâittirîya orthography of such words as *suvar*, *tanuvâ*, *aghniyâ* finds no occasion for mention in the Prâtiçâkhya; nor is the very strange change of a final labial in certain words to a guttural (as in *trishṭug indriye*, ii.4.11[2]; *trishtug yâjyâ*, ii.6.2[5]; *trishṭugbhiḥ*, v.1.4[5]) noticed anywhere; I presume (I have omitted to obtain distinct information upon the point) that in every such case the *pada*-text also has the guttural—which would take the whole matter out of the sphere of the Prâtiçâkhya.

found (under xx.3) for questioning whether in the *pada*-text belonging to the makers of the Prâtiçâkhya the peculiar rule followed by the known Tâittirîya *pada*-text as to the accentuation of its separable words was of force. The latter text is of a very peculiar, not to say an anomalous, character in many respects; in these it is supported by the Prâtiçâkhya, so far as the latter goes (I will instance as examples only the treatment of *yojâ* and *evâ*, and other cases noticed under iii.15, of *nîcâd*, v.8, and of *ekâikayâ*, v.19): whether it does not contain other peculiarities which are ignored by the Prâtiçâkhya, and which consequently prove it not to be the one which this presupposes, I cannot say; but, from an item or two of information received from Prof. Weber, I imagine that it does so. The question will, at any rate, be cleared up by the discussion of the Tâittirîya *pada*-text which Weber, as I rejoice to learn, intends to add to his transliterated edition of the Sanhitâ, now going through the press.

I attribute it only to a (very unusual) awkwardness of statement on the part of the Prâtiçâkhya, that it appears to leave a part of the words ending in an original *o* out of the category of *pragrahas* (see under iv.7), and so to deny them the right to be followed by *iti*, as they are in fact followed in the known *pada*-text.

The *krama*-text ("word-*krama*") appears to be mentioned in rules xxiii.20 and xxiv.5, and more unequivocally in xxiv.6 (all of them, however, of suspicious authenticity as original parts of the Prâtiçâkhya: see below); but it is only three times quoted in the comment (under vii.2, ix.17,20), and so makes but a small figure there as compared with the *jaṭâ*. Examples from the latter are given under iii.1, v.33, viii.8,12,16,35, ix.22, x.9,10,13, xi.9,16,17, xii. 7, xx.2, and sometimes in considerable number and at great length; and once (under xx.2), where the commentator has occasion to mention the various kinds of text, he specifies *saṁhitâ*, *pada*, and *jaṭâ*, ignoring the *krama* altogether. This seems strange, inasmuch as the *jaṭâ* is regarded* as a secondary form of *krama*, and founded upon it; but the simple explanation appears to be that the *krama* brings up no questions of *sandhi* which do not arise also in *saṁhitâ* and *pada*, and so needs no special attention where only methods of *sandhi* are taught; while the inversions of the *jaṭâ* bring new elements into contact, and so create new cases of combination which require to be settled. If we may trust the commentator's interpretation, rules viii.12,35 are given expressly for cases that arise only in *jaṭâ*-text; under viii.16, he commits an obviously false explanation in order to reach a *jaṭâ*-case; under v.33, he makes a *sandhi* which the Prâtiçâkhya certainly never intended, because it is required by the letter of the rule, in a case which the makers of the treatise had apparently overlooked; under xi.16,17, the *jaṭâ* is resorted to, apparently with reason, for counter-examples to justify the form of statement adopted in the rule. The weight of evidence, upon the whole, is decidedly in favor of

* See Dr. Thibaut's "Jaṭâpaṭala," Leipzig, 1870.

the assumption that the peculiar *jaṭā* combinations were had in view by those who constructed the Prâtiçâkhya—or, at least, by those who brought it into its present form. I would add, that it seems to me not unlikely that the term *vikrama* (in the sense of *kramavikṛti*) signifies the *jaṭā*-text in rules xxiii.20 and xxiv.5.

The names of the divisions of the Sanhitâ, *kâṇḍa*, *praçna* (not *prapâṭhaka*), and *anuvâka*, are found only in the commentary (see Index); respecting the absence of the subdivision of *anuvâkas* into *kaṇḍikâs* see above, p. 427 (also under viii.35 and xxiv.6, where this division is acknowledged by the commentator). But the Prâtiçâkhya itself gives names to certain parts of the Sanhitâ; which names, for the sake of convenience, I will put together here, with a reference to the rule under which the part designated by each is stated (for further details of their occurrence, see the Index): they are *agni* (iii.9), *ishṭi* (iv.52), *ukhya* (ix.20), *graha* (ix.20), *pṛshṭhya* (ix.20), *mahâpṛshṭhya* (xi.3), *yâjyâ* (iii.9), *rudra* (xi.3), *vâjapeya* (xi.3), *vikarsha* (xi.3), *viharya* (xi.3), and *hiraṇyavarṇîya* (ix.20).

A marked feature of the Prâtiçâkhya is its frequent citation of authorities by name. The list of names has been repeatedly put together by students of the Prâtiçâkhyas (in Weber's Indische Studien, iv.77–8, may be found notices respecting the historical and geographical indications derivable from them), but ought not to be omitted here also. It is as follows (including the cases of mention in the commentary, distinguished by an added *c*):

Âgniveçya, ix.4.
Âgniveçyâyana. xiv.32.
Âtreya, v.31. xvii.8.
Ukhya, viii.22. x.20. xvi.24
Uttamottarîya. viii.20.
Kâṇḍamâyana, ix.1, xv.7.8c.
Kâuṇḍinya, v.38, xviii.3,4c, xix.2; (*sthavira*). v.40c, xvii.4.5c.
Kâuhalîputra, v.40c, xvii.2: (Kâuhaleya, xix.4c, xxiii.17c).
Gâutama. v.38.
Pâushkarasâdi. v.37,38.40c, xiii.16. xiv.2.3c. xvii.6.
Plâkshâyaṇa, ix.6, xiv.11.17. xviii.5.
Plâkshi, v.38. ix.6. xiv.10,11c,17, xviii.5.
Bâḍabhîkâra. xiv.13.
Bhâradvâja. xvii.3: (Bharadvâja. v.40c).
Mâcâkîya (or Mâyikâya). x.22.
Vâtsapra, x.23.
Vâlmîki, v.36. ix.4, xviii.6.
Çânkhâyana. xv.7.8c.
Çâityâyana. v.40. xvii.1,3c.4c.7. xviii.2.
Sâṁkṛtya, viii.21, x.21. xvi.16.
Hârîta. xiv.18.19c.20c.21c,22c.

Of the three schools cited, the names have been already given (above, p. 427). And we have besides *âcâryâḥ* quoted in i.46; *eke âcâryâḥ* in v.30, ix.5, xiii.3, xiv.3,25; *eke* simply in i.47, ii.19, 27,47, v.39, viii.19, xi.19, xiv.33, xv.2,6, xviii.1. xix.3, xxi.13; *pûrve* in xv.9; and *sarve* in xviii.7.

The questions which all this array of authorities is called in to help settle may be classified as follows:

I. Matters of phonetic theory, with others of a general nature.

The nature of the tone of a circumflexed syllable, i.46–7; with this is combined an uncertainty of view of the Prâtiçâkhya itself, expressed in rules 44–5; there is nothing else like it in the treatise; perhaps we may best assume that rules 44–7 are a later intrusion. The mode of production of *anusvâra* and *svarabhakti*, ii.19. The quality of the *a*-element in *âi* and *âu*, ii.27. The phonetic character of *h* and *ḥ*, ii.47–8. The nature of the combination of *e* or *o* with (elided) *a*, xi.19. The occurrence of lingual *l*, xiii.16: this the comment vainly endeavors to make out an accepted doctrine of the Prâtiçâkhya. A denial of the enclitic circumflex, xiv. 32–3. Nasalization of final vowels, xv.6–8: the comment treats rule 8 as the direct teaching of the text-book. Accent of protracted vowels (?), xv.9. Corruption of the final theme-vowel of neuters in *as, is, us* in the nom. pl. before *ñ*, xvi.16. Utterance of *âi* final in a single case, xvi.24. Degrees of nasalization, xvii.1–5. Utterance of accents and alphabetic sounds generally, xvii.6–8. *Kampa* between two circumflex syllables, xix.3–5. Use of the term *yama* for the nasal counterparts, xxi.13. Utterance of the syllable *om*, xviii.1–7. *Yama*-tones held by certain schools, xxiii.14–19.

II. Matters of *sandhi* or euphonic combination.

1. The most important cases in this division are two or three in which the views of different authorities are reported without any clear expression by the treatise of the opinion held, or the rule to be followed, by its school. Thus, with regard to the combination of a final mute with an initial *h*, v.38–41; where, indeed, the view first stated, as that of certain specified teachers, is doubtless to be regarded as that of the Prâtiçâkhya, notwithstanding the equivocal way in which it is put forward. Again, at ix.1, the dropping of final *ḥ* before a sibilant followed by a surd mute must probably in like manner, though referred to the authority of a single teacher, be taken as a binding rule. And it is hard to believe that rule x. 19, prescribing the invariable omission of final *v*, was not meant to be modified by x.21. That the treatment of *anusvâra* as a distinct consonantal element is put by xv.2–3 upon certain dissidents, must not be looked at by itself alone; it stands connected with the general equivocal attitude assumed by the Prâtiçâkhya with reference to this vexed question in phonetics (see note to ii.30). Once more, the mode of duplication in groups beginning with *l* as reported in xiv.2–3, with reference to the authorities who teach it, seems to be acknowledged by a later rule (xiv.7) as binding: this interpretation, however, is not free from doubt.

2. In all other cases, the Prâtiçâkhya is liberal enough to record the opinions of respected authorities upon points as to which its own teachings are distinctly opposed to theirs. Thus, as to the treatment of *m* before *y* and *v*, v.30 and xiii.3 (the repeated mention of this shows it to be regarded as a view entitled to the most respectful consideration); the combination of *p* with *ç* and of *n* with *ç* before a consonant, v.36–7; the *sandhi* of *eshṭar* with *râyaḥ*, viii.19–22; the treatment of *ḥ* before an initial consonant, ix.4–6; the utterance or omission of final *y* and *v*, x.20–23; the insertion

of a surd mute between spirant and mute, xiv.10–11; aspiration of a mute before a sibilant, xiv.13; duplication in certain specified cases, xiv.17–22,25–8 (but the comment treats 28 as the direct prescription of the authors of the treatise); and *vikrama* accent after *pracaya*, xix.2.

Thus it is evident that, while this arraying of discordant opinions is a quite distinctive and a very interesting feature of our Prâtiçâkhya, it does not, except to a very limited extent, detract from the character of the latter as a consistent and positive record of the views of a school of Vedic study. Nor is it fairly to be brought into any relation to the peculiar character of the Black Yajur-Veda, as a text of which the constituent parts had been gathered together more miscellaneously, and less fully fused into conformity, than the other Vedic texts. No text could be so definitely constructed, and be made the object of so thorough and systematic study as the setting up of a text-book like the Prâtiçâkhya evinces, without assuming an established character, and being as authoritatively handed down and as accurately learned as any Vedic text.

It is by no means improbable that a part of these citations of authorities have been interpolated in the Prâtiçâkhya after the latter ceased to be a mere body of practical rules for the guidance of a school, and, in virtue of its thoroughness and comprehensiveness, gained more the character of a phonetic "treatise" on the Black Yajur-Veda, and was used in other schools than that which originated it. The commentator (as will be pointed out below) uses the citations as a cover under which to put upon the treatise certain doctrines which do not properly belong to it; and in other hands it may have undergone a like distortion in other directions.

Accretions of other kinds to the original text of the Prâtiçâkhya are plausibly to be presumed in various places. All the metrical rules (namely xvii.8, xxii.14,15, xxiii.2,14–15,20, xxiv.5,6) are to be set down without much question as unauthentic; they are proved such by their character not less than by their form; and several of them are found in other parts of the Prâtiçâkhya literature. We may include in the same category, indeed, with considerable show of reason, the seventeenth and eighteenth chapters, and all that follows the twenty-first, on the score of content alone: a part of their matter is inferior repetition of what had been given before; a part deals with subjects, and in a style, unsuited to a Prâtiçâkhya. That there is room at least to suspect the intrusion of rules in other parts of the work has been pointed out here and there in the notes: at this place, I will merely refer to certain rules which are put in strangely out of place, interrupting the natural connection of passages: such are i.25–7,60, vii.13,14, xiv.12–3, xv.6–9, xvi.24, xxii.3–8; of these, only vii.13,14 are indispensable parts of a treatise like the present.

Another notable characteristic of our Prâtiçâkhya is its sparing use of technical terms belonging to general grammar, consequent upon its refusal to deal with words or classes of words according to their grammatical character, its laborious definition of its subject-matter in the Sanhitâ by position and surroundings merely. There are but two cases of its departure from this method: namely, its use of *alopa* at xiii.15, and of *saṁkhyâsu* at xvi.25; and in neither one is its success precisely of a character to make us wish it had gone farther in the same direction. This peculiarity renders impossible any profitable comparison of its phraseology with that of other grammatical works.

The general character of the Prâtiçâkhya is that of an earnest, sensible, consistent treatise, thoroughly worked out and dealing with its proper task with completeness and accuracy, and confining itself quite strictly to that task. There is no labored feebleness and artificial obscurity, as in parts of the Vâjasaneyi-Prâtiçâkhya, nor any inclusion of matters pertaining to general grammar, as in the Atharva-Prâtiçâkhya. It has its minor inaccuracies and inconsistencies, its obscurities of *anuvṛtti* inseparable from the *sûtra*-style, and its rules that seem to defy interpretation: but these are inconspicuous blemishes; no one of the other works of its class is more thoroughly respectable throughout.

Turning, now, to the more special consideration of the commentary, we have to note, as the most important point, a break of continuity between it and the Prâtiçâkhya. The commentator is not the recipient of a certain tradition, that gives him surely and precisely the import of the rules which he has to expound; the text-book has come down to him as something authoritative and sacred, indeed, yet in some points obscure, so that he is in doubt as to what it means; in others imperfect, so that it needs emendation; in others not in accordance with the views held by him and his school respecting the text, so that these have to be interpreted into it.

Thus, in the first place, the instances are frequent in which, to his own interpretation of a rule, he adds a different view held by other interpreters: either without naming them (as under i.19,21, xiii.16, xiv.5,11, xvii.5, xxiii.7), or referring to one of his special sources and predecessors (as under ii.19,33), or setting off against one another the views of two of these, Vararuci and Mâhisheya (as under ii.14, iv.40, viii.19,20,22, xviii.7). In a large proportion of the instances, it is true, the difference of opinion is upon some utterly trivial point, turning on the interpretation of a *tu* or the like, and only illustrating the hair-splitting tendencies of the native exegetes; but in some cases it is of more consequence, and once goes so far as to question (under viii.20) whether an authority referred to is Uttamottarîya or Dvâvuttamottarîya. Again, where a rule is really obscure, the commentator has sometimes, palpably, nothing more than guesses to give at its meaning, and ventures two or three of them (as under ii.2, xiv.22, xv.9, xix.5, xxiii.17), among which it would be hard to choose the least acceptable; or, if he gives but one (as under xi.19, xviii.4, xxiii.18,19), it is no less unsatisfactory. There are yet other cases in which what seems to be the evident meaning of a rule is misapprehended and distorted, without reason (as under ii.52, iv.4, v.29, vii.11, xix.3). Occasionally, false interpretations, of every degree of violence, are committed, for the purpose either of correcting an oversight or inaccuracy of the Prâtiçâkhya (as under i.61, iii.1, viii.16, xi.3, xvi.26), or else of imposing upon the latter a doctrine which it was not intended to teach, but which is held by the commentator and his school (as under i.58, xiii.4, xxi.14,16). For this last purpose, too, advantage is sometimes taken of the citations of varying opinions so liberally made in the rules; the *dictum* of the quoted authority is declared to be approved in usage, or is even imposed upon the Prâtiçâkhya, to the setting aside of what the latter really prescribes. Thus, Pâushkarasâdi's doctrine of the conversion of *l* to *d* (xiii.16), which belongs neither to the Prâtiçâkhya nor to the Sanhitâ, is accepted; and the duplication of consonant-groups beginning with *l* which is ascribed (xiv.3) to certain unspecified teachers; and Plâkshi's mode of treatment of a spirant before a first mute (xiv.17), which has as further result a misinterpretation of xxi.16; and a part of rule xiv. 26, respecting the duplication of *l;* and rule xiv.28, to which a strange interpretation is given, prepared for by a yet stranger one of xiii.4; and rules xv.2,3, which require *anusvâra* instead of nasalization of a vowel; and the nasalization of a final protracted *a* (xv.8); and two rules (xviii.1,6) from among those which concern the utterance of *oṁ;* and rule x.21, as to the retention of final *v*, is given the preference over 19, which requires its omission; and the first rule (v.38) as to the combination of initial *h* with a preceding mute is ratified; and, in the variety of opinions respecting the circumflex tone, one (i.46) is selected for approval. In the few cases where the commentator does not express himself as to whether a rule is *ishṭa* or *anishṭa* (they are ii.19,27,47–8, xi.19, xix.2, xxi.13, xxiii.14–9), there may be question whether he means to have it regarded as approved, or thinks the matter of no consequence either way. There remain the majority of cases, in which he stands by the Prâtiçâkhya, rejecting the intruded doctrine (for further details, refer to the words *ishṭa* and *anishṭa* in the Sanskrit index).

Besides these more serious cases of misapprehension or intended modification of the teachings of his text-book, the commentator is not free from the ordinary and characteristic weaknesses of his craft in India: from feeble and puerile expositions, from attempts to find a wonderful pregnancy of meaning in some innocent particle or unintended difference of expression, from groundless etymologies, and the like; to these attention has been directed in the notes, and they are not of consequence enough to be recapitulated here.

For determining the personality of the commentator we have no data whatever, and for his place and period we have only the references to other authorities, which, though too few and indefinite to yield any statable result, need to be put together in this note. The three earlier commentators on whom the work is avowedly founded—namely, Vararuci, Mâhisheya, and Âtreya—are repeatedly appealed to, especially (as has been pointed out above) in the settlement of difficult or controverted points (for the details, see index). Vararuci is a name very common in grammatical literature; to identify our commentator with any other of the various individuals who have worn it would doubtless be daring in the extreme. Nor does Âtreya, probably, stand in any definable relation to the grammarian of that name who is (see p. 430) twice quoted in the Prâtiçâkhya itself. From Pâṇini, rules are directly quoted under ii.12, iii.9, v.1, xiii.16, xiv.4, xxiv.3; and the *pâṇinîyâḥ* or the *vyâkaraṇa* are farther referred to under i.15,53,57, ii. 47, xviii.1. Pâṇinean terms are, further, *nañ*, i.60, x.22, *ṇic*, ii.17, *hal*, ix.24, *yar*, xiv.4, and *lyap*, xxi.14. The Mahâbhâshya is professedly quoted under ii.7, v.2; but the passage given is actually from Kâiyyaṭa's gloss. A definition is taken from the Amarakoça under i.1. Kâuhaleya is quoted under xix.4, xxiii.17; and the Kâlanirṇaya under xviii.1. The Brâhmaṇa of the Vâjasaneyins is referred to under xiv.33, and extracts from the Mahâbhârata and various Purâṇas are set forth under xxiv.6.

But the authority most often appealed to is the "Çikshâ," by which the commentator intends a very different work from the *pâṇinîya* Çikshâ, and one much more comprehensive. He takes extracts from it, of a verse, or part of a verse, or more than one verse, under i.1 (three times), ii.2, xiv.5,28, xix.3, xx.12, xxi.1,15, xxii.13, xxiii.10,17. Among these extracts are (under i.1, ii.2, xxi.1, xxiii.10) several passages which are found also in the *pâṇinîya* Çikshâ; and among the metrical extracts which are now and then given without specifying their source (under xiv.23,26,28, xix.3, xxi.1,6,15, xxiii.17,19, xxiv.6) are likewise one or two (under xxiii. 17,19) which occur in the same treatise. That the commentator is inclined to regard his Çikshâ as of higher authority than the Prâtiçâkhya itself was pointed out under xx.12; that it was a work specially appertaining to the Tâittirîya-Sanhitâ may be inferred with probability from the words which it cites (under xxi.15) in illustration of the varieties of *svarabhakti*.

ANALYSIS.

I. Explanatory: terms and their use, interpretation of rules, etc.

1. *Terms and their use:*

kâra forms names of letters, xxii.4; of vowels, i.16; of consonants, i.17; exceptions, i.18.—*varṇa* forms names of letters, xxii.4; includes short, long, and protracted vowels, i.20.—*epha* forms name of *r*, i.19.—*varga*, with first mute, forms name of series, i.27.—*a* forms name of consonant, i.21; of a cited word, i.22.—*apṛkta*, a *pada* of a single letter, i.54.—*avagraha*, first member of a separable word, i.49.—*lopa*, loss, i.57.—*upasarga*, 'preposition,' includes what words, i.15.—offices of *ca*, *api*, *tu*, *atha*, *eva*, *vâ*. *na*, xxii.5–8.

2. *Interpretation of rules and forms, etc.:*

an increment, or word having euphonic change or elision, put in nominative, i.23; or in its text-form, i.24.—product of euphonic change put in accusative, i.28.—next element, or more, taken in case of doubt, i.25,26.—a cited *pada* means that *pada* only, i.50; but applies to it even when euphonically altered, or preceded by *a* or *an*, i.51–3.—rules for a specified passage apply only there, and peremptorily, i.59; but a series of three or more words, if repeated, reads as the first time, i.61.—*pûrva*, 'preceding,' and *uttara*, 'following,' designate a word only under the specified circumstances, i.29,30.—continued implication is of what stood last, i.58.—words to be combined, and rules to be applied, in their order, v.3.—a separable word treated as two words, except in enumeration, i.48.—an *apṛkta* treated as initial and as final, i.55.—elision and euphonic alteration affect single letters only, i.56; after elision of *y* or *v*, no farther combination made, x.25.—in *pragrahas*, and in enumeration of words containing *anusvâra*, a cause in another word maintains its force, i.60.

II Phonetic: enumeration, classification, description of alphabetic sounds, quantity, accent, etc.

1. *Enumeration and classification of alphabetic sounds:*

nine simple vowels [*a*, *â*, *â*3. *i*, *î*, *i*3, *u*. *û*, *û*3], i.2; sixteen vowels [the above, with *ṛ*, *ṝ*, *ḷ*. *e*, *âi*. *o*. *âu*], i.5; the rest consonants, i.6.—mutes, i.7; in five series, i.10; called "first" etc., i.11.—semivowels [*y*. *r*, *l*. *v*], i.8.—spirants [*χ*, *ç*, *sh*, *s*, *φ*, *h*], i.9.—surd consonants, i.12; *h*, i.13; sonants. i.14.

2. *Mode of formation of alphabetic sounds:*

general mode of production of articulate sounds, ii.2,3,7, xvii.7,8, xxii.1,2, xxiii. 2,3.—difference of surds, sonants, and *h*, ii.4–6.—mode of utterance of vowels, in general, ii.4,8,31,32; in particular, of *a*, *â*, ii.12; of *i*, *î*, ii.20–22; of *u*, *û*, ii.20,24,25; of *ṛ*, *ṝ*, *ḷ*, ii.18; of *e*, ii.15–17,23; of *âi*. ii.26–8; of *o*, ii.13,14; of *âu*, ii.26,27,29.—similar vowels, i.3,4—mode of utterance of consonants, in general, ii.33.34; of sonants, ii.8; of surds. ii.10,11; of *h* and sonant aspirates, ii.6,9; of nasality, ii.52; difference of nasal quality in different nasal sounds. xvii.1–4; of nasal mutes, ii.30.—mode of utterance of consonants in particular: of *k*-series, ii.35; of *c*-series, ii.36; of *ṭ*-series, ii.37; of *t*-series, ii. 38; of *p*-series, ii.39; of *y*, ii.40; of *r*. ii.41; of *l*, ii.42; of *v*, ii.43; of spirants, ii.44,45; of *h*. ii.6,9,46,47; of *visarjaniya*, ii.46,48; of *anusvára*, ii.19, 30; of *násikyas* (*yamas* etc.), ii.49–51; of *svarabhakti*, ii.19.

3. *Quantity*.

quantity of short and long vowels, i.31–3,35; of protracted vowels, i.36; of consonants, i.37; of *anusvára* (or nasalized vowel), i.34, xvii.5; of syllables ("heavy" and "light"), xxii.14,15; of pauses and hiatus, xxii.13; of *om*, xviii.1.

4. *Accent:*

general character of accents: acute, i.38, xxii.9; grave, i.39, xxii.10; circumflex, i.40–47, xvii.6.—varieties of independent circumflex: *nitya* or original, xx.2; its quality, xx.9: *kshâipra*. xx.1; its occurrence, x.16: its quality, xx. 9: *abhinihata*, xx.4; its occurrence, xii.9; its quality, xx.10: *praçlishṭa*, xx. 5; its occurrence, x.17; its quality, xx.11.—enclitic circumflex: its occurrence, xiv.29–33; its varieties: *prátihata*, xx.3; its quality, xx.11: *pádavṛtta*, xx.6; its quality, xx.12: *táirovyañjana*, xx.7; its quality, xx.12.—*pracaya* accent, xxi.10,11.—*vikrama*, xix.1,2; its quality, xvii.6.—*kampa*, between two circumflexes, xix.3–5.—accent resulting from combination of two syllables into one, x.10,12,16,17, xii.9–11.—accent of *om*, xviii.2,3,5–7.—accent of protracted vowel (?), xv.9.

5. *Syllabication:*

division of syllables, xxi.1–9.

6. *Mode and tones of uṭterance:*

general mode of utterance, xxiii.20; the three *sthânas* or qualities, xxii.11; the seven do., xxiii.4–10; the twenty-one *yamas* or tones, xxii.12, xxiii.11–19. —tone of *om*, xviii.4.

III. Sandhi or euphonic combination:

introductory, v.1–3; four kinds of combination, xxiv.1–4.

1. *Final vowels:*

final vowels not liable to combination, *pragrahas*, iv.1–54, x.24; special cases of uncombinable finals, x.13,18; protracted finals, x.24; their nasalization, xv.7,8.—nasalization of final vowels, xv.6.—the particle *u*, ix.16,17.—lengthening of final *a*, iii.2–6,8–12; of final *i* and *u*, iii.7,13,14.

combination of simple final vowels: with similar initial, x.2; of final *a* with initial vowels, x.4–9; exceptions, x.13; lost in certain cases before *e* or *o*, x. 14; *i*, *î*, *u*, final, x.15, ix.17; exceptions, ix.16, x.18.—combination of final diphthongs, ix.11,12,14,15; *e* and *o* with initial *a* (see also Initial vowels), ix.13; treatment of the resulting *y* and *v*, x.19–23; after their loss, no further combination, x.25.

accent resulting from combinations of final vowels, x.10,12,16,17, xx.1,5,9,11; resulting nasalization, x.11.

2. *Initial vowels:*

initial vowel lengthened, iii.15.—loss of *a* after final *e* or *o*, ix.13, xi.1; detail of cases of loss, and exceptions. xi.2–19, xii.1–8; resulting accent, xii.9-11, xx.4,10.—*ṛ* to *ar* in special case, v.9.

3. ***Final consonants:***

surd to nasal before nasal, viii.2; to sonant before all other sonant letters, viii.3; and. in a special case, before *m*, viii.4; to aspirate before spirant, xiv. 12,13.

visarjaniya to spirant before surds, ix.2–6; except before *ksh*. ix.3; to *sh* before *t*, in certain cases, vi.5.—omitted before spirant and surd mute, ix.1; also in *sa* etc., v.15–17; also before *r*, viii.7.16,17; special case before *r*, viii.18–22.—changed to *r*, viii.6; do. after *a* and *á*, viii.8–15; exceptional cases, v.10.—changed to *s* or *sh* before *k*, *kh*, *p*, in compound words, viii.23; do. in independent words, viii.24–35; exceptions, viii.32,33.—*aḥ* final to *o*, before *a* and sonants, ix.7,8; special exception, viii.18–22; before other vowels, ix.10; *áḥ* final, ix.9,10.

final mutes: *ṅ* doubled before vowel, ix.18; *ṅ* before *s*, *sh*, v.32.—*ṭ* before *s*, *sh*, v.33.—*t* before palatals, v.22,23; before *l*, v.25; before *ç*, v.22.—*n* before palatals, v.20,21,24,37, xv.1–3; before *t*, vi.14, xv.1–3; before *l*, v.25,26, 31, xv.1–3; before *ç*, v.24; before *s*, *sh*, v.33; changed to *r* or *y* [i. e. to *anusvâra*, xv.1–3]. ix.20–24; doubled before vowel, ix.19.—*m* before mutes and semivowels, v.27–31, xiii.3; before spirants and *r*, xiii.1.2. xv.1–3; unchanged before *rá*, xiii.4; special case of loss, v.18.

4. *Initial consonants:*

ç to *ch*. v.34–7.—*s* to *sh*, in words independent or compound, v.10. vi.1,2,4.6–13.—*t* to *ṭ*. vii.13.—*h* after a mute, v.38–41.—*n* to *ṇ*, vii.2,4.

elision of initial *m*, v.12; of *v*, v.13; of *s*, v.14.

5. *Interior consonants:*

t, *th* to *ṭ*, *ṭh*. vii.13,14.—*n* to *ṇ*. in same word with its cause, xiii.6–9,11,13–15; in other word, vii.3,5,6–12,15,16.—*s* to *sh*, vi.3.—*l* to *ḍ*, xiii.16.

6. *Abnormal insertions and elisions, duplication, etc.:*

insertion of *s* v.4–7; of *d*, v.8; of surd mute between sibilant and mute, xiv. 9–11; of nasal counterparts (*yamas* and *násikya*), xxi.12–14; of *svarabhakti*, xxi.15–16.

elision of initial *m*, *v*, *s*, see Initial consonants.—in composition of forms of *eka*, v.18,19.

duplication in consonant-groups, xiv.1–7,14–28; of initial *ch*, *kh*, *bh* in certain cases, xiv.8.

IV. Sundries:

enumeration and specification of cases of *ṇ*, otherwise than euphonic, in interior of words, xiii.9,10,12; of *anusvára*, do. do., xv.4,5, xxvi.2–31.

requirements in a scholar or teacher, xxiv.5,6.

INDEX OF CITATIONS

MADE IN THE COMMENTARY, FROM THE TÂITTIRÎYA-SANHITÂ.

THIS Index contains the references reported above in the body of the work, as made by the commentator to the fundamental text. If, however, a cited word or passage is reported as occurring more than once in the text, reference is given only to the first occurrence. It has been found impracticable to carry out any scheme of distinction of the value of the citations; and any one using the Index will have to turn back to the notes in order to determine whether a given passage is quoted merely as an example of some general class, or as one that was more or less probably had directly in view, as example or counter-example, by the makers of the treatise; whether it is a unique phrase, or one more than once repeated, or even a word of frequent occurrence—and so on.

TS. i.

1.1 i.21,33, ii.22, iii.1,3, ix.1, x.5,10,19, xiv.21, xvii.7, xviii.1,7, xx.3, xxi.7, xxii.13.
2 [1] xiii.2, xv.1, xxi.15; [2] x.2, xxiv.5.
3 iv.6, viii.8, xvi.27.
4 [1] viii.8.
5 [1] iv.44, ix.22, x.25, xi.16; [2] vi.11, xiii.7, xxiv.4.
7 [1] x.10.
8 vi.5, x.2,6, xi.8,16, xiv.1.
9 [1] vi.10, vii.14; [3] iii.15, v.2,21, x.13 *bis*, xi.16, xiv.12,13.
10 [1] vi.5, vii.14, xiv.10, xvi.2,27; [2] v.3, vi.4, xi.16; [3] ii.48, vii.13, ix.2, xvi.14.
11 [1] xiii.6.
12 iii.3, v.5, viii.8, xi.17, xiv.19.
13 [1] ii.20, ix.22 *bis*; [2] xiii.10 *bis*, xvi.26; [3] iv.12, ix.9, xii.8, xxi.12.
14 [1] i.61, iii.8,9,10; [2] viii.23, xi.3, xii.7; [3] i.61, xi.3, 9, xiii.16; [4] iii.12, v.17, vi.5 *bis*, vii.5,10, ix.22, x.10,25, xiii.3.
2.1 [1] ix.10, x.19,22,25, xi.8, xviii.7; [2] xi.18.
2 [1] iv.47, xiv.9; [1-2] iv.42; [2] xxi.3; [3] vi.12, x.2, 17.
3 [1] xi.13 *bis*; [3] iii.5, xi.8.
4 [1] xi.3, xxi.3; [2] xi.3.
5 [1] xiv.29; xx.1,7.
6 xi.10,17, xiii.10, xvi.29, xxi.6.
7 iii.5, iv.9 *bis*, xiv.28.
8 [1] ix.21,22, x.10, xi.16,17; [2] i.56, v.10.
9 iii.2, viii.27,28.
10 [1] iii.8, ix.21; [2] iv.52.
11 [1] viii.8,18–22,29, x.14, xvi.29; [2] xi.16.

TS. i.

2.12 [1] xi.11,17; [2] xvi.27.
13 [1] iii.2, iv.34; [2] iii.7, iv.15,22,33, xvi.2; [3] iv.46, xi.17.
14 [1] iii.8, ix.20,23, xii.7, xvi.15,27; [2] i.48, ii.47, iv.28, v.8, vi.5, viii.24, x.16, xiii.15, xiv.6, xvi.13; [2-3] i.56, v.15; [3] v.17, vii.10, xvi.14; [4] xiv.10, xvi.13; [5] viii.8; [5-6] iii.8; [6] vii.11, xi.4, xvi.2; [7] vi.2, viii.24, xvi.25.
3.1 [1] i.61.
2 [1] vii.11; [2] iv.12, vii.11, xiv.28.
3 i.51,60, iii.1, vii.6 *ter*.
4 [1] viii.26; xi.13,16.
5 xiv.26.
6 [1] iv.42; [1-2] iii.13; [2] i.33, x.10; end'g xxiv.6.
7 [1] iii.8, iv.11,47, viii.16; [2] viii.9. xi.16.
8 [1] iii.8; [2] iii.2, ix.22.
9 [1] i.37, v.38 *bis*, viii.2, xiv.12,20 *bis*, xxi.3.
10 [1] xi.17; [2] xiii.14, xvi.23.
11 xi.17.
12 ix.21, xi.18.
13 [1-2] v.13; [2] iv.20, viii.9.
14 [1] i.61, iii.12, ix.23, xiv.23, xvi.17, xx.12; [2] iii.10; [2-3] vii.12; [3] x.15, xii.7; [4] i.61; [5] vii.9, viii.28,34, xii.5; [6] iii.5; [7] iv.6, xvi.14; [8] viii.31, ix.22
4.1 [1] iii.5, ix.20, xiii.15; [2] iv.38, vi.13.
2 viii.27.
3 viii.10.
4 xi.10.
9 v.27, xxi.12.
10 iv.42, vi.4.
11 xi.16, xvi.25.
13 xi.17.

TS. i.

4.14 ii.44, ix.4.
16 xvi.13.
18 iv.41, xi.16.
19 vi.7, ix.20.
20 xv.1, xvii.4.
22 iii.12, iv.4,12, xvi.13,29.
24 vi.5, xi.13.
25 xiii.9.
26 iv.42.
27 vi.7, viii.27.
30 iv.11.
33 i.55, iii.14, vi.5, xi.3.
36 viii.32.
41 ii.49, xiv.24.
42 vii.16, ix.20.
43 [1] i.61, xi.9; [2] xvi.26.
44 [1] vii.2, xi.3, xii.5,7, xiii.4, xxiv.5; [2] viii.3, ix.22, xii.7, xvi.13 *bis*.
45 [1] iii.2, vi.5; [2] viii.24, xiii.12, xxi.4; [3] ix.21, xi.7, xv.4.
46 [1] xii.8, xiv.30,31, xx.3; [2] xiii.15.
5.1 [1] v.28,30, xiv.23, xvii.2; [2] ix.19, x.10,13; [3] v.28,30, xx.7.
2 [1] ix.20, xiv.23; [3] iv.16; [3-4] iv.15; [5] x.10.
3 [1] ii.48; [2] xiv.18; [3] iii.8, ix.22.
4 [3] xx.8; [4] v.28,31, xiv.28.
5 [1] i.33, xi.3 *bis*, xiv.9,19, 27; [3] xxii.13; [4] iii.4.
6 [1] x.10, xiv.23; [2] iii.8, viii.8; [3] iii.8, xi.13; [4] iii.5, v.32, xiv.5,12, 13, xxi.5.
7 [1] xi.18; [2] iv.38; [4] ii.49, v.15,37, xiv.24; [6] iii.5, vi.14, xvi.27.
8 [5] xi.16.
9 [1] ii.47, iv.33, xiv.1; [2] xiv.4, xvi.29; [3] ix.22; [4] vi.7, xiv.31, xvii.1; [6] x.9; [7] iv.11, v.20,24, viii.7, x.10.

TS. i.

5.10 [1]iv.17,38,42, xi.13,14, xx.8; [1-2]xi.16; [2]xi.16; [3]ix.22, xi.12; [4]ix.22.
11 [1]viii.33, xvi.2,19; [4]iii.2, xiii.14; [4-5]iii.14; [5]iii.10.
6.1 [1]ii.25.
2 [1]xi.11,17, xiv.32, xix.1, xxiv.5; [2]xi.16; [3]xvi.13.
3 [1]ix.21, xi.3, xiv.28; [3]xvi.19.
5 [1]vi.14, xi.16; [3]iii.7.
6 [3]xi.11; [4]ix.21 *quater*, 22, xi.16.
7 [1]iv.36, xxi.6; [3]v.13, x.16, xiv.11; [4]xi.16.
8 [1]xxi.15; [2]iv.49, v.18; [3]vii.3,11.
10 [2]iii.7; [3]xvi.15; [4]v.27, xiii.3, xvii.1; [5]x.8.
11 [1]vii.6; [2]vii.6; [4]xiii.9.
12 [1]iii.8, v.13, viii.24,32; [2]iii.12, xiii.12; [2-3]xii.7; [3]iii.10, iv.7, v.29, viii.15, x.22, xiii.4, xiv.4, xvi.21, xvii.5; [4]xii.5,11, xvi.29; [5]iii.10, ix.13, xii.8, xx.3; [6]ix.20,23, xii.7, xiii.12.
7.1 [1]ix.22; [2]iv.44; [4]xiv.9, 11, xxi.12,14.
2 [1]v.35, xv.7; [2]i.39, xvii.6, xix.2, xxiii.17, xxiv.5 *bis*; [4]v.13.
3 [3]iii.6, xxiv.5; [4]ix.21, xxiv.5.
4 [1]xiv.16 *bis*.
6 [7]vi.8.
7 [1]viii.27, xi.3; [2]viii.4, xi.3, xii.7 *bis*, xiv.23.
8 [1]xxi.5; [2]iv.20, xi.3, xii.4; [3]v.15, xii.7, xiii.12; [4]xvi.13 *bis*.
9 [1]i.30, viii.7,13,16; [2]viii.13,29, ix.22, xii.7.
10 [1]xiii.15; [2]xiv.27; [3]i.61, vi.4.
11 [1]v.25,31, ix.10.
12 [2]vi.2.
13 [1]iv.18, xiv.28; [3]iii.12; [5]vi.2, viii.8, xvii.4.
8.3 iii.14, vi.2, vii.2 *bis*.
4 [1]iii.12, vii.12, xv.6.
5 [1]iv.48, vii.16, ix.21, xiv.20, xvi.17; [2]ix.21, xiii.13.
6 [1]xii.11; [2]xiv.4.
7 [1]xiv 2, xx.2,8.
9 [1]xiii.15; [3]v.20, xv.1.
10 [3]iii.1,11, v.10, viii.13, xi.17.
11 vi.3, xiv.6.
12 [2]iv.11,13, xi.15 *bis*; [3]xiii.12.
13 [1]xiv 20; [2]iv.11; [2-3]xvi.29; [3]ix.1, x.10, xvi.29.

TS. i.

8.14 [2]iii.13, viii.24.
15 [2]vi.7, xvi.2.
16 [1]i.58, v.29, vi.4, xiii.4, xv.8; [2]i.58, ii.52, xv.8 *bis*, xvii.1.
18 xvi.13.
21 v.32, xi.17, xiv.12.
22 [1]vii.4; [3]iii.14; [5]xvi.14 *bis*.

TS. ii.

1.2 [1]iv.6, ix.7, xi.1, xii.9, xx.4,6,8; [2]iv.12; [3]ix.2,4,5,6, xiv.9,10,11, 15; [4]xiv.26, xxi.15; [5]vii.11, xiv.9 *bis*, 11 *bis*, xxi.14.
3 [1]xvii.2; [2]vi.12; [3]vi.12; [5]ix.2,6.
4 [7]iv.12,52.
5 [1]xi.7; [2]iv.14; [3]iii.7.
7 [2]v.25, xiv.23; [3]iii.4, viii.16; [7]xvi.21.
8 [1]xiv.21,26; [2]xiv.26, xx.2.
9 [2]xi.8; [3]iv.3,4,11,51.
10 [1]xvi.2.
11 [1]v.12, xiii.13; [2]iii.7; [3]iii.10; [4]iii.5, v.14, vi.5; [5]iv.40, ix.24, xiii.12, xvii.4; [6]iii.13, iv.10, v.12, xiii.15.
2.2 [1]v.9; [4]iii.7.
3 [3]ii.49.
4 [1]i.61; [5]ix.21; [7]xiv.15; [8]i.61, vi.13, xi.16.
5 [4]xiv.16, xxi.15; [5]iii 2; [6]xiv.5; [7]iv.40.
6 [1-2]iv.40; [5]xiii.12 *bis*.
7 [1]iii.5; [4]viii.15 *bis*, xi.4; [5]iv.52, xv.6.
8 [3]ix.1 *bis*; [6]v.32, ix.18.
9 [2]iv.2; [3-4]v.21; [7]iv.7, xv.6.
10 [2]i.43, iv.52.
11 [5]xix.3.
12 [1]viii.24, xiv.9,24,27; [4]v.38, xiv.20, xxi.3; [5]xii.7; [6]iii.7,12, vii.2,4; [7]iv.12; [8]iii.5, vii.2, viii.16, x.19,21,22, xv.6.
3.1 [3]ix.1, xvii.4.
2 [3]iv.53; [4]ii.44; [6]ix.4; [9]x.16.
3 [5]iv.53, xiii.13.
4 [1]xiii.14; [3]iv.52, vii.5.
5 [2]ix.10; [3]x.10, xvi.29, xx.2.
7 [4]ix.16.
8 [1]xiii.12; [2]iv.11.
9 [1]viii.26, xi.3.
10 [1]xx.3; [3]ii.48.
11 [4]iv.42, ix.11, x.22, xx.8, xxii.13; [5]viii.24.
12 [1]v.21.
13 [2]ii.44, xiv.9,10,11,15.
14 [1]iv.15; [3]v.17, xiii.9; [4]xii.7; [6]iv.34, v.8.

TS. ii.

4.1 [1]iii.7, v.24,33; [2]ix.19, xi.10, xxi.10; [4]xvi.13.
2 [2]ix.19; [3]vi.12, xiii.14, xvi.29.
3 [2]xx.4.
4 [1]xxii.13.
5 [1]v.2, vii.2, x.13,15.
6 [2]xiv.18.
7 [1]iii.5, viii.11; [2]viii.12, xi.16.
8 [2]iii.10 *bis*, 12.
9 [3]xvi.31.
10 [2]xiv.8,28; [3]iii.5, iv.24, ix.11, x.19, xxi.15.
11 [1]x.16; [2]vi.2; [4]vi.14; [6]iii.2, xiii.15.
12 [3]iv.6, vii.6, viii.8, ix.12, xv.6; [4]iii.9; [8]xv.7.
13 x.7, xiii.8, xiv.23.
14 [1]v.5, xii.8, xiv.11, xxi.14; [2]xii.7; [3]iii.8; [5]vi.2, viii.12.
5.1 [2]viii.8 *bis*; [3]ix.13, xi.1, xii.9, xx.4; [7]xiii.9.
2 [2]iv.2; [3]iv.53; [5]iv.28,29, 52, xvi.30.
3 [1]xvi.13; [6-7]xi.13; [7]vi.9, x.10, xvi.20.
4 [4]vii.2.
5 [2]iv.52, xiii.12; [3]x.4, xiv.7 *bis*; [4]xvi.11; [5]iv.11.
6 [1]iv.44; [3]ii.46, viii.8; [5]iv.42,44, x.24; [6]i.60, iv.11,44, xvi.11, xxiv.5.
7 [1]xxi.15; [1-2]xiv.16; [4]iv 33.
8 [3]xv.4; [5]xvi.13; [7]ii.14.
9 [1]ix.21, x.10 *bis*; [2]xvi.13, 26; [3]vi.14, ix 21, xiv.10; [6]ix.22.
10 [1]vi.14, xv.1, xvi.25.
11 [1-2]xvi.13.
12 [1]iv.52, vi.5, vii.13; [2]iii.3, xiv.28, xvi.13; [3]xvi.25; [4]v.2, x.13, xiv.33, xxiv.5; [5]vi.5, xii.8.
6.2 [1]iv.12,44, xiii.16; [2]ii.49, iv.30; [3-4]xix.2; [4]iv.53; [6]x.12.
3 [4]x.10; [5]iv.49.
5 [1]iv.25, x.10; [3]iv.25; [5]xiv.32, xix.1.
6 [1]xvi.13, xxiv.5; [2]viii.33; [3]iv.11, v.13, x.16.
7 [1]iv.39, viii.9; [3]iv.7, xv.8, xvii.2; [4]x.10; [5]iv.23.
8 [4]xvi.26.
9 [3]iv.44; [4]iii.7; [5]iv.29, ix.19, xiv.28; [8]viii.30.
10 [2]v.22, vii.3; [4]vi.7.
11 [1]iii.8,9, xiii.2, xx.8; [2]vi.2, xi.4, xiii.10, xvi.29; [3]iii.8, vii.2, viii.25, x.10, xiv.1; [4]iii.9, viii.24, xiii.2, xvi.20.

TS. iv.

5.9 [1] i.22, ix.3,5,6, xvi.26; [2] xiv.8.
10 [1] iv.7, xi.3; [2] iii.8, viii.26, xi.3; [3] iii.9; [4] iii.8, vi.5, vii.4; [5] xii.8; end'g xxiv.6.
11 [1] xi.17; [2] i.61, xi.16.
6.1 [1] vi.14, xi.3 *bis*, xii.8, xiv.9, xvii.2; [2] iii.14, xii.5; [3] xi.3, xii.7; [5] xvi.20 *bis*.
2 [1] xiv.8; [2] v.17; [4] iii.13, iv.38, vi.11; [5] viii.27, xvi.14; [6] iii.12.
3 [1] iii.8; [2] vii.9; [3] ix.21, 22; [4] ix.22.
4 [1] i.21, v.34, ix.3,4,5,6, xiii.15, xvi.26; [1-2] iii.12; [2] vi.12, ix.21, xii.8; [4] iii.10 *bis*, xvi.26.
5 [1] viii.24; [3] xii.6; [4] iii.10, ix.7; [6] xiii.9.
6 [1] ix.20, xi.3, xvii.3, xix.1; [1-2] x.13; [2] iv.20,21, v.2, vi.13 *bis*; [3] iii.7, 8, ix.20, xii.7, xiii.9, xvii.5; [4] iv.11, xi.3, xii.7 *bis*, xvi.20; [5] i.59, ix.20, xii.3,7; [6] v.17, x.10, xiv.27; [7] vi.4, xii.7.
7 [1] vii.8, ix.20, xi.3, xii.3; [3] iii.8, viii.8, xi.5 *ter*, xvi.13; [4] iv.38, xii.4, xvi.8; [5] iii.8, xvi.7.
8 [1] ix.8,20, xi.3, xiv.8; [2] xii.7, xvi.5; [3] xii.7.
9 [1] ix.20, xi.3, xvi.8; [2] iii.7; [3] iii.8,12, viii.32, xvi.5; [4] i.25, iii.14, iv.15 *bis*, v.4 *bis*, 38, viii.28, xii.7, xvi.13.
7.1 [1] xi.11.
2 [1] ii.44.
3 [1] v.20,27.
4 [1] xiv.15; [1-2] v.4, xiv.8; [2] xiii.12.
5 [1] iv.38, v.4, xiv.11, xxii.14, xxiv.5.
6 [1] viii.6, ix.2,6.
8 xiii.7.
9 [1] xxi.3.
10 [2] v.21.
12 [1] iii.10, xi.3 *bis*, xii.7 *bis*; [2] ix.22.
13 [1] iv.52, xvi.3; [2] iv.11, viii.25; [3] viii.33; [4] iii.12; [5] iii.6, iv.11, vi.14, xvi.13, xxiv.5.
14 [1] iii.3; [2] iii.12, xi.3, xii.7; [3] viii.8, xii.7.
15 [1] ix.20, xi.3, xiii.15, xvi.13; [2] iv.40, v.4; [3] iii.7, iv.52, xiv.23; [4] ix.23, xvii.1; [6] iii.10, iv.20 *bis*, 21, xvi.13,29; [7] iii.12,13, vi.2, xx.1.

TS. v.

1.1 [1] ix.20, xi.16; [2] v.18; [4] viii.33, ix.3, xiii.9 *bis*, xiv.26, xxi.12, xxiv.5.
2 [1] vii.8, x.9, xi.13, xviii.7; [3] xvi.13; [5] iii.6.
3 [1] i.61, xi.18; [3] i.61.
4 [1] xi.13,15; [4] iv.44.
5 [1] i.61, iv.25; [3-4] i.61; [4] iv.17,20; [5] xiv.16, xxi.16.
6 [3-4] iv.44,45; [4] vi.12,13, vii.16, ix.1.
7 [1] vi.2, xiii.13; [4] viii.8, xiv.8.
10 [1] x.10, xiii.7, xiv.4; [2-3] iv.52; [3] ii.49.
11 [1] vi.5, ix.7,13,20, xi.16; [2] iii.10, iv.20, vi.9, 13.
2.1 [7] i.21, iv.12, ix.3, xiv.15.
2 [5] xi.16,17.
3 [1] i.29; [2] xiv.18; [3-4] iii.5; [4] v.21,24; [5] iv.31; [6] iii.8.
4 [3] xvii.6.
5 [1] xvi.13; [2] xiii.9; [5] vi.12; [6] viii.8.
6 [2] vi.12; [3] vii.5,6.
7 [1] iv.25, xxi.8, xiv.9; [2] xvii.1,3, xxi.8; [3] ii.30, x.10, xiv.23; [4] iv.25,26; [5] iii.15, xiv.10, 11, xxi.9, xxiv.4.
8 [1] xiii.14; [5] xvii.1; [6] xxi.7; [7] xvi.2,13.
9 [1] xiv.11; [6] xvi.19.
10 [3] xvi.27; [6] xvii.3; [7] ix.21.
11 [1] ix.20, xiv.5,8 *bis*.
12 [1] ix.20; [2] xi.3,17.
3.1 [1] x.9; [2] xiv.28; [3] vi.12; [4] iv.50; [5] xvi.30 *bis*.
3 [1] vi.13; [3] xvi.25.
5 [2] iv.44,45; [3] vii.10; [4] x.14.
6 [1] vi.14; [2] x.18, xxiv.5; [3] vi.14, xiv.12.
7 [2] iv.42; [3] i.25, iv.11, 33.
8 [1] xvi.15; [3] xiv.8.
11 [1] xvi.13; [2] iii.5, vi.14; [3] x.16, xx.1,2.
12 [1] xx.7; [2] v.38, xi.17.
4.1 [1] iv.42; [4] xvi.14.
2 [2] v.38.
3 [3] vi.3, xiv.15; [4] xxi.9.
4 [1] vi.4; [4] iv.12, xxi.16.
6 [2] viii.29.
7 [3] iv.29; [7] xiii.9.
8 [5] i.31, iv.52, xiv.2,22.
9 [3] iv.11; [4] xi.5,6.
10 [2] xvi.14; [5] xvi.13.
11 [3] xxi.7.
12 [1] vi.5,14; [3] v.6.
5.1 [5] v.21; [7] xvi.16.
2 [4] v.17; [6] v.33, xiii.2.
3 [1] ix.21; [2] ix.18, xvii.2, xx.2,3, xxiv.5.

TS. v.

5.4 [1] ix.25 *bis*, ix.10; [2] iv.31; [4] iv.38, ix.16.
5 [1] xi.8,9; [2] vii.5,16, xvi.26; [3] xxi.2; [4] x.10, 17 *bis*, xvi.13, xx.5.
6 [1] iv.44; [2] iv.37
7 [1] iv.33; [3] viii.30, xi.5; [4] viii.23.
8 [1] x.18, xxiv.5.
9 [1] iv.11, xvi.26, xxi.10, xxiv.3,5; [2] i.22, ii.25 *bis*, 48, viii.2, xiv.23, xvi.26; [3] viii.16, xi.16,17.
10 [1] iv.32.
11 iv.39, xvi.26, xxi.8.
12 xvi.19.
15 iv.39, vii.13, xiii.12.
16 viii.17.
18 iv.28, ix.2.
19 viii.17, xiv.23.
20 iii.2.
21 x.4.
24 iv.12.
6.1 [1] iv.11, ix.20; [2] ii.47, iii.12, ix.15,20 *bis*, x.19, 21, xv.1, xvii.1,2, xx.2; [3] iii.15, vii.2, viii.8, xi.3,5; [5] vi.10.
2 [4] xi.18.
4 [1] iv.25 *bis*, xii.8, xvi.19; [4] xvi.27.
5 [3] ii.49, ix.19,21, xiii.12, xiv.24,27.
6 [1] v.22; [3] xi.17; [3-4] xvi.26; [4] v.6.
7 [3] xvi.8.
8 [1] xvi.2; [2] vi.12,13; [3] vi.13, xv.4; [4] iv.52; [6] iv.11.
9 [1] vii.3; [3] xiii.3.
12 iv.15.
14 x.14.
15 x.6.
21 i.59, iv.39,48 *bis*, xxi.8.
23 vi.12.
7.2 [1] vii.2; [3] vii.8, xi.17; [4] iii.10, xiv.11; [4-5] iv.7.
3 [1] vi.12, xi.13, xiv.9,17; [3] ii.25, iv.44, vi.14.
4 [2] x.12, xx.2,8; [3] iii.3; [4] xvi.22.
5 [2] vii.2; [7] iii.7
6 [2] viii.8, xiii.14; [6] vi.7.
7 [1] xi.16; [2] iv.11; [3] iii.15.
8 [1] xi.17.
9 [1] iv.7, ix.21,22,24, x.19, xi.9,16, xvii.1,6, xix.1, xx.2.
10 [1] xvii.1.
11 v.14, xiv.16, xxi.16.
12 i.22, v.37, x.14.
14 vi.7.
17 iii.7.
20 viii.13, x.12, xvi.8.
23 xiv.2,10, xvi.7,14,16.
26 ix.4, xx.8.

SANSKRIT INDEX.

The following Index contains the whole matter of the Prâtiçâkhya itself—both the proper vocabulary of the treatise, and the words and parts of words which it quotes from the Sanhitâ; the latter being distinguished by being printed with *spaced letters.* To this is added a very liberal selection from the vocabulary of the commentary; perhaps more liberal than may seem to some worth while, but I preferred to err in this direction rather than the contrary. The references to the commentary are designated by a prefixed *c;* and an added *v* indicates that the word is to be sought among the various readings given at the foot of the comment.

GENERAL INDEX.

The references by Roman and Arabic figures together are, as in the other Indexes, to chapter and rule; those by Arabic figures alone (with *p.* prefixed), to page of the volume.

ADDITIONS AND CORRECTIONS.

PART of these emendations are due to Prof. Weber, who has called my attention to them in private communications. A few slight misprints, of obvious character, are not noted here.

p. **2,** l. 25. The MS. used by Weber was another (No. 504) in the same collection, containing only the text (incomplete) of the Prâtiçâkhya.

p. **3,** l. 1. Dr. Rost's description of these MSS. has not yet appeared. It appears, however, that the rules of the Prâtiçâkhya are read interspersed in the commentary also, as well as prefixed to it in a body (with separate paging).

p. **3,** l. 4. The differences of reading in the Prâtiçâkhya text itself are more numerous than is here stated. They have been pointed out in the course of the work (either in the notes on the rules, or in the various readings to the comment)—namely, as occurring (with here and there an addition, omitted in its proper place) in i.61, ii.17,51, iv.11,39 (T. W. *ahne*, for *'hne*), v.13,20 (G. M. *çakâraç*, for *-raṁ:* a mere blunder), vii.8 (G. M. *yajush*, for *yajuḥ*), 12, viii.8 (T., it should be added, has dropped both *sanuta* and *stanuta*), 13,35, ix.21.22. x.11 (T. W. B. O. *anunâsikam*, for *'nun-*), 13 (G. M. *-pâ asiparo budhniyâ jyâ â pûshâ aminanta ârshe*, which is perhaps the more acceptable reading, since it gives the uncombinable finals their uncombinable quality in the rule also), 22, xi.16 (G. M. *adabdhâsa* and *ashâḍhaḥ*, with unelided *a*), 17 (G. M. *ahniyâ mâ "mbâli*), 18,19 (G. M. repeat the whole rule, instead of its last two words only), xii.4,9 (T. O. *asmin*, for *tas-*), xiii.4,13,14 (see farther on), 15, xiv.3,8 (G. M. *upasargaç ca pâtha:* a blunder only), 13,32, xvi.1,5 (G. M. *çaṅstân anant-:* a blunder), 7,13 (G. M. omit *pipivâ* in the rule, as well as its example in the comment; but they give the word in the rehearsal at the beginning of the comment), 16,19,22,26, xvii.2,4, xviii.5 (T. *svaritaç ca pl-*), xx.9 (G. M. substitute in the text-MS. rule xvii.6, except the word *pâushkarasâdeḥ*), xxi.5,6,14, xxii.7 (W. O. also have *-shakaḥ* in the rule, but not in the comment), xxiii.2,6,10,12,14,20, xxiv.4. The reading adopted for rule xiii.14 is that of T. G. M. (save that T. has *shṭha* for *shṇa*, and *râvṇṇa*, with *virâma* under the *v;* and G. M. have *râviṇṇa* in the text-MSS., and *rârâvṇṇa* in the MSS. with comment); W. gives *ṛṇṇ shaṇ shṭa mṇa râvṇ* (with *virâma* under both *v* and *n*); for O. the collator has noted nothing; B. reads *ṛṇ shaṇ'shṇa mṇa râvṇ grâvṇa.* Other evident copyists' errors occur, of too little account to be worth notice.

A reading has been adopted contrary to the authority of all the MSS. at ix.1,20 (where the MSS.-reading is *ikârâûkârap-*), xi.1,17. The writing of *iṅgya* for *iṅgya* was noted under i.48.

p. **9,** l. 16. The commentator, as will be seen under xxi.14, interprets out of existence the *nâsikya* as an independent element.

p. **11,** l. 7. The structure of *ṛ* is defined by the commentator under xxi.15.

p. **18,** l. 12. The commentator refers to some "different reading" (perhaps in his Çikshâ? there is no trace of it in the Prâtiçâkhya), beginning *pra parâ 'pa sam*, but declares it to have to do only with the addition to all these words of *iti* (in the *pada*-text, namely, which writes *e 'ti* for *â*, *ape 'ti* for *apa*, and so on) and not to their receiving the name *upasarga*. I still fail to see any reason for the limitation of the class to half its usual number.

p. **23,** l. 13. Dele the hyphen at the end of the line.

p. **33,** l. 16. One may conjecture that rule 43 formerly concluded the treatment of accent in this chapter, and applied to all the three kinds of accent; but, rules 44–7, on the circumflex, being later interpolated, the connection made it necessary to understand this also as applying to the circumflex alone.

p. **34,** rule 46. The same example (from iii.3.11 1) is quoted by the comment under this rule as under rules 43 and 47.

p. **37,** l. 19. Compare under rules xvi.26,29, where this claim is distinctly made. But it is not entirely well founded, for there are cases where combinations of sounds which are *padas* are quoted as *padâikadeças:* thus *han* in vii.11, *pâ* in xvi.2, *hi* in xvi.13, etc.

p. **42,** ll. 28,32,43, read iv.23 (for iv.25).

p. **46,** l. 3. Read (in part of the edition) *alteration* for *nasalization.*

p. **82,** last line. Restore (in part of the edition) the lost figure 6 before *na*, at the beginning of the line.

p. **83,** l. 2. The passage is found at iv.1.5 1.

p. **87,** rule 5. For *aghâ*, in rule and translation, read *adyâ;* and the example, on the next page, is *adyâçvâd* (p. *adya-çvât*). The St. Petersburg lexicon (in the Appendix) has this word in its proper form, but I unfortunately overlooked it.

p. **88,** l. 28, and p. **99,** l. 5. No division is made of *prâçṛṅga* in *pada*-text.

p. **96,** l. 28. Read *kaḥ* for *káḥ* (in part of the edition).

p. **101,** l. 20. I have little or no doubt that the interpretation here suggested is the true one.

p. **103,** l. 7 from below. *To* is not an independent word: see the St. Petersburg lexicon, s. v. *totaḥ.*

p. **104,** l. 24. So far as the vocatives in *o* are concerned. the existing *pada*-text appears to accord with the Prâtiçâkhya: we have them with *iti*, as *pragrahas*, for example, at i.3.8 1,14 7; 4.27, and without *iti* at i.2.13 2; 4.39. But *o, uto, upo*, and *pro* are followed by *iti* wherever they occur (for *to*, see the preceding correction), although this is not authorized by the Prâtiçâkhya.

p. **110,** l. 32. The *pada*-text divides *dyâvâ-pṛthivî.*

p. **121,** ll. 23,24. Read (in part of the edition) *áindrágni* and *indrágni.*

p. **123,** l. 18. Insert the omitted example *triṇi vratâ vidathe antar eshâm* (ii.1.11 5).

p. **124,** l. 12. Read (in part of the edition) *pâtam* for *patam.*

p. **132,** l. 15. But note the case reported under i.59 (p. 43).

p. **138,** l. 13. Read (in part of the edition) *nicâ* (for *nicâ*).

p. **153,** l. 27. I have omitted part of the passages in which *t* occurs before *sh*, namely vi.6.11 1,2: vii.2.8 7. It should have been added, too, that the Sanhitâ furnishes no example of *n* before *sh.*

p. **157,** l. 23. The citation is from vi.3.3 1, as under the two preceding rules.

p. **160,** l. 24. This is not correct, so far as the existing *pada*-text is concerned. I was not aware at the time of writing the note that that text treated the *avagraha*-pause as suspending the continuance of accentual influence (see p. 369, first marginal note). The application of the rule, however, is as stated, compound words having been already provided for by rule 2.

p. **167,** l. 14. The peculiarity of accentuation referred to in the preceding correction would allow of these examples being brought under rule 4.

p. **173,** l. 20. Read *-parâṇuttyâi.*

p. **176,** rule 11, translation. Read *havani.*

p. **179,** l. 12. The suggestion of *punarukti* here is not well-founded, the sphere of action of the rules in this and in the thirteenth chapter being different.

p. **183,** l. 10. *Ahorâtre pârçve* is found in Tâitt. Âraṇyaka, at iii.13.2.

p. **193,** ll. 9,10. References should have been given for the words *ahorâtrâbhyâm* and *ahorâtrayoḥ;* the former is found at ii.1.7 3 et al., the latter at vi.1.3 1. *Adhishavaṇe* occurs only at vi.2.11 4.

p. **194,** l. 14. The reference for *rukmo antar* is iv.1.10 4-5 et al.

p. **199,** l. 9 from below. The *pada*-text leaves *bṛhaspati'* undivided, so that the combination does not come within the ken of the treatise at all.

p. **199,** l. 13 from below. Read (in part of the edition) ii.1.5 7 for ii.1.57.

p. **205,** l. 14. The omission of *ḥ* before a spirant followed by a sonant consonant, here referred to as a doctrine held in schools of the Black Yajus, is practised in the manuscripts of our treatise and its commentary to a degree far beyond what can be regarded as merely accidental. G. M. observe it almost without exception, and it prevails also in the others.

p. **209,** rule 7. Doubtless *aḥsarvo* is to be understood here as an adjective, qualifying *visarjaniyaḥ* understood, '*ḥ* completed to *aḥ*,' as the comment clearly intends. This also removes the difficulty of *anuvṛtti* spoken of on pp. 210–11, so far as the implication of *visarjaniyaḥ* is concerned.

p. **216,** l. 2. Read *is* for *does.*

p. **218,** l. 5. The example *paçûn* etc. occurs first at i.5.2 1.

p. **222,** l. 12. Read (in part of the edition) *'gne 'vimân* (for *-mâñ*).

p. **224,** l. 4. Read *Also* for *Nor.*

p. **232**, l. 26. I have noted here all the cases in which the *samhitâ*-text shows *dhâ*, *mâ*, or *pâ* before *asi;* it appears, however, from Weber's edition of the Sanhitâ, that a part of them have *ḥ* in *pada*-text after the *â*.

p. **233**, l. 11 from below. Read (in part of the edition) *prape 've* (for *-pâ*).

p. **239**, l. 6. Read *o* for *a*.

p. **265**, l. 5. The combination *úrdhvo asthât* is in fact read first at iv.2.1[4], in an *ukhya*-passage.

p. **265**, l. 10. There is, however, a case in which *a* is omitted according to the general rules, when by the letter, though not the spirit, of i.61 it ought to be retained; see under i.61 (p. 47).

p. **273**, rule 12. I should doubtless have done better to adopt the reading *vâṇijâya* (for *bâṇ-*), in rule, version, and example.

p. **291**, l. 24. *Achâvâkaḥ* is found at vii.1.5[5].

p. **296**, l. 9. Read *ḥkshṇ* (by ix.3); and this would change the treatment of the group, since *ḥ* (i.9) is not a spirant.

p. **301**, l. 3. Read *ḥksh*, *ḥkshṇ*, *ḥkshv* (by ix.3); so that *jihvâmûlîya* occurs only in the four remaining groups.

p. **302**, l. 23. I can give no reference for *varshâbhyaḥ*, the reading at vii.4.13 being *varshyâbhyaḥ svâhâ 'varshyâbhyaḥ*

p. **303**, l. 9. I was heedless enough here to overlook the fact that a spirant never stands, according to the rules of this chapter, before either an aspirated surd or a nasal, since a first mute (by rule 9, above) is always inserted in such cases between the two. The groups *çch* etc., therefore, would be read according to this rule *çcch*, instead of *ççch*. The groups in which a nasal originally follows the spirant will be found catalogued under rule xxi.12 (p. 390). The example *tasmâd* etc., below, is therefore no counter-example, and it is G. M. that are in the wrong in so calling it; it is to be read *taspmât*, according to Plâkshi etc., instead of *tasspmât* (or, with *yama*, *tassppmât*).

p. **304**, l. 5. See also under xxi.16.

p. **308**, l. 6 from below. Read *dhakâre* for *-ra*.

p. **315**, l. 10. Prof. Hadley's paper may be found printed in full in the Transactions of the American Philological Association (vol. i., 1871, p. 1 ff. .

p. **334**, l. 7. Read vii.5.15[2] (for vii.5.14[2]).

p. **336**, l. 7. "Verbal forms"—that is, of course, all excepting *ṛjishi*.

p. **354**, ll. 17,25. See p. 426. Prof. Roth's MS. also ends with *samudraḥ;* he calls my attention, further, to the passage in the Bṛhad-Âraṇyaka (i.1.2), *samudra evâ 'sya* [i. e. *açvasya*] *bandhuḥ samudro yoniḥ*.

p. **356**, l. 3. For *dhṛta* as synonym of *pracaya*, see below, under xxiii.17 (p. 412).

p. **364**, l. 24. And accordant, it may be added, with the practice followed in the Vâjasaneyi-Sanhitâ, where there is no added figure, and no prolongation of the vowel.

p. **369**, marg. notes, l. 6. The *anudâtta*-mark under *çu-* (the second time) has fallen out.

p. **373**, l. 1. Read i.2.5[1] (for i.2.5[2]).

p. **386**, l. 18. The *e* sign has broken off in the *samhitâ*-reading of *âgne*.

p. **387**, l. 7. I have considered this point more fully in a paper on the Sanskrit accent in the Transactions of the Am. Philological Association (vol. i., 1871, p. 20 ff.).

p. **414**, l. 4. Read (in Devanâgarî) *kramavik-*, for *kramivak-* (altered in the type, by some mishap, after the last correction).

p. **425**, l. 29–30. *Achâvâkaḥ* is found at vii.1.5[5].

p. **428**, l. 37. But see, for the commentary, the additional note above to i.15 (or p. 18).

p. **429**, l. 26. The *krama*-text is also quoted under ix.24 (p. 224) by O. alone.

p. **438**, last line but one. Read xvi. for xxvi.